CENTRAL ASIA

Central Asia

A NEW HISTORY
FROM THE IMPERIAL CONQUESTS
TO THE PRESENT

ADEEB KHALID

PRINCETON UNIVERSITY PRESS
PRINCETON & OXFORD

Published by Princeton University Press
41 William Street, Princeton, New Jersey 08540
6 Oxford Street, Woodstock, Oxfordshire OX20 1TR

press.princeton.edu

All Rights Reserved

Library of Congress Cataloging-in-Publication Data

Names: Khalid, Adeeb, 1964– author.
Title: Central Asia : a new history from the imperial conquests to the present / Adeeb Khalid.
Description: First edition. | Princeton : Princeton University Press, [2021] | Includes bibliographical references and index.
Identifiers: LCCN 2020047138 (print) | LCCN 2020047139 (ebook) | ISBN 9780691161396 (hardback) | ISBN 9780691220437 (ebook)
Subjects: LCSH: Asia, Central—History. | Asia, Central—Ethnic relations. | Xinjiang Uygur Zizhiqu (China)—History. | Islam—Asia, Central—History. | Asia, Central—Civilization—Russian influences. | Asia, Central—Civilization—Chinese influences.
Classification: LCC DK856 .K47 2021 (print) | LCC DK856 (ebook) | DDC 958—dc23
LC record available at https://lccn.loc.gov/2020047138
LC ebook record available at https://lccn.loc.gov/2020047139

British Library Cataloging-in-Publication Data is available

Editorial: Priya Nelson, Thalia Leaf
Jacket Design: Pamela L. Schnitter
Production: Danielle Amatucci
Publicity: Kate Hensley, Kate Farquhar-Thomson

Jacket image: The Ark of Bukhara, Uzbekistan. Photo: Jeremy Sutton-Hibbert / Alamy Stock Photo

This book has been composed in Classic Arno

Printed on acid-free paper. ∞

Printed in the United States of America

10 9 8 7 6 5 4 3 2 1

CONTENTS

v

ILLUSTRATIONS

MAPS

TABLES

ABBREVIATIONS

CCP	Chinese Communist Party
CIA	Central Intelligence Agency
ETIM	East Turkestan Islamic Movement
ETR	Eastern Turkestan Republic
GMD	Guomindang (Chinese Nationalist Party)
GWOT	Global war on terrorism
KGB	Committee on State Security (Soviet political police)
NGO	Nongovermental organization
NYT	*New York Times*
PDPA	People's Democratic Party of Afghanistan
PLA	People's Liberation Army
POW	prisoner of war
PRC	People's Republic of China
RFA	Radio Free Asia
RGASPI	Russian State Archive of Sociopolitical History
SADUM	Religious Directorate for the Muslims of Central Asia and Kazakhstan
SCO	Shanghai Cooperation Organization
TCNU	Turkestan Committee of National Unity
TIP	Turkestan Islamic Party
UNESCO	United Nations Economic, Social, and Cultural Organization
XPCC	Xinjiang Production and Construction Corps

ACKNOWLEDGMENTS

MANY YEARS AGO, Brigitta van Rheinberg suggested that I write an accessible book on Central Asia for Princeton University Press. This, finally, is that book. It took longer than I expected and is longer than Brigitta expected, but it would not exist without her suggestion and encouragement. My thanks go to her for offering me the possibility both to think broadly about Central Asia's modern history and to address a wider audience.

This book synthesizes most of what I know about Central Asia. I therefore owe thanks to all of the friends and colleagues who have helped me over my career. But I owe a special round of thanks to those friends and colleagues who welcomed me to the study of Xinjiang and helped me get my bearings in it. James Millward, David Brophy, Rian Thum, and Max Oidtmann answered many questions, gave practical advice for my travels there, and saved me from many mistakes. Artemy Kalinovsky, Scott Levi, Susannah Ottaway, and Charles Shaw read different parts of the manuscript as it developed and gave invaluable advice. Max Oidtmann read the full draft of the penultimate version of this book and offered generous comments and many corrections. I also thank the two anonymous readers for Princeton University Press for their insights and their suggestions. These generous colleagues have made me clarify many arguments, step back from overstatements, and refine my writing. It should go without saying (but I will say it anyway) that none of these fine scholars bears any responsibility for the blemishes that remain in this book.

Big thank-yous go to David Brophy, Alexander Morrison, James Pickett, and Sean Roberts for sharing prepublication versions of their works. Darren Byler, Victoria Clement, Akram Habibulla, and Rinat Shigabdinov answered queries and provided sources. The staff of the Special Collections Reading Room at Lund University Library made my week there both pleasant and productive. I am grateful to Lisa D., Yulduz X., and Yahya al-Sini for research in Chinese-language materials. Many thanks go to Bill Nelson for the wonderful maps and Elizabeth Budd for the graphs.

At Princeton University Press, Eric Crahan shepherded the book through to production, and Priya Nelson took it to the end. Thalia Leaf bore the brunt of my questions and my neuroses with good grace and was amazingly thorough. Deborah Grahame-Smith at Westchester Publishing Services was patient and supportive. My gratitude goes out to all of them.

Carleton College supported the project throughout. A leave of absence in 2016–2017 allowed me to start writing this book, and a generous discretionary grant funded my trip to Xinjiang in the summer of 2019.

As always, the home front is the most important. Haroun was away, but Cheryl and Leila lived with this book for four years and showed remarkable patience with it and its author. Their love and support have been my most cherished possessions.

St. Paul, Minnesota
August 14, 2020

CENTRAL ASIA

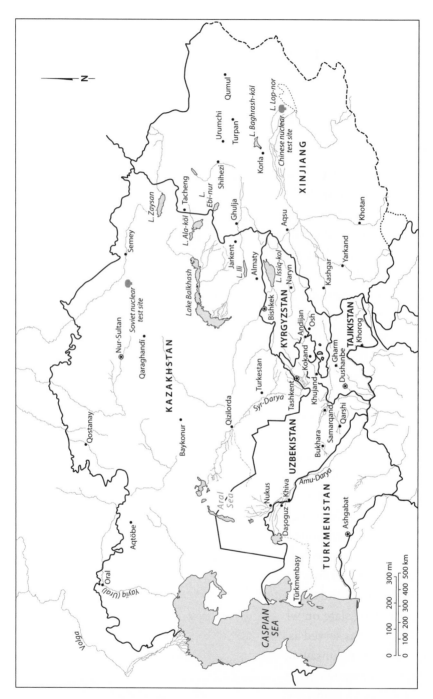

MAP 0.1. Central Asia today

INTRODUCTION

WHEN THE COLLAPSE of the Soviet Union hurled the republics of Central Asia onto the global stage, the region was all but unknown to the outside world. Its complicated modern history had transpired away from the gaze of that world, with its events little noticed and the sources hidden away under lock and key. There was little expertise on the region, and outside observers had few ways of making sense of it. Initial reactions cast the new states as artificial, weak, lacking in any history or legitimacy, and with a potential for insecurity and instability. Commentators pulled out references from the past to make sense of the unexpected present: hackneyed notions of the Silk Road and the Great Game were put to use to make sense of the newly emerged states, and exoticization was an easy fix. Commentary on Central Asia evoked vast, undulating grasslands filled with nomadic horsemen, the minarets and cupolas of medieval architecture, and natives in folkloric costumes. To be clear, this exoticization is not a peculiarly Western phenomenon. A Japanese documentary from the 1980s also cast the region in exotic light, with long shots of camels trudging into empty deserts to the New Age music of Kitaro. Today, Xinjiang is an exotic domestic destination for tourists from China proper, while in the wider Muslim world, the names Samarqand and Bukhara evoke medieval grandeur and luxury that again are not of the here and now. At its best, exoticism romanticizes Central Asia and places it beyond the reach of history. At its worst, it can render the region a blank slate on which one can inscribe anything one wishes. Central Asia has served as the locale of a number of Hollywood action movies featuring unsavory characters, while in the 2006 movie *Borat*, the British comedian Sacha Baron Cohen used the misadventures of a fictional Kazakh reporter visiting the United States to present a critique

1

of Western naïveté and gullibility. But the Kazakhstan represented in the film had nothing to do with the actual country. The ostensibly Kazakhstani scenes in the film were shot in Romania, and the film presented a completely made-up idea of Kazakhstan to its viewers. For Cohen, Kazakhstan's task was simply to embody the exotic, the inscrutable, the other.

Some of this was perhaps inevitable. For much of the modern period, Central Asia was invisible to the outside world. The Eurasian landmass had been divided up over the course of the nineteenth century between the two contiguous land empires of Russia and China. On the political map of the world, "Russia" and "China" appeared as singular entities. It was easy to see each of them as somehow homogeneous, rather than the highly variegated imperial spaces they were. This was indeed what happened. For most of the existence of the Soviet Union, the outside world knew it simply as Russia. On my first visit to Washington, D.C., I was surprised to see a sign in the metro pointing to "the Russian embassy." It was 1984 and the Cold War was getting quite hot, but American institutions—let alone the American public—could not tell the difference between Russia and the Soviet Union and remained oblivious to the multinational character of their main adversary. Xinjiang was, if anything, even more invisible, simply a part of an inscrutable (and exotic) domain called "China." Yet Central Asia was a distant backyard even within each empire, and little known even to those who specialized on one or both of the empires. The Tsarist regime treated Central Asia as a militarily sensitive region and restricted travel by foreign subjects there. Its Soviet successors were even more secretive, and for most of the Soviet period, Central Asia was inaccessible to outsiders. I grew up in Pakistan, on the other side of the Pamir Mountains from Central Asia. Tashkent, the biggest city in Central Asia at the time, was a mere 1,200 kilometers from my hometown of Lahore, but it might as well have been on a different planet. Travel was very difficult and news of current developments in short supply. It was this sense of wonder about a land so near, yet so far—one so familiar, yet very different—that first attracted me to Central Asia. The situation changed with the end of the Cold War and the dissolution of the Soviet Union. Central Asia is no longer isolated.

In fact, it occupies a pivotal place in the Belt and Road Initiative, China's hugely ambitious plan to remake the transportation and commercial infrastructure of Eurasia. Yet the view of the region as the distant heartland of Asia remains. Certainly in the public view, but also in policy circles, it remains an obscure place, the middle of nowhere, isolated from the rest of the world or caught in some sort of a time warp. This explains the constant invocation of the Silk Road, which heightens the sense that the region is best understood through its distant and exotic past, and the unstated assumption that its recent past and present are far less important or interesting.

Nothing could be further from the facts. Instead of being a place that time forgot and where one can forget time, Central Asia has been a crossroads of history. It has experienced every current of modern history, every achievement of modernity and every one of its disasters, and every extreme of the twentieth and the twenty-first centuries. The conquest of the region by the Tsarist (or Russian) and Qing empires marked a rupture in its history that needs to be taken seriously. Since then, Central Asia has experienced in succession colonial rule; many projects of revolutionary nation and culture building and of remaking of the economy and society under Communism; and, more recently, neoliberal globalization. For much of the twentieth century, Central Asia was a laboratory of modernity and a showcase for the Soviet model of development. These experiences have transformed the region and its people in fundamental ways. Its landscapes have been put to industrial use; its vast spaces domesticated by roads, railways, and airports; its cities reshaped; and its countryside brought under the plow as never before. The worldviews of its peoples and their ways of thinking about themselves, their communities, and their states have undergone enormous changes. The idea of the nation transformed notions of community in significant ways. The modern period has also seen major demographic shifts. The population has increased manifold, and the region has witnessed the influx of new populations through migrations, deportations, or state-sponsored settlement. The large numbers of Russians and Han Chinese who now live in Central Asia are the clearest example of such movements, but many other groups—Germans, Poles, Ashkenazi Jews,

Tatars, Hui (also known as Dungans), Koreans, and Chechens—have appeared in Central Asia during the modern period. The twentieth century brought universal literacy and massive transformations in the position of women in society. It also brought environmental disaster. The nuclear programs of both the Soviet Union and the People's Republic of China (PRC) were located in Central Asia, and both of them carried out open-air tests that had long-lasting effects on the population. In addition, the overuse of irrigation in Soviet Central Asia produced ecological disaster. The Aral Sea, once the fourth largest body of freshwater in the world, shrank drastically, transforming the climate and wreaking havoc on the health of those who live in its vicinity. For both good and ill, Central Asia is completely different from what it was in the middle of the eighteenth century. This book is an attempt to provide a coherent narrative of these transformations. Central Asia is not at all exotic or timeless. Rather, it is very much the product of history, a history it shares with all other societies that experienced colonialism, anticolonialism, modernization, and development in the past couple of centuries.

———

There are many ways to define Central Asia. The term coexists with others, such as "Inner Asia" or "Central Eurasia," each of which has a different inflection and scope. We could define Central Asia expansively to include the entire Eurasian steppe and its neighboring regions, extending from Hungary to Manchuria and stretching south to Afghanistan and even northern Pakistan and India. This is the definition adopted by the United Nations Economic, Social, and Cultural Organization (UNESCO). In Soviet parlance, however, Central Asia comprised only the four republics of Turkmenistan, Uzbekistan, Tajikistan, and Kyrgyzstan. I have chosen a middle position that defines Central Asia as encompassing the five post-Soviet states and the Xinjiang region of the PRC. This Central Asia encompasses those predominantly Muslim societies that came under the rule of the overland empires of the Romanovs and the Qing from the late eighteenth century on. These societies were interconnected before their conquest as well, but the conquest put them on a peculiar trajectory even as it distinguished them from those of their neighbors that were not conquered by those empires. In the twentieth century, of course, both the Russian and the Chinese empires underwent revolutionary transformations that transformed their Central Asian territories in significant ways. The experience of the past two centuries has left these societies with much more in common with each other than with their other neighbors. The historical contingency that the Russian conquest stopped at the Amu Darya River accounts for the radically different path that Afghanistan took in the twentieth century. For this reason, it does not belong in this story. For similar reasons, my Central Asia does not include the lands of the Tatars and Bashkirs, which are geographically connected to the steppe zone of Central Asia and inhabited by Turkic-speaking Muslims, but which have a much longer connection to the Russian state. I exclude Mongolia and Tibet from my purview for similar reasons. They are culturally quite different from the region that is the focus of this book, and their political histories have little in common with its history in the modern period.

For all that, the Central Asia that I examine is not homogeneous. It is a frontier zone between nomadic and agrarian populations, a division seen as axiomatic by the region's own peoples. The river valleys of Transoxiana and the oases of Altishahr boast some of the most ancient cities in the world. Much of the surrounding steppe was home to nomadic populations until the 1930s. Nomadic and sedentary societies interacted throughout history, but they had different trajectories in the modern period, with the imperial powers treating them differently and subjecting them to different policies. Another axis of difference was imperial. The "Russian" and "Chinese" parts of Central Asia have experienced regimes of power that were both similar and different. The PRC modeled many of its policies in Xinjiang on Soviet precedents in "Russian" Central Asia but took them in different directions. The book is an experiment in writing an integrated history of modern Central Asia. The different political regimes in the "Russian" and "Chinese" zones mean that most of the chapters focus on one or the other half of Central Asia. However, I do offer a comparison between Soviet and Chinese policies of managing national difference, economic development, and social transformation as they affected Central Asia.

———

This book argues that imperial conquest thrust Central Asia into a new era of its history. That conquest marked a rupture with the past, which grew less important and less helpful in understanding the new era. Empires have been the most common form of political organization in human history, and there had been plenty of empires in Central Asia's history. The conquests of the eighteenth and nineteenth centuries were different, however. They brought Central Asia under the control of large empires based outside the region. They completed the enclosure of the steppe that had been ongoing since the seventeenth century and reversed the long-term relationship between the region and its neighbors. In different ways, Russian and Chinese rule introduced new regimes of power to Central Asia. Imperial rule brought with it new institutional arrangements; tariff regimes; ways of entanglement in the world at large; and, ultimately, ways of seeing the world. The past did not disappear, of course, but the new order was significantly different. Central Asians related to the rest of the world in a different way. In the twentieth century, both empires were overthrown and replaced by regimes of social mobilization that aimed at modernization and development. Central Asia was swept into those processes. Its modern history tells us a great deal about modernity, colonialism, secularism, Communism, and development, some of the key phenomena that have shaped the world we live in. This book suggests that this modern history is worth understanding in its own right, and it offers a first attempt at such an understanding.

The period since the imperial conquests also produced new ways of thinking about self and community and created new forms of identification. The national labels with which contemporary Central Asians identify—Kazakh, Kyrgyz, Tajik, Turkmen, Uyghur, and Uzbek—emerged over the course of the twentieth century, displacing other forms of community. The labels have long existed, but they acquired new meanings in the modern age. The Uzbeks of the sixteenth century are not the same as those of the twenty-first, for instance, and the term "Turkmen" has a different meaning today than it did in the eighteenth century. The shifting meaning of these terms and the emergence of new ways of identification is a major concern in this book.

———

This book deals primarily with two imperial systems, those of Russia and China. They have shaped the context in which Central Asians have lived in the past two and a half centuries, but their mutual relationship has never been stable or symmetrical. Both systems have changed enormously. I trace the enormous transformations that the two polities experienced (imperial collapse, revolution, civil war, and state-led transformation), both individually and in relation to each other. In the middle of the eighteenth century, China's was much the wealthier and more powerful empire. The situation flipped in the nineteenth century, when Russia gained a military advantage as well as extraterritorial rights in China itself, while China—beset with threats both internal and external—risked being "carved up like a melon" by foreign powers, as the saying went. For much of the twentieth century, China was the recipient of aid and advice from the Soviet Union. Today, China is a world power and more firmly in control of its Central Asian possessions than ever before, while the Russian rule over Central Asia is no more. This imperial history also casts a long shadow on how we think and write about Central Asia. Overland empires did not have a formal separation between metropole and colony in the manner of overseas empires, a separation that makes the relationship between the imperial center and the conquered territories more nebulous. It is easier to see overland empires as somehow more homogeneous than overseas empires. In the twentieth century, Soviet rhetoric, seeking to minimize the imperial origins of the Soviet state, asserted that various non-Russian territories had joined the empire voluntarily and that the Soviet Union existed on the basis of a deep "friendship of peoples." Yet as we shall see below, Russia's possessions in Central Asia were thoroughly comparable to those of the overseas colonies of European empires. Since the demise of the Soviet Union, Central Asians have questioned the narrative to one degree or another, while the Russian public has been less receptive to the challenges. Today, it remembers the Tsarist empire with fondness and pride but is allergic to any mention of colonies or conquest. Soviet-era concepts thus create a post-Soviet amnesia about empire in Russia.

China is a different matter altogether. From the late Qing on, all Chinese governments, regardless of their ideological orientation, have insisted that China is not an empire but an indivisible nation-state with inviolable boundaries. The Qing dynasty collapsed in 1912 and was replaced by a republic, which only heightened the insistence on China's unity. Today, the People's Republic asserts that China in its current boundaries is the apotheosis of a Chinese nation-state that has existed throughout history as a single nation. This means that, in the words of an official proclamation of the State Council of the republic, Xinjiang has, "since the Western Han Dynasty (206 BC–24 AD), ... been an inseparable part of the unitary multi-ethnic Chinese nation."[1] According to this logic, Xinjiang is not part of Central Asia at all but constitutes the so-called Western Regions (*Xiyu*) of a transhistorical Chinese nation-state. This uncompromising and teleological view of China and its relationship to Xinjiang lies at the heart of the conflict in Xinjiang that is at a critical stage as I write these lines, with millions of Uyghurs in extrajudicial detention for not being loyal enough Chinese. Viewing China from Central Asia, as I do in this book, allows us to understand China in a new way. The "China" invoked by the Chinese government is a twentieth-century vision of the nation that subsumes a fraught history of numerous dynasties, many of which were established by peoples from Inner Asia, into a single narrative of an ever-present entity called China. This teleology does not fit well with the historical record, which is full of discontinuities and ruptures. One might equate China not with a single state, but with a political or cultural tradition—but even that continuity is problematic. Each new dynasty celebrated its novelty and its difference from its predecessors, rather than any continuity of a Chinese tradition. That tradition remained alien to lands beyond the central plains of China proper (*neidi*). More importantly for our purposes, the territorial extent of the various dynastic states varied enormously, and few of them controlled the whole territory of China proper, let alone everything within the current boundaries of the PRC. The Tang dynasty (618–907) had extended its rule to what is now Xinjiang. After the collapse of the Tang, no dynasty based in China proper controlled any part of Central Asia until the Qing conquests of the 1750s. The novelty of Xinjiang to the Qing imperium was underscored by its name, which means "New Dominion." The current boundaries of China were created by the eighteenth-century imperial conquests of a Manchu dynasty. It is with these conquests that I start this book.

Central Asia's history in the past two and a half centuries has been affected by transformations that often originated elsewhere (imperial conquests, the Russian and Chinese revolutions, and the neoliberal revolution). This book is about the ways Central Asians dealt with these transformations. I seek their agency both within and beyond the official institutions of the states that ruled them. People act in given circumstances, but they act in their own ways. Those ways differ and are always singular. Different groups of Central Asians had different notions of what ought to be done and how society had to act. The period I cover in this book has seen several monumental transformations—imperial conquest, revolutions, and both the building of socialism and its collapse—and each has produced new claims to leadership from new groups in society. There was plenty of contention within Central Asian societies, and I wish to convey that very clearly. In this book, we will see Central Asians arguing with each other as much as they argue with the Russians or the Chinese.

———

Central Asia stretches from the Caspian Sea in the west to the Altai Mountains in the east, and from the Köpet Dagh Mountains in the south to deep into the steppe in the north. It is an extensive area, about the size of the United States west of the Mississippi, and it encompasses

TABLE 0.1   Contemporary Central Asia

State or region	Capital	Area (km²)	Population (thousands)
Kazakhstan	Nur-Sultan	2,724,900	18,320
Kyrgyzstan	Bishkek	199,951	6,304
Tajikistan	Dushanbe	143,100	9,101
Turkmenistan	Ashgabat	491,210	5,851
Uzbekistan	Tashkent	448,978	32,476
Xinjiang	Ürümchi	1,664,897	24,870
Total		5,673,036	96,922

Source: Population figures for the five sovereign states are United Nations midyear estimates for 2018 (United Nations, *United Nations Demographic Yearbook 2018* [New York: United Nations, 2019], 693); figures for Xinjiang are for the end of 2018 (*China Statistical Yearbook 2019* [Beijing: China Statistics Press, 2019], table 2-6).

a great deal of geographic and environmental diversity. The fundamental fact about the region, however, is its great distance from open water. The continental pole—the point on the planet farthest from open water—lies at 46°17′ N, 86°40′ E, near the border between Xinjiang and Kazakhstan, 2,645 kilometers from the nearest coastline.[2] The climate is continental, with extremes of heat and cold, and water is generally scarce. It means that large parts of the region are grassland or desert and that agriculture and urban life are often dependent on irrigation. The region consists of a series of internal drainage basins—that is, areas in which rivers flow into inland seas or lakes rather than draining into oceans. (The only exception is the northernmost reaches of Kazakhstan, which drain into the Irtysh River that flows into the Arctic Ocean.) Central Asia has some of the tallest mountains in the world, but the rest of the terrain is rolling hills or flatlands. Snowmelt from the mountains gives rise to the rivers, which flow westward to the Aral Sea. The river valleys create the possibility of irrigated agriculture. As noted above, they were the sites of some of the most ancient cities in the world. The aridity also creates large areas of desert and, to the north, vast stretches of grassland. Central Asia has both areas of dense population and vast tracts of sparsely populated or uninhabitable land. Its population of over ninety million is unevenly distributed (see table 0.1 and map 0.2).

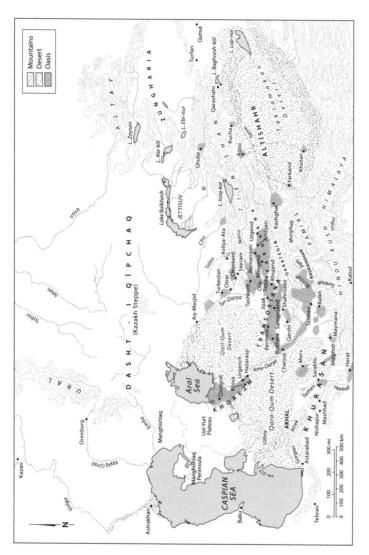

MAP 0.2. Central Asia: physical features and premodern geographic terminology

Before beginning the narrative, let us take a quick tour of the region to familiarize ourselves with the lay of the land and the geographic terminology used throughout the book. Let us fly west from the port city now known as Türkmenbaşy on the eastern shore of the Caspian Sea (it was known as Kransovodsk or Kizilsu until the 1990s). A vast desert called Karakum (or Garagum, "Black Sands") stretches out below us. To the south, running east to west is the Köpet Dagh mountain range, across which lies the Iranian plateau. Soon we reach the banks of the Amu Darya (Oxus to the Greeks and Jayhun to the Arabs). Once we cross it, we are in Transoxiana (the Land beyond the Oxus), which the Arabs called Mā warā' al-Nahr (or Maverannahr, the Land beyond the River). The term was used in all Islamicate languages to denote the region between the Amu and the Syr Daryas. A great portion of Transoxiana is also desert, called Kyzylkum (or Qizil Qum, "Red Sands"), but lands along the banks of the two rivers and others that flow into them (Zerafshan, "the Gold Bestower"; Vakhsh; Panj; and Surkhan Darya) support agriculture and have long supported urban life. Samarqand and Bukhara sit smack in the middle of Transoxiana. Downriver, where the Amu emptied into the Aral Sea, lies Khwarazm, another ancient city and for many centuries a major commercial and political center. Upriver, we find the fertile Ferghana valley, which today is the most densely populated part of Central Asia.

As we fly farther east, we spy the largest mountain system in the world. To the southeast lies the Pamir knot, called the "roof of the world," where a number of mountain chains come together. The Darvaz chain comes in from the southwest, the Karakorum and Himalayas stretch out eastward, and the Tien-Shan ("Celestial Mountains" in Chinese) range strikes out northward. This is inaccessible terrain that separates Central Asia from South Asia. The Tien-Shan also cleaves Central Asia longitudinally into western and eastern halves. Let us stick to the west for a while longer. To the northeast of the Pamir massif lies the Ferghana valley, which is surrounded on three sides by mountains. The western foothills of the Tien-Shan chain are a lush area watered by a number of tributaries of the Syr Darya, which give the area its name: Jettisuv in Kyrgyz and Kazakh and Semirech'e in Russian, meaning "seven rivers" in either case. North of the Syr Darya, we are on the steppe proper, a vast, mostly flat area of grassland or desert that stretches north until it blends into the Siberian taiga. In medieval Islamic sources, it was called the Dasht-i Qipchaq (the Qipchaq Steppe), named after a nomadic Turkic group that dominated it at the time. In the modern period, it makes sense to call it the Kazakh steppe, since in that era it has been inhabited by Kazakhs. Most of it is a plateau, the central part of which is known by the name Betpak Dala ("Hungry Steppe"), in testimony to the hardships that nature inflicts upon humans who try to live there. East of Jettisuv, however, we come upon another basin, called Zungharia after the nomadic people that occupied it until the eighteenth century. (The Zunghars play an important role at the beginning of the story this book relates.) They were Mongol and never became Muslim. Zungharia is a steppe grassland and the site of the continental pole of inaccessibility. Its southern boundary is formed by the Tien-Shan range, south of which is another large internal drainage basin—that of the Tarim River. The Tarim arises in the Karakorum Mountains and used to flow into Lop Nor Lake. Much of this basin is another desert, called the Taklamakan. It is dotted with fertile oases, which gave rise to cities in ancient times. The Tarim basin is also known as Altishahr ("Six Cities," a term for the oasis cities in the basin) as well as Eastern Turkestan. It is bounded on the south by the Kunlun Mountains, which separate it from the Tibet plateau. To its east lies the Turfan basin, a fault trough that houses the oases of Turfan and Qumul. Descending to 155 meters below sea level, it is one of the lowest depressions in the world. It has a very hot and dry climate, but the presence of underground water makes irrigated agriculture possible. Here we are at the other end of Central Asia, for to the east the Turfan basin connects to the Gansu corridor, a string of oases along a narrow path between the Kunlun Mountains to the south and the Gobi Desert to the north that leads down to the Yellow River (Huang He) valley and China proper. Central Asian sources used several terms for the lands beyond: Khitay for the area north of the Yellow River, once the land of the Khitans; Chin for the area south of that river; and Machin for the territory south of the Yangtze River. The Turfan basin at the easternmost edge of Central Asia had long been in commercial contact with China. For the rest of Muslim Central Asia, China remained a distant and culturally alien region.

As noted above, the Tien-Shan Mountains divide Central Asia in two, although the division has never prevented travel or other kinds of interaction, and the two regions are tied together by numerous cultural and economic links. Yet the two halves have often operated in different geopolitical arenas. Central Asia was often called Turkestan, "the land of the Turks," and its two halves referred to as western and eastern Turkestan. In the nineteenth century, after the imperial conquests, they were often called Russian and Chinese Turkestan. These were geographic terms, not names of political entities, of course, but they nevertheless acknowledged the commonality between the two parts. In addition to the east-west or Chinese-Russian division, we should also posit a north-south division between the steppe lands and the lands of the oases and irrigated agriculture. The division is very rough but nevertheless useful to keep in mind, for most the sedentary, agrarian population of Central Asia existed in Khwarazm, Transoxiana, Ferghana, and the oases of Altishahr, while the rest of the region—especially the steppe zone north of Transoxiana—remained predominantly nomadic until the 1930s.

This quick tour also confronts us with another important issue that everyone interested in Central Asia faces. Central Asian place names have changed over time, they often have more than one version, and there are numerous ways of spelling them. The same applies to Central Asian personal names. The spelling depends on whether one transliterates the name of a place or person from a Central Asian language or via Russian or Chinese. Transliterating names via Russian results in infelicities, so that *h* (which does not exist in Russian) becomes *kh*, and the sound represented by the English *j* is rendered by the unsightly (and, to non-Russian speakers, incomprehensible) jumble of *dzh*, while all sorts of vowels get bent out of shape. Chinese versions of Central Asian names, based on a syllabic transcription, often render the originals completely unidentifiable: Ahmad becomes Aimaiti, and Ibrahim turns into Yibulayin. In this book, I use the names of people and places as they appear in Central Asian languages, spelled according to Central Asian conventions (thus, I use Khujand, not Khodzhent, and Ürümchi, not Urumqi), but use well-established English spellings when they exist (thus, Kashgar, not Qäshqär, and Ferghana, not Fergana or Farg'ona). Occasionally, I give two versions of a place name, when both are in use. For the names of people, I use a common transliteration scheme for the period before the 1920s, when specific orthographies became established for different Central Asian languages. For the period after that, I transliterate names according to the language the person in question identified with most, recognizing all along that complete consistency is neither possible nor desirable.

Finally, a note about the term "Turkestan" and its variants. Turkestan (literally, the land of the Turks) was a generic term used in Central Asia and beyond for the territory north of the Amu Darya, where Turkic-speaking peoples predominated. The term was widespread enough that the Russians adopted it for the new province they established in 1865. From 1865 to 1924, Turkestan referred to a concrete administrative entity, but the older, more generic, sense of the term never disappeared. In the nineteenth and early twentieth centuries, conventional usage both locally and in Europe divided Central Asia into western or Russian, and eastern or Chinese Turkestan, roughly along the Tien-Shan. In the early twentieth century, the Turkic-speaking Muslim subjects of the Qing began to use Eastern Turkestan as the name for their region. None of this would be worth a comment were it not for the insistence of the PRC that Eastern Turkestan is a term invented by foreign imperialists with the aim of dismantling China and used today by alleged "separatists" and "extremists." The only term the Chinese government allows is Xinjiang. Even though the term contains the narrative of imperial conquest, it may not be translated into Uyghur. The Uyghur term for the region is Shinjang, the transliterated form of the Chinese name. Today, most Uyghurs use the term only under duress. In this book, I use the term "Xinjiang" to refer only to the administrative entity of that name. When referring to the region in other contexts, I use "Eastern Turkestan" or "Altishahr," and I usually follow the usage preferred by my sources.

1

The Multiple Heritages of Central Asia

MODERN CENTRAL ASIA has been shaped by a long history of interactions between the peoples of the Eurasian steppe and those of the agrarian societies (China, India, Iran, and Europe) that ring it. For environmental reasons, the steppe—the vast zone of grassland and desert that stretches from Hungary to Korea—cannot support a dense population. Early human societies discovered that the best strategy for survival on the steppe was pastoral nomadism, in which animals (camels, sheep, cattle, and horses) provide the basis of livelihood. Nomadic groups laid claim to distinct pasturelands and followed fixed migration routes between winter and summer pastures. Over the centuries, steppe nomads interacted with neighboring sedentary societies through raiding, trading, and conquest. The domestication of the horse gave nomads mobility and a military advantage for a millennium and a half. During this period, they built a number of empires on the steppe that could dictate terms to their sedentary neighbors and occasionally conquer them outright. Nomads were a constant presence on the frontiers of agrarian societies on Eurasia's edges, which found it almost impossible to control the vast spaces of the steppe. The agrarian empires saw nomads as barbarians and a problem to be solved. The Great Wall of China, built to keep the northern barbarians out (and Chinese peasants in), is an apt indication of this attitude. The wall is equally apt as a metaphor for the relationship between the two worlds, because it never succeeded in separating them. Instead, they remained intertwined in a symbiotic and permeable relationship. The Great Wall sat in a borderland that was a perpetual arena of interaction. Many Chinese states were founded by "barbarians" from the north or northwest, even if their foreign origins were often covered up in historical narratives. We pick up the story in the mid-eighteenth century, when this geopolitical relationship between the steppe and its neighbors began to flip as the sedentary empires on the fringes of the steppe began to first enclose and then conquer the steppe.

——————

For a millennium and a half, the steppe was ascendant. Beginning with the Xiongnu, steppe nomads created a number of empires that extracted trading rights or tribute from their neighbors and sometimes conquered them. Such empires had several features in common. They appeared around a charismatic leader who claimed divine sanction of his sovereignty and who was therefore able to knit various tribes (political units imagined along genealogical lines) into viable confederations. The first major steppe empire was that of the Xiongnu, whom we know through the name that Chinese sources use for them. The empire lasted for well over two hundred years (third century BCE–first century CE) and featured substantial urban settlements and a ramified administration. In the western steppe, the Scythians and Sarmatians built empires about the same time. In the sixth and seventh centuries CE, a group of nomads called the Türk established another empire in what is now Mongolia. Its center was in the Orkhon valley, and it left behind runic inscriptions that are the oldest surviving texts in any Turkic language. In the eighth century, another confederation of Turkic tribes formed the Uyghur empire. (Its name was to be revived in the twentieth century as the national name for the Turkic Muslim population of Xinjiang.)

River valleys and oases, where sufficient amounts of water were available, gave rise to sedentary societies and states built on agriculture. Transoxiana and the oases of the Tarim basin were part of this agrarian world. The so-called Bactria-Margiana Archaeological Complex dates back to 2200–1700 BCE and was a contemporary of civilizations in Egypt, Anatolia, and the Indus valley. In 539–330 BCE, the Achaemenid empire based in the Iranian plateau extended into Transoxiana, when the region was known as Sogdiana (Sughd). Alexander the Great defeated the Achaemenids, and Sogdiana became the easternmost part of his empire. He is supposed to have founded the city of Khujand as Alexandria Eschate ("Alexandria the Furthest"). Sogdiana was an independent Greco-Bactrian state in the third century BCE before it fell to nomadic groups from the east, which eventually established the Kushan empire that expanded south into India. Zoroaster was born in Sogdiana, and Zoroastrianism had a long career in Central Asia. The Kushans adopted Buddhism, and it was through them that it traveled to China. By the first century CE, these empires were linked by long-distance trade to China, India, and Iran.

This trade is the basis of our contemporary cliché of the "Silk Road." The term was coined in 1877 by the German geographer Ferdinand Freiherr von Richthofen, who used it to describe the routes along which Chinese silk was exported from the Han empire (206 BCE–220 CE) to Central Asia. Since then, however, the term has expanded to cover all trade that ostensibly linked "China" to "the West" for several centuries until it was displaced by maritime trade during Europe's Age of Discovery. This trade is supposed to have underpinned Central Asia's economy and made its civilization viable. There is much that is problematic about this view. The most lucrative trade moved along a north-south axis, and not from east to west, nor was "the West" (that is, Europe) a significant partner in the east-west trade. Few goods and fewer people traveled from one end of the road to the other. But more significantly for our purposes, the concept of the Silk Road turns Central Asia into simply a pathway, rather than a place of interest in its own right. The Silk Road works better as a metaphor of connectivity across cultures than as a description of a concrete historical phenomenon.[1] We will make little use of the term in this book.

The nomads of the steppe spoke a variety of languages belonging to the Altaic family, which includes Mongolian, Tungusic, and a host of Turkic languages. Most of the sedentary population spoke various

Indo-Iranian languages, which it shared with peoples in what are now Afghanistan and Iran. Transoxiana was always a frontier zone where the two linguistic families interacted the most intensely. It was the boundary between "Iran" and "Turan," the land of the nomads. The "Iran" here is much more expansive than the present-day nation-state of that name. Much of the action in the *Shahnameh* (The Book of Kings), the epic poem by Abu'l Qasim Firdausi (or Ferdowsi, ca. 940–1020) commemorating the pre-Islamic Persian kings, is set not in present-day Iran but in Transoxiana. Central Asia was also heterogeneous in its religious heritage. The nomads were shamanist—that is, they believed in the ability of certain individuals to travel back and forth between the material and the spiritual worlds, either to enlist the support of various spiritual forces in pursuit of success in war or to ensure people's health and well-being. Zoroastrianism and Buddhism were the prevalent religions among the sedentary population. In the eighth century, the Uyghurs adopted Manichaeism, and Nestorian Christianity flourished in the oasis cities of the region in the first millennium CE. The religious heritage of Central Asia was truly diverse.

––––––––

In the early eighth century, Transoxiana was conquered by Arab armies belonging to the Umayyad caliphate. Islam had emerged in the oasis cities of Arabia in the early seventh century, and its adherents, also pastoral nomads, embarked on a series of astonishing conquests that brought about the demise of the Sassanid empire in Iran, beat back the Byzantine empire into Anatolia, and created an Arab state that stretched from Spain to Transoxiana by the early eighth century. The Arabs conquered Merv in 671 and Bukhara in 709 and annexed Transoxiana to their empire. The Arab conquests coincided with the greatest expansion of any Chinese dynasty until that point. The Tang controlled much of what is now Xinjiang. The two armies came face to face in 751 at the Battle of Talas (in what is now Kyrgyzstan), where Tang forces were routed and the dynasty's westward expansion came to an end. In 750 the Umayyad dynasty was toppled by the Abbasids, a great deal of whose support came from insurgents in Iran and Transoxiana.

Conversion to Islam was a long-term process, however, and it took several generations for the majority of the sedentary, Persian-speaking population to become Muslim. Nonetheless, by the ninth century Transoxiana was solidly Muslim and had become an integral part of the Muslim world. Over the next two centuries, it produced a number of luminaries of the most fundamental importance in Islamic history. The sayings (*hadith*) of the Prophet Muhammad soon acquired a religious authority second only to that of the Qur'an, and their collection and categorization became a major preoccupation among scholars. Sunni Muslims hold six collections to be canonical. Two of the six compilers, Abu Isma'il al-Bukhari (810–870) and Abu 'Isa Muhammad al-Tirmidhi (825–892), were from Transoxiana, as were the influential jurists Abu Mansur Muhammad al-Maturidi (d. ca. 944) and Burhan al-Din Abu'l Hasan al-Marghinani (d. 1197). The mathematician Muhammad ibn Musa al-Khwarizmi (780–850), who founded algebra (and whose name, through its Latin corruption, gives us the word "algorithm"); the astronomer Ibn Kathir al-Farghani (d. 870); the great scientist Abu Nasr al-Muhammad al-Farabi (d. ca. 950), known as "the second teacher" (after Aristotle); the rationalist philosopher Abu 'Ali Ibn Sina (known in the West as Avicenna, 980–1037); and the geographer Abu Rayhan al-Beruni (973–1050)—figures of absolutely central importance in the history of Islamic civilization in its so-called classical age—were all born in the region. They were part of broader networks of travel and learning that served to make the cities of Transoxiana part of the heartland of the Muslim world. It was in this age that Bukhara and Samarqand acquired their reputation in the wider Muslim world. To a thirteenth-century historian, Bukhara was "the cupola of Islam" in the Muslim East, "like unto Baghdad" (the capital of the Abbasid caliphate), and "its environs are adorned with the brightness of the light of doctors and jurists and its surroundings embellished with the rarest of high attainments."[2]

Given its vast expanse, the caliphate was always largely decentralized, and regional governors had a great deal of leeway. By the middle of the ninth century, they had begun to act as they pleased, paying only the most nominal allegiance to the caliphate. It was in this context that a certain Ismail Samani, a local governor in Transoxiana, established his own dynasty with its capital at Bukhara. Ismail received investiture from the Abbasid caliph, but he was to all intents and purposes a sovereign ruler. The Samanid dynasty that he founded presided over the rebirth of Persian as an Islamicate language. The great scholars we just encountered all wrote in Arabic (and therefore are often misidentified as Arabs), but neither they nor their compatriots ever used Arabic as a language of everyday intercourse. After the Arab conquests, Persian, the language of Transoxiana, had sunk to the level of a vernacular. The Samanids reversed this trend and raised it to a language of administration and culture. Their court patronized the creation of a new literary language, which we now call New Persian (even though today it is over a thousand years old). Written in Arabic script, with a large number of Arabic loanwords, it was Islamic in its sensibility. Its first great poet was Rudaki (858–941), but it was the *Shahnameh*, composed at the Samanid court, that laid the foundations of Persian as an Islamicate language of high culture.

Islam spread more slowly in the neighboring steppe. The first historical reports of large-scale conversion among the Turks date from 960, when 200,000 tents (households) are said to have embraced Islam. By the end of the tenth century, Muslim Turks had become quite common and begun to assume political power. Turkic nomads belonging to the Ghaznavid and Qarakhanid dynasties conquered Transoxiana and launched campaigns of conquest far and wide, going south into India and competing with other Muslim dynasties in eastern Iran and what is now Afghanistan. Other Turkic groups entered military service in dynasties in the Middle East and became an integral part of the political landscape in that region. Over the ensuing centuries, Turks were to found a number of dynasties in the Muslim world. The Saljuqs fought the Byzantines and opened up Anatolia to Turkic settlement, where two centuries later the Ottomans established what became a mighty world empire. Yet the Islamization of the steppe was a long drawn out process that continued into the eighteenth century. Muslim societies interacted with non-Muslims along a long religious frontier that extended from Tibet to

Zungharia and beyond. The eastern oases of Turfan and Qumul were majority Buddhist as late as 1420, when a Muslim envoy to the Ming court noted "large idol-temples of superb beauty" in the two cities.[3]

———

Muslim sovereignty in Transoxiana and Altishahr was broken in the early twelfth century when the Ferghana valley and much of Altishahr were conquered by a new dynasty called the Qara Khitay. They were nomads, most likely of Tungusic speech, who had escaped from the collapse of the Liao empire in Manchuria and northeastern China in 1127. They imposed tribute on the cities and controlled the steppe for the next century, their only challenge coming from a new state in Khwarazm at the mouth of the Amu Darya. However, it was the irruption of the Mongol empire in the early thirteenth century that truly transformed Central Asia. At the dawn of the century, a certain Temüjin managed to unite all Mongol tribes behind him and launched on a series of conquests unrivaled in history. In 1206, he took the imperial title of Chinggis Khan (qa'an) and presided over a series of astonishing military campaigns that brought much of Eurasia under Mongol rule. He conquered China and Central Asia before he died in 1227. His sons continued the conquests, and at its zenith, the Mongol empire incorporated all of the steppe, Transoxiana, the Caucasus, all of Iran, and eastern Europe. Both China and Russia were part of a single imperium in the thirteenth century.

The Mongols achieved the apotheosis of nomadic empire building. Like all their predecessors, they used imperial charisma, a divine mandate, and an efficient system of military organization to achieve success. Unlike earlier nomadic empires, the Mongols conquered their sedentary neighbors and ruled them, commandeering bureaucrats from China and Iran to create systems of administration and taxation. The military campaigns were exceedingly violent, and Mongol brutality became proverbial across Eurasia, but the Mongol empire also created new connections. Historians speak of a *pax Mongolica* that turned most of Eurasia into a single economic zone and facilitated trade across it in an unprecedented fashion. The conquests also remade the politics of the region. They destroyed old elites and reshaped solidarities and affiliations across Eurasia. The Chinggisid family became the royal clan of all of Eurasia, and the principle that only descendants of Chinggis Khan through the male line had the right to rule was enshrined for a long time across the Mongol domains.

In the Chinggisid dispensation, sovereignty belonged to the Chinggisid family as a whole. There was no primogeniture, and all descendants of Chinggis Khan through the male line were eligible to rule and bear the title of khan. This turned out to be a built-in mechanism for instability. In his final testament, Chinggis had divided his realm into four parts (*ulus*) and bequeathed each of them to one of his four sons by his senior wife. The ancestral Mongol homelands and China went to his youngest son, Tolui, while Chinggis's grandson Batu (whose father, Jochi, predeceased Chinggis) received the western steppe, with its path to Europe. Chinggis had appointed his third son, Ögedei, as his heir and the great khan, the leader of the dynasty and symbol of the unity of the empire. The empire continued to expand. Batu's forces subdued the Slavic principalities of Kyivan Rus' and threatened Hungary before turning back unconquered. His *ulus*, which came to be known as the Golden Horde, ruled over the agrarian settlements of Rus' and the steppe north of the Black Sea. In 1258, Chinggis's grandson Hülegü invaded the Middle East and destroyed the Abbasid caliphate, bringing all of Iran and the Fertile Crescent under Mongol rule. Another grandson, Khubilai, expanded Mongol rule into southern China, finally defeating the Song dynasty in 1279. In 1260, during his campaigns, Khubilai became the great khan. He moved the capital to Beijing and adopted a Chinese dynastic title, Yuan, for his empire. There had been several contentious struggles for the title of great khan, and after Khubilai's death in 1294, the title lapsed. The different *ulus* grew apart and even came to blows.

Mongol rule reshaped Central Asia over the course of the thirteenth century. While the region escaped lightly in comparison with some other regions conquered by the Mongols, the damage to both Central Asia's economy and its cultural traditions was still great. The older dynasties were wiped out, and the infrastructure of Islam suffered greatly.

Chinggis Khan's actions in Bukhara in 1220 were emblematic of the initial phase of Mongol conquest. Having sacked the city, he rode into the main mosque and, mounting the pulpit, exclaimed to the assembled multitudes, "The countryside is empty of fodder; fill our horses' bellies." Ata Malik Juvaini, a Muslim historian in Mongol employ who is our best source for these events, recounts that the Mongols "opened all the magazines in the town and began carrying off the grain. And they brought the cases in which Korans were kept out into the courtyard of the mosque, where they cast the Korans right and left and turned these cases into mangers for their horses. After which they circulated cups of wine and sent for the singing-girls of the town to sing and dance for them; while the Mongols raised their voices to the tunes of their own songs. Meanwhile, the *imams, shaikhs, sayyids,* doctors and scholars of the age kept watch over their horses in the stable under the supervision of the equerries, and executed their commands."[4] In the end, however, the Mongols were largely indifferent to the religions of the people they conquered, and they did not actively persecute Islam. However, the religion was displaced from its position of authority, and Islamic law (*shariat*) replaced by the Chinggisid *yasa* as the framework for law and the political imagination.

Yet within a century, the Mongol empire had fragmented. In Central Asia, a new order emerged that preserved many aspects of the Chinggisid dispensation but that was thoroughly indigenized to a Muslim Central Asia. Chinggis had given his second son, Chaghatay, the lands of Altishahr, Zungharia, Transoxiana, and Khwarazm—essentially, the Central Asia we will discuss in this book—as his *ulus.* The name Chaghatay was to have a long career in Central Asia even if the trajectory of the actual *ulus* was turbulent, for Chaghatay's brothers and their descendants coveted his territory and fought for it constantly. Around 1330, the Chaghatayid khan Tarmashirin (r. 1331–1334) converted to Islam. He was not the first of his line to do so, but unlike his predecessors, he attempted to make Islam the official religion in his realm. That precipitated a revolt that overthrew him and caused a split in the khanate, as other Chaghatayids, loyal to Mongol traditions, raised a new khan in the east (Altishahr and the Turfan basin). Tarmashirin's line continued in Transoxiana in the west, with its solidly Muslim population. Thus, by the 1340s, the division between western and eastern Turkestan had become a reality. The east became known in Muslim sources as Mugholistan ("the Land of the Mongols"—that is, of non-Muslim nomads). That religious difference did not last long, however, for the eastern khan Tughluq Temür (r. 1347–1363) converted to Islam along with other princes when he ascended the throne. By the middle of the fourteenth century, the Chaghatay khanate had been divided in two, but in both east and west its rulers had become Muslim and adopted the Turkic speech of the majority of their subjects. They were also dependent on their Turkic subjects for their military force. Only men claiming direct descent from Chinggis could rule, but there was no shortage of those, and there were constant struggles among Chinggis's progeny. This provided leaders of non-Chinggisid tribes, mostly Turkic Muslims, with the opportunity to play kingmaker. Chinggisid princes often became puppets for ambitious Turkic military leaders, who were usually called emir. The most famous emir of all was Timur (1336–1405), who created his own world empire, with its capital at Samarqand.

Timur was a Muslim Turk of the Barlas tribe who by 1370 had defeated his Turkic rivals and reduced the Chaghatayid princes to figureheads. Yet he never claimed to be khan or a ruler in his own right but continued to rule in the name of the descendants of Chinggis Khan. After he married a Chinggisid princess in 1370, he took the title of *kürakän* (son-in-law), and he spent his career trying to emulate, if not surpass, Chinggis. He waged war on the various post-Mongol states, campaigning deep into the lands of the Golden Horde (in present-day Russia and Ukraine); Syria and Iran; and Mugholistan, which he invaded four times. Other campaigns of his broke new ground. He invaded Anatolia (where he defeated Beyazit, the sultan, and almost snuffed out the young Ottoman Empire) and India (where he infamously sacked Delhi in 1398). He was on a campaign against Ming China when he died in 1405. His career of conquest was comparable, both in its extent and its cruelty, to that of Chinggis Khan, and at its height, Timur's charisma had begun to rival that of Chinggis Khan. Yet this charisma was expressed in a different political language. To many contemporaries, and especially to his successors, Timur was Sahib Qiran (the Lord of the Auspicious Conjunction)—an astrological category most likely of Persian origin that had been thoroughly Islamized by the fourteenth century. Timur's birth was supposed to have coincided with an auspicious conjunction of Mars and Jupiter. He was thus a divinely ordained messianic ruler foretold by astrological phenomena. Metaphorically, he also represented conjunctions both of nomadic military prowess with the ethical and administrative ideals of sedentary civilization and of Mongol warrior traditions with Islamic civilization. Timur could embody both the Chinggisid dispensation and a revitalized (if transformed) Islamicate political tradition. He was a Muslim sovereign who adorned his capital with magnificent mosques and patronized Islamic learning. The booty from his campaigns funded the creation of a magnificent imperial capital, but he lived in the nomadic manner in luxurious tents outside the city. His persona had translated the Mongol heritage into an Islamic idiom. For this reason, he was to appeal to twentieth-century nation builders who could see the traditions of the steppe and the sown intertwined in his political legacy.

Timur's empire did not outlast him, but his descendants held on to a sizable chunk of territory on both sides of the Amu Darya. They also drew away from the Chinggisid heritage and emphasized their Islamic credentials. Over the course of the fifteenth century, the Timurid court—first in Samarqand and then in Herat (in present-day Afghanistan)—presided over an efflorescence of high culture, Islamicate in its sensibility and uniquely Central Asian. Timur's grandson Ulughbek established madrasas, hospitals, and an observatory in Samarqand. He was an astronomer of considerable accomplishment, who established the exact angle of the earth's elliptic plane and compiled the most comprehensive catalogue of stars since Ptolemy. The Timurid court also patronized the poet Jami (d. 1492), the painter Bihzad (d. 1535), and the poet and statesman Alisher Nava'i (d. 1501). The most remarkable thing about the Timurid court was the emergence of Turkic as a language of high culture. Turkic languages had been committed to writing in the Arabic script as early as the eleventh century. The Qarakhanid statesman Yusuf of Balasaghun (d. 1077) wrote *Qutadgu Bilig*

(Wisdom of royal glory), a mirror for princes, and Mahmud of Kashgar (d. 1102) compiled a *Compendium of the Languages of the Turks* in Arabic in Baghdad. However, it was at the Timurid court that Turkic became a fully respectable literary language, and Nava'i was its first exponent. This literary standard was called Chaghatay. At about the same time, a different literary variant of Turkic was crystallizing at the Ottoman court in Istanbul. Chaghatay and Ottoman developed in parallel, as eastern and western Turkic. They were both Islamicate in their sensibility and highly ornate, with large numbers of loanwords from Persian and Arabic. They operated as media for the expression of high culture rather than as modes of quotidian intercourse, with which they had little in common. Persian continued to be the language of expression in Transoxiana, but Turkic now took its place alongside it. The high culture—poetry, historiography, painting, and courtly manners—produced at the Timurid court in the fifteenth century was to have a lasting legacy in Central Asia and beyond.

———

The Timurid dynasty was overthrown at the dawn of the sixteenth century by a Chinggisid restoration brought about by a migration-cum-conquest by Chinggisid nomads from the *ulus* of Jochi, also known as the Golden Horde. That khanate had followed a trajectory similar to that of its Chaghatayid counterpart. In 1327, its khan, Özbek (or Uzbek), accepted Islam, after which the khanate became known as the *ulus* of Özbek. It began to weaken and fragment, as internecine warfare among various claimants to the throne destroyed all semblance of political cohesion. The Rus principalities became ever more independent, while Muslim and Turkic-speaking successor states emerged in the Crimea and on the Volga. The eastern part of the *ulus* of Uzbek remained predominantly nomadic. In the fifteenth century, Abulkhayr Khan (r. 1428–1468), a descendant of Jochi's fifth son, Shïban, had established himself as a powerful ruler, but his state fell apart upon his death, and his followers scattered. At the end of the fifteenth century, his grandson Muhammad Shibani Khan led between 200,000 and 400,000 followers south into Transoxiana, where they ousted the Timurids and established their own Uzbek state in Transoxiana. One of the Timurid princes who was driven out was called Zahiruddin Muhammad Babur (1483–1530). He escaped with a handful of followers to Kabul. He found fame and fortune in India, where he founded the Mughal empire that lasted until 1857. The Mughals called themselves Timurids and remained very conscious of their Timurid and Central Asian heritage.

Large-scale nomadic migrations that often turned into invasions and conquest had been a key feature of Eurasian history since antiquity. The Uzbek invasion/migration was one of the last. Shibani Khan's conquest had restored Chinggisid rule over Transoxiana, but it did not undo the cultural transformations of the Timurid era. Like the Timurids, the Shibanids were thoroughly Islamic and patronized Islamic elites. The Shibanid state was a highly decentralized tribal confederacy, but Bukhara was the capital and regained a sense of primacy in Transoxiana as a center of commerce and learning. The high point of the dynasty was the reign of Abdullah Khan II (r. 1583–1598), which saw the construction of a number of madrasas and caravanserais in Bukhara. The Shibanid conquest also transformed the demographics of Transoxiana, implanting a large Turkic population there—many of whose members sedentarized and took up agriculture. Persian remained the language of learning and administration, but the implantation of a Turkic population was to change the linguistic situation in the long term. The Shibanids were overthrown in their turn in 1598 by another Chinggisid dynasty from the Jochid *ulus*. That turn of events had everything to do with the final collapse of the Golden Horde. Muscovy had emerged as the most powerful among the Rus principalities conquered by the Mongols in the 1240s. As the Golden Horde weakened, Muscovy had begun to turn the tables on its former masters. As early as 1397, certain Tatar princes had become vassals of Muscovy. As the sixteenth century dawned, Muscovy was dictating terms to the khanate of Kazan on the Volga. Then, in 1547, Grand Prince Ivan IV ("the Terrible") of Muscovy took the title of tsar, with its imperial connotations—a clear sign of his renunciation of all connection to the steppe political tradition. In 1552, he stormed Kazan and annexed it. It was a Russian *reconquista*, and historians often see it as the founding of what became the Russian empire. Four years later, Ivan marched his armies down the Volga to Astrakhan, the seat of another successor state of the Golden Horde, and annexed it. Muscovy had gained a foothold on the Caspian. Some members of Astrakhan's ruling family fled to Transoxiana, where (a generation later, during a time of dynastic crisis) they managed to dethrone the Shibanids. Chinggisid rule continued in Transoxiana under a new dynasty.

Not everyone had agreed with Shibani Khan's move to the south. Other followers of Abulkhayr seceded and stayed behind in the north under the leadership of Janibeg and Giray Khans, both of Chinggisid descent. These followers came to be known as Qazaq or Kazakh. They remained nomadic and roamed over a large swath of territory north of the Syr Darya, from the Ural River in the west to Lake Balkhash in the east, where they were neighbors to the Zunghars, western Mongols who had adopted Buddhism. For two centuries, the Kazakhs were a major force in Eurasian politics, having relations with Muscovy in the west, the Zunghars in the east, and Transoxiana's Uzbeks in the south, as well as controlling the trade routes that linked them.

In the seventeenth century, then, Chinggisid dynasties ruled all of Central Asia except the Zunghar steppe. The new political order that took shape after the Chinggisid restoration was highly decentralized. In the Kazakh steppe, the leading khans controlled their followers in cooperation with other descendants of Chinggis Khan. By the early eighteenth century, the Kazakh steppe had been divided among three polities called *jüz*, usually translated as "Horde" in Western literature. They were the Junior Horde (Kishi Jüz), Middle Horde (Orta Jüz), and Senior Horde (Ulï Jüz). The city-based states of Transoxiana and Mugholistan were likewise decentralized. The khans were senior members of the Chinggisid dynasty. They had to deal with other Chinggisids as well as with the non-Chinggisid Turkic tribes, who provided the states' military manpower. The Turkic military elite (the emirs) expected a share of the revenues extracted from agriculture and trade, and they could always switch allegiance from one Chinggisid to another. This made for low state capacity and perpetual political instability.

The period after the Chinggisid restoration is often seen as one of isolation and decline. The rise of European maritime trade is supposed to have dealt the Silk Road a mortal blow by shifting trans-Eurasian trade to oceans and thereby consigned Central Asia to a centuries-long decline. The basic assumptions behind this paradigm have been thoroughly questioned in recent scholarship, but it retains a tenacious hold on our imaginations. Scholars have documented the continuing strength of Eurasian trade that linked Central Asia to India in the south, China in the east, Russia in the north, and Iran in the southwest.[5] Trade between Russia and China also passed through the steppe. Trade across the Eurasian steppe was, in fact, of long standing. The principalities of Rus had first emerged in the ninth century as trading stations established by mostly Scandinavian merchants to control trade that brought Central Asian and Middle Eastern silver to Europe. That trade never collapsed. In fact, protecting the trade routes was a major reason for Russian expansion on the steppe in the eighteenth century. For China, too, the Central Asian trade was significant—enough for the Ming dynasty, which replaced the Mongol Yuan dynasty in 1368, to control it by restricting the number of merchants allowed into China. Imperial attempts at controlling trade will play a large part in the story this book tells.

———

The Chinggisid dispensation held, but it was being challenged by other kinds of charisma. Timur was one example of this. Another resided in Islam. The traumas of the Mongol conquest and the destruction that accompanied it had given rise to numerous religious movements that ranged from pietistic through millenarian to antinomian. The fifteenth century saw the consolidation of Sufi networks across Central Asia. Sufism is a complex phenomenon—often problematically glossed as "Islamic mysticism"—in which initiates seek proximity to the divine through rituals of remembrance of God (*zikr*) and mediation (*muraqaba*). Sufism was communal: the seeker was initiated into a path (*tariqa*) by a master, whose authority lay in his lineage. The master-disciple relationship was all-important, and it created intense loyalties.

Across generations, the master-disciple links turned into multiple chains of transmission (*silsila*), each with its own rituals and modes of interpretation. The troublous times of the Mongol invasion produced all manner of Sufi orders. By the fifteenth century, such orders had emerged as forms of both religious practice and social organization. Sufi masters (shaykhs) could accumulate great influence as advisors to rulers, which could turn into landed wealth. Central Asia was the birthplace of some of the most prominent Sufi orders in the Muslim world. The Naqshbandi order founded by Baha'uddin Naqshband (d. 1389) was to spread around the world. His disciples were responsible for the conversion of many Chaghatayid rulers. The Sufis offered moral advice to the newly Islamized Chaghatayid rulers (and thereby gained political and monetary capital), but they could also present themselves as alternative sources of authority and vie for political power.

By the turn of the sixteenth century, the caravan of religions that had passed through Central Asia in the previous millennium was a thing of the past. The agrarian zones of Transoxiana and Altishahr were predominantly Muslim. The steppe remained a religious frontier, with Buddhism dominant in Zungharia, while Islam had made deep inroads among steppe nomads. Islam was thoroughly indigenized, however, and had become a crucial marker of community and identity. Communities remembered their conversion to Islam not through historical narratives of invasion, conquest, and conversion, but through myths of origin that conflated the conversion of rulers with the formation of a new Muslim community. The conversion was usually the work of holy men, usually Sufi masters, whose proximity to God endowed them with the ability to perform miracles. Satuq Bughra Khan (ca. 920–955), the Qarakhanid ruler of the Kashgar oasis, is reputed to be the first Turkic prince to convert to Islam. He secretly became a Muslim in his youth after contact with merchants from Transoxiana. He then rebelled against his uncle (the ruler), dethroned him, and converted his subjects to Islam. Özbek Khan, the Chinggisid ruler of the Golden Horde, was at a Mongol drinking ceremony when four holy men arrived and invited him to convert to Islam. The khan ordered his shamans to debate the newcomers. The debates turned into a competition of miracles. The two parties agreed to a trial by fire: one member of each party would enter an oven fired with ten cartloads of tamarisk branches, and "whoever emerges without being burned, his religion will be true." When the time came, Baba Tükles, one of the Muslim holy men, volunteered for the ordeal. He walked into the oven, reciting the Sufi *zikr* and survived, while his counterpart had to be forced into the oven and was instantly consumed by the fire. The khan and all those present became Muslims.[6] Tughluq Temür, the Chaghatayid khan of Mugholistan, met a certain Shaykh Jamaluddin when he was still as young man. Impressed by the meeting, he promised to become a Muslim if he ever became khan. By the time that happened, Jamaluddin had died, but his son Arshaduddin reminded the khan of his promise. Tughluq Temür kept his promise and became a Muslim, along with all but one of his princes. The one skeptic was a man called Jaras, who insisted that he would convert only if Jamaluddin could overpower one of his champion wrestlers. Arshaduddin duly defeated the man with a single blow, upon which "a great outcry arose among the assemblage. That day a hundred twenty thousand people shaved their heads and became Muslim. The Khan circumcised himself, and the light of Islam eradicated the darkness of heathenism and spread throughout the territory of Chaghatay Khan."[7]

In the eleventh century, Mahmud Kashgari had declared that the "Turks . . . all trace back to Turk, the son of Japheth, son of Noah,"[8] and that story became axiomatic in all Muslim societies in Central Asia. According to Islamic belief, Adam and Noah were the first among a large number of messengers that God has sent to humanity as bearers of divine guidance. They were part of a chain of divine intervention in human life that culminated with Muhammad, the "seal of the prophets." The children of Japheth were thus Muslims from the beginning, but they had fallen off the true path and ceased being Muslim. Their conversion at the hand of sacred figures then became merely a return to a prior condition. Other myths placed the mausoleum of Ali, the son-in-law of the Prophet Muhammad, in Mazar-i Sharif (in present-day Afghanistan) or in Shah-i Mardan in the Ferghana valley. A mountain peak near the latter site is called Solomon's Throne and reputed to be the place where

Solomon first turned to God. Such reliquary sites dissolved time and space and connected Central Asia to the core of the Islamic tradition.

It is important to remember that in this age, being Muslim was a matter of belonging to a community that was innately Muslim, not a matter of individual belief. What Islam meant in communal life was always open to interpretation and hence contestation. The social and political effects of Islam were always a matter of struggle between different forces. It was the ever-shifting relations between those who wielded political power and those who possessed the authority to interpret Islam—the scholars (*ulama*, "the learned") and the Sufis—that determined what Islam meant at a given historical moment. The changing interpretations of Islam and contestations over them are a major theme in this book.

———

This breakneck-speed overview of Central Asia's history up to the eighteenth century was meant to introduce certain key features of the heritage that Central Asians possessed as they entered the modern period. Multiple legacies—those of ancient urban life in the oases, steppe nomadism, Islam, and the Chinggisid empire—coexisted. Central Asians made sense of their own societies through a number of binaries: Turk versus Tajik, nomad versus sedentary, and the steppe versus the sown. These were important to the cultural imagination of Central Asia, but they should not be confused with social reality, which was always more complicated. In Transoxiana, not only did nomads and agriculturalists live in close proximity, but many nomads also practiced agriculture. The linguistic situation was equally complex. Persian had become a language of high culture by the eleventh century, as had Chaghatay Turkic by the fifteenth. In both cases, the written language was far from ordinary speech, which varied enormously across dialects. Writing was a specialized activity. Written texts were meant as much to show virtuosity and a mastery of cultural codes as to convey meaning. Persian and Chaghatay shared a number of cultural models, a common universe of meaning and symbolism, and a common vocabulary. It is more fruitful to think of Central Asian culture in the early modern age as Turko-Persian. Persian was far less important among the Kazakhs, and by the eighteenth century, its use was declining in Khwarazm and Altishahr as well. Many people—especially in Transoxiana—were bilingual, but it was the common set of cultural references and practices across the linguistic divide that made the culture Turko-Persian.

EMPIRE

ON A WINTRY DAY in February 1881, the Russian foreign minister Niko-lai Giers shook hands with the Qing diplomat Zeng Jize as the two signed a treaty bringing the so-called Ili Crisis to an end. The crisis had involved territory in the Ili region of Central Asia that was claimed by China but had been occupied by Russia in 1870 during an uprising that had vanquished Qing rule in Central Asia. The Treaty of St. Petersburg formalized the means of the region's return to China. The crisis is re-membered today mostly because it was the one occasion in the nine-teenth century when the beleaguered Qing empire came out ahead in a diplomatic tussle with a European power. However, the treaty was also a significant landmark in the history of Central Asia. By creating a stable border between the two empires, now subject to international law, the treaty formalized the division of Central Asia between them. The steppe had been enclosed.

The division of Central Asia between Russian and Chinese zones was to prove quite enduring. The boundary marked out in St. Petersburg exists, more or less, even today, though both the Russian and Qing em-pires are long gone. Yet the process that led to this division was long and complex, and we should start by making sense of it before exploring the implications of that division for Central Asia. We will be operating in a world in which empires were the normal form of political life—a world with its own logic that we will need to understand on its own terms. And we will see that very little about the rise of these two empires in Central Asia was foretold. Contingencies and accidents had as much as anything else to do with the shape that Central Asia took in the age of empire.

2

The Manchu Conquest of Eastern Turkestan

BETWEEN 1755 AND 1759, the armies of the Manchu empire overran Zungharia and Altishahr and incorporated the Muslims of Eastern Turkestan into a China-based political order. The Manchus had conquered China in the first half of the seventeenth century and established the Qing dynasty. At about the same time, the western Mongols of the Zunghar steppe had established one last steppe empire. The two contended for power for a century, before the Qing—which had far greater resources, extracted from the agrarian economy of China—was able to annihilate the Zunghars in a series of lightning-quick victories in the 1750s. The Zunghars had ruled over Altishahr for several decades at that point, but it now became part of the Qing empire. A conflict between two Inner Asian empires had thus made Xinjiang a part of China.

Bitter rivalries among Muslim elites of Altishahr had brought the region under Zunghar rule. By the middle of the seventeenth century, the Chinggisid dispensation was being challenged from a number of directions. The Sufi orders that had emerged after the upheavals of the Mongol conquest had acquired a great deal of wealth and influence. Sufi masters functioned as spiritual guides to rulers, giving them another layer of legitimacy. In return, the masters enjoyed grants of land and

revenue. The most important Sufi figures in Altishahr were the descendants of the Naqshbandi master Ahmad Kasani, known as Makhdum-i
A'zam ("the Greatest Master"), who moved to Altishahr from Transoxiana in the 1580s and acquired great influence at the Chaghatayid court
in Yarkand. Two lineages, coming from Makhdum-i A'zam's different
sons, soon began to compete for influence and followers. During the
1670s, Afaq Khoja, the eponymous head of the Afaqi branch, lost the
favor of the Chaghatayid ruler of Yarkand and was forced into exile.
He spent a decade proselytizing in Kashmir, Tibet, and Gansu. During
his travels, he is supposed to have met Ngawang Lobsang Gyatso, the
fifth Dalai Lama, in person. We learn from a much later hagiographical
account that the Khoja and the lama had a competition of miracles that,
unsurprisingly, Afaq Khoja won handily. Astonished, the Dalai Lama
asked Afaq Khoja who he was and where he came from. "I am a scholar
and a khoja of the Muslim tribe," he replied. "Specifically, the people of
Kashgar and Yarkand are my disciples and devotees. Recently someone
came and deprived me of these cities and drove me out. My request is
that you instruct someone to restore this homeland of mine into my
hands." The Dalai Lama was a forceful ruler who had unified most of
Tibet under a reformist brand of Buddhism and whose spiritual influence extended into western Mongolia. He told Afaq Khoja that while it
was very difficult for an army to go to Altishahr from Tibet, he would
be happy to have his Mongol disciples provide assistance. He wrote a
letter to Galdan Khan, the ruler of the Zunghars, asking him to deliver
the two cities to Afaq Khoja.[1]

The Zunghars were a loose confederation of western Mongol tribes
in the lands north of the Tien-Shan Mountains that had been united
into a single state by Batur Hongtaiji in 1635. They came to control the
long-distance trade among Russia, Transoxiana, and China. Fueled by
this trade, the new state succeeded quite spectacularly. Over the next
decades the Zunghars built walled cities, expanded agriculture and
trade, and accumulated enough resources to equip their armies with
cannons and gunpowder, much of which was produced locally. They
adopted Tibetan Buddhism and created a written language. Like all
steppe empires, they were expansionist. Galdan obliged the Dalai Lama

and drove out Ismail Khan, the last Chaghatayid ruler of Yarkand. He placed Afaq Khoja on the throne and left him to his own devices in return for an annual tribute. A later Eastern Turkestani source suggests that an annual tribute of 48,000 *tengas* (ounces of silver) was levied on Kashgar and was collected by Zunghar missions that arrived every harvest season. There does not seem to have been a permanent garrison stationed in Altishahr.[2] A Sufi figure thus acquired unprecedented temporal power in Altishahr under the tutelage of Buddhist nomads.

The enduring stereotype that religion and politics are completely intertwined in Islam is historically untenable. For most of Islamic history, religious and political authority have resided in different groups, and the relationship between Islam and power has been quite fluid. Religious authority belonged to individuals distinguished by their learning and lineage, which created a certain charisma. By the seventeenth century, the earlier divides between legal scholars (*ulama*) and the Sufis had largely been bridged by the rise of Sufi orders such as the Naqshbandiya that emphasized engagement with the world, rather than its renunciation, as the correct path to God. Kingship, however, retained its aura. The possession of the throne could often be its own justification, and especially in the post-Mongol dispensation, Chinggisid descent was a basic requirement of legitimacy. The *ulama* were willing to consider legitimate all rulers who permitted them to enforce the *shariat*. But the situation was always dynamic. The Khojas of Altishahr had gained their wealth and influence by advising Chinggisid rulers but had then developed greater ambitions. Afaq Khoja, therefore, represents one end of the spectrum, in which the Sufi *ishan* (master) became the king. Sufi ritual became part of public life, and Sufi shrines and lodges the prime of political power, all under the suzerainty of the Zunghars.[3] Things fell apart pretty quickly after Afaq Khoja's death in 1694, however, as his two sons from different marriages fought for control. The Chaghatayids attempted a comeback, but it was the Ishaqi Khojas, the great rivals of the Afaqis, who came out ahead. The Zunghars placed their leader Daniyal Khoja on the throne and deported members of Afaq Khoja's lineage to the Zunghar capital in Ghulja, where they remained as hostages. The Zunghars were happy to extract revenue from

Altishahr but otherwise let it be. But if the burden of Zunghar rule sat lightly on Altishahr, the Zunghar state was keen to develop agriculture in its heartland to have a regular source of grain. It moved a group of peasants from Altishahr north to Zungharia, where they constructed irrigation channels and worked the land. This community acquired the name of Taranchi ("agriculturalist") when its members settled in the north, which was largely nomadic and non-Muslim. They were the first Turkic-speaking Muslim population in the steppe lands of Zungharia.

———

The Zunghars' expansion also brought them into conflict with the Qing. Manchu warriors had established the dynasty when they overthrew the Ming and conquered China at about the same time as the Zunghars were consolidating their state. The Manchus shared many Inner Asian traditions with the steppe. During the early stages of their conquest, they had subdued eastern Mongol tribes and incorporated them into the empire as a military elite. Nurhaci, the founder of the Qing, married the daughter of a Mongol chief, and intermarriage between the imperial family and Mongol nobles became common. The Qing came up with a fascinating synthesis of Inner Asian political ideology and Chinese methods of organization to run the most populous empire of the time. The Qing was a dynastic empire run by a coalition of Manchu and Mongol warriors who saw themselves as distinct from the various subject populations they had conquered. Their relations with the Zunghars began amicably enough, with the Zunghars sending a diplomatic mission to Beijing in 1653, but the relations soon deteriorated. The Qing expected the Zunghars to behave as vassals, but Galdan (r. 1677–1697), the conqueror of Altishahr, had greater ambitions. Matters came to a head, and the first of many Qing-Zunghar wars began in 1687. The Qing, with the resources of a vast agrarian empire at its command, held the advantage, but distance and space, as well as speed and mobility, favored the Zunghars, who were able to ward off the Qing time and time again. The Zunghars were a constant thorn in the side of the Qing, but the latter realized the danger of imperial overreach and spent several decades building up defenses and laying out military routes in the west. This consolidation took Qing influence into eastern Turkestan. The Muslim *begs* of Qumul and Turfan became vassals and were incorporated into the banner system of military administration.

The death of the Zunghar ruler Galdan Tsereng in 1745 touched off a succession struggle that gave the Qing an opening. When Amursana, one of the contenders, sought Qing help in 1755, the Qianlong emperor was happy to oblige, and Qing armies defeated Amursana's rival, Dawachi. However, Amursana was not content to be a Qing vassal and rose up in revolt. At this, Qianlong seems to have come to the end of his patience. He ordered a full-blown invasion of Zunghar lands with the aim of solving the problem once and for all. "Show no mercy at all to the rebels," he commanded. "Only the old and weak should be saved. Our previous military campaigns were too lenient. If we act as before, our troops will withdraw, and further trouble will occur."[4] It was an enormous campaign, with immensely long supply lines across inhospitable territory, but the Qing armies pulled it off. A series of battles over the next two years destroyed the Zunghars as a people. Qing armies killed a fifth of the male population and distributed Zunghar women and children as servants to the commanders. Another two-fifths of the Zunghars died of smallpox, and the rest fled westward. Zungharia was largely depopulated and annexed to the Qing. "With this policy," Peter Perdue, the leading historian of the era, writes, "the Qing succeeded in imposing a 'final solution' to China's northwest frontier problems."[5]

Qing expansion might have stopped at this point, but circumstances conspired to keep it going. The Zunghars held Afaq Khoja's grandsons Burhan ud-Din and Jahan as hostages in Ghulja. The Qing freed them and gave them logistical support to establish them as Qing vassals in Altishahr. Upon Amursana's revolt, however, the brothers also renounced their allegiance to the Qing and sought to establish power in their own names. The Qianlong emperor authorized a punitive expedition, and over the next two years Qing armies chased the Khojas and their supporters across Altishahr and into western Turkestan. The brothers found refuge with Sultan Shah, the ruler of Badakhshan (in what is now northern Afghanistan), but that proved only a temporary reprieve. As Qing armies arrived in hot pursuit, Sultan Shah dragged his feet, but he ultimately had the brothers killed and delivered up the head of Khoja Jahan to the Manchus. The trophy was taken to Beijing and ceremonially presented to the emperor before being put on display on the main gate of the Forbidden City.[6]

Chasing the two Khojas had brought Qing forces farther west than any China-based armies had gone in a thousand years. Qing armies camped on the outskirts of Tashkent, while one unit reached the town of Talas, the scene of the famous battle a millennium earlier between Chinese and Arab forces. Qing forces sought submission from local rulers wherever they went. By the time the campaign was called off, several Kazakh and Kyrgyz tribes; the ruler of the new state of Khoqand, in the Ferghana valley; and numerous petty rulers from as far away as Badakhshan, Chitral, and Baltistan had offered submission. The Qing did not occupy these lands, and the submission often remained notional. However, Zungharia and Altishahr were occupied and tied to a state based in China. The territory of the Qing empire had tripled in size.

————

The Qing state was based in China, but to what extent was it a Chinese state? A cohort of so-called New Qing historians have argued persuasively in recent decades that the Qing was not simply another dynasty that had thoroughly assimilated to Chinese culture. Rather, it was an Inner Asian empire of conquest, and China was only one part (although a very important part) of a much wider empire. The Qing drew on both Inner Asian and Chinese political traditions. In common with any number of Inner Asian empires, the Qing took difference for granted and used different methods of rule for different groups of subjects, each of which had an equivalent relationship to the ruling house. The Chinese subjects of the Qing constituted the vast bulk of the population, but they remained only one of several cultural entities in the empire. As James Millward writes, "Though the empire [was] centripetal, at the center [lay] neither an abstract 'Chinese civilization,' nor even the Confucian Son of Heaven, but rather the Aisin Gioro house, in the person

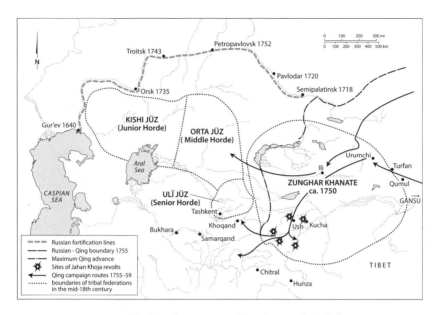

MAP 2.1. The Manchu conquest of Zungharia and Altishahr

of the many-faceted Qing emperor."[7] The emperor presented himself differently to different groups of his subjects. To Han Chinese, he was the *huangdi*, the emperor and the bearer of the Mandate of Heaven. To Manchus and Mongols, he was a khan in the Inner Asian tradition, and to Tibetans, he was the *chakravartin*, the turner of the wheels of Buddhist law. In Muslim Central Asia, the emperor presented himself as a ruler in both Chinggisid and Islamic terms, as the upholder of justice and order.[8] This imperial ideology led to differentiated practices of rule across the empire. In China proper (*neidi*), the Qing assimilated the Chinese bureaucracy, examination system, and Confucian cosmological order, even as they kept the Han Chinese population at a distance. In Chinese cities, Qing garrisons lived in walled compounds that spatially differentiated them from the local population. In non-Chinese areas, the Qing aspired not to assimilation to a Chinese core, but to the maintenance of power through the recognition of difference. The vast territories of the Zunghar empire were incorporated into the Qing empire on these terms.

The Qing called the territory they conquered Xinjiang (meaning, as noted above, "New Dominion"). It was occupied by Manchu and Mongol banner forces and ruled indirectly through local elites. Qing interest was focused on the north, where the steppe provided sufficient fodder for the cavalry and where geopolitical competition with Russia had become an urgent issue. It was the seat of the Ili General, governor of the new territory and leader of the vast bulk of the army of occupation (which numbered around forty thousand until the middle of the nineteenth century, divided evenly between Manchu and Mongol bannermen and ordinary Han soldiers). The Qing also sponsored the settlement of Chinese peasants on state farms to fill the land that had been left largely unpopulated by the genocide of the Zunghars. Settlers each received thirty *mu* (about two hectares) of land, tools, seeds, a horse, and a loan of two silver taels to establish themselves.[9] The response was not overwhelming, but early on the north emerged as the bastion of Qing power in the region. In the east, the oases of Qumul and Turfan occupied a special place. They had long historical connections, both commercial and political, with China proper, and their Muslim rulers had submitted to the Qing well before the defeat of the Zunghars. The situation was rather different in the south (which the Qing called Huibu, "Muslim region"). The military presence was thinner and largely restricted to troops on three-year rotations. Each oasis was overseen by superintendents (*banshi dachen*), who were answerable to councilors based in Kashgar and Yarkand, and eventually to the Ili General in Ghulja. These superintendents were mostly Manchu or Mongol bannermen, and they were concerned primarily with defense. Civil administration—the business of tax collection, adjudication of disputes, supervision of bazaars—was given over to Muslim officials, while the local Muslim population continued to be subject to Islamic law, administered by the *begs* and *akhunds*. Many of these Muslim officials came from Qumul and Turfan, eastern regions with a longer history of connection to the Qing. Emin Khoja, the *beg* of Turfan, was given the hereditary rank of *junwang* ("commandery prince") and appointed as the first superintendent in Altishahr, with headquarters in Yarkand. He was responsible for much of the correspondence with the Qing's outer vassals in the immediate aftermath of the conquest and instrumental in having the remains of the two Khojas delivered to Beijing.[10] Under Qing military occupation, Altishahr was run by a Muslim elite.

Qing power was based in walled fortresses built across Xinjiang. (Qing garrisons in China proper were walled off as well.) In the north, Qing fortresses grew into substantial towns with a significant Chinese presence. Ürümchi developed quite early as a commercial center. A traveler in 1777 described it as "the most prosperous and populated place outside the Pass."[11] In the oasis cities of the south, the Qing built fortresses alongside existing cities. These were called new cities (*xincheng*) or Manchu cities (*Mancheng*). In Kashgar, the walled compound—built two *li* (one kilometer) northwest of the old city—contained barracks, the armory, and government buildings. The walled garrisons were essential for defense, and they also inscribed in space the distinction between the rulers and the ruled. The rulers were Manchu and Mongol, while the ruled were the local Turkic Muslims. Han Chinese occupied a unique place in this dispensation. Chinese peasants were settled in the north. In the south, they came mostly as merchants. Supplying the armies was big business, but Han merchants also acquired interests in retail trade across the region and in the trade with Russia. The Qing did not permit Han merchants to reside permanently in Altishahr or to bring their families there with them. This was a mixture of caution—an effort not to destabilize the nascent order by overburdening the compact Muslim populations in relatively densely populated oases—and a lack of interest in the south. Han merchants lived outside the old cities, in or near the citadels built by the Qing. A significant part of the Chinese population that arrived in Xinjiang was Muslim. Chinese-speaking Muslims, now called Hui, had formed a distinct community in China for centuries. In Xinjiang, where they were called Dungan or Tungan in local Turkic, they had a double identity, sharing their faith with the Turkic population of the new frontier and their language with the Han merchants and other settlers. The Qing considered them a subset of the Han and made them subject to Qing, not Islamic, law. Given that Xinjiang was ruled by Manchu military officials, not the Han, the Dungan did not have a clear intermediary role in the region. Indeed, they were much closer to Han merchants or peasants and often served the Qing. Islamic solidarity did not define their relationship to the Turkic-speaking Muslim population of the new Qing frontier.

Members of the Turkic Muslim elite bore many different titles, but collectively they were called *wang*. The highest ranking among them were regularly received at court in Beijing, their biographies were included in official records, and their portraits were displayed in the Hall of Purple Radiance in the Forbidden City. The *wang*s of Qumul ruled their district as practically autonomous lords, enjoying the right to the corvée labor of their subjects. Other *wang*s were less magnificent but nevertheless part of the aristocracy of the empire. The system of indirect rule made it possible for local Muslims to imagine that they were still part of an Islamic order. Muslim *wang*s presented two different faces to the Qing and to local Muslim society. To the Qing, they spoke in Manchu and later in Chinese and celebrated their subjugation in the vocabulary of Qing ceremonial. To Muslim society, they presented themselves as servants of Islam and seldom mentioned the Qing. After Emin Khoja's death, his son, Sulayman *wang*, built a madrasa in Turfan to honor his memory. Its façade bears inscriptions in both Chinese and Turkic. The Chinese inscription openly expresses Emin's status as a "returned servant" of "Emperor Qianlong of the Great Qing."[12] The Turkic inscription makes no mention of the Qing and gives thanks only to God. When the Qing emperor was mentioned in Muslim sources, he was called "Khaqan-i Chin" ("the emperor of China"), using a Chinggisid term long indigenized in Central Asia. Indirect rule made it possible for Muslim elites in Qing Xinjiang to imagine that they still existed in an Islamic order. There were also other ways of pretending that Altishahr had not been conquered by non-Muslims. Writing at the beginning of the twentieth century, Molla Musa Sayrami asserted that the first *wang*s had actually asked for the responsibility from the Qing in the face of local disorder. A number of men had gathered to discuss the crisis in the country, he wrote. Because of the incompetence of the Khojas, "the land and the people have been ruined," they argued, and they decided to ask the "*khaqan* of China" for military help. "If some troops come and take the government from the Khojas, and Altishahr becomes a part of the khanate of

China, then our land will prosper and our children will be tranquil."
Seven men went to the *khaqan* of China to petition for help. The emperor
not only sent a large number of troops to bring order to Altishahr but
also rewarded the seven men for their services with high posts and titles.
Sayrami also recounted a legend claiming that the emperors of China
had been Muslim in the past.[13] Such a construal of history softened the
reality of Altishahr's incorporation into a non-Muslim empire.

Yet for all that, the legitimacy of Qing rule in Xinjiang remained precarious. The *beg*s might project their authority in Islamic and Central
Asian terms, but the Qing could never fully co-opt Islamic authority.
Discontent with maladministration and abuse of power by both Manchu officers and Muslim *beg*s combined with anxieties about the fate of
Muslim women to fuel a number of rebellions. The first one broke out
in the far western town of Ush (or Uch Turpan) in 1764. The Qing did
not allow troops or Chinese merchants to bring their families with
them. Prostitution therefore flourished, and Qing administrators and
banner troops took Muslim women as wives or concubines.[14] In Ush in
1764, the Qing superintendent Sucheng and his son were abducting
local women, while Abdullah, the local hakim *beg*, extorted money from
the population. Sucheng's dragooning of 240 men to carry his luggage
on an official caravan to Beijing sparked a rebellion in which the town's
population slaughtered Abdullah, Sucheng, and the Qing garrison. The
walled city then held out for several months against the punitive expedition that arrived. Qing vengeance was severe. When the city finally surrendered, some 2,350 men were executed, and about 8,000 women and
children were transported to Ili as slaves. Yet many other rebellions followed. Others were to be connected to developments in western Turkestan, beyond the Qing borders.

3

Khoqand and Qing Silver

ONE OF THE PETTY PRINCES whom Qing generals encountered in their sweep through Central Asia was Erdene Biy, the ruler of the newly established state of Khoqand in the Ferghana valley. Erdene had little choice but to welcome the Qing envoys and to submit to the Qianlong emperor. The submission imposed few constraints upon him, however. Indeed, he and his successors used the Qing connection to ensure immense growth that was to make Khoqand into a regional power and even allow it to dictate terms in Altishahr for a brief period.

Khoqand had emerged at the beginning of the eighteenth century in the context of a long-term regional crisis that had weakened the Chingissid Tuqay-Timurid dynasty that ruled Bukhara. Chinggisid legitimacy still required a great deal of generosity on the part of the rulers to keep their followers happy. A long-term financial crisis had made it increasingly difficult for the dynasty to keep its non-Chinggisid Uzbek emirs loyal and obedient. The emirs' discontent took the form of refusal to remit revenues to the capital or answer summons when the khan declared war. In this process, the Ferghana valley slipped out of the dynasty's control. Into the political vacuum stepped a group of Khojas, related to those of Altishahr, who aspired to political power. At some time around 1706, an Uzbek emir called Shahrukh massacred them and took power in his own name. Shahrukh and his descendants were lucky in a way, for the Ferghana valley escaped a number of calamities that struck the rest of Transoxiana in the first half of the eighteenth century and allowed their state to take hold.

The Zunghars' expansion had led them into conflict with the Kazakhs. In 1723, a major Zunghar victory saw the Kazakhs scatter south and west in what came to be called a "Barefooted Flight"—a desperate retreat toward Transoxiana, where their arrival brought the Tuqay-Timurid dynasty close to collapse. But it was the unconnected invasion by the armies of Nadir Shah, the Turkmen conqueror from Iran, that sounded the death knell of the Chingissid order in Transoxiana. Nadir had started out as the small-time head of a band of raiders near Mashhad. As the Safavid dynasty crumbled as a result of a revolt by warlords from its eastern periphery (in present-day Afghanistan), Nadir consolidated his power and eventually took the crown himself. He campaigned far and wide—west into the Ottoman Empire; east into India, where his sack of Delhi began the end of the Mughal Empire; and north into Transoxiana, which his armies invaded in both 1737 and 1740. Nadir's strength lay in his command of a huge multiethnic army and his use of cannons and firearms. Estimates of the size of his army range from 80,000 to 200,000 troops, an enormous number. Composed of men levied from the many territories he had conquered, the army was paid regularly and organized on a decimal system. His gunpowder weaponry was unlike anything Central Asia had seen before. A single battle convinced Abulfayz Khan of Bukhara to submit rather than fight. Although Nadir left Abulfayz on his throne as a vassal, the former's conquests had sealed the dynasty's fate. When Nadir was assassinated in 1747 by one of his followers, an Uzbek officer in his army, Muhammad Rahim of the Manghit tribe staged a coup in Bukhara. He had Abulfayz assassinated and replaced by a puppet khan of Chingissid origins. A decade later, Muhammad Rahim gave up the charade and assumed full power in his own name. The Manghit dynasty he founded was to last into the twentieth century.[1]

Nadir Shah's campaigns in Transoxiana had plunged the region to its nadir. Samarqand had been depopulated, leaving its trade collapsed, madrasas desolated, and agriculture and irrigation damaged. Bukhara fared a little better and quickly saw a considerable revival. The Manghits made up for their lack of Chingissid legitimacy by turning to Islam. They patronized the *ulama* and the madrasas, so that by the middle of the nineteenth century, the city had become known as *Bukhara-yi sharif* (Bukhara the Noble) and was considered a major center of Islamic learning—drawing students from across Central Asia as well as from the Volga-Urals lands to the north.[2] Long-distance trade with Russia continued, and the emirs of Bukhara also undertook the modernization of their military. The Manghits sought to undermine the power of the tribes by creating a standing army directly answerable to the palace and promoting to high positions outsiders (usually Iranian or Zunghar slaves captured in battle) personally beholden to them. In Khwarazm to the north, the Qonghirat Uzbeks ruled in their own name. They fostered a close relationship with the neighboring Turkmens, which allowed them to beat back rival Uzbek tribes. Khiva prospered as an entrepôt, and the nineteenth century saw considerable construction in the city. Neither the Qing nor the Russians played a significant part in these developments. Transoxiana remained part of a different diplomatic theater, much more closely tied to the south.

The Ferghana valley escaped the attentions of Nadir Shah. In fact, the general strife in Transoxiana produced a large-scale migration into the valley, which gradually became a densely populated center of agricultural life and saw its population increase steadily throughout the eighteenth century. It was in this context that the Qing drew Khoqand into its orbit. Erdene's submission to the Qing imposed few constraints on him, however, and brought him many advantages. He was allowed to send tribute missions to the Qing that returned with lavish gifts from the emperor and could be accompanied by merchants exempted from the usual tariffs. Erdene began the custom of sending as many tribute missions to the Qing as the latter would allow. By one count, Khoqand dispatched forty-eight missions to Kashgar between 1761 and 1821, eight of which were allowed to proceed to Beijing.[3] Submission also brought the right for Khoqandi merchants to trade in Xinjiang at favorable tax rates. Ferghana merchants had long traded in Eastern Turkestan. Now, Khoqand's relationship with the Qing brought a massive expansion in their activity. Over the next two or three generations, Khoqand's Andijani merchants established vast networks in Eastern Turkestan and cemented an intermediary position in the trade between Russia and the Qing.

Commercial growth fueled significant territorial expansion.[4] By the turn of the nineteenth century, Khoqand had become a significant regional power. Erdene's great-grandson Alim Khan (r. 1799–1811) implemented a series of military reforms—including the creation of a standing army—that allowed Khoqand to increase its territory manifold. Khoqandi forces pushed northward into land held by Kyrgyz and Kazakh nomads to better control the trade routes. The troops built fortresses along the Chü River and far down the Syr Darya and acquired a stronger hold over the steppe than any sedentary state had managed since the time of Timur. The Ferghana valley became a magnet for immigration from both Transoxania and Altishahr. The khans of Khoqand also oversaw the construction of irrigation canals, which led to massive growth in agriculture. The Ferghana valley became a densely populated center of agricultural life.

Alim also took the lofty title of khan, which was by custom reserved for those who could claim Chingissid descent through the male line. Alim presided over the creation of a new legitimizing myth that connected the Shahrukhid dynasty to Timur via Zahiruddin Muhammad Babur, the founder of the Mughal empire in India. Babur was a princeling of Timurid origins who was ousted from his ancestral homeland by the conquering armies of Shibani Khan's Uzbeks. According to the legend, he had left behind an infant son in a golden cradle, who was saved by local villagers and became the progenitor of the Ming tribe to which the Shahrukhid dynasty belonged. Along with advancing a fictive claim to Timurid lineage, Alim's brother and successor, Umar Khan (r. 1811–1822), created a court culture modeled explicitly on that of the Timurids by offering patronage to poets, artists, and historians from across Central Asia. Umar himself was a poet of some accomplishment. His senior wife, Nodira, also wrote poetry, and both held literary salons. Khoqand became the center of a literary renaissance in Chaghatay. Alim also cultivated his Islamic credentials. He sponsored the construction of a major mosque and a number of madrasas and provided sinecures for the learned. He took on the title of *amir ul-muslimin* ("commander of the Muslims") to go with that of khan. Chroniclers were kind to him, giving him the reputation of a pious ruler and remembering his reign fondly.

Umar died at the age of thirty-six, his fondness for wine being partly responsible for his early demise. His son Muhammad Ali (or Madali) was fourteen and quite headstrong when he came to the throne in 1822. He liked his pleasures, and he made little effort to keep his proclivity for gambling, drinking, and womanizing a secret. But it was his infatuation with one of his father's younger wives that caused a true scandal. Madali was only a little younger than Khan Padishah, the woman his father had married near the end of his (admittedly rather short) life, and Madali was smitten with her even before she was widowed. Once he became khan, Madali broke all taboos and married his stepmother.[5] He even found some *ulama* to sanction the marriage on the grounds that Madali had a penis when he came out of his mother's womb, and if his penis had touched her vagina then, there was nothing objectionable with it touching his stepmother's vagina. Such flexibility of interpretation did not impress many people, but Madali remained in power for over two decades, during which Khoqand continued to grow.

———

The saga of the Khojas of Altishahr had continued meanwhile and was to shape Khoqand's destiny after the turn of the nineteenth century. The Qing had managed to have the sultan of Badakhshan deliver the two brothers who had defied them in 1763, along with three of the four sons of Burhanuddin Khoja. (His brother Jahan had no children.) But the fourth son, Sarimsaq, had survived. Retainers took him to safety, and he eventually turned up in Khoqand. In 1788, the Qing demanded that he be extradited, but Narbuta Biy, then ruler of Khoqand, refused. Khoqand's submission to the Qing had never resulted in any real interference in its affairs. Now, the refusal to extradite Sarimsaq was an indication that Narbuta did not consider himself to be a vassal of the Qing in any meaningful way.[6] The tribute missions continued, but the Qing had no control over Khoqand. As the nineteenth century got going, the balance of power shifted in Khoqand's favor. It was a substantial military power now, and its merchants had a dominant role in the trade of Altishahr.

Sarimsaq Khoja seems to have lived out his days in golden captivity in Khoqand. The khans had always been wary of the unchecked author-ity of religious elites, and they did not want him disturbing their fruitful relationship with the Qing. Sarimsaq's son, Jahangir Khoja, was less ac-commodating to his hosts. In 1814, he slipped out of Khoqand in the dark of night and, gathering more than three hundred Kyrgyz tribesmen around him, attacked Kashgar. Altishahr had only four or five thousand troops stationed there, but they proved enough to repel Jahangir's incur-sion. He lost many men but managed to escape back to Khoqand, where Umar Khan chastised him for his actions but left him alone. The failure does not seem to have shaken his resolve, however, for he repeated the effort in 1820 and was repelled again. Umar now put him under house arrest. Two years later, soon after Umar's death brought his young son to the throne, Jahangir escaped again, this time to Kyrgyz nomads, where he spent two years building up a following.

In 1826, he launched a full-blown invasion of Altishahr, leading a force of several hundred men that included Kyrgyz nomads and other follow-ers from Khoqand and Bukhara. He made his way to the mausoleum of Satuq Bughra Khan, the first Turkic ruler to accept Islam, in the town of Atush, near Kashgar. There, he was confronted by a Qing force that surrounded his men. A few of his followers managed to escape to a nearby settlement where they sought help, while Jahangir hid in the graves of the mausoleum complex all night with two companions. Just when his cause seemed lost, help arrived. Hearing that Jahangir had returned, local villagers, many of them members of the Afaqi order, made their way to the mausoleum. A bloodbath ensued in which the Qing troops were routed. Jahangir left the graves only after the fighting was over. Once he was found, "the entire army of Islam," we are told by a Khoqandi chronicler, "approached Jahangir Khoja at the graveyard and fell to their knees before him. Then, with great respect and honor, they put Jahangir Khoja on a fast and noble horse. As people heard this news, everyone, young and old alike, came out to welcome Jahangir Khoja as he was on his way toward Kashgar."[7] Jahangir was greeted as a liberator, and his men captured Gulbagh, the fortified Qing garrison, while Qing forces fled eastward. By autumn, Jahangir had taken the title of Sayyid Jahangir Sultan and had extended his control to Yarkand and Khotan. For Jahangir, this was simply a matter of regaining his rights. "Kashgar and those [other] places are the lands of my ancestors," he later told the Qing.[8] Stories of wealthy merchants from various cities sending Jahangir men and money indicate that his arrival was seen by many as a restoration of Khoja rule that had been usurped by the Qing sixty years earlier. Khoja power had been restored through a popular uprising.

The Qing court was taken aback by the scale of the uprising. During the winter of 1826–1827, it redeployed thousands of troops from the north and retook Kashgar with great violence in March 1827. Jahangir escaped, and it took thousands of Qing troops many months to hunt him down. He was finally captured in February 1828 and taken to Beijing with an escort of two thousand men. There he was questioned and then executed by being sliced to death. The restoration of Qing rule had been costly and humiliating and led to a debate on the place of Altishahr in the empire. Manchu councilors in Xinjiang argued for retrenchment in Altishahr, citing the high cost of occupying the region. "The four western cities have enemies on all sides, the territory is not worth guarding and the people are not worth making into subjects," wrote Wulonga, the councilor at Kashgar. "It is basically a burdensome and cancerous part of Altishahr."[9] Indeed, Xinjiang had always been expensive to maintain. Revenue raised locally had never been enough, and Qing rule there had been possible only through the annual transfer of vast amounts of silver from the central government. Known as *xiexiang* ("shared pay"), this system of revenue sharing was a common practice in China, and Xinjiang had always depended on these transfers. By 1828, the annual *xiexiang* sent to Xinjiang was 830,000 taels.[10]

Wulonga had a point, but his views were vociferously opposed by a number of literati and bureaucrats in Beijing who had long argued the opposite—that Xinjiang, including Altishahr, should be integrated more closely into the empire and the administrative structure of China proper introduced there. A Statecraft school had emerged as a result of the new challenges faced by the empire. In 1820, Gong Zizhen (1792–1841), a young member of the school, had written "A Proposal for Establishing a Province in the Western Regions," in which he argued forcefully against "the stupid scholars with shallow views and the degenerate students from lowly hamlets" who considered Xinjiang to be a drain on the empire's resources. Heaven had brought the Qing to the west, and the sacrifices of Manchu bannermen and ordinary Chinese soldiers could not be called a loss. "If we wish to continue on with the already established merit and add to it and extend it, then nothing would be better than weighing and considering the principle of loss and gain," Gong wrote. "And what is the principle of loss and gain? It is nothing more than two sentences: 'Taking people from the center to benefit the west,' and 'Taking wealth from the west to benefit the center.'" Gong suggested that a combination of land improvement and colonization by private Chinese farmers, both financed by the empire, would make Xinjiang productive and relieve the overpopulation of China proper. These measures were to be combined with the installation of a civilian bureaucratic administrative system to replace the military and *beg* system in Xinjiang. Gong acknowledged that his proposals would require "extremely large" expenditures, but he was confident that in twenty years, the return would be "ten thousand-fold." Gong implicitly repudiated the basis of Qing policy in Xinjiang, which was based on the region's maintenance as a Manchu preserve, distinct from China proper. The civilian administration Gong envisioned would have authority over the bannermen, whose distinction would be a lower tax rate and the fact that when "they commit offences, they must not be caned by any official below the rank of a district magistrate."[11] Xinjiang would be settled by Han Chinese and governed by them as well. When Gong wrote this proposal, he had not passed his examinations and was not entitled to submit his essay as a memorial to the court. The essay was published only in 1827, just as the debate over retrenchment was going on. None of its suggestions was implemented then, but the essay was nevertheless prescient. A century and a half later, Chinese policies were to bear an uncanny resemblance to what Gong had suggested.

In 1828, the Qing response was to increase troop levels in Altishahr, expel Khoqandi merchants, and confiscate their property. This backfired. With nothing much to lose now, Madali Khan (the man who had married his stepmother) showed up in Kashgar in 1831 with the older brother of Jahangir Khoja in tow. Madali launched another jihad, this time for his own benefit. The population was less enthusiastic now and did not rise up on behalf of the Khoja. The Khoqandis could not dislodge the Qing, but they were able to leverage their retreat into a commercial and diplomatic triumph. The Qing agreed to allow Khoqandi merchants back in and compensate them for the loss of their property during the expulsion. More remarkably, they allowed Khoqandi merchants the privilege of tax-free trade and granted Madali the right to have his own *aqsaqals* (community elders) oversee Khoqandi merchants in Altishahr and collect taxes on his behalf. Khoqand had gone from being a vassal to having extraterritorial privileges in Xinjiang.

———

The rest of Transoxiana also recovered from the crisis of the mid-eighteenth century, but the political situation remained thoroughly unstable. Rulers could claim sovereignty by minting coins and having their name invoked in the sermon that preceded the Friday afternoon prayers, the most important weekly ritual of worship. The actual exercise of power was a different matter. It always required cutting deals with those who were supposed to be subservient to the would-be ruler. Ranks and titles were granted by rulers as markers of status and authority, but they did not correspond to stable offices, for these did not exist. Those who governed provinces shared in the ruler's sovereignty (as well as in the revenue that they raised), and they could easily transfer their loyalty to someone else or assert power in their own right. Tribes and regional governors jealously guarded their freedoms, and the dynasts had to resort to a combination of coercion, exhortation, and bribery to maintain their claims to supremacy. Rulers' control of territory was never absolute and uncontested. Conventional wisdom sees Central Asia in this period as divided into the three states of Khiva, Bukhara, and Khoqand. The reality was more complex. An Indian Muslim traveler who visited Central Asia in 1812–1813 enumerated eight major rulers in Transoxiana, with varying degrees of authority and sovereignty.[12] In this fragmented theater of politics, state capacity was limited and there were numerous, overlapping centers of power. The level of bureaucratization remained very low. Dynastic rulers attempted to centralize power by forming standing armies, bringing in new forms of command, and acquiring firearms, but none could completely vanquish the power of the tribes. Military reform was carried out by imported soldiers. Iranian soldiers, many of them slaves captured in war or by Turkmen tribes, provided most of the manpower for the newly organized standing armies.[13] Russian captives, often traders who had been abducted by nomads and sold into slavery, were another source of military expertise. Similarly, several Indian Muslims with experience in the armies of the East India Company served in Khoqand, one of them rising to be governor of Tashkent for several years.[14] The British traveler Joseph Wolff was "most agreeably surprised" when a military band struck up "God Save the Queen" for him one evening in Bukhara in 1844.[15] The levels of technology remained low: the firearms were largely imported, there was no industry, and the printing press never appeared in the region.

Khoqand's luck ran out in the 1840s. The Manghits in Bukhara had long been wary of Khoqand's growth. In 1842, Emir Nasrullah seized on the general revulsion caused by Madali's marriage to his stepmother to challenge Khoqand. Nasrullah marched into the Ferghana valley, occupied the city of Khoqand, and captured and executed Madali along with his mother, the poet Nodira, and other members of the royal family. Although Bukharan success did not last long (the invaders were driven out after only a few weeks), Khoqand never recovered from the crisis. The new khan was at the mercy of his military elites. After 1842, Khoqand's history is one of continuous upheaval in which factional struggles among warrior elites produced a number of palace coups and countercoups. The strife was intensified by constant conflict with Bukhara, as its emirs sought to recoup their victory of 1842. The confusion in Khoqand left the Khojas free to act on their own. In 1847, seven descendants of Jahangir Khoja invaded Altishahr in the company of Kyrgyz warriors. Katta Khoja was proclaimed ruler in Kashgar, and the Khoja forces spread out toward Yengisar, Yarkand, and Aqsu. It was three months before Qing reinforcements ousted the Khoja. This failure did not persuade the Khojas to give up on their quest. Different Khojas invaded Kashgar in 1852, 1855, and 1857, without any support from Khoqand. The last invasion, led by Khoja Wali Khan, was particularly gruesome. Wali Khan and his men rode into Kashgar and advanced deep into Altishahr in multiple directions. The initial enthusiasm that the invasion aroused among the local population soon evaporated, however, as Wali Khan proceeded to pillage not just Chinese merchants but also the Muslims. His men raped women indiscriminately and killed enough people to build a tower of skulls on the banks of the Qizil River. It was seventy-seven days before Qing reinforcements arrived to retake the city. During this short period, Wali Khan had done much to diminish the allure of Khoja legitimacy. When Qing reinforcements did arrive, Wali Khan's forces scattered, and the troops wreaked their own vengeance on the local population. Altishahr was in as great a disarray as Khoqand. Meanwhile, other powers—Russia and Britain—were becoming interested in Central Asia. The region's greatest asset, its distance, was about to lose its value.

4

A Kazakh Ethnographer in Kashgar

THE CARAVAN THAT arrived in Kashgar in October 1858 from Semi-palatinsk (now Semey) was as usual composed of Turkic-speaking Muslims who were Russian subjects. The Russian trade with Central Asia and China had long been dominated by Muslims from the Volga basin, people who are today called Tatars. That trade had survived the upheavals experienced by Altishahr, including the recent invasion led by Khoja Wali Khan. But among the merchants was a young man who called himself Alimbay. If he had been searched, interrogators would have found on him papers with notes written in Russian. The young merchant was a military officer in disguise, tasked with gathering intelligence about the state of affairs in Altishahr. The reason he could blend in with the rest of the caravan was that he was a Kazakh who answered to the name of Shoqan Wälikhanov (or Choqan Valikhanov) in real life.

Born in 1835, Wälikhanov was the great-grandson of Ablay Khan, who had ruled the Middle Horde of the Kazakhs in the eighteenth century. He had graduated from the Siberian Cadets Corps in Omsk and become an officer in the Russian army, a scholar, and a government servant. As adjutant to the governor-general of Western Siberia, he had participated in a number of expeditions in the Kazakh steppe, around Issiq Köl and into Ghulja. In 1857, he had been elected to the Russian Imperial Geographic Society, and it was that body that funded his incognito trip to Kashgar. Wälikhanov spent six months in Kashgar, during which he escaped discovery. He acquired a collection of local manuscripts and coins, which he took back with him to Russia. Wälikhanov was the toast of St. Petersburg society when he spent fifteen months there in 1860–1861. He became a part of Russian academic life and a friend of Fyodor Dostoevsky, whom he met during the latter's exile in Semipalatinsk. Wälikhanov published widely in Russian, and some of his descriptions of Eastern Turkestan were translated into English in 1866. Sadly, his life was cut short by tuberculosis, which claimed Wälikhanov before he completed his thirtieth year.

Exploration and espionage went hand in hand with science and conquest in the age of empire. What was unusual about Wälikhanov was his position as a Kazakh officer in the Russian army who was exploring and spying on Central Asia. Wälikhanov's all-too-brief career offers insights into the nature of both the Russian empire and the geopolitical conjuncture of the mid-nineteenth century. His visit to Kashgar came at a point when the Qing empire was faltering, Russia was ascendant, and the British Indian empire was emerging as a factor in Central Asia.

———

Russia had no natural boundaries separating it from the steppe and its inhabitants, and competition with steppe nomads had been a perennial feature of Russian life ever since the first Slavs had appeared on the far western edges of the Eurasian steppe in the seventh and eighth centuries CE. The principalities of Rus' had been subjugated by the Mongols and brought into the same imperium as China, the Middle East, and Central Asia. As Mongol power receded, Muscovy emerged as the preeminent power among the eastern Slavs. Initially, it was a Mongol successor state, but by the sixteenth century, it had begun to see itself differently. Ivan IV (the Terrible) took the title of tsar, with its Christian connotations, upon his coronation in 1547, and he soon launched a campaign of reconquest against Muscovy's former overlords. Muscovite forces took the khanate of Kazan, the Muslim successor to the Golden Horde, in 1552, and Astrakhan in 1556, giving Muscovy a large number of Muslim subjects and a foothold on the Caspian. A second wave of expansion in the

1580s saw Russian freebooters and the military caste of the Cossacks expanding Muscovite rule into the forest zone north of the steppe. The defeat of Küchüm Khan of the Chingissid khanate of Sibir in 1582 was a landmark, after which Cossacks imposed tribute on the indigenous peoples of the forest. Slavic settlers followed, overwhelming the small indigenous populations. Fur was the main commodity to be extracted (either as trade or tribute—the difference was slight and often invisible to the native peoples) from the forest zone, and much of this extraction was done by state-authorized private merchants, none of whom were more famous than the Stroganov family. This combination of free enterprise and freebooting extended Muscovite rule across the vast expanses that we now call Siberia to the Pacific. The Russian presence in Siberia was weak and distant from the imperial center, but it outweighed any other presence. In 1689, Muscovite forces met up with the Qing in the Far East. The two empires signed the treaty of Nerchinsk (drafted in Latin by Jesuit missionaries at the Qing court), which drew boundaries between the two in the Far East. No one noticed it on the steppe, but the linking of two agrarian states on the periphery of the steppe was ominous. The treaty marked the beginning of the end of the steppe's autonomy.

Peter the Great (r. 1689–1725) shook up Muscovy at the dawn of the eighteenth century with a series of top-down reforms. Peter transformed Muscovy's army and state and the way its elites thought, worked, and looked. He was fascinated by northern and central Europe, and his reforms self-consciously copied European phenomena. The military reforms were meant to bring his armies up to par with those of Sweden, with whom he fought a twenty-year war, and to put Russia on the map of Europe. They were accompanied by a cultural reorientation away from the Muscovite past and toward the central European present. Peter renamed Muscovy the Russian empire, with its pretensions to universal rule and the heritage of Rome. The empire was to have a new capital, and its servitors were to act and dress as Europeans. Peter ordered his nobles to shave off their beards (he was not above using scissors himself to cut off the beards of those who tarried), the women to mingle with the men, and all to follow current best practices from the courts of

Europe. Peter's real ambitions lay in Europe, but he realized that imperial expansion was much easier in the east. With characteristic aplomb, he set out to explore new trade routes, sources of revenue, and territories to annex. Rumors of the existence both of a river route to India from the Caspian and of gold in the Amu Darya led Peter to order a mission to Khiva in 1714 to assess the political situation there and search for gold. The news brought back by the mission was positive enough that Peter dispatched a second mission in 1716, under the command of Prince Aleksandr Bekovich-Cherkassky, with the tasks of building a fort on the southern shores of the Caspian, looking for gold, and talking the khan of Khiva into sending a joint Russian-Khivan commercial mission to India. When Bekovich-Cherkassky showed up with a body of 2,200 men, the Khivans, unsurprisingly, saw the mission as an invasion and challenged it in battle. The Russians won the initial skirmish but were later massacred almost to a man. A different mission inspired by the lure of gold—this time to Yarkand in Altishahr—was no more successful, if less disastrous. The Zunghars, who controlled Yarkand at the time, shooed away the armed mission from Tobolsk led by Lieutenant Colonel Ivan Bukgoltz (Buchholtz). However, Bukgoltz managed to establish a fort on the Om River that later became the town of Omsk.[1] The visionary projects of Peter produced little immediate result, but there was no question that Russia had become a presence on the steppe by the time of his death, with Russian fortresses strung along the steppe.

Russian trade with Central Asia and China was of long standing.[2] Caravans connected Russia to markets in Transoxiana and China. This trade involved steppe nomads—Kazakhs and Zunghars—who charged fees for transit and protection and thus became enmeshed in long-distance political ties. On the Russian side, much of the trade was run by Tatar merchants. The Tatars' passage to Muscovite rule was traumatic in the beginning. Muscovite conquest was followed by campaigns of forced conversion that wreaked havoc on Tatars, but Muscovy soon reached a modus vivendi with its Muslim population. It incorporated Tatars and Bashkirs into the empire-wide system of ranks and standings that defined the rights and obligations of each group. Russia's frontier on the steppe took the form of lines of fortifications that offered a defense against the nomads and helped pacify the land behind them.[3] The fortifications often existed at great distances from the center of Russian power and were manned by Cossacks. Until the early nineteenth century, the area in front of the lines remained a borderland in which the Russian state and its agents did not have a decisive advantage in power. Rather, the lives of the Cossacks were intertwined with those of their Kazakh neighbors in multiple ways, from trade to intermarriage.[4] This should not be surprising. The term "Cossack" (*Kazak* in Russian) comes from the Turkic term *Qazaq*, which is also the original of "Kazakh." Both the Cossacks and the Kazakhs emerged as part of a broader steppe-based phenomenon of brigandage.[5] By the late eighteenth century, the Russian state had brought the Cossacks to heel and made them do imperial work. The land behind the lines they manned was opened up to Russian peasant settlement, which drastically altered the way the land was used.

Zunghar expansion began a cycle of immensely bloody wars with the Kazakhs in which the Zunghars came to hold the advantage. In 1723, a major Zunghar victory saw the Kazakhs scatter south and west in a "Barefooted Flight"—a desperate retreat toward Transoxiana, where their arrival shook the agrarian states of the region to the core. Other Kazakh leaders turned to Russia for help. In 1730, Abulkhayr Khan, the ruler of the Junior Horde, sent an embassy to St. Petersburg seeking Russian protection against the Zunghars and the construction of a fort of his territory. The empress Anna was only too happy to oblige. Abulkhayr swore an oath to her in 1731, promising to serve her, pay tribute (*yasak*), and protect Russian traders passing through his territory. Shemeke (Shah Muhammad) Khan of the Middle Horde followed suit in 1732, and the sultans of the Great Horde took oaths of loyalty to Anna in 1733.

The oaths meant different things to the two sides.[6] The Russians assumed that the Kazakhs were submitting to their sovereignty in taking the oath. The Kazakhs saw the oaths as temporary alliances rather than permanent submission. When the Russian envoy—a Bashkir Muslim called Muhammad Tevkelev—arrived to accept Abulkhayr's oath of allegiance, he found intense dissension among Kazakh notables, who thought that they had requested Abulkhayr to ask for a peace treaty, rather than to become an imperial subject.[7] With the Qing conquests in Zungharia, the Kazakhs now found themselves wedged between two empires. Many Kazakh leaders who had sworn oaths of allegiance to the Russian empire now submitted to the Qing, which allowed them to send embassies to Beijing and gave them presents and titles and trading privileges in border cities.[8] For the Kazakhs, the oaths to the Qing were practical measures undertaken with short-term concerns in mind, not an offer of long-term fidelity. Distance and the boundlessness of the steppe offered some comfort, and neither empire was in a position to force the issue. In the south, in their dealings with the states of Transoxiana or the armies of Nadir Shah, Kazakhs acted as sovereign actors, not in any way constrained by their oaths to the two empires. Into the nineteenth century, the Kazakhs were able to maneuver between the Russians and the Qing, seeking the best advantage. The Russians could ensure Kazakh loyalty only through the practice of holding as hostages children of the rulers who submitted. These children were given Russian educations, and some of them turned into intermediaries between the Kazakhs and the Russian state. Even so, the Kazakhs rebelled often and failed to pay their tribute, and their leaders often had to retake their oaths.

Things changed as the nineteenth century progressed. Faced with fiscal problems, the Qing largely retreated from the steppe beyond the pickets on the Xinjiang border, while the Russians consolidated their control through the construction of forts ever deeper into the steppe. In 1822, they sought for the first time to assert real administrative control over the Kazakhs of the Middle Horde. The Statute on the Siberian Kazakhs imposed taxation and an administrative structure on them. It also abolished the position of the khan and replaced the khan with a number of sultans to be elected by the elders of different administrative units. It also forbade Middle Horde Kazakhs from having any contact with the Qing. The Russians introduced similar statutes in other parts of the Kazakh steppe in the decades that followed and built more and more fortresses, but the process of the integration of the Kazakhs into the Russian empire was far from smooth. There were frequent revolts, as various groups of Kazakhs refused to pay taxes and raided Russian settlements and fortifications. Qenesarï Sultan wanted to be recognized as khan and to rule on his own behalf. Between 1837 and 1847, he kept Russian forces in check and created a de facto state in the steppe. This episode is usually called a revolt against Russian rule, but it might more accurately be called the existence of an independent state. It was only after the midpoint of the century that the Russians could be certain of their occupation of the Kazakh steppe.

In the 1840s, the Russians had begun to expand south of that region. A campaign against Khiva in the winter of 1839–1840 ended in disaster, when a force led by General Vasily Perovsky ground to a halt well before reaching Khiva and returned to base in Fort Emba north of the Aral Sea, having lost half of its camels and with half its men either dead or grievously wounded. The fiasco did not dent Russian ambitions, however. Over the next few years, the Russians built a number of forts on the Aral Sea and the lower reaches of the Syr Darya in territory claimed by the khans of Khiva. In 1853, Perovsky used one of these to capture the Khoqandi fortress of Aq Masjid on the Syr Darya and thus acquire a foothold in Transoxiana. The fortress was renamed Perovsk in honor of the conqueror. In the meantime, the Siberian Line had moved south, as Russian forces established fortresses in Kopal at the foot of the Alatau Mountains in 1847. Another fortress, established at Vernoe (now Almaty) in 1854 brought Jettisuv (Semirech'e) under Russian control. Perovsk and Vernoe were separated by a thousand kilometers, but Russia had become a major presence in the region.

––––––––

The 1822 Statute on the Siberian Kazakhs was typical of Russian imperial legislation. The Russian empire was a dynastic empire of conquest that took difference for granted and sought to accommodate it. The empire incorporated new territories and groups on specific terms inscribed in charters or legislation unique to each new conquest. The Statute on the Siberian Kazakhs did not apply to Siberian Cossacks, for instance, even if they lived on the same territory as the Siberian Kazakhs.

This was the hallmark of a particularist empire in which each group had a unique—different and unequal—relationship to the tsar. The recognition of difference was codified by Catherine the Great in 1773 in an Edict of Toleration of All Faiths that allowed the practice of all religions in the empire. This was not the same thing as the freedom of religion, let alone the freedom of conscience, but it was significant. Subjects had to belong to one religion or another, and the state oversaw the functioning of each religious community. Peter had subjugated the Orthodox Church to the state, replacing the patriarch with a Holy Synod that was subject to secular authority. Catherine extended that principle to Islam, creating the Muhammadan Spiritual Assembly at Orenburg. In many ways, it was a church for Islam, a hierarchical institution that organized religious authority on behalf of the state. Catherine saw it as a way of bringing order to Islam among the sedentary Tatar population. She also hoped that Islam would "civilize" the Kazakhs, who were giving the empire a difficult time. To this end, she sponsored the construction of mosques on the Kazakh steppe and used the Spiritual Assembly as a diplomatic tool. At that time, such an institution was unique in the Muslim world, and the first mufti had to struggle to have his authority acknowledged. But gradually, the Spiritual Assembly came to be an integral part of the religious landscape of the Volga-Urals region.

Finally, the Russian empire did not rule on behalf of the Russians—no such category officially existed until late in the nineteenth century. Ethnic Russians did not enjoy any privileges as a result of being Russian. Most Russians were in fact serfs until emancipation in 1861, while serfdom did not exist outside the Slavic heartland of the empire. Rather, the empire was run by a multinational noble elite that served the dynasty. The elites of each new territory could be inducted into the Russian imperial nobility, which in addition to Russians included Baltic Germans, Poles, Georgians, Ukrainians, and not a few Tatars and Bashkirs. Loyalty to the dynasty, not ethnic belonging, was the key here.

This is what allowed Shoqan Wälikhanov to serve the empire in the ways that he did. The Russian empire sought intermediaries in each region that it conquered, but Wälikhanov was more than an intermediary. He was an imperial servitor who was at home in the ranks of the empire's multinational bureaucratic, military, and academic elites. He was also the exception in Central Asia. As we shall see below, Central Asia was conquered on different terms. Central Asians were not incorporated into the Russian nobility, and no other Central Asian rose to the rank that Wälikhanov had achieved.

The geopolitical balance in Eurasia had shifted greatly since the time of the Qing conquests. The Qing empire was in a different place than it had been a century earlier, when it had taken Central Asia by storm. Population growth and an economic depression had weakened imperial oversight, while rebellions had begun to crop up in many places. The most significant of these was the Taiping uprising, the immense upheaval that ravaged China proper from 1850 to 1864 and cost the Qing an immense amount of human and financial resources. At the same time, terms of trade with increasingly assertive European powers had begun to shift, and the Europeans had begun to flex their military muscle in defense of their trade. Matters came to a head with the First Opium War (1839–1842), imposed by Britain in defense of its right to sell opium in China, which dealt the Qing a devastating defeat. The peace treaty signed at Nanjing in August 1842 extorted from the Qing the first of a series of unequal treaties in which the Qing signed off their right to set import tariffs on goods sold by British merchants in China. British subjects were also to enjoy extraterritoriality—that is, they could be tried only according to British laws in consular courts, even for criminal offenses committed in China. Finally, Britain was able to open consulates in so-called treaty ports that were open for free trade. The United States signed a similar treaty in 1843, France followed in 1844, and eventually all European powers (including Russia) would benefit from such treaties. The Qing empire had become a victim of imperialism. This was the beginning of what would later be called the Century of Humiliation for China, and it was to shape the intellectual and political history of China in very significant ways.

By the 1850s, then, the Qing's relationship with the Russian empire had flipped, with the Russians in the ascendant. A 1727 treaty required all trade between the two empires to pass through Kiakhta, a small border town south of Lake Baikal. However, by 1840, Russian subjects had started trading in Xinjiang without permission. This activity was formalized by the Treaty of Ghulja in 1851, which allowed Russian merchants to trade freely in the Ili valley and Russia to open consulates in Ghulja and Targabatay. For the Russians, the turmoil in Altishahr represented both a threat and an opportunity.

Meanwhile, another empire had appeared on the scene—that of the British. The East India Company had begun to conquer territory in the middle of the eighteenth century, and by the nineteenth, India had become the most valuable British colony. Along with possession came a constant worry about the colony's security. Debate among British policy makers centered on the best way to defend the empire's Indian possessions from possible attack instigated or perpetrated by Britain's European rivals. During the Napoleonic Wars, Bonaparte had occupied Egypt as a way of cutting Britain off from India, while Paul I, emperor of Russia during a period when it was aligned with Bonaparte, had ordered a speculative overland invasion of India. To address the fear of invasion, the British surrounded India with a series of client states that would provide a buffer against potential invaders. Where the Indian border should lie proved to be a matter of great contention among British policy makers. Ultimately, what was known as the Forward School won out, and in the first half of the nineteenth century, British territory expanded massively toward the northwest at the same time as Russia was consolidating its hold on the Kazakh steppe.

The British search for security also required geographic exploration and intelligence gathering. Central Asia's geography was little known to outsiders at this time. British authorities in India also organized missions of military and geographic exploration in the mountainous regions to the north of India. Beginning in the 1810s, British agents (many of them Indian) scoped out the terrain, looking for passages into Tibet, Afghanistan, and Transoxiana. In 1825, William Moorcroft, a veterinarian in the service of the East India Company, reached Bukhara in the company of a small expedition. He was Superintendent of the Stud for the East India Company's armies and was primarily looking for horses, but his mission was also to find out more about the routes that linked India to Central Asia. Moorcroft spent six months in the emirate as a guest of Emir Haydar. He did not find the breeding horses he was looking for, but he took copious notes about the routes that he discovered. He had been on the road for six years when he arrived in Bukhara. He was sick when he left Bukhara and died on the return journey near Andkhoy, in what is now Afghanistan.

In the years that followed, other British missions arrived in Central Asia, seeking intelligence, trade, and a defense against what the British viewed as Russian intrigues. The missions were often met with suspicion, and their members found themselves embroiled in political struggles in the region. In 1842, Emir Nasrullah of Bukhara imprisoned two British agents and then had them executed. Nasrullah's subjects called him *amir-i qassāb* (the Butcher Emir), and the executions both made Bukhara notorious in Britain and laid the foundations of a tenacious narrative of Central Asian barbarity in the West. They also gave rise to the myth of the Great Game, a long-drawn-out imperial rivalry that is supposed to have driven imperial expansion in Central Asia. The myth has spawned a vast literature, "based on the same narrow group of (mostly published) English-language sources, and consisting largely of a series of anecdotes of adventure and derring-do by heavily-moustachioed officers and explorers against a picturesque but badly-drawn Central Asian backdrop."[9] Based on an uncritical reading of self-interested nineteenth-century accounts, this literature exaggerates the significance of the British role in Central Asia and mischaracterizes the geopolitics of the age. Britain's primary concern was the defense of India, not territorial conquest in Central Asia. British policy makers had an often irrational fear that the Russians might invade India. British agents searched for mountain passes that the Russians might use and wanted India to be ringed by friendly states that could act as a buffer between India and Russia. But the real issue was Anglo-Russian rivalry in Europe and the potential of a crisis in Europe to spill over into India. As the Russian empire expanded, it had to take into consideration British concerns about India, but those were not the primary motor of Russian expansion in Transoxiana.[10]

———

Wälikhanov's visit to Kashgar combined espionage with geographic and ethnographic discovery and was part of a broader phenomenon that had begun to encompass Central Asia by the middle of the nineteenth century. Altishahr and Transoxiana were beginning to attract the attention of outside empires. The Russians had a clear advantage over the British or the Qing in that respect. They had traded with the region for longer and had longer-standing contacts with it. And they were to emerge as the victors in the imperial contest.

5

Imperial Conquests

THE THREE DECADES after Shoqan Wälikhanov's visit to Kashgar brought profound changes to Central Asia. Russian armies advanced swiftly into Transoxiana, subjugating the sedentary states of the region. Simultaneously but independently, Qing rule collapsed in Xinjiang, throwing the geopolitical situation wide open. This upheaval gave Yaqub Beg, a warrior from Khoqand, the opportunity to establish one last Central Asian state in the ruins of Qing rule. In the process, he became the first Central Asian global press sensation. The Qing collapse and the Russian advance drew the British into the region, which produced a number of diplomatic crises between the British and Russian empires. Yet the confrontation between the Russian and the British empires never came to a head, while the Qing, against all expectations, came back and reconquered Eastern Turkestan. By the mid-1880s, a new imperial order had arisen in Central Asia in which the region was divided between the Russian and the Qing empires, while the British had withdrawn to an observer status. The new division of Central Asia was based on international law—itself a nascent phenomenon, but one which enabled global recognition of imperial claims. In this chapter, we will try to make sense of this tumultuous era and examine the sense that Central Asians made of it.

———

The consolidation of Russian rule over the Kazakh steppe during the first half of the nineteenth century brought the empire into contiguity

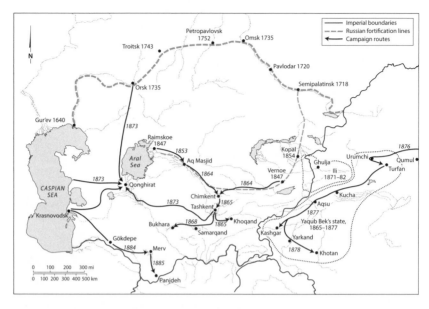

MAP 5.1. Imperial conquests of the mid-nineteenth century

with Transoxiana and set it on a collision course with the sedentary states of the region. The fundamental reason behind the Russian advance was strategic. There were no natural barriers to separate Russia from its neighbors. Having finally brought the vast expanses of the steppe under control, the Russian military hoped to find a "natural frontier" that would be easy to demarcate and defend. Such a frontier had to lie beyond the steppe, in the fertile lands of Transoxiana.[1] This, along with the desire to maintain Russian prestige on the steppe, drove Russian expansion. Rivalry with the British and a desire to grab Central Asia before the British got there played almost no role in the Russian advance. Nor did a hunger for cotton. Soviet historians assumed that there was an economic motive for the conquest, and the cotton argument has often been made by Western historians as well. Indeed, cotton had been part of Central Asia's exports to Russia before the conquest, but Russia's fledgling textile industry depended largely on cotton imported from the United States. The American civil war disrupted those supplies and threw the industry into a crisis. But there is no evidence that cotton featured as a concern among Russian policy makers as they debated

Russia's course in Central Asia.[2] Trade followed the flag and was a secondary consideration in Tsarist thinking.

The Russian advance south of the Kazakh steppe had begun from two directions. In the west, after the fiasco of the Khivan campaign of 1839–1840, the Russians built forts on the Aral Sea and the lower reaches of the Syr Darya on territory claimed by the khans of Khiva. In 1853, General Vasily Perovsky took the Khoqandi fortress of Aq Masjid on the Syr Darya, giving the Russian empire a foothold in Transoxiana. Aq Masjid was renamed Perovsk. Simultaneously, from the east, the Siberian (Irtysh) line began moving south, with the construction of forts at Kopal at the foot of the Alatau Mountains in 1847 and Vernoe (now Almaty) in 1854, the year after the sack of Aq Masjid. This new extension brought most of Jettisuv (Semirech'e) and the wooded foothills of the Alatau Mountains under Russian territorial control, but a thousand-kilometer gap remained between Perovsk and Vernoe. There was talk of uniting the two lines of fortresses, but further action was largely suspended by the Crimean War (1853–1856). Although Russia suffered a humiliating defeat at the hands of Britain and France, the war heightened the allure of Central Asia for Russia's military. Russian prestige needed to be resurrected, and Central Asia provided ample opportunity for relatively easy victories—especially as the great uprising in India in 1857 had distracted the British. By 1860, Russian armies had resumed their activity in Transoxiana. The initial advance was at the expense of Khoqand, which lost the fortresses of Toqmaq and Pishpek (now Bishkek) to the Russians. In 1864, Russian armies led by General Mikhail Cherniaev took the towns of Turkistan, Chimkent, and Avliya Ata and made an unsuccessful attempt to capture Tashkent.

Tashkent had risen to prominence in the eighteenth century as an entrepôt of the steppe trade. Its merchants had deep connections with Russia. In the latter part of the eighteenth century, the city's notables had invited a Kazakh of Chingissid ancestry to run the city. Alim Khan had conquered it for Khoqand in 1809, and the city had been fought over by Bukhara and Khoqand since then. It was also on the Russian radar. By 1860, Russian strategists were talking about making Tashkent the anchor of a "natural frontier" where the Orenburg and Siberian lines of fortifications could be connected. Tashkent would be wrenched away from Khoqand and made into a vassal state under a pliant ruler. The vassal state would serve as a buffer between Russia and the rest of Central Asia and provide Russia with a natural frontier.

Khoqand had never recovered from the Bukharan invasion of 1842. The Shahrukhid dynasty had been restored, but it had lost effective power, and politics in Khoqand had turned into an eternal struggle between the various constituencies that the Shahrukhid dynasty had brought together. After the restoration, these factions—Kyrgyz and Qipchaq tribes and the sedentary populations, both Turkic- and Tajik-speaking—fell out quite spectacularly.[3] The Russian advance on the steppe robbed Khoqand of its resources and made any resolution of the chaos almost impossible. The two decades after 1842 witnessed a number of coups and countercoups, as different factions placed their candidates on the throne. Instability in Altishahr and Russian encroachment in the north exacerbated the crisis by depriving Khoqand of the revenues that had fueled its growth. Emir Nasrullah of Bukhara was more interested in defeating Khoqand than in preparing for the Russians. In 1854, Khudayar Khan of Khoqand had sent a diplomatic mission to the East India Company, seeking military assistance. "I confidently hope," we read in the translation of his missive made by British bureaucrats, "that you will send one or two persons of . . . skill and wisdom in the arts of chemistry, and of the smelting of metals, with instruments of mining; and also a few military engines and weapons which might be the means of expelling this tribe of evil-doing Russians, who are always subverting order."[4] He received no response. The British might have been worried about Russian advances in Central Asia, but they had little interest in military intervention across such great distances. In any case, Khudayar Khan was more occupied with internal strife and the never-ending struggle with Bukhara.

By the time Russian armies approached Tashkent, Khudayar had been ousted for the second time, and Khoqand was under the control of the Qipchaq warlord Alimqul. He came from Khoqand to face the Russians but was fatally wounded in battle. There was plenty of internal dissension among Khoqandi forces, and they eventually fled, leaving the inhabitants of Tashkent to deal with Cherniaev. On June 29, 1865, the notables of the city opened the gates and surrendered. But instead of turning the city into a vassal state, the Russians made it the capital of a new Russian district that included all the territory conquered in the previous decade down the course of the Amu Darya. They called the new district Turkestan. The term ("land of the Turks") had already existed as a generic description of the region. Now it became the name of a concrete administrative entity, one that was to grow over the next quarter of a century.

————

As the Russians pressed down in Transoxiana, Qing rule came crashing down in Xinjiang in the face of a popular rebellion. The rebellion began not in Altishahr—which had always given the Qing trouble—but in the north, and it was connected to upheavals farther afield in the Qing empire. Defeat in the First Opium War was accompanied by a number of rebellions across the empire that weakened the hold of the central government on its provinces. One of those was among the Hui (Chinese-speaking Muslims) of Shaanxi and Gansu provinces in 1862. Rumors began to fly that the Qing had ordered the extermination of all Hui (much as they had in fact done with the Zunghars a century earlier), and in June 1864 these rumors arrived in Xinjiang. The revolt began on the night of June 3–4, 1864, in the small town of Kucha, where the Hui burned down a bazaar outside the city and attacked government buildings, murdering Manchu and Han officials and troops. The local Turkic Muslim population joined in. Another uprising took place in Ürümchi, and in the months that followed, the revolt spread across Xinjiang. In city after city, crowds often armed only with axes, hoes, and clubs stormed citadels and assaulted the local Han populations. While many cities revolted independently, a hastily formed Muslim army set out from Kucha and succeeded in taking many cities as far east as Turfan. Qing rule had ceased to exist in Xinjiang.[5]

The revolt was unusual in that Dungans (as the Hui were known locally) and Turkestanis acted together. In that sense, it was a Muslim revolt against the Qing. The unity did not last for very long, however. The collapse of the Qing order threw open the region to intense competition for leadership, as many different actors—*begs*, Khojas, Dungans, and nomads—vied for power. In Ili, the alliance between the Dungans and the Taranchi broke down very soon after victory. After open warfare, the Taranchi emerged triumphant and raised a man called Abu'l Ala Khan to the office of sultan in 1866. In Kashgar, the rebellion took its own course. The Dungan uprising was repulsed both by the Qing citadel and the Muslim old city, where Qutlugh Beg, the local Qing governor, massacred the Dungans. The subsequent course of events is not entirely clear, but it seems that Qutlugh Beg asked the Kyrgyz tribe of Turaygir Qipchaq for help against the Dungans and then quailed at the prospect that its chieftain, Siddiq Beg, might take the town himself. In the ensuing stalemate, Siddiq made the fateful decision to ask for help from Alimqul, the de facto ruler of Khoqand. This set the scene for one final Khoja incursion into Altishahr.

Although he was besieged by Russian forces in Tashkent, Alimqul sent Buzurg Khoja, the leading Afaqi Khoja of his generation, to Kashgar with a small entourage under the command of a trusted companion called Yaqub Beg. Buzurg Khoja was under strict orders not to interfere in the business of "taking and giving, punishment and execution, dismissal and appointment, and affairs like these"—that is, the actual running of the government.[6] His job was to be the symbol of unity for the insurgents in Kashgar. The old connections between Khoqand and Altishahr had taken on a new form at the moment of the Qing collapse. Buzurg Khoja arrived in Kashgar in January 1865 and was welcomed by the population, which then turned on the Kyrgyz and drove them out of the city. But the real beneficiary was Yaqub Beg. Immediately after his arrival, he set about capturing power himself. His success was startling, and in a few months he had not only taken control of Kashgar but also launched on a career of conquest that ultimately brought all of Altishahr under his control. The Kucha army, composed as it was of volunteers with minimal military experience, stood no chance against Yaqub Beg's warriors, and he also put to the sword the Kyrgyz of Siddiq Beg and the Dungans of Kashgar. Yaqub Beg's cause was helped by the arrival of forces fleeing the Russians in Ferghana. By 1867, he had consolidated his rule over all of Altishahr. In 1870, conflict with the Dungans led him east, where he sacked Ürümchi and Turfan and added them to his state. A Khoqandi warrior had managed to create a new state in Altishahr.

———

The Russians had originally planned to turn Tashkent into a vassal state to serve as a natural frontier. These plans evaporated in the face of military opportunity. Instead, the city became the base for Russian expansion into the rest of Central Asia. It was to remain the center of Russian power until the end of the Soviet period, a century and a quarter later. The Russian advance after the conquest of Tashkent was lightning quick. A small Russian force routed a massive Bukharan army in the battle of Irjar in May 1866, which opened the road to Samarqand. The emir Muzaffar finally sued for peace in 1868. Khudayar Khan of Khoqand accepted Russian suzerainty later in the same year. The Russians now turned their attention to Khiva again. Two earlier invasions of the khanate (in 1717 and 1839–1840) had ended in ignominy. Now there was to be no room for error. In 1869, a Russian force landed on the eastern shore of the Caspian Sea and established an outpost called Krasnovodsk (Kizilsu). An attack launched from there on Khiva was repulsed in 1872, but a more determined effort the following year succeeded. In a three-pronged attack, Russian columns marched on Khiva from Krasnovodsk, Orenburg, and Tashkent. The city fell easily, and the khan sued for peace. Three years later, in 1876, a rebellion broke out in Khoqand against Khudayar Khan that then took an anti-Russian turn. The Russians launched a "pacification" campaign of great brutality and annexed the khanate. By 1876, Russia had conquered or subjugated all of Transoxiana.

The defeat had been rapid and massive. Russian casualties were minuscule, while local armies suffered huge losses. Central Asian commentators were dismayed and blamed various shortcomings of the armies. They were not entirely wrong. The military modernization project had not gone far enough, and the new armies proved to be no match for the Russians. Transoxiana's distance had been its greatest asset in the nineteenth century, but now that became a liability. Its rulers looked for help against the Russians and found none. In 1864, Alimqul had dispatched embassies to the Ottoman sultan and the British in India, as well as to the rulers of Afghanistan and Kashmir.[7] After his defeat at Irjar, Muzaffar also sent a mission to the British in India and another to the Ottoman Empire, but again to no avail. The British had little interest in intervening at such distances, while the Ottomans had little prior connection to Central Asia and had enough problems of their own with the Russian empire to be able to do anything. Central Asians were left to face the Russians on their own.

Yet only the military could be wholeheartedly enthusiastic about the progress of Russian arms in the region. The ministries of finance and foreign affairs took a different view of the matter, with the former worrying about the expense of administering vast new territories in a period of fiscal restraint, while the latter feared "complications" with Britain. These considerations shaped the final arrangements of Russian rule in Central Asia. Large swaths of territory were annexed and incorporated into the empire. In 1865, recent territorial acquisitions were formed into a new Russian district called Turkestan, with Tashkent as its center. Two years later, Turkestan was raised to the level of a province under the command of a governor-general. But St. Petersburg was hesitant to completely swallow the states in the region. Khudayar Khan had been ousted in a power struggle in Khoqand. Russian forces placed him back on the throne once he accepted Russian suzerainty. Similarly, the Russians annexed a large chunk of Bukhara's territory (including the city of Samarqand) but left the emir on his throne in return for reparations and a treaty granting Russian merchants equal rights in the country. The emir "acknowledged himself to be the obedient servant of the Emperor of All the Russias" and "renounced the right to maintain direct and friendly relations with neighboring rulers and khans and to conclude with them any commercial or other treaties [or to] . . . undertake any military actions against them without the knowledge and permission of the supreme Russian authority in Central Asia."[8] In 1873, Muhammad

Rahim Khan of Khiva was obliged to accept Russian suzerainty on similar terms. He promised to pay 2.2 million rubles in reparations, renounced the right to conduct foreign affairs, and allowed Russian shipping free movement on the Amu Darya and Russian merchants full
access to his markets. Khoqand, Bukhara, and Khiva had been turned
into protectorates of Russia. They remained formally distinct from the
empire, with their rulers free to govern as they pleased. The arrange-
ment with Khoqand collapsed in 1876, when an uprising against the
khan sent him fleeing to Russia. The former khanate was then annexed
to Turkestan, but Bukhara and Khiva remained protectorates down to
the end of the Tsarist regime.

———

The last wave of Russian expansion took place in the Turkmen desert,
the territory between the newly formed protectorates and Iran and Afghanistan. Its conquest cost the Russians more lives than that of the rest
of Central Asia put together and saw the greatest Russian brutality. In
1879, a force under General Nikolai Lomakin used the fortress of Krasnovodsk to launch an attack on the Ahal-Teke Turkmens. As Russian
troops advanced, the entire population of the oasis took refuge in a
mud-walled fortress near Gökdepe. Lomakin bombarded the fortress
with artillery and rocket fire, and when noncombatants fled, he ordered
them attacked as well. About two thousand men, women, and children
were killed before Lomakin ordered the fortress stormed. In a final desperate move, the Turkmens rushed their attackers and drove them back,
killing almost two hundred Russians and forcing them to retreat. This
was by far the biggest loss of life the Russians suffered in their conquest
of Central Asia. The Russian government decided that this loss had to
be avenged to protect Russian "prestige." The tsar personally oversaw
the organization of a new expedition, for which no expense was spared
and which was designed to be fail-safe. He commissioned the construction of a railway, the first in Central Asia, to facilitate the mobilization,
even though the railway was not finished in time. He gave the command

to General Mikhail Skobelev (1843–1882), who was the toast of Russian society at the moment for his feats in the recent Russo-Ottoman War of 1877–1878. Skobelev had made his name in Central Asia, where he had taken part in numerous campaigns—culminating in the ruthless final conquest of Khoqand in 1876. His career had taught him some lessons. "I hold it as a principle," he told a British journalist, "that in Asia the duration of peace is in direct proportion to the slaughter you inflict on the enemy."[9] In November 1880, fourteen months after the massacres carried out by Lomakin's troops, Skobelev led another Russian army to Gökdepe. The Turkmens again sheltered in the fortress and resisted just as stubbornly as they had the year before, but Skobelev mined the walls of the fortress and, on January 12, 1881, launched an all-out assault on the fortress. As the walls gave way, the defenders fled. Skobelev's soldiers pursued them far into the desert and slaughtered 8,000 of them, regardless of their sex or age. Another 6,500 corpses lay in the fortress itself.

The massacre at Gökdepe can hold its head high in any company of colonial atrocities. The slaughter broke Turkmen resistance, and Skobelev's armies marched deep into the desert, taking Ashgabat and several other settlements. Over the next four years, Russia annexed the oases of Tejen, Merv, and Yolatan, meeting with varying degrees of resistance, and eventually reached the eastern boundaries of Afghanistan. The British, who counted Afghanistan as a client state, were concerned enough that in 1884 they initiated the formation of an Anglo-Russian Boundary Commission to demarcate Afghanistan's boundaries with Russia. The flash point was the oasis of Panjdeh, which Afghanistan claimed and where Afghan and Russian forces faced each other through the winter of 1884–1885, with the British members of the boundary commission present with an escort of five hundred Indian troops. In March 1885, mutual provocations led to a Russian assault that pushed the Afghans back across the Kushka River, with considerable loss of life. This assault provoked a serious diplomatic crisis between Britain and Russia. For a while it looked as if the two empires might go to war in Central Asia, but the crisis was averted. Over the next year the commission laid out a boundary, guaranteed by a treaty between the two European powers and hence subject to international law, that marked the limits of the Russian empire in Central Asia.[10] The boundary needed some tweaking, mostly in the Pamirs, and adjustments were not finished until 1895, but this was the end of Russian expansion to the south. It had ended not at a natural frontier but at a political one, where the presence of another great power had constrained it.

———

As Muslim rule was collapsing in the west, Yaqub Beg was establishing a Muslim state in the east (see figure 5.1). His life before his arrival in Kashgar quickly became the stuff of legend. We know relatively little about it, but it is clear that he was born to a middling family and rose through the ranks in the chaos that engulfed Khoqand in the 1840s. He served as governor of Aq Masjid but was recalled before Perovsky's assault on the fortress in 1853. By 1865, Yaqub Beg was a trusted advisor of Alimqul and was chosen personally by him to mastermind the intervention in Kashgar. Alimqul's death soon afterward made Yaqub Beg a free agent. His conquests were nevertheless remarkable, for he did not possess any of the usual forms of legitimacy. He did not use the title of khan, contenting himself with the more modest titles of *badavlat* and *ataliq ghazi*. *Badavlat* meant "the possessor of fortune." *Ataliq* was the military rank that Yaqub Beg had in Khoqand, while *ghazi* can be translated as "warrior for the faith." Yaqub Beg positioned himself as a defender of Islam and made his service to Islam the main source of his legitimacy. He enforced strict forms of Islamic law and patronized madrasas and mausoleums of the major Sufi figures in Altishahr, while he sidelined the living Sufis. Buzurg Khoja had been Yaqub Beg's key to Kashgar, but the former quickly lost all influence and returned to Khoqand. Yaqub Beg's conquest of Kashgar finally put paid to the khojas' influence in Altishahr. At the same time, he showed no inclination to help the cause of Khoqand or to oppose the Russian onslaught. Instead, he strengthened the frontier with Khoqand and sought to find some sort of accommodation with the Russians.

FIG. 5.1. Yaqub Beg. Undated photograph. Published in *Zapiski Vostochnogo otdeleniia Russkogo arkheologicheskogo obshchestva*, 1899, no. 11: 89.

The Russians were wary of him. They had witnessed the collapse of Qing power in Central Asia with mixed feelings. That collapse might open up possibilities for further Russian expansion or the acquisition of vassals in Xinjiang, but dangers also lurked. The upheaval might spill over into their territory. The Muslim rebellion had already produced a wave of refugees fleeing into Russian territory from the Ili valley in the north. Dungans and Taranchis (sedentary Turkic Muslims) acting together had overthrown Qing rule in the Ili valley, but the coalition had fallen apart soon afterward, and a Taranchi named Abu'l Ala Khan had declared himself sultan in the valley. The Russians feared that this Muslim statelet might become a magnet for Kazakhs who were Russian subjects or be annexed by Yaqub Beg. To preempt those possibilities, they seized upon the flight to Ili of a Kazakh who was a Russian subject accused of murder to invade the valley. Abu'l Ala Khan's forces could offer little resistance, and on June 22, 1871, he offered the keys to the city of Ghulja to General Gerasim Kolpakovsky, the governor of Semirech'e and leader of the military expedition. Publicly, the Russians asserted that the occupation was to help the Qing maintain order in its borderlands and that as soon as the Chinese government had restored order, Ili would be returned to the Qing. However, since no one expected the Qing to retake the province, the promise of returning Ili was largely hypothetical when it was made. The Ili valley was integrated into the Russian empire, linking its trade ever more tightly with that of Jettisuv.

Once they had secured Ili, the Russians entered into communication with Yaqub Beg to secure the status of Russian subjects who traded in Altishahr. Russian officials were careful not to recognize Yaqub Beg as a legitimate ruler and conducted all communications with him through the governor-general of the newly established province of Turkestan rather than through the Russian Foreign Ministry. Nevertheless, Russia signed a commercial treaty in 1872 with Yaqub Beg that addressed him as the "honorable ruler" of his domains. The treaty gave Russian subjects the right to trade in what it referred to as Yettishahr (Seven Cities, a variant of Altishahr), establish their own caravanserais, and appoint commercial agents.[11] These were more or less the same terms that Russia had imposed on Bukhara in 1868. As far as the Russians were concerned, Kashgar was now a vassal state on their frontier.

Yaqub Beg was pleased that the Russian treaty provided him with security and recognition, but he wanted to be more than a Russian vassal. He dispatched a mission to India, seeking the establishment of commercial links and inviting a diplomatic mission in response. The British had been alarmed by the Russian expansion into Transoxiana and wanted to block Russian influence in Eastern Turkestan. They also hoped to include Yaqub Beg's domain in the system of friendly (and pliant) states with which they had long sought to ring India. Altishahr would thus be an eastern counterpart to Afghanistan. Yet British officials in India knew very little about Altishahr. A few intrepid private travelers were the first Britons to show up in Kashgar. R. B. Shaw visited Kashgar in 1868–1869 and after his return wrote a highly exaggerated account of the commercial potential of Altishahr as well as its strategic significance.[12] Lord Mayo, the viceroy of India, then dispatched a mission to Yaqub Beg whose members spent the winter of 1873–1874 in Kashgar. In February, the mission signed a commercial treaty that paralleled the one Yaqub Beg had signed with the Russians. However, the British recognized Yaqub Beg as "the Ruler of the territory of Kashgar and Yarkund" and appointed a representative to his court. Yaqub Beg was also allowed to buy weapons in India.[13]

Yaqub Beg also reached out to the Ottomans. The Ottoman Empire was the most powerful Muslim state of the time, and its sultans also claimed the title of caliph, the spiritual head of the world's Sunni Muslims. Muslim sovereigns from around the world had occasionally turned to them for assistance. Yet by the mid-nineteenth century, the empire was experiencing the same kinds of diplomatic and military problems as the Qing. It was pressed by European powers who imposed unequal treaties on it and threatened its territory. Russia had emerged as the primary antagonist in this regard. The Ottomans had therefore studiously ignored a number of approaches from Central Asian rulers in previous decades. This time the situation was a little different. A concatenation of circumstances allowed the Ottomans to offer help to Yaqub Beg. The nascent Ottoman press was abuzz with excitement about the Muslim uprising and the establishment of independent Muslim states in China, even if the details remained murky. Eastern Turkestan was a safe place for the Ottomans to exercise their claim to be the spiritual heads of the Muslim world. They had no relations with the Qing and could intervene in eastern Turkestan without antagonizing either Russia or Britain, which were otherwise wary of potential Ottoman influence over their own Muslim colonial subjects.

Alimqul had initiated contact with the Ottomans as a desperate eleventh-hour measure in 1864. By the time his envoy arrived in Istanbul, Alimqul was dead and Tashkent had fallen to the Russians, but the news of Yaqub Beg's victories had begun to reach the Ottoman Empire. The envoy, Sayyid Yaqub Khan, happened to be a nephew of Yaqub Beg, and on his own authority, he requested that the sultan send an imperial letter and an Ottoman medal to Yaqub Beg. In addition, he requested a supply of rifles and military instructors for Kashgar. The Ottomans sent the rifles but not the letter. Upon his return to Kashgar in 1869, Yaqub Khan convinced his uncle to seek additional Ottoman help. As a result, Yaqub Beg dispatched a formal mission of his own to Istanbul in 1873, which procured the requested letter. The Ottomans also sent four military officers as instructors for Yaqub Beg's army, as well as six cannons and twelve hundred rifles. When the mission returned to Kashgar, Yaqub Beg performed a solemn ceremony at Afaq Khoja's mausoleum in which he girded himself with the sword that the sultan had sent him, had the imperial letter read aloud, and ordered that the sultan be mentioned in the Friday sermon and that his name appear on the coinage of the land. At least officially, he had accepted the sultan as his suzerain.

This was a win-win situation for the two sides. Yaqub Beg's acceptance of the caliph as a suzerain did nothing to constrain him in any way, but it was useful for showing his subjects that he was tied to a major outside power. It was also a new basis of legitimation that went beyond the Chingissid or local Islamic sources that had been conventional in Central Asia. The Ottomans, for their part, could bolster their claim to be supporters of a distant Muslim community without incurring too many diplomatic risks. Yet this modest intervention was the most concrete step the Ottomans ever took to provide aid to another Muslim country. Nor was it to be repeated. The episode is more significant for other reasons. It was indicative of collapsing distances and the incorporation of Central Asia into broader global politics. And it marked the emergence of the Ottoman Empire as a factor in Central Asian history. The Ottoman Empire might not have intervened directly in the region after the dispatch of the four military advisors, but it was to retain a certain allure in the minds of Central Asian elites, as we shall see in the chapters that follow. It was to be a model for emulation, an interlocutor, and a node of loyalty, even as colonial rule was consolidated in the region.

There were many novelties to the state that Yaqub Beg built. It had a conscription-based army, something that only Alim Khan had attempted before in Central Asia. The army was trained in modern ways by the four Ottoman instructors as well as a number of Afghan and Indian Muslim officers. Yaqub Beg was the first Central Asian ruler to establish links with powers outside the region. Yet many of his methods were rooted firmly in the Central Asian tradition. The state had minimal institutionalization. It was built on conquest and funded through the harsh extraction of revenue from the population. Meanwhile, Yaqub Beg's entourage, the ruling circle, was composed largely of men who had come over from the Ferghana valley. Many Altishahris came to see Yaqub Beg's rule as a regime of occupation. The experiment was unsustainable, and it ran into trouble soon enough.

––––––

The loss of Xinjiang had given rise to intense debate in Beijing about the region's place in the empire. The question of Xinjiang's worth to the empire had been raised ever since its conquest in 1759, and it now was repeated with force. Important voices at the court argued for abandoning distant, troublesome, and barren Xinjiang and focusing instead on strengthening the coast against the very real threats from European powers and especially Japan. Others argued that recovering Xinjiang was essential. No one formulated that argument better than General Zuo Zongtang. A scholar from Hunan, he had failed three times to acquire a worthy rank in civil examinations but had made his name by organizing a local army to fight against various rebellions in the south. He had then been made governor-general of Shaanxi and Gansu, where he had pacified the Dungan rebellion. Now he argued that while defending the coast was important, the Eurasian frontiers were more important to the empire's security. In the northwest, there were "no natural boundaries that serve to hamper the advance of enemies," and everything depended on the strength of the armed forces stationed there. "Therefore," he argued, "Xinjiang is important for the sake of defending Mongolia; and to defend Mongolia is to secure the capital. Beijing and the Northwest are connected to each other just like fingers are connected to the arm. When they are solidly united and connected, security can be guaranteed. However, if [our control over] Xinjiang is not solid, the various tribes of Mongolia would also become an unstable factor."[14] Yet, the present danger arose not from the indigenous population but from Russia and Britain. "When it comes to the management of the affairs of Xinjiang," Zuo wrote to a colleague, "the most important task is to prevent Russia's collaboration with Britain in violating our interest, rather than to suppress the Muslims."[15] He combined this pragmatic point with the argument that abandoning Xinjiang would be a betrayal by the present emperor of his ancestors, who had first brought the region into the empire. Zuo's arguments won out, and in 1875 the Tongzhi emperor appointed him imperial commissioner for military affairs in Xinjiang, with the charge of recovering Xinjiang for the Qing. Zuo became the first Han to be in charge of the region, which had hitherto been a preserve of Manchu and Mongol warriors.

Zuo made meticulous preparations for his campaign, assembling an army of sixty thousand troops trained according to modern methods and armed with imported weapons. The soldiers established farms to ensure a supply of food, which Zuo supplemented with a vast logistical apparatus for purchasing grain in Gansu and Qumul and from Russian merchants in Ili. The court provided substantial funding and allowed Zuo to raise two foreign loans totaling 8.5 million taels from the Hong Kong and Shanghai Banking Corporation. The campaign ended up costing the

FIG. 5.2. The conquerors of Central Asia: Zuo Zongtang (left, a photograph from 1875) and Mikhail Cherniaev (right, a photogravure from 1882). One of many generals who contributed to the Russian conquest of Central Asia, Cherniaev took Tashkent in 1865 and returned as governor-general of Turkestan for a brief stint between 1882 and 1884.

Qing 26.5 million taels (the equivalent of 1,060 tons of silver), which amounted to one-sixth of the annual expenditure of the Qing treasury.[16] Zuo moved his headquarters to Suzhou in April 1876 and began what turned out to be an inexorable surge across the northwest. Qing armies took all of Zungharia in three months in 1876, before turning south in the autumn. Yaqub Beg had hoped to avoid a military confrontation and reach a diplomatic solution that might leave him in control of Altishahr as a vassal of the Qing. He had raised the matter with a British envoy in 1873–1874 and in 1877 and had sent an envoy to London to negotiate, with British help, with Qing representatives. The British favored such a solution, which would have been beneficial to their strategic goals in Central Asia. The Qing court had initially expressed some interest, but by 1877, as Zuo's armies advanced rapidly, it saw no reason to leave Yaqub Beg in power, even as a vassal. All that was rendered moot when Yaqub Beg died suddenly, most likely of a cerebral hemorrhage, in May 1877. After his death, his state collapsed in a heap as infighting broke out among various groups in his entourage. Zuo's forces marched in and took over all of

Altishahr with relatively little resistance. The last city to yield was Khotan, which fell on January 2, 1878. Against all odds, the Qing had reconquered Xinjiang. Yaqub Beg's adventure was over, as were British hopes of a buffer state to the north of India.

———

The second conquest of Xinjiang by the Chinese brought the Ili question back to life. The Russians had asserted that their occupation of the valley was temporary. Now their bluff had been called. Some Russian officials wanted simply to keep the territory, but ultimately the Russian government decided to return it and extract concessions from the Qing. In negotiations at Livadia in the Crimea in 1879, the Qing diplomat Chonghou agreed to a treaty that offered Russia five million rubles as reimbursement for the cost of the occupation, the right to open seven consulates in Xinjiang and Mongolia, and the right to engage in duty-free trade across the two regions. Moreover, Russia was to retain western Ili as well as the Muzart and Talki passes that allowed entry to Altishahr. The Qing court was stunned by the concessions that Chonghou had made and refused to ratify the treaty. It managed to bring Russia back to the bargaining table and renegotiate the deal at St. Petersburg in 1881, where the Qing obtained much better terms. In exchange for a higher indemnity (nine million rubles), they were able to retake the mountain passes, reduce the number of new consulates to two, and shrink the free-trade area to a hundred-*li* (fifty-kilometer) border zone. The treaty also allowed those residents of Ili who preferred to remain Russian subjects to move to Russian territory.[17] Ten thousand households of Taranchis—the vast majority of the community—and many Dungans availed themselves of this opportunity. They had no love for the Qing and anticipated reprisals when Qing rule returned. They were settled in compact communities in the Vernyi and Jarkent districts in Jettisuv (Semirech'e). The Russians were clearly delighted to have their new frontier populated by groups who were fiercely anti-Qing.[18] In Altishahr, many members of Yaqub Beg's regime as well as many locals poured into the Ferghana valley, preferring life under Russian rule to an

MAP 5.2. Imperial Central Asia

The map shows administrative boundaries at the end of the period of imperial conquest.
Russian Central Asia included the two protectorates of Khiva and Bukhara and nine districts
(*oblasts*). While Uralsk and Turgay were freestanding districts, the rest were grouped in larger
units (*krais*) headed by governors-general. Semirech'e was part of the Steppe *Krai* between
1884 and 1899. Transcaspia was administered from Tiflis (now Tbilisi) in the Caucasus until
1898 (hence its name), when it was made part of Turkestan. Xinjiang was divided into four
circuits. Altay was added to it in 1912.

uncertain future under the resurgent Qing. This was to be the first of
many movements of populations across the Russian-Chinese border
that the treaty established.

The Treaty of St. Petersburg formalized the means of Ili's return to
China. It is remembered today mostly because it was the one occasion
in the nineteenth century when the beleaguered Qing empire came out
ahead in a diplomatic tussle with a European power. However, the treaty
was also a significant landmark in the history of Central Asia. By creating a stable border between the two empires that was subject to international law, the treaty formalized the division of Central Asia between
them. The steppe had been fully enclosed. In 1867, the Russians turned
the district of Turkestan, established two years earlier, into a region

(*krai*) divided into districts (*oblasts*), a part of the Russian empire sub-ject to Russian imperial legislation and run by a Russian bureaucracy (see map 5.2). The region expanded as Russian conquests continued until 1889. In 1868, the Russians introduced new administrative forms on the steppe, dividing it into four districts. In 1881, the two eastern *oblasts*—Akmolinsk and Semipalatinsk, the lands of the Middle Horde—were joined together in the Steppe *Krai*. Both Turkestan and the Steppe *Krai* were headed by governors-general, who were respon-sible directly to the tsar. The governor-general of Turkestan in particular enjoyed wide authority, including the responsibility for dealing with the protectorates of Khiva and Bukhara as well as other indigenous states along Turkestan's borders. Locals called him *yorim podishoh*, which liter-ally means "half-king," although "viceroy" would be an apt translation. Meanwhile, the Qing turned Xinjiang into a province in 1884 and began to introduce into it the administrative structures of China proper. Xin-jiang was no longer a zone of military occupation or a preserve of Man-chu and Mongol bannermen. Yet both empires took the heterogeneity of their populations as a given. The point was to manage difference rather than to enforce homogeneity. In practice, this meant that differ-ent jurisdictions were governed by their own statutes, and different re-ligious communities continued to be judged by their own laws. In both empires, Central Asian territories remained distinctive.

6

A Colonial Order

IN 1873, EUGENE SCHUYLER, the secretary of the American legation in St. Petersburg, packed his bags and went off to visit Russia's new conquests in Central Asia. He was often critical of what he saw, even if he thought that Russian rule was an improvement over "native despotism." His first impressions of Tashkent, however, were quite striking. "As I sat in the porch in the bright moonlight, the first night of my arrival at Tashkent," he wrote, "I could scarcely believe that I was in Central Asia, but seemed rather to be in one of the quiet little towns of Central New York. The broad dusty streets, shaded by double rows of trees; the sound of rippling water in every direction; the small white houses, set a little back from the streets, with trees and a palisade in front; the large square, full of turf and flowers, with a little church in the middle—all combined to give me this familiar impression." Schuyler was describing the new city that the Russians were building across the Anhor River from Tashkent's citadel. "By daylight," he continued, "Tashkent seems more like one of the Western American towns—Denver, for instance, though lacking in the busy air which pervades that place, and with Sarts, in turbans and gowns, in place of Indians and miners."[1] Schuyler instinctively saw Russian Tashkent as a frontier town. That description would have been even more apt for the cities that appeared on the steppe, most of them built around points in Russian lines of fortification. Orsk, Semipalatinsk, Vernyi (now Almaty), and Pishpek (now Bishkek) all started as Russian forts and were frontier settlements. But Schuyler's instincts were right. They both remind us that Russia's conquest of Central Asia took place at the same time as the U.S. conquest of the American West and help us think of the two events in a broader framework of colonialism. Like the United States, the Russian empire did not have formal colonies that would be territorially or juridically distinct from the imperial metropole, but both were equally part of nineteenth-century colonialism.

Russia's expansion into Central Asia was an integral part of European colonial expansion around the globe in the nineteenth century, and both the Russians and their rivals saw it as such. In 1864, as Russian armies pressed south from the Syr Darya, Prince Alexander Gorchakov, the Russian foreign minister, sent a memorandum to Russian ambassadors abroad that laid out the official rationale for Russian expansion in Central Asia. "The position of Russia in Central Asia is that of all civilised States which are brought into contact with half-savage nomad populations, possessing no fixed social organisation," he wrote. "In such cases it always happens that the more civilised State is found, in the interest of the security of its frontier and its commercial relations, to exercise a certain ascendancy over those whom their turbulent and unsettled character make most undesirable neighbours." This, he was at pains to point out, was also the experience of all other great powers: "The United States of America, France in Algeria, Holland in her Colonies, England in India—all have been irresistibly forced, less by ambition than by imperious necessity, into this onward march, where the greatest difficulty is to know when to stop." The civilizational difference was key here, for, as Gorchakov argued, "it is a peculiarity of Asiatics to respect nothing but visible and palpable force; the moral force of reason and of the interests of civilisation has as yet no hold upon them."[2] British observers found plenty of parallels between Russian Central Asia and British India. Lord Curzon, the future viceroy of India and British foreign secretary, traveled through Central Asia in 1888–1889 partly to explore "how [the Russians'] methods and their results compare with those of England in India."[3] Russian authors agreed with the comparison, even if they argued that Russian rule in Central Asia was more humane than British imperialism in India. Such parallels were commonplace in Russian public life as well, with Turkestan seen as more comparable to

British India or Algeria than to other parts of the Russian empire.[4] Central Asia was a colony of the Russian empire.

While colonialism, like any other term in the human sciences, has no universally agreed upon definition, we will use it to refer to a cluster of practices and concepts that emerged in the seventeenth century, when European empires began to conceptualize vast unbridgeable differences between the metropole and colonies and colonial subjects. The differences were conceived of in terms of civilization, race, and ethnicity, and they were increasingly authorized by science. Colonial empires also claimed a civilizing mission that would bring order and good governance to the natives and raise them to a civilized state. There remained a tension between the claims of civilizing the natives and a sense that the difference was unbridgeable—that no matter how much progress the natives achieved, they still needed more. It was this understanding of difference that Gorchakov had in mind when he offered his justification for Russian expansion.

The Russian empire was no stranger to the business of managing difference. Its various territories were governed by statutes particular to them, while a ramified system of "ranks and standings" placed different social groups in a complex hierarchy. The Muslims of the Volga-Urals region, conquered in the sixteenth century, were integrated into the empire according to such principles. But the difference that set Central Asia apart was far greater, and it was conceptualized using the language of nineteenth-century European colonialism, not older Russian idioms of difference. This understanding of difference shaped the way Central Asia was governed. The region's indigenous population was never assimilated to the empire-wide system of ranks and standings. Legally, it remained *inorodtsy* ("alien"), a category that signified backwardness and moral distance. In Turkestan, the indigenous population was called *tuzemtsy* ("natives"), with all the colonial connotations of that term. Central Asians were exempted from compulsory military service, which was an important sign of imperial belonging. The protectorates imposed on Bukhara and Khiva were also unique in the Russian empire and borrowed from nineteenth-century European imperialism. They were empire on the cheap, for the colonial power left indigenous rulers on the throne to rule their subjects according to their own lights and at their own expense, while denying the rulers any rights to economic independence or to make foreign policy. The British used the method widely in Africa as well as in India, where hundreds of princely states coexisted with provinces under direct British rule. Rulers of these princely states were answerable to British agents (appointed by the viceroy) who usually took up residence at court. It was this model that the Russians adopted for Bukhara and Khiva. A "political agent" stationed in the town of Kagan, a short distance from Bukhara and part of a Russian enclave, was Russia's interlocutor with the emir. The khan of Khiva dealt with a Russian functionary stationed in Petro-Aleksandrovsk, a Russian township eighty kilometers away.

Colonial difference was inscribed in space, social practice, and law. Tashkent's new Russian city was part of a widespread phenomenon of colonial urbanism. The British and the French also built new cities in their colonies, which were meant to display the civilizational superiority of the conquerors. Russian Tashkent, with its wide, orderly boulevards, provided a sharp contrast to the labyrinthine alleys of the old city. It was a little bit of Russia implanted in Turkestan. Already in 1875, with construction less than a decade old, a Hungarian visitor noted that "one can live for years in Russian Tashkent without even suspecting the existence of the Sart part of town."[5] Tashkent was the first and most important, but Russian "new cities" also developed outside Samarqand, Kokand (as the city of Khoqand came to be known now), Marghilan, and Khujand. There was no apartheid, however, and many affluent Central Asians built houses in the new cities even though they were clearly Russian spaces. Tashkent acquired a municipal assembly, gas lighting, a tramway (which was mechanized in 1912 by a Belgian company), theaters, parks, and restaurants. In 1917, at the end of the imperial era, it had half as many people as the old city did.

The Russian administration of Turkestan was headed by the military. All governors-general and all governors of the various districts were military officers. Below them was a two-tiered bureaucracy. The higher levels operated only in Russian and were staffed almost entirely by Russians or other Europeans from the Russian empire. The members of the

lower-level administration, where the empire interacted with local society, were recruited from the local population and operated in local
languages. In areas of settled population, property owners chose elec-
tors (*ellikboshi*), who in turn elected village elders (*aqsaqqal*) and police
chiefs at the county (*volost'*) level. A similar elective system of administration emerged among the nomadic population.[6]

The colonial order produced a dual society in which Russian and
Muslim societies existed side by side with only limited interaction.
There was no apartheid or legal segregation, but there was a clear division between Russian and native spaces. The Russians had found their
earliest interlocutors among merchants who already had commercial
interests in the Russian trade. Soon after the sack of Tashkent, Mikhail
Cherniaev, the conquering general, decorated thirty-one men for
"assiduous service and attachment to the Russian government."[7] Said
Azim-*bai*, a merchant with extensive trading interests in Russia that
predated the conquest, was one of the Russians' first interlocutors in
Tashkent. He received the rank of "hereditary honorable citizen" from
the tsar himself in St. Petersburg, and his family became an important
pillar of Muslim society in Tashkent. But the main burden of dealing
with the natives, including those employed in the lower rungs of the
administrative order that the Russians built, fell to Tatar or Kazakh interpreters who came with the conquering armies. Konstantin Kaufman,
Turkestan's first governor-general, established Russian schools in the
main cities, but he was disappointed in his hopes of attracting Central
Asian students to them. Almost no parents were willing to send their
sons to Russian schools, for fear that they would lose their religion or
culture. In 1884, Kaufman's successor, Nikolai Rozenbakh, established
so-called Russian-native schools, which offered a basic Russian curriculum in the mornings and, to win the trust of the parents, lessons from a
mullah in the afternoon. Even these had a rocky beginning. Local notables who were expected to send their sons to these schools often hired
poor children of the neighborhood to attend instead. The situation
changed only gradually. By the turn of the twentieth century, as a knowledge of Russian became increasingly important in everyday life, these
schools had become quite popular. In the last years of Tsarist rule,

prominent citizens of the cities of Turkestan were petitioning the government to open more such schools. Graduates of these schools formed
the class of intermediaries that the Russian empire needed in Turkestan.
Beyond their still small ranks, however, Russian was little understood.

———

Modernity arrived in the wake of empire in many parts of the world, and
Central Asia was no exception. The Russian empire brought new forms
of power, technologies, and ways of seeing the world that were to prove
highly subversive of the status quo in Central Asia. Backed by a modern
army and a bureaucracy, the Russian empire had substantially greater
state capacity than indigenous Central Asian states had ever managed
to acquire, and it reshaped power relations in the region in significant
ways. The Russian conquest put an end to the perpetual tussles between
rulers and warrior clans and the political fragmentation that they created. Kazakh elites had a much longer experience of Russian rule. New
regulations in 1881 formalized this relationship further, turning Kazakh
sultans into elected officers. In Turkestan, Russian rule meant the demise of the tribal elites—the local governors and petty rulers who had
long challenged the dynasts from below. The elites lost their ability to
control local resources and the power that came with that control. Some
were exiled to other parts of the Russian empire, others emigrated
(mostly to Afghanistan), and still others sank to the status of landlords
if they were lucky. In any case, Russian legislation granted de facto property rights in land to those who cultivated it and curtailed the power of
landlords. They were never to have a major impact on local life. Turkestan and the Kazakh lands became unified political spaces as never before,
and it became possible to imagine a community of Turkestanis for the
first time. The rulers who remained (the khan of Khiva and the emir of
Bukhara) also benefited from this consolidation of power. In Bukhara,
the protectorate transformed the relationship between the emirs and
the local governors, who no longer had the option of rising up in revolt
against the emir, for that would invite Russian intervention. This is most
clearly visible in the case of the Keneges emirs of Shahr-i Sabz who had

been the Manghits' archrivals since before the foundation of the Manghit dynasty. The Keneges had vied for power as the Chaghatayid rule of Abulfayz Khan faltered in the middle of the eighteenth century, and they had retained a sturdy independence from Bukhara the whole time, with a dynasty based in Shar-i Sabz that the Manghits could never fully subjugate. It was the Russians who finally broke the power of the Keneges and handed the city to Bukhara.[8] (The Russians also handed over territory in the Pamirs to Bukhara after the final delineation of the boundary between the Russian empire, Afghanistan, and British India was formalized in the 1890s.) Under the protectorate, Bukharan emirs had far greater control over their territory than their predecessors had ever enjoyed when they were independent. Over the ensuing decades, new notions of community and solidarity were to arise around these new spaces.

The railway, steamship, telegraph, and postal system tied Central Asia to the rest of the world as never before. The first printing press in Central Asia was established in Tashkent in 1870, the telegraph arrived there in June 1873, and the first bank opened in May 1875. After a slow beginning, the region was also linked to Russia by railway. Railway construction in Central Asia began for military, not economic, reasons. The first track was laid in the Turkmen desert during the final conquest of the Turkmens. It extended eastward over the years, reaching Tashkent in 1898 and extending into the Ferghana valley. It also connected Central Asia to steamships on the Caspian and, via other rail links, to those on the Black Sea. A direct line to inner Russia via Orenburg was completed in 1910. Over a generation, the conquest utterly transformed Central Asia's economy. The biggest impact was in agriculture. New crops appeared in Central Asia that brought about important changes in people's diet. Potatoes, tomatoes, and beets were all new to the region and quickly became staples of the local cuisine. Other crops were developed more intensively. Sericulture took on a heightened importance, and industrial mining appeared for the first time. But it was cotton that was the main motor of transformation of the region and its economy.

Cotton had been grown in Transoxiana since time immemorial, and by the nineteenth century it had become an important export item in the region's trade with Russia. Even before Tashkent was taken, certain Russian merchants were traveling, at great risk and discomfort, to Central Asia to scope out the possibilities. Cotton also drew the attention of Kaufman—Turkestan's governor-general for fourteen decisive years between 1867 and 1881—who dispatched two experts to Texas to investigate contemporary American methods of production and to look for new strains of cotton. The cotton traditionally grown in Transoxiana was a short-fiber variety that could produce only poorer varieties of yarn. American varieties had longer fiber that was easier to turn into fabric. Kaufman's emissaries brought back several new varieties of cotton, and one, Upland cotton (*Gossypium hirsutum*), succeeded beyond all expectations in Turkestan. The first export shipment was made in 1884, after which more and more peasants took to growing cotton with enthusiasm. Initially, textile mills in Moscow and Łódź sent their own buyers to acquire cotton directly from the growers, but specialized firms that did the buying quickly arose. The profits to be made from the trade in cotton were substantial, and the cotton trading firms laid the foundations of a new urban merchant class in Turkestan. Cotton also provided the basis for the first emergence of modern industry in the region. Cotton gins cleaned the cotton before it was shipped to textile mills in Russia or Poland (then part of the Russian empire). The finished goods were then sent back to Central Asia. Cotton fibers knit Turkestan's peasants into the world economy and created a typically colonial relationship between Russia and Central Asia.

The first printing press in Central Asia was established by Kaufman, but printing was soon also taken up by local booksellers, who began to produce printed versions of the books they had long sold. Print quickly became ubiquitous. Trains and steamships brought books from far and wide to Central Asia's bookshops. Along with the books came a greater novelty, the newspaper. The first newspapers were official organs: *Turkiston viloyatining gazeti* (Turkestan gazette), published in Tashkent beginning in 1870, and the *Dala wilayatïnïng gazeti* (Steppe gazette), published in Omsk beginning in 1888. They aimed to provide "useful information" for the native population, but they nevertheless became venues for the expression of new ideas. Other newspapers in various

Turkic languages or Persian arrived from farther afield—the Crimea, the Ottoman Empire, Iran, and India—and brought news and ideas from faraway places. New patterns of the circulation of goods, people, and ideas reshaped the horizons of Central Asians. The world shrank as the new order made possible new kinds of journeys, in terms of their range, speed, and direction.

Conquest also brought people from the rest of the Russian empire to Central Asia. They came as soldiers, peasant settlers, administrators, merchants, and job seekers. Most of the newcomers were Russian or Ukrainian, but Baltic Germans, Poles, Ashkenazi Jews, and Armenians also appeared in the region. So did Tatars, Turkic-speaking Muslims from the Volga-Urals region, which had been under Russian rule since the 1550s. A few Tatars were officers in the army, but most came as translators or merchants. Over the next several decades, the Tatars were to play many different roles in Central Asia. Many of the newcomers settled in cities, whose character changed (as we shall soon see), but there were also many peasant settlers among them. The settlers' main destination was the steppe. The first colonists were Cossacks, who were members of the military caste that had become a main pillar of the Tsarist empire and whom the empire settled on the frontier to provide a first line of defense. Once the steppe was subdued, peasant settlers followed, first on their own and then, after 1896, in an organized manner. This settlement was part of a larger movement of Slavic peasants that saw well over five million people move to Siberia or Central Asia between 1885 and 1913. In the Kazakh steppe, it was settler colonialism, not cotton, that produced the greatest transformation. As Russian settlers put more and more land under the plow, they disrupted the nomadic way of life, forcing many Kazakhs to settle and take up agriculture or, in many cases, to become wage laborers for the settlers (see figure 6.1). Peasant settlement had begun to alter the demographic and ecological balance on the steppe. It also led to great dissatisfaction among the Kazakhs. The land question was to emerge as the central issue for Kazakh elites in the twentieth century.

Russian rule in Central Asia was a curious mixture of hubris and paranoia. Russian administrators were fully confident of the superiority

FIG. 6.1. A Kazakh settlement, ca. 1900. Postcard (author's collection).

of the European civilization that they represented. Enlightened rule, good government, orderly taxation, and modern technology would transform the region and civilize its people. The first years after the establishment of the new administrative order saw a number of utopian plans of transformation. In 1873, Ferdinand de Lesseps, the builder of the Suez Canal, proposed a railway from Calais to Calcutta that would pass through the new Russian territories before going down to Peshawar via Kabul. Others sought to change the course of the Amu Darya to make it flow into the Caspian, which would both irrigate the desert and create a water route to India.[9] In the 1890s, after a terrible famine had ravaged inner Russia, the imperial government began a project of planned settlement of Slavic peasants in Central Asia. The main destination was the Kazakh steppe, which was supposed to contain large amounts of unused land. A number of expeditions set out to measure the amount of land the nomads needed. Not surprisingly, surveys decreed that there were large amounts of land in excess of the nomads' needs and thus available for peasant settlement. In Turkestan, with its denser population, the local administration remained wary of large-scale settlement except in Semirech'e (Jettisuv) in the northeast and the northern parts of Syr Darya district. Local officials routinely denied that suitable land was available in Turkestan, and the region was closed to settlement by the governor-general in 1897. Yet after the turn of the twentieth century, the Resettlement Administration, the agency responsible for peasant settlement, set its eyes on Turkestan as well. The head of the administration and future minister of agriculture A. V. Krivoshein hoped to create a "new Turkestan" in which Slavic settlers would plant cotton on lands newly irrigated through government-sponsored schemes. Although the project was still in its infancy when the imperial regime collapsed, Central Asia had become a colony of both occupation and settlement, with a substantial Russian presence in the region.

This hubris was always accompanied by fear that Russian rule was thin and the population too "fanatical" to be reconciled to it. For Turkestan's new rulers, Islam represented the main threat to Russian rule in the region. They deemed it synonymous with fanaticism, which predisposed Muslims to irrational hatred of the conquerors. It had to be dealt with carefully. For Kaufman, the solution was to pursue a policy of disregard (*ignorirovanie*) toward Islam. Islam and Islamic institutions were to be left alone—for curbing them would only inflame fanaticism—but Islamic dignitaries were to have no official functions or positions under Russian rule. Kaufman hoped that deprived of state support, Islam would decay. The nomads were quite different. Their way of life was deemed to be "based on natural and still primitive principles" and they were therefore considered to "have no specific religious faith."[10] Russian policy was therefore to handle fanaticism carefully and keep it from spreading to the nomads. That had not always been the case. A century earlier, Catherine the Great had seen the nomads as the problem. For her, the nomads' propensity to raid and pillage could be curbed only by encouraging the spread of Islam on the steppe, which would have a civilizing influence on the nomads. Catherine oversaw the construction of several mosques on the steppe and the establishment of Islamic educational institutions (staffed by Tatars) among the Kazakhs of the Junior Horde. Islamic institutions thus facilitated the consolidation of Russian power in the Kazakh lands.[11] By the mid-nineteenth century, however,

Russian views of Islam had changed. Kaufman established distinct patterns of administration for each type of population and even suggested redrawing administrative boundaries in Turkestan to perpetuate the "natural demarcation" of the settled from the nomad.[12] While the boundaries were not redrawn during the Tsarist period, nomads and sedentary Muslims were subjected to different legal regimes. In the sedentary zones of Turkestan, the population remained subject to the *shariat* as interpreted by the Muslim judges (*qazis*). The competence of the *qazis* was restricted, their procedures modified, and their decisions subjected to review by Russian officials, but the *shariat* remained in operation. Among the nomads—Kazakhs, Kyrgyz, and Turkmens— personal law was to be based on custom (*adat*), and it was to be adjudicated by elected judges called *biy*. Nomads and sedentary people had always seen each other as different, but the Russians crystallized the distinction into law.

The policy of disregard also rested on certain basic characteristics of the Russian empire. Resources were scarce, and the administrative machinery was stretched thin. As in other colonial situations across the world, the Russians ruled Central Asia with a small number of men. The lowest tiers of the administration—headmen, irrigation controllers, tax collectors—were all staffed by locals, while Russians staffed only the higher levels of administration. Since only a very few Russian administrators knew any local languages, Central Asia remained alien to them. One of the few competent Orientalists in government service was N. P. Ostroumov, who arrived in Tashkent in 1877 with a degree in Islamic Studies from Kazan University and went on to serve in numerous capacities for the next forty years. He was editor of the official local-language newspaper, censor, confidant of governors-general, and font of advice on all things Central Asian to Russian officials. In 1911, he confided to a visitor that he thought Russian rule would not last a single day in Turkestan if the Russian armies were withdrawn.[13] This sense bred caution among officials, who were loath to provoke local sensibilities and who saw the maintenance of social peace as their highest priority.

Not surprisingly, none of the utopian programs of transformation were realized in the imperial period. While the traditional network of irrigation channels continued to function and was meticulously maintained, the imperial period saw only very modest gains in the construction of new irrigation works. Only two large-scale irrigation projects came to fruition in Turkestan in the Tsarist period. The first, along the course of the Murghab River in Transcaspia, was an attempt to reconstruct the thirteenth-century irrigation network that had fed the Merv oasis. In 1887, all land along the river was proclaimed to be the personal property of the tsar, who lavished funds on it to create a model of planned development. The Murghab Imperial Domain, as the property was called, came to include a series of canals and reservoirs that, by the eve of the First World War, could irrigate 25,000 *desiatina* (27,500 hectares) of land. It also featured hydroelectric stations, experimental farms and orchards, and the planned city of Bayram Ali. Most of the land in it was rented out to Russian settlers. The second major irrigation project was in the Hungry Steppe, where Kaufman's early failures were redeemed in small measure by other projects. In part, it was the work of Grand Duke Nikolai Konstantinovich, a nephew of Alexander II who had ended up in exile in Tashkent as a result of his dissolute life: after having stolen diamonds from his mother to pay for his many affairs, he was declared insane ("diseased moral dissipation" was the official diagnosis) and packed off to Tashkent to live out his disgraceful life in the obscurity of the imperial frontier. In Tashkent, he seems to have found a mission, for he threw himself and his considerable funds into irrigation schemes. He too devoted a lot of effort to trying to redirect the course of the Amu Darya, but he eventually settled for smaller projects. The most successful involved enlarging an old irrigation channel to form the Nicholas I canal that extended deep into the Hungry Steppe. It was acquired by the Russian treasury and later formed the basis of a larger system of irrigation that emerged in the final years before the war. The first major canal built with modern technology, the Romanov, opened in 1913 and was expected to irrigate 45,000 *desiatina*s (50,000 hectares). Yet for a half-century's effort, these were very modest results. Russian observers were aware of the paucity of Russian achievements, especially when compared to what the British were doing in Punjab. "In comparison with what the English engineers have done," wrote one commentator in 1906, "our weak and largely unsuccessful attempts to irrigate a small area of land in Central Asia appear positively pitiful and insignificant."[14] Other projects bore similarly sparse fruit. Turkestan remained a land of small peasant holdings. There were no plantations or significant industry, and the cotton boom was based on peasant smallholders.

―――――

The Qing reconquest of eastern Turkestan was underwritten by a different civilizing mission. Zuo Zongtang harked back to the Statecraft school, which drew its inspiration not from the European Enlightenment but from Confucian classics—although it allowed ample space for technical modernization. Zuo may not have read the memorial penned in 1820 by another member of the school, Gong Zizhen (whom we met in chapter 3), but the two men's hopes for Xinjiang were similar. The indigenous population was to be won over to Confucian moral values. This was to be accompanied by substantial investment in land reclamation, the settlement of Han and Hui peasants, the introduction of a Chinese administrative system, and the establishment of Confucian education, all of which would turn the new province into a lush garden that would pay for its own upkeep.[15] These hopes were soon dashed when the new arrangements failed for lack of resources, and the Statecraft school's vision was soon supplanted by a new program of thoroughgoing reform based on European ideas, as the Qing sought a remedy for its predicament.

Zuo's vision became official policy when the newly reconquered territory was made a province in 1884, with its capital at Ürümchi. Provincialization meant that the old military administration run by Manchu and Mongol bannermen with their Muslim intermediaries (*wangs*) was to be replaced by a fully bureaucratic system of circuits, prefectures, and counties, to be staffed by Han Chinese functionaries. In practice, the new regulations made a number of exceptions for Xinjiang. The bureaucrats running it were not part of the general rotation of jobs in the imperial civil service, nor were they required to pass the same examinations. The new bureaucracy was filled by members of the conquering army.

Zuo had organized it as a modern army outside the banner system of the Qing. It was staffed by Chinese soldiers (both Han and Hui) and a close-knit circle of officers, largely from Hunan province. Zuo did not spend much time in Xinjiang after the end of the campaign, but Xinjiang became a place for opportunity for the Hunanese officers of his army, who dominated the province until the end of the empire in 1912. The second Qing conquest of Xinjiang was thus quite different from the first.

Yet, it turned out, provincialization was much easier said than done. The roads in Xinjiang were poor, and there could be no question of railway construction or of establishing Chinese education for the population at large. Since few of the new bureaucrats spoke Turkic, the old Muslim intermediaries remained in place, despite being demoted to the status of "official servants" rather than "officials." Han settlement also proved difficult to organize. Many soldiers demobilized from Zuo's conquering army staffed land reclamation projects, but few showed the inclination to become hardy homesteaders. The Chinese proportion of Xinjiang's population remained minuscule, while the distance between the rulers and the ruled was as great as in Russian Central Asia, if not greater. In Altishahr the Qing had built their fortified cities some distance away from the old cities, although here the concern was security more than the assertion of civilizational superiority. That did not alter after Xinjiang became a province. In the north, most cities developed around forts, much as they had in the Russian empire. Ghulja and Ürümchi were as ethnically distinct from their hinterland as Vernyi or Pishpek.

A bigger reason for the weakness of Qing rule in eastern Turkestan was that the Qing empire was itself being imperialized. Since the Opium Wars, its geopolitical weakness had allowed other empires to force it to sign unequal treaties and extort extraterritorial privileges from it. Both Russia and Britain possessed such rights, and they were strengthened in the diplomacy that accompanied the reestablishment of Qing rule in Xinjiang. The Treaty of St. Petersburg gave Russia the right to open four consulates in Xinjiang and for Russian subjects to be able to trade freely in the region. Britain had also acquired a presence in the area during Yaqub Beg's rule. After the reconquest, it extracted from the Qing the right to operate a consulate in Kashgar and to have its subjects trade in the province on the same terms as Russian subjects. Extraterritoriality and the right to tariff-free trade by subjects of European states were key features of nineteenth-century imperialism around the globe. What was unusual about Xinjiang was that for both the Russian and the British empires, the beneficiaries of extraterritoriality were imperial subjects who were racially and culturally distinct from the imperial rulers. The Russian subjects who operated in Xinjiang were largely Tatars in the north and "Andijanis" in the south. The "Andijanis" had enjoyed privileged status in Xinjiang as subjects of Khoqand. They had become Russian subjects after the Russian conquest of Khoqand, even if they had had nothing to do with the Russian empire in the past and although most of them were not even born in western Turkestan. Yet they found their new status to be quite advantageous. In addition to not paying taxes, they also had the protection of Russian consuls and exemption from being tried in Qing courts of law. The consulates—in Tarabagatay, Ghulja, Ürümchi, and Kashgar—became centers of Russian influence. The consuls appointed headmen (*aqsaqqal*) for their subjects who resided in different places. The headmen mediated between Russian subjects and Qing authorities as well as resolving disputes among them. The headmen diffused extraterritoriality much farther afield than the limited number of consuls would have been able to. The British subjects who traded in Xinjiang were all Indian, and most of them were Hindus. The British consulate in Kashgar took over existing networks of headmen of Indian communities and gave them consular protection. Qing functionaries chafed at the appointment of these headmen, for the relevant treaties made no explicit mention of them, but there was little the Qing could do about it.

British influence was restricted to the south of Xinjiang, but the Russians had a presence throughout the new province, and Russian trade came to dominate the new province. Russian subjects imported raw materials, including cotton, from Xinjiang, and exported fabrics, metal goods, watches, cigarettes, and liquor, all of which were much cheaper than their Chinese counterparts—which were taxed in multiple ways. Chinese merchants had to pay internal tariffs (*lijin*) when crossing provincial boundaries. Xinjiang authorities, deprived of the revenue from the Russian trade, also often had to forgo the *lijin*, since full collection ran the risk of driving Chinese merchants into bankruptcy. Xinjiang's administration therefore remained dependent on subsidies from the central budget (which was increasingly strained by the demands of indemnities to be paid to great powers, especially in the aftermath of the Boxer Rebellion in 1900). Russian economic dominance in Xinjiang took many forms. Well before the turn of the twentieth century, the ruble had become the most stable and widely accepted currency in the bazaars of Xinjiang. Given the weakness of the infrastructure in the Qing empire, even Chinese goods traveled to Xinjiang on Russian railways. The Trans-Siberian Railway, completed in 1894, and the Chinese Eastern Railway, a Russian concession in Manchuria completed in 1896, provided the quickest means of transportation from the Chinese seaboard to Xinjiang. It was cheaper and quicker to transport cargo from, say, Shanghai to Kashgar around Asia and through the Russian empire (by steamship to Odessa or Batumi on the Black Sea, then by the Transcaspian railway to Andijan, before a short caravan hop to Kashgar) than overland across the Qing lands.[16] A Chinese postal service was established only after the fall of the Qing. Before then, Russian post offices remained the only way to connect to the global postal system. There was also no telegraph in Xinjiang. News from abroad was likely to come faster via Russian Turkestan than through China. The new merchant class in Xinjiang was much more closely tied to Russia than to the rest of China and looked west for its opportunities and its inspiration. Nor was the cross-border traffic only one way. Many landless or poor peasants, primarily from Kashgar, traveled to Russian Turkestan in search of work and higher wages. This labor migration had begun in the 1870s, but it took on significant proportions after the turn of the twentieth century. Rough estimates suggested that 13,000 people made the journey in 1905, 28,000 in 1908, and perhaps as many as 50,000 annually during the years of the First World War. Some migrants went to Semirech'e (where there was already a sizable Taranchi population whose members had migrated from Ili at the time of the area's return to the Qing), but Ferghana was a more popular destination. Kashgari labor was an important part of the development of Russian Turkestan, especially its cotton boom. While the migration was largely seasonal, many stayed for the long term, often acquiring Russian papers. This community of Kashgaris was to play an important part in the emergence of Uyghur national identity in the twentieth century.

Xinjiang was also a colony, but in a number of important ways it was a colony of the Russian empire much more than that of the Qing. As the twentieth century dawned, Eastern Turkestan was precisely that: an eastern extension of Turkestan, poorer and less developed, and a backyard of Russian Turkestan, with which it interacted much more intensively than it did with China proper.

7

New Visions of the World

"THE EUROPEANS, taking advantage of our negligence and ignorance, took our government from our hands, and are gradually taking over our crafts and trades. If we do not quickly make an effort to reform our affairs in order to safeguard ourselves, our nation, and our children, our future will be extremely difficult." This was the diagnosis of the current state of Turkestani society offered in 1906 by Munavvar-qori Abdurashidxon-oghli of Tashkent in the first issue of the *Sun*, a newspaper that he launched when the political liberalization following the Russian revolution of 1905 had made it possible for Central Asians to publish newspapers. According to Munavvar-qori, the situation was dire: "All our acts and actions, our ways, our words, our maktabs and madrasas, our methods of teaching, and our morals are corrupt. If we continue in this way for another five or ten years, we are in danger of being dispersed and effaced under the oppression of developed nations." The solution was for society to undertake reform to pull itself up by its bootstraps: "Reform begins with a rapid start in cultivating sciences conforming to our times. Becoming acquainted with the sciences of the present age depends upon the reform of our schools and our methods of teaching." Cultivating sciences necessary to meet the needs of the new age would allow Turkestanis to ward off the bleak future that otherwise beckoned. Society had to be exhorted to reform, but the task was not easy: "The curtain of ignorance has so shut our eyes that we don't even know to what extent we have fallen behind. . . . There are many [among us] who, having spent all their lives as if in a dark house, isolated from everybody, consider all reform to be corruption, and portray all reformers as mischief-mongers."[1]

The Russian conquest posed new questions even as it made possible new ways of posing them. By the turn of the twentieth century, an entirely new discourse of reform had arisen in Turkestan. Its proponents sought answers to the predicament their society faced. Why had Central Asia been conquered? What gave the Europeans the military and economic superiority that allowed them not just to rule the world but also to invent new things? How were Muslims to survive in the new world into which colonialism had plunged them? Nor were these questions simply of abstract philosophical import. The challenges and temptations provided by the colonial presence in Muslim societies made the questions a matter of practical concern. The gas-lit streets of new Tashkent and its fancy stores, and yes, its taverns and brothels, asked questions that had to be answered, at least by those who interacted with these phenomena. The advocacy of reform took place in public spaces (newspapers, charitable organizations, and eventually the theater) that were new to Central Asia. Reform was articulated by groups that were new in society, and it was underpinned by a view of the world that was substantially new. And the ideas were linked to similar movements far away. The trains, steamships, and mail that tied Central Asia to the world economy brought printed books and newspapers from far afield. The *Turkistan Gazette* had published "useful information" since 1870, but it was soon joined by newspapers in various forms of Turkic or Persian from the Crimea, the Ottoman Empire, Iran, and India. These newspapers connected Central Asia to faraway places as never before. Newspapers, books, and modern maps and globes made many of their users "aware of world," as they reported time and time again in later autobiographical accounts. Strikingly, none of these newspapers was in Russian, and Russia did not provide models of action and emulation. These came from other Muslim societies in the Russian empire and beyond. Often, these connections were new, and made possible by the new links built by the empire.[2]

The most important links were with other Muslim societies of the Russian empire, which had been part of the empire for much longer

FIG. 7.1. A new-method school in Samarqand, ca. 1911. Pupils sit at desks laid out in neat rows. Schools did not hold classes outdoors. The subjects might well have been posing for Sergei Prokudin-Gorskii, a pioneer of color photography who traveled around the Russian empire on an imperial commission to document its diversity. Prokudin-Gorskii photograph collection, Library of Congress, Prints and Photographs Division.

than Turkestan. Among the Tatars of the Volga and the Crimea, a modernist reform movement with a focus on elementary education had emerged in the last quarter of the nineteenth century. Its biggest champion was Ismail Bey Gasprinsky, a Crimean *murza* (noble) who had received a Russian education and spent time in Moscow, Paris, and Istanbul. Gasprinsky had come up with the idea of a "new-method" school, in which Muslim children would be taught the alphabet using the new phonetic method, which in turn would produce functional literacy more efficiently than the traditional *maktab* did (see figure 7.1). New-method schools were to combine functional literacy with new kinds of knowledge—arithmetic, general science, geography, and history—to ensure that Muslim children were equipped for operating in the modern world. The new-method (*usul-i jadid*) school gave the movement its name of Jadidism. The school was the centerpiece, but Gasprinsky's reform project encompassed a great deal more. In his vision, once Muslims of the Russian empire achieved civilization, they would have newspapers, books, and theater in their own languages, as well as teachers, doctors, and businessmen. In 1883, Gasprinsky received permission to publish a newspaper. Called *Tercüman* (Interpreter), it pushed the message of reform to its readers, who were to be found across the Russian empire, in Eastern Turkestan, and in the Ottoman Empire. Gasprinky's message found fertile ground among the Tatars of the Volga-Urals region, where a robust merchant class was interested in modern education. Philanthropists established reformed madrasas in cities such as Kazan, Ufa, and Orenburg, while Tatar publishing took off in the last quarter of the nineteenth century, and a robust periodical press emerged after 1905. By the turn of the twentieth century, Tatar publishing houses were producing large quantities of original works as well as translations into Tatar of the writings of Russian and other European authors.

The Ottoman Empire was another major source of models of reform. It was the only reasonably powerful Muslim state left at the turn of the twentieth century. Ottoman sultans claimed the title of caliph, the spiritual leader of the world's Muslims and the symbol of Muslim unity. They had done so since 1517, when they had conquered the Middle East. Few Muslim rulers had acknowledged that status, but as more and more Muslim societies fell under colonial rule, many in the Muslim world began to look at the Ottoman Empire with renewed respect, projecting on it their own hopes and seeing in it a model for the modernization of Muslim societies. Of course, the Ottomans were in dire straits at this time. Much like the Qing, the Ottoman Empire faced internal upheavals along with foreign encroachment that made even the empire's continued existence uncertain. In response, since the early nineteenth century, Ottoman statemen had sought ways to strengthen the state through centralization and the creation of new institutions. In the process, the empire had tackled questions of creating modern Muslim education and new institutions within an Islamic framework. The Ottomans had begun to emphasize their claim to the caliphate in the middle of the nineteenth century. As various European powers appeared as protectors of non-Muslim populations in the Ottoman Empire, the Ottomans sought some diplomatic leverage by claiming to be the spiritual leaders of the world's Muslims, most of whom were by that point colonial subjects of one European empire or another. The Ottomans' ability to do anything substantial to protect or help other Muslims was practically negligible (the mission sent to Yaqub Beg that we encountered in chapter 5 was highly exceptional), but the claim to the caliphate created new bonds of affective solidarity with Muslims as far afield as Bengal and Aceh—and Bukhara, Tashkent, and Yarkand. Meanwhile, the Ottoman press and other Ottoman publications began to appear in Central Asia, where they were easily comprehensible to the educated public. The Ottoman appeal was even stronger in Bukhara. The emirs presented themselves as the last Muslim sovereigns in Central Asia and as guardians of Islam. The result was a deeply conservative cultural policy that kept the new method of schooling out of Bukhara. However, Bukhara's merchants, increasingly tied to the Russian empire and beyond, wanted modern education for their sons. In 1909, they established a benevolent society to send students to Istanbul to receive the education that the emirs would not allow in Bukhara.

In Turkestan, reform appealed to a new generation of men who had a foot in the new world that the Russians had forced upon Central Asia, even if they had emerged from the old world. Munavvar-qori, for example, came from a family deeply rooted in Islamic learning. He had studied in madrasas in Tashkent and Bukhara and was a religious scholar in his own right (the qori in his name is an honorific indicating that he had memorized the Qur'an), but his reading of newspapers and other contemporary works had convinced him of the need for reform. He was twenty-eight when he penned the editorial quoted above. Mahmudkhoja Behbudiy, his counterpart in Samarqand, was a mufti (jusrisconsult), a position that continued to exist under Russian rule. He came from a family of solid means that also had some commercial interests

FIG. 7.2. Leading Jadid figures: Mahmudkhoja Behbudiy from Samarqand (left) and
Abdurauf Fitrat of Bukhara (right), both ca. 1913.

and he had spent eight months traveling in the Caucasus and the Ottoman Empire in 1899–1900 on his way to the hajj. He had seen the institutions of modern education that the Ottoman Empire and Egypt had
pioneered in recent decades. He became an avid proponent of reform
upon his return to Samarqand, when he was not quite twenty-six. Abdurauf Fitrat of Bukhara had a traditional madrasa education before he
received a scholarship from Bukhara's benevolent society to study in
Istanbul (see figure 7.2). The choice of Istanbul was fateful. The
Bukharan merchants did not think of sending students to St. Petersburg
(the imperial capital) or Tehran (the capital of Iran, whose language
Bukhara shared), let alone the Tatar cities of Kazan or Orenburg. They
chose Istanbul because it was the capital of the only powerful Muslim
state in the world and the place where new ideas of coping with the
modern world were being put into practice. Fitrat arrived in Istanbul in
1909 in the immediate aftermath of the Young Turk Revolution to find
the city abuzz with debates about the future. His four years in Istanbul
shaped his outlook for the rest of his life.

Many Jadids, as the proponents of reforms are usually called, had
Islamic credentials, but they were also young. They saw their own society

with new eyes and found much about it wanting. Their advocacy of reform was the assertion of power of a new generation. That brought its own difficulties, as we shall see below, but reform became part of the social landscape of urban Turkestan in the last decade and a half of the Tsarist era. The reformers opened new-method schools and wrote primers and textbooks for them. They established bookstores, public reading rooms, benevolent societies, and (after 1906) newspapers of their own. These newspapers struggled financially, but they were often killed by censorship before they could succumb to the market. Nevertheless, these new phenomena created a public space in Turkestan for the first time and reordered the way culture was produced and talked about. New genres of writing—the newspaper feuilleton, the fictional travelogue, and the stage play—produced a new language of critique, while satire and its visual counterpart, the cartoon, reshaped the parameters in which culture and society were discussed. The new literature was earnestly didactic and profoundly moralizing, and it featured a great deal of criticism of the existing state of affairs in Turkestan.

The Jadids were fascinated by modernity. They admired Europe (to which Russia also belonged) for its technological prowess, wealth, and might, even as they feared the consequences of that might for their own society. They had appropriated the ideas of progress and civilization as well as their cognate, advancement. These Enlightenment ideas came to them more through Ottoman or Tatar translations than from Russian texts, and the ideas radically transformed the Jadids' worldview. Progress and civilization for them were universal phenomena, achievable by and necessary to all societies. Societies that fell behind because of "negligence and ignorance" were conquered and marginalized. The Jadid project was therefore directed inward, at Muslim society, rather than at the Russians. It was not just because criticism of the empire was impossible, but also because for the Jadids, it was up to Muslim society to reform itself. The Jadids sought to lift "the curtain of ignorance" that they thought prevented their compatriots from seeing the bitter truth. Jadid authors criticized the wealthy and the *ulama* for dereliction of their duties to society. The intensely didactic theater (seen as a "house of admonition" where society could take stock of its ills) criticized wealthy merchants who spent their money hosting feasts to celebrate circumcisions or weddings rather than establishing schools or scholarships and took the *ulama* to task for not guiding people to reform. The old life became an object of ridicule—it was archaic and could not meet the needs of the age. The crisis extended to Islam. Muslims were in a state of crisis because over the ages, they had strayed from the true teachings of Islam and mired themselves in customs and traditions that had nothing to do with their faith. The corruption of the faith had thrown Muslims off the path to progress. Muslims needed to understand Islam properly, disavow various "accretions" to the faith, and ditch customs and traditions that they had acquired over the centuries. Reform involved nothing less than rethinking Islam and its place in society.

Progress and the quest for civilization required that society heed the call for reform. The Jadids, in common with the members of many other movements, were fond of the metaphor of awakening. The community had to awaken from its slumber of ignorance and heedlessness to take its rightful place in the world. Reform also involved a radical reimagination of community. Jadid reform was aimed squarely at Muslim society, not at the colonizer. Turkestan's Jadids addressed their appeals to their compatriots, fellow inhabitants of a homeland (*vatan*) that they usually identified with Turkestan. *Vatan* had long signified the place of origin, usually the place of one's birth. The Jadids came to use it in a much broader, more abstract way to describe all of Turkestan. They also began to talk about the *millat*, an old term now resignified to mean "the nation." Historically, Central Asians had identified themselves with lineage, locality, religion, or dynasty, and the idea of a nation was quite new. The nation can be imagined in many different ways—along lines of territory, ethnicity, or confession—but it represents a new kind of community based on "a deep, horizontal comeradeship," as Benedict Anderson puts it, of all its members.[3] For the Jadids of Turkestan, the nation usually encompassed "the Muslims of Turkestan," a community delineated by geography and confession. Reformers in Bukhara had come to see the protectorate as a homeland. Fitrat rhapsodized about Bukhara: "My homeland! The place where my body and my soul prostrate / My haven, my honor, my glory / my Ka'ba, my *qibla*, my garden."[4] Such sentiments would have been unimaginable to people of his grandparents' generation.

Yet beneath these territorial notions of identity, a different understanding of community was creeping into the imaginations of the Jadids. The idea that humanity was divided into distinct nations, each defined by a common culture and heritage that found their expression in language, had emerged over the course of the nineteenth century and rearranged notions of legitimacy and solidarity in Europe. It arrived in Central Asia from multiple sources—Russian officials categorizing people according to ethnic criteria, Muslim reformers in other parts of the Russian empire who began to see ethnic difference as significant, and Ottoman debates about the best way to save the state. Ethnicity (rather than lineage or locality) was a new way of imagining community. It then led to the idea that the various peoples who spoke Turkic languages were related and that their language, culture, contributions to the Islamicate past should be a point of pride. European research in ethnography and philology in the latter half of the nineteenth century had discovered links between the various Turkic groups of Eurasia that were now divided between the Ottoman, Russian, and Qing empires. This produced complicated dynamics. Turkic-language newspapers circulated across the Russian and the Ottoman Empires and had much in common. The vast majority of the Muslim subjects of the Russian empire used a Turkic language, and the community of the Muslims of the empire could now also be seen as a linguistic community. For Gasprinsky, the founder of the new-method school, Russia's Muslim subjects needed to act in concert to achieve their goals. The masthead of his newspaper carried the motto "Dilde, fikirde, işte birlik" ("Unity in language, thought, and deed"). Gasprinsky hoped to establish a common Turkic language that would be comprehensible to all Turkic speakers, from the shores of the Bosporus, as he put it, to the sands of Kashgar. Neither political nor linguistic unity ever came about, but the aspiration was there. More important than a common language was the understanding that one's ethnic origin was a point of pride and an efficient form of solidarity. We might call this new form of understanding community "Turkism."

Turkism was to wreak havoc on older ways of understanding community and to reshape discourses of identity among Turkic populations in all three empires, as we shall see below. However, it was not the same thing as pan-Turkism—the idea that all Turkic populations should unite in a single state—which became the bugbear of both the Russian and British empires. (The idea of a pan-Turkic threat was to have a long career in the twentieth century, informing policies first of the British and the Russian empires and then of the Soviet and Chinese Communist regimes.)

————

Not surprisingly, the call for reform was bitterly opposed by those who did not see the world the same way as the Jadids. Many of Turkestan's merchants were only lukewarm about the reform project. They wanted their sons to learn Russian, but they had little interest in the kind of thoroughgoing reform that the Jadids prescribed. Most of Turkestan's *ulama* were profoundly inimical to reform. The Russians left Islamic law alone but got rid of the local ruling classes that had always given the *ulama* competition. Now, the latter could assert their authority unperturbed by challenges from the khans and *beks*. At the same time, they could pretend that Russian rule had been established through a process of negotiation in which they had had a say. In Tashkent, Mikhail Cherniaev had given charters to the elders of each of the four quarters of the city, promising that the Muslim population would be allowed to continue using its old customs and practicing the *shariat*.[5] After Samarqand was taken by Russian forces, the city's mufti, Mulla Kamaluddin Kuzfalak, appeared before Konstantin Kaufman to profess allegiance to Russia and cede the city to the empire. His intent was to avoid further bloodshed, a historian of the defeat tells us, but—being "a wise and ingenious man, knowledgeable of the arts of conversation, and having no equal in the matter of flattery and deception"—he did an excellent job of buttering up the conqueror. "We Muslims know," he told Kaufman, "that Christians are compassionate and benevolent toward Muslims and that of all nations, this group has the closest love for the people of Islam.

Therefore, we, the people of Samarqand, are seekers of union with the Russians, and desirous of their arrival. Without hesitation, we want to draw ourselves under the shadow of the sovereignty and support of the Emperor."[6] There was more to this speech than flattery and deception. Kuzfalak was expressing a position with deep roots in the Central Asian Islamic tradition. At the close of the Chingissid era, with its many upheavals, the *ulama* had come to see order and stability as absolute necessities. They were willing to see all rulers as legitimate, no matter how they came to power, as long as they did not oppose the *shariat* or hinder the work of the *ulama*. With the Russian conquest, this argument was extended to non-Muslim rulers as well. Indeed, in the age of colonialism, when most of the world's Muslim societies ended up under the rule of some European empire, most *ulama* came to accept imperial rule as Islamically legitimate as long as the imperial power did not obstruct the practice of Islam. The *ulama* were at peace with the Russian empire and loyal to it.

Russian administrators worried constantly about "Islamic fanaticism," but Russian rule faced remarkably little opposition in the name of Islam. After the dust from the conquest had settled, the population remained largely peaceful, and with one exception, there were no revolts against Russian rule until 1916. That exception was an uprising headed by a Sufi master named Madali Eshon, who in 1898 led several hundred of his followers in an assault on Russian barracks in Andijan. The crowd, armed only with knives, cudgels, and talismans, killed twenty-two soldiers while they slept. Once the garrison had regrouped after its surprise, it was able to disperse the insurgents. Russian retribution was swift and severe. Over the next few days, Russian forces hunted down the insurgents and anyone associated with them. Eighteen of the insurgents, including Madali, were hanged in public, and 360 were exiled to Siberia. Mingtepa, the village where Madali lived, was razed to the ground, its inhabitants expelled, and a Russian settlement called simply Russkoe ("Russian") founded on its site. The uprising did not have any resonance for the rest of society. The *ulama* were uniformly hostile to Madali, whom they ridiculed as an illiterate imposter whose ignorance and egotism had led not just to the deaths

FIG. 7.3. "The State of Affairs in Bukhara." Bukhara had become a byword for heedlessness
and backwardness in the modernist press of the Russian empire. This satirical cartoon from
the popular illustrated satirical magazine *Mulla Nasreddin*, published in Azerbaijani in Tiflis,
depicts Bukharans as oblivious and conceited while the city crumbles around them.
Such criticism was a common feature of the conflict between reformers and conservatives
that raged in Central Asia (and many other Muslim societies) at this time.
Mulla Nasreddin, August 8, 1911.

of many of his followers, but to the worsening of relations with the
Russian state.[7]

The *ulama* had no questions about Turkestan's new predicament, let
alone any answers. As far as they were concerned, everything was fine.
Existing madrasas were packed with students (many of whom had come
from far away), new ones were being built with the riches produced by
the cotton economy, and the *ulama* had unprecedented prestige and
authority in society. The Muslim rulers of Turkestan had kept them on
a tight leash. Now, in those rulers' absence, the *ulama* were the keepers
of morals and guardians of Islam, while the Russians gave them plenty
of leeway. They administered Islamic justice to members of their society.
Islamic institutions flourished under Russian rule. The Ferghana valley,
the heart of cotton country, became a major center of Islamic learning.

That learning took off even among the Kazakhs, whom Kaufman and his followers had hoped to save from Islam. Orenburg, Tobolsk, and Semipalatinsk became centers of Islamic learning, with several madrasas, usually staffed by Tatars, producing a kind of book learning that had previously not existed among the Kazakhs. The *ulama* kept society away from the temptations offered by the new order and on the path of proper behavior by policing the boundaries that separated Muslims from their conquerors. There was no need for wholesale reform of custom and tradition. So what if some half-educated youths had begun to find fault with the old ways, or Muslims from beyond Central Asia had begun to question the value of the education offered by the old madrasas? That behavior represented folly and risked blurring the lines between Muslims and non-Muslims. The *ulama* firmly opposed reforms, declaring the new method of schooling to be *haram* (that is, impermissible according to Islamic norms). The more zealous among them also pronounced reading newspapers or going to the theater *haram*. The lines were drawn clearly, and the advocacy of reform created immense discord in urban society in Turkestan (see figure 7.3).

———

Zuo Zongtang had ambitious plans for establishing a network of Confucian schools in Xinjiang to inculcate Chinese norms and a knowledge of the Chinese language among the local population, but—much like Kaufman's Russian schools—they failed to attract many students.[8] As in Russian Turkestan, elite families in Xinjiang dodged the requirement to send their children to official schools by hiring the children of poor families to go in their place. By the early twentieth century, the Qing empire had given up on Confucian education. In 1907, as part of an empire-wide reform, these schools were replaced by a new kind of Chinese school that offered a modern curriculum without emphasizing Confucian precepts, but the new schools fared no better with local families. A small group of interpreters emerged who acted as intermediaries between local society and the new administration (and, it seems, were viewed with scorn by both sides), but a Chinese-educated Muslim elite never materialized. Chinese rule, embodied by small numbers of Chinese *ambans* and a slimmed down military presence, remained far distant and spatially segregated from the Muslim population. A sign of the distance between the rulers and the ruled was the commonplace usage of the term *chantou* ("turbaned head") to denote the region's Turkic Muslim population in official correspondence.

Modern education in eastern Turkestan therefore came from Muslim, not Chinese, sources, and there were many similarities with the experience of western Turkestan. Yaqub Beg had broken the power of the Khojas in the region and thus given merchants an opportunity to assert their authority in society, and they had a more prominent role in the movement for the new method than was the case in Russian Turkestan. New-method schools first appeared in Ghulja in the Ili valley in the 1890s. Ghulja was the center of the Russian trade in Xinjiang, most of which was dominated by Tatar merchants. The city had become an outpost of Tatar culture, and the first new-method schools there were tied to Tatar networks in the Volga region, rather than to Russian Turkestan. By the turn of the twentieth century, many local merchants had also become interested in modern education. The wealthy Musabayev brothers, whose commercial links with Russia were strong enough that they had added Russian endings to their names, founded the first local new-method school in Ghulja in 1898. On one of his trips to Russia, Husayn Musabayev had met the Tatar industrialist and philanthropist Ahmed Bay Höseyinov, who had established the new-method Husayniye madrasa in Orenburg. Höseyinov convinced Musabayev to support modern education in Eastern Turkestan. Musabayev hired Masum Efendi, a teacher from a Tatar school in Jarkent in Russian Turkestan, and sent him to Istanbul for further study. On his way to Istanbul, Masum Efendi made sure to visit Gasprinsky in the Crimea. He returned to Ghulja in 1904 with a degree from the Imperial School of Civil Administration, one of the modern institutions created by Ottoman reforms, and was appointed principal of the school. Things were more difficult in Altishahr, where the first new-method school opened only in 1912. It was the brainchild of Abdulqadir Damulla, a scholar with full Islamic credentials who had traveled far and wide, studying in madrasas in Kokand and Bukhara and visiting India, the Ottoman Empire, and Egypt. He also wrote a number of textbooks that he had printed in Kazan.[9]

Printing had a difficult time in Eastern Turkestan. Zuo, much like Kaufman, had established a printing press to disseminate useful knowledge to the Qing's newly reconquered subjects, but it does not seem to have lasted very long. The first indigenous press was established in Yengisar in 1893 by Nur Muhammad Haji, who had traveled widely in India and the Ottoman Empire. He published a few works from Altishahr's Sufi tradition and did some contract work for the authorities, publishing two didactic works by Qing emperors. The Musabayevs seem to have taken the press over and named it the Brilliant Rising Sun Press, but it soon folded. The Musabayevs also launched Altishahr's first Turkic newspaper in 1911, but it too rapidly came to grief.[10] Another press was established in 1910 by Swedish missionaries who had worked (largely unsuccessfully) in Kashgar since 1892. It published some Christian texts (translated from Swedish or Arabic) and did contract work for the government and the Russian and British consulates. It also published Altishahr's first almanacs, but otherwise all printed books came from Russian Turkestan or Kazan. Theater, that great hope of the Jadids in the Russian empire, never appeared in Xinjiang. Eastern Turkestan did not witness the same intensity of debate that took place in Russian Turkestan, yet a reform project did take form, and its gaze was firmly fixed westward, to the Russian and the Ottoman Empires.

Turkism arrived in Eastern Turkestan from two different directions. In the north, Ghulja was part of the Tatar world, and Tatar ideas of Turkic identity began to appear in its schools at the end of the first decade of the twentieth century. In Kashgar, Turkism came directly from the Ottoman Empire. In 1913, the Society for the Promotion of Education, organized by local philanthropists led by the Musabayevs, decided to invite a teacher from the Ottoman Empire to teach at the local new-method school. The person who arrived to take up the job in March 1914 was Ahmed Kemal, a native of Rhodes and a member of the Committee for Union and Progress. Kemal took over as director of the Musabayevs' school in Artush, where he flew the Ottoman flag and taught students Ottoman military marches in addition to the usual new-method curriculum. The teaching was intensely national in intent. "Kashgar is a city that belongs to us, the Turks of Chinese Turkestan," read one passage in the primer that Kemal wrote for the school (it was printed in Kazan in Russia). "It is a great place, where the Turkic race, to which we belong, was born and grew up."[11] Kemal represented a direct link to Turkism as it had developed in the Ottoman Empire. Such connections to the Ottoman Empire were inconceivable in the Russian empire, but Chinese authorities had no issue with allowing an Ottoman teacher to teach. With the First World War starting in Europe, however, the Russian and British consuls saw red and managed to have the school shut down in August 1915. However, Turkism was there to stay.

————

Reform took a rather different course among the Kazakhs. The administrative reforms of 1822 had imposed a Russian administrative structure on large parts of the Kazakh steppe and reduced the Kazakh khans to the status of sultans, to be appointed by Russian officials. In the middle of the nineteenth century, members of the Kazakh aristocracy had begun sending their sons to Russian schools. Shoqan Wälikhanov was one of the earliest (and most unusual) products of this schooling. Others followed in his footsteps, although it was only at the turn of the twentieth century that a self-conscious group of like-minded individuals emerged to form a Kazakh intelligentsia. Älikhan Bökeykhanov (b. 1866), the grandson of the last khan of the Bökey horde, attended the Omsk Technical School and then graduated from the Forestry Institute in St. Petersburg. Muhammetjan Tynyshbayev (b. 1879) studied at the gymnasium in Vernyi and went to the Imperial Institute of Transport Engineers in St. Petersburg, from which he graduated in 1905. Mustafa Choqay (or Shoqay, b. 1890), born in a village near Perovsk (Aq Masjid), also came from an aristocratic family. Having graduated from the Tashkent Gymnasium, he went to the University of St. Petersburg, where he obtained a law degree. Other members of the Kazakh intelligentsia were educated on the steppe, but quite often in Russian institutions. Ähmetjan Baytursïnov (b. 1872) attended a Russian-native school before attending the Orenburg Teachers College. He taught in country schools for Kazakhs for a decade and a half before becoming a

FIG. 7.4. Kazakh leaders: Älikhan Bökeykhanov, Ahmetjan Baytursïnov, and Mirjaqïp Dulatov in Orenburg, 1913. Members of the Kazakh intelligentsia had different backgrounds and orientations than the Jadids of Turkestan (see figure 7.2). Wikipedia.

writer and politician. Mirjaqïp Dulatov (b. 1885) similarly attended a Russian-native school and worked as a village schoolteacher. Along with Baytursïnov, he was one of the major reformers of the Kazakh language, men who formalized its grammar and orthography and put it to use in the classroom and the press. Both men were also fluent in Russian (see figure 7.4).

The Kazakh intelligentsia faced less opposition than reformers in Turkestan. There were no Kazakh merchants to speak of, and the *ulama* were a small group without the same clout that they had in the agrarian zone to the south. The intelligentsia's main competition came from the *aqïn*, the traveling bards who were the custodians of the past. A group of such bards who called themselves the *zar zaman* ("troubled times") poets evoked the past as a pastoral utopia that had been destroyed by the Russian conquest. They laid the blame for the conquest on the moral decay of Kazakh rulers, rather than on any backwardness in Kazakh society. This was a very different vision of the world, to be sure, but it did not produce the same conflicts that the call for reform did in Turkestan.

The most pressing issue for the Kazakh intelligentsia was the land question. Cossacks and Russian peasants had been settling on Kazakh lands for a couple of centuries, but the settlement had taken on different dimensions since the conquest of Turkestan had turned the Kazakh steppe into an internal territory of the Russian empire. The government viewed the steppe as an underpopulated area that could accommodate settlers from inner Russia. Even before a devastating famine in 1890–1891 brought fears that the Russian heartland was overcrowded, official commissions had been surveying the Kazakh steppe to determine the amount of land that was in excess of the needs of its current inhabitants. Peasant settlement (or resettlement, as the imperial authorities called it) would relieve population pressure in inner Russia and Russify the alien steppe by implanting a loyal population in it. For the Kazakhs, massive settlement would not only take their land away and alter the demographic balance but make nomadism unviable. Kazakhs had to shape up to meet the challenge. Progress was just as important a goal for the new Kazakh intelligentsia as it was for the Jadids of Turkestan and Bukhara. The Kazakh intelligentsia also viewed their society as weak and in need of transformation. Progress for them entailed the eventual sedentarization of the Kazakhs, both because they saw agrarian life as a higher form of civilization than nomadism, and because sedentarization would reinforce the Kazakhs' claim to their land and might reduce the amount of Russian settlement.[12] They came to imagine the Kazakhs as a nation. This meant writing new histories that departed from the way the past had been recounted by the *aqïn*. The new history saw all Kazakhs as part of a single national community and having a common descent over time. It also meant locating the Kazakhs in their proper ethnic context, as a Turkic group instead of one tied to the mythical history of the Mongol empire. The new Kazakh intellectuals also were invested in Turkism. Mirjaqïp Dulatulï liked to write under the pen name of Turïk Balasï ("Child of the Turks"). In 1909 he issued a clarion call to his fellow Kazakhs, now imagined as a nation:

> Open your eyes, awaken, O Kazakh, hold up your head
> Don't waste your life in vain!
> The land is gone, faith has weakened, life has become illicit,
> My Kazakh, now the time for lying around is past![13]

The metaphor of awakening, of becoming aware of the world and preparing for the struggle, was common in national thought of the era. What we need to note here is that the (still imagined) Kazakh nation existed alongside and parallel to the Muslims of Turkestan being imagined by intellectuals in Transoxiana. There were at least two different conversations about nationhood and two different national projects in Russian Central Asia when the Tsarist empire collapsed.

There was debate among Kazakh intellectuals about the cultural orientation of Kazakh society—whether or not Kazakhs should be subject to the Orenburg Spiritual Assembly and what role Islam should play in their society. However, the *ulama* had a minor role even in this debate. Islamic book learning had increased in significance in Kazakh society after the Russian conquest, as the pacification of the steppe made it easier for madrasa students from Transoxiana and the Volga-Urals region to work in the Kazakh steppe and for young Kazakh men to study in madrasas. A group of Kazakh *ulama* had emerged, but the social prestige it enjoyed remained limited. Muslim cultural reform was a much smaller phenomenon among the Kazakhs than in Turkestan, and cultural debates took place within different parameters.

———

The Russian revolution of 1905 opened up some political space for the reformers. An unsuccessful war with Japan over imperial influence in Manchuria, the ancestral lands of the Qing, produced widespread political mobilization across urban Russia. On Sunday, January 9, 1905, soldiers guarding the Winter Palace in St. Petersburg massacred a crowd of workers who had come to deliver a petition to the tsar. This "Bloody Sunday" transformed the situation and led to wave after wave of strikes and ever-increasing demands for political liberalization. Nicholas II dragged his feet, but he was forced to grant civil liberties by October. The following spring, he granted a quasi-constitution and allowed the creation of a representative body, the State Duma. These developments ushered in a new era in Russia's history, with legal political parties, a much freer press, and popular representation (albeit unequal and restricted). Even though Nicholas began trying to take back the concessions he had granted as soon as the revolutionary turmoil began to die down, he could never completely vanquish these freedoms.

Much of the drama of the first Russian revolution played out in Russia itself. In Central Asia, the Russian population mobilized quickly, with railway workers carrying out large-scale strikes and some soldiers mutinying, but the Muslim population remained largely aloof. After the proclamation of civil rights, Muslim notables organized various petitions asking for minor reforms and, among the Kazakhs, for curbing the settlement of Russian peasants on the steppe. The revolution had accentuated the divide between Russians and natives in Central Asia and given the Russians the sense that they were the only political actors in that corner of the Russian empire. In any case, the quasi-constitutional order that emerged after 1905 did not abolish the rule of difference according to which the Russian empire had long functioned. Elections to the State Duma were conducted on a weighted franchise, and different groups voted in separate curiae. Turkestan was represented in the Duma by six "native" and seven Russian deputies, while the Steppe *Krai* had four Kazakh deputies and ten Russian ones. A conservative reform of the electoral law in 1907 disenfranchised Turkestan completely, denying even its Russian population the right to vote and confirming the colonial position of the province. Yet the rights to a free press and to assemble were never completely revoked. The following decade saw the consolidation of Jadidism in the cities and the emergence of a Kazakh national movement on the steppe.

Yet until 1917, reformers in Central Asia took aim at their own societies and eschewed political claims. Both in Turkestan and on the Kazakh steppe, the modernists wanted their societies to be included in the empire as equals, to overcome the rule of difference. However, Tsarist authorities were uncomfortable with any expressions of independent opinion. They mistook for separatism the striving for inclusion and looked upon the modernists with great suspicion. They surveilled modernists' newspapers, raided their schools, and monitored their benevolent societies. Tsarist authorities were much more comfortable dealing with the conservative *ulama*, who were happy with the rule of difference and did not make any demands on the state.

8

Imperial Collapse

THE IMPERIAL ORDER established in Central Asia proved short-lived, as both the Russian and Qing empires collapsed in the face of war and revolution in the 1910s. Although the two revolutions were quite different and neither started in Central Asia, they both affected the region in profound ways. A Han national revolution brought down the Qing in 1911–1912 and set in motion three decades of turmoil in China, during which Xinjiang was often only loosely connected to the rest of the Chinese state. Two years later, the Russian empire went to war with other powers in Europe. The Great War (now known as the First World War) was the suicide of empires. Russia's was the first one to collapse—the Romanov dynasty collapsed in the third year of the war, and the empire had largely disintegrated by the fourth. But the first cracks had appeared earlier, in a massive uprising in Central Asia in 1916. Tsarist rule ceased to exist in parts on Central Asia in the summer of 1916 and had not been restored by the time revolution in the imperial capital put paid to the dynasty in February 1917.

———

The Chinese revolution of 1911–1912 was rooted in a growing discontent with the Qing dynasty, which had faced internal turmoil and external humiliation for several generations. Foreign powers were "carving China up like a melon," as the expression went, and the Qing seemed incapable of doing anything about it. Ironically, the discontent was articulated by new groups that emerged in Chinese society as a result of efforts by the Qing to reform the state. Thousands of students had gone abroad to study—to Britain and France, and especially Japan—and they acquired a new vocabulary of thinking about politics. By the turn of the twentieth century, many had come to see the overthrow of the dynasty as the only solution to China's predicament. Secret societies aimed at overthrowing the regime proliferated in China's cities.

The discontent was cast in a political vocabulary new to China. Concepts such as democracy, representation, race, nation, and revolution appeared in Chinese discourse for the first time, mostly through terms appropriated from Japanese or with older Chinese terms given new meaning. Out of these new concepts emerged modern Han Chinese nationalism. Modern Chinese intellectuals reread older notions of lineage in the light of new theories of race and came up with the idea of a racially defined Chinese nation that was descended from the Yellow Emperor. The critique of the Qing took on racial connotations. The dynasty was not just incompetent but also alien, a foreign occupying force and barbarian to boot. In the words of the young firebrand Zou Rong (1885–1905), "Their tribes lived beyond Shanhaiguan [that is, beyond the Great Wall] and fundamentally are of a different race from our illustrious descendants of the Yellow Emperor. Their land is barren; their people, furry; their minds, bestial; their customs, savage."[1] For Zhang Binglin (1869–1936), the Manchus were an alien race who had committed many crimes against the Han Chinese. They had also refused to assimilate to Chinese culture, although Zhang's new racial categories meant that he saw cultural assimilation as a chimera: Manchus would remain Manchus even if they assimilated. The revolt against them was to be an act of revenge through which the Han Chinese would regain their collective honor and dignity. The Han had a right and an obligation to recover their own state from foreign occupation, just as the Greeks and the Poles were trying to do. Zhang saw the anti-Manchu struggle as part of a universal plan of ethnic or racial liberation in which old civilized peoples would overthrow their occupiers.[2]

A single incident on October 9, 1911, set in motion a concatenation of events that led to the fall of the dynasty and the end of the two-millennia-old tradition of empire in China. A group of young revolutionaries belonging to a secret society in Hankou in Hubei province were making a bomb when it exploded. The authorities swooped in and summarily executed three of the bomb makers and confiscated papers that included membership records of their society. Afraid that their whole organization would be destroyed, the revolutionaries decided to launch an uprising right away. A series of mutinies took place in units of the New Army, the military corps formed by the Qing as part of a last-ditch modernization effort, across several provinces in the weeks that followed. By the end of the month, the government had accepted key demands for a parliament and a constitution. This move toward a constitutional monarchy was accompanied by continued violence between revolutionary and loyalist troops. Sun Yat-sen, the most prominent leader of the revolutionary opposition, was overseas when the revolutionary events began. By the time he returned to Shanghai on December 25, 1911, the mutinies had been joined by considerable political mobilization, often based in civil society organizations that were products of the late Qing reform efforts. Delegates from sixteen provincial assemblies met in Nanjing and proclaimed Sun the provisional president of the republic. Sun took office on January 1, 1912, while the Qing remained in power. It was only on February 12 that the mother of the five-year-old emperor Puyi announced his abdication, having negotiated a deal that allowed the imperial family to stay in the Forbidden City, retain its property, and receive a substantial stipend from the state. China had finally become a republic in the aftermath of what came to be called the Xinhai Revolution.

The Qing dynasty was gone, but what of the empire it had built? The Mongols had been partners of the Qing and now saw little reason to stay in the republic. In Outer Mongolia, a group of prominent nobles and Buddhist clerics declared Mongolia independent under the kingship of Agvaanl Uvsanchoijinyam Danzan Vanchüg, the Tibetan-born head of the Buddhist hierarchy in Mongolia, who took the title of Bogd Khagan. In seeking to distance itself from China, the new theocratic monarchy sought Russian protection. Not willing to alienate China, the Russians negotiated a far-reaching autonomy for Mongolia within the Chinese

orbit but with substantial Russian influence. Meanwhile, an armed rebellion expelled Chinese troops from the province of Tibet. The Dalai
Lama declared that the patron-priest relationship that had linked Tibet
to the Qing had "faded like a rainbow in the sky" and sought to maximize
his independence.[3] He turned to the British in India for support. The
new Chinese government attended a trilateral conference at Simla, where
the Tibetans sought to negotiate an agreement whereby the Chinese republic would grant Tibet internal autonomy under British watch. This
led to persistent Tibetan attempts to gain independence during the next
four decades. In Xinjiang, however, the revolution had little effect. As had
happened in Russian Turkestan after the 1905 revolution, the Central
Asian population remained largely aloof from the upheaval among the
Chinese, in which various factions of the occupying army fought each
other. Han troops of the New Army were the biggest champions of the
republic, but they could not overthrow loyalist troops. For several
months in 1912, different military groups contended for power. Out of
the chaos emerged the figure of Yang Zengxin. When the Qing fell, Yang
was the circuit intendant and commissioner of judicial affairs at Ürümchi. He had served in Gansu and Ningxia (both of which had large Hui
populations) before being posted to Xinjiang. When Yuan Dahua, the
last Qing governor, fled during the fighting between Qing and revolutionary troops, Yang was able to seize power with the help of a small force
of Hui that he raised locally. Beijing formalized his position and appointed him civil and military governor of Xinjiang. Yang spent the next
three years consolidating his power in the province. He used his Hui
troops to bring to heel revolutionaries of various stripes. There was discontent with him among the officer corps of the New Army. He took
care of that in the time-honored fashion of inviting many of the officers
to a banquet and having them massacred. Yang also oversaw the end of
the power of Manchu and Mongol warrior elites in the province. Zuo's
reconquest of Xinjiang had begun the marginalization of the old banner
elites in Xinjiang. Under Yang, Han bureaucrats and military officers,
mostly from his home province of Yunnan, completely took over.

The new republican leaders in Beijing faced different issues. They
were nationalists who wanted to get rid of the Qing but keep the

multinational empire the dynasty had built. The new leaders declared
the old multinational empire to be a single nation-state with an alien-
able territory and inviolable boundaries. Faced with encroachment by
foreign powers, the Qing had begun to assert the inviolability of its frontiers. Increasingly, it had reinterpreted the term Zhongguo ("Central
State"—more commonly rendered as "Middle Kingdom" in English) to
make it synonymous with their holdings. Geography textbooks for the
new schools established in the first decade of the twentieth century
conflated "Qing" and "China" and represented both as indivisible
wholes.[4] Zhongguo had acquired the connotations of the European
term "China." The nationalist leaders took this argument in a new direction. There was much at stake in ensuring the territorial integrity of the
empire they had inherited. There was pride, but there were also the vast
natural resources in the non-Han parts of the empire that were crucial
to the well-being of the country, as well as the strategic consideration
that a small China would be easier prey for imperial powers—especially
China's neighbors, Japan and Russia. The strident racialist nationalism
of the kind articulated by Zuo or Zhang that spoke of the oppression of
the descendants of the Yellow Emperor by alien races was scarcely us-
able as a legitimizing tool for a multiethnic republic. Sun therefore conceptualized the new republic as a union of five so-called races: Han,
Manchus, Mongols, Tibetans, and Muslims, the last category including
the Sino-Muslims (Hui or Dungans) and the various Turkic groups of
eastern Turkestan (most significantly, Kazakh nomads and the sedentary population we now call Uyghurs). Other non-Chinese groups,
mostly in the southwest, were not considered numerically significant or
culturally advanced enough to be considered as separate races. The new
republic adopted a five-striped flag to signify this union. Yet even Sun's
ideas were premised on the fundamental assumption that the five races
were still part of a greater Zhonghua people, a united community of
people who belonged to Zhongguo, the state. The idea of the essential
unity of the state, the inviolability of its frontiers, and the inalienability
of its territory has been the lodestar for all Chinese elites, regardless of
their political leanings, in the century since the Xinhai Revolution. All
Chinese governments, Nationalist and Communist alike, have insisted

on this principle, even in the interwar decades of the twentieth century, when China was politically fragmented. They have been remarkably successful in this. Successive governments have laid claim to Xinjiang, Tibet, and Taiwan. Mongolia was the only Qing territory to escape, and its road to independence was long and hard: only in 1949 did the Chinese state recognize its independence, and only in 1965 did it join the United Nations.

It is important to remember that the idea of the unity of five races was purely a Han project. The elites of the other four "races" were not consulted. Few of them were invested in the maintenance of the territorial unity of the empire without the dynasty. As the elites of Outer Mongolia and Tibet showed by their actions, they did not want to stay in the empire. In Eastern Turkestan, the ideas of Islam and Turkism were far more compelling than those of belonging to China. The notion of the inviolable unity of the Chinese state has appeared as a colonial imposition in the non-Han borderlands of the former empire of the Qing.

———

The Chinese revolutionaries in Ili began publishing a newspaper in several languages, including Turkic, in an attempt to politicize the population and convey their enthusiasm about the new possibilities opened up by the fall of the Qing. The newly appointed commander-in-chief of provincial forces in Kashgar, Yang Zuanxu, told locals in his first speech: "As long as the laws are obeyed, then you may implement reforms as you see fit, nothing will stand in the way. . . . The age of ignorance has ended—all peoples and nations must open their eyes."[5] It was this enthusiasm that led Muslim reformers in Kashgar to organize their benevolent society and invite Ahmed Kemal to come from Istanbul to direct the Musabayevs' school in Artush. But the enthusiasm rapidly gave way to chaos throughout the former empire. The republican government was soon engulfed in conflict. Sun was supplanted as president by Yuan Shikai, a Qing grandee and profoundly conservative figure who dissolved parliament and ruled by decree. In 1915, he attempted to restore the monarchy and had himself crowned emperor. He died soon after, leaving too many questions unresolved for an orderly transition. While the national government remained, state power became increasingly fragmented, and many provinces passed into the hands of warlords. Xinjiang's fate was in many ways unique. The annual subsidies (officially, interprovincial transfers, or *xiexiang*) from the central government that had kept its finances afloat had vanished after 1912.[6] Now, unrest in China proper cut Xinjiang off from the capital, leaving Yang to his own devices. Through a combination of skill and bloodthirstiness, Yang ensured the territorial integrity of the province; stability within it; and most importantly, the security of Chinese rule in the province, even if its links with China were cut off. For the next three decades, Xinjiang was ruled by Han governors who acted in the name of China but often had very little connection with the central government and indeed often defied its commands outright. It is difficult to find similar examples in the history of colonialism. The Unilateral Declaration of Independence by the white settlers in Rhodesia in 1965, issued against the wishes of London to keep white power secure in that settler colony, may be the closest historical parallel to events in Xinjiang after the ascent of Yang, and even that is not very close.

———

As the new Chinese republic disintegrated, the sun was beginning to set on the age of empire in the rest of Eurasia. The Great War that erupted in Europe in the summer of 1914 pitted vast, sprawling multiethnic empires against one another. The crowned heads of Europe found themselves making unprecedented demands on their subjects. As the war dragged on, its devastation consigned the legitimizing principle of dynastic empire, already under attack, to its grave. The first one to fall was the Romanov dynasty, which collapsed in the war's third winter.

Although Central Asia was far from the front lines and its indigenous population was exempt from military service, it was nevertheless deeply affected by the war. Russian authorities were worried about the loyalty of their Muslim subjects—especially after November 1914, when the Ottoman Empire entered the war on the side of Germany and the

Habsburg Empire. The fear of pan-Islam lingered in Russian minds throughout the war. Secret police records are full of intimations of danger: of Ottoman emissaries roaming through Central Asia at will, collections being taken to benefit the Ottoman war effort, and alleged *mujahidin* ("those who undertake jihad") stockpiling arms in secret depots in Ferghana to prepare for an uprising. Yet there was little basis for this fear. Every power in the Triple Entente fielded colonial Muslim soldiers in the war. Russia mobilized about a million Muslim soldiers (mostly Tatars and Bashkirs) during the war.[7] In Central Asia, Muslim political elites showed enthusiasm in gathering donations for the war effort and clearly expressed their loyalty to the empire, which they proclaimed was the *vatan*. "There is nothing to be done," Mahmudkhoja Behbudiy wrote after the Ottoman Empire entered the war, "except expressing sorrow that the fires ignited by the Germans have engulfed Russia and Turkey. . . . We, the Muslims of Turkestan, are subjects of Russia and co-religionists of the Turks. Our common religion and common race [with the Ottomans] cannot hinder our friendship with Russia, because this war is not a religious war, but one for political gain, indeed a German war."[8] He hoped that loyalty and participation in the war effort would lead to political concessions and the full inclusion of Turkestan's Muslims in the imperial order after the war. Kazakh leaders went even further. In February 1915, Ähmetjan Baytursïnov and Älikhan Bökeykhanov traveled to Petrograd (the suitably un-German name that the imperial capital had acquired after the onset of war) to petition the Ministry of War to conscript Kazakhs for the war effort. Their hope was that conscription would lead to the abolition of the alien (*inorodets*) status of the Kazakhs and thus pave the way for them to be represented in the Duma and have some voice in the policy debates about settlement and land policy. The ministry considered the Kazakhs too backward to be useful in modern warfare (their nomadic lifestyle was a major shortcoming, as was their lack of Russian), and nothing came of this petition.[9] While many Central Asians retained sympathy for the Ottomans, none rebelled on their behalf.

It was the immiseration and devastation of war that brought about the end to the colonial peace in Central Asia that had largely held since the conquest. Extra taxes and levies and "voluntary" contributions to the war effort bit into the local economy. The war also exacerbated relations between settlers and the indigenous population. Early German victories had created a massive refugee crisis in the Russian empire, as people displaced from the front line fled to the safety of the interior. Many of them headed to Central Asia. In addition, Tsarist authorities placed tens of thousands of prisoners of war (POWs)—mostly Habsburg subjects—in Central Asia. By the autumn of 1915, Syr Darya district alone had more than a quarter of a million displaced persons (including POWs) officially registered as living there, and doubtless many more had arrived without papers.[10] The influx of such large numbers of Europeans rendered many of the debates over settlement moot; it also created a major food crisis in Turkestan that quickly developed a sharp ethnic dimension. Tashkent saw major food riots. On February 28 and 29, 1916, Russian women ransacked the main bazaar in the new city and beat up Muslim traders, whom they accused of hoarding and speculation. The municipal government established a food supply committee and instituted rationing, but it provided ration cards only to the European population.[11]

———

The unrest exploded into full-blown rebellion in July 1916. Desperate for manpower in a military effort that had turned catastrophic, Nicholas II revoked the exemption from conscription that Central Asians had enjoyed since the conquest and decreed a massive mobilization for work in labor and supply battalions behind the front lines. The government had ambitious goals. It expected to mobilize 250,000 men ages 19–43 in Turkestan and another 230,000 from the Steppe region (8 percent of the male population of the region). The political elites in both Turkestan and the Steppe *Krai* supported the decree and began to help in the recruitment. They were blindsided by the surge of popular opposition. The announcement of the mobilization had come out of the blue and resulted in all manner of rumors about what awaited the recruits. Assurances that they would not see military action backfired, for many groups saw work in labor battalions as a sign of dishonor. The announcement was made in the middle of the harvest season, when labor was all important. It was immensely unpopular and led to a massive uprising across Central Asia, by far the most serious challenge to Russian rule in Turkestan.

The uprising began on July 4 in Khujand and spread across the agrarian regions of Turkestan in the weeks that followed. Angry crowds targeted police stations or the houses of the *ellikboshi*, who had been tasked with drawing up lists of those to be recruited. In case after case, crowds attacked the stations and houses to destroy the lists. The most violent episode took place in Jizzakh, a town near Samarqand, where the insurgents recognized an *ishan* by the name of Nazir Khoja Abdusalomov as their *bek*. Nazir Khoja proceeded to declare a jihad against the Russians. The insurgents destroyed sixty-five versts (seventy kilometers) of rail track and cut telegraph lines. It took a punitive expedition from Tashkent consisting of thirteen military companies and three *sotnia*s ("hundreds") of Cossacks, all armed with cannons and machine guns, to win back control of the railways. By September, Russian forces had brought the sedentary population under control, and convoys of conscripts began to be sent to the front. Eventually, some 123,000 men were recruited and sent to forced labor behind the front lines.

In the nomadic areas, the uprising took on an altogether larger scale. In large swaths of territory, Russian rule collapsed. Kazakhs pitched their yurts and began to gather in large numbers, the better to fight. In many locations, they proclaimed new khans. In Torghay district, the uprising took a much more organized form. The insurgents elected two khans, one each for the Qïpchaq and Arghïn lineages, and established a modicum of statehood in the form of tax collectors, judges, a governing council, and an organized army that involved as many as 50,000 people under the leadership of Amangeldi Imanov.[12] They laid siege to the town of Torghay and had not been defeated when the revolution of February 1917 toppled the monarchy. But the greatest violence came in Jettisuv (Semirech'e), where opposition to mobilization coalesced with long-standing frustrations with Russian settlement and the loss of land. Initially, the insurgents attacked government offices and indigenous functionaries, but they soon turned on Russian settlements, where they burned houses, destroyed farm inventory, and murdered or kidnapped the settlers. The insurgency was far less organized than in Torghay. The high point of organization came in mid-August when a force of 4,000–5,000 under the leadership of Qanat Abukin laid siege to the town of Toqmaq for almost a week. Otherwise, the uprising in Jettisuv was decentralized.

The empire's response was far more violent and merciless. On July 21, the tsar appointed Alexei Kuropatkin governor-general of Turkestan with a brief to quell the uprising. Kuropatkin, a former minister of war, was an old Turkestan hand. As a young lieutenant, he had taken part in many battles during the conquest of Turkestan, including the infamous assault on Gökdepe, and had then served in Turkestan in various capacities for almost a quarter of a century. Now, he returned to restore order as he liked to see it. He issued orders to arm Russian settlers in Jettisuv, who were to fight alongside the regiments being brought in from the front. Russian settlers in Jettisuv were subject to conscription, and some 25,000 of them had been mobilized since 1914. In the autumn of 1916, soldiers from settlements that were seriously affected by the uprising were released from the army and sent back to Jettisuv as part of paramilitary militias. Across Europe, the Great War had been exceptionally brutal, and the lines dividing armed soldiers from the civilian population had often been dissolved. Returning soldiers brought the violence of the front and its methods to Jettisuv.[13] Soldiers and armed settlers repaid the violence of the nomads with usurious interest, wreaking vengeance on the nomads who remained, putting whole villages to the sword, stealing cattle, destroying irrigation channels, and occupying the land. Kuropatkin made formal plans to confiscate all land where "Russian blood had been spilt" and to separate Russian and Kyrgyz populations in large parts of Jettisuv. The area around Issiq Köl and the Chü River was to be cleansed of its Kazakh and Kyrgyz population and given to Russian settlers, while a nomad-only district was to be established in the Narïn region.

Faced with this violence, more than a quarter of a million Kazakh and Kyrgyz nomads fled with their herds across the imperial boundary to Xinjiang. The flight brought disaster. The trek was difficult and caused many deaths. Those who survived found themselves living in terrible conditions. The sudden arrival of such numbers of refugees sent food prices skyrocketing, while the Russian ruble fell in value. The bazaars of Xinjiang were clogged with belongings sold by their owners for a pittance out of desperation. The winter was terrible, and large numbers of refugees died of disease and starvation, as did their livestock. In the spring, they began to trek back to Jettisuv, only to find their lands occupied by settlers—who responded to their return with more violence. The final balance sheet for the uprising is difficult to draw up. Total Russian losses were substantial but mostly concentrated in Jettisuv. Official figures put the number of Russian deaths at 2,246, of which 2,108 took place in Jettisuv. In typical colonial fashion, however, Kazakh and Kyrgyz casualties far outnumbered Russian deaths but were not counted in any systematic way. Estimates for nomad deaths are between 40,000 and 100,000, with the worst losses in Jettisuv. According to early Soviet figures, 20 percent of the people of the district, 50 percent of the horses, 39 percent of the cattle, 55 percent of the camels, and 58 percent of the sheep were lost. Irrigation channels, orchards, and farmland lay in ruins. The economic destruction was accompanied by the complete breakdown of relations between Russians and nomads. The consequences were felt for many years.

The uprising of 1916 was the biggest revolt that any belligerent power faced on the home front during the First World War. In Torghay district, the Tsarist order was never reestablished, for the monarchy collapsed before it could subdue the uprising. The uprising of 1916 was in fact the opening act in the collapse of the Russian empire, the first of a series of uprisings and civil wars that were to last well into the 1920s. Yet Kuropatkin's ruthlessness saved Russian rule from total collapse in Central Asia. His plans for ethnic cleansing, however, were cut short by monumental events far away. In February 1917, as the imperial order collapsed, Central Asia was already in upheaval. Settler-soldiers in Jettisuv continued the bloodshed all through 1917, with the fall of the monarchy barely making a difference. There was no clear break between the uprising and the revolution, but the demise of the monarchy ushered in not just years of upheaval but radical new visions for politics and society and a new kind of state. The revolution unleashed by the collapse of the Russian empire was to change the world.

REVOLUTION

ON FEBRUARY 23, 1917, riots broke out on the streets of Petrograd as women workers protested against the food shortages that had become chronic across the Russian empire. Food riots were inherently political, and the demands went from "we want bread" to "down with autocracy" within a couple of days. Seven days of demonstrations were enough to bring down the monarchy. After some waffling, Nicholas II abdicated in favor of his brother Michael on March 2. The following day, when Michael refused the throne, the three-hundred-year-old Romanov dynasty ceased to exist. "The dynasty fell by shaking, like rotten fruit," as Lev Trotsky put it memorably. The rot was caused as much by the war as anything else. The huge demands on subjects' resources and loyalty created by the war destroyed the legitimacy that had knit the empire together. Political revolution soon turned into a thoroughgoing social revolution, as various groups across the empire sought to redefine their relationship to each other and to power. In Russia itself, the revolution was articulated along lines of class: ordinary workers and soldiers organized spontaneously in soviets (councils) in parallel to the organizations of privileged society, which took the form of committees of public safety. Among the non-Russian populations of the empire, however, the revolution was a moment of national liberation. Non-Russians organized along national lines and demanded various kinds of autonomy or, in some cases, outright independence. The result was a massive convulsion that gripped the lands of the Russian empire and spilled over into its neighbors, including Xinjiang. Out of the rubble came the world's first socialist state and a global challenge to the imperial order that had structured politics for the previous several centuries. Born of the crisis of the global capitalist order, Communism posed a particular challenge to it. It promised an alternative path to progress and modernity that exercised a great fascination for colonial peoples around the world, who saw in it a road to national salvation. In Russian Central Asia, the Jadids hoped that revolution would allow them to implement the reforms they had long advocated. For similar reasons, Communism found fertile ground in China as well, where it came to be seen as the path to national salvation. After the cataclysms of the Second World War (known in China as the War of Resistance against Japan) and a brutal civil war, the Chinese Communists swept to power in their own Communist revolution of 1949.

9

Hope and Disappointment

THE HEAVENS ABOVE Tashkent had never witnessed a scene like it. On March 13, 1917, thirty thousand men, a large chunk of the city's population, crammed into the Friday mosque—not to pray, but to hear speakers explain the import of stirring events in the Russian imperial capital. Crowds of this size had never gathered in Central Asia outside of wartime. The abdication of the tsar, however, produced an unprecedented mobilization. A new Russia was being born. What was Central Asia's place in it going to be?

Hope abounded, and enthusiasm for the new era was palpable. "Praise be that the epoch of freedom has arrived. The sun of justice has lit the world," wrote the Tashkent poet Sirojiddin Makhdum Sidqiy in the preface to a long poem titled "The New Liberty" that he published on March 12. Freedom, justice, and equality were the main fruits of the new era for him, and they required action: "The time of love and truth has come. . . . Now, we have to set aside our false thoughts; . . . the most important aim must be to give thought to how we will live happily in the arena of freedom."[1] He was not alone. The independent Uzbek-language press that emerged quickly was full of such sentiments. The gathering in Tashkent's mosque was proof that the enthusiasm was widely shared. Nor was the excitement limited to Tashkent. It spread across Central Asia and among Central Asians everywhere. Far away, in a labor regiment behind the war's front lines, a group of Kazakhs who had been conscripted as a result of the 1916 decree, similarly proclaimed: "The sun of liberty, of the equality and fraternity of all peoples of Russia, has arisen. Kazakhs need to organize to support the new order and the new government. It is necessary to work in contact with all nationalities supporting the new order."[2]

Much of the promise seemed to materialize in the first weeks after the fall of the monarchy. In a series of sweeping legislative acts, the Provisional Government that replaced the tsar abolished all legal distinctions between citizens on the basis of rank, religion, sex, or nationality and granted every citizen, including women, over the age of twenty the right to vote. (Central Asian women thus received the vote earlier than their counterparts in Britain or the United States.) The Provisional Government also guaranteed the absolute freedom of the press and assembly. Russia was the freest country in the world, and the Provisional Government had raised former colonial subjects to full citizenship and legal equality. The rule of difference was over.

———

The spring of 1917 saw an unprecedented political mobilization in Central Asia, accompanied by a frenzy of organization in which activists created dozens of cultural and political societies. The Samarqand Muslim Education Union, the Enthusiasts of Education in Andijon, and the Turan Society in Tashkent had primarily educational and cultural goals, while other organizations brought together students and artisans. Activists formed the Muslim Council (the Shuroi Islomiya) as an umbrella organization and traveled around Turkestan, organizing local branches or bringing local initiatives into the fold. More practical steps included the opening of new-method schools in large numbers and the creation of crash courses for those who would teach in them. Theater groups sprang into action as well. The culmination of this activity was the convocation of the Congress of Muslims of Turkestan that opened in Tashkent on April 16. Similar national congresses were meeting across the empire. Like them, the Tashkent conference was not strictly representative, but it welcomed delegates nominated by various public organizations from across Turkestan. It had a lengthy agenda, but its most important resolutions concerned the future of Turkestan. After six days

of debate, the congress resolved that Turkestan should be an autonomous part of a federal republic of Russia.[3]

We might stop to note one peculiar feature of the spring of 1917. The
euphoria expressed above was widely shared across the former empire.
For most national movements in that empire, the question was how to
find a new and better place in a new and better Russia. Almost no one
wanted independence or secession. The language of liberty, equality,
democracy, progress, autonomy, and nation took hold in Muslim politics in 1917. A mere half-century separated 1917 from the time of the
khans, when politics was imagined in a completely different vocabulary.
The new vocabulary was accompanied by new rituals of public life.
Gatherings large and small began by choosing, often by acclamation, a
presidium, chair, and secretary. Records were kept and duly published
in the vernacular press that sprang up out of nowhere. The official *Turkestan Gazette* was given over to the public and renamed *Najot* (Redemption). The overthrow of the Russian monarchy was seen as a moment
of opportunity that could reshape not just Central Asia's relation to Russia but Central Asian society itself.

All of this was too good to last. Dark clouds of conflict appeared from
a number of directions. The initial meetings had been organized by a
coalition of Jadids and a small number of Muslims with a Russian education. (The opening up of the political system had put a renewed emphasis on the knowledge of Russian.) These men had assumed that their
knowledge of the modern world made them the natural leaders to lead
their community through the possibilities of the new age opened up by
the demise of the monarchy. They were delighted by the promise of
liberty and equality, which would allow the nation to progress in the
modern world. Other groups in society had a very different take on the
situation. As we have seen above, the *ulama* did not view the reform of
the whole existing way of life as necessary, let alone desirable. They
found the universalism of the new order, with its erasure of distinctions,
threatening. The imperial order had defined clear boundaries between
Muslims and non-Muslims and given the *ulama* a role in guarding those
boundaries. The new order, in which those boundaries would be erased,
was not desirable. Liberty meant disorder. For them, "the meaning of

liberty was just that there would be no veil or modesty for women, [who would] walk around the streets and bazaars bareheaded like the women of the Christians and mingle with unrelated men, while the meaning of equality was that there was no difference between the *ulama* of Islam and Jews or Hindus, and that Jadids would remove turbans from the heads of the august *ulama* and replace them with the Russian *shapka* or the Jewish *telpak*."[4] Above all, they bitterly resented the challenge to their authority in society posed by the youth. By late April, conservative elites had organized under the leadership of the *ulama* and established their own political party, called Ulamo Jamiyati (the Society of Ulama). The two sides quickly came to be at daggers drawn and spent the rest of 1917 in bitter disputes that frequently descended into physical violence. The rhetoric sharpened rapidly, so that by June, the *ulama* were routinely issuing fatwas against the youth for being "infidels," and the Jadids accusing the *ulama* of being "traitors to the nation."

Bukhara was a different kind of battlefield. Reform-minded Bukharans decided to seek the intervention of the Provisional Government in the cause of liberal reform in Bukhara. "Great Russia, through its devoted sons, has irretrievably overthrown the old despotic regime, and founded in its place a free, democratic government," they telegraphed Petrograd. "We humbly ask that the new Russian government in the near future instruct our government to change the manner of its governance to the bases of freedom and equality, so that we may [also] take pride in the fact that we are under the protection of Great Free Russia."[5] The Provisional Government did work with the emir to come up with a manifesto of reform, which was proclaimed at a public meeting on April 7. But the emir saw other possibilities in the revolution. Rather than liberalizing his regime and devolving power, he wanted to wrest full sovereignty from the Russians. He acquired support from the conservative *ulama* in the city and turned their ire on the Jadids. The Jadids had organized a demonstration both to "thank the emir for his manifesto" and to assert their presence on the streets. That demonstration was brutally assaulted by a counterdemonstration, whose participants accused the Jadids of being infidels and traitors. The government then arrested a number of the most active reformers and chased the others out of the emirate. Sadriddin Ayni (1878–1954), a professor at one of the most renowned madrasas in the city, was given seventy-five lashes of the whip.

The battle lines thus drawn were to shape the contours of Central Asian politics for years to come. In 1917, the *ulama* bested the Jadids in a number of municipal elections. It was clear that the Jadids were not the dominant force in society. They learned from this experience a robust disregard for public opinion. If the nation did not know its own best interests, then it had to be led to its salvation by force, if necessary. Revolution came to mean to them a modality of rapid, forceful transformation.

———

The Provisional Government had proclaimed the equality of all citizens, but the burdens of the past could not be shed so easily. Russians in Turkestan were surprised at the extent of the mobilization among the Muslim population. They had assumed that 1917 would be a replay of 1905 and not threaten their privileged position in the colony. There were plenty of divisions among the settlers—between the privileged and the poor, between urban dwellers and peasants, and between long-term settlers and soldiers who had just arrived—but all of them started with the assumption that they would not have to share power with the natives. In Tashkent, liberal Russians sought to establish the Russian city as a completely separate entity, with its own budget and political representation. But the most fateful development was the rise of the soviets, the councils that had emerged as the most potent form of lower-class mobilization in Russia after the fall of the monarchy. In Turkestan, soviets were formed by Europeans. They included a few workers, but they were outnumbered by soldiers, many of whom were also settlers in the region. On March 31, the Tashkent Soviet, acting on its own, arrested Alexei Kuropatkin, the governor-general, and deported him from Turkestan. The Provisional Government appointed a Turkestan Committee that included several Muslim members (but only one from Turkestan), but it could never acquire any real authority. For the next two and a half years, Turkestan was largely independent of central control, and events there often had a logic of their own. Indeed, across the empire, a massive social revolution unfolded in which different social groups sought to renegotiate the social order. Over the course of 1917, central power evaporated across the empire, as the enthusiasm of the early weeks of the revolution gave way to state collapse and unrestrained ethnic conflict.

Things were made worse by a struggle over the food supply in a situation of massive shortages. All across the empire, "hoarding" and "speculation" had become signs of counterrevolutionary activity. In Turkestan the struggle against these phenomena took on a nakedly ethnic dimension. Over the course of the summer, raiding and requisitioning of food from Muslims by Europeans acting in the name of the revolution became common in cities. In the countryside, events took a far more radical turn. As Kazakh and Kyrgyz nomads who had fled to Xinjiang in 1916 began to return in the spring, they were attacked by soldiers and armed settlers and often murdered in cold blood. At the same time, settlers felt empowered by revolutionary slogans of the "socialization of land" and "power to localities" to grab land from their neighbors. In the colonial context of Jettisuv, punishing rebellion and seeking social justice for the (Russian) downtrodden could coincide. As Niccolò Pianciola puts it, these settlers likely "saw their actions both as an ongoing wartime measure against treacherous ethnic groups and as part of the peasants' revolution in the Empire."[6]

In October, the Tashkent garrison mutinied and grabbed power in the name of the Tashkent Soviet. The move had more to do with local food supply questions than with any deep commitment to socialist ideology or to proletarian power. The Tashkent Soviet proceeded to explicitly exclude Muslims from its ranks. "The inclusion of Muslims in the organ of supreme regional power," it stated, "is unacceptable at the present time in view of both the completely indefinite attitude of the native population toward the power of the Soviets of soldiers', workers', and peasants' deputies, and the fact that there are no proletarian class organizations among the native population whose representation in the organ of supreme regional power [we] would welcome."[7] The Tashkent Soviet proclaimed a proletarian revolution, and the only proletarians were colonial settlers. (The fact that most of them were settlers and soldiers rather than proletarians in the Marxist sense of the word seemed almost irrelevant.) The language of class was being used to assert colonial privileges. In Marco Buttino's apt phrase, the revolution had been turned upside down in Turkestan.[8] In Xinjiang, a Chinese official had taken power after collapse of the Qing had severed the region from the capital. In Turkestan, Russian soldier-settlers had claimed power for themselves.

———

The seizure of power by Europeans drove the Jadids to create an alternative center of power within the framework of the freedoms promised by the Provisional Government. In November 1917, a Muslim congress declared Turkestan autonomous in a liberal democratic Russia and established a Provisional Government of Turkestan in the city of Kokand. The government promised the election of a regional parliament, with guaranteed representation for the European population of Turkestan. A mere fifty years after the defeat of the khans, Central Asian sovereignty was declared in terms of the will of the people, to be backed by a popularly elected assembly. And while the government was to be autonomous within a liberal Russia and was envisaged as a territorial government, the rhetoric surrounding its proclamation clearly saw it as a national government for people of Turkestan. In a poem he wrote for the occasion, the poet Cholpan (Abdulhamid Sulaymon) spoke rapturously of a new beginning:

> Open your eyes, look around!
> Brothers, look what an age has dawned!
> The world is filled with happiness
>
> May life be sacrificed for such days.
>
> REFRAIN:
> Turkestaniness is our pride, Turanian-ness is our title
> The Homeland is our Life, may our blood be sacrificed![9]

The Turkiston Muxotriyati (Turkestan Autonomy), as the government called itself, was clearly an attempt at national statehood, even if it was seen as within a Russian political orbit.

It is hard to imagine a less propitious time for such a political experiment. Political order had melted away throughout the Russian empire, and a civil war was already incipient. The government had no money or arms, and its stakeholders had no experience in running a government. As soon as the Tashkent Soviet could spare arms and men, it stormed Kokand and destroyed large parts of the city, as well as its attempt at statehood. The Turkestan Autonomy had lasted for only seventy-eight days, but it was to loom large as a villain in the Soviet imagination for decades to come. It was the first of many abortive attempts at national statehood in Central Asia in the interwar period. We will encounter similar attempts in Bukhara and Eastern Turkestan in the chapters that follow. In February 1918, however, Turkestan's Russian settlers seemed to be conquering the region for themselves in the name of the proletariat.

Developments took a rather different course in the Kazakh lands. The Kazakh intelligentsia had already mobilized around the issue of conscription in 1916, and it redoubled its efforts in the direction of mobilizing the Kazakh population for the elections to the Constituent Assembly. Here, too, the focus was on the Kazakhs as a nation, with the hope of making use of the opportunities opened up by the revolution to acquire national unity and national rights for the Kazakhs. A series of local conferences culminated in the First All-Kazakh Congress in Orenburg in July, which drew delegates from all Kazakh communities—including those in Turkestan. Political organization was difficult because of the distances involved and the overwhelmingly rural nature of the Kazakh population, but its leadership was not challenged by the *ulama*. The Islamic learned class was much smaller among the Kazakhs, and its cultural capital was no match for that of the aristocratic elites that comprised the intelligentsia. The congress voted for national and territorial autonomy for the Kazakhs in a democratic, federal Russian state. However, when the Bolsheviks seized power in Petrograd in October, all of that became moot. The Second All-Kazakh Congress that met in December hastened to proclaim an autonomous national government, to be called Alash Orda (the Land of Alash), on the territory of the Steppe *Krai* and Ural'sk and Turgay *oblasts* with the ultimate goal of uniting the Kazakhs living in Turkestan with the republic. The executive body for this government was to have guaranteed representation for non-Kazakh inhabitants of the republic. Nevertheless, Alash Orda was to be the national state of the Kazakhs. The congress also paid attention to the formation of a national militia, which was necessary given that "the [Russian] state is living through an extremely difficult time, with murder and robbery everywhere as a sign of general disintegration and anarchy, from which the Kazakhs are not immune," and to creating a commission to produce Kazakh-language textbooks, without which national schools could not be established.[10] With civil war brewing, the Alash leadership set up its capital in Semipalatinsk and attempted to establish national autonomy. Like the Turkestan Autonomy proclaimed the previous month in Kokand, Alash Orda sought territorial autonomy within the parameters of the February revolution. And like the Kokand government, it was led by modernist intellectuals, and it faced insurmountable obstacles in turning its proclamations into political reality. Alash Orda struggled to raise revenue and build institutions, but circumstances, as we shall see below, gave it a longer lease on life than its Turkestani counterpart. It was not abolished until 1920.

————

By spring 1918, then, the euphoria of the previous year had become a distant memory. The state had ceased to exist in Central Asia. Red Guards—militias formed by soldiers who had drifted back to their villages, taking their arms with them, after the Russian imperial army had largely demobilized itself by the autumn of 1917—took power in the name of the soviets in a number of towns across Turkestan and the Steppe *Krai*. The murder and dispossession of the nomads continued in Jettisuv. In spring 1918, Jettisuv was full of returning settler-soldiers who were often bent on revenge. They were also self-proclaimed revolutionaries. Jettisuv witnessed a settler revolution that acted against both Russian elites and the indigenous population. But the soviets' power was challenged from a number of directions. To the north, the Cossack Ataman Aleksandr Dutov had declared Bolshevik laws null and void in the territory of the Orenburg Cossacks and established a government of his own in Orenburg, the town that had been the center of the Kazakh political movement throughout 1917. The Dutov regime cut the only direct rail link between inner Russia and Turkestan. Alash Orda continued to exist, even though it barely controlled its territory. During 1918 and 1919, Alash Orda raised a militia and fought alongside the Whites. It also passed a substantial amount of legislation within the legal framework of the Provisional Government and held out hope for the convocation of the Constituent Assembly. In Transcaspia, Russian Mensheviks and moderate Socialist Revolutionaries ousted the Bolsheviks and established a parallel government in Ashgabat. In Bukhara, the emir used the revolution to attempt to regain the independence his ancestors had lost to Russia in the nineteenth century. He tried to keep the war out of his domains and made cautious approaches to Afghanistan and the British for help.

This intense conflict played out against the backdrop of a devastating famine. Cotton cultivation had boomed during the war and made Turkestan dependent on imported food. The winter of 1916–1917 was harsh, and in 1917 the rains failed at the same time as political turbulence disrupted transport networks and grain shipments from Russia. "In Jizzakh county, the populace died like flies," we read in a report. "There was no one to gather up the corpses, which were to be found at every step, half eaten by dogs and jackals. It was possible to gather the bones of these unfortunates only in 1919. . . . Hungry death reigned."[11] In the winter of 1917–1918, refugees in search of food began arriving in Tashkent, where they huddled in front of factories and other enterprises, asking for work so they could feed themselves. Many collapsed and died in the streets. Others never made it to Tashkent and died en route. The famine was exacerbated by accompanying epidemics of cholera, typhus, and typhoid. Buttino has combed through the statistical evidence to delineate the full scale of the catastrophe brought about by the combination of war and famine. Between 1915 and 1920, the amount of cultivated land declined by half, the livestock population decreased by 75 percent, and cotton production practically ceased. The losses were not uniform across social groups: while Russian peasants saw a decline of 28 percent in their cultivated land and lost 6.5 percent of their livestock, the indigenous population fared much worse. The sedentary Muslim population shrank by 39 percent and that of the nomads by 46 percent.[12]

———

As the Russian state collapsed and different groups sought security and access to food, local forms of solidarity emerged. In the Turkmen desert, various groups of nomads came to control the countryside. In Semirech'e, the bloodletting from 1916 continued unabated. Russian settlers continued to kill nomads and usurp their land. Ferghana descended into chaos as Russian settlers, not very numerous but armed, began to confiscate the land of their Muslim neighbors and requisition their supplies of grain. The main issue was the famine, but land seizures had perfect revolutionary credentials. The rural population organized in self-defense. A number of warlords (*qo'rboshi*) emerged to rally the population, although they soon acquired a logic of their own. These warlords often resorted to the military vocabulary of the khanate of Khoqand— even though no one claimed the mantle of the khan of Khoqand, so thorough had been the dismantlement of the old elites.

The Soviets called the insurgents "Basmachi." The term, which meant "bandit" or "highwayman," had long been in use to describe men who stalked travelers in rural Ferghana before the revolution. Other writers have seen in the Basmachi a national revolt or anti-Soviet resistance. None of these characterizations is entirely accurate. The Basmachi began to provide armed self-defense against the settlers, but they also fought all forms of state power based in the cities. In their vocabulary, modes of mobilization, and forms of leadership, the Basmachi represented a very different form of politics than what had gripped the urban populations during 1917. One of the first *qo'rboshi* was Ergash, an outlaw who had led a band of highwaymen in Ferghana before the revolution.

He had been arrested and exiled to Siberia for that activity. In 1917, a massive empire-wide amnesty allowed him to return to Ferghana, where he was promptly appointed chief of police in the old city of Kokand. In February 1918, desperate to establish some sort of an armed force, the Turkestan Autonomy appointed him commander in chief of its largely nonexistent army. After the destruction of Kokand, Ergash fled to his native village, where he organized a band of armed men to defend it against the depredations of the settlers. Its leaders had little in common with those who operated in the political realm in 1917–1918: neither the Jadids nor urban *ulama* had anything to do with the Basmachi. In fact, many Basmachi leaders saw "Jadid" and "Bolshevik" as synonyms and fought against both equally bitterly. Many *qo'rboshi* in Ferghana were men like Ergash: former outlaws who had spent time in exile in distant parts of the Russian empire. Some of them were descended from Khoqand's old military elite, but almost none had any connection to the public life that had emerged in urban Central Asia under Tsarist rule. Their areas of operation were strictly local, as were their concerns. And they often found themselves living at the expense of the very people they were defending: their exactions of food, forage, and livestock and their forcing villagers to join the armed bands all added to the misery of rural society.

———

The Bolsheviks were virtually absent from the scene in February 1917. Their rise to popularity was a sign of the radicalization of opinion in the Russian heartland as the year progressed. The revolution of 1917 might have been seen by most non-Russians as a moment of national liberation, but it had no clear national dimension for the empire's Russians. The Xinhai Revolution in China was about liberating the Chinese nation from the rule of an alien dynasty. In contrast, for Russians the revolution of 1917 was about liberating the oppressed classes from the tyranny of an unjust social order. The dominant language that emerged in Russia was that of class. From the beginning, when the Provisional Government was challenged by the Petrograd Soviet as the voice of the lower classes, the revolution played out as a struggle of ordinary people against the privileged strata. Positions became radicalized over the course of the year, and by October the most radical parties were in ascendance in Petrograd and Moscow and at the front. As noted above, the Bolsheviks overthrew the Provisional Government in October and claimed power in the name of the soviets.

The Bolshevik vision was utterly universalist. Karl Marx had provided a basic outline of history as progress toward a classless society free of oppression or exploitation. The Bolsheviks hoped to turn this vision into reality. They aimed to do nothing less than to remake the world and usher all of humanity into the utopia of a classless society. They were the agents of History (with a capital h), and their mission had been foretold and their goals foreordained. The appalling cruelty and violence of the Bolshevik era was underwritten by this millennial vision. The vision allowed them to undertake projects of social and cultural engineering that other regimes would have balked at. They did not always succeed, and the unintended consequences of their actions were often more important than the intended ones. Nevertheless, their triumph altered the course of history. The twentieth century would have been very different if the Russian revolution of 1917 had turned out differently.

In 1917–1918, of course, all of this lay in the future, and none of it had been foretold. The Bolsheviks established their power only after a prolonged period of violent conflict. Their seizure of power in Petrograd was deeply resented by people across the political spectrum and led almost immediately to armed conflict, which turned into an extremely brutal civil war that lasted into 1921. Civil war is perhaps a misnomer. The Russian state had largely collapsed by the end of 1917, and a bewildering array of forces struggled for power. The Russian civil war is usually understood as a conflict between the "Reds" and the "Whites." While the Reds were the Bolsheviks and more or less cohesive, the term "Whites" lumps together a vast number of forces that had little in common beyond their hatred of the Bolsheviks. There were Cossacks and generals of the imperial army who fought to revive the empire; socialists and liberals who fought in the name of the Constituent Assembly, the great dream of the revolution that had been abolished by the Bolsheviks; armies of various non-Russian peoples who fought for autonomy or independence; and local groups that fought for control of food supplies and land. As armies chased each other across farmland and steppe, they laid waste to crops and destroyed irrigation channels and railways. Both the human and the material costs were enormous. The bitter struggle for victory shaped Bolshevik attitudes in significant ways.

The establishment of Soviet power in Central Asia was a long process, with many twists and turns. To a certain extent, it was built on a second conquest of Central Asia, as the Red Army fought its way into the region. Central Asia saw machine guns and aircraft fire for the first time during this war. But the military conquest was also accompanied by political work that brought Central Asians into the new order. Curiously, the Bolsheviks, the party of class-based revolution, were also the only ones in Russia to offer support for national rights in 1917. Both Vladimir Lenin and Joseph Stalin believed that national and linguistic differences in a multinational empire could not be wished away; rather, they were objective facts that had to be dealt with. Class struggle and the ultimate victory of the proletariat would be easier if national grievances were dealt with first. Granting national autonomy would allow the oppressed non-Russian nationalities to be able to see clearly the class oppression of their own bourgeoisies, and revolutionary propaganda was most effective in one's own language. These abstract views were tested by the realities of 1917. The Bolsheviks were taken aback by the strength of national movements in the empire. The task then became to harness these grievances to achieve the Bolsheviks' ends. One of the earliest decrees of Soviet power was a proclamation "To All Toiling Muslims of Russia and the East," in which Lenin and Stalin exhorted Muslims to support the new government: "All you, whose mosques and shrines have been destroyed, whose faith and customs have been violated by the Tsars and oppressors of Russia! Henceforward your beliefs and customs, your national and cultural institutions, are declared free and inviolable! Build your national life freely and without hindrance."[13] The Bolsheviks wanted to distance themselves as much as possible from the burdens of the imperial past. Soviet power had to appear to the non-Russians as their own power, not that of the Russians. "It is devilishly important," Lenin wrote in 1921, "to *conquer* the trust of the natives; to conquer it three or four times; *to show* that we are *not* imperialists, that we will *not* tolerate deviations in that direction."[14] In practice, these ideas were to shift shape multiple times, often in unexpected ways. But the Bolsheviks did acquire a nationalities policy that they used to balance national difference with class universalism. Over the course of the twentieth century, many of its postulates would be borrowed, appropriated, and applied by a number of socialist regimes, including that in China.

Still, what was socialism to look like in the colony? If socialism was the triumph of the proletariat, what did it mean for a region such as Central Asia that had no industry and hence no proletariat? The Tashkent Soviet gave one answer: if the indigenous population had no proletariat, then it could have nothing to do with revolutionary power. Bolshevik leaders in Moscow were appalled by the practical consequences of this line of argument. The conquest of power by Russian settlers in Turkestan was not the way the leaders hoped to establish Soviet rule in Turkestan. With civil war raging, however, they could assert their authority over the Tashkent Soviet only by sending plenipotentiaries who, through a combination of threats and moral suasion, attempted to bring the self-proclaimed Soviet power of the settlers in line with the desires of the center. Petr Kobozev, the first such plenipotentiary, arrived in Tashkent in April 1918 and set about loosening the settlers' grip on power. In a telegram that announced his appointment, Stalin advised Tashkent's Soviet rulers "to attract to [political] work [even] adherents of [Alexander] Kerensky from the natives if they are ready to serve Soviet power—the latter only gains from it, and there is nothing to be afraid of in the shadows of the past."[15] Soviet power was to have a broader base than just the proletariat, and loyalty and support for Soviet power was to be the most essential criterion. This drove Kobozev's work. He oversaw the creation of soviets among the Muslim population and forced the Tashkent Soviet to accept Muslim representatives. In May, he presided over a congress of soviets of all of Turkestan that declared Turkestan an autonomous Soviet republic within a socialist

Russia. This was a Soviet counterpart to the autonomy declared by the Muslim national movement in Kokand half a year earlier. Kobozev faced a great deal of pushback from Tashkent's settler socialists, and it was not until the Red Army arrived in November 1919 that their power was finally broken. A Turkestan Commission of the Central Committee of the Communist Party that arrived in the wake of the Red Army assumed control of Soviet and party organizations in the region. One of its targets was the settlers, many of whom were removed from office and deported to Russia.

The situation was even messier with Alash Orda. The Kazakh steppe was the scene of some of the fiercest battles of the Russian civil war. Alash Orda had first sided with the Whites, but its relations with them remained difficult. By late 1919, the Red Army had turned the tide and put White forces to flight, and Alash Orda switched sides after the Bolsheviks offered the Kazakh population amnesty in return for acceptance of Soviet rule. Alash Orda's hope of collaborating as equals with the Bolsheviks was dashed, however. The Bolsheviks were little inclined to form such alliances. As agents of History, they could make tactical concessions to other forces, but alliances and collaboration were anathema. "We do not know of any Alash Orda government and do not recognize it, and cannot enter into treaty relations with it," Kirrevkom, the revolutionary committee in charge of ruling land conquered by Bolshevik forces, informed the Red Army command on December 31, 1919. "The government as such is dissolved."[16] The most the Bolsheviks could offer Alash Orda were a few jobs for its members in the Soviet administration. In its place, the Bolsheviks created their own version of an autonomous Kazakh republic. Officially proclaimed on August 26, 1920, it brought together in one entity the Kazakh population of the four steppe oblasts, the Manghïshlaq peninsula of Turkestan, and Astrakhan oblast. Much as had happened in Turkestan, Moscow had trumped bourgeois autonomy with its Soviet counterpart. Communism had been established on the ruins of national movements in Central Asia.

10

The Threshold of the East

"COMRADE LENIN IS A GREAT MAN, who has understood the Eastern question very well and who has begun the attempt at awakening and uniting the East."[1] Thus wrote Abdurauf Fitrat, the Bukharan thinker and activist, in spring 1919. The "Eastern question" for him concerned liberating "the East" from European imperialism. Fitrat had long been an ardent supporter of cultural and political reform, which he felt alone could ensure the survival and prosperity of Central Asia's Muslims in the modern world. Eight years earlier he had published *A Dialogue between a European and a Bukharan Professor*, a pamphlet that gained much renown in Central Asia. In it, a Bukharan professor of the old stripe, traveling to the hajj via India, discusses new-method schools with an Englishman he encounters. The professor is hostile to the new schools, and it is the Englishman who argues that it is necessary for Muslims around the world to cultivate new learning so they can meet the needs of the modern age. In 1911, Fitrat had seen Europe as a model to be emulated, but the Great War had changed everything. To Fitrat, who had spent four formative years in Istanbul, the utter defeat of the Ottomans brought a sense of desperation. The Jadids, along with the overwhelming majority of the Muslims in the Russian empire, had remained loyal to Russia when the Ottomans joined the war on the side of Germany and Austria. Nevertheless, the Ottoman Empire had long exercised an emotional pull on Muslims under colonial rule, who saw in its existence hope that Muslims could create modern forms of statehood in the age of European domination. Now, with the Ottoman

Empire lying prone in abject defeat, the downfall of the Muslim world seemed complete and the need for change all the more urgent. The new situation altered Fitrat's assessment of Europe, which now appeared to him as a vicious exploiter of the rest of the world. His earlier fascination with the liberal civilization of Europe was replaced by a radical antico- lonial critique of the bourgeois order. The Bolsheviks—more precisely, the idea of revolution—now appeared to be the heralds of a new age, models of emulation of a different kind. The Bolsheviks had successfully challenged the old order of empire and shown the power of mobiliza- tion and organization. They appeared to Fitrat to be agents of a new world order that contained the possibility of national liberation and progress for the entire Muslim world.

The Russian revolution of 1917 was a decolonizing moment. Many anticolonial actors beyond the Russian empire came to see in the tri- umph of the Bolsheviks a new way of combating their oppression. American historians have spoken of a "Wilsonian moment" in world politics, when in the aftermath of the Great War's slaughter, many na- tional movements in the colonized world pinned their hopes on the ideas of national self-determination and territorial sovereignty that the American president Woodrow Wilson espoused for Europe. The hope of remaking the world in this image foundered quickly on the indiffer- ence of European empires and Wilson himself, who had no intention of extending his ideas to the world beyond Europe.[2] This is a somewhat narcissistic view of the world. The Wilsonian moment, such as it was, coexisted with a Leninist moment, which occurred when other anti- colonial actors staked their hopes on rather different methods of achieving liberation from colonial servitude. The Bolshevik model of revolution inspired them. They saw in Communism a path to national salvation and modernity, as well as a formula for reorganizing society to better fight colonial rule. Indeed, Communism, anticolonialism, and nationalism were to be closely intertwined for the rest of the twentieth century. That connection was first made in the years after the Russian revolution, and Central Asia lay at the epicenter of this activity. For a short while, Tashkent in particular became the crossroads of world revolution.

As soon as Kobozev loosened the Russian settlers' hold on the new Soviet regime in Tashkent in the spring of 1918, significant numbers of Turkestanis flocked to the new organs of power. Some of them were Jadids, still smarting from their defeat at the hands of the *ulama* in 1918. They used their new access to power to attack the *ulama*. Municipal soviets run by them dismantled the *ulama*'s organizations and confiscated their property in the name of the revolution. They also used the revolutionary methods of requisitioning and extorting "contributions" from the wealthy to build new-method schools, theaters, and public libraries. But Soviet institutions also attracted a different group of local actors, those with no prior record of involvement in Muslim cultural reform. One such actor was Turar Risqŭlov (1894–1938), a Kazakh from Jettisuv who had attended a Russian-native school and then the school of agronomy in Pishpek (as Bishkek was then called). In October 1916, he matriculated at the Tashkent normal school. In March 1917, after the revolution, he made his way back to his hometown of Merke, where he became involved in the new Soviet institutions as they were established. He returned to Tashkent in mid-1918 as a Soviet delegate and rose rapidly in the ranks, becoming the commissar for health by late 1918. In 1919, he was to become the head of the newly established Bureau of Muslim Communist Organizations (Musburo)—which, under Kobozev's patronage, challenged Russian settlers for control of the local party organization. Most members of the Musburo had attended Russian-native schools, and their knowledge of Russian was a crucial asset in the new age. Most of them also came from prosperous backgrounds, and all were young (Risqŭlov was twenty-four when he became a commissar). The revolution had empowered the youth and given them the opportunity to shake up their society.

Risqŭlov came up with a new theory of revolution in the colony. "In Turkestan," he wrote to Lenin in May 1920, "as in the entire colonial East, two dominant groups have existed and [continue to] exist in the social struggle: the oppressed, exploited colonial natives, and European capital."[3] Imperial powers sent "their best exploiters and functionaries" to the colonies, people who liked to think that "even a worker is a representative of a higher culture than the natives, a so-called Kulturträger."[4] Colonial exploitation took place along national, not class, lines. Revolution, Rïsqŭlov was arguing, had to be reimagined in the colonial peripheries of the empire and redirected toward undoing the injustices and inequalities of the colonial order. In this reading of the revolution, the nation supplanted class as the primary category of analysis and the locus of political struggle. Rïsqŭlov had mapped the Marxist scheme of history onto the nation. There were policy implications of this shift in emphasis. For example, the new order needed to empower the colonial population at the expense of the settlers and build the new order around the former's needs. In January 1920, Turkestan's national Communists, having acquired a majority in the Fifth Congress of the Communist Party of Turkestan, declared Soviet Turkestan a national republic for its indigenous population. Turkestan was renamed the Turkic Republic, and the Communist Party of Turkestan became the Turkic Communist Party. The resolutions were quickly overturned by Moscow's plenipotentiaries, but they give an insight into what communism meant to the first Muslim Communists. It was a path to national salvation that could deliver the nation from enemies, both internal (such as the *ulama*) and external (Russian settlers).

———

Many other groups in the colonial world made the same connection between national salvation and communism. Few of them cared about the class rhetoric of the Bolsheviks, but they were all fascinated by the idea of revolution and national liberation. Central Asia lay at the nexus of a series of overlapping crises that emanated from the end of the First World War. Britain had emerged triumphant—especially in the Middle East, where it acquired a dominant role in Iran and the Arabian peninsula. Iran had been in turmoil since before the war, when Britain and Russia had divided it up into spheres of interest. Yet British paramountcy was not without its blemishes. In Anatolia, defeated Ottoman forces rose up against the possibility of occupation and fragmentation of what was left of the empire. By 1919, Mustafa Kemal Pasha (who took the name Atatürk in 1934) had galvanized a resistance movement against the Allies. Afghanistan had long chafed under British control. In 1919, a new emir declared war on British India and managed to win recognition of his independence, after which he immediately established relations with Soviet Russia. And then there was India. There had long been a small contingent of Indian activists abroad who aimed to overthrow British rule in their country. A group calling itself Ghadar ("Mutiny," the term the British used to describe the great uprising of 1857) had formed in San Francisco. Other activists had plotted with Germany and the Ottomans during the war and formed a Provisional Government of India in Exile in Afghanistan. India witnessed political upheaval in the aftermath of war. Many Indians had hoped to receive greater political rights, if not home rule, as a reward for their contribution to the war. Indian Muslims additionally campaigned for the British to preserve the Ottoman caliphate. British stonewalling, if not outright repression, led to political radicalization and a fascination with alternative ways of solving India's problems.

In 1919–1920, hundreds of Indians, the vast majority of them Muslim, began arriving in Tashkent. They had different trajectories, but they all aspired to overthrow British rule in India through armed incursions from outside. They received help from the fledgling Soviet regime and formed themselves into the Indian Revolutionary Association. They encountered many other groups in the city. Tens of thousands of former Ottoman POWs, liberated but left to fend for themselves after the Bolsheviks withdrew from the war, wanted to make their way back to Anatolia to fight against its occupation. Mustafa Suphi was an Ottoman dissident who had escaped internal exile by fleeing to Russia in 1913. When the war began, he was arrested as an enemy subject and interned in a prison camp in the Urals. He became a Marxist in prison and joined the Bolsheviks. After the revolution, he was active in various Soviet efforts to mobilize Muslims of European Russia. He arrived in Tashkent in early 1920 to organize Turkish POWs into a Communist party and give their anti-British sentiments properly revolutionary moorings. Avetis Mikaelian (Sultanzadeh), an Armenian from Iran, had come to Russia in 1907 to attend an Armenian seminary but got involved in radical politics and joined the Social Democratic Party in 1909. He was active in underground work for that party in the Caucasus as well as Iran. After 1917, he was part of the same circles as Suphi, but focused on the large Iranian migrant population in the Caucasus. In 1919, he was one of the founders of Adalat (Justice), an Iranian Marxist party in exile. He was also in Tashkent in 1920, hoping to recruit Iranians into both the party and a voluntary brigade to fight the British in Iran. Finally, Afghan citizens of various stripes and labor migrants from Eastern Turkestan added to the ferment in Tashkent.

———

The Bolsheviks wanted to remake the world, not just Russia, and that gave them anticolonial credentials. They had used anticolonial rhetoric from the beginning. They had published the secret treaties signed by the Tsarist empire and renounced the extraterritorial rights and privileges extracted by the empire from China, Iran, and the Ottoman Empire. Throughout 1917, they had hoped that revolution in Russia would lead to revolution in other advanced industrial states of western Europe. By the winter of 1918–1919, it was clear that that revolution was not forthcoming and that the bourgeois order had survived the war. Lenin had long argued that exploitation in the colonies tempered the exploitation of workers in the metropole and dampened their revolutionary fervor. It was now clear to the Bolsheviks that the way to bring revolution to western Europe was to deprive European powers of their colonies. As Trotsky famously put it in 1919, "the road [to revolution in] Paris and London [lay] via the towns of Afghanistan, the Punjab and Bengal."[5] The task at hand, then, was to foment revolution in the colonies. "Eastern policy" became all the rage in Moscow, and the peoples of the East (a generic Russian term that referred to all of Asia and bits of northern Africa)—long thought of (if thought of at all) as benighted and backward—now became beacons of hope for the future of Europe. There was, of course, no blueprint for how colonial revolution was to be achieved. The next few years witnessed a number of different initiatives, some of them quite speculative and all of them imagined on the fly, for revolutionizing the East. The moment passed soon, as other considerations took precedence, and the enthusiasm for world revolution diminished, though the goal was not abandoned completely.

Turkestan occupied a central place in these initiatives. It was to be the threshold to Asia, the place from which India and China would be revolutionized. Already in December 1919, the Turkestan Commission had established the Council for International Propaganda in Tashkent to spread the message of revolution to India. The council was the main source of support for the Indian revolutionaries who arrived in Tashkent. The following summer, the Eastern Question took pride of place in Moscow at the Second Congress of the Communist International (Comintern), the organization of Communist parties around the world established by the Soviets in 1919. The Comintern congress convened a Congress of the Peoples of the East in Baku in September 1920. It also created a youth league, the Bureau for Propaganda and Activity among the Peoples of the East, and the Turkestan Bureau in Tashkent. The last bureau was headed by Manabendra Nath Roy (1887–1954), an Indian revolutionary of a rather different stripe. He had begun his political life as an Indian patriot, having become increasingly convinced that only an armed struggle would rid India of British rule. When the Great War broke out in 1914, Roy had left India in search of German help. That quest took him to Java, Japan, and China, before he arrived in the United States. It was there that he discovered socialism. When U.S. entry into the war led to a crackdown on anti-British organizations, Roy escaped to Mexico, where he was one of the founders of the Socialist Workers' Party. In 1920, he attended the Second Congress of the Comintern as a Mexican delegate. Nationalism had led him to anticolonialism and world revolution. He was sent to Tashkent to open the bureau as well as a military school that was to train Indian revolutionaries. He represented a more orthodox, Marxist approach to revolution than the other Indian revolutionaries who had arrived in Tashkent earlier in the year.

The enthusiasm unleashed by the idea of revolutionizing the colonial world was real, and it came from the peoples of the East themselves. The Bolsheviks tried to harness this sentiment, but they were seldom able to control it. The would-be revolutionaries continued to imagine revolution according to their own lights. The Bolsheviks were unhappy with this ideological heterodoxy, and they had other concerns as well. The hope of spreading revolution always coexisted with the need to safeguard the security of the nascent Soviet state, and these more realistic interests soon came to take precedence. Since its inception, the Soviet state had been the object of opprobrium by the Allies, who had intervened militarily in the Russian civil war and imposed an economic embargo on the new regime. In March 1921, Britain agreed to sign a trade agreement with the Soviet government to end the blockade. One of the conditions imposed by the British was that "the Russian Soviet Government [would refrain] from any attempt by military or diplomatic or any other form of action or propaganda to encourage any of the peoples of Asia in any form of hostile action against British interests or the British Empire, especially in India and in the Independent State of Afghanistan."[6] The Soviets disbanded the Indian military school in Tashkent and sent the Indian revolutionaries to Moscow to study at the newly founded Communist University for the Toilers of the East. The Turks and Iranians also moved on. The idea of fomenting revolution in the colonial world did not go away entirely, but its locus moved away from Central Asia.

———

Yet, there was plenty of revolutionary action left in Central Asia. Military adventurism on the part of Soviet forces combined with enthusiasm for the idea of revolution among local groups saw the creation of three revolutionary republics in and around Central Asia in 1920. In February, freshly arrived Red Army units occupied the khanate of Khiva and established a people's republic in its place. (The term "people's republic" was to have a long career in the twentieth century. Khiva was one of the first such republics.) The khanate had experienced internal strife since 1916 for reasons not directly connected to either the uprising of 1916 or the Russian revolution. Given that turmoil, Red Army units seized the opportunity to overthrow the khan and proclaim a republic. In June,

Bolsheviks from the Caucasus proclaimed a soviet republic in Gilan, in northern Iran, which had been the scene of a local insurgency since 1915. The insurgents, led by Mirza Kuchuk Khan, sought land reform and the end of corruption in Iran's central government. After the Russian revolution, their views became radicalized, and they established ties with Soviet officials in the Caucasus—who were only too happy to show up in Gilan in the company of Iranian exiles and establish the Soviet Republic of Iran. Moscow was always less enthused by this adventure than the revolutionaries on the ground, and it abandoned the republic soon after signing a treaty of friendship with Iran's central government in February 1921. However, the brief existence of the republic was proof of the appeal of the idea of revolution beyond the boundaries of the Soviet state.

Finally, at the end of August 1920, Red Army troops under the command of Mikhail Frunze invaded Bukhara, toppled the emir, and established the People's Soviet Republic of Bukhara (see figure 10.1). Since the fall of the monarchy in February 1917, the emir had sought to maximize his independence from Russia and to hold both reform and revolution at bay. He had chased Bukhara's Jadids into exile in Soviet Turkestan, where they became increasingly radicalized. The Young Bukharans, as Bukharan Jadids had taken to calling themselves, came to see revolution through the prism of the nation. According to them, the salvation of Bukhara lay in getting rid of the oppressive and traitorous emir and establishing a republic in his place. The Soviets were both afraid that outright annexation might antagonize Britain and deeply uncertain of their ability to run the state themselves. They therefore put in place another people's republic, this one headed by the Young Bukharans. The fall of the emirate marked the end of the tradition of Central Asian statehood: Bukhara was the last indigenous Central Asian state to fall.

Frunze had made the Young Bukharans join the tiny Bukharan Communist Party that already existed, but he could not turn them into instant Bolsheviks. Rather, the Bukharan republic brought the Jadids into political power in a way that never happened in Turkestan. The Young Bukharans pursued an agenda that had far more to do with national salvation and self-strengthening than anything that Marx ever wrote or that the Bolsheviks might have recognized as proper policy. Its government

FIG. 10.1. The Third Congress of the Bukharan People's Soviet Republic, August 1921. The
banner on the left hails the Comintern and the Bukharan Communist Party, while the
one on the right celebrates the nation (*khalq*) and the homeland (*vatan*).
Among those seated are Abdurauf Fitrat (far left), Fayzulla Khojayev (center),
and Usman Khoja (second from right). Photo courtesy of Timur Kocaoğlu.

was headed by Fayzulla Khojayev (1896–1938), a scion of one of the
wealthiest families in Bukhara who was a committed reformist. Fitrat
returned to Bukhara and eventually became finance minister (his signature appeared on the banknotes issued by the government) and minister of education. The Young Bukharan government acted like many
modernizing states of the past: it sought to introduce new systems of
administration, public health, and modern education (creating a network of new-method schools and reforming the city's famed madrasas).
It also made an effort to regulate Islam and to bring the *ulama* to heel.
And it attempted to establish direct diplomatic relations with other
countries, establishing an embassy in Kabul, sending a diplomatic mission to Turkey, and opening a trade representation in Berlin. It also
joined a long list of modernizing regimes—from eighteenth-century
imperial Russia to Egypt, Iran, and Japan in the nineteenth century—that

sent students abroad to acquire a modern education. From 1922 on, the Bukharan republic sent forty-seven students (some of them as young as ten) to Germany and a larger number to Turkey.[7] Germany was particularly important to the Jadids, who saw western Europe as the seat of modernity and sought an indirect connection with it.

Yet the Young Bukharans could never shake off their dependence on the Soviets, who had no interest in helping a Muslim modernist state flourish in Central Asia. The Soviets tried their best to restrict Bukhara's direct contacts with the outside world. They blocked a visit to Bukhara by a Turkish delegation, while Soviet ambassadors in Kabul and Berlin asserted control over Bukhara's representations. The Young Bukharans chafed at Soviet control. Usmon Khoja, a cousin of Fayzulla's and the chair of the Central Executive Committee of the republic, took the most radical step of all. In December 1921, during a tour of inspection in the mountainous eastern regions of Bukhara, he led the military units under his command in an assault on the Red Army barracks in Dushanbe and declared war on all Russian troops in the republic. The Red Army units survived the scare and Usmon Khoja fled to Afghanistan. He eventually moved to Turkey and became a prominent figure in the Central Asian emigration. Others attempted to resist Soviet pressure from within the government. In May 1923, the Soviet plenipotentiary representative in Bukhara (the successor of the Tsarist political agent) forced four Bukharan ministers (including Fitrat) out of the government and had them exiled to Moscow. This little purge rendered the Bukharan republic much more docile, a shadow of its former self.

———

In Turkestan, Moscow moved to institutionalize its authority. The Turkestan Commission was replaced by a permanent Turkestan Bureau based in Tashkent. Its members were appointed by the Central Committee of the Russian Communist Party and included Central Asians from the beginning. In 1922, the republics of Bukhara and Khiva were also put under the commission's jurisdiction, and it was renamed the Central Asia Bureau. In the summer of 1920, the new bureau oversaw an overhaul of local party organizations. Rïsqŭlov was assigned to a desk job in Moscow, and a new leadership was installed in Turkestan. The men who replaced Rïsqŭlov in leading party positions were more circumspect but not very different in terms of background: they all had Russian educations and experience in Soviet work since 1917, but few had participated in cultural reform before the revolution. For the party, the fundamental problem was finding a cohort of native cadres that it could speak with and that would have some standing with the local population. Given the paucity of indigenous cadres with modern educations and a command of Russian, party authorities had little choice but to look to the same kinds of individuals. Still, Moscow's emissaries remained wary of the ideological shortcomings of such men, even as they worked with them.

Bringing Turkestan under control also meant doing something about the Russian settlers. The bloodbath in Jettisuv had continued. Most settlers had seen the revolution as an opportunity to grab land from the nomads. The conflict that began in 1916 had continued unabated and done much to galvanize Turkestan's Muslim Communists into action. In one of their major successes, they managed to force the party to act. In 1921, it decided to implement a thorough land reform in Jettisuv that involved disarming the settlers, expropriating their land (including the land they had grabbed since 1916), and expelling them to Russia. Over the course of 1921–1922, perhaps as many as 30,000 settlers were deported from Jettisuv and another 10,000 from other parts of Turkestan. Here, Soviet power came closest to embracing the process of decolonization.[8] It was also the most explicit attempt by Soviet authorities to show in deeds and not just words that Soviet power was not a direct descendant of Tsarist colonial power. Georgy Safarov, appointed to the Turkestan Commission in August 1920, initiated the process in dramatic style. In June 1921—accompanied by Sultanbek Qojanov, a Kazakh activist—Safarov went on a tour of Russian settlements in Jettisuv, with the goal of punishing Russian settlers for their misdeeds since 1916. In village after village the two men gathered settlers in public meetings, where Safarov harangued and manhandled them. In the village of Koltsovka in Karakol (Przhevalsk) county, the site of the worst settler excesses in 1916, Safarov ordered a Kyrgyz attendee to beat a certain Komarov in front of the assembled public, while Safarov berated Komarov and threatened to "send him to the moon" with his revolver. In Prudki, he made settlers stand on chairs and shout, "I'm a fool!" as they were beaten by Kyrgyz bystanders.[9]

This was political theater at its rawest. It helped that some party officials who arrived from Moscow had a low opinion of the settlers. For Grigory Broido, head of the department of external relations of the Turkestan Commission, the Russian settlers in Jettisuv were "land-rich kulaks" who had no sympathy for the revolution. According to him, "The norms of the Soviet constitution and of Soviet decrees have become in the hands of this bestial kulak a mere weapon for plundering the nomads."[10] But Safarov and Broido were outliers. Their colleagues in the Turkestan Commission did not share this dark assessment. Rather, they tended to see the Russian population of Turkestan, even the *kulaks* ("rich peasants") among them, as the major pillar of support for Soviet rule in the region. Safarov's actions produced stiff opposition from his colleagues and his victims, who accused him of abuse of power before the Party Control Commission (it is because of this case that we have the detailed account of his actions against the settlers). Safarov was acquitted, but nothing like his actions was ever repeated. The episode remained unique in Soviet history.

———

The convulsions besetting the Russian empire spilled across its porous boundaries in Eurasia. Mongolia became enmeshed in the Russian civil war when White forces fleeing the Reds invaded the country in 1921. China had sought to take advantage of the chaos in Russia to reassert its claim over the country and had stationed troops there in 1917. The Whites scattered these garrisons and installed Bogd Khagan as the ruler of an independent Mongolia. The Reds soon chased out the Whites and put the Mongol People's Party, a small group of modernist urban elites, in power, with Bogd Khagan confirmed as a constitutional monarch. The Russian civil war had led to Mongolian independence.

The new constitutional monarchy soon became a Soviet satellite whose further political development was shaped by its Soviet connection.

Xinjiang fared better than Mongolia. It too was buffeted by waves of humanity crashing across its boundaries, but its governor, Yang Zengxin, managed not just to keep the worst of the chaos out of his domain but also to acquire a degree of power in it that no previous governor of Xinjiang had commanded. Through a combination of skill and bloodthirstiness, Yang ensured the territorial integrity of the province; stability within it; and most importantly, the security of Chinese rule in the province. Although he had been appointed by the Republic, Yang was a Confucian official of the old stripe. For him, the world worked best if it maintained order, and he was therefore wary of the ideas of revolution, anticolonial struggle, and national self-determination that emanated from the Soviet Union. "It is frightening to see these Muslims and Turbans handling their own affairs of state during this time of chaos," he once wrote of the situation in Soviet Central Asia.[11] Yang feared that similar ideas in Xinjiang might lead to the Han being driven out and the province being lost to the Soviets. He therefore did his best to keep such frightening phenomena out of his domain. He controlled the borders with the rest of China to ensure that unsuitable ideas did not enter Xinjiang and banned all newspapers from it. He also shut down many of the new Chinese schools that had opened since the beginning of the twentieth century and allowed conservative Muslims to attack Jadid schools. He combined these measures with thorough vetting of all officials and creating a network of spies that reported to him.

Yang could not keep the outside world out, of course. The uprising of 1916 in the Russian empire brought a quarter of a million desperate Kazakh and Kyrgyz refugees to Xinjiang. The following year, tens of thousands of Taranchis and Dungans, buffeted by both Cossacks and Kazakhs, fled from Semirech'e into Xinjiang.[12] They were followed a couple of years later by defeated White armies. First came the army of Ataman Aleksandr Dutov, which crossed the border in February 1920 with many civilians in tow. A little later, General Andrei Bakich crossed the border at Tarbaghatay with eight thousand soldiers and five thousand civilians, and a month later, his commander, Ataman Boris Annenkov, arrived in Ghulja with a thousand men. Yang tried his best to scatter and disarm the troops, sending Annenkov's men to Dunhuang (in Gansu) and interning the followers of Bakich in a camp in the steppe. The two generals were not reconciled to defeat, however, and set about preparing a counterattack on Soviet territory. By this time the Soviets were largely in control of Turkestan and the Steppe region and were pressuring Yang to do something about the presence of their enemies in his domain. In May 1921, in return for a payment in gold, Yang allowed Soviet forces to enter Xinjiang and deal with the Whites. However, the Red Army assault was less than fully successful, for Bakich escaped with two-thirds of his soldiers and made his way to Mongolia, where he sought to regroup with White forces. The subsequent Red victory in Mongolia meant that Bakich was pushed back into Xinjiang, where a second Red Army assault in September led to his final defeat. Meanwhile, Annenkov was arrested by Yang's forces and delivered to the Soviets. The so-called Xinjiang Front of the Russian civil war was over, but it had left 30,000–40,000 Russian refugees behind.[13] Some of them trickled back into Semirech'e, where they often reignited struggles with Kazakhs over land; others stayed behind and laid the foundation of a Russian émigré community in Xinjiang. However, unlike in Mongolia, the Red Army did not stay on after its victory and Xinjiang remained legally a part of China.

Yang showed that for all his dislike of revolution he could deal with the Soviets to get rid of his unwelcome guests, the White troops. He could also cooperate with them to resume cross-border trade, which had collapsed during the revolution and the civil war. Famine in Soviet Turkestan and acute shortages of food in Russian cities drove Soviet authorities to look for food supplies in Xinjiang. In May 1920, the Turkestan government sent a delegation to Ghulja to negotiate the resumption of trade with Yang. It was a remarkable agreement, signed between regional authorities from the edges of two empires acting largely on their own. The Soviet government soon regained control of Turkestan's foreign affairs, but Yang remained free to conduct his own relations with the Soviets. For the Soviets, it was a matter of revolutionary pride that agreements with neighbors be made on equal footing. They renounced the extraterritorial claims that Russians had enjoyed in Xinjiang since the Treaty of St. Petersburg and, in return for maintaining consulates in Xinjiang, they allowed the opening of "Chinese" consulates in Soviet Central Asia. Although these consulates were nominally answerable by the Foreign Ministry in Beijing, their actual operation was left entirely to Yang, who appointed his relatives or close collaborators to the consulates in Tashkent, Andijon, Zaysan, Semipalatinsk, and Almaty, which he used to keep a watchful eye on labor migrants from Xinjiang who now returned to Turkestan in large numbers.[14]

Xinjiang was largely spared the attentions of Soviet enthusiasts of world revolution. There were those in Soviet Central Asia who wanted to spread revolution into Xinjiang, but they did not get their way. Many members of the large Eastern Turkestani diaspora in Soviet lands—the Taranchis, Dungans, and Kashgaris of long residence as well as those who were recent labor migrants—were indeed enthused and radicalized by the revolution, and as we shall see in chapter 11, many of them wanted to return to their homeland and liberate it. Jānis Rudzutaks, the Latvian Bolshevik who headed the Turkestan Bureau in 1920–1921, prepared a plan for establishing Soviet republics of Kashgaria and Zungharia on the pattern of Khiva and Bukhara. He was adamantly opposed by Georgy Chicherin, the commissar for foreign affairs, who was always averse to the unbridled revolutionary adventurism of his colleagues. Nothing came of Rudzutaks's plans, and the Soviets continued to deal with Yang.

———

The Soviets' hesitation to interfere in Xinjiang had much to do with their assessment of the situation in China. Postwar developments had produced widespread radicalization in China as well. Many in China had hoped that the postwar settlement would lead to the abolition of foreign concessions and the unequal treaties on which they were based. Instead, the victorious powers decided at Versailles to maintain the status quo and award Germany's concessions in China to Japan, instead of abolishing them. The Wilsonian moment was over. The news of this decision led to widespread protests across urban China that began a period of cultural and political renewal. It was also a moment of disillusionment with bourgeois liberalism, and some intellectuals turned to Marx to find answers. His work was then little known in China: it was the triumph of the Bolsheviks in Russia that put the spotlight on Marx. The first discussion circles in China devoted to the study of Marx appeared only in 1918. There, Chinese intellectuals read Marx through the prism of the nation. Li Dazhao, one of the earliest Chinese Marxists, argued that foreign imperialist powers had exploited China as a country and that "the whole country has gradually been transformed into part of the world proletariat."[15] China thus was a proletarian nation. This was the same argument that Risqŭlov (and many others) had made. The connection between nation and revolution was never to disappear from Chinese Communism. Later Chinese Marxists would come up with the idea of communism with Chinese characteristics, but the poor fit between Marx's categories and Chinese concerns was present at the birth of Chinese Communism.

The Comintern was early interested in China and in 1919 sent two emissaries to investigate the situation in the country. They helped organize various Marxist study groups into the Chinese Communist Party (CCP), which held its founding congress in Shanghai in July 1921. But given the virtual absence of an industrial proletariat in China, the Comintern and the Soviets saw little immediate prospect for a Communist revolution in the country and put their bets instead on the Guomindang (GMD), the Nationalist Party founded by Sun Yat-sen. They argued that a national democratic revolution was a prerequisite for any future Communist revolution in the semicolonial conditions in China. These conditions required a united front that obligated the CCP to work with the Nationalists. The Comintern declared the GMD to be a revolutionary party and provided it with substantial aid, in the process reshaping it in the Bolshevik image. By 1923, the GMD had been restructured as a centralized party with a revolutionary mission. China thus boasted two Leninist parties that, for all their ideological antagonisms, shared a common organizational model. They were also both committed to ensuring the territorial integrity of China, which they saw not as an empire but an indivisible nation-state.

The Comintern and the Soviets accepted this claim because the global struggle against imperialism required a strong and united China. The fate of China's colonial peripheries had to be tied to that of revolution in China as a whole, and the Soviet Union sought to guarantee the territorial integrity of the Chinese republic. There could be no talk of Chinese colonial rule in Xinjiang, let alone of Xinjiang's liberation from it.

11

A Soviet Central Asia

THE DECADE AFTER the collapse of the Tsarist empire was a tumultuous period in Central Asia, as two different projects of radical change sought to transform the region. The Bolsheviks were motivated by a vision—utopian and brutal at the same time—of remaking the world, overcoming "backwardness," and dragging all peoples to the brilliant future of Communism. The Jadids, shaken by opposition from conservatives in their own society, had become fascinated by revolution as a means of bringing about the change that they desired. Their vision was radicalized by the upheavals of the civil war (as well as broader, global transformations of the era after the First World War), and they were willing to experiment with ideas that they might not even have contemplated before 1917. The two projects had considerable overlap: they shared the rhetoric of progress, anticolonial struggle, and the liberation of the East. For different reasons both favored a cultural revolution, which included mass education, land reform, women's liberation, and (perhaps paradoxically for the Bolsheviks) the creation of national identities. Both took aim at traditional society, which they equated with backwardness and stagnation. Yet the two projects operated on different logics, and they coexisted uneasily for a decade while Soviet control over Central Asia remained tenuous. But precisely because of this uncertain control, the decade produced unprecedented cultural ferment that created modern Central Asian culture.

———

By late 1923, the dust had begun to settle in Central Asia, and the Soviet order was taking shape. The Soviets had brought settler violence under control and subdued the Basmachi insurgency. Central Asia was again part of the Russian state, but under new conditions. The Soviet order was built on the mobilization of society by an activist state, spearheaded by a party with a self-proclaimed mandate to transform the world. Society was to be reshaped and pushed along the path of progress to classlessness. In significant ways, the Soviet Union was the world's first developmentalist state. The party—now called the Russian Communist Party (Bolshevik)—was no ordinary party. It saw itself as the agent of History, the seer of the future, and the vanguard of society. A pyramidal structure of ostensibly elected councils (soviets), ranging from the village through counties and districts and up to the level of the republic, provided the basic administrative structure of this order, while trade unions, cultural and political societies, labor cooperatives, women's clubs, and youth leagues provided other ways of bringing people into politics. All of this would have been inconceivable under the Tsarist order, which was based on the exclusion of people from politics. The Soviet Union was one of a new variety of what might be called mobilizational states that emerged in the interwar period, in which the state sought to reshape society by using modern means of social intervention in a number of realms. It was not simply new forms of organization that were necessary. People had to be taught to see the world in the Bolshevik way. They had to be taught to see inequality as exploitation, class as fundamental, and revolutionary struggle as the path to salvation. In 1919, Stalin, then the people's commissar for nationalities affairs, wrote that the main task of Soviet power in "the East" was "to raise the cultural level of [its] backward peoples, to build a broad system of schools and educational institutions, and to conduct . . . Soviet agitation, oral and printed, in the language that is native to and understood by the surrounding laboring population."[1] The party spent a great deal of energy on political education, sending out teams armed with posters, newspapers, film, and theater to propagate the new political message. Marches, demonstrations, and public meetings, all orchestrated by the party or its agents, became the new norm of public life. A network of red tea-houses, red yurts, and red corners sprang up across Soviet Central Asia. Campaigns for the "liquidation of illiteracy," to promote public health and hygiene, and to introduce new agricultural techniques sought to reshape old habits and customs and transform culture. Although Soviet power still barely existed in the region, its agents set out to shake up local society.[2]

But who was to do this work of mobilization, agitation, and propaganda in Central Asia? Few Russians knew local languages or had enough connections in local societies to have any hope of being effective. A few activists arrived full of missionary zeal, but the leg work had to be done by members of indigenous societies. The Soviets had their greatest success in the margins of society, among people who did not have major stakes in the established order. There were plenty of fractures in society, and they had been greatly magnified by war, famine, and economic collapse. The new order found a footing among landless or land-poor peasants; nomads without adequate livestock; women who had escaped abusive families or been cast out by them; and perhaps most crucially of all, among youth eager for change. In 1923, the party launched the policy of *korenizatsiia* ("indigenization") in all non-Russian regions of the Soviet Union. This entailed the use of local languages in schools, courts, and workplaces; the hiring of locals to fill administrative positions; and giving preference to locals for jobs in the workplace. The historian Terry Martin has called this the world's first affirmative action program.[3] It did not quite deliver on its promises and ground to a halt in the 1930s, but the promise was important. Combined with territorial autonomy, indigenization promised a radical transformation of the balance of power between the imperial metropole and its colonial peripheries, and it did much to attract enthusiastic young people to the Soviet side.

The authorities also worked to create a new group of local party members they could trust. The first Central Asians to join the party had been accidental Communists. Public figures from before the revolution, who had their own agendas, joined the party because they had no

choice once the Bolsheviks had taken power and proclaimed a monopoly over public life. In Bukhara and the Kazakh republic, the Bolsheviks incorporated members of the older political elites into the party.
Men such as Turar Rïsqŭlov saw the party's goals through the prism of
their own concerns of fighting settler violence and eradicating the legacy of colonial rule in Central Asia. They did yeoman's work in establishing party cells among the indigenous population and recruiting Muslims. But party authorities were eager to create a cohort of indigenous
communists with proper ideological training. In 1922, they began sending young Central Asians to Moscow to study at the Communist University for the Toilers of the East, the Sverdlov Communist University,
and eventually the Institute of the Red Professoriate, institutions of
ideological education for the party elite. Others were educated at party
schools that began to appear in Central Asia. By the mid-1920s, a new
group of Muslim Communists had begun to appear.

———

Stalin's list of the goals of Soviet power in Central Asia had many reso-
nances for the Jadids. Building "a broad system of schools and educational institutions" and "raising the cultural level" of their compatriots
were dear to their hearts. There were grounds for cooperation. There
had been little love lost between the Jadids and the Bolsheviks in 1917,
but things had changed fairly quickly since then. Opposition from conservatives in their own society in 1917 had made the Jadids lose faith in
gradualism and exhortation, while the abject defeat of the Ottoman
Empire in 1918 created a feeling of desperation. "Many among us," Abdurauf Fitrat wrote in 1920, "say, 'Rapid change in methods of education,
in language and orthography, or in the position of women, is against
public opinion and creates discord among Muslims. [Therefore,] we
need to enter into [such reforms] gradually.'" Fitrat disagreed. "The
thing called 'public opinion' does not exist among us," he continued.
"We have a 'general' majority, but it has no opinion. . . . The thoughts
that our majority has today are not its own but are only the thoughts of
some imam or *akhund*. [Given all this,] no good can come from gradual-

ness."[4] The nation was too ignorant and too heedless to know its own good; it had to be dragged into the modern world, kicking and screaming if need be. The new revolutionary regime seemed to promise radical change, especially after Moscow broke the settlers' grip on Soviet power. Some Jadids joined the Communist Party. Most did not, but they seized the opportunities created by the new order to implement their newly radicalized goals.

The decade after 1917 witnessed a number of revolts among the Jadids—against the authority of the past, the authority of the elders, literary conventions and conventions of sociability, the authority of the *ulama*, and ultimately the authority of Islam. The theater exploded with activity. The winters of 1919–1920 and 1920–1921, beset with famine and civil war, saw hectic activity in Tashkent's theaters. A new journalism came into existence. The press that emerged in 1917 did not survive, but new vernacular newspapers, funded (if only modestly) by the party, began appearing in 1918. The new press featured Soviet content— translations of speeches by Bolshevik leaders, political messages, and official analyses of current affairs—but it was also a vehicle for social criticism and new genres of writing. These genres (the newspaper report, satirical feuilleton, short story, memoir, novel, bureaucratic form, and eventually technical manual) had begun to appear in Central Asia before the revolution, but it was in the first decade after it that they really took hold. The new prose literature was novel in both form and content. Poetry remained king, but it too was transformed. Poets rejected the old poetry of the rose and the nightingale, of God, love, and wine, and insisted on introducing new topics. And the new poetry came in new forms, as poets rejected Persianate conventions of form and genre and used new systems of prosody and meter. The master of this new poetry was Cholpan. He had begun writing before the revolution, when he was still a schoolboy, but he found his voice and passion in 1917. Over the next several years, he created a body of work that was new in its form, vocabulary, and sensibility.

Publishing took off in the Kazakh republic as well. Kazakh activists had already standardized the Kazakh language before the revolution, but the 1920s saw unprecedented publishing efforts. Turkmen and

Kyrgyz both really became written languages for the first time in this decade. Both societies were largely oral and used the elaborate form of Chaghatay Turkic for any written communication. Now, the creation of a written language demanded standardization. The creation of new, modern literary standards also raised a host of questions. A language needs a new lexicon to represent new phenomena (both new inventions, such as the telephone and the railway, and new concepts, such as exploitation and revolution). Should this vocabulary come from other Turkic languages, Persian or Arabic (the traditional sources of loanwords for Islamicate languages), Russian, or French? Or should new words be invented from purely indigenous sources? And how should the new language be written? Since the late nineteenth century, many reformers in Turkic-speaking societies had argued that the unmodified Arabic script was not suitable for writing Turkic languages and that this unsuitability lay behind the high rates of illiteracy in those societies. The Arabic script does not indicate short vowels, while Turkic languages are rich in vowels, having anywhere from six to ten of them. The Arabic alphabet also contains a number of letters to indicate sounds specific to Arabic. In other languages, those letters were pronounced differently, so that spelling bore little relation to pronunciation. For those who saw universal literacy as the surest path to progress, a purely phonetic script was the desired goal. Even before the revolution, Kazakh activists had created a phonetic orthography for their language through a substantial reform of the Arabic script. In 1919, a conference in Tashkent came up with an even more radical reform for the orthography of Uzbek that involved modifying the Arabic script to indicate all vowels, dropping the Arabic-specific letters, and spelling everything phonetically.[5] The proposals put forward by the conference were not universally accepted, but change was afoot. The next few years saw a great deal of ferment in Uzbek, as writers experimented with spelling and vocabulary, coining new terms to go with the new genres of writing that had begun to appear.

Women too had to change if society were to progress. Nomadic women did not veil, but women in sedentary communities wore a particularly onerous form of full body covering called *paranji* that was ac-

FIG. 11.1. Women in *paranji* and *chachvon,* old city of Tashkent, 1920s. Photo by Max Penson.
© www.maxpenson.com.

companied by a head covering made of horsehair called *chachvon,* which covered even the eyes (see figure 11.1). The *paranji-chachvon* combination seems to have become widespread after the Russian conquest as a way of drawing boundaries between the Muslim community and its conquerors. It underpinned a fairly rigid system of seclusion and a set of gender norms that defined social practices. In 1917, the Provisional Government had given women the right to vote and turned Central Asian women into full, rights-bearing citizens. This did not go down well with conservative forces in the region, and women's participation in elections in that year was spotty, with women completely barred from polling stations in many locations. For the Jadids, this was madness, for it denied the Muslim population its proper representation. The question of voting soon became moot, but the bigger issue of women's proper place in society remained. The Jadids saw the question through the prisms of nation and progress. They argued that women had to be educated because the nation needed good mothers. Their ideal of companionate marriage similarly underlay a new vision of a national community based on autonomous nuclear family units. The convulsions of the era of the revolution made this goal seem both more urgent and more achievable. The debate centered on the issues of bride wealth (*qalin*), which the groom's family paid to the bride's family; ending women's seclusion and bringing them into educational institutions and the workforce; and, in the sedentary areas, the question of veiling. As in many places around the world, the "women's question" was largely debated among reformist men, but a small number of women activists, mostly from Jadid families, had emerged by the early 1920s. Many of them stopped wearing the *paranji-chachvon* combination when they left the house. Such unveiling was a major public statement that provoked the fury of the rest of Muslim society. It was easier to do in the Russian spaces of the new cities. Although the vast majority of women did not unveil, the presence of the new woman became an inescapable part of urban life.[6]

The debate extended to Islam itself. Jadidism, we should remember, had begun as a movement of religious reform. The opposition of conservative *ulama* in 1917 had radicalized the Jadids, who increasingly tied their critique of customary practices to the idea of the nation. They now characterized their opponents as enemies of and traitors to the nation, who used religion for their private gain and ended up keeping the people backward. What emerged was a peculiarly Muslim form of anticlericalism, in which the *ulama* were reviled as duplicitous, selfish, greedy, and ultimately as religionmongers (*dinfurushlar*). The theater and the new press mocked the *ulama*, with cartoons in the new satirical magazines poking brutal fun at them. The Tashkent magazine *Mushtum* (Fist) was edited by Abdulla Qodiriy, a man of impeccable Islamic credentials (he had studied in madrasas in Tashkent), who nevertheless published cartoons that depicted the *ulama* as two-faced, cunning creatures, often showing them as animals. In a long-running series of satirical sketches, Qodiriy lampooned the *ulama* through the character of Kalvak Makhzum ("Friar Simple"), a mullah of the old stripe who combined ignorance, conceit, superciliousness, and bigotry in his person. The *ulama* retained considerable authority among the population but had been excluded from the new institutions of power. Their moment of prominence in 1917 had not lasted. They were also excluded from the new press and left to fulminate in the mosques and on the streets. They routinely hurled accusations of apostasy and infidelity at their opponents, and matters often descended into violence. When the Young Bukharans entered Bukhara as its rulers, the first targets of their wrath were the city's leading religious functionaries who had played a large part in the persecution of reformers since 1917. Some of the most august personages were made to clean toilets around the city before digging their own graves, into which they were swiftly consigned by a revolutionary tribunal.[7] In return, *ulama*-led mobs commonly attacked new-method schools and cultural clubs in urban neighborhoods, while women who attended schools (let alone those who unveiled) were routinely harassed and assaulted. Turkestani society was in the midst of serious contestation over its past and future, as well as its tradition and religion.

The slope from reform to revolution was slippery, and criticisms of the *ulama* could shade into criticisms of Islam itself. Fitrat traveled the greatest distance here. Before 1917, he had published a number of works of Islamic piety in a modernist vein, including a biography of the Prophet and a long work that presented the Qur'an, if understood correctly, as the guide to salvation. The confrontation with the *ulama* that began in 1917 transformed his views. In 1923 and 1924, he published two short works that took anticlericalism into the realm of irreligion. In a novella called *Qiyomat* (Resurrection), Fitrat retold the Islamic story of the afterlife in a sardonic fashion that shows up its contradictions and ultimately subverts its meaning. Pochomir, an opium addict in withdrawal, hallucinates that he has died and is in his grave. There, he beats back the attempts of Munkar and Nakir, the two angels who visit the dead in their graves, to question him on his deeds and sends them packing. He then sleeps peacefully until the trumpet sounds for the resurrection. The resurrection is a scene of pure chaos in which people, all stark naked, jostle with each other for years as they wait for their sins and good deeds to be weighed. The angels who work the scales are a combination of brutish policemen and incompetent Soviet bureaucrats.

Pochomir talks his way into paradise, where he has a bejeweled house and a posse of nubile young men and women waiting for him. However, the pleasures of paradise pale very quickly, especially when he discovers that heavenly wine does not lead to inebriation. Pochomir wakes up just as his disgust at the idea of a wine that does not inebriate sets in.[8] In *Shaytonning tangriga isyoni* (Satan's revolt against God), Fitrat subverted the standard Islamic story of Satan's refusal to obey God by turning the refusal into a heroic revolt against a capricious, malicious God who expects only absolute obedience. Satan emerges as a heroic figure because of his revolt. In the climactic final scene, Satan taunts God:

> My guide is science, my prophet is knowledge.
> My aides are my brain and my tongue.
> . . .
> Get lost with your wisdom, your throne,
> With your power, your majesty, your world.[9]

A starker reversal of the Islamic order of things is scarcely imaginable.

———

How do we make sense of Fitrat's revolt against God? Some historians have read these works as veiled critiques of the Soviet order, viewing the former as mocking Bolshevik claims of leading humanity to its utopian future and the latter as a refusal to accept the godlike claims of the party. A critique of the Soviet order is certainly present, but it is not the only thing going on in Fitrat's texts. There was no reason for Fitrat to cast his critique in a language so subversive of Islam. It is important to read between the lines, but what the lines say cannot be ignored. Fitrat clearly is disenchanted with his religion. He subverts Islamic narratives from within: all his references come from the Islamic tradition, even as he upends their accepted understandings. We might call what Fitrat accomplishes here an Islamicate critique of Islam. Such a reading also recognizes the cultural radicalism of the 1920s, which extended far beyond Soviet Central Asia. In Tatarstan and Azerbaijan, too, radicalized

Muslim reformers were moving from reform to irreligion. The Turkish Republic that arose from the ruins of the Ottoman Empire initiated a series of radical reforms that in many ways paralleled events in the Soviet Union. Atatürk beat back the authority of the *ulama*, nationalized Islam, and instituted a lay political order that pushed Islam out of the public sphere. In Iran, Reza Shah, founder of the Pahlavi dynasty, likewise established a secularizing state, banned veiling, and curtailed religious education, all in the name of the Iranian nation. The difference was that in Turkey and Iran, radicalized modernist intellectuals were aligned with newly powerful states, while in Central Asia the Jadids were in an uncertain collaboration with a radical state that they did not control.

Fitrat's radicalism did not make him a Communist either. One bit of conventional wisdom about this period, asserted often but without much evidence, has it that there was a straight path from Jadidism to Communism—that the Jadids either became communists or, at the very least, formed an alliance with the communists. Fitrat, like most Jadids who had appeared in public life before 1917, never joined the party. They worked in Soviet institutions (mostly in the realm of culture), but that work did not amount to an alliance. The Bolsheviks could contemplate tactical collaboration, but they did not form alliances with other forces. Rather, what transpired was an uneasy coexistence made possible by the Bolsheviks' poor control of Soviet institutions.

———

By the middle of the 1920s, Central Asian communists had begun to consolidate in a new group. Most of them had entered public life in or after 1917 and had no prior experience of work in cultural reform. Many of them had studied in Jadid schools, but they had gone on to attend Russian-native schools—those imperial institutions established to create a set of intermediaries between the Tsarist empire and its native subjects. Instead the schools helped produce if not the gravediggers of the empire, certainly a cohort of people who were happy to dance on the empire's grave. The new communists' knowledge of Russian was a key factor in their rise. They tended to be very young, entering the highest offices of the party and Soviet hierarchies in their twenties and rising through the ranks at great speed. They were invested in the vision of the bright future the party purveyed. Communism, they hoped, would lead Central Asia to development and progress and make it a beacon for the rest of the Muslim world. Membership in the party also represented an opportunity for the communists, for they saw themselves as the agents who would pull their society out of its backwardness. They were even younger and even more impatient than the Jadids, with whom they had an awkward relationship. The two groups agreed on the kinds of reform they wanted to effect, but the communists were sure that the new ideology would allow them to bring about what their elders had been unable to achieve. Membership in the party gave them power in their own society, even as it freed them from Islamic moral strictures and, often, the bonds of their families and gave them a sense of beguiling freedom. Central Asian communists were the foot soldiers of most of the campaigns for political and cultural transformation that remade Central Asia in the interwar decades (see figure 11.2).

Yet the place of indigenous communists remained an awkward one. They were subject to party discipline, which functioned along ethnic lines in Central Asia. The Soviet regime could not quite dismantle the dual society that had taken shape during the Tsarist period. As noted above, in 1923, the Soviet state launched with much fanfare a campaign of indigenization that was supposed to make Soviet power indigenous in the non-Russian parts of the Soviet Union. The campaign was largely a failure, both in its language and personnel dimensions. Local languages did not become dominant in government paperwork except perhaps at the lowest levels of village administration, where there were no Russians. The party in Central Asia remained a segregated space, with Muslims and Europeans forming separate cells, and the Europeans having a sense of ownership that they would not relinquish. Many high-ranking indigenous communists chafed at the domination of the Europeans and the habit of men sent from Moscow of not listening to them. This mutual distrust shouts out from the pages of the party's internal

FIG. 11.2. A group of Uzbek cadres during the land-water reform of 1925–1927 (see chapter 13).
Photo courtesy Elyor Turakulov (Musabayev).

correspondence, and it often spilled out into the open. In December 1925, eighteen members of the Central Committee of the newly formed Communist Party of Uzbekistan asked to be relieved of their duties since "conditions [in the party were] not suitable for friendly and fruitful work."[10] A group of thirty Kyrgyz Communists had signed a similar petition earlier in the year, and other such scandals continued to emerge.

The party was a band of brothers in which leading cadres were linked not just by bureaucratic chains of command but also by friendships that went back to their days in the underground. They found newcomers, especially those from exotic parts of the country, not entirely trustworthy. In Central Asia, European cadres, whether those born in the region or recent arrivals, had a very different take on the goals of the Soviet regime in the region. They ranged from those with unreconstructed views of the irredeemable backwardness of the "natives" to those who wanted to bestow on them the gifts of progress and uplift—but they were to be gifts. In contrast, indigenous communists saw the Soviet order as a way of promoting their societies on their own terms. They had a fundamentally different stake in the system. That difference was to lead to catastrophe for many of them. In 1924, however, Central Asian communists experienced the moment of what was surely their greatest triumph: the redrawing of the political boundaries of Central Asia along national lines.

12

Autonomy, Soviet Style

IN 1924, the Soviet government transformed the political map of Central Asia. In a matter of months, Turkestan, Bukhara, and Khiva disappeared and were replaced by a number of republics—each bearing the name of a national group. This reconfiguration of Central Asia's political geography is perhaps the most lasting legacy of the Soviet period. Without the "national-territorial delimitation" of 1924, Central Asia would look very different today. Yet the process is also deeply misunderstood. Most of the writing on the subject outside the former Soviet Union sees it as a classic example of a divide-and-rule policy through which the Soviets broke up the unity of Central Asia. The argument has the force of simplicity on its side and has proved to be unshakable. "The potential for political solidarity among Soviet Muslims was attacked by a deliberate policy of divide and rule," goes a typical assertion. "Central Asian states of today owe their territorial existence to Stalin. He responded to the threat of pan-Turkish and pan-Islamic nationalism by parceling out the territories of Russian Turkestan into the five republics."[1] This resulted, we are told by another writer, in the "artificial creation of new national entities" along completely arbitrary criteria, in a process in which the Soviets "amused themselves by making the problem even more complicated."[2] Central Asians had no role to play in the process other than being its victims.

The problem with this narrative is that it is entirely wrong. The actual process of the delimitation was a lot more complex than such simplistic and ill-informed accounts claim. The national delimitation of Central

Asia was the result of the implementation in the region of a policy that the Bolsheviks had applied everywhere else in their state by 1924, and it reflected certain basic assumptions they made about national difference. In 1913, when the revolution was only a theoretical possibility, Lenin had asked Stalin—himself a Georgian—to articulate the Bolshevik position on the "national question." Stalin took for granted that nations existed. "A nation," he wrote, "is a historically constituted, stable community of people, formed on the basis of a common language, territory, economic life, and psychological make-up manifested in a common culture."[3] No contemporary nationalist in Europe would have raised an eyebrow at this combination of history, language, and culture as the basis of a national community. Stalin did argue that nations were transient: they arose during the capitalist stage of development and would wither away once Communism arrived. In the present, however, they were all too real and had to be contended with. Stalin proposed national territorial autonomy as the ideal form of organization of a multinational socialist state of the future.

That future arrived faster than anyone had expected in 1913. In 1917, Stalin was the people's commissar for nationalities affairs, and he had to deal with an explosion of national mobilization in Russia's imperial borderlands during the civil war. In response to the various declarations of autonomy by national movements, the Bolsheviks developed a nationalities policy that promised autonomy, but on Soviet terms. The autonomy would be proletarian and exercised by the party, and the autonomous region would be loyal to the Soviet state. The autonomous governments proclaimed at Kokand and by Alash Orda in late 1917 were supplanted by properly Soviet versions. Nevertheless, Soviet territorial autonomy did open up the possibility of nationally or linguistically homogeneous political units. In December 1922, a new constitution transformed the Soviet state into a federal union based on national territorial autonomy. Territorial autonomy existed at various levels, from that of a republic that was a member of the union through autonomous republics within union republics and to more modest autonomous *oblasts* and districts for less numerous or "culturally backward" national groups. By the end of 1923, boundaries in the rest of the Soviet state had been transformed according to the national principle: a Ukraine and a Belarus had been carved out of the Slavic heartland of the empire, and a number of other autonomous republics had been proclaimed across the Soviet state. Central Asia was the last part of the country where this general Soviet policy was implemented.

In this case, the redrawing of the boundaries had nothing to do with a fear of Central Asian unity, for such a thing did not exist. We have seen in the last few chapters plenty of evidence of the absence of any overarching unity of the region. Rather, for the Soviet government, the problem was quite the opposite: Central Asia was too fragmented and heterogeneous to be ruled effectively. For the Soviet regime, the main task in the non-Russian parts of the former empire was to win the trust of the people and to make them think that Soviet rule was different from its Tsarist predecessor. To do this, Soviet authorities had to speak to the non-Russians in their own language, and that task would be much easier if administrative entities were linguistically homogeneous. Then administration, education, and propaganda could all be carried out in the same language. But Central Asia was divided into three multilingual republics (Turkestan, Bukhara, and Khiva). Nor was the linguistic issue the only one. There were very real tensions between nomadic and sedentary populations in all three republics, and the conflicts crept into the party. Party authorities worried about factionalism among local cadres. Turkestan's Soviet leadership was divided between Kazakh and Uzbek leaders. "National relations here are extraordinarily sharp," Juozas Vareikis, the Latvian head of the Central Asia Bureau of the party, reported to Stalin in early 1924, "for the simple reason that there is a constant struggle between Uzbeks and Kazakhs [in the party] for the right to be the ruling nation [in Turkestan]."[4] To the Soviets, all of this was evidence of factionalism and fragmentation, rather than of some overarching unity that threatened them. Nor did the Soviets concoct these nations out of thin air. The nations into which Central Asia was divided in 1924 had been imagined by Central Asians in the previous decades. The Soviet decision to demarcate new boundaries in Central Asia crystallized national projects that had been ongoing. The process of the national delimitation of Central Asia is one of the unexpected triumphs of local national projects in Soviet conditions and through Soviet institutions.

The delimitation of national boundaries in Central Asia took place only a few years after a very similar process had taken place in Central Europe. In the aftermath of the defeat of the multinational Habsburg Empire in the Great War, its lands had been divided up on the national principle into a number of homogeneous states. The Wilsonian principle of self-determination had legitimized the creation of the new states of Poland, Hungary, Romania, Czechoslovakia, and Yugoslavia, a process that involved the redrawing of boundaries and the creation of linguistically homogeneous states. The Soviet national delimitation in Central Asia and elsewhere was premised on similar understandings of the efficacy of nationally and linguistically homogeneous spaces, even if the political goals were different. The Soviet nationalities policies had a prophylactic goal—to contain nationalism and put it at the service of building socialism—but they nevertheless created nationally homogeneous spaces and gave currency to the notion of national self-determination.

———

Abdurauf Fitrat was in Bukhara when the tsar abdicated. He had returned from Istanbul in 1913 with a new vision of the world and a clear appreciation of the necessity of reform. He continued to write—he published two major works on Islamic reform as well as several shorter books for use in new-method schools—and was involved in the city's secret societies. He also continued to express the hope that the emir would fulfill his duty as a monarch and initiate reform in the emirate. After the fall of the Russian monarchy, Fitrat was part of the secret society that asked the Provisional Government to push the emir toward reform, and he duly suffered from the emir's persecution of the reformers. He escaped to Samarqand, where he began to write for *Hurriyat* (Liberty), the Uzbek-language newspaper that Mahmudkhoja Behbudiy had launched after the revolution. In his columns in *Hurriyat*, Fitrat commented on current developments, but he also wrote a great deal of poetry that expressed the sense of possibility and opportunity he and his fellow reformers felt. The emir had completely discredited himself by his actions, but there was nevertheless a great deal of hope for Central Asia. Fitrat published three poems titled "Sorrows of the Homeland." The first of them proclaimed:

> O great Turan, land of lions!
> What happened to you? What state are you in? What days have
>   fallen upon you?
> O glorious cradle of Chinggises, Timurs, Oghuzes, [and] Attilas! . . .
>
> How did you fall into the pit of your slavery?[5]

The newly liberated discourse of 1917 included an intense concern with Turkism. The homeland whose sorrow Fitrat expressed was not just Bukhara. Rather, it was Turan, a far more expansive concept. The term was of Iranian provenance and expressed the opposite of the concept of "Iran." In the *Shahnameh*, Turan is the land of Iran's enemies, even if the constant interaction between the two made them frenemies more than enemies. The term "Turan" had been appropriated by Turkic groups and now appeared as a synonym for the common homeland of all Turkic nations. Fitrat here evoked the history of not just Muslim Central Asia but of the nomadic steppe. There was a lost greatness to be accounted for. Now was the moment of opportunity, if the heirs of past greatness could see it. He wrote:

> You are not helpless, you are not alone! Today, you have eighty
>   million children in the world.
> The blood in their veins is the blood of Chinggises and Temurs.
>   Their might is your might!
> O Great Turan, land of lions!
> Don't grieve! Your old empires, your old kingdoms, your old
>   braves, your old lions are all there, no one has disappeared.
> Only . . . ah, only . . . they have all scattered.[6]

The "eighty million children" referred to all Turkic peoples in the world, who were scattered over a vast area stretching from the Balkans to Turfan and divided among three empires. In the rest of his writings, Fitrat was to have a less expansive view of the national community he championed, limiting it to Central Asia. There was nevertheless an enormous shift here. Previously he had spoken on behalf of the "noble nation of Bukhara." In Turkestan, the nation had been imagined as "the Muslims of Turkestan." Now, in the summer of possibilities, the rhetoric had shifted to a much greater community evoked along lines not of territory but of ethnicity. Fitrat spoke of the children of Turan, not of a community defined by dynastic conquest. The idea of an ethnically defined nationhood had never before been expressed quite so explicitly. The liberty of 1917 and the sense of the possibilities it brought had unleashed a new national imagination.

The Jadids used the terms "Uzbek" and "Turk" synonymously in 1917, although "Turk" dropped out soon afterward. At the time of the Russian conquest, "Uzbek" denoted the nomadic Turkic groups that had ousted the Timurids from Transoxiana, but the term's scope broadened during the Tsarist period, and it had increasingly come to signify the entire sedentary Turkic population of Turkestan. Now, the sedentary population of Turkestan was being reimagined as the Uzbek nation. This was clearly a different sense of the term than had prevailed before, for it was Timur who emerged as the central figure in this new national imagination. For outsiders, he might have been synonymous with violence and cruelty, but Turkist authors since the late nineteenth century had repeatedly invoked him as a great figure. He was the node that tied the nomadic heritage of Central Asia firmly to its Islamicate high culture. All nations required a great past and a glorious high culture to be legitimate. The Uzbek nation could find both in Timur's empire—which was, after all, based in Transoxiana. We may call this a Chaghatayist vision of the Uzbek nation.

Fitrat invoked Timur repeatedly in 1917, summoning his spirit to come to the rescue of and rejuvenate the nation:

Great Sovereign! The honor of Turkdom has been pillaged
The state you established for the Turks is gone, the sovereignty
    you established under the Turks has gone to the enemy.

My Sovereign!
To shed the blood of those who betrayed Turkdom, even if they
    are Turks themselves, is your sacred habit—arise!
Crush, beat, kill those who betrayed your legacy![7]

The sons of the homeland had to be gathered and set to the task of re-building the lost greatness. This required not the re-creation of the past but the implementation of the agenda of reform that the Jadids had long ago identified. Reform was absolutely necessary for the nation, but the nation was also indispensable to the cause of reform, for only a properly national form of reform would meet the needs of the age. To secure its place in the world, the nation had to acquire modern knowledge and skills; to be educated, organized, and rendered healthy; but also to re-main true to itself. The new national culture would be both modern and national. (All national movements in the world faced this dialectic be-tween modernity and authenticity, between catching up with the powerful and retaining one's sense of self, but the answers they have come up with have varied enormously.)

————

Fitrat spoke of Turan and its many million children, but his was not the only national project in Central Asia at this time. A Kazakh national movement had long existed in parallel. In 1917, it had aspired to unite all Kazakhs in one territorial unit, which clearly meant changing the boundaries of Turkestan. It had its own imaginary and priorities. Timur and the high culture of the Timurid courts had no resonance for the Kazakhs. Far more pressing were questions of Russian colonization and the loss of land. The Kazakh national leadership had an easier time with its own society. The *ulama* were not a major force, and the battles that rocked Uzbek society did not have the same significance among the Kazakhs. However, education and cultural transformation were top pri-orities. Alash Orda had made the creation of primary school textbooks one of its main tasks, even when its survival was not guaranteed. After the dissolution of the government in 1920, its members devoted their energy to education, creating new textbooks for schools and a new literature. A distinct Kazakh language, with an orthography that reflected Kazakh pronunciation, had emerged before the revolution. The issue for Kazakh intellectuals was the creation of a modern written literature that was their own.

Indeed, this was the period when a number of other national projects crystallized in Central Asia. As we have seen above, the idea of a nation defined by a common language and heritage had arrived in Central Asia from several directions in the aftermath of the Russian conquest. The Russian state sought to classify the population along ethnic lines. Although Russian ethnographers never came up with a standard classification of the region's population, the idea of ethnic classification left a lasting impact. This was accompanied by the prevalence of Turkist discourses among Muslim intellectuals in both the Russian and Ottoman Empires, who had come to see nationhood as a prerequisite for progress. Any number of groups began to reimagine their collective identities as national. Nationhood and modernity were deeply intertwined in this new imagination. Turkmen activists came to think of the Turkmens as a nation rather than just a conglomeration of tribes.[8] A distinct sense of Kyrgyzness can be discerned in narratives from before the revolution.[9] In 1922, a number of Kyrgyz party members demanded the recognition of the Kyrgyz as a nation separate from the Kazakhs and the creation of an autonomous Kyrgyz region in Turkestan. Karakalpak activists similarly sought status as a nation separate from the Kazakhs. Writers from the small community of so-called Bukharan Jews developed a sense of national identity and self-expression. Each of these national ideas was accompanied by attempts to delineate a national language and draw cultural boundaries against neighboring peoples. Turkmen and Kyrgyz became written languages for the first time in this period. Activists codified formal grammars and rules of orthography in each case. New national schools and the new Soviet vernacular press became the sites where these new written languages began to develop.

The Uyghur national project emerged in Soviet Turkestan rather than in Xinjiang. The Turkic-speaking sedentary Muslim population of Alt-ishahr had long thought of itself as Muslim (*musulman*) or local (*yerlik*) and thus distinct from other neighboring communities, Muslim and non-Muslim. It had drawn boundaries against other Muslims, including nomads such as Kazakhs and Kyrgyz, the Chinese-speaking Dungans, and those living outside of Altishahr.[10] In the early years of the twentieth century, the arrival of Turkism turned the older discourses of Altishahr identity into a national project. Writers began imagining the population of Altishahr as the descendants of the Uyghur nomads who had established a state in eastern Turkestan in pre-Islamic times. Nazarkhoja Abdusamadov, a Taranchi of Jadid sympathies from Jettisuv, had adopted Uyghur Balisi (Child of Uyghur) as his pen name as early as 1914. The Congress of Kashgarian and Jungharian Workers in Tashkent in June 1921 established the Revolutionary Union of Altishahri and Jungharian Workers–Uyghur, which was the first time the term "Uyghur" was used to denote a community. The congress included representatives from a number of communities with roots in Xinjiang: the Taranchi and the Dungans of Jettisuv, who were Russian subjects; and the Kashgarian communities of Ferghana, most of whose members were labor migrants and retained their status as Chinese subjects. Eventually, the Taranchis and the Dungans went their separate ways, and the Uyghur title was inherited by the Kashgaris.[11] The term "Uyghur" increasingly came to be used in Soviet documents. Little of this mobilization had an immediate effect on Xinjiang, which Yang Zengxin sought to keep hermetically sealed from subversive ideas, but this national idea was to find traction in Xinjiang in the 1930s.

Finally, there is the curious—and for posterity, highly controversial—case of the Tajiks. The large Persian-speaking population of Turkestan was divided by many fault lines. The largest portion of it was urban, constituting the bulk of the population in the cities of Bukhara, Samarqand, and Khujand, but there was also an entirely rural portion that inhabited the inaccessible mountainous redoubts of eastern Bukhara and that had always resisted external rule, whether from Bukhara or Tashkent. The Persian-speaking population of the cities never imagined their language to be a major node of identity, something that would make them into a separate nation from their Turkic-speaking sedentary Muslim neighbors. In fact, many Persian speakers were bilingual, and many were enthralled with Turkism and the promise of modernity it entailed. After all, Fitrat, the main theorist of Chaghatayism, grew up in a Persian-speaking family and wrote exclusively in Persian until the revolution, even when he lived in Istanbul. But it was in Istanbul that Fitrat picked up the idea of Turkism, and he returned to Bukhara convinced of the Turkist belief—with no basis in fact—that the Persian speakers of Central Asia were really Turks who had forgotten their mother tongue under the baneful influence of courts stricken with a cultural cringe. With most politically and culturally active Persian speakers invested in the Chaghatayist project, there was no mobilization for the recognition of a Persian-speaking nation in Central Asia. A Tajik movement arose only after Tajikistan was created in 1924 as a residual category to accommodate the Persian-speaking population of eastern Bukhara—a rural society marked by practically universal illiteracy and low on every indicator of progress, and thus quite the opposite of the historical image of the Persian speakers as the original city dwellers and culture producers of Central Asia. We will return to that story below.

To be sure, what existed in 1924 were national ideas that excited individuals who were invested in them and willing to mobilize resources around them. The bulk of the population remained indifferent to the national ideas and continued to identify itself along different, more parochial, axes. This should not surprise us or make us think of the national projects as inauthentic or fake. Nations never arise fully formed to demand their rights but are always shaped by national movements and then by states. National movements always work on two fronts: one against the outside world to demand recognition and autonomy or independence for the nation; and another against the nation itself, which they seek to constitute and reshape. For most national movements, the task is as much to reshape the nation, transform it, and educate and mobilize it so that it can adequately face the challenges of the present as it is to celebrate it. Members of the nation have to be taught to think of themselves as belonging to a single nation (this is primarily the task of mass education) and to abandon antiquated customs and traditions that are deemed to have been the cause of the nation's decline. The authenticity of the nation is affirmed by an appeal to a past greatness (often reimagined) that was sullied by foreign borrowings. As noted above, all national movements deal with this dialectical relationship between modernity and authenticity. We will witness this in the case of Central Asia in the following chapters, but it is useful to keep in mind that it is hardly unique.

———

In January 1924, party authorities in Moscow decided "to initiate a preliminary discussion of the possibility and expediency of the delimitation of Kazakh, Uzbek, and Turkmen districts [in Turkestan] according to the national principle."[12] That preliminary discussion turned into a full-blown debate that moved very quickly. Commissions representing different nationalities elected from among party members presented proposals for creating their republics. By June, the delimitation had been agreed upon and approved by Moscow. Over the summer, territorial commissions hammered out the new boundaries, and the process was complete by November 18, when the governments of Turkestan, Bukhara, and Khiva met to dissolve those entities and create the new republics.

Moscow had no intention of opening up the debate to the public. Rather, it was the vanguard party that was to decide the question. Central Asian party members jumped at the opportunity with surprising alacrity and largely drove the debate as it unfolded. They were invested in the national projects mentioned above. All sides took the existence of different nations in Central Asia as an obvious fact. The surprisingly acrimonious debate revolved around the question of how to divide Central Asia, not whether to divide it. No one opposed the idea of delimitation. A number of participants put forward the idea of a Central Asian federation: instead of a number of separate republics, each dealing directly with the center, Central Asia would join the union as a federation of national republics. The argument was based not on a notion of Central Asian unity but on the principle of retaining the economic coherence of the region. That idea was voted down. What took center stage was the question of where the boundaries, both ethnic and territorial, lay between the various nations of Central Asia. There was no preexisting standard classificatory grid for the region's ethnic composition. The initial discussion involved only three nationalities. Several other national categories that are current in Central Asia today crystallized during the process of delimitation, a process in which local national projects and modern practices of ethnographic categorization intersected in complex ways with the political interests of the Soviet regime, which was still finding its feet.

The claims for the Uzbek nation were formulated by the Bukharan Communist Party, which came up with the idea of "creating [an] Uzbekistan on the basis of Bukhara." The argument it made in its basic document was simple: "The Uzbek people, earlier united in the state of Timur and his successors, disintegrated in recent centuries into various parts. Over the course of centuries, this disintegration was characterized by the weakening of economic forces and of political structures, the final stage of which is the economic decomposition, the loss of state unity, and the physical destruction of the people under the domination of khanates, emirates, and Tsarism." The document asserted that the Timurid state was the national state of the Uzbeks—a key Chaghatayist point—and saw the loss of a unified state as the cause of decline, cultural backwardness, and even exploitation. But now that the revolution had "put the Uzbek people at a new stage of historical development," it was necessary to give "all peoples bearing a single name their own Soviet political units on a national basis, according to the specificities of their way of life and economic habits."[13] These national units would allow the party to "undertake integral economic and cultural work" and ease the work of socialist construction. The author of the document was Fayzulla Khojayev, the Young Bukharan prime minister of the Bukharan People's Republic and a self-proclaimed disciple of Fitrat. Khojayev turned the project of reestablishing the national unity of the Uzbek people into a significant revolutionary task of the Soviet state. In another sense, the new Uzbekistan was Bukhara redux, with the entire sedentary population of Central Asia gathered into it and excluding the nomads whom Bukharan rulers had never been able to subdue. This was the culmination of the Chaghatayist project that imagined the sedentary population of Central Asia as a unified nation. It was also, in a manner, the reconstitution in Soviet conditions of Timurid statehood.

The biggest challenge to the Bukharan project for Uzbekistan came from the Kazakh commission. It was led by Sultanbek Qojanov (1894–1938), who had a complicated past. In 1917, he had collaborated with Mustafa Choqay on a Kazakh-language newspaper he published in Tashkent and had helped organize a Kazakh movement. In 1921, having joined the Communist Party, he had accompanied Georgy Safarov on his decolonizing tour of Jettisuv. Initially, Qojanov favored a Central Asian federation, but once that idea had been abandoned, he and his colleagues pursued the goal—common to all Kazakh elites in the early twentieth century—of uniting all Kazakhs in one political unit. This meant uniting the Kazakhs of Turkestan with those of the Kazakh autonomous republic that had existed since 1920 on the territory of the former Steppe governorate-general. To this end, they laid claim to all of Jettisuv and the Syr Darya district, including the city of Tashkent, which they argued was the center of Kazakh economic life and should belong to the Kazakhs. Kazakh representatives also mocked Uzbek claims and argued that the Uzbeks were not a real nation at all, but an aggregation of different groups with no claims to nationhood. The Turkmens sided with the Kazakhs, mostly to escape the economic dominance of Uzbeks. Kyrgyz representatives successfully argued that they were a nation distinct from the Kazakhs (a view strenuously opposed by Kazakh delegates), as did the Karakalpaks.

The sharpness of the disputes among the different commissions seemed to take Moscow and its emissaries by surprise. The European leaders of the Central Asia Bureau tried to set the ground rules, and Moscow had the final say on the most contentious issues. It was Stalin himself who ruled that Tashkent should form part of Uzbekistan, not Kazakhstan, but the verbatim records of the debates make it clear that Central Asia's Communists shaped the debate.[14]

The delimitation abolished Turkestan, Bukhara, and Khiva and instead created a number of new national territories. Uzbekistan and Turkmenistan became union republics—that is, signatories to the treaty that formed the federal union. The Kazakhs did not get Tashkent, but a large part of Syr Darya district and all of Jettisuv were transferred to the Kazakh autonomous republic that had existed since 1920. The Soviet process of national delimitation fulfilled a dream that the Kazakh political class had had since at least 1917. Kazakhstan became an autonomous republic within the Russian Republic, while the Karakalpaks and Kyrgyzes acquired autonomous districts, also in the Russian Republic. Finally, a Tajik autonomous republic was created within Uzbekistan. Over the next twelve years, some territorial adjustments were made, and various territories were elevated to higher degrees of autonomy: Tajikistan became a union republic in 1929, as did Kazakhstan and Kyrgyzstan in 1936. The Karakalpak autonomous district was raised to the level of an autonomous republic and transferred to Uzbekistan in 1936. By that year, the political map of Central Asia had taken its present shape.

The most significant thing about the delimitation was the triumph of the idea of the nation, which became the default manner of identification. Soviet policies recognized and codified nationality, even as they averred the universality of History. All nations were destined to tread the same path of progress to the final destination of a classless society, but they were to do so in their own languages and wearing their own costumes. All Soviet citizens were officially categorized by their nationality. Nationality was not just an abstract sense of cultural belonging but a part of one's legal identity. It was inscribed on identity documents and was of consequence as Soviet citizens negotiated their way through life. The promise of national self-determination was to be a large part of Soviet self-representation in the decades that followed. The Soviet regime had turned various national projects of Central Asian intellectuals into political reality. The process also froze the national divisions as they existed in 1924, recognizing six nations. Some of them (the Uzbeks and Kazakhs) were perhaps obvious, while others (such as the Kyrgyz and Karakalpaks) were less so. The Kazakh intelligentsia had seen the latter two groups as subgroups of the Kazakh nation, but activism on behalf of Kyrgyz and Karakalpak autonomy made sure that they appeared as separate nations. However, no one had mobilized on behalf of groups such as the Sart or Qipchaq, which therefore disappeared from official nomenclature and came to be seen as part of the Uzbek nation.

Thus was created a new map of Central Asia with its putatively national republics. The new republics were put together from different parts. Kazakhstan combined the lands of the former Steppe region with those of Jettisuv and Syr Darya districts of Turkestan. The political activists from the two regions had operated in different networks, and it took some time for them to gel into a single political elite. Uzbekistan and Turkmenistan both included lands from Turkestan, which had been under direct Russian administration for several decades, and from the protectorates of Bukhara and Khiva, which had never been administered by Russia. The various republics were not identical. Uzbekistan, which became a union republic in 1924, included the major cities of the region and claimed the bulk of its heritage. The other republics largely defined themselves in contrast to it. Kazakhstan, however, occupied almost as large an area as British India. It was formed as an autonomous republic within the Russian Republic, which strengthened the steppe zone's longer and deeper connections to Russia. Later in the 1920s, when Soviet economic planners divided the Soviet Union into a series of economic zones, Kazakhstan became an economic region in its own right, separate from the other four republics of Central Asia. (This was the logic behind the Soviet locution of "Central Asia and Kazakhstan," which was often mistaken in the West as another attempt at divide-and-rule.)

Ethnonational boundaries are never god given but always emerge in political struggles between national movements and states. The point to remember is that these struggles took place among Central Asians and were not simply imposed by the Soviets (let alone by Stalin himself). Once the national territories had come into being, national belonging took on new relevance for everyday life. It mattered that one was classified as an Uzbek in Uzbekistan or as Kazakh in Kazakhstan. Nations had a title to their territory, and "titular nationals"—the common Soviet term for members of nations living in their own territory— were supposed to enjoy certain preferences in employment to promote the indigenization of the non-Russian parts of the Soviet Union. More significantly, now that national territories had emerged, certain key processes of nation building could proceed: the creation of standardized national languages, as well as the cultivation of distinct national cultures, literary pantheons, and historical traditions of each nation. These processes took place in such institutions as public schools, the press, and museums, each of which was funded by the Soviet state but staffed in large part by Central Asians. The golden age of Soviet nations was to come after the Second World War, but the creation of national republics was the crucial step in that history.

13

Revolution from Above

THE CREATION of new political boundaries signaled the Soviet state's growing confidence in its control over Central Asia. Over the next decade and a half, it unleashed a series of campaigns that utterly transformed the region. The transformations came in three waves. The first began in 1925, when the party opened an "ideological front" to assert its control over cultural policy. The second wave was connected to pan-Soviet developments. In 1929, Stalin, the Georgian who was then general secretary of the All-Union Communist Party, announced a "Great Break" from the policies of the previous decade and launched the country, full steam ahead, on a course of rapid industrialization. In 1917, a revolution in society had brought the state down; between 1929 and 1933, the state shook up society and remade it in significant ways. The openness and uncertainty of the first decade after 1917 gave way to a strident celebration of the new order. The revolution from above removed most of the prominent figures of the first Soviet decade and replaced them with a new generation of local cadres who were products of the Soviet order. The third wave brought the Great Terror of 1936–1938, which decimated this new cohort as well. By the time the terror wound down, Soviet Central Asia had become unrecognizably different from what it had been in 1929, let alone in 1917.

None of these developments was straightforward or predetermined. The Soviet leadership faced several fundamental conceptual problems as it set out to transform Central Asia. Fitting Central Asian reality to Marxian categories had always taxed the Bolsheviks. How did a proletarian

215

revolution unfold in an area with no industry or proletariat? Where did nomads fit in the evolutionary scale that Marx (and many others) espied in human development? How did one read the internal divisions of nomadic society? Were the wealthy clan elders the equivalent of feudal lords or of the bourgeoisie? Were merchants who made their wealth in the bazaar trade really the bourgeoisie? Were artisans proletarians or something else? Soviet theorists sought to find local equivalents of general Bolshevik categories that often derived from Russian realities. If the Russian countryside had rich peasants called *kulaks* who ostensibly exploited their poorer neighbors, the Kazakh nomads had to yield an equivalent category. If Russian cities had their bourgeois who exploited the workers, then Central Asian cities had to produce an equivalent category. It was the *bais* ("the wealthy") who came to serve as the Central Asian equivalent of the bourgeoisie, even though they had made money in trade rather than in industry. *Bais* in the countryside could also stand in for *kulaks*. Ultimately, categories mattered little. In the chaos of the Great Break, nothing was clear: everything was up for grabs.

Filipp Goloshchekin arrived in Qïzïlorda, then the capital of Kazakhstan, as the first secretary of the republic's Communist party in October 1925. Goloshchekin was not new to Central Asia: he had been a member of the Turkestan Commission that had formalized Soviet rule in Turkestan in 1919–1920. Now, upon his arrival in Kazakhstan, he did not like what he saw at all. Everywhere he looked, he found *bais* whose wealth and influence seemed not to have been reduced by the revolution and life going on as if the revolution had never taken place. As far as he was concerned, there was no Soviet power in the republic. Kazakhstan needed a "Small October," a revolution carried out by the party to overthrow the power of the *bais* and establish the conditions for Soviet rule. Goloshchekin initiated a campaign of confiscations against "large stockholders" and "semi-feudals" that targeted seven hundred households, before being broadened to larger groups.[1] An analogous campaign for the so-called demanapization of Kyrgyz society targeted *manaps* (clan elders), who had come to stand in for *kulaks*. In the same year, the party launched a land-water reform in Turkmenistan and Uzbekistan, which redistributed land and rights to irrigation water to landless or land-poor farmers. The wealthy could face any number of fates, from deprivation of rights (to vote, conduct business, or send children to school) through the confiscation of property to arrest and deportation. The redistribution of land was meant to empower the poor and create support for Soviet power. We still do not have a clear idea of how successful land reform was in Uzbekistan, but we can be sure that it helped widen cleavages that already existed in society.

The party also began to flex its muscle in the field of cultural policy. The range and variety of opinions expressed in the press started to shrink, and the language of national reform that had coexisted uneasily with its Bolshevik counterpart began to disappear from the printed page. The party also took control of long-standing cultural debates in Central Asia. The question of orthographic reform took on a new shape in 1926, when the party decided that it favored a switch to the Latin alphabet for all "Eastern" languages in the Soviet Union. Latinization as a radical solution to orthographic reform had been championed by Azerbaijani activists since the revolution. Their basic argument was that Latin characters were easier to teach and their use would help reduce illiteracy. Latin characters were thus progressive and, above all, international. In 1922, Azerbaijan's government had officially adopted the Latin script. Since then, Azerbaijani enthusiasts had pushed Latinization as a panacea for overcoming not just illiteracy but all forms of backwardness. According to the linguist and activist Semed Ağa Ağamalı oğlu, Latinization was "the cultural revolution in the East." In 1926, he organized a Turkological Congress in Baku that pushed for the Latinization of all Turkic languages in the Soviet Union. The idea had no support in Central Asia, where orthographic reform had revolved around the reform of the Arabic alphabet. But in 1926, the party threw its weight behind Latinization and adopted it as official policy. By 1928, all languages of Central Asia had been equipped with Latin alphabets, and the languages transitioned to the new script over the next three or four years. The party had requisitioned for its own goals an argument first made by Muslim proponents of national progress.[2]

The party used a similar tactic in the campaign against veiling and female seclusion in Uzbekistan and Tajikistan. The question of women's position in society had been around since before the revolution. For the Jadids, education and companionate marriage were supposed to make women better Muslims and better mothers of the nation. In the autumn of 1926, the party decided to "intensify work among women" and to shift the focus from organization and education to an all-out assault on the established norms that underpinned women's position in society. The campaign—launched on March 8, 1927, International Women's Day and the tenth anniversary of the beginning of the revolution—began with thousands of women taking off their *paranjis* and throwing them into bonfires. In the rhetoric that accompanied the campaign, unveiling meant liberation not just from seclusion and oppressive customs, but from economic exploitation and Islam itself. The campaign was called *hujum* ("assault"), and it was meant to symbolize an assault on backwardness itself. By liberating women from the *paranji* and the *chachvon* and bringing them into public life and the job market, the party would push Central Asian societies along the path of progress, toward development and socialism (see figure 13.1).[3]

At the same time, the party finally acted to extirpate religion from Central Asian society. The Bolsheviks' Marxist convictions led them to see religion as an impediment to the full development of human potential. Its focus on the afterlife and the supernatural flew in the face of the hard-core rationalism that the Bolsheviks had inherited from the Enlightenment, while its institutional strength and worldly power made it a dangerous competitor in the political field. In Russia itself, antireligious campaigns had emerged during the civil war. The Russian Orthodox Church had its wealth confiscated, its churches desecrated, and its clergy persecuted. In Central Asia, the Soviets were keenly aware of the weakness of their hold on power, and therefore they held back on antireligious policies in the region, citing its "cultural backwardness" and the "fanaticism" of its inhabitants as reasons for caution. That caution had dissipated by 1927, and the party began a frontal assault on Islamic

FIG. 13.1. Unveiled women celebrate their liberation by Soviet power. This semantically dense poster, published by the Bezbozhnik (Godless) publishing house in Moscow in 1930, repays close examination. Three unveiled women hold a red banner as they stride forward into the brilliant future of Communism, indicated here by tractors and a building flying a red flag. In the background, men attack a mosque (on the right), while another man attacks a book with pseudo-Arabic lettering on it with a dagger (on the left). A man in traditional garb, implying religious authority, cowers in the front. The party here completely appropriates the meaning of unveiling and casts women's liberation as a struggle against Islam and a victory for socialism. The mood is triumphalist. Yet note that the unveiled women still cover their heads with a scarf. In Kemalist Turkey, such women would still be considered veiled. Soviet unveiling was about getting rid of the *paranji* and *chachvon*, ending women's seclusion, and bringing them into "productive labor." Poster collection, RU/SU 1979, Hoover Institution Archives.

institutions. Many of them had weakened in the decade since the revolution, even in the absence of full-blown antireligious campaigns. The
number of Islamic courts had shrunk, and their competence had been
reduced by successive rounds of Soviet legislation. Pious endowments
(*waqfs*) had continued to exist but had been brought under state control
and their revenues diverted to public education. Madrasas had also suffered, as their sources of income shrank or disappeared, while religious

publishing had basically stopped with the revolution. But the antireligious campaign that began in 1927 was nevertheless new. It saw the abolition of Islamic courts, the closure of madrasas, and the final confiscation of all remaining *waqf* property. The last space for the *shariat* in public life had been eliminated. The campaign extended to shrines and mosques, which were attacked, desecrated, and shut down in large numbers. Many *ulama* were arrested and persecuted, others fell silent, and many more emigrated to Chinese Turkestan or Afghanistan. A mere ten years after the fall of the Tsarist order, the Muslim society of Central Asia found itself in radically transformed circumstances.

The destruction continued for much of the following decade and came to a stop only in 1941, when in the face of total war, Soviet authorities called a truce with religion. This was the greatest assault on Islam in Central Asia since the Mongol invasions seven centuries earlier. Its effect was to disestablish Islam in Muslim society. The immense damage to the infrastructure of Islam, especially the abolition of Islamic education and publishing, reshaped patterns of authority in society for the rest of the twentieth century.[4] The Soviet experience of the battering of religion by the party-state occupies little space in general histories of secularization, which continue to focus on the gradual differentiation of the realms of religion and the state through long-term social change. The Soviet method of violent repression of religion was to be replicated in several other places in the mid-twentieth century, mostly by socialist states driven by a vision of creating a fully rational society (and destroying opposition). That violence is also a part of the history of secularization in the modern world and the one most relevant to Central Asia.

The "ideological front" directly targeted the Jadids and others connected with public life outside the party. They were derided as "old intellectuals," men whose time had passed and who now represented only reaction. It was a new crop of young (in fact, very young) men, calling themselves cultural workers to avoid the odium of the term "intellectual," who took the battle to their elders. They dug up the Jadids' writings from before the revolution or its early years to prove that they were bourgeois nationalists, interested only in justifying the domination of the local bourgeoisie over the population, and pan-Islamists and pan-Turkists to boot. Little did the Jadids know when in the Tsarist period or the throes of the revolution they had exhorted their society to change in the name of national progress that they would later be held accountable for their words according to criteria that did not then exist. But such was the case. All those connected with the Turkestan Autonomy of 1917–1918—which included almost everyone of any note at that time—were now considered ardent nationalists who had conspired to break away from the land of the revolution and to place Turkestan under a British protectorate. The old intellectuals began to be pushed out of public life. Some sought to mollify the Soviets by writing on revolutionary themes, others retreated into scholarship, and still others fell silent.

The campaign moved into a higher gear in 1929 when the OGPU, the Unified State Political Administration, as the political police was then called, began arresting people on often quite fantastical charges—of bourgeois nationalism, counterrevolution, working with foreign intelligence agencies to seek the breakup of the Soviet Union, and so on. A number of highly publicized trials purged the national intelligentsias in all republics. The OGPU purged a secret organization called the Union of the East (Ittihodi Sharq) in Tajikistan and one called Turkmen Independence (Türkmen Azatlygy) in Turkmenistan. The accusations carried away to labor camps or their graves many intellectuals with a record of public life before 1917. In Kazakhstan, Goloshchekin presided over a purge that similarly took away all Kazakh activists with past connections to Alash Orda as well as the Kazakh communists, who had proved surprisingly obstreperous. This purge spared some of the biggest names of the prerevolutionary generation, but it decisively transformed the cultural landscape. The ebullience of the previous decade was gone. Those who survived lived under constant threat of arrest and were subject to ongoing vituperative attacks in the press. Abdurauf Fitrat took shelter in academic life, while Cholpan and Abdulla Qodiriy took up freelance translation work—and they were luckier than many others. The Jadids had been largely pushed out of public life by the early 1930s.

———

It would be too facile to see these campaigns as simply an attack of the Bolsheviks on Central Asian society. The Bolsheviks were not external to Central Asia. The foot soldiers in all these campaigns were Central Asian Muslims. Kazakh *bais* were dispossessed by Kazakh activists, and it was poor peasants and radical urban youth or members of village soviets who went around confiscating the property of the *bais* or closing mosques and shrines. Their motivations varied, no doubt, but the campaigns did much to mobilize the indigenous population to support the Soviet cause. Those who participated in these campaigns acquired a new sense of loyalty to the new order and a new vocabulary for thinking about politics. The campaigns also created enormous conflicts within society. Land reform was not always popular. There were plenty of stories of poor peasants who refused to take their neighbors' land, which they deemed to be against the *shariat*, or surreptitiously returned it. The desecration and closure of mosques and shrines often produced a backlash. In the most famous case, the poet and playwright Hamza Hakimzoda Niyoziy was stoned to death by a mob as he led an effort to dismantle a shrine attributed to Ali, the son-in-law of the Prophet.

Perhaps not surprisingly, the greatest opposition arose to the *hujum*, the unveiling campaign in Uzbekistan. Unveiling struck at the heart of Uzbek gender norms and produced the greatest wrath from society. The initial campaign was driven in large part by activists of the Women's Division of the party. They included Russian women with a sense of missionary paternalism and a small number of dedicated Uzbek women who had served as delegates (*vakilas*) of the Women's Division in their neighborhoods and villages. They tended to be women who had escaped abusive marriages and were thus rebels in their own right. Their numbers proved insufficient to sustain the *hujum*, and the party handed over the responsibility for unveiling to men in its ranks and in the state apparat. Unveiling "their" women became a measure of loyalty for party members. From the beginning, the *hujum* faced a violent pushback from society. Activists were threatened, and they often had to flee for their lives. In Chust in the Ferghana valley, a protest turned violent, and the crowd killed a policeman and ransacked the town council building. But it was unveiled women who paid the highest price. They became the targets of abuse and horrible brutality. They were beaten, raped, and—in countless cases—murdered for violating the gendered moral order of society.

At a time when the state and its foot soldiers who had been recruited from the margins of society were turning the established order upside down, men drew the last line at the veil. Women who unveiled thus bore the brunt of patriarchal wrath. Upholders of the moral order claimed that unveiled women had become prostitutes and forsaken their religion and therefore deserved the worst punishment. Marianne Kamp, the preeminent historian of the *hujum*, argues that the rapes and murders that became common during it were not spontaneous crimes of passion but "premeditated, incited, and often involved groups of people. . . . [They] were intended to terrorize other women. They were a demonstration—often deliberately gruesome, involving cutting, dismemberment, and the disposal of the body with symbolic dishonor."[5] Women activists were a particular target, but many women were murdered by their husbands, fathers, or brothers. The young actresses Tursunoy Saidazimova and Nurxon Yo'ldoshxo'jayeva were both murdered by their relatives for dishonoring their families. This conflict was indigenous to Uzbek society and not simply directed at a state that was external to it.

The violence stopped only when the party wound down the campaign in 1929. It had achieved modest results at great cost. The total number of women murdered is difficult to establish, for not all murders were reported. However, it is safe to say that the cases numbered in the thousands. The Soviet state claimed the victims of the violence as its own. In 1928, it classified the murder of unveiled women as a terrorist act and persecuted the murderers, some of whom were given show trials with all the publicity that came with them. Saidazimova and Yo'ldoshxo'jayeva (along with Hamza) became martyrs of the new life.

———

By this time, Stalin's revolution was well under way. One of his major arguments in the struggle for power had been that with world revolution stalled, the Soviet regime needed to build socialism in one country before it could think seriously about revolutionizing the world. Building socialism in one country meant a no-holds-barred drive to industrialize it as rapidly as possible. The economy would be developed not through the chaotic impulses of the market, but according to a plan of action established by the state. A planned economy required the integration of the countryside, for agricultural surpluses were to fund the drive for industrialization. Most of the agricultural sector remained in private hands, however, and the state had to use economic incentives to procure the produce it needed to feed the cities and to export. It often struggled to meet its procurement goals. The solution was to collectivize the agricultural sector, amalgamating small holdings into large collectives that would enable economies of scale and the introduction of mechanization. The process would stir up the "sea of peasant stagnation" and elevate backward peasants to a higher level of civilization. What went for Russian peasants also went for the "culturally backward" peoples of the former empire. The planned economy was supposed to lead backward nations to socialist modernity.

Across the Soviet Union, collectivization was carried out with great violence. Urban youth—many of whom were members of the party or its youth branch, the Komsomol—descended on villages, where they held meetings in which people classified as *kulaks* were dispossessed and their property given to the collective. These outside agitators banked on the support of poor and landless peasants in the village, though violence always trumped exhortation. As with all campaigns of the era, collectivization ran out of control, with local activists behaving with little regard to rules or guidelines. Overachieving was the ideal (the goals of the first five-year plan were supposed to be met in four years—so much for planning!), and in that pursuit Soviet activists recognized few boundaries. There was little method to the madness, as Stalin himself recognized when he stated in a famous speech that Soviet activists were "dizzy with success" and thus committing "excesses" in their dizziness. Collectivization authorized the exercise of raw, arbitrary power in the localities.

Few peasants wanted to give up their land or livestock. There were uprisings aplenty and violence against agitators and their local accomplices. For the OGPU, such resistance amounted to terrorist acts of *bais* and *kulaks*, and it resurrected the term "Basmachi" to attach to the unrest. The Red Army was back in action, for local police could seldom cope with the opposition. In Turkmenistan, armed rebellion spread to fourteen of that republic's thirty-eight districts, with its epicenter in the Karakum Desert. Soviet rule could be restored only after massive use of force, including aerial bombardment by Red Army and OGPU paramilitary forces.[6] There were other forms of resistance, too. Tens of thousands of Turkmens fled across the border to Afghanistan or Iran. Others slaughtered their livestock rather than yield it to the state. But the state rode out the upheaval. Once the dust had settled, the Central Asian countryside had been transformed. Collectivization had forced peasants onto large farms to work for the state, but very little of the infrastructure necessary for running large-scale farms existed. There were very few technicians, accountants, or agronomists and almost no technology. Tractors—those ubiquitous symbols of Soviet progress—were exceedingly rare, and their scarcity was matched only by that of mechanics who could service them. But the collectivized farms were nevertheless obliged to deliver produce according to orders issued by the state and at prices that it set. Many peasants in Russia saw collectivization as the return of the serfdom that had been abolished only in 1861. Central Asia had never experienced serfdom, and in that region, the state's stranglehold on the rural economy was entirely unprecedented. Peasants had always been subject to the exactions of khans and *beks*, but they had never been made to work directly for the state or been tied to its insatiable demand for a cash crop.

———

Collectivization in Uzbekistan was directed at cotton. The Soviets had been keenly interested in Turkestan's cotton from the beginning. In 1918, with civil war still raging, Moscow began sending cotton-buying

missions to Central Asia and investing funds in resurrecting the irrigation infrastructure that had collapsed during the revolution. In the decade that followed, Moscow pushed to increase the acreage under cotton and raise the yield. This meant considerable investment in irrigation
as well as rebuilding the entire credit infrastructure from scratch, for the
banks and cotton-buying firms that had supported cultivation before
the revolution were gone. From 1921, the Main Cotton Committee, a
federal institution based in Moscow, became the sole provider of credit
for cotton production and buyer of cotton. The procurement price for
cotton was set by the party and was not subject to negotiation, despite
demands from republican leaders. Over the next decade, the ratio between the price that the state paid for cotton and the price it charged for
grain steadily declined, and after the famine of 1917–1920, many peasants
were wary of devoting too much land to cotton. The Main Cotton Committee could offer access to cash and grain, which it often used as a form
of payment, but otherwise peasants had to be coaxed into producing
cotton. Komsomol activists began organizing Cotton Days as important
holidays and exhorting peasants to grow more cotton as a form of struggle against the *bais* and for building socialism. Meanwhile, the regime's
appetite for cotton only grew. In 1929, it pronounced "cotton independence" to be a major economic goal and declared the maximization of
cotton production to be an integral part of socialist construction. Cotton became a matter of such importance that directives about it came
straight from the Politburo, the highest organ of the party in Moscow,
often over the signature of Stalin. For example, Stalin telegraphed
Isaak Bauman, the head of the Central Asia Bureau, about shortages
in the output of two cotton ginning factories in Uzbekistan. "Such inat-
tention to the basic production of raw material for the struggle with
saboteurs of cotton is particularly inadmissible for the Central Asia
Bureau since it tears away at the most important measures for the defense of the cotton harvest," Stalin thundered. "The Central Committee places personal responsibility on you for the timely fulfillment of
the plans for [the two factories]."[7] The Central Asia Bureau had become the central government's agent for the procurement of cotton.
For its part, Uzbekistan became synonymous with cotton. The cotton

boll was to remain the republic's symbol in Soviet visual language until the end of the Soviet period.

In Kazakhstan, collectivization took on an altogether more cata-strophic turn. The vast majority of the Kazakh population was still no-madic, and society was ravaged by the demands placed by the state dur-ing collectivization. The disasters of collectivization produced a famine that consumed 40 percent of the Kazakh population. Famine led to disease and flight that further wreaked havoc on Kazakh lives. The re-sults were devastating and permanent. In three short years, nomadism ceased to be a viable option. The sedentarization of nomads had long been talked about by various reformers. Now it was accomplished as an unanticipated consequence of collectivization. The famine also altered the demographic balance of Kazakhstan, reducing the Kazakhs to a minority in their own republic. Collectivization had devastated many parts of the Soviet Union. Ukraine was particularly badly hit. A famine, now memorialized as the Holodomor ("Hunger-Death") carried away millions of peasants. The proportional devastation was highest in Kazakh-stan, particularly among the Kazakhs.[8]

Kazakhstan was part of a different economic zone of the Soviet econ-omy than the other four republics of Central Asia. It was tasked with providing grain and meat, rather than cotton, to the industrial heartland of the Soviet state. The onset of collectivization led to a sharp rise in the procurement targets set by the state, which rose tenfold between 1929 and 1931.[9] Deprived of the grain they needed for food, nomads began selling their livestock to buy grain (either to fulfill the procurement quo-tas levied on them or to feed themselves) or slaughtering animals (to feed themselves, avoid being labeled bais, or prevent the livestock from being confiscated). The situation was made worse by the state's decision to begin requisitioning meat and livestock from nomads. In the summer of 1930, the Politburo decreed the requisitioning of almost one-quarter of the Kazakhs' livestock during the 1930–1931 fiscal year. The two cities of Moscow and Leningrad alone received 80 percent of the meat from the republic.[10] For the Kazakhs, the results were catastrophic. Lands they had used for pasture were collectivized and put under the plow. Their livestock was confiscated, collectivized, and handed over to grain-growing collective farms, where workers could not tend the animals. According to the party's estimates, nine-tenths of the livestock in the republic perished during collectivization.[11] Without livestock, land could not be sown or plowed. Requisitioned grain rotted in warehouses because there were no draft animals left to carry it away. Nomads could neither eat nor move.

Kazakhs in three different regions of the republic—the Manghïshlaq peninsula in the west, the Turghay plateau in the north, and the Syr Darya region in the south—rose up in armed revolt in early 1930. The horrors of 1916–1917 were still fresh in people's memory. But the rebels' arms were light and their organization weak, often revolving around certain lineages. The OGPU put down the uprisings with great brutality. By the autumn of that year, hunger had raised its head in several areas. Over the course of 1931, famine spread across the republic, bringing its companions of disease and epidemics. The lack of food affected all segments of society, Russian peasants as well as Kazakh nomads—although the impact varied across national lines, with Kazakhs suffering far more. However, the onset of famine did not reduce Moscow's appetite for grain and livestock, and the quotas kept increasing. Faced with hunger and the limitless demands of the state, nomads fled. They went to the Volga region to the west, Siberia in the north, and Uzbekistan in the south, where the streets of Tashkent were once again flooded with starving Kazakhs, a sight that had been only too common in 1919 and 1920. Perhaps as many as 200,000 people crossed into the Ili valley of Eastern Turkestan. As we shall see below, Xinjiang was experiencing a period of turbulence of its own, and the Soviet government was wary of the motives of those who fled there. Soviet border guards and the OGPU shot and killed thousands of people, but many more managed to cross the border.[12]

The first waves of refugees brought their cattle with them, some of which they tried to sell. As a result, prices of livestock plummeted in bazaars across Central Asia. Later arrivals came with nothing except disease. They found little sympathy in the places where they ended up. Railways refused to let them board, the police treated them as outlaws, and the factories and city centers they flooded looked upon them as a menace for fear of disease. Europeans on the steppe had always disdained the nomads as backward and uncivilized, and now they blamed the nomads for their own misery. Everywhere, the refugees were seen as an unwelcome burden on local resources. In their utter destitution, many families abandoned their starving children, and inevitably there were cases of cannibalism.

The situation began to improve only in 1934, when Moscow lowered procurement quotas and delivered some food aid. It then began the process of repatriation and resettlement of the survivors into "labor-deficit" areas of Kazakhstan. By the time the catastrophe was over, 1.5 million people had died in the republic and another 1.1 million had left it, many of them never to return. Although European peasants suffered in the famine, its impact on the Kazakhs was much greater. They had constituted 57.1 percent of the population of the republic in the 1926 census but accounted for 90 percent of the victims of the famine. Those who survived found themselves living in a completely different part of the republic, without the possibility of practicing pastoral nomadism. Collectivization had spelled the end of nomadism on the Kazakh steppe.[13]

———

The introduction of the planned economy also meant the final closure of the bazaars in Central Asia and the demise of its merchant class. The tenor of public life changed sharply. The cult of Stalin pervaded everything. The flux of the 1920s was a thing of the past, replaced by the absolute certainty of the party's current line—which, however, had a disconcerting habit of slithering around like a viper. The state had conquered all spaces for the production of culture. Writers, musicians, and painters were now all to belong to official unions, without which their work could not be published. Membership in the unions brought its perks but also serious restrictions on what could be written or composed. Terror and fear—of counterrevolutionaries and of "enemies of the people" who might be operating publicly while wearing the mask of loyalty to the Soviet project—became real, backed as they were by a political police free of any oversight. (To make matters worse, political police were immune from pressures of indigenization. In Central Asia, the force remained solidly European. Complaints about the lack of indigenization in the political police were common among Central Asian cadres and provided the OGPU with yet more proof of their "political unreliability.") Since by definition there was nothing wrong with the system, anything that went wrong—such as a furnace that melted down because of overuse, cotton fields that failed to yield the outrageous amounts expected of them, and construction projects that were delayed—had to be the work of "wreckers" and saboteurs who were enemies of the revolution, and hence of the people. Such enemies became more cunning the closer socialism came to attaining its goals. They had to be dealt with mercilessly. The 1930s saw an enormous expansion of the Gulag, the countrywide network of forced labor camps that served both as a means of punishment and a source of labor.

Soviet citizens also had to be protected from the dangers and temptations of the outside world. In 1923, the state had created a border zone twenty-two kilometers wide along all its land and sea borders that was subject to the special jurisdiction of the border police. The state's control of those vast spaces, especially in Eurasia, remained tenuous for much of the 1920s, but by the time the 1930s began, the border had effectively been sealed. Mass flights of desperate citizens could still breach the border, although as many Kazakhs discovered in 1932, those flights did not go unchallenged. A few people managed to escape illegally. The mountainous route to Kashgar contained enough byways for experienced guides to dodge the border guards and convey individuals or small groups into Xinjiang. Yousof Mamoor was thirteen in 1930, when his father, formerly a prosperous merchant from Kokand, arranged for him and three other family members to be smuggled into Kashgar. The journey took twenty days on foot, during which Yousof got frostbite. The party had a close encounter with border guards but managed to cross into Chinese territory. Yousof's father had escaped previously and managed to bring some funds with him in the form of gold bullion. Over the next year, he managed to gather almost all of his family in

Kashgar.[14] Yousof's family was one of hundreds that took this route. But even this escape route was eventually plugged, and by the middle of the 1930s, the Soviet Union was effectively cut off from the rest of the world. Participating in the hajj was banned, and foreign travel became a privilege granted to a very few trusted figures of the regime. There were almost no Central Asians among them. If Jadidism had emerged through the flow of ideas from around the Muslim world, and if revolutionaries from far afield had gathered in Tashkent in the heady years of 1919–1922, that was all ancient history by 1930. No foreign publications arrived in Central Asia, and the only destination left for Central Asian intellectuals was Moscow.

And yet, there was something exhilarating about the transformation going on across the Soviet Union. While the capitalist world suffered through the Great Depression, the Soviet Union seemed to be a continent-size construction site. It liked to showcase the great experiment it was undertaking and invited sympathetic figures from the West to visit. Central Asia was important in this regard, for there it seemed that the inequities of the colonial order were being erased, colonial subjects were becoming citizens, and backwardness was being conquered. We have a small corpus of travel literature from the 1930s that captures this sense of excitement. Joshua Kunitz, an American Communist who traveled to Central Asia in 1934, met a young Tajik member of the State Planning Commission, who told him:

> If you ever write about Tadjikistan, please don't fall into the error of most of the Europeans who visit us, don't descend to exoticism, don't become worked up over the magnificence of chaos. . . . Please don't expatiate on the beauty of our apparel, the quaintness of our villages, the mystery hidden beneath our women's *paranjas*, the charm of sitting on rugs under shady plane trees and listening to the sweet monotones of our bards, of drinking green tea from a *piala*—and eating

pilaf with our hands. Really, there is little that is charming about all that. Take any cultured Central Asian, cultured in the modern sense, that is, and to him most of the local customs mean simply backwardness, ignorance of the most elementary rules of sanitation and prophylactics.[15]

Overcoming backwardness, catching up with the rest of the world, eradicating harmful customs—the Jadids would have been fine with these goals. Many nationalists and many nation-states in the twentieth century have pursued similar goals. The Soviets claimed to achieve them better than anyone else had done. Langston Hughes, the great American poet, spent several months in Central Asia (for him, the Soviet Union's own "dusty, colored, cotton-growing South") in the winter of 1932–1933. He saw Soviet Central Asia through the prism of race. For him, the most remarkable thing about Central Asia was the absence of a color line. "I am riding South from Moscow and am not Jim-Crowed, and none of the darker people on the train with me are Jim-Crowed," he wrote. He met a "man almost as brown as I am," who turned out to be the mayor of Bukhara. "But I learned in the course of our conversation that there are many cities in Central Asia where dark men and women were in control of the government—many, many such cities. And I thought about Mississippi where more than half of the population is Negro, but one never hears of a Negro mayor."[16] He found the new order inspiring for its abolition of difference:

> The gentlemen ... who wrote lovely books about the defeat of
>   the flesh and the triumph of the spirit ... will kindly come
>   forward and
> Speak about the Revolution—where flesh triumphs (as well as
>   the spirit) ... and the young by the hundreds of thousands
>   are free from hunger to grow and study and love and propagate,
>   bodies and souls unchained without My Lord saying a
>   commoner shall never marry my daughter or the Rabbi
>   crying cursed be the mating of Jews and Gentiles or Kipling
>   writing never the twain shall meet—
> For the twain have met.... [17]

Such sentiments are an important reminder to us of the fascination exercised on millions in the colonial world by notions of progress and culture and by hopes of tossing out the old and doing away with inequality and difference. They also illustrate the contrast between the Tsarist and the Soviet orders.

Soviet Central Asia also looked good from across the border in Xinjiang. For many Eastern Turkestanis, the autonomous republics, language rights, and presence of Central Asians in positions of power contrasted sharply with the realities of Han rule in their homeland. Xinjiang was the only exception to Soviet Central Asia's isolation from the rest of the world. The labor migration from Xinjiang had picked up again after 1921, and Soviet Central Asia was still the best bet for Eastern Turkestanis seeking a modern education. From the mid-1920s on, small numbers of students had been coming to Soviet institutions from Xinjiang and witnessing a society that was increasingly different from theirs.

All of this was ironic because as the 1930s began, Stalin lost interest in the anticolonial enthusiasms that had animated imaginations in the early years of the revolution. Talk of exporting the revolution had disappeared, as had that of industrializing Central Asia. Soviet economic policy increasingly came to focus on a model of self-sufficient development based on regional specialization within the Soviet Union. Central Asia's lot was to supply raw materials (cotton from the south and meat and grain from the north) to industrial enterprises in Russia. Central Asia did not witness any of the great construction projects (the *stroiki*) that defined the Soviet 1930s. The decade's only major project in the region was the Great Ferghana Canal, built entirely by manual labor in 1939. To many Central Asian Communists, this was unreconstructed colonialism. The promise of decolonization and equalization had been a large part of the appeal of Communism to them, and many were disheartened by these developments. In Kazakhstan, a number of leading Kazakh Communists argued forcefully against economic plans that would keep Kazakhstan in the role of supplying raw materials to Russian industry. "Whereas the imperialist Russian bourgeoisie would only strip raw materials from outlying regions while planting numerous factories and industrial works in their own backyard," wrote Smaghŭl

Sädwaqasov, the commissar for education and editor of the main Kazakh-language newspaper, "socialist industry should develop according to the principle of economic expediency," meaning that "industry should be situated as close as possible to the sources of raw materials."[18] In Uzbekistan, the emphasis on cotton made many party members grumble about "red colonialism." OGPU agents began reporting whispered statements by party members and others that Uzbekistan, as a supplier of cotton, was merely a red colony, no better (and perhaps worse) than Egypt or India under British rule. A certain Mirzo Rahimov resigned from the party in 1928 because he disagreed with key policies. "Uzbekistan is a socialist colony," he stated, "and has no independence. It would be independent if it were like Egypt or Afghanistan."[19]

───────

The party could do no wrong, of course, and if errant members thought its policies were colonial, then the problem lay with them. Dissent was a clear sign of ideological impurity that had to be purged. The party had always been wary of the lack of ideological steadfastness among its members and had regularly cleansed its ranks. For much of the 1920s, with qualified personnel in short supply, especially in Central Asia, purges usually led to demotion, reassignment to remote locations, or expulsion from the party. By 1929, deviant party members faced jail or, worse, the Gulag. The 1930s saw wave upon wave of purges that shook up society throughout the Soviet Union. The population of the Gulag surged as all sorts of people were hauled in on scarcely believable charges of anti-Soviet or counterrevolutionary activity. The purges struck at the highest levels of leadership in all Soviet institutions: the army, the people's commissariats, academic institutions, and the party itself. The culmination of the process was the Great Terror of 1936–1938, in which a series of show trials in Moscow saw some of the most famous Old Bolsheviks confess to a series of fantastical crimes against the revolution, the state, and the people, and be duly executed.

The terror reached Central Asia in 1937. In Uzbekistan, Fayzulla Khojayev, the chair of the council of people's commissars, and Akmal

Ikromov, the first secretary of the republic's party organization, were discovered to be members of "nationalist counterrevolutionary organizations" that had from their beginning sought to separate Uzbekistan from the Soviet Union and to turn it into an English protectorate.[20] They were among the defendants in the last of the three major show trials in Moscow and were executed in March 1938. In Turkmenistan, Gaýgysyz Atabaýev, the chair of the republic's council of people's commissars, and Nedirbaý Aýtakov, the head of its executive committee, met the same fate, although in less prominent company. They too were accused of being members of a counterrevolutionary nationalist organization and shot.[21] Turar Rïsqŭlov, having spent fifteen fairly peaceful years in government jobs in Moscow, was arrested in May 1937 and shot in February 1938.[22] Along with these political figures went the cultural intelligentsia. A wave of arrests in 1937 swept up what was left of the prerevolutionary intelligentsia as well as many who had entered public life after the revolution. They were all accused of nationalism that had led them to treasonous anti-Soviet activity. Two generations of the modern Central Asian intelligentsia were executed in 1938. In Uzbekistan, a great many of the executions took place on the single night of October 4–5 in the political police prison on the northern outskirts of Tashkent. Among its victims were Fitrat, Cholpan, and Qodiriy, the great stalwarts of Uzbek literature of the 1920s. That massacre marked the passing of the age of revolution and revolutionary enthusiasms, as well as a changing of the guard in both politics and culture. The names of those executed disappeared from use, some for decades. Those who replaced them were fully a product of Soviet rule, with no experience of public life in non-Soviet conditions. They also had a much greater sense of caution and a greater appreciation of the new rules of the game.

————

As the Great Terror wound down in 1939, the Soviet Union was a very different place than it had been a decade earlier. Its economy had been transformed, its society turned upside down, and its cultural life brought under the stultifying ideological control of the party. In Central Asia, nomads had become peasants, and peasants had been corralled into collective farms and rendered subservient to the state in unprecedented fashion. The Soviet Union was a single economic space in which workers searched for jobs. It was also a single space in which the outcasts of the Soviet order—prisoners, internal exiles, and "special settlers"—were scattered. Uzbek *bais* were deported to Ukraine or the north Caucasus, and Kazakhs scattered in all directions during the famine. But the inflow of people into Central Asia was much greater than the outflow. Soviet Europeans came to Central Asia as industrial or political experts. They also came as manual laborers to work in the factories, mines, and construction sites that sprungup, or fleeing misfortune or political calamity back home. And they came as victims of the Gulag. Karaganda, one of the largest camps in the Gulag archipelago, occupied almost eighteen thousand square kilometers in northeastern Kazakhstan, atop one of the largest coal basins in the country. It was built in 1931 at the height of the famine and filled up with deportees from Russia. Once the system of forced labor was largely abandoned after Stalin's death, prison camps tended to turn into company towns, and the inmates who had survived stayed there. Deportees became settlers and helped change the demographic balance of Kazakhstan.

The triumph of the idea of Socialism in One Country also reshaped the nationalities policy of the Soviet state, producing a set of formulations that were to last until the end of the Soviet era. There is no better moment at which to pick up the story of this transformation than a reception Stalin hosted at the Kremlin in 1935 for "progressive kolkhoz workers"—those who had performed wonders in picking cotton—from Tajikistan and Turkmenistan. The kolkhoz workers came bedecked in their "national" folkloric dress and paid the requisite homage to Stalin for having made their life more joyous. Their dress marked them as national, while their service to the Soviet economy made them Soviet. In his speech, Stalin affirmed the fact that one could be both national and Soviet at the same time as he trotted out a new formula that was to redefine the Soviet Union until its end. "But comrades," he said, "there is one thing more valuable than cotton—that is the friendship of the peoples of our country."[23] The Soviet Union was now not just a union of national republics but the living embodiment of the friendship of peoples. All of the more than a hundred officially recognized nationalities lived in perpetual friendship. They were committed to the same goals and trod the same path to make the same progress. Some nations were farther along the path than others, but otherwise the differences between them were ones of culture—language, dress, and cuisine—rather than anything more significant. As the different nations became modern and socialist, their cultures would also change but remain national. The Stalinist understanding of nations took for granted that differences among them were rooted in something real ("objective") that would never completely disappear. Each Soviet nation would acquire a culture that was national in form and socialist in content (another Stalinist slogan that was to have a long life). The socialist content was shared by all Soviet citizens, but national forms varied. For non-Russians, national form came to be symbolized by folkloric features, particularly traditional national costume. Nothing was more typical of Soviet iconography of nationality than peasants in folkloric costumes singing in the fields or dancing "national" folk dances. Nationality continued to be represented by the folkloric past, even as socialism ushered the various nations into the bright future of modernity (see figure 13.2).

But official proclamations increasingly paired this celebration of national identity with a Soviet patriotism common to all nations inhabiting the multinational Soviet state. Official rhetoric was full of references to "the Soviet people," united in their common loyalty to the Soviet homeland (called both *rodina*, "motherland," and *otechestvo*, "fatherland," in different contexts). The name of the country—the Union of Soviet Socialist Republics—was unique in the world for having no national or geographic reference. It was rooted in the utopian impulses of the revolution that were now challenged by the new realities of socialism in one country. The new emphasis on a common Soviet patriotism brought to the fore the question of the relationship between the Russians and the Soviet state. Lenin had been eager to distance the new regime from its imperial heritage, and the 1920s had seen virulent

FIG. 13.2. National in form, socialist in content? A classic image by the famed photographer Max Penson, 1930s. The photograph is a work of socialist realism in that it presents the future as the present. An Uzbek family, clad in national costume, feasts on plentiful national cuisine provided by socialism. The family is nuclear, the women unveiled, and everyone sits at a table in a room equipped with windows and curtains—signs of modernity. The portrait on the wall firmly places the modernity as Soviet and socialist. The boy is in modern clothes, but the *doppi* (the Uzbek "national" hat) nationalizes him. © www.maxpenson.com.

critiques of Tsarist imperialism. By the 1930s, however, ideological winds were blowing in a very different direction. The Russians emerged as the leading nation, the most advanced and progressive, of the Soviet state. They were officially designated the "elder brothers" of all other Soviet nationalities, with their language used as the language of communication between the various groups and as the latter's gateway to civilization and world culture. Russian was introduced as a compulsory subject in all non-Russian schools in 1938, and symbols of old Russia— its poets and artists, its explorers and scientists, and even its generals— became symbols of the new Soviet Union. The term "conquest" (*zavoevanie*) disappeared from the historical lexicon, to be replaced by "unification" or "annexation" (*prisoedinenie*). The story of the expansion of the Russian empire as told in official histories that appeared in the rest of the Soviet period downplayed military conquest in favor of various stories of the annexation, often called voluntary, of different principalities and kingdoms to the Russian state. In the case of Central Asia, the annexation by Russia actually did the locals a favor, it was now argued, by keeping them from being conquered by the much more rapacious British and by bringing them under the influence of progressive Russian thought and the Russian revolutionary tradition.

Each nation in Central Asia was free to celebrate its past and develop its future, but it had to do so on the basis of the enduring friendship with other peoples of the Soviet Union, in which Russians were the main interlocutors. Russian became the language of contact with modernity and the outside world. One effect of this shift was the replacement of the Latin alphabets of Central Asian languages by Cyrillic in the second half of the 1930s. A decade earlier, the Latin script had been celebrated for being international and cosmopolitan (there was even talk of switching Russian to Latin orthography). But in the late 1930s, all Turkic languages in the Soviet Union dropped the Latin script, without any debate, in favor of Cyrillic. The internationalism and cosmopolitanism of the previous decade gave way to Soviet patriotism.

Yet, for all that, Russians still did not own the Soviet state. It was always clear that the Soviet people would remain multinational—a collection of nations united in a common cause—rather than a single, homogeneous entity. The Russians' domination of the union (they accounted for 58 percent of the population in the 1939 census) came with a lot of dilemmas and paradoxes that were never fully resolved. The major nationalities, the ones with union republics, came to be tied to their territories and given ownership over them, with that ownership projected as deep into the past as the available evidence could bear. Official narratives emphasized the longevity of each nation's occupation of its territory and its devotion to it, as evidenced by the numerous wars each nation had fought against foreign invaders other than the Russians. This had the clear effect of making citizens think of their republics as national homelands to which they had a title ("titular nationality" was the common Soviet term to designate the status of members of nationalities living in "their own" republics). The Russians, in contrast, identified with the whole Soviet state, but by design specifically Russian national institutions remained poorly developed. The relationship between the Russians and the non-Russians was neither symmetrical nor stable, but the Russians never had an exclusive claim to the Soviet Union.

The place of Central Asian nations in the Soviet Union was thus redefined. Let us take the example of Uzbekistan. In 1941, the four-hundredth anniversary of the death of Alisher Nava'i, the Timurid court poet and the founder of Chaghatay letters, was celebrated at the all-union level. Nava'i was celebrated as an Uzbek national hero. The celebration included the publication of a pamphlet by Aleksandr Yakubovsky titled *On the Question of the Ethnogenesis of the Uzbek People*, which laid out a history of the Uzbek people and their claim to the territory of Uzbekistan in a way that made it the foundational text of Uzbek identity for the rest of the Soviet period and beyond. Ethnogenesis was a concept just being formulated in Soviet anthropology. It posited that different ethnic or national groups had evolved through genesis—that is, actual flesh-and-blood mixing—over historical time. Its completely un-Marxist premises notwithstanding, the concept was to have a strong career in later Soviet times. In 1941, Yakubovsky argued that "contemporary Uzbeks, building a Communist society in fraternal collaboration with other peoples of the USSR, . . . have a long and uninterrupted history of their development on the territory of Uzbekistan." For Yakubovsky, this was clear in the ethnic history of the region. "Philology and linguistics," he wrote, "give us the same uninterrupted line of development that passes from the language of Khoja Ahmad Yasavi, through that of Lutfi and Alisher Nava'i, to the contemporary Uzbek literary language."[24] The Uzbeks had always been on their land and were tied to it. In the years that followed, Uzbek textbooks told of repeated attempts by outsiders (Arabs, Mongols, and Iranians) to conquer the lands that were now Uzbekistan, each of which was beaten back by patriotic Uzbeks. Uzbekness was thus projected deep into the past. The creation of a national state of the Uzbek people now became yet one more of the great achievements of the

Soviet state. Nationality and Sovietness could coexist. We might note the bitter irony that what Yakubovsky had dressed up in the garb of ethnogenesis was precisely the Chaghatayist vision of Uzbekness that Fitrat had articulated in the 1910s. Fitrat would have wholeheartedly agreed with Yakubovsky, had he not been lying in an unmarked grave by that time. He and his generation had paid with their lives for the vision that, sans Timur, came to be entrenched as the official version of Soviet Uzbek identity in the 1940s.

14

A Republic in Eastern Turkestan

IT WAS NOVEMBER 12, 1933. Flags bearing a crescent and star on a pale blue field fluttered and banners waved as twenty thousand men gathered on the banks of the river Tuman outside Kashgar. Amid the hubbub, Abdulbaqi Sabit Damulla, a respected Islamic scholar, stepped up to the podium and proclaimed the creation of the Eastern Turkestan Republic (ETR). Troops gave a forty-one-gun salute, and students sang a national hymn: "Our flag is a blue flag, our horde is a golden horde. Turkestan is the homeland of our Turkic people, it has become ours."[1] Sabit Damulla then led a parade back to the center of the city, where the crowd listened to further speeches outlining the structure of the government and the policies it wanted to pursue. The government had a constitution and a fifteen-member cabinet. Sabit Damulla was elected its prime minister. The government aspired to bring peace and prosperity to the region, and it spoke the language of national self-determination and anti-imperialism. A few weeks earlier, the activists who proclaimed the republic had begun publishing *Eastern Turkestan Life*, Kashgar's first newspaper. "Praise be that these days the oppressed country of Eastern Turkestan has been liberated from the imprisonment of oppression and national rule established," its first issue exclaimed. "There is no more accursed thing in the world than living imprisoned under the thumb of an alien nation. Along with that, it is not possible to imagine a greater blessing than national sovereignty and the independence and dignity of the homeland [*vatan*]."[2] A half-century after the collapse of Yaqub Beg's state, the new state was based on a very different vocabulary of politics.

Republic, nation, homeland, constitution, and anticolonial struggle—concepts that would have been inconceivable to Yaqub Beg and his contemporaries—now underpinned the secession of Altishahr from the Chinese empire.

A severe crisis of Han Chinese rule in Xinjiang had made the proclamation of the republic possible. The same crisis engulfed it in a paroxysm of violence and led to its swift destruction. Yet its fleeting existence provides insights into developments in Muslim society in Eastern Turkestan under the surface of the political stability of Yang Zengxin's rule.

———

Yang had sought to inoculate Xinjiang against the warlords of the rest of China and the revolutionary upheaval that beset Soviet Central Asia in the decade after 1917. He had established an authoritarian regime that kept most features of modernity at bay. Unlike in Soviet Central Asia, there was no modern education or press, let alone land redistribution, and no campaigns for unveiling, attacks on religion, or creation of mass organizations. Instead of mobilization, Yang preferred people to keep in their place in a hierarchical political order. If the Soviets spoke in terms of the will of the people and national self-determination, Yang preferred a paternalistic political order in which the people were taken care of by solicitous officials. He cut some deals with Muslim elites—the prince of Qumul retained his privileges, as did some Kazakh chiefs—but there could be no question of the people making political demands, let alone seeking sovereignty. While all along Yang professed his loyalty to the Chinese republic, his political instincts were those of the imperial era. The politics of difference remained firmly in place.

Nonetheless, Yang could not keep the twentieth century out of Xinjiang. Unauthorized ideas filtered in, despite his best efforts to contain them. He was perhaps more successful at keeping the rest of China out of his domain. It was the Soviet Union that became the channel of ideas and indeed a source of inspiration. Xinjiang's trade with the Soviet Union picked up after 1922 and was soon many times greater than its trade with the rest of China. In 1925, the seasonal labor migration from Xinjiang to the Soviet Union began again. Yang worried about it: "If I let Xinjiang's Turbans cross the Soviet border with impunity and without any restrictions whatsoever, the ten thousand seasonal expatriate laborers of today will become the ten thousand agitating returnees of tomorrow."[3] He set up forms of surveillance at the Xinjiang consulates in the Soviet Union, but the Soviets were more interested in the cheap labor provided by the Eastern Turkestanis than in mobilizing them for revolution. Political agitation directed at Soviet Uyghurs was not to be directed at the labor migrants. In fact, by 1927, the Soviets had decided that "any agitation toward splitting Xinjiang from China [was] entirely harmful and impermissible,"[4] and that their geopolitical goals were best served by working for a united China. Yang might have worried more about the wealthy merchants who traveled not just to Central Asia but also to Nizhny Novgorod and Moscow. Many of their sons spent time in the Soviet Union and learned Russian. More significantly, they also were swept up in the enthusiasms of the Central Asian intelligentsia in the 1920s. The ideas of the nation, national progress, and cultural transformation began to seep into Xinjiang from Soviet Central Asia despite Yang's best attempts to cordon his domain off from them.

One such affluent merchant's son was Abdukhaliq Abdurahman oghli (b. 1901), whose father was from Turfan. Abdukhaliq traveled with his grandfather to Russian Turkestan in 1916, where he studied at a Russian-native school in Semipalatinsk. After his return to Xinjiang, he enrolled in one of the few *xuetang*s, the modern Chinese schools established in the late Qing period, still allowed to function by Yang. In 1923, Abdukhaliq returned to the Soviet Union, where he stayed for three years. Back in Xinjiang, he sought to establish a printing press and a magazine, but he was denied permission. In 1927, he established a benevolent society for the propagation of education.[5] This was precisely the kind of activity the Jadids of Russian Turkestan had engaged in before the revolution. Abdukhaliq was backed financially by Maqsut Muhiti, one of the town's leading merchants and the founder of a Jadid school. Few of these efforts bore fruit, however, for the government would not allow them. But if Yang could deny permission for the establishment of a press and a magazine, he could not keep Abdukhaliq from composing poetry. In 1917, Abdukhaliq began writing verse that was new in style and content and centrally concerned with the nation. He also turned to the trope of awakening. In 1920, in a poem titled "Awaken!," he diagnosed the critical state of his community:

> O poor Uyghur, awaken, enough of your slumber,
> You have nothing, the next thing to go will be your life.
> If you don't save yourself from this death,
> Ah, your situation will be dangerous, so dangerous.[6]

His choice of pen name, Abdukhaliq Uyghur, is indicative of his outlook. The term "Uyghur" had been coined in the Eastern Turkestani diaspora in the Soviet Union, but Abdukhaliq was perhaps the first person in Xinjiang to use the term or use it to denote the Muslims of Eastern Turkestan as a nation, a community with common political interests and a common future. And the course of action was clear to Uyghur:

> What state is the nation in
> Open your eyes, descendants of Uyghur.
> Make some effort, pay attention,
> Arise, get rid of your empty words.[7]

Elsewhere he wrote: "Take your life in your hand, arise! / You will find no other way!"[8]

Others followed a different path. Mehmed Emin Bughra (b. 1901) came from a family of madrasa teachers in Khotan and followed the usual course of madrasa education. He did not travel overseas but still acquired a keen sense of the injustice of the situation in Eastern Turkestan. Writing in exile in 1940, he recalled how in his youth he had become aware of the fact that "Eastern Turkestan . . . was a colony of the Manchu Empire [whose] people were forced by Chinese functionaries to live in medieval darkness, deprived of contemporary knowledge and training."[9] A more conventional case was that of Masud Sabri (b. 1886), a scion of a prosperous family from Ghulja who had gone to the Ottoman Empire to study at the beginning of the twentieth century. He trained as a medical doctor but also acquired a deep commitment to

Turkism. He returned to Ghulja on the eve of the First World War and threw himself into public life. He established a hospital and a pharmacy, as well as a number of modern schools. This activity ran afoul of Yang, who repeatedly closed schools founded by Masud and jailed him for "revolutionary activities." Even in the absence of newspapers and magazines or a functioning telegraph or postal system, ideas of the nation and national rights and national struggle had contaminated Yang's earthly paradise.

———

Yang was assassinated at a banquet on July 7, 1928. There was some poetic justice in the fact that his career ended at a banquet as it had taken off at one, but his death threw Xinjiang into a period of prolonged turmoil that brought Han rule in the province to the brink of extinction. We still do not know who ordered the assassination, but the beneficiary was Jin Shuren, Yang's second in command, who managed to take over the province. In his last months, Yang had been worried about challenges from warlords from neighboring provinces who threatened to encroach upon Yang's turf as they were pressed by the GMD, which had launched a military expedition in 1926–1927 to root them out. Had he lived, he would have faced the need to buttress his military forces and find a way to pay for them, since subsidies from the center were still not forthcoming. That task was left to Jin, who went after it with single-minded purpose. He tripled the size of his army within five months of taking power and doubled it again in the year that followed, reaching a total of sixty thousand men—all Han recruited from the neighboring provinces of Gansu and Shaanxi. This buildup was accompanied by a program of road building and weapons acquisition from the Soviet Union and British India.[10] To pay for all this, Jin printed unbacked paper currency with abandon while also seeking to extract as much revenue as possible from the province's slender resources. He increased existing taxes and introduced new ones, including levies on butchering livestock and cutting down trees. This new extraction was not backed by any political program that might give it

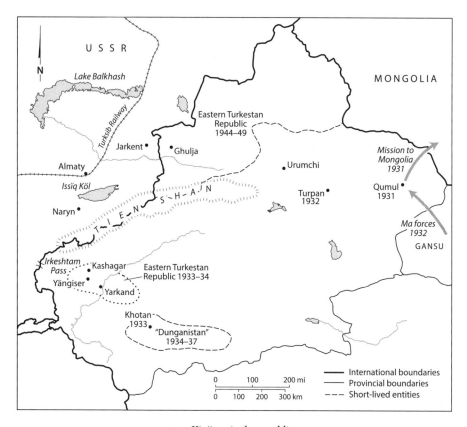

MAP 14.1. Xinjiang in the republican era

a veneer of legitimacy. Collectivization in the Soviet Union was also a form of heightened extraction from the countryside, but it was accompanied on the one hand by political mobilization in the name of a bright future and on the other hand by the coercive violence of the OGPU. Jin, like Yang, had nothing to offer in this regard. Instead, Jin made matters worse by dismantling many of Yang's arrangements with local elites and replacing many indigenous officeholders with Han bureaucrats as a way of maximizing his reach into society. None of this sat well with the local population.

A number of rebellions broke out simultaneously. The first took place in Qumul in the far east of the province in February 1931 (see map 14.1). Qumul was the part of Xinjiang with the deepest ties to the Chinese state. Its rulers had aided the Qing to conquer Xinjiang in the 1750s and in Zuo Zongtang's reconquest in 1880–1881. For this, they were given the hereditary title of *wang* and left to rule their domain as they pleased. Their autonomy had not been curbed when Xinjiang became a province in 1884. Among other privileges, the *wang*s enjoyed the right to corvée labor from Muslim peasants who lived on their land. But when the reigning *wang*, Maqsut Shah, died in 1930, Jin abolished the principality and confiscated the *wang*'s land. Any relief that Maqsut's serfs might have felt at the abolition of their obligations was offset by the increased taxes that Jin imposed, as well as by his decision to settle Han peasants from outside Xinjiang on some of the land. It was in this atmosphere that a Chinese tax collector called Zhang coerced a Muslim father in a village outside Qumul to give the collector his daughter in marriage. This affront to local religious and gender sensibilities set off a rebellion. As Zhang and his men were carousing at the wedding, a group of angry locals attacked and killed them. The insurgents then turned their fury on police garrisons across the county as well as recent Han settlers, murdering almost a hundred families and burying their heads under the fields they had recently acquired. The rebellion spread rapidly, and soon the Muslim part of Qumul had fallen to the insurgents. Although an armed force from Ürümchi retook the city, largely destroying it in the process, many of the insurgents retreated to the surrounding mountains.

At this point, the uprising was taken over by men from the court of Maqsut Shah who sought to turn the jacquerie into a political movement. Khoja Niyaz, head of the palace guard; Yolbars Khan, the *ordabegi* (chancellor); and Bäshir Wang, a claimant to the abolished throne, assumed positions of leadership and made contact with forces beyond Qumul. A letter to the Mongolian government articulated their grievances: "For several hundred years, we, the Chantou people, have carried out impositions under the hand of the Chinese, laboring in the place of dogs and donkeys. Now, for the last ten or twenty years the tyranny of these Chinese has increased, and [they have taken] by all variety of means the proceeds of our lands and waters, the wealth and goods in our hands, and by placing officials everywhere and stationing troops,

and forcing us to provide them with feed and firewood, food and suste-
nance, they have carried out countless injustices beyond limit."[11] This
was anticolonial language at its most direct. Noteworthy is the use of
the term "Chantou people." *Chantou*, "turbaned head," was the pejorative term used by Qing and Han officials for the Turkic Muslim population of Xinjiang. It was also used in Mongolia, however, which might
have been why the authors of the letter used it. That self-designation was
to change over the course of the rebellion, as much of it was fought in
the name of the Eastern Turkestani nation. The mission to Mongolia
was successful, and the rebels received two trucks full of arms and am-
munition, which allowed the rebels to carry on. The Mongolian aid was
not to be repeated, for the Soviets, the paramount power in Mongolia,
had no enthusiasm for the rebellion.

Yolbars also made contact with Dungan warlords from Gansu. That
province had long been the bastion of a number of Chinese Muslim
warlords (all surnamed Ma) who commanded poorly trained but numerous armies. Ma Zhongying, the youngest of them, offered help:
"First I shall alleviate the suffering of the Uyghurs of Hami [Qumul],
then I shall drive Jin Shuren from the stage by force of arms," he is supposed to have promised Yolbars.[12] Ma invaded Xinjiang with a motley
group of about five hundred soldiers, but his force bore the formal title
of the 36th Division of the Chinese National Army—a title granted to
it by the GMD, which considered Jin to be a rebel. Ma's men laid siege
to Qumul but encountered fierce resistance from the local Han garrison.
Meanwhile, Jin was able to muster a military response, putting together
a force made up of the soldiers of the Han general Zhang Peiyun from
Ili, as well as a regiment raised from the White Russian émigrés who had
stayed in Xinjiang. This regiment was able to raise the siege at the beginning of November and send the rebels back to the mountains. Ma withdrew to Gansu to recuperate from some serious wounds he had received
in the battle. The following year, another uprising broke out in Turfan,
a mere two hundred kilometers from the capital, Ürümchi. It was initiated by a secret society organized by a number of local figures with Jadid
leanings. The uprising was led by Mahmut Muhiti, whose brother Maqsut had long been active in Jadid activities and had been a friend to and

patron of the poet Abdukhaliq Uyghur.[13] However, warlords soon took over. From his sickbed in Gansu, Ma Zhongying dispatched an officer named Ma Shiming to lead the rebels. Ma Fuming, the Dungan commandant of the Turfan garrison, went over to the rebels with his troops, while the Qumul rebels also made haste for Turfan, which now became the center of the uprising. This coalition of Turkic and Dungan troops led by Khoja Niyaz and Ma Shiming, respectively, harassed provincial troops through the winter of 1932–1933 and managed to lay siege to Ürümchi. Jin's power—and perhaps the Chinese hold on Xinjiang—seemed to be on the brink of collapse.

———

Jin was saved by the Soviet Union. The rise of Japan and its ambitions for empire had rattled the Soviet leadership. In 1931, Japan had occupied Manchuria and transformed it into a puppet state, and there was talk of Japanese expansion in areas under Han Chinese rule. The Soviets feared that Japan might likewise install a Turanian state in Xinjiang under a pliant Dungan warlord. Stalin was all too aware of the Soviet Union's geopolitical vulnerability and military weakness and was not willing to take any chances. Soviet thinking about foreign policy had also undergone a sea change with the triumph of Stalin's slogan of building socialism in one country, which made the defense of the one country under socialism synonymous with the defense of socialism worldwide. Old-fashioned geopolitical thinking made a comeback in Soviet foreign policy. By the end of the 1920s, the enthusiasm for revolutionizing the East was a distant memory, and the search for defensive cordons, natural resources, and military advantage had come to guide Soviet policy. Moscow had sold armaments (including two military aeroplanes) for hard cash to Jin in 1931 and made a secret trade deal with him. Soviet border guards also took part in joint operations with Xinjiang troops to both protect the Soviet border and keep the peace in Xinjiang. Now, as Ürümchi lay besieged, the Soviet government transported there some two thousand Chinese troops who had fled to the Soviet Far East after the Japanese invasion of Manchuria in 1931. This Manchurian Salvation

Army arrived in Ürümchi just in time to relieve the city. The Soviet Union had saved the day for Han rule in Xinjiang.

Ürümchi survived, but Jin did not. He was ousted in a coup on April 12, 1933, soon after the siege was lifted. The man who emerged triumphant from the coup was Sheng Shicai (b. 1887), the chief of staff of the provincial army. Like Yang and Jin, he ruled Xinjiang in the name of China but in open defiance of the central government. When Nanjing sent Huang Musong, its vice-minister for foreign affairs, as "pacification commissioner" to Ürümchi to assess the situation, Sheng put him under house arrest and released him only on condition that Nanjing confirm Sheng as *duban*, military commander in chief and de facto governor. Instead, Sheng turned to the Soviets. One of his first acts after taking power had been to meet with the Soviet consul in Ürümchi. The Soviets did not have a hand in the coup that brought Sheng to power, but they certainly benefited from its outcome and quickly acquired a stake in Sheng's retaining his position. In September, when Nanjing sent Luo Weng'an, the minister of foreign affairs, to officially confirm Sheng as *duban*, it still had hopes of displacing him from his perch. Right after the ceremony, Luo approached both Zhang Peiyun, a Han general in Ili, and Ma Zhongying, the Dungan warlord, asking for help in dislodging Sheng. Zhang responded favorably and in December set out to attack Ürümchi. However, his advance was halted by a Soviet force of several thousand men with tanks and aeroplanes that decimated his troops. Two weeks later, Soviet planes bombed Ma's remaining troops as they besieged Ürümchi and forced them to retreat. Sheng's hold on power was guaranteed in rather brazen fashion by Soviet intervention.

As Sheng attempted to establish himself in power, he entered into negotiations with Khoja Niyaz, the leader of the Qumul uprising. Over the summer of 1933, the two worked out an agreement to partition the province in a way that would result in an "East Turkestan" that "would be an independent and autonomous Islamic country stretching from Qumul to Kashgar. It [will] not recognize Ürümchi as the center. Muslims will administer their own affairs." The border between the two would be the Tien-Shan Mountains, and "the Chinese would not extend beyond them."[14] Khoja Niyaz was to be the ruler of this Eastern Turkestan.

———

Events in Altishahr had taken their own course during the previous year. There was no single spark, let alone coordination, for the events that led to the proclamation of ETR. We can find the first seeds of the ETR in an uprising in Khotan in February 1933 that was the work of a secret society founded by Bughra. As noted above, Bughra was the scion of a scholarly family and had come to see Eastern Turkestan's situation as one of colonial servitude. After finding employment at a madrasa, he had traveled around the province to get a sense of the "condition of the land, the spiritual state of the nation, and the power of the enemy." Bughra found a soul mate in Ghulja. Sabit Damulla—a native of Atush, near Kashgar, who is introduced above in this chapter—had studied in Kashgar and Bukhara before the First World War and then traveled extensively in Turkey, Egypt, and India. After he moved to Khotan, the secret society launched its uprising. We know little about the number of its members or the amount of its resources, but the uprising drove Chinese forces out of Khotan and its environs. The society established what it called an Islamic government in the town, whose officials included two of Bughra's younger brothers as well as Sabit Damulla. The leaders of the government styled themselves emirs, a term that had clear Islamic connotations. They formed a small army, being helped in this endeavor by the arrival of a Kyrgyz warlord called Janibek, a former Basmachi from Soviet Turkestan who had been living a quiet life of exile in Keriyä. Despite their lack of training and poor weaponry, the Khotan armies took Yarkand and a number of smaller towns and put to the sword a force of Dungans that arrived from Kashgar to relieve the Han regiments in the new city of Yarkand. They then moved toward Kashgar.

Meanwhile, Sheng's Soviet-backed victory at Ürümchi drove many of his surviving opponents southward. They were a motley crew, including both Turkic and Dungan forces. The Kyrgyz of western Xinjiang also rose up, under the leadership of Osman Ali. By May 1933, this coalition had taken Kashgar. However, success led only to a fracturing of the coalition. The position of the Dungans, for instance, was quite different in Altishahr than it was in the north. From the beginning, the Dungans had been central to the maintenance of Qing rule in Altishahr, a tradition that had continued into the republican era. Dungan officials saw themselves as supporters of and partners in the empire. As a result, there was little love lost between them and the local Muslim population. Ma Fuxing, whom Yang Zengxin had appointed military commander of Kashgar between 1916 and 1924, had been famous for the brutality of his reign. His successor, Ma Shaowu, also ruled with a strong arm. The tension between the Dungans and the local Muslim population surfaced again when Muslim armies took Kashgar and it was instrumental in the breakup of the coalition. Ma Shaowu and his Chinese troops found themselves besieged in the new city. The Dungans accompanying the insurgents from the north decided to side with Ma and broke with their Turkic partners. Meanwhile, other factions of the coalition skirmished with each other constantly, and the Muslim old city changed hands among them a number of times over the summer of 1933.

It was in the midst of this chaos that civic activists began working toward independence. Merchants and Jadid-leaning *ulama* from Kashgar constituted the core of this group. It was strengthened by the arrival of members of the Khotan government. News of the upheaval also drew back to Kashgar several exiles from Soviet Central Asia and beyond. One of the first institutions to be created was a ministry of education, which commandeered the only printing press in town (owned by a Swedish Christian mission that had existed for several decades) and began publishing a newspaper, *Eastern Turkestan Life*. It was edited by Qutluq Haji Shävqi, a local Jadid of long standing whose name had appeared twenty years earlier in Ismail Gasprinsky's *Tercüman*, the Crimean newspaper that had been the flagship of Islamic reform in the Russian empire. On September 10, activists, spearheaded by Sabit Damulla, established the Istiqlal Jamiyati ("Independence Association"), which began preparations for the proclamation of the republic on November 12.[15]

Bughra and his brothers had proclaimed themselves emirs in Khotan, but in Kashgar the secessionist state was proclaimed as a republic. The new state used many names. The coins it minted bore the names Republic of Uyghuristan and the Islamic Republic of Turkestan, while its passports were issued in the name of the Sublime Islamic Republic of East Turkestan,[16] but it is most commonly known as the ETR. Nation, homeland, and Islam were inextricably intertwined in the vision of the republic's founders. The extent of the homeland was never spelled out, but "Eastern Turkestan" most likely meant the stretch of predominantly Muslim country from Qumul to Kashgar, excluding Zungharia in the north. In fact, the republic controlled only the oases of Kashgar, Yarkand, and Khotan—and it did not fully control them. The first article of the constitution simply stated, "The Eastern Turkestan Republic is established on the basis of the Islamic shariat and acts in accordance with commandments of the Wise Qur'an, which is the source of our happiness and the embodiment of immutable divine law."[17] Other articles of the constitution used "president" interchangeably with "commander of the faithful." Yet as the theater of its proclamation makes clear, the republic was based on the politics of participation and national self-determination. Its leaders saw "Eastern Turkestan" as part of a broader community of Turkic peoples, who were by definition Muslim. The republic did not use the term "Uyghur." Emblazoned across the masthead of *Eastern Turkestan Life* was Gasprinsky's classic Jadid slogan, "Unity in language, thought, and deed."

The ETR was a Jadid republic proclaimed at the farthest reach of the Turkic world. Its government was a coalition of modernist *ulama* and men who had long been active in Jadid activities in Kashgar. It combined a modernist understanding of Islam with concerns of anticolonial nationalism in a Turkist vein. Its rhetoric was rooted in Central Asian Muslim modernism, as the use of Gasprinsky's slogan clearly showed. The constellation of forces was quite different from that of Russian Turkestan in 1917, where the *ulama* and the Jadids had been mortal enemies. In Eastern Turkestan in 1932–1933, reformist *ulama* were at peace with the idea of progress for the sake of the nation and homeland, nor did they feel threatened by the youth as their Tashkent counterparts in 1917 had. The government was based in Kashgar, but only six of the fifteen cabinet members came from Kashgar or the nearby town of Atush. The others were from Turfan or Khotan. Sabit Damulla had been born in Atush but spent most of his adult life in Ghulja. The cabinet represented a broad coalition of modernist forces from across Eastern Turkestan. Yet its members made the fateful decision to offer the presidency of the republic to Khoja Niyaz, whom they did not know and with whom they had little in common. His possession of military might and his agreement with Sheng made him attractive to the ETR leaders. He was celebrated in the pages of *Eastern Turkestan Life* as a "great victor" and a kind ruler.

The new republic had all the trappings of modern statehood—a constitution, cabinet, flag, currency, and passports—but it had been born in extremely difficult circumstances. As a landlocked state with no developed resources, the ETR would have faced insurmountable challenges in any case. And it did not even fully control its own territory, for Dungan forces continued to occupy the new city in Kashgar. The new government hurried to make contact with foreign states. The leaders of ETR were not fond of the Soviets, for by 1933, the idea that Jadid goals might be accomplished by Soviet means had been put to rest in Soviet Central Asia. A telegram announcing the establishment of the ETR to the government of Turkey provoked some exuberance in the Turkish press but drew no reaction from the government, which was avowedly noninterventionist at the time. An approach to Afghanistan produced similarly scanty results. The only remaining hope was Britain. A delegation dispatched to New Delhi was quickly rebuffed when it finally arrived in February 1934. Chinese historians routinely claim that the ETR was a British puppet, created to undermine Chinese sovereignty, but nothing could be further from the facts. Britain in the 1930s was committed to the territorial integrity of China and saw Nanjing as the sole authority in Xinjiang. It had no intention of intervening on behalf of the ETR.[18] Extorting extraterritorial rights in Xinjiang from the Chinese government and even selling arms to quasi-independent governors of the province was one thing; providing support to a secessionist state was quite another. Officials at the British consulate in Kashgar chronicled the tumultuous events of the era but did nothing to intervene in them.

The other power in the region, the Soviet Union, was resolutely opposed to the idea of another independent Muslim state on its border.[19] The Soviet state had just purged Soviet Central Asia's cultural elites for fear of nationalism, and it was not about to allow the creation of an independent state in Eastern Turkestan. The Soviets did not need to intervene directly, for they acquired the support of none other than Khoja Niyaz, the president of the ETR. In the autumn, he had entered into negotiations with the Soviets, seeking arms for his forces from them.[20] When he finally arrived in Kashgar in January 1934, he brought only misfortune with him. Over the summer, he had broken with Ma Zhongying, the Dungan warlord he had invited into Xinjiang in 1932. Ma had battled Sheng on behalf of Nanjing but been defeated by Soviet intervention, just as Khoja Niyaz began to negotiate with the Soviets. Now Ma pursued Khoja Niyaz to Kashgar. In February 1934, Ma's Dungan troops sacked Kashgar in the name of the GMD. The assault on Kashgar was followed by a pogrom in which most shops in the city were looted and perhaps as many as 4,500 people killed.[21] The leaders of the republic had decamped to Yengisar before the Dungans arrived in Kashgar and had tried to reestablish the government there. The Dungans followed them and took the city. Sabit Damulla escaped to Yarkand, but Ma's men executed Abdullah Bughra, one of the Khotan emirs, and sent his head to be displayed outside the main mosque in Kashgar. Khoja Niyaz had escaped the carnage in Kashgar because he was meeting with Soviet officials in Irkeshtam, the border post with the Soviet Union. There he promised to work with Sheng and disassociate himself from the ETR. After his return, he told Sabit Damulla, the prime minister, to dissolve the government. When Sabit Damulla refused, Khoja Niyaz marched with his men to Yarkand, arrested Sabit Damulla, and delivered him to the provincial authorities in Aqsu, who unceremoniously hanged him. That was the end of the ETR. Sheng was rid of it without having to fight it. His work had been done by Dungan troops ostensibly loyal to Nanjing and by the ETR's own president.

The ETR had lasted about as long as the Turkestan Autonomy founded at Kokand in 1917–1918. Both were attempts at statehood by cultural elites who were unprepared and underresourced for such an adventure. In the case of the ETR, the intellectuals were sidelined and outflanked by the military men on their own side, who acted according to their own interests. Both republics provide a glimpse of the aspirations that motivated their leaders and of the political vocabulary (of nation, constitution, self-determination, and modernity) that had gained traction among Central Asian populations. Both became symbols of those aspirations, and both were reviled by the regimes that destroyed them. In the official Chinese imagination, the ETR occupies a place similar to that of the Turkestan Autonomy in Soviet historiography—a precedent that was dangerous because of the possibilities it contained and hence to be constantly denigrated or, better yet, forgotten. For Uyghurs, however, the ETR represents something completely different. Its proclamation gave a boost to a sense of nationhood in Eastern Turkestan. Today Uyghurs see it as a failed attempt at national statehood. The light blue flag of the republic is now the symbol of Uyghur self-assertion and is used widely in the diaspora.

————

By 1934, Sheng Shicai was in control of most of Xinjiang. He was cut of very different cloth than Yang or Jin. A native of Liaoning province in Manchuria, Sheng had studied not in the Confucian tradition but at universities and military academies in Japan. His worldview had been shaped by his wariness of Japanese designs on China and the sense that China needed to adopt new methods for self-strengthening. Like all Han Chinese thinkers, he saw Xinjiang not as a colonial possession of China but as an integral part of the country. However, in his view retaining Xinjiang as a Chinese possession required the use of unusual tactics. Sheng had no patience for interference by a central government that was not in a position to provide any material assistance. Xinjiang had been on its own since the proclamation of the Chinese republic. Instead, Sheng sought Soviet support and adopted a new political language and style of rule. In place of the highly conservative political style of Yang and Jin, Sheng introduced the rhetoric of mobilization and inclusiveness to Xinjiang that borrowed heavily from Soviet practices. Chinese imperialism in Xinjiang would now use the language of Soviet anticolonialism.

The Soviets were eager to cultivate Sheng as a client. Gone were the days when the Soviet government published secret agreements and renounced the unequal treaties signed by its predecessor. Socialism in one country required the use of all tactics available to ensure national security. Xinjiang was important both as a buffer against the threat of Japanese expansion and as an economic resource. The Soviets' relationship with Sheng was built on the exploration and exploitation of Xinjiang's natural resources for the cause of Soviet industrialization. The Soviets offered Sheng two loans totaling 7.5 million gold rubles to revitalize Xinjiang's financial sector and develop its infrastructure, and to allow Sheng to purchase Soviet arms. In return, Soviet organizations acquired the right to explore the mineral resources of the province on a concessionary basis and to trade in Xinjiang on a tax-free basis.[22] Over the next decade, Soviet organizations established a number of mining operations and oil production facilities in northern Xinjiang. In addition, the Soviet military stationed three thousand troops and an air squadron near Qumul. In effect, the Soviet Union had regained the extraterritorial privileges that the Tsarist empire had extorted from the Qing. Xinjiang had become a Soviet satellite.

Soviet advisors poured into the province. They staffed all sorts of government offices and helped establish the Xinjiang Provincial Public Security Bureau, a political police organization modeled on the OGPU. Many of the advisors were Chinese citizens, either Han or Turkestani, who had lived in the Soviet Union as exiles. Soviet Central Asia played a significant role in this extension of Soviet influence: the central committees of the Communist parties of Uzbekistan and Kazakhstan were routinely tasked with providing logistical and personnel support for Soviet efforts in Xinjiang. Sheng also started sending large numbers of students to educational institutions in Soviet Central Asia. This produced a generation of Eastern Turkestani Muslim intellectuals who were far more familiar with Russian than with Chinese and felt an affinity for the Soviet Union. The Uyghurs who studied in Tashkent in the 1930s—known as the *Tashkentchilär* ("Tashkenters")—were to play an outsize role in Xinjiang politics over the next two decades.

Sheng sought to ingratiate himself with Stalin. In June 1934, he wrote Stalin a lengthy letter in which he boasted of his long study of Marxism and his firm faith in socialism. The GMD was founded on a "completely bankrupt teaching having no philosophical or scientific basis," Sheng wrote. "Therefore, there remains only one way to save China and Xinjiang, to overthrow the bloodthirsty, dissolute Nanjing government, create a Soviet Government, and fight imperialism in a common front with the USSR under the leadership of the Comintern."[23] He also expressed a wish to join the Communist Party of the Soviet Union. Stalin found the letter "depressing," for "only a provocateur or a hopeless 'leftist' having no idea about Marxism could have written it."[24] He later instructed Garegin Apresov, the Soviet consul in Ürümchi, to tell Sheng that "the Sovietization of Xinjiang in whatever form . . . does not enter into our plans and we consider any idea about the Sovietization of Xinjiang . . . dangerous." This was because "we consider the territorial integrity of China to be advisable and desirable, not only from the point of view of China, but also from the point of view of the USSR."[25] Stalin would work with Sheng but would not take any nonsense from him.

Sheng's flattery did not work, but he still borrowed a great deal from the Soviet political repertoire, both in form and in content. The vocabulary of rule changed. The coup against Jin on April 12, 1933, became a "revolution," and the language of progress, unity, and anti-imperialism was ubiquitous. The changes went beyond mere vocabulary. Sheng created a Soviet-style official culture based on political mobilization. In Kashgar, his government took over *Eastern Turkestan Life*, the newspaper of the ETR, and relaunched it as *New Life*. Its first issue informed readers that "the new government established in the country is a civilized government that works to unite under equal rights and justice all children of the homeland residing in the province, such as Uyghurs, Han, Mongols, Dungans, Kyrgyz, and Kazakhs. With an eye to rights and the nourishing of humanity, it abolishes estrangement and creates friendship among the various peoples, and works for the well-being and comfort of all."[26] The vocabulary of equal rights, of "children of the homeland," and of "friendship among the various peoples" was new to Xinjiang and rooted in Soviet discourses. Sheng issued a series of slogans—the Eight Great Proclamations and the Nine Tasks, which ultimately boiled down to the Six Great Policies of Anti-Imperialism, Peace, Ethnic Equality, Clean Government, Construction, and Friendship with the Soviet Union.[27] In August 1934, Sheng presided over the formation of an organization called the Xinjiang People's Anti-Imperialist Union. It was supposed to "lead people from all walks of life [and] from all nationalities to conduct the new government's Six Great Policies," to "resolutely fight against any imperialists and other lackeys who alienate the different nationalities in Xinjiang and who want to undermine peace in Xinjiang," and to "support the construction of new Xinjiang."[28] The union organized "anti-imperialist training courses" for officials, teachers, and military officers as well as public meetings, and it frequently posted slogans, wall newspapers, and fliers on the streets.[29] Anti-imperialist mobilization would ensure that Xinjiang remained a part of China and indeed become a model for the rest of the country.[30] For Sheng, meeting that goal required recognizing the fact that Xinjiang was inhabited by multiple nationalities and according each of them language and cultural rights.

In 1934 and 1935, Sheng organized two Congresses of People's Representatives in Ürümchi. The second one proclaimed nationality to be an officially recognized category. The ETR had referred to "our Turkic people" as constituting the nation it served. The Second Congress of People's Representatives instead recognized fourteen different nationalities living in Xinjiang. These included Han Chinese and Dungans, Manchus, Mongols, and the small Tungusic groups of the Sibe (a Manchurian group settled in the Ili valley by the Qing) and Solon, as well as immigrant groups such as Tatars, Uzbeks, and Russians. Eastern Turkestan's Muslim population (the ETR's nation) was now seen as a multinational group consisting of Uyghurs, Kazakhs, Kyrgyz, Tajiks, and Taranchis. With the exception of the last group, this classification adhered to Soviet categories. The term "Uyghur" thus entered the official vocabulary as the designation for the sedentary Turkic-speaking population of the province. The term had come into use among the Eastern Turkestani diaspora in Soviet Central Asia and had been adopted by progressive intellectuals in Xinjiang, but it had never been accepted by Ürümchi authorities—which had continued to use the pejorative term *chantou*. Now, "Uyghur" was established as the official term, and its transcription in Chinese characters standardized.[31]

This was Soviet nationalities policy, minus any notion of autonomy or indigenization. Sheng did appoint a few locals to prominent positions (for example, Khoja Niyaz was made deputy chairman of the province), but he made no commitment to nurturing an indigenous political elite. Abdughafur Damla, Kashgar's chief *qazi*, put it bluntly: "Just because you make up 90% of the population of Xinjiang, don't think that positions will be given to you proportionally. The positions will go to those who study and serve the government."[32] Nevertheless, recognition of nationality as a category was a major shift in official policy. It underpinned a new way of thinking about Xinjiang and its people. A key feature of the new policy was the creation of state-funded "enlightenment associations" and cultural clubs that promoted various languages and published materials in them. The Uyghur Enlightenment Association, established in August 1934, came to have branches all over Xinjiang, while analogous associations for Kazakhs and Mongols also appeared. The Uyghur association launched Ürümchi's first Uyghur-language newspaper, the *Shing Jang gäziti* (Xinjiang Gazette). The enlightenment associations also created a network of local-language schools. If Yang had actively suppressed modern education for Muslims, Sheng presided over the creation of the first network of vernacular public educational institutions in the province's history. This was accompanied by a spurt in book publishing in Uyghur. While Sheng's speeches and proclamations, as well as new laws and regulations, accounted for the bulk of the new material, the Sheng era also saw the appearance of primers and textbooks for schools, "useful books" (such as manuals for sericulture and accounting), and histories. Print culture had finally arrived in Eastern Turkestan.

The destruction of the ETR had not brought the south under Sheng's control. The Dungan army of Ma Zhongying, ostensibly loyal to the GMD, was still active. In a move that remains unexplained, Ma went to Irkeshtam to meet with Soviet officials and never returned. His fate is still unknown. Most likely, he was arrested by the Soviets and held hostage for future negotiations with Dungans, whom the Soviets wanted to cooperate with Sheng.[33] His followers, led by his brother-in-law Ma Hushan, retreated to Khotan, which they proceeded to occupy and rule as a military colony for the next three years. Ma Hushan imposed viciously high taxes and press-ganged peasants into his army in the hope one day of taking on Sheng. He liked to be called *padishah* (king), even as he professed loyalty to Nanjing. This little corner of Xinjiang, sometimes called Dunganistan by contemporary observers, had remained beyond Sheng's grasp, but it was, as Andrew Forbes has rightly noted, a loyalist "bastion of Chinese colonialism, and not of Muslim separatism, in Xinjiang."[34] Kashgar was occupied by a small force loyal to Sheng, who appointed Mahmut Muhiti deputy commander of the Southern Xinjiang Military Region. Muhiti had a long record as a Jadid activist in Turfan. He had been one of the organizers of the Turfan uprising against Jin Shuren. Since then, he had worked with Khoja Niyaz, which was the reason for his appointment. Muhiti proceeded to rule Kashgar with a great deal of autonomy, guaranteed by its distance from Ürümchi.

By 1937, however, the relationship had frayed. Muhiti, unhappy with Sheng's embrace of the Soviets, instigated large-scale street demonstrations in Kashgar.[35] As the situation worsened, Muhiti fled to India. His abrupt departure led to uprisings among the troops he had controlled in Yarkand and Yangiser, who executed all Soviet-trained officials (or those suspected of Soviet sympathies) and set up their own Turkic government. At this point, Ma Hushan, the self-proclaimed king of Dunganistan, showed up with his forces. His goals remain uncertain: he claimed to be "putting down the rebels" in the name of the Nationalist government in Nanjing; he was in contact with the Soviets, promising to bring peace and stability to the south; and he claimed to the British consulate to be "acting in covenant with the Turkis with a view to over-throwing the Provincial Government and replacing it by an Islamic Government offering strict allegiance to Nanjing."[36] At this point, the Soviets intervened in force. On September 1, the Osh and Naryn Regiments of the Soviet Army, both based in Kyrgyzstan, went into action alongside Sheng's forces, with air cover provided by the Soviet air force. The Dungan forces were routed, and the Soviets occupied Kashgar, Yarkand, Yengisar, and Khotan. The aerial bombing was deadly (some émigré sources put the death toll at eighty thousand people) and the political aftermath even bloodier. Sheng's political police arrested and executed thousands of Dungan and Turkic troops.[37] Soviet power had finally put Sheng in control of all of Xinjiang.

Sheng then unleashed a very Soviet-style purge against "traitors," "pan-Turkists," "enemies of the people," imperialist spies, and Japanese agents. This wave of arrests and executions took thousands of lives, including large shares of the Uyghur and Dungan intelligentsia. Khoja Niyaz, the president and betrayer of the ETR, who had since 1934 served as Sheng's deputy in Xinjiang, was now accused of being a Japanese agent and executed. Several White Russian generals who had helped Sheng come to power in 1933 also lost their lives. After that, the weak pretense of giving positions to members of the local population was abandoned, and Sheng came to rule solely on the basis of Han power.

His alliance with the Soviets had led Sheng to form a partnership with Chinese Communists, many of whom had been sent to work in Xinjiang. Yet he remained wary of them and attempted to free himself of their influence. In 1938, as the threat of a European war escalated, Sheng was granted a visit to the Kremlin, where Stalin himself received him on three occasions. Sheng was now enough of an asset that Stalin agreed to his admission to the Communist Party of the Soviet Union. After Sheng returned, he asked Moscow to "grant my request that the Comintern order the officials of the Chinese Communist Party in Xinjiang to liquidate the Party organization and abolish the secret meetings of the cells." He justified the request by arguing that "the culturally backward nationalities of Xinjiang [that is, its indigenous population] will find out about the arrival in Xinjiang of Chinese Communists and this will provide an opportunity for imperialist agents to spread rumors and provocations."[38] On the eve of the Second World War, Sheng had positioned himself as a Soviet Communist, the guarantor of a secure border to the Soviet Union, but an opponent of both the Nationalists and the Communists in China. As the 1930s departed, Xinjiang was tightly knit to the Soviet Union, a solid buffer between Soviet Central Asia and Japanese expansionism. The Japanese invasion of China proper in 1937 only strengthened Sheng's dependence on the Soviets. Yet the Second World War was to bring many twists and turns in that relationship, as it transformed the Soviet Union itself.

15

The Crucible of War

THE SECOND WORLD WAR finally came to the Soviet Union on June 22, 1941. Stalin had sought to avoid armed conflict with Germany at all costs, even signing a treaty of nonaggression with the Nazi regime in 1939. He had good reason to believe that the Soviet Union was not ready for war. The blood that the Soviet regime had spilled in the 1930s meant that it could not take the loyalty of its citizens for granted. In addition, the purges that had devastated the political elites had also reached into the upper echelons of the armed forces, and many generals had been demoted, imprisoned, or shot. For all of the forced industrialization of the decade, the country was in no shape to fight a war. Stalin even signed a treaty of non-aggression with Nazi Germany to stave off involvement in a war. Hitler, however, made the decision for Stalin when, two years into the war, he unilaterally terminated the pact and launched a frontal assault on the Soviet Union.

The beginning of the war was inauspicious for the Soviets. Nazi forces drove deep into Soviet territory, destroying large chunks of the Soviet armies and occupying major sections of the country's industrial heartland. In the first six months, more than 800,000 Soviet troops were killed, 1.3 million were wounded, and 2.3 million were taken prisoner by the Nazis. The Soviet regime, its hands drenched in the blood of its own citizens after a decade of trauma, faced a major crisis of morale. Defeatism was rampant among citizens who had been victims of collectivization and other forms of state terror. Nevertheless, the regime launched a desperate, all-out effort that mobilized the country's resources and eventually led to victory. That war effort changed much about the country and the minds of its citizens.

Central Asia was far away from the front lines, and it did not suffer the devastation that the front did. Nevertheless, the effects of the war in Central Asia were transformative at many levels. Central Asians of all backgrounds went off to war, where they fought alongside members of all Soviet nationalities. In marked contrast to the First World War, where the Tsarist regime's attempts to mobilize the indigenous population had led to the massive uprising of 1916 and heightened Central Asia's difference from the rest of the empire, the Second World War integrated the region into the Soviet state. The war brought the Soviet Union to Central Asia and made Central Asians Soviet.

———

In many ways, war brought liberation—from the economy of distribution, the dictates of cotton, the ideological straitjacket that had suffocated all public discourse, and even the campaign against religion. With all resources devoted to the war, the Soviet state gave up its monopoly on food distribution, assigning the responsibility for the food supply to localities and local organizations. Given that 40 percent of the Soviet Union's arable land had been occupied by the Germans in the first weeks of the war, food production took precedence over even cotton, whose acreage plummeted. The breakdown of the central supply system brought enormous hardships but also a revival of older practices that had been outlawed for a decade and a half. The political police noted with alarm the reappearance in the Ferghana valley of feasts celebrating life-cycle events such as births, weddings, and funerals in Muslim families.[1] The ideological ardor of the political police was not always shared by the state, which very early on decided to fight the war on patriotic, not ideological, lines. The slogan of Socialism in One Country had rendered socialism and Soviet patriotism synonymous in important ways. Now, the war became the Great Patriotic War, in which all the various peoples of the multinational Soviet state fought shoulder to shoulder for the defense of their common homeland. That common homeland was socialist by definition, but the war effort had little place for talk of proletarian solidarity or the international class struggle. Heroism was to be measured by loyalty to the state and the Soviet people.

———

The state even made peace with religion. It permitted the reopening of places of worship and co-opted religious rhetoric for the war effort. From the outset, the Russian Orthodox Church issued patriotic proclamations summoning believers to the defense of the homeland. In July 1941, Abdurahman Rasulev, the head of the Central Spiritual Administration of Muslims, the successor to the Orenburg Spiritual Assembly founded by Catherine the Great in 1788, called on all Soviet Muslims "to rise up in defense of their native land, to pray in the mosques for the victory of the Red Army and to give their blessing to their sons who are fighting in a just cause."[2] In Uzbekistan, imams in several mosques supported the war effort in the first Friday sermons after the outbreak of war.[3] Central Asian *ulama*—a group that had barely survived the 1930s—threw their energies into the war effort, mobilizing support at a time of low morale and gathering donations for the front. The regime appreciated these efforts but also sought to oversee them. To this end, it decided to allow the creation of a spiritual administration in Central Asia on the pattern of the Central Spiritual Administration of Muslims.[4] A group of *ulama* in Tashkent was then tasked with petitioning the state to allow the convocation of a conference of ulama from across Central Asia with the goal of establishing such an organization. The lead in this was taken by the octogenarian Naqshbandi shaykh Ishan Babakhan ibn Abdulmajid Khan of Tashkent. Babakhan was a scholar of some prominence who had suffered along with all other *ulama* in the 1930s. His house had been confiscated, and he had been in and out of prison in the late 1930s. Now, he was eager to help in the war effort. He was summoned to Moscow, where he evidently met with Stalin—who offered him tea and asked about the mood of the Muslim population.[5] Babakhan returned to Tashkent to host a conference of *ulama* from across the five republics of Central Asia, which then established the Spiritual Administration for the Muslims of Central Asia and Kazakhstan (or SADUM, as it was commonly known after its Russian initials). In September 1943 the Bishops' Council of the Russian Orthodox Church met for the first time since the revolution and elected members of the Holy Synod of the Church. The wartime Soviet state was mobilizing all religious forces for the war effort.

SADUM, like the Tsarist-era Orenburg Spiritual Assembly, was half church and half ministry of religious affairs. Its establishment was a significant landmark in the history of Islam in Central Asia, for such an institution had never before existed there. Konstantin Kaufman had ensured that Turkestan remained beyond the assembly's jurisdiction. However, reformers had come to see some sort of a bureaucratic institution as necessary for the implementation of reform, and in the years after the revolution they had therefore established *mahkama-yi shar'iya* (*shariat* administrations) at the local level. Soviet authorities had never allowed these local administrations to coalesce into a single unified entity and had dismantled them in 1927. Now, at the height of the Second World War, the authorities did an about-face and allowed the *ulama* to establish something much more centralized and more extensive, with a jurisdiction that spanned all five republics. For the first time in the history of Muslim Central Asia, its *ulama* had come together in a ramified bureaucratic institution.

The *ulama* who worked to establish SADUM hoped to mark out a space in which Islam and Islamic practice could exist legally and be tolerated. To achieve this goal, they were quite willing to help with the war effort. One of the first acts of SADUM was the publication of the "Appeal to All Muslims of the Soviet Union," in which Babakhan exhorted "the Muslims of Turkestan and Kazakhstan" to

> join hands in union with the brother-nations of our state, and, in perfect friendship and with the zeal and intensity of lions, struggle against Hitler's accursed [army]; annihilate the vile fascists without mercy; wipe them from the face of the earth; protect every last inch of the Soviet land with every last drop of your blood; fight with perfect loyalty and intensely, that it will not fall into the hands of the

enemy; make your battle lines firm like iron; be steadfast in your military discipline; follow the orders of your commanders, never shrinking from [your duty], and execute your orders with all haste and perfect loyalty.[6]

The appeal used specifically religious vocabulary, declaring the war to be a "general and sacred jihad, [a] holy war," and asserting that "every Muslim who sacrifices himself for God in the path of religion is a martyr. And every single Muslim who slays the accursed and seditious enemy is a warrior for the faith."[7] The *ulama* remained loyal to the state, despite all that they had suffered in the previous decade and a half. They were motivated by a fundamental faith in the necessity of order and the legitimacy of those who upheld order. It was the same faith that had allowed them to accept Tsarist rule. Now, in much harsher conditions, they remained loyal to the Stalinist state.

———

But if war brought some sense of liberation, its overriding effect was one of immense privation and sacrifice. Central Asians were full participants in the war: the region sent men to fight at the front and contributed to the war effort through extra labor and taxation. The hardship of war was felt across society, for it left few families untouched. The experience transformed the identities of the men who fought, and it brought the elderly and women into Soviet life as never before.

Military service was still new to the region. Central Asians had been drafted into so-called national units of the Red Army since the 1920s. These were units with commanders fluent in the local language that were deployed at home to defend Soviet borders and maintain law and order (and to fight "bandits"). They were not interchangeable parts of the Red Army. Universal conscription into the Soviet army was decreed only in 1938, as Stalin prepared for the possibility of war. Few Central Asians had previous experience of service in the army when, in 1941, the state declared a general mobilization of the population, calling up all male citizens between the ages of 18 and 50 regardless of their ethnicity or place of residence. Over the course of the war, 3.4 million Central Asians were drafted into the army, where they served alongside men of all Soviet nationalities. They saw action at the front, and many of them were among the troops that liberated eastern Europe from the Nazis and hoisted the Soviet flag on the Reichstag in Berlin.

Over the course of the war, the Soviet army called up 1.5 million people from Uzbekistan out of a population of 6.5 million. Some 500,000 never returned.[8] Kazakhstan, where the horrors of the collectivization famine were very recent, yielded 1.2 million soldiers, of whom approximately 450,000 were ethnic Kazakhs.[9] By the time the war ended, an estimated 314,000 people of Central Asian nationalities had lost their lives in combat.[10] There were noncombat deaths as well, though of course they were not as heavy as the casualties at the front. The departure of so many men to the front forced women to work outside the home. In Uzbekistan, the war finally unveiled women and brought them into the labor force, even as it made them more vulnerable to the excesses of administrative control over them.[11] Central Asians also mobilized to fund war matériel and to contribute goods that were sent to the front. The army requisitioned large numbers of horses and practically the entire supply of transport vehicles in Central Asia, while existing industry switched to producing material for the war.

———

Faced with the alarmingly rapid German advance in the first weeks of the war, the Soviet government ordered the evacuation of important personnel and whole sectors of the economy to the interior. The evacuees included political figures, academics, and intellectuals, some as individuals and others as parts of research or artistic organizations. In addition, factories were disassembled, put on trains, and moved to cities in the Volga-Urals region, Siberia, and Central Asia. In 1941–1942, Kazakhstan received 532,000 civilians and 50,000 skilled technical workers who had been evacuated from the war zone. The numbers were greater in Uzbekistan, which received over a million people, including 200,000 orphaned children. Tashkent was a major destination for evacuees, and for two years it hosted some of Russia's foremost poets and artists, who created a set of literary salons for the duration. The Leningrad Conservatory also moved to Tashkent, as did a number of research institutes. But the main goal of the evacuation was to preserve the defense industry of the country, and it was the factories transplanted to Central Asia that were the central concern of the managers of the evacuation. More than 300 factories were established in Kazakhstan during the war, and over 280 in Uzbekistan.[12] Until the war, industrialization had been very light in Central Asia, as the emerging model of regional specialization had consigned the region to the role of producer of raw materials. Now, heavy industry appeared overnight, with considerable investment in new construction and infrastructural projects such as hydroelectric plants. Nevertheless, evacuation was a logistical nightmare. There was little infrastructure in Central Asia to establish heavy industry. For example, factories often found their new locations insufficient and energy sources vastly inadequate. The influx of large numbers of people put a strain on housing and supplies of food and water—particularly in Tashkent, whose population swelled to well over a million during the war (the 1939 census had counted 585,000 people in the city).

The impact of the evacuation was mixed. Evacuated people and institutions tended to displace existing local institutions in the priorities of the planners. Nor did the new industry create many new jobs, since factories arrived with their own workers. But the evacuation also brought the Soviet Union to Central Asia in meaningful ways while simultaneously brining Central Asia into the Soviet Union. For many of the evacuees, their time in Central Asia was their first encounter with the Soviet East. Many of them returned home with fond memories of the kindness and hospitality they had received. They also brought back with them knowledge of the culture and the cuisine of Central Asia that reshaped the region's image in broader Soviet culture. Many factories returned to their original locations after 1944, but some remained in Central Asia, including the giant Moscow Aviation Factory no. 84 that had relocated to Tashkent, where it continued to operate until 2015. Visiting academics also helped establish Uzbekistan's Academy of Sciences in 1943. And the evacuation had led to the construction of power plants and hydroelectric projects. In general, the unexpected wartime evacuation laid the foundation of heavy industry in Central Asia, something that had not been in Soviet plans before the war.

————

The biggest impact of the war was on the way Central Asians thought about the Soviet Union; their place in it; and, ultimately, themselves. The war transformed people's sense of self and belonging and made them into Soviet citizens in a way that few Central Asians had been before the war. The families of those who did not return from the front were of course profoundly affected. Kyrgyz or Uzbek peasants who did return came back as Soviet citizens, the experience of fighting shoulder to shoulder with men from across the union having broadened their horizons. But the war also involved those who donated voluntarily to the war effort, whose organizations gathered money to pay for war planes or tanks, who wrote letters to soldiers at the front, who suffered food and housing shortages, and who took in Russian or Ukrainian orphans as foster children. It brought Central Asians into a new community of Soviet citizens—not a community based on any sense of global revolution or socialism, but "a community of suffering and heroism created by the war."[13]

In 1942, official Soviet rhetoric began to present the war as a national war for each of the many nations inhabiting the Soviet Union. Party officials and writers of each nation drafted letters from "the people" to their warriors at the front that were published locally and in the central newspapers *Pravda* and *Izvestiia*.[14] These letters depicted German malevolence as directed against all Soviet nationalities, not just Russians. They used powerful poetic language and invoked each nation's geography and history. The letter from the Uzbek nation, composed by a number of leading Uzbek writers, was read out at multiple public meetings, and a total of 2,412,000 people signed it. It was then published in both Uzbek and Russian in *Pravda*. In the letter, "the Uzbek nation" informed its soldiers that

The enemy wants to develop slave markets where it will sell free Uzbeks like cattle. It wants to turn our canals built with love into rivers of blood, to bring about an age worse than that of the Manghit emir of Bukhara or the bloodthirsty khans of Khiva and Khoqand. It wants to raze to the ground the Samarqand of the great Uzbek poet Navoiy and the astronomer Ulughbek, the Ferghana of the Uzbek poet Muqimiy, the Bukhara of Turobiy, the hero who fought against the Mongol invaders. . . . Hitler intends to destroy our literature and our pens, our books and our poetry, our songs and our music, our cozy homes and our silken nights, the beauty of our women, the peace of our elderly, the quiet sleep of our children.[15]

The Tajik nation's letter was published only in Russian, but it reminded Tajik soldiers that "when we speak of the Motherland, we think not only of the lush abundance of the Vakhsh valley, not only of the apricot and apple orchards of Leninobod, the snow-covered peaks of the Pamirs that reach out to the sky: our Motherland is also the green forests and wide rivers of Russia, the fertile fields of Ukraine, the picturesque shores of the Black Sea . . . and the cradle of the revolution—the great city of Lenin."[16] The national and the Soviet were deeply intertwined in these letters.

The letters were an important feat of political mobilization. Officers recalled how effective they were in boosting morale among soldiers, and there were stories of Uzbek troops keeping these letters with them as talismans. Wartime literature and theater similarly sought suitably local and national heroes to inspire Central Asians. It glorified Central Asian figures of past generations who had struggled against (non-Russian) foreign invaders. Muqanna, the "veiled prophet" who fought Arab armies in Merv in the eighth century, was cast as an Uzbek national hero, and Temur Malik, who defended Khujand against Chinggis Khan's armies in the thirteenth century, became a Tajik national hero. Both were the subjects of several novels and plays that appeared during the war. Along with the use of religious vocabulary by SADUM, this nationalization of the war effort welded the Soviet and the national together. It made it possible to be Uzbek or Kazakh or Tajik and Soviet and Muslim at the same time.

There was another side to the war, however. Over the course of the war, German armies captured more than 5.7 million Soviet soldiers as prisoners of war. Most of them were treated with remarkable cruelty (an astounding 3.5 million of them died in captivity), but the Nazis also made a deliberate attempt to recruit non-Russian soldiers in national units to fight against the Soviets in a quest for national liberation. The result was the organization of a number of so-called Eastern Troops (*Osttruppen*), units commanded by German officers but composed of soldiers from a number of non-Russian nationalities. One of these was the Turkestan Legion, recruited from Soviet Central Asian prisoners of war.

The first Central Asians started arriving in Nazi concentration camps in the late summer of 1941. Their path from their kolkhoz to the prison camp had been remarkably short. Most of them had never held a rifle in their hands before they were conscripted, put in a uniform, and (with the slightest modicum of military training) dispatched to the front, where they were promptly taken prisoner if they did not get killed. The chance of getting killed did not diminish with captivity. The Soviet Union had not signed the 1929 Geneva Convention on the Treatment of Prisoners of War, so Soviet troops did not have the legal protection of POW status. Over the summer and autumn of 1941, Schutzstaffel (SS) squads—and, apparently, ordinary soldiers—executed many Muslim prisoners of war because they were circumcised, which to the Nazis proved that they were Jews. In another instance, a group of Central Asian prisoners was transported to a concentration camp in the Netherlands to be exhibited to skeptical Dutch communists as examples of the *Untermenschen* ("subhumans") to be found in the Soviet Union. Many did not survive the maltreatment and the winter, and the seventy-seven who did were marched into the woods in April 1942 and executed.[17]

Even as these executions continued, Nazi authorities took the first steps toward organizing the Turkestan Legion. They sought collaborators in the tiny Central Asian émigré community. One figure was Vali

Qayum-Khan, one of the students sent to study in Germany by the Bukharan republic in 1922–1923. Qayum-Khan had managed to stay behind when the Soviets canceled the students' stipends and recalled them to the Soviet Union. In 1941, he attracted the attention of German authorities. The Nazis also sought out Mustafa Choqay, the head of the short-lived autonomous government of Turkestan in 1917–1918. Choqay had been living in the Paris suburb of Nogent-sur-Marne, where he published *Yosh Turkiston* (Young Turkestan), a modest journal for the émigré community, and through his lecturing, he had become the sole voice of the Central Asian emigration in Europe. He was arrested after hostilities with the Soviet Union began and placed in a camp in Compiègne with other émigrés from the former Russian empire. From there he was summoned to Berlin to work with Central Asian POWs. He was curious to meet Central Asians for the first time in a generation and to take stock of the situation. He was dismayed by what he saw. Food, clothing, and shelter were all inadequate, while summary executions for being circumcised continued. "It is not possible to relate all the various cases of senseless executions in Dębica," he wrote to Qayum-Khan after visiting a concentration camp in Poland. "Every time I left the camp, I saw several corpses with smashed skulls. . . . One wonders how much of this is because of the 'Asiatic contagion' about which loudspeakers scream everyday all over Germany."[18] He had no sympathy for the Nazi cause, but he was moved by the idea that a Nazi triumph would destroy the Soviet Union and liberate Central Asia: "Yes, we have no path, other than the anti-Soviet path, other than the wish for victory over Soviet Russia and over Russian Bolshevism. This path, regardless of our will, is laid through Germany. And it is strewn with the corpses of those executed in Dębica."[19] This "small and pitiful speculative trade in human misfortune" was necessary to achieve the goal of national liberation.

Choqay contracted typhus in one of the camps and passed away in Berlin on December 27, 1941, but Qayum-Khan lived to see the establishment of the Turkestan Legion on January 13, 1942. He became chair of the Turkestan Committee of National Unity (TCNU), an ostensible government in exile that was established as the political wing of the legion. It published a magazine titled *Millij Turkistan* (National Turkestan) that was distributed to the recruits and preached the goal of national liberation: "In order to obtain the independence of Turkestan, it is necessary to gather the might of all Turkestanis in one place and to use it for struggle," declared the TCNU.[20] "Turkestan" here meant the five republics of Central Asia, which was more extensive than the Turkestan that had been declared autonomous at Kokand in 1917. It is difficult to say whether that idea had any purchase on the imaginations of those who enlisted in the legion. Men joined for a variety of reasons. The thirst for national liberation was often combined with the much more practical concern of escaping the creeping death promised by the prison camps. Estimates for the numbers of men in the Turkestan Legion range from 110,000 to 180,000 over the course of the war. Some of them participated in the Nazi invasion of the Caucasus in 1942, and others fought U.S. forces in northern Italy in the last stages of the war. Six battalions of *Osttruppen* were part of the last-ditch defense of Berlin in 1945. But most of the time, the legion was tasked with fighting partisans behind Nazi lines or providing security in occupied zones in Ukraine, Slovakia, and France.[21] Tens of thousands of members of the legion lost their lives in battle.

———

Had the war ended differently, we might be writing about the Turkestan Legion in a different vein. In the event, however, there is no question that among Central Asians loyalty to the Soviet Union won out over the temptation to defect. If some *Osttruppen* defended Berlin, there were a great many more Central Asians among the Red Army troops that took the city, as well as others in Nazi-occupied Europe. The story of the sons of Central Asian villages who stormed European capitals to deliver their residents from the Nazi yoke is usually forgotten, but it is an important one nevertheless, for it capped a period of rapid transformation. The millions of Central Asians mobilized in the war produced many remarkable figures who were widely celebrated as both Soviet and national heroes. Sabir Rahimov (1902–1945), a Kazakh from Tashkent, rose to the rank of major general, the first Central Asian to achieve that rank.

He died in battle on the eve of victory while commanding a division that had taken Danzig (Gdańsk) in the final Soviet push into Nazi Germany. The members of the Panfilov Division, a multinational unit, were recruited in southern Kazakhstan and Kyrgyzstan at the beginning of the war. The division took part in the Battle of Moscow in late 1941, where twenty-eight of its fighters were supposed to have died in action after destroying eighteen German tanks and otherwise helping stop the German attack. In post-Soviet times, some of the details of the story turned out to have been fabricated, but the Twenty-Eight Panfilovtsy passed into legend and were celebrated throughout the Soviet Union as exemplars both of Soviet multinationalism and of Central Asia's contribution to the war. A small number of Central Asian women also saw combat. Among them were two recipients of the title Hero of the Soviet Union, the highest military honor in the country (and awarded to only ninety women during the war): the sniper Äliya Moldaghülova (1925–1944) and the machine gunner Mänshuk Mämetova (1922–1944), both Kazakhs. There were many other heroes. The Kazakh pilot Talghat Begeldinov (1922–2014) flew 305 combat missions and was made a Hero of the Soviet Union twice (a very rare feat). Hundreds of Central Asians received that title. Their deeds were celebrated widely and made them part of both a pan-Soviet pantheon of heroes as well as a national one.

The millions of ordinary veterans who survived returned home with their sense of the world and of themselves transformed. They had seen the world far beyond their villages, formed friendships with comrades from across the Soviet Union, and learned Russian. Some of them had taken Russian nicknames or married Russian women.[22] But all of them came back with a sense of themselves as Soviet citizens, part of a greater whole. For the rest of the Soviet period, the Great Patriotic War functioned as the node around which a Soviet patriotism emerged that knit together the various Soviet nationalities. Common sacrifice and struggle became the primary locus for Central Asians' entry into full-fledged Soviet citizenship. Participation in the war worked at the level of individual lived experience and became the most common trope in Soviet public discourse for asserting common citizenship for Central Asians.

Down to the end of the Soviet period, service and sacrifice in the war remained the foremost form of asserting a common Soviet identity for the country's multinational population. In Central Asia, this trope appeared in thousands of novels, films, and plays. Central Asian veterans wore their medals just as proudly as any other Soviet citizen. The Great Patriotic War had made Central Asians into Soviets.

―――――

But the Soviet victory was not a simple tale of moral triumph. It came at a great cost, and the victors suffered great tribulations. Once the Germans were beaten back, the Soviet state turned its wrath on those whom it accused of collaboration. The indictment was collective—it was not individuals, but whole national groups that stood accused of treason to the socialist motherland—and so was the punishment. Entire populations of the accused nations were deported and their republics dismantled. The deportations involved several nationalities of the north Caucasus (Chechens, Ingushes, Karachays, Balkars, Meskhetian [Ahıska] Turks, and Kalmyks) and the Crimean Tatars. Modern states have frequently used deportations and forced population movements as a tool for fashioning a perfect body politic. Deportations excise harmful elements from the state and, by putting them to useful labor, give them a chance at redemption. The Soviets had embraced this technique from the beginning, although many of the deportations of the 1920s were justified in terms of class enmity (alleged *kulaks* constituted a large group of deportees during collectivization). By the 1930s, the logic had turned national, and it was national, not social, groups that were being deported. In 1937, almost 172,000 Soviet Koreans had been forcibly removed from the Far East and resettled in Central Asia. In the first weeks of the war, the entire population of Volga Germans, descendants of farmers invited in the eighteenth century by Catherine the Great to settle on the land, had been deported to the Soviet interior. The deportations after the German retreat were part of this broader phenomenon. Central Asia was the main dumping ground for this round of deportations as well.

The deportations of 1943–1944 involved more than a million people. They were hurried, brutal affairs, in which people were given only a few hours to gather their belongings before being put on cattle trains and sent east. Large numbers of people died in transit, as did many more in the first year in exile. Once they arrived in Central Asia, they found little sympathy from host societies, their common Muslimness and Turkicness notwithstanding. The deportees were extra mouths to feed, and they were also perceived as traitors. Uzbek villagers grumbled that, having sacrificed for the war, they now had to live alongside enemies of the state. The Uzbek man who complained that such "traitors" should not have been "sent to a good place like Uzbekistan, they at least should have been sent to a place in Siberia for their crime against the Motherland,"[23] spoke as a Soviet patriot. In their own perverse way, the deportations strengthened Central Asians' identification with the Soviet state.

The Soviet state also treated returning POWs with suspicion and great cruelty. At the beginning of the war, the Supreme High Command of the Soviet Army had, over Stalin's signature, issued the infamous Order No. 270, according to which "commanders and political officers who, during combat tear off their insignia and desert to the rear or surrender to the enemy, [were to] be considered malicious deserters whose families are subject to arrest as a family for violation of an oath and betrayal of their homeland."[24] This equation of being taken prisoner with having deserted and committed treason never went away. Returning POWs passed through "filtration camps," where they had to convince the political police that they had not collaborated. They could be redrafted, sent to labor battalions, or even end up in the Gulag. Some Central Asian POWs, both those who had fought in the Turkestan Legion and those who had not, managed to avoid repatriation. They joined the small Central Asian diaspora in Turkey, Saudi Arabia, and Western Europe. Several members of the Turkestan Legion survived. Vali Qayum-Khan stayed in Germany and continued to publish *Millij Turkistan*. Baymirza Hayit earned a PhD in Central Asian history from the University of Cologne in 1950 and became a prominent historian. The onset of the Cold War improved things for the former legionnaires, for the transition from Nazi anti-Communism to its American variant proved all too easy. Many of them found work at Radio Liberty, the U.S.-funded propaganda service aimed at the Soviet Union. Ruzi Nazar, another leading light of the Turkestan Legion, worked his way into the favor of American occupation authorities and joined the Central Intelligence Agency (CIA) in 1951. He spent the rest of his career fighting Communism for the United States, all the way up to the war in Afghanistan in the 1980s.[25] Another lasting legacy of the Turkestan Legion was the vision of Central Asian unity articulated by the TCNU. Largely through the work of scholars such as Hayit, that vision became axiomatic among the few scholars in the West who concerned themselves with Central Asia, although it had no traction in the region itself.

16

Another Republic in Eastern Turkestan

IN OCTOBER 1944, hundreds of armed rebels stormed the garrison in the small town of Nilka in the far northwest of Xinjiang and forced the Han troops stationed there to withdraw. The rebels then marched on Ghulja, the capital of Ili district, and assaulted it on November 7. According to émigré accounts, the Muslim population of the town and neighboring villages rose up and, armed with old rifles or knives, came to the aid of the insurgents.[1] The rebels took Ghulja after three days of fighting and drove out the Han troops garrisoned there. The rebels had achieved stunning military successes, and over the next nine months, they pushed Chinese forces out of the three northwestern districts of Ili, Altay, and Tarbaghatay.

Even before they had full control of the city, the rebels had proclaimed a republic. The second ETR was established in Ghulja on November 12, the eleventh anniversary of the foundation of the first ETR in Kashgar. The new government, whose members were announced in the same month, included religious dignitaries, prominent merchants and landholders of Ghulja and its environs, and modernist intellectuals.[2] The government was headed by Alikhan Tora Shakirjanov (b. 1885), an Islamic scholar of great renown in Ghulja. Much like the *ulama* who were involved in the first ETR, he had a modernist bent and had been profoundly influenced by Turkist ideas. More surprisingly, he was an

Uzbek born in Toqmaq (in what is now Kyrgyzstan), who had fled the Soviet Union in 1931 after an arrest for "anti-Soviet work." The republic's earliest proclamations combined Islamic and national themes in much the same way as the first ETR had done. An example is this text in a translation made by the U.S. consulate in Ürümchi: "The Turkestan Islam Government is organized: praise be to Allah for his manifold blessings! . . . We will not throw down our arms until we have made you free from the five bloody fingers of the Chinese oppressors' power, nor until the very roots of the Chinese oppressors' government have dried and died away from the face of the earth of East Turkestan, which we have inherited as our native land from our fathers and grandfathers."[3] Other statements claimed Eastern Turkestan as the homeland of its indigenous population and disavowed any historical links to China: "Of the fourteen nations living in East Turkestan, the ten nations accounted the most numerous have had no national, racial or cultural relationship nor any community of blood with the Chinese, nor did any ever exist."[4] Although this proclamation spoke of fourteen nationalities living in Turkestan, using the Soviet-style classificatory scheme introduced by Sheng Shicai, other statements spoke of "the peoples of Eastern Turkestan" as a single nation, going back to the rhetoric of the first ETR. Like the first, the second ETR was explicitly secessionist. It used the language of anticolonial nationalism to protest the Han Chinese occupation of Eastern Turkestan.

Yet the circumstances of the second republic differed substantially from those of the first. The new republic had been proclaimed not in Altishahr but in the Ili valley in the northwest of Xinjiang. Kazakhs formed the largest part of its population, and there were substantial populations of Mongols and the Sibe, in addition to the Uyghurs. Many Kazakh groups had been in revolt in Altay before the November 1944 uprising, while the Mongols and Sibe had their own grievances. The Ili National Army, as the republic's forces were called, included recruits from several nationalities, including a Sibe cavalry company.[5] If the first ETR had risen amid a general crisis related to Han rule over Xinjiang, the second was proclaimed against the central government, which had regained control of the province and was asserting its authority there.

And while the first ETR had been opposed by the Soviet Union, the second had its full support. The second ETR lasted for five years, rather than the three months that the first had managed. While its leadership changed and its rhetoric evolved over these five years, it exercised all the duties of a government. It organized a new administration at the county level, issued its own currency and revenue stamps, carried out campaigns for land reform, oversaw infrastructure growth in its territory, and maintained armed forces that allowed it to exercise real sovereignty over the three districts it controlled.

———————

These differences between the two republics were the result of massive geopolitical transformations in Xinjiang set in motion by the Second World War. Sheng reconsidered his options when the war came to the Soviet Union in 1941. His need for outside help in maintaining his regime remained, but the massive reverses the Soviet Union suffered in the first months of the war made him wonder about the viability of continued Soviet support. The entry of the United States (a wealthy, powerful ally of the GMD) into the war also altered Sheng's calculus, for it made the GMD appear to be a safer bet than the Soviet Union. Furthermore, Stalin had upped the ante for Sheng. In 1940, with war imminent, Stalin imposed a new agreement on Sheng, according to which the Soviet Union leased Xinjiang's tin mines for a period of fifty years and Soviet specialists acquired the right to unfettered exploration and exploitation of the province's resources. Sheng began grumbling to the members of his inner circle that Lenin and Stalin had no understanding of Marxism and that the Soviet Union was simply engaged in "red colonialism."[6] Then on March 19, 1942, Sheng's younger brother Shiqi, a Soviet-trained general in the Xinjiang provincial forces, was murdered in mysterious circumstances. Sheng Shicai blamed the murder on a "Communist plot" that had been concocted in Soviet institutions in Xinjiang with the aims of "disrupt[ing] the rear area of the defensive war of China [against Japan]" and "overthrow[ing] the existing government of Xinjiang," and he claimed that the Soviet consul general Bakulin had

led the conspiracy.[7] Sheng broke off relations with the Soviets, suspend-
ing all trade with them, closing the border with the Soviet Union, and
asking Soviet advisors and technicians to leave Xinjiang. He also persecuted the many Chinese Communists who had been sent to work in
Xinjiang. Among the victims was Mao Zemin (the younger brother of
Mao Zedong), who had served as provincial treasurer. He was accused
of having masterminded a vast conspiracy that "had penetrated every
organ of government and was directed jointly by Moscow and Yenan,"
the headquarters of the CCP, and executed.[8] Sheng then reached out
to the GMD and began the process of reintegrating the province into
the Chinese state. By the summer of 1942, the GMD had begun moving
its troops into Xinjiang and had established a branch of the party there
for the first time.

There was one more twist in the story. In the spring of 1943—after
the Soviet victory at Stalingrad, when the tide had turned in the favor
of the Soviet Union—Sheng attempted to switch sides again. He arrested GMD representatives in Xinjiang and asked Stalin for help
against the "Japanese conspiracy" that he had just crushed. Stalin had
had enough. He leaked Sheng's letter to Chiang Kai-shek and washed his
hands of Sheng. Sheng was removed from office by the GMD and sent
to Chongqing to take up the position of minister of agriculture and forestry. He was rumored to have avoided execution only by giving a massive donation to the GMD treasury from the funds he had accumulated
in his decade in power in Xinjiang. (Things worked out fine for Sheng.
He worked for the GMD until its defeat in 1949, when he retreated to
Taiwan with the rest of the party's leaders. He died in his bed in 1970.)
The GMD appointed Wu Zhongxin to succeed Sheng as governor of
Xinjiang. For the first time in the republican era, the province was under
at least the nominal control of the central government.

How was the GMD to integrate the province into China? In its early
years, under Comintern pressure, it had recognized the right of self-
determination for all *minzus* (nationalities) in China, but without accepting the notion of territorial autonomy.[9] The Japanese invasion of
China in 1937 changed things dramatically, leading the GMD to emphasize unity above all else. A racialist vision of the nation that harked back

to the anti-Manchu racism of the early twentieth century emerged. This view was best articulated in a little book titled *China's Destiny* that appeared under Chiang Kai-shek's name in 1943 and became required reading for all party members. The book had in fact been ghostwritten by the historian Tao Xisheng, who asserted that a single Chinese nation (*Zhonghua minzu*) had existed as a whole for five thousand years, during which time it had "grown by a gradual amalgamation of various stocks into a harmonious and organic whole." The various "stocks" (*zongzu*) had scattered across the land, from the Pamirs to the Amur River basin, and "due to their different geographic environments, they had developed different cultures." But despite their diversity, "they had either a common ancestry or were related to one another through many generations of intermarriage."[10] Non-Han peoples were not minorities or frontier peoples, but part of a single ancient and homogeneous Chinese nation. This vision underlay GMD policies as the party set out to "recover sovereignty over Xinjiang." It planned to "develop" the northwest by implanting in it as many as one million Han settlers (the total population of Xinjiang at that time was around four million). In addition, the government hoped to maintain 100,000 Han and Hui troops in the province. This outlook—that Xinjiang could be integrated into China by Chinese settlement, administration, and military occupation—had a long history in Chinese statecraft, although no previous government had been able to accomplish its goals. Xinjiang's problems lay not in the imposition of Chinese rule over an alien population but merely in "shoddy infrastructure and incessant foreign meddling."[11] The foreign meddling was Soviet, of course. One way of rolling back Soviet influence was to invite the United States and Great Britain to open consulates in Ürümchi. Both powers accepted with alacrity. The United States was a completely new presence in Central Asia, and this was the first time that Britain had been able to open a consulate in the north of Xinjiang.

Not surprisingly, GMD's assimilationist policies did not sit well with the local population. The grievances were of long standing. They ranged from unhappiness with the callous behavior of Han officials and widespread police repression to concerns about Chinese troops' treatment of local women. The Sheng era had seen expansion of Uyghur-language education and of the press. The latter was under Sheng's political control, but it nevertheless created a reading community that spanned the province and made the population politically aware. Sheng's closure of the border with the Soviet Union cut both nomads and agriculturalists off from their primary markets and created a shortage of manufactured goods in Xinjiang. The GMD printed unbacked Xinjiang dollars to pay for the resulting deficits but then decided to replace the local currency with the even more inflationary Nationalist dollar at fixed rates of exchange. This came on top of a long list of exactions that Sheng had put in place before his departure. In 1943, the settlement of Han refugees on grasslands near Gucheng (Qitai) led to the forcible eviction of Kazakhs from their lands. By that autumn, Kazakhs in the Altay district and on the northern slopes of the Tien-Shan range were in revolt, under the leadership of the chieftain Osman Batur. The uprising that proclaimed the Ghulja republic in 1944 built on this dissatisfaction.

———

The extent of Soviet support for the ETR was a matter of conjuncture at the time, but the opening of Soviet archives leaves no doubt about the matter. We now know that the Soviets rendered substantial military aid to the ETR, providing everything from armaments and uniforms to military advisors and soldiers. In fact, Soviet generals commanded all military operations and were largely responsible for the successes of the ETR army. After Sheng turned on the Soviet Union, the Politburo resolved that "the Soviet government cannot tolerate such provocative activity of the *duban* which is hostile to the Soviet Union and cannot give him aid to pursue his current policy directed at oppressing the peoples of Xinjiang." Instead, the Politburo laid out a different course of action. The Soviet government was to "lend support to the non-Chinese nationalities of Xinjiang (Uyghurs, Kazakhs, Kyrgyz, Mongols, and others) in their struggle against the repressive colonial policy of the *duban* and the Xinjiang government." This support was to take the form of establishing "illegal groups ('Groups of National Revival') among each nationality in Xinjiang" and to give them help in forming "military and political cadres . . . and to provide them with the necessary armaments." The responsibility for executing this plan was assigned to the Communist parties of Kazakhstan, Kyrgyzstan, and Uzbekistan.[12] Over the next year, a substantial amount of Uyghur-language material was printed in Almaty and Tashkent and smuggled into Xinjiang. In addition, Soviet cadres, both Russian and Central Asian, poured into the northwest of Xinjiang.

This was a reversal of the long-standing Soviet policy to seek the unity of China and treat the country as a whole as a victim of imperialism. Stalin's newfound enthusiasm for supporting the anticolonial struggle of Xinjiang's non-Chinese people was rooted in nakedly geopolitical considerations as he pondered the postwar future. At the Yalta Conference, Stalin had promised Franklin D. Roosevelt and Winston Churchill to join the war against Japan after Germany was defeated. In return, he had received assurances that the Soviet Union would receive all of the privileges that Tsarist Russia had enjoyed in Manchuria before they were "violated by the treacherous attack of Japan in 1904"—including control of the port of Darien (Dalian) and the Chinese Eastern and South Manchurian railways. Gone was the early Soviet aversion to secret pacts and unequal treaties. China was not consulted. Stalin also undertook to sign the Sino-Soviet Treaty of Friendship and Alliance aimed against Japan. Soviet involvement in the ETR was a way of putting pressure on the GMD to sign the treaty without complaining about Soviet extortions in Manchuria. More broadly, the Soviets hoped to create a buffer zone around their border in which they might retain long-term strategic influence. At the same time as the Soviets intervened in Xinjiang, they also supported the secessionist Republic of Azerbaijan in northern Iran and pressured Turkey to grant Soviet shipping the right of free transit through the Dardanelles. As the Azerbaijani historian Cemil Hesenli notes, the three interventions were deeply intertwined for the Soviets.[13] They were part of a single strategy of ensuring the security of Soviet borders by implanting friendly states along them. This was good old-fashioned imperial thinking, in which the language of anticolonialism served only Soviet geopolitical goals.

Soviet support did not mean that the second ETR merely did Moscow's bidding. Even Stalin did not have a magic wand that could conjure up uprisings out of nothing. The grievances were there. They were based on the brutal military occupation that formed the basis of Chinese rule in Xinjiang and the economic hardship imposed by policies that refused to recognize the existence of non-Han peoples in Xinjiang or acknowledge that they might have any collective rights. Nor was the aspiration for nationhood and independence summoned out of nothing by the Soviets. In fact, the collaboration between the Soviets and the ETR had plenty of tensions and paradoxes. It may be less surprising that Alikhan Tora, who had fled the Soviet Union to escape persecution, worked with the Soviets in the cause of national liberation of the place of his refuge than that the Soviet government was willing to work with a former Soviet citizen—of clerical background, no less. In the 1930s, many Soviet citizens had been executed after merely being accused of wanting to leave the country. But times had changed. As the Politburo explored the possibility of fomenting an uprising, reports from the field by Soviet consular officials stressed both the profound alienation from Chinese rule in Eastern Turkestani society and the necessity of working with the clergy.[14] Stalin could be quite flexible in pursuit of his geopolitical goals. He had made peace with religion in the Soviet Union. In fact, Alikhan Tora's brother, Alimkhan, had been appointed to a leading position in Kyrgyzstan under SADUM, which had been established in 1943.

The ETR scored a number of military successes, and by the summer of 1945, its momentum seemed unstoppable. Alikhan Tora hoped that the offensive would continue and lead to the liberation of all Xinjiang. In June, he wrote to a Soviet field commander: "I hope that you will undertake all measures for speeding up an invasion of the south. Not a single minute is to be wasted. The decisive moment has arrived, it is necessary to strike the iron when it is hot."[15] Several weeks earlier, he had written directly to Stalin, "the creator of the culture and equal rights of all peoples, the great leader of the Soviet Union":

I, and the peoples of East Turkestan recently liberated from oppression, hope in you, Chief Marshal, that the peoples of East Turkestan will be liberated . . . with the aid of the Great Soviet Union, which is giving us comprehensive aid in this cause. Millions of people of East Turkestan constantly look to you as their leader, protecting the interests of oppressed peoples. We are deeply confident that we will always receive the legitimate and necessary assistance from you. We will thereby be able to expel all our oppressors from our homeland. I hope that the colonizers will be expelled if we have the aid we need from the Soviet Union.[16]

But Stalin had other concerns. Once he had signed the Treaty of Friendship and Alliance in August 1945, Stalin had little use for the rebellion in Xinjiang. He forced the ETR to sue for peace and negotiate a ceasefire. The GMD had seen the uprising simply as "the treachery of the Ili nationalities" and a result of Soviet machinations, but it was relieved at the offer and happy to begin peace negotiations.

Alikhan Tora was unhappy, and he persisted in his demands for the continuation of military action. Eventually, the Soviets got sick of him. In June 1946, he was summoned to the Soviet military headquarters in Ghulja and told that Usmon Yusupov, the head of the Uzbek Communist Party, wanted to meet him. Alikhan Tora was put in a Soviet military vehicle, driven across the border to Almaty, and flown to Tashkent, where he received an official welcome. After the welcome, however, he was taken into custody and interrogated for several months. It was not an auspicious time in the Soviet Union for people under interrogation, but Alikhan Tora survived. He was eventually allowed to live in a neighborhood in Tashkent's old city, where he spent his time practicing traditional medicine, writing, and teaching. He gave lessons on Islam in underground settings and wrote "for the desk drawer"—that is, works that could not be published in Soviet conditions. His books included a biography of the Prophet Muhammad and a memoir of his time in Eastern Turkestan that unfortunately stops short of his ascension to power. He died only in 1976.[17] We know all this now, but at the time, Alikhan's disappearance from Ghulja was completely unexplained.

Even before his removal from the scene, Alikhan Tora had lost a great deal of his influence within the government to younger men of a more

secular and modernist bent—many of whom had lived and been educated in the Soviet Union. The most prominent among them was
Äkhmätjan Qasimi (b. 1914). Details about his life are few, but he was
born in Ghulja and orphaned at an early age. An uncle took him to the
Soviet Union in 1926 and placed him in a boarding school for orphans
in Jarkent. He attended educational institutions in Almaty, Tashkent,
and Moscow, although there are conflicting reports about which university he attended in the Soviet capital.[18] He returned to Xinjiang only
in 1942, just as Sheng broke with Moscow. Qasimi was promptly arrested and spent over a year in various jails. He was released by Wu in
1944 and eventually made his way to Ghulja, where he began to work
for the newspaper published by the ETR. His colleagues soon discovered his education and mastery of Russian, and he rose rapidly to prominence. He led the ETR delegation when it began holding peace talks
with the GMD in the summer of 1945, and he inherited the unques-
tioned leadership of the government after Alikhan Tora's disappearance
the following year. By the autumn of 1945, overt references to Islam had
disappeared from the proclamations of the ETR.

———

The negotiations for a peace treaty began in October 1945 and dragged
on until the following summer. The central government's delegation
was headed by Zhang Zhizhong, a former commander of the Northwestern Military Headquarters of the GMD, who had first arrived in
Ürümchi to head the military response to the uprising. In March 1946,
Zhang was appointed governor of Xinjiang. Eventually, an agreement
was hammered out, according to which the province was to have a government of twenty-five officials, ten of whom (including the chair) were
to be appointed by the central government, while the other fifteen were
to be chosen from among figures recommended by the districts. The
three districts of the ETR were to recommend six members of the government. More importantly, the three districts were also to maintain
their military forces of up to twelve thousand men, only half of whom

were to be under the command of the National Army in Xinjiang. Peace Preservation Corps were to be established in the other seven districts of the province, and those in Aqsu and Kashgar were to be recruited from the Muslim population and commanded by a Muslim officer. The agreement also provided for elections of county-level officials, full freedom of religion, and the official use of local languages in government, business, and education.[19] These arrangements were unlike any others in force in China and had far-reaching consequences for the future of Xinjiang. The first government envisioned under these accords was to be headed by Zhang, who was to be backed by two Muslim deputies: Burhan Shähidi, a provincial appointee, and Qasimi, nominated by the ETR. Of the council's twenty-five members, only six were to be Han.

The agreement was never implemented, and the coalition government never took power. Alikhan Tora was about to disappear, and Osman Batur, the Kazakh warlord, had grown wary of the ETR's alliance with the Soviets. Zhang also faced opposition from the army, many of whose leaders were adamantly opposed to his concessionary line. In contrast, ETR leaders were always suspicious of the central government and its heavy military presence in the rest of the province. The leaders made little effort to restore transportation links between the ETR and the rest of the province or to unite Xinjiang's currency, but they did mobilize support in the rest of the province. The Eastern Turkestan Youth League established branches throughout the province, and at the height of its popularity it had 300,000 members.[20] The league spread an intensely national message, underwriting demands for expansive autonomy within the Chinese state. In the spring of 1947, when Zhang undertook a tour of the south, he was confronted with massive demonstrations demanding the withdrawal of Chinese troops from the province, the promulgation of self-rule, and his own ouster.[21] Mass mobilization took many other forms as well. In Ürümchi, large crowds gathered on several occasions in February 1947 to demand the full implementation of the peace accords and to hear remarks by Qasimi and other ETR leaders. The urban population across Xinjiang had galvanized around the national idea pursued by the ETR.

Faced with this mobilization, the GMD backtracked from its message about the racial unity of all Chinese citizens and turned for advice and support to three Eastern Turkestani Muslims who had been working with it, often against substantial odds, to seek greater rights for Xinjiang within a Chinese state. The most important of the three was Isa Yusuf (b. 1901), who had worked with the GMD since 1932. The son of a local *beg* in Yengisar, near Kashgar, Isa had studied in a local Chinese school at the same time as he acquired the usual madrasa education. He picked up the usual Jadid notions of nation and progress and acquired a strong sense of discontent with the place of Xinjiang's Muslim society in the Chinese state. At the age of twenty-five, he was appointed interpreter at the Xinjiang consulate in the Soviet Uzbek city of Andijan, where he spent six crucial years. He learned Russian but also imbibed the national ideas then current among the Uzbek intelligentsia. His sojourn also coincided with Stalin's revolution from above and the assault on the Central Asian intelligentsia that accompanied it. The experience turned him into a committed anticommunist and gave him a lifelong suspicion of Russian geopolitical motives. He decided that Eastern Turkestan could not be truly independent, for any independent state would buckle under Soviet hegemony. The solution for him was for the region to seek maximal autonomy within a Chinese state. With this goal in mind, he traveled to China proper in 1932 and began making contacts in the government. He had unusual enough qualifications to succeed, and the time was right: the GMD was trying to work out ways of keeping the country together. Isa was invited to join the Border Affairs Commission, the organ that dealt with the country's non-Han populations. In return, he collaborated with the GMD, going on a tour of the Middle East and India in 1938–1939 to garner diplomatic and public support for China in its confrontation with Japan.[22]

During this trip, Isa visited Afghanistan, where he met the second of the three men, Mehmed Emin Bughra—the leader of the first ETR, who had been living in exile in Kabul for several years. Bughra had been forced to forgo political activities as a condition for being allowed to live

in Afghanistan. As a result, he had turned to scholarship and was working on a general history of Eastern Turkestan. Isa convinced him to
come to Nanjing to work with the GMD in the quest for autonomy for
his homeland. Getting the requisite paperwork took a while, but Bughra
arrived in Chongqing, the GMD's wartime capital, in April 1943. The
fact that the leader of a secessionist rebellion would now collaborate
with (and be accepted by) the central government was a sign of the
complexity of the geopolitical situation of Eastern Turkestan and the
paucity of choices that were available to all sides. The third man was
Masud Sabri (b. 1886), a scion of a prosperous family from Ghulja. He
had spent over a decade at the beginning of the century in the Ottoman
Empire, where he trained as a medical doctor. In addition to medical
training, Sabri had also acquired a deep commitment to Turkism. Back
in Ghulja, he established not just a hospital and a pharmacy but also a
number of modern schools. This activity ran afoul of Yang Zengxin,
who repeatedly closed schools founded by Sabri and jailed him for
"revolutionary activities." During the upheavals of 1933, Sabri found
himself in Aqsu, where he was involved in the ETR. He had to escape
to India when the republic was destroyed. He made his way to Nanjing
in 1934 and joined the GMD for reasons similar to those of Isa. Sabri
went far in the party, being elected to its Central Committee and named
to the State Council of the Republic of China.[23]

The three men worked with the GMD because they saw no other
alternative for Eastern Turkestan. They hoped to push the central government in the direction of recognizing the region's national specificity
and granting it greater autonomy. They were deeply committed to a
Turkist view of Eastern Turkestan and thus had no fondness for Chiang
Kai-shek's notion of the Chinese nation as a racially homogeneous entity. Isa had organized the Eastern Turkestan Association, a society for
Eastern Turkestani students and residents in Nanjing, and published
the newspaper *Chiniy Türkistan avazi* (The Voice of Chinese Turkestan)
as a mouthpiece for his program. All three had pushed for the official
recognition of the Turkic population of Eastern Turkestan as a distinct
national community. They had engaged in spirited polemics against
Chinese scholars who argued that the inhabitants of the province were

not Turks but part of a single and racially homogeneous united Chinese nation. In 1941, at the eighth congress of the GMD, Sabri had argued against the use of the generic term Hui ("Muslim") for the inhabitants of Turkestan, for the term confused religion with nationality. He argued that while Eastern Turkestan was an integral part of China, it was nevertheless the homeland (*vätän*) of a distinct nation (*millät*), a fact that should be officially recognized. He also insisted that the province be called Eastern Turkestan, not Xinjiang.[24]

In 1945, circumstances forced the GMD to listen to the three men. They were appointed to official positions in Ürümchi, where they came to be known as *Üch äpändi*, the Three Gentlemen. Their appointment inaugurated a short period in which the Chinese state acknowledged that the indigenous population of the province had political rights and was entitled to self-determination. Zhang, who had been appointed governor of Xinjiang in 1946, said at a press conference in Ürümchi: "We Chinese comprise only five per cent of the population in Sinkiang. Why have we not turned over political power to the Uighurs and other racial groups who constitute the other 95 per cent? In many respects, the policies adopted by the Sinkiang government in the past were entirely wrong—no different, in fact, than the policies of imperialist nations toward their colonies. These mistakes we must correct, as we must remove and atone for the many evils and bloodstains left behind by ex-Governor Sheng."[25] Such a statement was unprecedented in the history of Qing or Chinese rule over Eastern Turkestan, and it was not to be repeated. Zhang recognized Turkic as an official language in the province, local history became part of the school curriculum, and the official press was told to use the term "Eastern Turkistan" instead of Xinjiang. And Zhang allowed the Three Gentlemen to organize cultural and political work among the indigenous population. Isa established a publishing house called Altay that issued a journal of the same name and a newspaper titled *Erk* (Liberty). On its masthead was Gasprinsky's Jadid slogan, "Unity in language, thought, and deed," as well as the following proclamation: "We are nationalists. We are democrats. We are humanists. Our race is Turkic. Our religion is Islam. Our homeland is Turkestan." Attached to the publishing house was a library and a scientific commission that set out to create a common language for all the Turkic groups of Turkestan and to publish useful books in that language.[26]

Much of the Three Gentlemen's work was organized against the ETR, which made for an intriguing political conflict. We see here two different versions of Turkism arrayed against each other, with very different political and geopolitical implications. The ETR's rhetoric changed after 1946, with its proclamations increasingly using the Soviet vocabulary of struggle against imperialism, unity of the people, and class struggle. More significantly, ETR proclamations spoke, Soviet-style, of multiple nationalities in Eastern Turkestan. The Association for the Defense of Peace and Democracy in Xinjiang, established by the ETR to work toward the implementation of the peace treaty, spoke of Eastern Turkestan as the native land of a number of nationalities: "We genuinely believe that peace and friendship between the peoples of Xinjiang, justice and real freedom will be established if the Uyghurs and Kazakhs, Kyrgyz and Mongols, Chinese and Dungans, Uzbeks and other peoples inhabiting our territory join together to finally put an end to lawlessness, the denial of rights, slavery, poverty, and ignorance. We will build a life on our native land in the interests of peoples who engage in useful work and in this life there will be no place for animosity between different nationalities or the humiliation of small ethnic groups."[27] The ETR shelved talk of a single Eastern Turkestani nation (*millät*) and appeals to Islamic legitimacy.

The Three Gentlemen preferred to speak of a single Turkic nation of Eastern Turkestan. This explains Isa's attempts to codify a common Turkic language for the region. The Three Gentlemen were rooted in a Jadid framework of Turkic Islamic identity, but by 1947 the ETR was using a Soviet framework to articulate its Turkic identity. This led to mutual suspicions and the pursuit of different political strategies. Bughra, the leader of the first ETR, was now arguing against the second ETR. Decades later, Isa recalled a private conversation with Qasimi in which the latter told him, "The Chinese have oppressed us greatly." Isa's response was: "The Chinese oppressed us. I agree. Did they oppress us as much as the Russians have oppressed the people of Western Turkestan?" He saw China as the lesser evil. Qasimi also assured him, "More than any-thing else, and despite everything, I am an Uyghur!" Isa noted, sourly, "He said he was an Uyghur. He did not say he was a Turk."[28] Herein lay the major difference between their positions. Isa considered Qasimi to be simply a Soviet agent (he suspected that Qasimi had actually been born in Russian Turkestan), while Qasimi saw the Three Gentlemen as agents of imperialism—"smoking English tobacco, drinking American beer, dressed in the garb of colonizers"—who intended to sell out their own nation.[29] Both sides were nationalist and Turkist, but they imagined very different futures for Eastern Turkestan.

————

By 1947, intense political mobilization against Chinese rule in the seven districts still under GMD control had led the GMD to take its most des-perate action. The central government removed Zhang from office in June 1947 and replaced him with Masud Sabri, who became the first Turkestani to head Eastern Turkestan since its conquest by the Qing. Sabri was in a difficult position. There was determined opposition within the GMD to the granting of autonomy to national populations, and his authority was constrained in significant ways. He could do little about the massive problems plaguing the province: a deteriorating economy marked by massive shortages of basic necessities and rampant inflation, the rou-tine interference in political life by the overwhelmingly Han GMD army, and strident dissent by the local population against the policies of the central government. For all his national credentials, Sabri came to be seen as a figurehead who only followed Chinese orders. In January 1949, the central government decided to take the poisoned chalice away from Sabri and pass it to another local, Burhan Shähidi. Shähidi was a different sort of figure than Masud. Shähidi—a Tatar from the village of Aksu, in what is now Tatarstan—had arrived in Xinjiang in 1912 at the age of eigh-teen to work as an accountant for a Tatar firm in Chuguchak. After sev-eral years, Shähidi launched himself on a career in Xinjiang's government service. He was an interpreter for Yang Zengxin, and Jin Shuren sent him to Germany as a trade agent. Sheng Shicai appointed him to a diplomatic post in the Soviet Union in 1937, only to recall him the following year and imprison him for being a Trotskyite. Shähidi remained in jail until 1944, when he was released and again put to work for the government. He was appointed as Zhang's deputy in the coalition government of 1946.[30] His career had taught him a great deal of flexibility. He was sympathetic to the Soviets but also acceptable to the Chinese, whom he had long served. He spoke Russian better than Chinese and had been the head of the Association for the Defense of Peace and Democracy. His appointment was a last-ditch attempt by the GMD to mend fences with the Soviets as the CCP closed in on the GMD in the Chinese civil war. Shähidi was to be the last governor of republican Xinjiang.

———

Xinjiang's fate was sealed by events beyond its borders. Japan's defeat in the war had reanimated the conflict between the GMD and the CCP, and China had been in the grip of a full-blown civil war since 1946. By 1949, the Communists were on the brink of victory. The brutal civil war never reached Xinjiang. By the summer of 1949, Communist forces were assembling in Gansu and Qinghai provinces, and the GMD was in full retreat. In August 1949, Zhang, who had defected to the Communists, urged Shähidi and Tao Zhiyue, the commander of GMD forces in Xinjiang, to surrender. Chiang reportedly ordered Tao to resist. Meanwhile, the Three Gentlemen plotted with Ma Bufan and Ma Jinshan, Chinese Muslim generals in the GMD army, to overthrow Tao and fight the Communists.[31] They also urged the GMD to declare Xinjiang independent, so that the Communist invasion of it could become an international incident. Nothing came of these initiatives, for the GMD preferred to lose Xinjiang to the Communists than to declare it independent. Tao allowed those of his officers who wanted to leave to do so, before he surrendered his remaining eighty thousand troops by cable in late September 1949. The following day, Shähidi telegraphed his allegiance to the CCP. Such was the "peaceful liberation" of Xinjiang. It had surrendered to the Communists even before the arrival of the People's Liberation Army (PLA).

The Communist victory in China altered Stalin's calculus about the ETR. His support for the republic was premised on his need to bargain with the GMD. Now he had little need for the republic, and he was happy to sacrifice it. He helped the PLA occupy Xinjiang: when it turned out that the PLA did not have the resources to occupy the province, the Soviet government airlifted a division of the PLA to Ürümchi in mid-October, two weeks after the PRC had been proclaimed in Beijing.[32] In addition, the Soviets shipped one thousand tons of aviation fuel and ten thousand tons of grain to Xinjiang to see the PLA through the winter.[33] Stalin had been worried that a power vacuum in Eastern Turkestan would pave the way for British or U.S. gains in the region, so he was eager to help the Communists occupy it.[34] The "peaceful liberation" of Xinjiang was facilitated in great part by Soviet help.

The new situation put the ETR in an awkward position. Its rhetoric had been frankly anti-Han and for independence, and it had no prior links with Chinese Communists. But it was also allied to the Soviets, who supported the CCP. Mao squared the circle by declaring the revolution in the three districts of the ETR to be an integral part of the Chinese revolution. A self-proclaimed revolutionary regime could scarcely object to the victory of the Chinese revolution, nor could it put up a fight now that Stalin, its patron, had thrown his support behind the CCP. Qasimi consequently renounced the ETR's claims to independence and welcomed the new regime. The PLA treated the three districts of the ETR gingerly. It took its time reorganizing the ETR army and purging it of those suspected of national separatism. But the biggest political problem was solved in mysterious ways. In late August, Mao invited a delegation from the ETR to attend the National People's Consultative Conference in Beijing, a gathering of various political parties and nationalities to demonstrate solidarity with the CCP. The five-member delegation from the ETR left for Almaty, where it boarded a plane that was to take it to Beijing. The plane never arrived. Four months later, Beijing announced that the plane had crashed near Irkutsk, in Siberia, killing all aboard. The ETR leaders had disappeared. A new delegation, headed by Säypidin (or Sayfiddin) Äzizi, was hastily assembled and sent off to attend the consultative congress.

It disavowed all demands for autonomy for Xinjiang or its three northern districts.

The mystery surrounding the plane crash remains unsolved to this day. The demise of the ETR leaders was too convenient for too many sides to be understood simply as an accident. The archives have yielded no smoking gun (they seldom do), and in the absence of documentary evidence, all sorts of explanations have been put forward. Some authors have claimed that the delegation had arrived in Beijing, but its members were arrested and imprisoned. More recently, scholars have pointed the finger at Stalin. The ETR had outlived its usefulness to the Soviet Union. Stalin wanted a secure border with a Xinjiang that was firmly part of what he hoped would be a friendly and pliant Communist regime in China. He had suggested to the Central Committee of the CCP that after the Communists took Xinjiang, they should raise the share of the Han Chinese in the population from 5 percent to 30 percent as a way to secure Chinese control over "such a large and rich region and for the defense of the frontiers of China."[35] The ETR leaders were an inconvenient obstacle to that goal. But no matter what caused the plane crash, it solved a problem for both Mao and Stalin.

Thus ended the second attempt in the second quarter of the twentieth century to assert the national rights of the Turkic peoples of Eastern Turkestan. Both the ETR and the Three Gentlemen had been defeated. For the latter, this was the end of the road. Isa and Bughra fled to India and ended up in exile in Turkey. They had no illusions left about the ability or the willingness of the GMD to accommodate any national demands. Of all the Eastern Turkestanis who had worked with the GMD, only Yolbars Khan—the servitor of the former *wang* of Qumul who had led the first uprising against Jin Shuren in 1931 and hung around ever since, never rising to any great prominence—followed the GMD into exile in Taiwan. He lived on until 1971 as a token of the GMD claim to Xinjiang.

Russian Turkestan had experienced the full brunt of the social upheavals unleashed by the Russian revolution, and the Soviet power that emerged there had some roots in the region. Chinese Turkestan had suffered grievously since the proclamation of the republic, but it had remained terra incognita for the Chinese Communists. True, several hundred of them had worked in the province during the brief period when Sheng was aligned with the Soviets, but that brief episode—which had ended in the disastrous persecution of the Communists by Sheng—had left little trace on the party's conceptions of the world. Conversely, for all the Soviet influence in the three districts of the ETR, there was not a single Muslim member of the CCP in Xinjiang at the moment of its "peaceful liberation."

———

The second ETR was effaced in Chinese Communist historiography by being assimilated into the general history of the Chinese revolution led by the CCP against imperialism and its lackeys, such as the GMD. Chinese scholarship studiously avoids the term "Eastern Turkestan Republic" and refers to the ETR simply as the "Three Districts Revolution." The indigenous peoples of Xinjiang play only a passive role in it. They and their leaders were "under the influence of the Soviets," "manipulated" or "seduced" by them, and "thus caused the social and political situation in Xinjiang's border regions to become increasingly nervous, chaotic, and agitated."[36] The complete liberation of the region required the tutelage of Han and the CCP. Uyghurs remember the two ETRs very differently, seeing both as failed attempts to achieve national independence that point to futures that might still be possible. To be sure, the Ghulja ETR embodied many contradictions. It was dominated by Uyghurs, but the population of the three districts ruled by the ETR was largely composed of Kazakh nomads, and the majority of the sedentary Muslim population of Eastern Turkestan remained beyond its grasp. Soviet support allowed it to exist and even thrive but also limited it in many ways. Yet there can be little question that the government enjoyed legitimacy in the eyes of the population over which it ruled or that it performed the tasks of governance adequately over the five years of its existence. It was above all a reminder to China of the colonial nature of its rule in the province.

COMMUNISM

THE FOUR DECADES between the Chinese revolution and the collapse of the Soviet Union were a period of actually existing Communism. For Central Asia, these were transformative years. In Soviet Central Asia, the years after Stalin's death saw a turn away from terror, as the Soviet state opted instead for rule through institutions. The decades that followed saw little of the upheavals and violence that had marked the years since the First World War. In the Stalinist decades, the destruction of the old had overshadowed the creation of the new. Postwar reconstruction led to stability and long-term economic and demographic growth that transformed Central Asia in significant ways. Large-scale investment in infrastructure and industry led to economic and demographic growth, while the stability favored by the new leadership allowed the consolidation of indigenous political elites within the Soviet framework. The Soviet Union had always been a developmentalist state—rapid industrialization and human development were major planks of the regime's legitimacy—but it was only in the years after the Second World War that Central Asia ceased to be a periphery of the Soviet state and became fully integrated within it. Soviet policies in Central Asia had much in common with policies in the decolonizing world, where there were substantial inputs into development. The construction of canals, dams, and industry brought Central Asia into the Soviet mainstream, while developments in education meant that Central Asians came to think of themselves as Soviet.

The absence of massive upheavals or campaigns of transformation in this period means that we will relate the history of this period differently.

Instead of the concern with different political campaigns that shaped the narrative in the previous section, now we will focus on long-term developments in the economy and society. We will have more tables and graphs as we trace the evolution of Central Asian societies in a period of stability. The 1960s and 1970s were in many ways a golden age of Soviet Central Asia, and they are remembered as such—even if that memory occludes the dark clouds that hung over the future. For better or worse, it was these decades that shaped the societies that emerged after the collapse of the Soviet Union in 1991.

Xinjiang followed a rather different course. Its incorporation into the PRC inaugurated a period of often violent transformation that had much in common with the fate of Soviet Central Asia in the 1930s. The province was swept into the catastrophes of the Great Leap Forward and the Cultural Revolution that bruised its society and transformed its economy. Then, after the Sino-Soviet alliance went up in flames, the province became a tense borderland where the two Communist powers faced off (and where they exchanged fire in 1969). It experienced little of the economic development that Soviet Central Asia saw in the same period. The two parts of Central Asia were farther apart in this era than at any other time in history.

17

Development, Soviet Style

ON AUGUST 29, 1949, villagers in the Semipalatinsk district of north-eastern Kazakhstan felt the earth tremble and saw the heavens turn red as a mushroom-shaped cloud occupied the sky. The nuclear age that dawned with the end of the Second World War had arrived in Central Asia right away, and it was Kazakhstan's lot to host it. As the Soviet government pursued the nuclear bomb, it located its nuclear testing facilities on the Kazakh steppe because of its remoteness. The Soviet nuclear program embodied many of the paradoxes of the Soviet Union's postwar status as a global superpower. Its facilities were built by forced labor from the Gulag, using technologies that would have been familiar to the builders of the pyramids in Egypt. (The fact that a top-secret installation of the highest state importance was built by men who were accused of treason and antistate activity was the least of the ironies of the Stalinist era.) Nevertheless, the Semipalatinsk Test Site, an area of about eighteen thousand square kilometers to the west of the town of Semipalatinsk and the epicenter of the Soviet nuclear program, pushed Central Asia inexorably into the modernity of the nuclear age. In the forty years after the first Soviet nuclear explosion in 1949, the Soviet Union conducted 456 nuclear tests on the site, 116 of them above ground. Semipalatinsk, the capital of the short-lived Alash Orda government in 1918–1919, became a continental counterpart to Bikini Atoll in the 1950s. Later tests were moved underground, but they were so routine that announcements about them were broadcast on local radio stations alongside movie show times and weather forecasts.[1] Almost no

Kazakhs worked on the site, but they were recipients of its radioactive bounty. Shrouded in state secrecy and legitimized by calls to Soviet patriotism, the site was active until 1989, by which time it had become the center of potent antinuclear and environmentalist movements.

The war effort had integrated Central Asia into the Soviet Union as never before and made Central Asians into Soviet citizens. These processes continued in the decades that followed. In addition to military service, the Communist Party and the Komsomol provided channels for the creation of an indigenous political elite, now thoroughly Soviet, that grew in self-confidence and influence. Exponential growth in the educational system reshaped Central Asian societies and created a new intelligentsia, again thoroughly Soviet, that was firmly ensconced in Soviet institutions. Substantial economic growth accompanied by sizable investments in the economy underpinned these developments. Heavy industry had arrived in the region during the war, when factories close to the front were evacuated, and quite a lot of that industry stayed. The postwar period saw a rapid expansion in mineral extraction and the creation of metallurgical and chemical industries in Central Asia, but most significant was a considerable growth in infrastructure: new roads, railways, irrigation projects, and hydroelectric dams transformed Central Asia and its relationship to the Soviet state.

———

The immediate postwar years had been anything but auspicious. The Soviet state sought to reestablish control, taking back the little freedoms that had slipped from its control during the war. For the southern republics of Central Asia, this meant insistent new demands to bring back the focus on cotton that had been weakened by the need to produce grain during the war years. In July 1945, only a couple of months after the fall of Berlin, Moscow issued a decree ordering the restoration of prewar levels of cotton production in Uzbekistan. The Uzbek leadership had already volunteered to do this, but it had hoped that Moscow would supply funding, machinery, and technical assistance to make the change possible. Little help was forthcoming, but the pressure to fulfill quotas continued. With food in short supply, Uzbek peasants dragged their feet in switching to cotton, and prewar levels of production were not achieved until 1949. By that time, Moscow had foisted a plenipotentiary official on Uzbekistan with the powers of hiring and firing at the highest level. That official, S. D. Ignat'ev, proceeded to shake up the republic's leadership and force through another purge of the Communist Party of Uzbekistan, which saw the dismissal of thousands of members on accusations of corruption, nationalism, or careerism. Usmon Yusupov, who had been first secretary of the party since the great purge of 1937, was kicked upstairs to head the freshly minted Ministry of Cotton Production in Moscow, while several members of his cohort were demoted, and many low-ranking officials were fired from their jobs and expelled from the party.[2] This was not the Great Terror redux, however: demotions, expulsions, and sinecures were much better than the executions that had been the fate of the victims of the purges of 1936 and 1937. Still, the assertion of central power was menacing and put the republic's leadership in its place.

This shake-up was accompanied by a renewed campaign for ideological purity. Headed by Andrei Zhdanov, the campaign began in 1949 with an attack on "rootless cosmopolitanism." The term was a thinly veiled reference to Jews—a people not rooted in the Soviet Union and whose loyalty the Stalinist regime had come to doubt. The campaign was part and parcel of Soviet patriotism as it had developed under the slogan of Socialism in One Country, but the war had reshaped that patriotism. Patriotism had to be rooted, but not all rootedness was acceptable. It turned out that writing rooted too much in Central Asian soil was also suspect, not of cosmopolitanism but of "bourgeois nationalism"; "feudal-*bai* backwardness"; and that ever-present bogeyman, "pan-Islamism." Stalin might have briefly supported the anticolonial nationalism of the Muslim population of Eastern Turkestan, but he saw the situation inside the Soviet Union quite differently. During the war, Stalin had come to see the Russians as the main pillar of the Soviet state. At a victory reception for Red Army commanders at the Kremlin on May 2, 1945, Stalin had proposed a toast to "the health of our Soviet people, and in the first place, the Russian people. I drink in the first place to the health of the Russian people because it is the most outstanding nation of all the nations forming the Soviet Union. I propose a toast to the health of the Russian people because it has won in this war universal recognition as the leading force of the Soviet Union among all the peoples of our country."[3]

Non-Russians could relate to the Soviet Union only by affirming the tutelage of the Russians. Patriotic works produced during the war that glorified local heroes fighting against foreign invaders now smacked of nationalism. A play by Hamid Olimjon titled *The Revolt of Muqanna* was deemed to be saturated with Islamic symbolism, while it turned out that Maqsud Shaykhzoda's 1941 play *Jalaluddin*, an account of the heroic defense of Khwarazm against the Mongols, had actually proclaimed the slogan of Greater Uzbekistan. In 1951, it was the turn of epic poetry. Such poetry had been nationalized over the previous decades, so that *Alpamish* had become the Uzbek national epic and *Manas* was claimed as a Kyrgyz national treasure. The Turkmen epic *Gorkut Ata* was denounced as "a bloodthirsty chronicle of the Oghuz feudals, a poem of religious fanaticism and of brutish hatred of non-Muslims." *Alpamish* was "impregnated with the poison of feudalism and reaction, breathing Muslim fanaticism and hatred towards non-Muslims," while *Manas* was "dangerous from the standpoint of educating Kyrgyz youth in the spirit of proletarian internationalism, of the Stalinist friendship of nations and of Soviet patriotism."[4] The Central Asian musical establishment was attacked for its emphasis on national peculiarities and its resistance to European musical influences (via a Russian musical canon whose use had become a form of orthodoxy), while Central Asian music was denigrated for its "primitiveness" and its monophony. Barely a dozen years after the Central Asian intelligentsia had been massacred in the Great Terror of 1937–1938, here was another assault on it. This time, the victims were sent to prison, not to their graves, but the fear was back. And non-Russians, even those rooted in the Socialist Motherland, found that any expression of their national specificity could be a crime. Stalin, himself a Georgian, had come close to turning the Soviet Union into a new Russian empire.

But even Stalin had to die, which he did on March 5, 1953. He left behind a number of daunting problems: scandalously low standards of living, poor agricultural productivity, and the need to compete with a vastly richer United States in a global struggle for power and influence. It was clear to his successors that Stalin's methods of rule, based on terror and violence, could not continue in his absence. Postwar reconstruction had focused on heavy industry, leaving items of everyday use almost nonexistent. Nikita Khrushchev, who emerged victorious in the power struggle that followed Stalin's death, denounced Stalin for his crimes against the party and began to move the country away from Stalin's legacy. This process of de-Stalinization was built on decentralizing the economy and campaigns for improving food production and the living conditions of Soviet citizens. Khrushchev faced much opposition from entrenched elites, whom he worked diligently to remove from office. In Central Asia, he managed to pry out many Stalin appointees, especially those at the highest levels, and replace them with those more amenable to reform.

Khrushchev also rolled back the cult of Stalin and began reducing the ideological frigidity of his rule. The "Thaw" saw censorship scaled back and many of the ideological strictures of late Stalinism repudiated. Khrushchev also initiated the process of rehabilitating the victims of the purges. Special courts reviewed the accusations that had sent so many people to the Gulag or their graves and voided most of the charges. Survivors could now resume their careers, and in the case of those who were rehabilitated posthumously, their families were now rid of the odium of accusation. However, Khrushchev was not a liberal but a true enthusiast who felt that the Soviet Union had lost its revolutionary moorings under Stalin. His goal was to recover the enthusiasms of the revolutionary period, which he did through a number of mobilization campaigns.

The first of these campaigns targeted the massive problems in agriculture. Collectivization had not been a success, and food remained scarce. Khrushchev sought to improve yields and general efficiency, as well as to put new land under the plow. There were vast open spaces in Kazakhstan and Siberia that had never been used to produce food. Now rid of their nomadic populations, they were imagined to be virgin lands, awaiting impregnation by enthusiastic Soviet citizens driven by re-newed revolutionary zeal. In 1954, the party spearheaded a campaign to put this land to agricultural use. The Virgin Lands campaign appealed to revolutionary enthusiasm, and over the next several years it brought forty million hectares under the plow, half of them in Kazakhstan. More than 300,000 people, mostly members of the Komsomol, answered the call to settle the steppe and make it productive. Over the years, they were joined by tens of thousands of others who came to provide techni-cal support and staff the infrastructure of the new towns and settlements being built. The vast majority of the immigrants came from Russia and Ukraine with dreams of pioneering a bright Communist future. The lands where nomads had roamed until a generation earlier now became state farms growing wheat and raising livestock in nonnomadic ways. The campaign transformed the demographics of Kazakhstan. By 1959, Slavs constituted 52 percent of the republic's population, while the Kazakhs made up only 30 percent. The settlers of the Virgin Lands campaign were not the only cause of this demographic shift. The depor-tations of Poles before the war and of Chechens and other peoples of the Caucasus during it, combined with the arrival of hundreds of thou-sands of inmates of the Gulag system, had already altered Kazakhstan's population balance. Once Khrushchev began dismantling the Gulag, the camps became industrial or mining cities across the Soviet Union.[5] Many inmates had nowhere to go and no jobs to find, so they stayed put. Karaganda, the site of a notorious camp, was Kazakhstan's second city in the census of 1959. Kazakhstan's integration into the Soviet Union took the form of a demographic deluge.

Moscow's obsession with cotton remained. Khrushchev pressed for ever higher production targets, without offering any new incentives. Many of the men Khrushchev raised to positions of leadership in the republics were loyal to him because of the promise of decentralization, which gave the republics greater control over decisions. In 1957, these leaders helped Khrushchev stave off a revolt against him by Stalin-era stalwarts who were skeptical about the direction of Khrushchev's poli-cies. However, having consolidated his position, Khrushchev turned on his allies and began to pursue a policy of centralization that brooked little opposition. Between 1959 and 1962, he forced out of office the lead-ers of all five Central Asian republics for "shortcomings" in economic or nationalities policy. In 1959, Sobir Kamolov, the first secretary of the Communist Party of Uzbekistan, was removed from office for his failure to fulfill quotas for cotton as well as for other shortcomings. He was replaced by Sharaf Rashidov, a war hero and writer who had been very much a compromise candidate.[6] In 1961, Tursunbay Uljaboyev, the first secretary of the Communist Party of Tajikistan, was removed from of-fice in the wake of a scandal that found local officials padding their re-ports on the production of cotton. Turkmenistan's first secretary, Suhan Babayev, was forced out for nationalism. His Kyrgyzstani counterpart, Ishak Razzakov, a survivor from the Stalin era, was also removed. The following year, Dinmuhammed Kunayev was forced out of office in Ka-zakhstan for his opposition to the transfer of irrigated lands in the south to Uzbekistan and to Khrushchev's wish to move the republic's capital of the republic to Akmolinsk, in Virgin Lands territory.[7] (The irony here is that in 1996, the government of independent Kazakhstan moved the capital to Akmolinsk, then called Aqmola, for a different set of reasons.) By 1962, all five of the new leaders of Central Asian republics were pre-cariously placed and apparently at the mercy of the center. Yet a little luck and new developments in Moscow meant that this cohort was to to have a long run in power. Although they might not have suspected it when they came into office, they were to oversee the most stable and prosperous part of the Soviet era in Central Asia.

———

Engineers broke ground for the Karakum Canal in Turkmenistan in 1954. This grandiose project aimed to draw water from the Amu Darya to irrigate the wastelands of the Karakum Desert. Construction contin-ued into the 1980s, by which time the canal, touted as the River of Hap-piness, totaled 1,375 kilometers in length and was irrigating 600,000 hectares planted with cotton. The Karakum Canal was one of a number of ambitious projects that the Soviet government launched in the years after Stalin's death that were meant to conquer nature and make it productive. The Hungry Steppe development project in Uzbekistan involved building a number of reservoirs along the Amu Darya and constructing the Southern Hungry Steppe Canal, which was meant to irrigate 300,000 hectares. The Amu-Bukhara Canal, built during the 1960s, brought water from the Amu Darya to the Qarshi steppe near Bukhara, with the goal of irrigating 1,000,000 hectares. A series of dams harnessed the region's rivers to produce hydroelectricity. Perhaps the most significant project was the Nurek Dam on the Vakhsh River in Tajikistan, built over the course of the 1960s. The Tajik leadership had long pressed Moscow for the construction of the dam, but the project was approved only in 1959 and then passed through a period of uncertainty. At the time of its completion in 1972, the 300-meter-high Nurek was the tallest dam in the world. It had a capacity of 2,700 megawatts, which was to support the creation of heavy industry in the republic and lead to the transformation of its economy. Many of these projects had been dreamed up in the Tsarist era in the first flush of hubris of imperial conquest. They were now being realized in the postwar Soviet Union. The early Soviet decades in Central Asia had seen an immense amount of dislocation, characterized by a great deal of haste and waste, and had little to show for it. The great construction projects of the 1930s had largely passed Central Asia by. Now, in the mid-1950s, the center was willing to invest greater resources in its projects in Central Asia.

The turn to greater investment in the region was also driven by the global situation created by decolonization in the aftermath of the Second World War. The Soviet Union presented itself as an alternative model of economic development to the countries of Asia and Africa that were achieving independence, and it made much of the fact that Central Asia, a former colonial periphery, had now become a part of the metropole. Yet huge disparities still remained between the industrialized zones of the former imperial heartland and the largely agrarian periphery of Central Asia. Central Asia's party leaders argued with some insistence for major funding on infrastructural projects, often using explicitly anticolonial arguments and the need to forestall diplomatic embarrassment on account of Soviet disparities. Tursun Uljaboyev, Tajikistan's first secretary in the Khrushchev years, argued for the Nurek Dam because its construction would allow Tajikistan to export electricity to Afghanistan and be an example to neighboring countries. "The East needs such light," he told Khrushchev.[8]

Developments in Soviet Central Asia in the post-Stalin years bore an uncanny resemblance to what was going on in newly independent countries in Asia and Africa. Dams and the hydroelectric power they produced were the most potent symbols of development in the twentieth century. From the Tennessee valley in the United States to the Volta Dam in Ghana, the Aswan High Dam in Egypt, and the Tarbela Dam in Pakistan, hydroelectric projects were seen as agents of human mastery over nature, the embodiments of the promise of modern technology to deliver progress and higher living standards, and mechanisms for improving national economies. Soviet Central Asia saw its share of such projects. As Sergei Abashin suggests, the region, much like many parts of the "Third World," witnessed a "green revolution" in the 1950s, with increasing mechanization of the agricultural sector, improvements in agronomic support, and the use of fertilizers to raise yields.[9] The Khrushchev era was a moment of decolonization in Soviet Central Asia.

———

Khrushchev's enthusiasm eventually wore thin on his colleagues in the party leadership. Having survived the upheavals of the 1920s, the Great Terror of Stalin, and the Second World War, they wanted stability more than anything else. In October 1964, they ousted Khrushchev for his failures in foreign policy and his "hare-brained schemes." The new leadership began a period of rule by committee that lasted into the mid-1980s. "Trust in cadres" (rather than Stalin's perpetual suspicion of them) became the new slogan. The theoretical basis for this new order had been provided by Khrushchev himself. In 1961, at the Twenty-Second Party Congress, he had pushed through a new program for the party that unabashedly promised that "the current generation shall live under Communism." More importantly, it declared that the Soviet Union had reached the stage of "mature socialism," the penultimate stage before full Communism. The arrival of mature socialism meant that all contradictions within society had been resolved and that mutually hostile social classes had been replaced by three groups (workers, peasants, and intellectuals) that lived in harmony. Class struggle was thus rendered obsolete, and the Communist Party was now "the party of the entire [Soviet] people." Its task now was to organize the people for the gradual ascendance to full Communism. In some ways, this was the final triumph of Stalin's notion of Socialism in One Country. The Communist Party went from being the vanguard of the proletariat to a mass party whose task was to oversee production. In 1988, the Communist Party of the Soviet Union had more than nineteen million members across the country, or a full 8 percent of the country's population. The party had become a political machine for the distribution of power and resources. (The numbers were lower in Central Asia, but the basic point remained: joining the party paved the way to opportunity.)

The period of 1964–1982, when Leonid Brezhnev was general secretary of the Soviet Communist Party, was Soviet Central Asia's golden age. The economy grew, standards of living rose, and Central Asians across the five republics came to identify with the Soviet state as never before. Brezhnev's aversion to upheaval led him to strike a tacit bargain with national leaderships in the republics. National Communist elites could run their republics without undue interference from the center as long as they met their production quotas, did not make radical demands on the center, and kept nationalism in check. In Central Asia, Brezhnev worked with the men who had come to power late in the Khrushchev era. The only change he made was to bring Kunayev back into office in Kazakhstan. Brezhnev had become friends with Kunayev when the former had been first secretary of the Kazakh Communist Party in the mid-1950s, and the personal bond was to be important in the relationship between Moscow and Almaty. The Brezhnev era was a period of unprecedented stability in Central Asia (as well as in the rest of the Soviet Union): four of the five republics were run by the same men throughout the period, and three of them died in office (see table 17.1).

TABLE 17.1 Brezhnev-era first secretaries of Communist parties in Central Asia

Republic	First secretary	Dates in office
Uzbekistan	Sharaf Rashidov	1959–1983
Tajikistan	Jabbor Rasulov	1961–1982
Kazakhstan	Dinmuhamed Kunayev	1960–1962 and 1964–1986
Kyrgyzstan	Turdakun Usubaliyev	1961–1985
Turkmenistan	Balyş Övezov	1960–1969
	Muhammetnazar Gapurov	1969–1985

The one exception proves the rule. It was a revolt among Turkmen cadres, not directives from Moscow or party discipline, that ousted Balyş Övezov as the first secretary of Turkmenistan's party in 1969. His successor, Muhammetnazar Gapurov, then stayed in power for the rest of the Brezhnev period.

This was a new political elite, whose members were Soviet and national at the same time. The first generation of Central Asian communists had been destroyed by Stalin in 1937. The generation that replaced them had learned the political game of the Stalin era the hard way. They could read signals from Moscow, but they lived in perpetual fear and knew not to make too many demands of the center. The men put in place by Khrushchev at the beginning of his rule were slightly younger but thoroughly Soviet in their political instincts, comfortable in the party, and free of the fear that had been ingrained in their predecessors. The men who took over after Khrushchev's reshuffling of officeholders between 1959 and 1962 belonged to the same generation. Now, freed from the fear of arbitrary intervention from Moscow, they came to see themselves as the leaders not just of their republics, but also of their nations.

Rashidov left a deep imprint on Uzbekistan, which he ran for twenty-four of the sixty-seven years (from 1924 to 1991) it existed as a Soviet republic. Born in November 1917, Rashidov could be the personification of Soviet rule. He came from a humble family in Jizzakh, near Samarqand, and he attended a teacher's training college in his hometown before earning a degree in philology at the Uzbek State University in Samarqand. He taught in middle schools for a few years before becoming a journalist for *Lenin yo'li* (Lenin's path), the official newspaper of Samarqand province. Then came the Second World War. He participated in the Battle of Moscow and was badly wounded. Invalided back to his hometown, he took up journalism and writing full-time. He had joined Uzbekistan's Communist Party in 1939, and he rose through the ranks, becoming the secretary of the Samarqand provincial party organization in 1944 and appointed editor of *Qizil O'zbekiston* (Red Uzbekistan), the party's newspaper, in 1947. In 1950, he became the chair of the republic's Writers Union and was elected chairman of the Presidium of the Uzbek Supreme Soviet, the nominal legislative organ of the republic. He was also recruited to be the face of Soviet diplomacy in the decolonizing world, and over the next nine years he traveled overseas several times. He was clearly from a different mold than those who had preceded him as presidium chairman. Akmal Ikromov, the first Uzbek to head the republic's party, was an accidental Communist; Usmon Yusupov, who succeeded him in 1937, benefited from the opportunities opened up by the Great Terror, but he did not have a Soviet education, nor had he served in the army. Rashidov cultivated personal relations with the leadership in Moscow, while in Uzbekistan he sat atop a vast network of patronage that ensured the distribution of resources and influence and was responsible for the fulfillment of economic plans, with cotton as the kingpin (see figure 17.1).

Kunayev had a slightly different trajectory in Kazakhstan. Born in 1911 in Vernyi (now Almaty) to a Kazakh functionary, Kunayev received a technical education, graduating from the Institute of Non-Ferrous and Fine Metallurgy in Moscow in 1936, and worked as an engineer in a number of mining operations in Kazakhstan. He joined the party in 1939 and prospered, becoming deputy chairman of the republic's Council of People's Commissars in 1942. He also served as head of the Kazakhstan Academy of Sciences between 1952 and 1955 and then returned to the Council of Ministers until his appointment as first secretary of the party in 1960. He differed from Rashidov not only in his technical background (which was typical of most Soviet leaders of his generation), but also in heading the Communist Party in a republic where Russians outnumbered the indigenous population. He was only the second Kazakh to

FIG. 17.1. Sharaf Rashidov (fourth from right) accompanies Leonid Brezhnev, general
secretary of the Communist Party of the Soviet Union (fifth from right), and Alexei Kosygin,
chair of the Council of Ministers, on a visit to Sovkhoz (State Farm) No. 19 in Mirzacho'l,
1978. Rashidov, like other Central Asian leaders of his cohort, enjoyed personal relations with
leaders in Moscow, and agriculture was a matter of state import.
Photo: Sharaf Rashidov House Museum, Jizzax; sharafrashidov.org.

lead the party in Kazakhstan, but Moscow's claims of offering autonomy
and self-determination meant that it had no choice but to appoint a
Kazakh to the highest office in Kazakhstan. His friendship with
Brezhnev was a key asset, and it ensured that Kunayev stayed at the
helm of the only Soviet republic where the titular nation did not make
up a majority of the population.

The new Soviet Central Asian political elite was entrusted to run its
own republics, but Moscow nevertheless retained certain levers of control. Behind the first secretaries sat second secretaries who were usually
Russians seconded from Moscow. In most Central Asian republics, the
leadership of the political police (now called the KGB) remained in the
hands of Russians, while the armed forces stationed in each republic
were answerable to central authorities, and their command remained in
the hands of career officers who were Russians. Kunayev was admitted
to the Politburo in 1971, and Rashidov remained a candidate (that is,

nonvoting) member from 1961 to his death in 1983. Kunayev was one of only two Central Asians (the other was the Uzbek Nuriddin Muhitdinov, who served in the Presidium, as the Politburo was then called, between 1956 and 1961) to sit in the highest organ of the Soviet party-state in the seven decades of its existence. As trusted leaders of the republics, they could—and did—argue for investment in their republics and defend the interests of those republics (and of their citizens) in all-Union forums, which in turn strengthened their claims to national leadership. Rashidov received large amounts of central funding for the reconstruction of Tashkent after a devastating earthquake in 1966. He was also instrumental in the construction of a metro system in Tashkent, whose lavishly decorated stations opened to the public in 1977, the sixtieth anniversary of both the October revolution and Rashidov's birth. Sovietness and nationality coexisted without friction.

———

The fate of the three southern republics of Uzbekistan, Tajikistan, and Turkmenistan was determined by Moscow's insatiable appetite for cotton. Cotton defined not just the structures of the economies of these republics, but it also explained much about power and authority in those societies. The three decades we have been talking about also witnessed the peak of the "cottonization" of Central Asia, which had fundamental implications for politics, society, and the environment.

The party had declared the goal of "cotton independence" back in 1929. In the postwar period, not only was that independence achieved, but cotton also became an important export commodity for the Soviet Union. By the 1970s, it was the second largest earner of foreign exchange in the agricultural sector. The procurement goals were set by the state, which also set the price at which it would buy the cotton from the producers. That price had no relation to the price cotton commanded on the world market. In return, the state promised in the postwar era to invest in irrigation, mechanization, and other infrastructure, even though there always remained a gap between what Central Asian leaders expected in terms of investment and what the state provided. By the

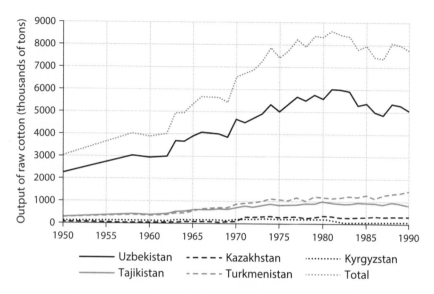

FIG. 17.2. Cotton production in the postwar period. *Source: Narodnoe khoziaistvo SSSR* (Moscow, various years).

end of the Soviet period, Uzbekistan alone produced more cotton than all of the United States. The increases in production were made possible by expanding the area under cultivation. The vast new tracts of land brought under cultivation by the massive irrigation projects described above were mostly devoted to cotton. Land sown with cotton increased massively during the postwar period. By the end of the Soviet period, cotton occupied 46 percent of all the cultivated land in the three southern republics (in many districts, that share was above 70 percent). Sixty percent of Uzbekistan's irrigated land was planted with cotton.[10] Southern Central Asia had become a cotton plantation (figure 17.2).

The comparison with plantation economies is not merely a rhetorical device. There were striking parallels between a plantation and a cotton-producing collective farm in Central Asia. Cotton farms produced a cash crop for export, employing large numbers of unskilled workers under the supervision of small numbers of overseers. The focus on the cash crop discouraged the production of food crops or livestock and skewed resource allocation in general. Central Asia's cotton farms, just like plantations in the American South or elsewhere in the colonial world, were vertically integrated into a production process centered elsewhere. Decisions about prices, wages, production schedules, or capital investment were made far away with no input from the producers.[11] All through the Khrushchev period, the ever-increasing demands were not matched by sufficient incentives. Khrushchev indeed seemed to be convinced that Central Asian cotton farmers were living off the bounty of others and not contributing enough to the Soviet state. Moscow was always hesitant to increase the prices it paid for the cotton it commanded to be grown, although the production always increased when prices were periodically raised. Yet as with much of the Soviet economy, the price had little connection to the cost of production, since that remained difficult to calculate. The official price for cotton paid no attention to the costs of the depreciation of land, transporting food to Central Asia, and other opportunities of production that were forgone in favor of cotton. More importantly, the price paid for cotton had shrunk greatly relative to the price of grain or other items of consumption. Measured in terms of work hours required to produce cotton, productivity in the Soviet cotton sector remained low.

The state's single-minded focus on raising output produced unexpected results, often the very opposite of what was intended. Cotton is a very labor-intensive crop. In principle, the Soviet state was committed to mechanization. The cotton harvester was developed in the United States in the 1930s, and the Soviets began producing their own models by the late 1940s. By 1950, the machines were being produced in Uzbekistan. The hope was that the mechanization of cotton picking would free up labor that could then be diverted to industry. Things turned out differently. Farm machinery proved to be expensive (after 1958, collective or state farms were expected to buy their own equipment) and difficult to maintain, as trained mechanics remained scarce and spare parts were difficult to obtain. Many farm managers therefore found it easier and cheaper to use manual labor. In fact, the proportion of the cotton crop that was mechanically harvested declined from the late 1970s on. The burden of labor fell unevenly across rural society. The Soviet liberation of women had allowed them to enter the workforce, where they often ended up doing the hardest work. Men found picking cotton to be de-

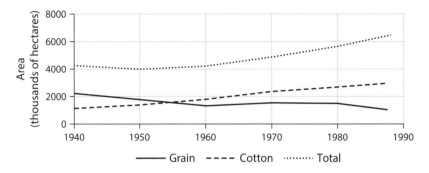

FIG. 17.3. Cotton and grain production in Turkmenistan, Uzbekistan, and Tajikistan, 1940–1990. Cotton had first call on the land opened up for cultivation by the massive irrigation projects in the region, while land sown with grain decreased in both absolute and relative terms. *Source:* Robert Craumer, "Agricultural Change, Labor Supply, and Rural Out-Migration in Soviet Central Asia," in *Geographic Perspectives on Soviet Central Asia*, ed. Robert A. Lewis (New York: Routledge, 1992).

meaning and worthless and found all sorts of ways of dodging the task and passing it along to women.[12] The responsibility for mobilizing for the harvest fell on local party organizations, which could be quite ruthless in holding collective farms responsible for their quotas. Cotton brought the power of the state into the village.

Cotton came at the expense of food crops and pasture for livestock (see figure 17.3). Most farms abandoned crop rotation involving alfalfa or a season of fallow to keep up with the ever-increasing demand for cotton. Central Asia had early become dependent on food shipped in from elsewhere, and shortages were chronic. Per capita consumption in the region of meat, eggs, and milk remained well below the Soviet average.[13] However, cotton was ever-present in Central Asia. Not only did cotton bolls decorate everything from teapots to façades of apartment buildings, but villagers also used cotton stalks for fuel and cottonseed oil for cooking. The one thing missing was a textile industry. Cotton was ginned on location but then sent off to mills in Russia to be turned into textiles. In 1984, Uzbekistan produced 70 percent of the Soviet Union's cotton but only 4 percent of its textiles.[14] As far as cotton was concerned, Central Asia remained a colony.

In other ways, Central Asians were full-fledged citizens of the Soviet Union, with all the rights and obligations that came with that status.

TABLE 17.2   Urban population as a percentage of the total, 1959–1989

Nationality	1959	1970	1979	1989
USSR total	47.9%	56.3%	62.0%	65.9%
Uzbeks	21.8	24.9	29.2	31.0
Tajiks	20.6	26.0	28.1	28.3
Kazakhs	24.1	26.7	31.6	38.7
Kyrgyzes	10.8	14.6	19.6	22.2
Turkmens	25.4	31.0	32.3	33.4

Source: Robert J. Kaiser, *The Geography of Nationalism in Russia and the USSR* (Princeton, NJ: Princeton University Press, 1994), 203.

Men were subject to compulsory military service, but Central Asians, like all Soviet citizens, benefited from universal free education and almost free health care. In addition, state social expenditures (for guaranteed employment, pensions, and paid maternity leaves) expanded substantially in the Brezhnev years. By the 1980s, social expenditures had risen to 12 percent of gross domestic product and were largely covered by transfers from Moscow.[15] Yet Central Asia's development in the postwar period had many peculiarities. The industrialization planned in the Khrushchev years stalled. The early hopes that the mechanization of cotton harvesting would free up labor for industrialization came to very little, and Central Asia remained predominantly rural (see table 17.2). There was an element of choice in this. Key features of the late-Soviet state ensured that the flight of impoverished rural populations to the cities that marked the rest of the developing world in the mid-twentieth century did not happen in Central Asia. Most villages had access to electricity and elementary education, and social spending by the state on salaries and pensions reduced poverty. Living space was abundant and familiar, and inhabitants could count on the support of family members and friends. The countryside was familiar, a national space where there were few Russians. In contrast, the cities remained an alien space dominated by Europeans. Few young Central Asians felt compelled to leave the countryside. Economic planners had trouble getting rural Central Asians to move to the cities in their own republics, let alone to those in other parts of the Soviet Union.[16]

Still, from the late 1950s on, cities grew substantially in Central Asia and took on a new physiognomy. Khrushchev's push for the expansion of urban housing brought a proliferation of apartment blocks built on a standard design (many of them prefabricated) that cropped up across the cities of the Soviet Union. From Tallinn to Vladivostok and across Central Asia, identical five- or nine-story buildings transformed the urban landscape. Urban living changed quite drastically as more and more of the population moved out of traditional *mahallas* (urban neighborhoods) and into apartment blocks. Significant differences remained between the rhythm of life in the *mahallas* that survived and in the new, Soviet-era developments, as well as between large cities or republican capitals and smaller cities, where Europeans predominated to a lesser extent. The most substantial transformation took place in Tashkent. The center of Russian power in Central Asia ever since the conquest, it had become the largest city in the region well before the beginning of the twentieth century. In 1930, its old and new cities were finally amalgamated into a single municipality, but the stark differences between them remained. Much of the new construction—of structures housing government and party offices, parks, and squares—took place in the new city. The old city did acquire electricity and running water, but it lagged behind the new city in the provision of utilities and social services. For Soviet planners, the stark contrast between the two parts of town was as unwelcome as were the narrow, winding alleys of the old city. Beginning in 1937, the authorities had begun planning a radical redesign of the city that would demolish much of the old city and replace it with wide avenues and apartment blocks. Nothing much came of the plan, as the war intervened. The evacuation reshaped the city in unexpected ways, but the dichotomy between the old and the new cities remained. In the postwar years, the city expanded, with new planned developments coming in along the edges of the new city, while the old city gradually diminished through demolitions. A long-term plan for its modernization was in the works.[17]

The situation was transformed on April 26, 1966, when Tashkent was hit by an earthquake measuring 5.1 on the Richter scale, with its epicenter directly underneath the city center. Miraculously, the loss of life was small, but much of the city lay in ruins. Moscow acted with alacrity. Brezhnev and Alexei Kosygin, the prime minister, flew to Tashkent on the day of the earthquake and promised to provide generous funding for reconstruction. The rebuilding of Tashkent became a Union-wide project: construction crews arrived from around the country to help with the rebuilding. Over the next three years, the city was rebuilt—or rather a new city was built. The scale of destruction and the availability of funding gave Soviet planners carte blanche to create a model Soviet city. The Tashkent that emerged was a city of wide boulevards, extensive parks and green spaces, and massive apartment blocks. The city center was redesigned as a showpiece of Soviet modernity. The old city had suffered extensive damage. Now, large parts of it were bulldozed and replaced by new construction, leaving only a few *mahallas* behind. The new master plan moved industry to the outskirts of town and had a long-term plan for transportation infrastructure that included a metro, which opened in 1977. While the first constructions after 1966 were built according to generic Soviet patterns, starting in the early 1970s, "national" elements began to crop up. These were mostly limited to decorative elements, but they also included architectural innovations that took account of Tashkent's hot summers and bright sunshine.[18]

But the unwillingness of Central Asians to move out of the countryside remained and it ensured that the dual society that had taken shape during the Tsarist period was never really dismantled. This situation produced a peculiar ethnic division of labor, whereby Central Asians worked primarily in agriculture, service sectors, and light and food industries, and Europeans continued to dominate heavy industry and technical fields. A Central Asian technical intelligentsia did emerge, as did an industrial working class, but these groups remained small. Most Central Asians in higher education tended to gravitate toward the human and social sciences. In 1987, only 53 percent of industrial jobs in Uzbekistan were held by Uzbeks, while Tajiks accounted for 48 percent of the industrial workforce in their republic and the Kyrgyz only a quarter.[19] At the same time, the generous benefits for childbearing that the state began offering in the 1960s produced high birth rates. Central Asia witnessed massive population growth in the postwar period that re-

TABLE 17.3   The growth of the Central Asian population by nationality, 1959–1989

Nationality	1959	1970	1979	1989	Change, 1959–1989
Uzbeks	6,015,416	9,195,093	12,455,978	16,697,825	277.5%
Kazakhs	3,621,610	5,298,818	6,556,442	8,135,818	224.6
Tajiks	1,396,939	2,135,883	2,897,697	4,215,372	301.8
Turkmens	1,001,585	1,525,284	2,027,913	2,728,965	272.5
Kyrgyzes	968,659	1,452,222	1,906,271	2,528,946	261.1
Karakalpaks	172,556	236,009	303,324	423,520	245.4

Source: Census figures from demoscope.ru.

Notes: Figures refer to passport nationality throughout the Soviet Union. However, 98% of Central Asians continued to live in the five Central Asian republics.

shaped the demographic balance not just in the region but in the Soviet Union as a whole (see table 17.3). The share of Central Asian nationalities in the total Soviet population nearly doubled over this period, from 6.3 percent in 1959 to 12.3 percent in 1989. Central Asian Muslims accounted for 28 percent of the increase in the total Soviet population in those three decades. The population growth also made Central Asia more Central Asian. The years after the revolution had seen an influx of Europeans into the region. Millions had been dumped in the region through exile and deportation, and others had come in search of jobs. The post-Stalin period saw another influx of Europeans into Central Asia. The Virgin Lands campaign was unusual in its scale and the intensity of immigration that it produced, but many more Europeans came in search of jobs or were sent by the center to serve in various capacities. European immigration continued through the 1970s, but after that it tailed off, and in the 1980s—before the collapse of the Soviet Union— the direction of population flows had reversed. The overall percentage of the European population had declined since the war because of the high birth rates of Central Asians. The decline in European immigration magnified the domination of titular nationalities in their republics. Even Kazakhstan, which had been flooded by settlers to a much greater extent than the rest of the region, had an indigenous plurality in the population by 1989 (see table 17.4).

TABLE 17.4   National composition of the Central Asian republics, 1959–1989

Republic	1959		1970		1979		1989	
	Titular	Russian	Titular	Russian	Titular	Russian	Titular	Russian
Uzbekistan	62.1%	13.5%	65.5%	12.5%	68.7%	10.8%	71.4%	8.3%
Kazakhstan	30.0	42.7	32.6	42.4	36.0	40.8	39.7	37.8
Tajikistan	53.1	13.3	56.2	11.9	58.8	10.4	62.3	7.6
Turkmenistan	60.9	17.3	65.6	14.5	68.4	12.6	72.0	9.5
Kyrgyzstan	40.5	30.2	43.8	29.2	47.9	25.9	52.4	21.5

Source: Robert J. Kaiser, *The Geography of Nationalism in Russia and the USSR* (Princeton, NJ: Princeton University Press, 1994), 174.

None of this is to say that rural Central Asia remained untouched by Soviet life. Quite the opposite: the state was present in the village in many ways. Cotton production was the most important, but in addition the people who staffed schools, clinics, and the local police were all locals who represented the state in the village. This "rural intelligentsia" was funded by the state, and its members saw themselves as bearers of Soviet values. The countryside was thoroughly Sovietized, to the point that being Soviet and being national became completely intertwined. The refusal to move to the cities and the persistence of customary ways of life were not acts of resistance to Soviet rule but were made possible by it.

———

The Brezhnevite golden age had begun to lose its luster by the time the 1980s rolled around. Economic growth had slowed considerably by the late 1970s. The slowdown was endemic to the whole Soviet economy, but it had local peculiarities in Central Asia. The rapid population growth undermined many of the gains. Investment in the industrial sector had begun to decline, both in absolute terms and per capita. Even the agricultural sector suffered. The new land being put to use was often of marginal quality that could not produce at the same level as older land. Cotton yields stagnated, the level of mechanization declined, and the amount of cotton fiber produced per ton of raw cotton fell. More cotton was picked by hand in the 1980s than in the previous decade. Infant mortality increased over the 1970s. At the end of the Soviet era, Uzbekistan's infant mortality rate was almost twice the Soviet average, and the figures for Tajikistan and Turkmenistan were even higher (and the figures were doubtless worse for the indigenous nationalities).[20] Soviet planners had also begun to be concerned about the oversupply of labor and the de facto unemployment that it produced, but rural Central Asians still refused to migrate to the cities, let alone to other parts of the Soviet Union. Attempts to mobilize Central Asian labor for long-term projects in other parts of the Soviet state had little success. In 1976, a multiyear project to reclaim tracts of agricultural land in the Novgorod region of Russia contracted its labor supply from Uzbekistan, for instance, but such initiatives did not even make a dent in the demographic problem.[21]

This relentless pursuit of production brought about ecological catastrophe, the full scale of which was becoming clear as the 1980s began. The abandonment of crop rotation had led to the detriment of soil quality, while irrigation had brought salinity and waterlogging in its wake. Water use was generally inefficient: most irrigation channels were not lined and lost a great deal of water through seepage and evaporation in the desert sun. Irrigation withdrew so much water that the rivers ran dry. By the early 1980s, the outflow from the Amu and Syr Daryas into the Aral Sea had dwindled to almost nothing, with the inflow being zero in 1982–1983 and again in 1985–1986.[22] The Aral Sea had begun to shrink already by 1970 (see map 17.1). Between 1960 and 1987, its water level fell by thirteen meters, and its surface area shrank by 40 percent.[23] Until 1960, the sea had supported a thriving fishing industry, which completely vanished. The salinity of the water more than doubled, killing off much of the marine life, while the reduction of the sea altered the regional climate, making the temperature range more extreme and the precipitation less abundant, as well as unleashing dust storms of unprecedented intensity.

These challenges did nothing to dent Soviet planners' boundless confidence in the ability of science and technology to conquer nature. They had in fact foreseen the decline of Central Asia's rivers, and their answer

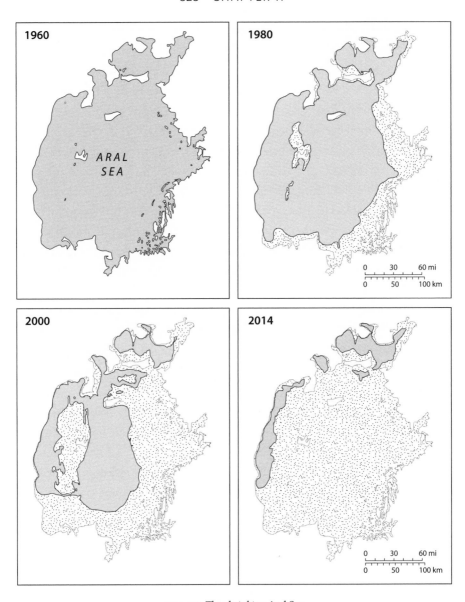

MAP 17.1. The shrinking Aral Sea

to that change was an even more audacious recourse to technology. A "project of the century" would divert water from the rivers in Siberia the flowed north to the Arctic, through a canal 2,500 kilometers long. The water would be pumped over watersheds and other barriers to Central Asia, where it would supplement the water of local rivers and open up new lands to irrigation. The idea had first been floated in 1869, in the hubris of the Tsarist conquest of Central Asia, but like many such ideas, it had remained a dream until the Soviet era. It reemerged in the 1950s and was pushed by a number of constituencies: the federal Ministry of Land Reclamation and Water Resources, Central Asian political elites, and many scientists and engineers in Russia. In 1984, the Communist Party approved the project, and construction on the first phase was set to begin in the late 1980s. The project would have reduced the flow of the River Ob into the Arctic by 32 percent and brought about unimaginable changes to the Arctic Ocean and the tundra on its shores, and thus on global climatic patterns. The project had always had its skeptics—both within the technical community and without—who accused the proponents of the project of underestimating its cost, technical difficulties, and impact on the climate. Opposition to the project united a nascent environmental movement with Russian nationalists who mobilized around the pillage of Russian nature and Russian resources. The timing was right: Mikhail Gorbachev had just ascended to power and pushed for greater openness in public debate. The project of the century was the first victim of this glasnost. The party leadership did an about-face in 1986 and canceled the project. Glasnost was eventually to lead to the demise of the Soviet Union, but it also spared the planet from one of the more audacious assaults on nature dreamed up in the Soviet period.

Science had always been central in the Soviet quest for cotton, and chemicalization was one of its main goals. If nature would not cooperate, then chemicals in various guises—used as fertilizers, pesticides, and defoliants—would help convince it to yield more "white gold," as cotton was known in Soviet rhetoric. Large-scale use of fertilizers for Central Asian cotton began in the 1950s and was quickly followed by large-scale use of defoliants (to remove the leaves of the cotton plant and thus make picking easier) and pesticides. By the 1980s, the use of chemicals averaged 20–25 kilograms per hectare.[24] Over the decades, so many chemicals were pumped into the cotton fields of Central Asia that the land itself became toxic. Once the Aral Sea began to recede, its former bed, now thoroughly polluted, was exposed to the elements, and yielded up its chemicals to dust storms and rain. Pollution literally rained down upon the population and caused widespread disease and birth defects. Through it all, the regime's appetite for cotton never diminished. There was no movement toward reducing the region's devotion to cotton. Instead, projections in the 1980s called for annual cotton production in Central Asia to be raised to over eight million tons.

Environmental catastrophes were not limited to the Soviet Union. As the California drought of the 2010s showed, irrational use of natural resources can take place under capitalism as well, and radical shifts to new patterns of land use are just as difficult under free-market conditions as under a command-administrative system. Capitalism did not stop almonds, say, with their enormous thirst for scarce water, from becoming a major crop in arid California, and once established, that industry found it as hard to move to other crops as did Uzbek kolkhozes. Nor was the Soviet faith in the power of science and technology to master nature unique. Soviet planners shared that faith with all other heirs of the Enlightenment. A lot of the plans that the Soviets implemented or thought of implementing—such as irrigating the Hungry Steppe, maximizing cotton production, and diverting Siberian rivers—were first conceived of in the imperial age. After all, the Soviet conceit was to accomplish what mere bourgeois planners could not. The Soviet specificity lay in the combination of a hypercentralized economy and a completely opaque political system with Central Asia's peripheral location in it—which made Central Asia's political elites complicit in the cottonization of their republics.

18

Soviet in Form, National in Content?

TASHKENT'S METRO OPENED IN 1977. It was part of the urban development plan for Tashkent adopted after the earthquake of 1966, but it was also a prestige project. Inaugurated in the year of the sixtieth anniversary of the revolution, it began with two lines that intersected in the new ceremonial center of the city at stations called Paxtakor (Cotton Grower, of course, but in this case referring to Tashkent's football team, which played in a stadium nearby) and Alisher Navoiy (named after the great poet of the Timurid era). Metro stations in the Soviet Union were "palaces of the proletariat," richly decorated with scenes appropriate to the name of the station. The Alisher Navoiy station was one of the most ornate in the entire Soviet Union. It was decorated with mosaics depicting scenes from Navoiy's poetry, created in the style of the Central Asian miniature painting of his era. The Soviet state had lavished resources on celebrating the work of a court poet who wrote works of mystical content steeped in the Islamicate literary tradition of Central Asia.

Navoiy (or Nava'i) was the central figure in the pantheon of Uzbek cultural heroes that crystallized in the Soviet era. The Uzbek national opera house was also named after him, as was the most important boulevard that stretched eastward from the center of Tashkent, and several statues of him were to be found around the city. He was joined in this public display of national pride by a host of luminaries from the past, who represented the magnificent cultural heritage of the Uzbek nation. Tashkent might have had more Russians than Uzbeks in it, but as the capital of the republic, it showcased Uzbek heritage in its public spaces. The symbols of the Uzbek past were inscribed in space: in metro stations, parks, and streets, as well as on the façades of new buildings. They were also ever present in the literature of the period and history books, in film and on the stage, and in museums across the republic. What was true for Uzbekistan was also true for all other Soviet republics. The Soviets had always taken the existence of nations for granted and recognized that each nation had a distinctive culture and history. How the nations could speak about that past varied over the Soviet period. The late Stalinist era tended to be deeply suspicious of any expressions of national distinctiveness not couched in terms of slavish gratitude to the Russians. In contrast, the Khrushchev and especially the Brezhnev periods were a golden age for national narratives and the celebration of national heritages. Limits to national expressions still remained, to be sure, and nationality coexisted with a Sovietness common to all Soviet citizens, but in these decades national identities crystallized and became meaningful to ordinary people.

These phenomena fully nationalized the region—that is, they divided up Central Asia's past and present along national lines. Each nation was seen as distinct, housed in its republic (which was its national homeland), with its distinctiveness firmly rooted in the past. Most people outside the Soviet Union assumed that these national designations were artificial constructs of the Soviet state that meant little to Central Asians, who were supposed to have retained a sense of themselves as only Central Asian or Muslim. But that view was far off the mark. Central Asia's national projects predated the revolution, but they crystallized in the Soviet period and on the Soviet state's dime. National categories were an important part of people's lives. Listed on their identity documents, the categories were politically relevant, and they gave meaning to people's sense of self. Ordinary citizens took these categories for granted and invested them with a great deal of meaning. Yet, crucially, these national identities were not subversive to the Soviet order but rather made it familiar and natural. Vincent Fourniau has called this process the "silent indigenization" of Soviet rule in postwar Central Asia.[1]

———

Soviet culture was to be socialist in content and national in form. The slogan was Stalinist, but it expressed a challenge that all societies have faced in the modern world: how to be modern and yet retain a sense of the self. How was, for instance, Japan to adapt to the new practices, goods, and ideas that came with modernity? How was U.S. society to cope with new ideas or new configurations of gender that stemmed from industrialization and urbanization? What was the modern Indian family to look like? What did it mean for Iranians to become modern? Modernity always produced anxieties and contestation, and everywhere the dialectic between change and authenticity played out in peculiar ways. In the Soviet Union, the party-state claimed the right to define both modernity (which was to be socialism) and the national. The limits of the latter varied over time. As we have seen, Stalin's suspicion of nationalism had circumscribed the limits of national expression. Central Asian elites had been decimated in the 1930s on charges of nationalism, and expressions of any national sentiment had come under attack again in the postwar deep freeze of late Stalinism. However, the Thaw under Khrushchev reshaped the cultural landscape and expanded the limits of what was permissible for national expression. The new and newly confident national Communist elites that emerged in this period, combined with a new generation of national intelligentsia in each republic, transformed the situation. The national cultures and national identities were not subversive to the Soviet order; rather, they took shape in Soviet conditions and were made possible by them.

Nationality was an official category in the Soviet Union. Belonging to one nationality rather than another had practical consequences, from the choice of schools open to one's children to preferences in employment. National belonging thus became part of the everyday behavior of Soviet citizens. A vast array of practices reified nationhood. Food was marked as national. Each nation had its own cuisine, which centered on one dish that was its pride—*pulov* for the Uzbeks (the Tajiks had their own distinctive variant), *besparmak* for the Kazakhs, *işlykly* for the Turkmens, and so forth. Each also had its own dress. National style was ubiquitous. This process of nationalization also involved standardization and, to a certain extent, simplification. National forms for each nation were identified, codified, and preserved. The study of their national heritage had been part of the national projects of Central Asian intellectuals in the 1920s. After that generation was destroyed, the task of determining national forms fell into the hands of mostly European ethnographers and even party functionaries. That role was reclaimed by national intellectuals of the new generation. The Soviet command economy had space for the production of national goods for each republic—not only works of art meant for display, but also (and more importantly) items of everyday use, such as clothing, crockery, and furniture available in distinct national styles. Over the course of the Soviet period, but particularly in the post-Stalin years, each nation claimed ownership of distinctive patterns and motifs. The production of national goods often shifted to factories, but artisanal production never disappeared. National goods provided a niche in the Soviet command economy where masters of traditional crafts could survive in radically new conditions.[2]

Soviet policy and Soviet scholarship took nations to be natural phenomena. In the late 1930s, Soviet ethnographers and historians had begun using the concept of ethnogenesis, which posited that each nation had a specific genetic composition that had emerged through various permutations of mixing over the centuries. Each nation had its own set of traits and its own record of cultural achievement that stretched into the past. Not all aspects of heritage were worthy of celebration—feudal, religious, or other retrograde features of the past were to be condemned—but each nation also had popular (hence progressive) elements that could be celebrated. What was progressive and what not was open to a surprisingly expansive debate. The recent past was problematic because it was tied up with the messy origins of the Soviet order. Those who had lost out in the cultural and political battles of the 1920s and 1930s could not be celebrated. Thus, Kazakh history was to be written without any mention of the generation of intellectuals who were involved in Alash Orda, and the history of Uzbek literature could not mention the names of Abdurauf Fitrat and Cholpan. The process of rehabilitation during the Khrushchev years had its limits. Many of the earliest critics of the Bolsheviks were never rehabilitated, and there were gradations in the rehabilitation of the others. In Uzbekistan, for instance, Abdulla Qodiriy was rehabilitated and given a suitably proletarian biography. His novels reappeared in print in 1957, published for the first time in Cyrillic script, and bookstores could scarcely keep the works in stock. Qodiriy never lost his position as the most beloved author of Uzbek prose, but little about the context in which he wrote could be mentioned. Fitrat and Cholpan had a different fate: they were legally rehabilitated, but their works were not republished, and their names could be mentioned only in the context of their being exemplars of counterrevolutionary bourgeois nationalism.

The amnesia imposed on recent history did not extend to the deeper past, which was nationalized everywhere with gusto. Intellectuals of each nation created canons of their national literature and art and pantheons of their great cultural figures. The great oral epics attacked in the late Stalin period returned as parts of proud national origin myths and fonts of modern literature. Kyrgyz intellectuals raised the epic *Manas*, the 500,000-couplet-long epic first written down in the Tsarist period, to the status of a national monument and the fount of the Kyrgyz language and nationhood. Kazakh folklore similarly served as the origin of the written literature that had emerged only in the nineteenth century. Turkmen scholars outlined a path of Turkmen literature that led from the earliest Turkic-language poetry composed in Turkmen lands through the work of the poet Makhtumquli (or Magtymguly, 1724–1807) to the Soviet period. Uzbek and Tajik scholars could lay claim to a much longer tradition of written literature: they claimed the entire tradition of Turkic and Persian letters, respectively, of Central Asia. The anthologies of Uzbek literature published from the 1950s on began with the works of Mahmud Kashgari and Yusuf Khass Hajib, the first men to write in Turkic, and passed through the Eastern Turkic poetry of Ata'i, Yasavi (the great Sufi master), and Lutfi before reaching Nava'i. The

canon then continued through the post-Timurid period to the twentieth century. The pantheon of Uzbek cultural heroes included Sufi figures such as Ahmed Yasavi and Nava'i and imperial figures such as
Timur's grandson Mirza Ulughbek (1394–1449), who was a leading
astronomer and the builder of an observatory in Samarqand, and Zahiruddin Muhammad Babur (1483–1530), the Timurid prince who
founded the Mughal empire in India. The Tajik canon was outlined as
early as 1926 by Sadriddin Ayni, who—in his monumental *Samples of
Tajik Literature*—proclaimed all Persian-language poetry created in
Transoxiana to be Tajik. Since it was in Bukhara that Persian had re-
emerged as a literary language after the devastations of the Arab conquest, Tajik literature reached back to the very origins of what is called
New Persian.

There remained limits to what could be said. Khrushchev's Thaw did
not touch many fundamental tenets of Stalinist nationalities policy, and
such orthodoxies as the views that the Russian empire had been built
on the basis of the accession of various regions, not by military conquest; the Russians were the elder brothers in the fraternal family of
friendly nations; and Russian was the language of international communication, survived until the end of the Soviet era. Yet within these
constraints, Soviet Central Asian intellectuals had considerable scope
for cultivating national culture and celebrating the nation. Large numbers of literary scholars and historians worked away on these tasks,
backed by an extensive system of research and publication. Each republic had literary and research journals in its own language, while well-
staffed departments of history, literature, ethnography, and folklore in
universities and institutes produced the research. Museums catalogued
and displayed the material heritage of each nation, while publishers put
out works by the cultural heroes of their republic in massive editions.
In addition, historical novels became a popular vehicle for celebrating
the past. A Soviet joke was that historians wrote fiction, while writers of
fiction wrote history. In Uzbekistan, the Timurid era became the focus
of the loving attention of a number of writers. Pirimqul Qodirov's novel
Yulduzli tunlar (Starry Nights, 1978) painted a panorama of the age of
Babur, while a sequel, *Avlodlar dovoni* (The Crossings of Generations,

1988) recounted the exploits of his successors, the Mughal emperors Humayun and Akbar—all of whom were seen as great Uzbek heroes. Odil Yoqubov, in *Ulug'bek xazinasi* (Ulughbek's Treasure, 1974), wrote lovingly of Ulughbek. Both these novels were critically acclaimed and translated into several foreign languages. The Tajik writer Sotim Ulughzoda similarly wrote novels celebrating Rudaki and Ferdowsi, the first poets in New Persian who were active in Transoxiana; a play on Abu 'Ali ibn Sina; and a novel titled *Rivoyati Sughdî* (A Sogdian Tale), about the Arab invasion of Sogdiana.

This reclamation and celebration of the cultural heritage was selective. The great cultural heroes of the past were celebrated for their contribution to the world's cultural heritage, patriotism, humanism, and freethinking. Their work was unmoored from its historical and cultural origins. The Sufi poetry of Nava'i and Makhtumquli was read in a national vein, its Islamic background largely disregarded. This secularization of heritage happened under Soviet conditions, but it was hardly unique to them. All sorts of national movements have claimed past heroes on national terms by rereading their works for contemporary purposes. What is more important in the Soviet case is that such narratives asserted the antiquity of each nation, its existence across the ages, its ancient claim to its territory, and its place in a global (not just Soviet) comity of nations. They also nationalized culture and divided up the past among the various nations that were now deemed to have always existed as distinct entities. Historical figures were thus claimed by one nation or another, and great works of art or literature became not merely the works of individual genius but the common patrimony of the entire nation. Again, this is hardly unusual in a global context. This is the same process through which Bach and Beethoven came to belong to Germany (and to the West in general) and Vivaldi became an Italian genius. In Central Asia, the national narratives bore an uncanny resemblance to the visions of the 1920s, even though the visionaries of that decade lay in unmarked graves and their names could not be mentioned. This is most clearly the case with the way Uzbek heritage was imagined. The Jadids in the 1920s had imagined the Uzbek nation as the heir to the entire tradition of Muslim statehood and the culture of sedentary Central

Asia. In a series of learned volumes published between 1926 and 1928, Fitrat had outlined a canon of Uzbek literature that stretched from the earliest writings in Turkic; through the emergence of Eastern Turkic, its efflorescence in the courts of the Timurid era, and its transformations in the Uzbek period; to the emergence of modern forms of expression with the Jadids. Fitrat was viciously attacked in the 1930s for "pan-Turkism" and all sorts of other sins, and those charges were prominent in the indictment that led to his execution in 1938. Fitrat was vindicated after his death, for the late-Soviet narratives of the Uzbek nation drew precisely the same connections across the centuries that he had made.

All this work of national celebration was funded by the Soviet state and was perfectly aboveboard. The remarkable expansion of the Soviet educational system in the post-Stalin years made this possible. The expansion was both horizontal and vertical. Elementary schools appeared in every village and neighborhood, and a dense network of secondary and vocational schools spread throughout the five republics. Universal schooling not only produced universal literacy—a phenomenal achievement, given the very high rates of illiteracy that prevailed at the time of the revolution—but was also an important vector of socialization into Soviet citizenship. School curricula were largely homogeneous across the country. At the same time, higher education expanded. At the beginning of the Second World War, there were only three universities in the region, two in Uzbekistan and one in Kazakhstan. By the end of the 1950s, each republic possessed multiple universities, as well as numerous teachers colleges and vocational schools. There was a parallel structure of research institutions: each republic had its own academy of sciences, with a ramified system of research institutes in the humanities as well as the sciences. This vast infrastructure of educational and research organizations produced a new generation of specialists as well as providing large numbers of jobs for those engaged in intellectual work. While the technical and scientific fields continued to be dominated by Europeans, the humanities were monopolized by members of each republic's titular nation. The Soviet educational system produced and then employed large numbers of historians, literary scholars, ethnographers, folklorists, and musicologists who came to see themselves as the creators and curators of distinctive national cultures.

The Soviet Central Asian intelligentsia was professionalized and ensconced in Soviet institutions. It was thus quite different from the *ulama* and the Jadids, the older groups of intellectuals that had been destroyed in the 1930s. There were elements of continuity with previous generations, to be sure. A few survivors of the Gulag were able to find academic work again after their rehabilitation. The new intelligentsia also contained a remarkable number of children of those who had been purged. They were helped by extended family networks, but they also had to reinvent themselves, keeping quiet about their backgrounds and emphasizing their notable families' commitment to serving the people. But they were able to do so, and many found niches for themselves in Soviet institutions after the war. Muhammadjon Shakuri (or Shukurov, 1925–2012)—the son of Sadr Ziyo, a Bukharan notable who had been supportive of the Young Bukharans and died in a Soviet prison—became a leading scholar of Tajik literature, defending his dissertation in Moscow and being elected a member of Tajikistan's Academy of Sciences in 1981. Baroat Hojiboyeva—the daughter of Abdurahim Hojiboyev, the first head of Tajikistan's government who was purged in 1933—also defended her dissertation in Moscow (in 1968) and became a prominent scholar in Tajikistan. The father of Chingiz Aitmatov (1928–2008), Kyrgyzstan's most famous writer, who won acclaim across the Soviet Union, was an early Kyrgyz Communist who had been shot in 1938. There are many other examples of children of the purged who did not turn their back on the Soviet order. Their stories indicate not just survival but adaptation. Other members of the new Soviet intelligentsia came from humble backgrounds. They were the beneficiaries of the massive expansion of education in the postwar years and of the Soviet order. They discovered the world of learning in Soviet institutions and were profoundly shaped by them. They were fully Soviet, even as they remained Central Asians. The late-Soviet intelligentsia in Central Asia was closely connected to national party elites as well, through bonds of friendship and sometimes marriage. Many politicians were writers themselves. Sharaf Rashidov, we will remember, was a novelist who had headed

Uzbekistan's Writers Union for two years before he ascended to the heights of political power. The close ties between the cultural and political elites shaped the contours of Soviet Central Asian life in significant ways.

———

Nor was nationality simply a matter of narratives and celebration. It came to be grounded in everyday social practice. If nationalities policy recognized and, in many ways, affirmed national customs and traditions, then the command economy laid the framework for the consolidation of customary ways of life, especially in the countryside. The Soviet economy, with its perpetual shortages, made social networks based on families and communities essential to the procurement of goods and services that money alone could not obtain. Combined with the emphasis on agricultural production, the Soviet system generated deep social conservatism in Central Asian society.

The Communist values of collectivism mapped onto the rhythms of agricultural labor to reproduce local solidarities that had been shaken up in the upheavals of the 1920s and 1930s. Collective farms became nodes of community. Collective farm directors and local party officials, who were responsible to the state for fulfilling quotas, acted as agents of both the state and local community building.[3] The authoritarian rule of collective farm directors re-created an order that was surprisingly patriarchal and drew its legitimacy from local custom. In *mahallas* and on kolkhozes, respect for age, community and family, and communal practices made a stirring comeback. The family emerged triumphant as the main locus of Soviet Central Asian life (see figure 18.1). It was through the family and its connections that individuals negotiated the Soviet economy. Crucially, this conservatism was intimately linked to national identities. It was the national custom of Uzbeks or Turkmens, say, to respect elders, celebrate life-cycle events, and be hospitable. Respect for customs and traditions marked the boundaries of the nation.

The party-state had its own list of Soviet values. Soviet citizens were supposed to value hard work, collectivism, and respect for the community

FIG. 18.1. Socialist in form, national in content? The family of Nishanali Avazov, the chairman of Lenin collective farm, 1983. Nothing could be more Soviet than being chairman of a collective farm, and nothing could be more Uzbek than the *dasturxon* (tablecloth) groaning under the feast here. The family is multigenerational, and Avazov is clearly the patriarch. Compare this with the vision of the future presented in figure 13.2. Photo: Sputnik Images.

and to avoid narcissism, self-indulgence, and socially irresponsible consumption. Society had been turned upside down in the 1920s and 1930s by rebellious, impatient youth. Now, the members of that generation who had survived began to see the wisdom of respecting the old. In the Soviet Union as a whole, the government had come to see youth as the object of nurturing and grooming, not as a revolutionary force in its own right. The Khrushchev years also saw the emergence of a nonconformist youth subculture that copied Western fashions and modes of behavior. The critique of this subculture, both in official sources and among the respectable members of the public, centered on its self-indulgence, disruptiveness, lack of social consciousness, and lack of respect for the community. This critique blended very well with traditional Central Asian norms and made Soviet values consistent with local traditions.

Tradition, however, is a tricky thing to talk about. Traditions claim to be links to the past, but they are immensely mutable. Many traditions disappeared in the turmoil of the Stalin era. The grotesque horsehair veil worn by women in sedentary areas was gone, religious observance had declined markedly, and the entire way of life based on nomadism had vanished. The traditions that had survived the Stalinist era or re-emerged after it were not exactly the same as those of previous generations but bore the signs of times in which they existed. Take, for instance, the life-cycle celebrations that were perhaps the most important markers of national identity in this era. Celebrations of births, circumcisions, and weddings involved music (both national and contemporary Soviet pop) and were awash in a sea of vodka, the drinking of which also became part of national traditions. Weddings assimilated many European elements (the bride wore white, and cake was often involved). At the end of life, only the most diehard Communists were buried with no Islamic ritual, but many Muslim graves were topped by busts of the deceased in typical Soviet style. Central Asian traditions were not frozen in time. They were significant not as proof of the continuity or immutability of society but as markers of boundaries. They also distinguished Central Asians from outsiders: Soviet Europeans, Koreans, Armenians, and other Muslims. The traditions celebrated in late-Soviet Central Asia were not relics of the past, as the Soviet phrase had it, not things that stood outside the Soviet order, but things that were very much a part of it and indeed shaped by it.

This confluence of Soviet and customary values also shaped gender relations. Veiling had disappeared by the war, and in the postwar period all girls went to school and most women worked. However, these phenomena could not shake up the gender order in society. There were a number of urban women who held high-profile positions in academia and politics. Uzbeks took great pride in the fact that Khadija Sulaymonova, who was the republic's minister of justice from 1956 to 1958, was the first woman to occupy such a post anywhere in the world. She was a member of the Uzbekistan's academy of sciences and ended her career as head of the republic's high court. Yodgor Nasriddinova headed Uzbekistan's Supreme Soviet from 1959 to 1970, when she was elected chair of the Soviet of Nationalities in Moscow, the upper chamber of the Soviet Union's legislature. Women were elected to legislatures in the republics in small numbers and occasionally led collective farms or enterprises. Yet these successes coexisted with a hardening of gender roles across Central Asian societies (with Kazakh and Kyrgyz societies being partial exceptions). The number of girls, especially in the countryside, who stayed in school beyond the compulsory eight years remained low, and the vast majority of girls continued to be married off by their families in arranged marriages in their teens. Most families practiced gender segregation, even as women worked outside the home (which in the countryside often included the most physically demanding labor). They had many children, which heightened the value attached to motherhood. While public spaces remained resolutely mixed and all schooling was coeducational, family life took on a highly gendered form in most segments of society, and socializing took place along segregated lines. The Soviet liberation of women had abolished veiling and put women in the workforce, but other Soviet policies had enabled the consolidation of new gender hierarchies in Central Asia.

All Soviet women faced the double burden of working and being the primary caretakers at home, but Central Asian women had added responsibilities. In a pattern observed in many parts of the world, women came to be seen as guardians of the faith and the inner values of the community. Men were supposed to go out and engage in the rough-and-tumble of the world, while women guarded the chastity of the home and community. They were also the guardians of tradition and of religious observance on behalf of the whole community. The British anthropologist Gillian Tett, who did fieldwork in a village in Tajikistan in the twilight years of Soviet rule, once asked a village notable whether he felt any contradiction in being both a Muslim and a Communist. "'Not at all,' he laughed. 'I am a communist. I cannot fast or pray at work. But my wife and *kelin* [daughter-in-law], they are sitting at home, so they must fast and pray! So we will not suffer from sins. We are a Muslim home!'"[4] This, of course, placed peculiar burdens on women that often flew in the face of official Soviet proclamations. More intriguingly, female modesty came to be asserted as an official Soviet value in

Central Asia. The most natural target was women whose dress or behavior was deemed antisocial and hence anti-Soviet. These norms were articulated in the local-language press, with satirical and lifestyle magazines being the main channel of dissemination. In a short story from 1956, Abdulla Qahhor, a prominent Uzbek author, narrated the social death of a respected schoolteacher who, perhaps in an effort to reclaim his youth, transforms himself. He shaves his white beard off, starts dressing in hipster fashion, and marries a young woman who dresses immodestly, wearing sleeveless blouses and high heels. This transformation shocks the *mahalla* community, which reacts with anger and ostracizes the couple. The anger falls most heavily on the young woman, who "had robbed the mahalla of its warmth and extinguished the light that had always shone in people's hearts." When the teacher dies suddenly from "overexertion," a month after his wedding, no one comes to his funeral.[5] Qahhor's sympathies lie entirely with the community, and his satire is directed wholly at the old man and his garish young wife. The community and its conservative values, outrage, and policing of its members' behavior are taken as being entirely in the right. Women were being celebrated as the upholders of Soviet values three decades after communities wreaked enormous violence on them in response to the Soviet campaign of unveiling. Central Asians had become Soviet—being Uzbek or Kyrgyz or Tajik, being Soviet, and even being Muslim were not mutually exclusive. They came to coexist more or less happily in the later Soviet period.

———

The dual society continued to exist. In the Brezhnev era, it took the form of a broad division between two umbrella groups, Europeans and Muslims. The term "Muslim" in this context indicated not religious belief or practice, but communal belonging within the Soviet context. It was a sign of localism, applied to those who practiced local customs and were seen to belong to local communities. It was not a homogeneous category, and distinctions between people belonging to different nationalities remained important. Tatars or Chechens inhabited the outer limits of Muslimness, for they did not practice the same customs as Central Asians. The term "Europeans" denoted all outsiders in Central Asia—Russians, Ukrainians, Poles, Germans, Ashkenazi Jews, Armenians, Georgians, and even Koreans. Europeans all used Russian as their main (if not only) language. The countryside was solidly Muslim (except in Kazakhstan), while cities tended to be European. In 1979, when Tashkent was the fourth largest city in the Soviet Union (behind only Moscow, Leningrad, and Kyiv), 45 percent of its population was European, while only 41 percent was Uzbek. The proportion of Europeans was even higher in other capital cities: Almaty's population was three-fourths European, as was Frunze's; Ashgabat and Dushanbe were almost half European. Other than in Kazakhstan, which had a substantial rural Russian population, the vast majority of Russians in Central Asia lived in cities (for example, 96 percent of the Russians in Uzbekistan were urban dwellers). In the major cities, the language of the street was Russian, and the European population had a sense of ownership of urban space.

We should not overstate the point. The European–Muslim distinction existed in the realm of social practice and had no legal basis. The Soviet state consistently used an antiracist discourse and policed equality among its citizens, while notions of the friendship of peoples and internationalism had real meaning for Soviet citizens. Central Asian urban life was characterized by a mingling of nationalities that was taken as normal by participants and that many remember with great fondness.[6] The dichotomy between European and Muslim encompassed a number of fine gradations. Ashkenazi Jews who ended up in Central Asia often found better professional positions than they might have had in Russia. Tatars, Armenians, and Koreans, all Russian-speaking by the later Soviet period, had a significant role in public life, and their presence muted the sharp divide between Russians and locals.

The European–Muslim dichotomy was modulated in other ways as well. Official rhetoric encouraged and celebrated mixed marriages as living proof of the friendship of peoples. Intermarriage across the divide was not widespread, but it certainly existed and was a noticeable part of society. Mixed marriages in Central Asia overwhelmingly involved

Muslim men marrying European women, but they were not limited to any particular stratum of society. Young men returning from service in the Soviet Army (which always took place in other parts of the Soviet Union) sometimes brought back European wives. Some found their mates at universities or research institutes, while others lost their hearts in the Komsomol. Interethnic marriages were unusual because they were always based on mutual attraction in a society where most marriages continued to be arranged by parents.[7] Beyond mixed marriages, urban life in Central Asia was multinational. People of different nationalities interacted in residential compounds, workplaces, schools, and universities. Ambitious parents sent their children to Russian-medium schools, which were more prestigious and imparted fluency in the most important language of the country. By the 1980s, many elite Central Asians, especially in Kazakhstan and Kyrgyzstan, were using Russian as their primary language.

———

Oljas Süleymenov (b. 1936) was perhaps the most prominent Kazakh man of letters of the later Soviet period. In many ways, his life encompassed the twists and turns of the Soviet period. His father, a military officer, was executed in the purges when Süleymenov was only a year old. Süleymenov's family survived, and he was able to train as a geologist, getting a degree from Kazakh State University. He then turned to literature and had a prolific career as a poet and literary historian. In 1966, he wrote the script for *Land of the Fathers*—a film directed by Shaken Aymanov, one of the first generation of Kazakh filmmakers and a war veteran. The film tells the story of fourteen-year-old Bayan, who accompanies his grandfather to Russia "in the first summer after the war" to retrieve the body of Bayan's father, who had died at the front near Leningrad. The grandfather wants to bury his son on the Kazakh steppe, in the land of his fathers, as custom requires. But when Bayan finally reaches his destination, he finds that his father is buried in a communal grave with others of all Soviet nationalities, who had died alongside him. Bayan realizes that the whole of the Soviet Union is the land of the fathers, equally sacred to all its citizens. If Bayan's father is buried in Leningrad, then Leningrad is his land too, and the Kazakh nation has a claim on Leningrad. But there is more to the film. Bayan's father has, of course, given his life for the Soviet Union, and his Sovietness is beyond doubt. Bayan represents the future. He will become (or has become, since he is the narrator) a Soviet citizen. The grandfather represents the past, with its customs and traditions. Not everything about him is portrayed in a positive light. He is suspicious of Russians and adheres to Islamic rules of ritual purity that prevent him from embracing the multinational community of friendship. Yet his grasp of tradition imparts to him the quiet dignity that is his defining characteristic in the film. The final scene shows Bayan and his grandfather—the future and the past—in a loving embrace.[8]

Superficially, the film hews to the official slogan of the friendship of peoples, but it nevertheless pushes against a fundamental asymmetry in Soviet nationalities relations. Soviet nationalities policy had favored the creation of national republics for the non-Russians of the former Russian empire as a way to win their trust and undercut nationalist sentiment. Each republic was the national homeland for its titular nationality within the Soviet whole. The Old Bolsheviks who had won the civil war and created the Soviet state were a multinational lot, with Georgians, Latvians, Ukrainians, and Jews overrepresented among them. After Stalin's revolution from above, that cosmopolitanism was dented, but it never disappeared. The Russians therefore had a complicated relationship with the Soviet Union. They imagined the entire Soviet Union as their space, where they could roam and settle and about which they had a sense of ownership. For most Russians, Central Asia was theirs, although different and somewhat exotic, and many could not always tell the different Central Asian republics apart. Even the highest officials tended to know little about Central Asia. Khrushchev had once famously greeted "the people of Tajikistan" at a rally in Tashkent, the capital of Uzbekistan. Decades later, Gorbachev spoke of "Uzbekia" and "Tajikia," terms that were never used in Central Asia. Official rhetoric presented Russians as first among equals and the elder brothers in the Soviet family of nations. Russian was the default official language of the country. While the Soviet state recognized all sorts of languages, it did not mandate their use on an equal footing (unlike, say, the official bilingualism in Canada or Belgium). Russians carried their language with them and had minimal need to learn other languages, while non-Russian elites had to be fluent in Russian to succeed in life. And there were Russian chauvinists who would have liked to see the Soviet Union be acknowledged as a Russian state, although they were never ascendant. In any case, the Russians accounted for only a little over half of the Soviet population (54.6 percent according to the 1959 census, and 52.4 percent in 1979) in the postwar period and could not have easily dominated the multinational state.

Yet, the Soviet Union was never conceptualized as a Russian state. It was a union of national republics, the only country in the world not to have either a geographic or an ethnic indicator in its name. Sovietness was ethnically neutral and never straightforwardly synonymous with Russianness. It indicated modernity, socialism, and a commitment to equality and justice. Soviet patriotism—that is, an allegiance to the multinational Soviet state—was a significant force, enacted in numerous rituals of public life. It could and did coexist with national identities. By the later Soviet period, there was undoubtedly a common Soviet culture in existence with common practices and understandings that could be expressed in any number of languages. Central Asian urbanites saw participation in this common Soviet culture as the adoption of a universal culture of modernity, or as Europeanization rather than Russification, even if they acknowledged that this broader European culture had come to Central Asia via Russia.[9]

Of course, the relationship between the national and the Soviet was never without tension, for not all aspects of Soviet modernity were assimilable to the national. Soviet medicine considered male circumcision to be a dangerous and unhealthy practice, as well as a sign of backwardness. Central Asians refused to see the foreskin as a sign of enlightenment and modernity, and the practice of male circumcision remained nearly universal in the region throughout the Soviet period. Other questions were more fraught. The balance between the national and the Soviet, or between tradition and modernity, was always in flux, especially for urban professional families. The need to show status and wealth, socialize with Europeans, and assert one's taste and culturedness led to all kinds of choices. If one could be too modern (such as a woman who dressed in miniskirts or a man who wore his hair too long), one could also be too national—especially in cities, which remained European spaces. How to dress, eat, and decorate one's home were all questions that required careful answers. Individuals and families placed themselves on a spectrum ranging from local, traditional, and national to European, modern, and Soviet. Often the choices were contextual: one could wear European dress for work or school and national dress at home or for visiting friends. Many urban families maintained two dining or living rooms, one in the European and the other in the national style. Of course, societies around the world faced similar questions. What was peculiar in Soviet Central Asia was the self-consciousness of the choices, because the binary of national and European was ever present, and both the national and the Soviet were in large part official categories. The national or traditional was as Soviet as the European the modern (see figure 18.2).

The 1980 novel *The Day Lasts More than a Hundred Years* by the Kyrgyz writer Chingiz Aitmatov is many things: a science fiction fantasy that depicts a utopia in the future; a reflection on Soviet life; and a meditation on memory, identity, and history. The novel is set at a railway station on the Kazakh steppe—"where the trains went from East to West, and from West to East"—and one of the main narrative axes of the novel is provided by the attempt of Yedigey Jangeldin, an old Kazakh man, to bury his friend with the proper ritual at an ancestral cemetery thirty kilometers away. Giving the dead man a proper burial is necessary for the maintenance of memory in the face of progress and change. The ritual is Islamic, but the memory is ancestral and national, and it does not conflict with being Soviet. Jangeldin gets the news of his friend's death in the middle of the night while he is manning a railway signal station. He calls his supervisor, who says:

"What can you do—it's night."
"I will pray. I will lay out the dead man. I'll say prayers."

FIG. 18.2. Tashkent State University, 1970. Urban Central Asia was a multinational space.
Note the variety of faces and styles in women's dress on September 1, the first day of
the academic year. Photo: Sputnik Images.

"Say prayers? You?!"

"Yes, me. I know all the prayers."

"And this after sixty years of Soviet rule?"

"What's Soviet rule got to do with it? People have been pray-
ing over the dead for centuries. It's a man who's died, not some
beast."[10]

Jangeldin was a good Soviet citizen: he had served in the Great Patriotic War and had worked all his life after that on the railways (which signified modernity, progress, socialism, and Sovietness). Yet he was concerned about keeping national memory alive through Islamic ritual. The Soviet, the Muslim, and the national coexisted easily within him.

Jangeldin is a good metaphor for the place that Islam occupied in late-Soviet Central Asia. Stalin had made peace with religion during the war, and the repression of the 1930s never returned. But neither was the destruction of that decade undone. Public space, both physical and intellectual, was thoroughly de-Islamized. The great mosques of Samarqand and Bukhara were preserved as "architectural monuments," but they did not host any worship. Islam and its moral commandments played no role whatsoever in public proclamations, which all had to make sense in a Marxist-Leninist framework. The Soviet public space remained hostile to religion. The scaling back of active repression of religion during the war did not mean that the state gave up on the basic goal of creating a secular society in which religion would be expunged from people's minds. But the methods were different. The League of the Militant Godless, whose members had gone around desecrating churches and mosques in the 1930s, was dismantled after the war. It was replaced by the Knowledge Society, a Union-wide organization that organized lectures and exhibitions on "scientific atheism" and provided rational explanations for the world. By contrast, there was no religious education or publishing. As generation after generation came of age without any religious education outside the family, fewer and fewer people were left in possession of Islamic knowledge. I do not mean here a formal command of points of theology or textual interpretation (which in all societies is the province of small learned elites) but everyday ritual practices, such as proper worship, the prayers said on various occasions, rules of ritual purity, and so on. In all Muslim societies, the observance of ritual varies greatly, from those who seldom perform ritual worship or keep the fast to those who perform the five daily prayers punctiliously and fast during (and even outside of) Ramadan. In late-Soviet Central Asia, very few people performed everyday rituals. Dietary taboos largely disappeared. Alcohol was a casual feature of life across society, and even the consumption of pork—which could not be avoided in many situations, such as in army service, on trains, and in cafeterias—became common. The routines of everyday life bore little relation to Islamic ritual.

This did not mean that people stopped thinking of themselves as Muslims. Far from it. Rather, the meaning of being Muslim changed. For most Muslims in the Soviet Union, belonging to Islam became a marker of national identity, for which no personal piety or observance was necessary. Islam was an indispensable part of national customs and traditions that served to set Central Asians apart from various kinds of outsiders. A certain kind of "proxy religiosity" emerged, in which certain groups in society—a few families of august lineage, women, and old men—performed rituals more diligently and were understood to have fulfilled the obligations for the whole community, which thus remained Muslim. Most Central Asians related to Islam through the concept of Muslimness (*musulmonchilik* in Uzbek, *musïlmanshïlïq* in Kazakh): a communal identity centered on a set of cultural and behavioral patterns in which faith and ritual observance are not the central features. A number of ethnographic studies of the post-Soviet period have noted that most Central Asians see Islam as residing in domestic rituals and customary practices, not in public life. We can call this form of religious minimalism Soviet Islam or national Islam. Jangeldin represents this perfectly.

The learned tradition of Islam survived in a few precarious spaces. One was SADUM, created in 1943 as an officially sanctioned organization to both facilitate and monitor Islamic activity. It was allowed to reopen the Mir-i Arab madrasa in Bukhara, which began teaching a thoroughly modernized curriculum in 1948. A second institution, the Imam al-Bukhari Islamic Institute, opened in 1971 as a postgraduate adjunct to the Bukharan madrasa. Mir-i Arab had an enrollment of eighty-six in 1982, while the institute had only thirty-four places, and the two institutions served the entire Soviet Union. This was the extent of formal Islamic education available. SADUM also operated officially registered mosques, whose numbers remained small (in 1981, there were about 180 such mosques in all of Central Asia), and it maintained a small number of shrines. In the 1960s it began sending students to study at religious institutions in Muslim countries friendly to the USSR, such as Egypt, Syria, and Libya. This ability to maintain some sort of contact with Muslims outside the Soviet Union was particularly precious in Soviet conditions. In return, SADUM served Soviet foreign policy aims in the Muslim world. Its leaders welcomed visiting dignitaries from Muslim countries and attended international conferences on peace or religious freedom. SADUM also published a quarterly magazine called *Muslims of the Soviet East* in several languages (English, French, Arabic, and Dari) for foreign consumption.[11]

SADUM's founders were bona fide *ulama* who had survived the horrors of the 1930s. They worked in the hope of preserving some semblance of a tradition of Islamic learning and perhaps of asserting some influence on local society. One of SADUM's first actions was to establish an office to issue fatwas on questions sent in by people from throughout its domain. Although SADUM's founder Ishan Babakhan was a Naqshbandi shaykh in the conventional Central Asian mold, his successors at SADUM acquired an affinity for modernist and rigorist currents of Islam that bore some relation to the Jadids but were closely tied to contemporary developments in the Arab world. On questions of ritual, a number SADUM fatwas contradicted the consensus of the Central Asian Islamic tradition. SADUM also issued fatwas at the request of the Soviet state. These fatwas represented some of the most radical stances of the organization. For instance, SADUM decreed performing honest work to be an Islamic virtue, the fulfillment of which required Muslims to avoid absenteeism and drunkenness (both of which were perennial problems for the state). Other fatwas went further, declaring fasting during Ramadan not to be obligatory for those involved in physical labor or that the sacrifice of livestock for the Feast of Sacrifice (*Qurban hayit*), the celebratory breaking of the fast during Ramadan (*iftar*), and the collection of alms for the poor were no longer obligatory in Soviet conditions. Yet other fatwas condemned as un-Islamic such customs as visits to shrines, seeking intercession from the dead, the wearing of the *paranji*, the activities of Sufi masters, and excessive expense at feasts celebrating life-cycle events. This opposition to tradition put

SADUM's *ulama* in a precarious position, since they appeared to be critics of traditions that could be defended on both religious and national grounds. The *ulama* remained liable to marginalization in society on both of those grounds.[12] SADUM, we should keep in mind, was a minor Soviet institution. Its fatwas had no legal force, its officials had no public profile or presence, and they did not take part in official functions at home.

A great deal of religious activity went on outside the control of SADUM. This unofficial Islam was by definition illegal but was largely tolerated in the later Soviet period. Much like the shadow economy, which flourished in the same period, unofficial Islam was not subversive, nor were the lines dividing it from the official Islam of SADUM clear. SADUM's *ulama* sought to provide guidance, rather than to bring all unofficial activity under their control. Unregistered mosques, existing on the sly in warehouses and supply sheds in collective farms or urban neighborhoods, outnumbered official ones. Numerous shrines attracted pilgrims, and life-cycle celebrations often involved the recitation of the Qur'an or of benedictions, which was performed by elders from the community. Many of the shrines belonged to locally esteemed families of august lineage, who managed to maintain Islamic learning across generations. In the late 1950s, some of them began offering lessons in secret to selected students. Called *hujra* (literally, a cell in a madrasa where students lived), such study circles were among the few venues for the preservation of formal Islamic learning in Central Asia. Most of the teachers were *ulama* who had survived the mayhem of the 1930s and were concerned with conserving Islamic knowledge in their society. They had little interest in either the iconoclastic critiques of the Jadids or the new currents of political Islam that had emerged in the Middle East in the period after the Second World War.

The most important of these teachers turned out to be Muhammad-jon Rustamov (ca. 1892–1989), known to his students as Domla Hindustoniy, "the Indian professor." A member of the Jadids' generation, Muhammadjon had a very different life. He studied in madrasas at Kokand and Bukhara at the time when the Jadids were formulating their critique of traditional education in Central Asia. He had little sympathy with it, and during the upheaval of the Russian civil war, he left Turkestan in search of education. He ended up in India (hence his epithet), where he studied at the resolutely nonreformist Usmania madrasa in Ajmer. He returned home in 1929, just as Stalin was launching his revolution from above, and of course he promptly got into trouble. He was incarcerated for more than eight years in three different stints over the next quarter-century, although he served in the Soviet army during the Second World War and was wounded at the western front in Belarus. Afterward, he briefly worked as an official imam for SADUM in Tajikistan. After his retirement, he started teaching informally in a *hujra*. He also wrote a six-volume commentary on the Qur'an that remained unpublished. Another major figure in the *hujra* circuit was Alikhan To'ra Shakirjanov, the erstwhile leader of the second ETR who was kidnapped by Soviet authorities for his recalcitrance and brought to Tashkent. As was the case with Hindustoniy, his concerns were purely conservationist: he wanted to preserve Islamic learning, not to subject it to the kind of critique the Jadids had been fond of. Soviet rule for him was a test for believers, in which success had to be achieved through reliance on God and patience, rather than political or military struggle. Islam for him was not a matter of politics.[13]

19

Xinjiang under Chinese Communism

XINJIANG EXPERIENCED the four postwar decades very differently than Soviet Central Asia. The Chinese revolution arrived in Xinjiang in the form of a military takeover by the People's Liberation Army (PLA) in October 1949. In the decades that followed, Party policy alternated between watchful accommodation to local conditions and radical phases, reminiscent of the Soviet 1930s, of brutal repression. Underneath all the mayhem, Xinjiang was integrated into the Chinese state as never before. Soviet influence, so important in the Sheng era, disappeared over the course of the 1950s. By the end of the decade, when the Sino-Soviet alliance gave way to a bitter split, the border was heavily militarized and the Soviet Union became enemy territory. For the next three decades, the two parts of Central Asia were isolated from one another.

———

The "peaceful liberation of Xinjiang" was not entirely peaceful. Guomindang (GMD) forces surrendered without a fight but other forces in the province were less pliant. The men under Osman Batir, the Kazakh chieftain who had broken from the ETR, continued to fight the PLA for autonomy and the nomadic way of life. It took the PLA over a year to break their resistance. Osman was surrounded and captured in the lands along the Gansu-Qinghai border in February 1951 and publicly executed in

Ürümchi on April 29. Many of his followers voted with their feet. Four thousand families set out on a trek across Xinjiang and Tibet to Kashmir. They were pursued by the PLA and dogged by the elements, and only 350 families made it across the border. They found refuge in Turkey. This "Kazakh exodus" garnered international attention at the time and put Xinjiang in the headlines one last time, before the rest of the world largely forgot about it for several decades.[1] Large-scale resistance was largely over by 1952, but more localized acts of rebellion and violent protest continued for many years. Khotan alone saw eight violent protests between late 1954 and May 1956, some of them involving thousands of men.[2]

The PLA trod carefully in the first years after its conquest of the province. It left the territory of the second ETR, defended by the Ili National Army, alone, occupying it only in late 1950, when it incorporated the national army into its ranks. It accompanied public executions with "political work" to bring the followers over to the new order. Osman's son Sherdiman eluded the PLA for another eighteen months, but finally surrendered. He and his followers were settled in the Altay region and provided material support, with Sherdiman becoming director of animal husbandry in the city of Altay. The new regime left private trade largely alone and carried out only a modest land reform that involved the organization of mutual aid teams among poor peasants with the goal of eventually organizing them into cooperatives. Nomadic areas in the north felt the weight of the new order even less. The land reform did affect the larger landowners and the endowed (*waqf*) properties of mosques and other Islamic institutions. Much more significant was the policy of systematic settlement of the land by Han Chinese that began with the arrival of the PLA in the province. In 1950, it demobilized 110,000 men and settled them along the edges of the oases and the path from Ürümchi to China proper. These demobilized soldiers engaged in agriculture, animal husbandry, land reclamation, and capital construction. They also helped out with local policing and provided auxiliary support for the border police. An archipelago of large-scale farms and ranches emerged across Xinjiang. These so-called "soldier farms" (*bingtuan*) were formalized in 1954 as the Xinjiang Production and Construction Corps (XPCC), a paramilitary organization subordinate directly to the Ministry of Agriculture in

Beijing.[3] From the initial Qing conquest of Xinjiang, the policy of settling military units on farms so that they became self-sufficient had frequently been mooted but never implemented with any success. Under Communist auspices, however, the system prospered and expanded massively over the next decades. The XPCC exists to this day as an entity largely independent of the regional government. Organized along military lines, it runs a parallel administrative system that encompasses whole districts.

Xinjiang remained under direct military rule until 1954. Ultimate authority belonged to the Xinjiang Military District, formed in December 1949, and commanded by the First Field Army whose cadres provided the main source of leadership in the new organs of power. Wang Zhen, the commander of the First Field Army, was the de facto ruler of the province. In 1952, he was recalled to China proper and replaced by General Wang Enmao, who was to be the commander of the Xinjiang Military Region and the head of the Xinjiang Committee of the CCP until 1967. Military personnel, overwhelmingly Han, staffed the new organs of power. For all the turmoil that Xinjiang had seen in the decade and a half preceding its "peaceful liberation," the Chinese Communist Party had hardly a trace of influence among the indigenous population of the region. The few Muslim Communists in Xinjiang were oriented to the Soviet, not the Chinese, Communist Party. The CCP therefore had little choice but to coopt non-Communists into the new organs of power it created. Burhan Shähidi, the last GMD governor of Xinjiang, became the chair of the provincial "people's government" formed on December 18, 1949. The leadership of the ETR provided another pool of indigenous cadres. Säypidin Äzizi, the most senior surviving member of the ETR after the mysterious plane crash, became the most prominent Muslim Communist in the region. He was to live a charmed life and survive in office until his retirement in 1978. However, both Shähidi and Äzizi were in large measure figureheads, for their prominence at the top was not accompanied by sizable recruitment of indigenous cadres at lower levels. Han officials dominated the party and the government.

Increasing integration into China meant the diminution of Soviet influence in Xinjiang. One of Mao's first acts after winning power was to travel to Moscow for a summit with Stalin. It was the first time that Mao had left China in his life. Stalin treated him haughtily, but deigned to sign a Treaty of Friendship, Alliance and Mutual Assistance with the new Communist power. For a decade, the Sino-Soviet alliance flourished: the Soviets pledged $300 million in aid over five years and sent thousands of advisors and experts to China, helping to guarantee the survival of the Communist regime. Stalin did squeeze a number of concessions out of China. A supplementary agreement created two Sino-Soviet joint stock companies to exploit Xinjiang's oil and nonferrous metals and allowed the Soviets to retain their consulates in Ürümchi and Ghulja. China needed Soviet support and Mao went along with the concessions, but they irked him greatly. Bizarrely, the alliance remained strong while Stalin lived, but began to crumble when Khrushchev began to move the Soviet Union away from Stalin's legacy. By 1959, Sino-Soviet relations were in bad shape and in 1962 the two sides had come to blows, with numerous border skirmishes. Xinjiang was at the epicenter of this dispute. Even before that happened, the Chinese state tried its best to reduce Soviet influence there. It bought out the Soviet share in the joint-stock companies soon after Stalin's death and sought to curtail Soviet economic reach in the province. Even in the heyday of the alliance, CCP authorities were deeply suspicious of Xinjiang intellectuals and party members with Soviet connections. That suspicion was to figure large in the "rectification campaign" that shook Xinjiang in 1958.

———

"From now on, China's nationality problems enter a new historical stage," Säypidin Äzizi proclaimed in 1951. "The minority race problems are no longer concerned with the struggle for freedom and equality from the pan-racialists . . . but rather how to safeguard and build the fatherland and how to shake off the yoke of feudal exploitation."[4] The CCP had proclaimed a program of recognizing the rights of non-Han peoples that extended to autonomy, which it began to put into practice after its victory in the Chinese civil war. While the rhetoric and the policies bore a certain resemblance to Soviet nationalities policies, from which they had originated, in practice the space for recognizing national difference in the PRC was far more modest than it was in the Soviet Union. China remained a unitary national state. Autonomy existed within strict limits and was subordinated to an intense emphasis on national unity. Federalism was never an option.

From its beginning, the CCP had been a movement for national salvation. It was the most significant of the many movements in colonial and semicolonial lands that understood Communism primarily as anti-imperialism. Mao's "knowledge of the West in general, and of Marxism in particular was . . . rather limited," according to Xiaoyuan Liu. For Mao, "communism was first and foremost one of several 'methods' that could be used to solve China's problems."[5] The CCP shared more with the GMD in its thinking about nationalities policy than it ever acknowledged. Both parties saw China as a victim of colonialism, not a perpetrator of it. China's non-Han territories were an integral part of the national body, and their separation from China could not be contemplated. The GMD had gone through a number of formulations of the national question, from imagining China as a union of "five races" to insisting that all citizens of China were of the same racial stock. Communist formulations used a different vocabulary but were equally insistent on the unity of the state.

In the 1920s, the Comintern had forced the nascent CCP to include the concept of national autonomy in its platform. The constitution of the short-lived Chinese Soviet republic in Jiangxi province (1931–1934) recognized the right of minority nationals (shaoshu minzu) to self-determination (zijue). It asserted that "the Soviet has always recognized the right of small and weak minzus to secede from China and establish their own independent state."[6] Yet the Comintern's influence on the party was waning, and soon afterward the CCP backed away from any commitment to independence or self-determination. During the 1930s, CCP proclamations were more equivocal, speaking of the "goal of national freedom for all minority nationals within China."[7] The Japanese invasion of China forced Mao to reevaluate many things. Even class struggle was put on the back burner, and the Chinese people (Zhonghua minzu) emerged as the subject of the struggle. While GMD theorists had insisted on racial unity and the common descent of all Chinese, Communist writers instead talked about the "interconnected historical evolution of a composite yet organically unified Zhonghua minzu."[8] The route to national unity might have been different for Communist writers, but the unity was just as important and nonnegotiable as it was for the GMD. For the Communists, too, it was incumbent upon "the various minzus [to] unite into a single body to jointly resist the Japanese invaders." *Minzu*s were to have equal rights and "the right to manage their own affairs," but they were to exist in a single state. On the eve of the Communist victory, Stalin sent Anastas Mikoyan to China to confer with the CCP leaders. Mikoyan met with Mao several times at his field headquarters. During a discussion of the national question, Mikoyan suggested that the CCP should not "go overboard in the national question by means of providing independence to national minorities and thereby reducing the territory of the Chinese state." He was passing along Stalin's preference that resolving the "national question" be subservient to broader political goals. Mao did not need to be told this. "Mao Zedong was glad to hear this advice," Mikoyan noted, "but you could tell by his face that he had no intention of giving independence to anybody whatsoever."[9]

For Mao, the question was clear. "China is a country vast in territory, rich in resources and large in population," he noted in 1956. "As a matter of fact, it is the Han nationality whose population is large and the minority nationalities whose territory is vast and whose resources are rich, or at least in all probability their resources under the soil are rich."[10] The territory with the vast, untapped resources was inhabited by non-Chinese. The CCP formulated its nationalities policies in this context. China was to be a "unified, multinational state" in which all nationalities were to enjoy equal rights and be "masters of their own house" through a system of autonomy (*zizhi*). However, autonomy was to have nothing to do with self-determination. "All national regional autonomous areas," according to a position paper from 1956, "are parts of the Chinese People's Republic and cannot be separated from it; national regional autonomy is a local autonomy exercised under the unified leadership of the central people's government, and the organs of nationalities autonomy have the status of local government, depending on superior, national organs for leadership. This provides protection for the areas where the national minorities live together and fully manifests their right to be 'masters in their own houses' (the right to establish their residence and to manage their own affairs)."[11] At the same time, the state attempted to classify and categorize the various non-Han peoples of the country on an ethnographic grid. Sun Yat-sen had spoken of five races inhabiting China, but now the state recognized fifty-six nationalities. The Han accounted for well over 90 percent of the population, and the other fifty-five nationalities were "minorities." Thus, the Uyghur were a minority nationality even in Altishahr, where they formed the overwhelming majority of the population. The Han were the most advanced *minzu* and had the obligation to lead the minorities to progress and socialism. This formula of "55 minorities + the Han = the PRC" (or "55 + 1 = 1," for short) became the basic paradigm of the management of national difference in the PRC.[12] This was a fundamental difference from the Soviet Union. The Russians had a dominant role in that country—officially they were designated as elder brothers to all other nationalities and the leading force in the union—but the state was never conceptualized as a Russian state or as having existed across the centuries as a single entity. In contrast, the PRC is a Chinese state that is imagined to have existed across time as a unified state. It belongs to a single Chinese people, which also has existed across time. The non-Han nationalities are minorities in that nation who do not have an ancestral claim to the territory on which they live.

The PRC declared Xinjiang autonomous in 1955. Initially, the autonomy was to be purely territorial. However, Äzizi argued that "autonomy is not given to mountains and rivers. It is given to particular nationalities." Mao seemed to agree, and Xinjiang was designated the Xinjiang Uyghur Autonomous Region.[13] Yet its connection to the Uyghurs was limited, and its autonomy was severely circumscribed. Xinjiang became a patchwork of multiple autonomies built from the ground up (see map 19.1). At the lowest level are numerous autonomous counties nestled within larger divisions. The territory controlled by the second ETR became the Ili Kazakh Autonomous Prefecture. There are also Hui and Kyrgyz autonomous prefectures, as well as two Mongol autonomous regions—one of which, the Bayingolin Autonomous Prefecture, oc-

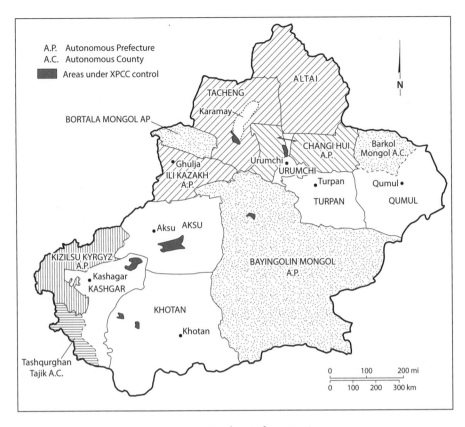

A.P.   Autonomous Prefecture
A.C.   Autonomous County
▨   Areas under XPCC control

BORTALA MONGOL AP

ALTAI

TACHENG

Karamay

CHANGJI HUI
A.P.

Barkol
Mongol A.C.

Ghulja

Urumchi

ILI KAZAKH
A.P.

URUMCHI

Turpan

Qumul

TURPAN

QUMUL

Aksu   AKSU

KIZILSU KYRGYZ
A.P.

BAYINGOLIN MONGOL
A.P.

Kashagar

KASHGAR

KHOTAN

Khotan

Tashqurghan
Tajik A.C.

0   100   200 mi
0   100   200   300 km

MAP 19.1. Xinjiang's nested autonomies

cupies almost half of Xinjiang's territory. These arrangements are over-
lain by the archipelago of *bingtuan* farms that form part of a parallel
administrative system and are answerable directly to Beijing. Thus, even
though it carried the Uyghur name in its official title, Xinjiang was not
conceptualized as a national homeland of the Uyghurs, and the Uyghurs
did not have any title to it (unlike the way, say, the Uzbeks had a title to
Uzbekistan in the Soviet period). Xinjiang is instead simply a place
where "thirteen nationalities live together in peace."

Xinjiang was unique in China in that it had experienced Soviet-style
nationalities policies since the mid-1930s. Sheng, we will remember, had
recognized fourteen nationalities in Xinjiang and established cultural
advancement associations for each of them. While he never entertained

the idea of territorial autonomy and his interest in nationalities cooled after 1937, the idea of national rights remained. The years of GMD rule in Xinjiang had seen heightened mobilization among the urban Muslim population around the national idea, and the ETR had been deeply invested in it. Therefore, the CCP's nationalities policies, with their minimalist conception of autonomy, came as a bitter disappointment to national elites, who continued to press for more. A meeting of fifty-one intellectuals held in Ghulja in 1951 voted for the creation of an Uyghuristan as an autonomous republic in a federal China. A parallel meeting of Kazakh activists demanded the creation of an autonomous Kazakh province in Xinjiang that would bring together the Kazakh populations of the Ili valley, Ürümchi, and Inner Mongolia. Both proposals foresaw the passage of power from both party and government organs to Uyghur and Kazakh figures, following the Soviet model.[14] Soviet territorial autonomy was born at the grave sites of national movements of the civil war era and was always meant to be preemptive, but to Xinjiang's indigenous elites, many of whom had studied in Tashkent (the 1930s generation of Tashkenters remained the backbone of the indigenous political and cultural elite in Xinjiang into the 1950s), it appeared far superior to anything the CCP was willing to grant.[15] Nor was the fascination with the Soviet model simply a matter of elite sympathies. Up until the mid-1950s, all textbooks for Uyghur and Kazakh schools in Xinjiang came from the Soviet Union. "Among the local residents," two Chinese historians complain, "this situation even led to confused conceptions about the motherland. As of the 1950s, ethnic minority children in the Ili Region knew something about the USSR and Moscow but had no idea about China and Beijing. Many intellectuals, ethnic minority cadres, and members of the masses regarded the USSR as their motherland and saw China only as their secondary motherland."[16]

These grievances came out into the open when Mao issued his famous proclamation: "Let a hundred flowers bloom and a hundred schools of thought contend." This campaign, launched in 1956, was meant to elicit reactions from society to the Communist regime. The torrent of criticism that followed took the party by surprise, and it then launched an anti-Rightist campaign to persecute the critics. In Xinjiang, Muslim intellectuals complained that Xinjiang was autonomous in name only and had no real rights. They also expressed deep discontent with the scale of Han settlement and the Han domination of key posts in the party and industry, as well as a sense that Xinjiang's natural resources were being exploited for the benefit of China proper. At a plenary meeting of the Xinjiang party organization in January 1958, Muslim cadres argued vociferously in favor of Soviet-style autonomy: "Why do we need Han people's help to become socialist? The Soviet Union has a federal system, and every ethnic group became socialist, didn't they?" Others went further. Ziya Sämädi, the head of the Department of Culture of the provincial government, demanded the creation of an Uyghuristan separate from the PRC.[17] He had considerable support at the meeting, but Äzizi, the most senior Uyghur Communist, pushed back in a four-hour speech titled "Firmly Oppose Local Nationalism and Struggle for the Grand Victory of Socialism." Eventually, the plenum ratified "A Plan for Carrying Out Rectification among Non-Han Cadres and Intellectuals," which accused the dissidents of "local nationalism," "splittism," and sympathy for the Soviet Union. This was a tremendous blow to the small indigenous elite whose members had held positions in the new organs of power since 1949. Abdurehim Äysa (or Isa), deputy chairman of the People's Committee of the Ili Kazakh Autonomous Prefecture, committed suicide after his views were denounced. The blooming flowers were replaced by a fierce "anti-rightist and anti-local nationalism" campaign that saw many indigenous leaders fired. More than 1,600 cadres were accused of "local nationalism." Ninety-two of these fled to the Soviet Union, and the rest were sent off to labor camps for "thought reform."

———

The campaign against local nationalism was intertwined with two major developments. The first was the worsening of relations with the Soviet Union. The tensions that had always existed in the Sino-Soviet alliance came to the fore after Khrushchev shifted course in 1956. Mao took on the mantle of Marxist orthodoxy and accused Khrushchev of being a revisionist and capitulating on class struggle at home and struggle with the capitalist bloc abroad. In Xinjiang, sympathy with revisionism became a sign of political unreliability and counterrevolution. The second was the launch of the Great Leap Forward, a campaign of rapid and forced transformation of China's rural economy to an industrial one. It was akin to the Stalinist mobilization of the 1930s in its hope of jump-starting industrialization. In Xinjiang, the campaign involved abandoning moderate policies of accommodation of local national peculiarities. If China was to leap forward, all forms of backwardness had to destroyed, regardless of their national or cultural origins. Official rhetoric now insisted that the national problem was a class problem, to be solved by bringing the struggle against oppressing classes to each nationality, using universal methods. Any defense of local peculiarities merely signified local nationalism. The earlier caution against "Great Hanism" vanished. Now, the situation was crystal clear: Han represented modernity; all other cultures were backward by definition, and the overcoming of their backwardness required the copying of Han practices. The radicalism of the Great Leap Forward licensed Han chauvinism in Xinjiang.

The Leap transformed Xinjiang's rural sector. All of Xinjiang's peasants were bundled into 562 communes, averaging 5,500 households each, while the pastoral areas were finally subjugated into the new order. Nomads in the north were formed into 24 communes in 1958, their animals pooled, and the profits shared.[18] Although the state remained cautious and paid for the animals that were communized, the intent was to turn pastoral nomads into ranchers obligated to the state and producing on its behalf. Communes featured mess halls that replaced individual kitchens (family kitchen utensils were melted down in "backyard furnaces" to produce steel for industrialization). The assault on backwardness particularly targeted Islam and Islamic institutions in a way that again recalled the Stalinist campaigns of 1927–1941, although the Xinjiang episode is far less well documented. Attacks on "religious and conservative thinking" led to mosques and shrines being closed and in many cases destroyed, the celebration of Islamic holidays being banned, and travel for the hajj proscribed.

The Great Leap Forward produced even worse disasters than collectivization had in the Soviet Union. It created a famine of even greater magnitude—estimates of total casualties range from 30 million to 45 million—although its epicenter was in China proper and it largely spared Xinjiang. Nevertheless, provincial authorities exhorted people to eat less and send grain to other parts of the motherland.[19] Communal mess halls were to "popularize the advanced method of planned use of grain through mixing coarse grain with fine grain, making delicate dishes out of coarse grain, and serving solid food and porridge alternately."[20] Food shortages in Ürümchi led to the closure of universities in December 1959. The Leap also provoked one last mass population movement across the Sino-Soviet border.

As a result of the various population movements we have seen in this book, Xinjiang in 1949 contained large numbers of recent immigrants and exiles from the Soviet Union. They included both those who had fled the Soviet Union in terror and those who had come to Xinjiang as Soviet officials. There were also many Xinjiang natives who had spent time in the Soviet Union and acquired Soviet papers. Even when Sino-Soviet relations were warm, the CCP was suspicious of this group. By 1954, Zhou Enlai, the prime minister, was suggesting to Soviet diplomats that Soviet citizens either take Chinese citizenship or be repatriated. The Virgin Lands campaign that had just been launched needed extra hands, and Soviet consulates across China began to recruit Soviet citizens for repatriation. They were quite successful in this endeavor. In 1955, 115,000 Soviet passport holders were repatriated to the Soviet Union, including 68,000 from Xinjiang.[21] The Chinese seem to have worried about the exodus from Xinjiang, and in a change of mind, they asked the Soviets to stop accepting Uyghur and Kazakh repatriates to avoid harming Xinjiang's economy. Emigration to the Soviet Union slowed down for a while. By 1959, however, the Sino-Soviet alliance had crumbled, and the radical policies of the Great Leap Forward were in full swing. Uyghur-language radio broadcasts from Tashkent and Almaty criticized Chinese nationality policies and presented a picture of plenty in the Soviet Union. Many Uyghurs and Kazakhs—often with no prior connection to the Soviet Union—began to emigrate to the Soviet Union. Initially, Soviet border guards would return those they intercepted, but soon that stopped, and those escaping Xinjiang were allowed entry into the Soviet Union. At the same time, Soviet consulates in Xinjiang began issuing Soviet papers almost indiscriminately, causing the emigration to turn into a torrent. In late spring of 1962, the Soviet Union opened its border at Khorgos, a mere sixty-five kilometers from Ghulja, and allowed anyone who wanted to cross it, with or without a passport. News of this development spread like wildfire in Ghulja, and large numbers of people dropped everything and made a beeline for the border, using the public buses that were the only form of transport. Estimates of the number of people who crossed the border in those weeks vary from 60,000 to 100,000. Then, on May 29, Chinese authorities stopped selling bus tickets. An angry crowd gathered at the bus station and marched on the local county administrative offices, which it ransacked. As it moved to the CCP building, it was met with machine-gun fire that killed many protesters and wounded many more. A campaign against this "counterrevolutionary" movement ensued, in which large numbers of people were arrested. The border was closed and militarized. It was not to open again for a quarter of a century.

The Soviet Union had closely guarded borders, and it did not usually take in refugees. The opening of the border in 1962 to Uyghurs and Kazakhs from Xinjiang was highly unusual. The opening was in part meant to be a rebuke to the Chinese leaders for their treatment of non-Han nationalities, but it was also rooted in long-term Soviet connections with Xinjiang. The immigrants mostly remained in Kazakhstan: the Kazakhs among them were settled on collective farms around the republic, although many went where they had family connections. The Uyghurs were settled just across the border in Semirech'e, the old hub of Muslim immigrants and exiles from Qing and Chinese rule, although many of them ended up in Almaty, where there was a long-established Soviet Uyghur community. The newcomers were distinct in their lack of Russian and their greater propensity to be observant Muslims. Over the years, however, these distinctions tended to diminish. In contrast, the anti-Chinese feelings did not, and Almaty became a bastion of anti-Chinese Soviet Uyghurness.[22] There was little reckoning with the causes of this exodus on the Chinese side, where it was seen as a result of Soviet machinations and added to the already long list of grievances against the erstwhile ally.

———

The Great Leap Forward had been called off in 1961 amid the disaster that it had provoked, and in Xinjiang, the more moderate policies of the pre-Leap years returned for a while. The calm was shattered again in 1966 with the launch of the Great Proletarian Cultural Revolution. If the Great Leap Forward had parallels in the Soviet experience, the Cultural Revolution was unique to China. It was an attempt by Mao to reclaim his authority in the party, which had been damaged by the disaster of the Leap, by unleashing a grassroots uprising against the party itself. Mao called on the youth of the country to attack the Four Olds—old ideas, culture, customs, and habits—wherever they could find them. Schools and universities shut down as students fanned out across the country to revolutionize it, and China descended into chaos as armed factions of Red Guards fought their elders and each other. In Xinjiang, the Cultural Revolution was a fight between different Han factions. Wang Enmao and his cohort from the First Field Army lost their positions in 1968 when the regional government was replaced by a ten-member revolutionary committee, eight of whose members were Han. Wang was demoted to vice-chair and removed from Xinjiang in the following year. Xinjiang was in turmoil that even the threat of a Soviet invasion could not contain.

If the political aspect of the Cultural Revolution in Xinjiang can be narrated simply as a series of pitched battles over control of the region, its cultural aspect was very different. It was aimed squarely at "minority" nationalities. There has been little accounting of the terrors of the Cultural Revolution in Xinjiang, and almost no archival research has been conducted on the subject. From what we know, there is little indication that Uyghur or Kazakh youth mobilized in defense of Mao Zedong Thought or sought to revolutionize their own societies. Rather, it was Han revolutionaries who sought to extirpate the Four Olds from Xinjiang's Muslim cultures. This is a fundamental difference between the

Soviet campaigns of the 1920s and 1930s in Central Asia, where all the foot soldiers were radical youth of local nationalities, and the events in Xinjiang, where the nationalities as a whole were objects of suspicion and disdain. Mosques, shrines, and cemeteries were shut down and often desecrated. Decades later, one émigré recounted a memory from his childhood in Yengisar, near Kashgar: "Several black and white pigs were kept in a building people called 'mosque'. . . . When I grew older I found out that almost all the mosques in our region were turned into pig houses. Even Uyghur songs were written in praise of pigs."[23] Cultural revolutionaries shut down madrasas, burned copies of the Qur'an, prohibited the wearing of local dress, and forcibly cut off the long hair of Uyghur women in public. Non-Han intellectuals, religious figures, and disgraced cadres were arrested and subjected to public humiliations known as struggle sessions, in which they were often forced to eat pork. Such attacks on Islam and local culture continued into the late 1970s, well after the political turmoil had stopped. The Cultural Revolution was disastrous for indigenous cadres, who lost what little presence they had in leadership ranks. Other than the ever resilient Äzizi, there were hardly any Uyghurs in the revolutionary committee that was established in 1968 to restore order in Xinjiang. Nationality had ceased to matter in policy.

———

Mao's death led to the end of the Cultural Revolution. Within a month, the party leadership arrested his main followers—the Gang of Four, which included his widow—and distanced itself from the policies of the previous decade. In 1978, the CCP elected Deng Xiaoping, a former comrade of Mao's who had been disgraced during the Cultural Revolution, as its first secretary. Deng inaugurated an era of reform, in which the pendulum swung back toward moderation in the PRC's relations with China's minorities. The State Commission on Nationalities Affairs, the main body that oversaw the implementation of nationalities policy, was revived in May 1978 after more than a decade of inactivity, and the issue of recognizing and accommodating national difference made a cautious return to official rhetoric. For Xinjiang, the reform era opened up new possibilities. The repression of Islam stopped, and in the early 1980s, the state even paid for the repair or restoration of mosques that had been damaged or destroyed during the Cultural Revolution.[24] It reestablished the China Islamic Association and permitted the provision of religious education again, even paying for a small number of local imams to be sent for higher education to the China Islamic Institute in Beijing (some were even sent to Egypt).[25] Language rights became real again, and a new space emerged for the articulation of local national cultures. The 1980s and 1990s appear now to have been a golden age of modern Uyghur culture, in which new forms of expression appeared and Uyghur intellectuals were able to create a cogent narrative of an Uyghur national past.

The Communist regime had established Uyghur academic and cultural institutions in the early 1950s and tasked them with standardizing the Uyghur language, gathering and systematizing Uyghur folklore and other aspects of cultural heritage, and creating academic work suitable for the modern age. The Xinjiang Committee for Orthographic Reform worked out a standard orthography based on the reformed Arabic script that had been pioneered in the Soviet Union in the 1920s. In 1956, Beijing decided to switch all minority languages to the Cyrillic script, but before anything could be done in that regard, the Soviet alliance came to an end, and Latinization became the preferred option. In 1957, Uyghur and Kazakh were switched to the Latin script, with the Latin letters having the same values as the newly adopted pinyin transcription for Chinese. (Thus, the letter *q* stood for "ch" and *x* for "sh.") The switch took place at the same moment as the Great Leap Forward, and thus no dissent was permissible. "To oppose the adoption of the new writing systems based on the Plan for the Phonetic Spelling of Chinese (Pinyin) and to oppose the development of minority languages along with Chinese is to oppose socialism and communism of the Chinese peoples, and to oppose the reform of writing systems of minority languages based on the Plan is to oppose the unity of all Chinese nationalities and the unification of the motherland," Äzizi wrote in 1960.[26] Work also began on the collection and preservation of Xinjiang's cultural heritage, with the corpus of *muqam* music and the songs that accompanied it as its most important feature. But this cultural work largely disappeared during the mayhem of the Great Leap Forward and the Cultural Revolution, when Uyghur intellectuals were dismissed from their jobs in large numbers, subjected to struggle sessions, and often arrested. The fate of Ibrahim Muti'i is quite typical. A linguist, he had published a modern edition of an eighteenth-century five-language dictionary. He was arrested in 1960 on charges of "Rightism" and spent fifteen years in prison. Once the Cultural Revolution started, he was subjected to struggle sessions, in which his interrogators dropped volumes of his dictionary on his head.[27] He lived to see the reform era, when the Uyghur academic world was put back together.

Uyghur-language publishing had been limited to official newspapers and magazines, with very little literary content. A new era began in 1978, when a number of new literary and scholarly journals began publishing and the Uyghur novel made its belated appearance. The Uyghur language was accorded a guaranteed official status again. The Latin alphabet introduced in 1957 had never been fully implemented. A renewed push for Latinization began in 1970, when the dust had settled a bit. "The reform of Uygur and Kazakh characters is a revolution that breaks the old and establishes the new," Äzizi now proclaimed. "It is an event of great practical and far-reaching historical significance in the political and cultural life of Uygur and Kazakh peoples."[28] Yet the new letters never caught on, and the plan was finally scrapped in 1982. The last signs in the Latin script had disappeared by 1986. Since then, Uyghur and Kazakh have been written in the reformed Arabic script that was, as noted above, first used in the Soviet Union in the 1920s. It was very much a Jadid project, introduced in the years of the Russian civil war. Xinjiang's Arabic script is one of the few real legacies of Jadidism that remains intact in the twenty-first century. Alongside orthographic reform came the development of new vocabulary and the standardization of grammar. In common with other projects of language reform in the modern world, literary Uyghur was brought closer to the spoken language, with the dialects of the Ili region becoming the basis for the modern standardized language. This meant the replacement of many Arabic and Persian terms by vernacular, Turkic equivalents, as well as the creation of new terms for objects and concepts that were new to the region. Official pressure to use Chinese loanwords for the new vocabulary produced few results. Uyghur writers had absorbed a great deal of Russian vocabulary—especially, but not solely, for political terms—during the interwar years. That lexicon was never displaced by Chinese equivalents. Today, written Uyghur retains a substantial trove of Russian borrowings. (The full Uyghur-language title of the region, *Shinjang Uyghur Aptonom Rayoni*, contains two Russian loanwords.)

Uyghur intellectuals had greater latitude in the 1980s and 1990s than before or since, and they created a cogent narrative of an Uyghur nation that had continuously existed in Xinjiang across the centuries. The main vehicle for the articulation of this identity was the historical novel, which experienced a boom in the 1980s and 1990s. As was the case in the Brezhnev period in Soviet Central Asia, novelists could write more freely than historians, and it was writers such as Abdurähim Ötkür, Säypidin Äzizi, and Abduväli Äli who penned panoramas of Uyghur history. Ethnographic and musicological research created a set of national cultural heroes who could be claimed by all Uyghurs. They ranged from Satuq Bughra Khan, the tenth-century Qarakhanid prince of Kashgar, who was the first Turkic ruler to convert to Islam; Yusuf Khass Hajib, the eleventh-century poet and author, whose *Wisdom of Royal Glory* is one of the earliest written works in Turkic; his contemporary Mahmud Kashgari, the lexicographer who compiled the first compendium of Turkic languages (in Arabic); Amannisa Khan, the concubine of the sixteenth-century ruler of Yarkand who is credited with collecting the Twelve Muqam. These figures all had lived and worked in Eastern Turkestan and represented the Uyghur nation's claim to the territory of Xinjiang. The Uyghur vision of their own history is thus in fundamental conflict with the vision of the Chinese state. Such histories were implicit rebuttals of official Chinese pronouncements that declared Xinjiang to have eternally been a part of China.

This sort of canon-building was almost exactly what the intelligentsias of Soviet republics accomplished in the post-Stalin period. The Soviet intellectuals were however backed by self-confident national political elites, ensconced in Soviet institutions and the party. Uyghur elites had much less room for maneuver. The career of Äzizi shows up the difference in all its specificity. Born to a wealthy Uyghur family in 1915, Äzizi was one of the Tashkenters, the cohort of Uyghur youth educated in Uzbekistan in the 1930s. He was minister of education in the Ghulja ETR. When the entire senior leadership of the republic died in the mysterious plane crash, Äzizi was left as its senior member and one of the few intermediaries for the CCP in the province. Over the next quarter-century, he was the most prominent Uyghur Communist, chairing the Xinjiang government from 1955 to 1967 and then again from 1972 to 1978. During that second stint, he was also the secretary of the Xinjiang Committee of the CCP, the only time the office was occupied by a non-Han person. In later life, from 1993 to 1998, he served as the vice-chairman of the Chinese People's Political Consultative Conference, the advisory body with which the CCP consults on matters of legislation. He died in his bed in 2003. Äzizi was a master survivor, having navigated all the twists and turns of those decades, mostly by being Beijing's mouthpiece. He denounced "Rightism" and "local nationalism" in 1958 and throughout the Cultural Revolution, he faithfully echoed Mao's pronouncements and served as the Party's enthusiastic spokesman on nationalities issues. His paeans to Mao resembled the words of Soviet republican leaders from the 1930s, not the language Äzizi's contemporaries might have used. For Äzizi was no Rashidov. The Uzbek first secretary had to fulfill quotas and toe the line in many ways, but he sat atop an Uzbek political elite that controlled the republic and had grown very self-confident in its place in Soviet life. Uzbek elites could—and did—celebrate their heritage and take pride in belonging to the Soviet family of nations. There was no equivalent space for Uyghur elites; indeed, there was no equivalent Uyghur political elite.

Äzizi was also a writer, playwright, poet, and historian, and his creative work was concerned with elaborating a vision of the Uyghur national past and celebrating Uyghur national heroes. In the 1950s, he had been involved in the collection, notation, and publication of the corpus of *muqam* music and the songs that accompanied it. After a hiatus of two decades, when he was busy navigating the Cultural Revolution, he picked up his pen again in the more relaxed 1980s, when he had retired. He authored one of the first historical novels of the era, a thousand-page epic chronicling the life of Satuq Bughra Khan, as well as an opera on the life of Amannisa Khan, other historical works, and a substantial body of poetry. He also published a lengthy memoir that spends over a thousand pages describing his early life but ends in 1949. Among this vast corpus, a short allegorical tale that he published in a Kashgar literary magazine in 1983 deserves attention. The story tells of a frog who lived in a pond in a barnyard ruled by a rooster. The frog crawls out of the pond and aspires to be king of the whole barnyard. He works his way up by flattering the rooster, singing songs that praise him fulsomely. The rooster is impressed enough to appoint him *beg* of the pond. The inhabitants of the pond, having witnessed his obsequiousness, lose all respect for him and refuse to accept his authority. In desperation, the frog tries to climb up the tree on which the rooster lives, only to lose his grip and fall to his death. The rooster is shocked but recovers enough to say, "You got what you deserve. . . . How can a frog be equal to a rooster?" Äzizi had written a bitter satire of his own life: Äzizi (the frog) could flatter Mao (the rooster) all he wanted, but Mao had no intention of raising Äzizi to any heights. The flattery also cost Äzizi the respect of other denizens of the pond (Xinjiang). "This Uyghur *Animal Farm* skewers the Chinese regime's puffery and patronage and, ultimately, its racism," writes Gardner Bovingdon. "The emphasis on speciation and on biology as destiny echoes Great Han chauvinism in the larger society."[29] In his retirement, Äzizi seems to have realized the limits to the possibilities offered by the Chinese regime to its minorities.

In the 1980s, China began to open Xinjiang to foreign travelers. The region had been almost completely closed to the outside world (with the exception of Soviet experts who had worked there during the heyday of the Sino-Soviet alliance) since the Communist takeover. The turbulent years of the republican period had seen a number of European travelers pass through, and they had left behind a small library of travelogues.

That traffic came to an abrupt halt in 1949, and the next four decades saw hardly any foreign visitors to Xinjiang. The Soviet border was heavily militarized and sealed by the early 1960s, as was the border with India—with which China fought a war in 1962. Now, in the mid-1980s, China opened up an overland route to Pakistan. Sino-Pakistani friendship had blossomed because both countries were enemies of the Soviet Union and India. Part of the strategic relationship between the two countries was the construction of the Karakorum Highway that traversed the Karakorum Mountains and connected Kashgar to northern Pakistan. The route was opened in 1986 and brought Pakistani traders to Kashgar, the first foreigners to visit the region in any number for decades. At the same time, Xinjiang began to be opened to tourist travel. Its main draw at the time was its natural beauty and the caught-in-time feeling of its cities. I visited Kashgar in 1986 and was struck both by the poor standards of living and the way in which the old city still functioned as a living whole. Kashgar felt very remote: the Soviet and Indian borders were closed, the only crossing into Pakistan was a mountain pass five thousand meters above sea level, and travel beyond the city was still very difficult. I did not know it then, but Central Asia was just about to change dramatically.

20

On the Front Lines of the Cold War

"*POEKHALI!*" (Off we go!), said the man in the space suit as the countdown neared zero. It was April 12, 1961, and Yuri Gagarin, the man in the space suit, was about to become the first human being to go into space. The Soviet Union had already won the Space Race three and a half years earlier when it launched Sputnik 1, the first artificial satellite, into orbit on October 4, 1957. However, the journey of the first human being into space was an altogether more significant milestone. News of Gagarin's orbit of earth set off spontaneous celebrations around the Soviet Union. Space exploration became a central mythology of the late Soviet Union and a point of immense pride for Soviet citizens. It is important to remind ourselves, then, that the Soviet space program was based in Baikonur on the Kazakh steppe. Both Sputnik 1 and Gagarin began their journeys in Kazakhstan. The Space Age started in Central Asia.

The Space Race was an integral part of the Cold War, and Central Asia was at its center. The Berlin Wall might have been the most potent symbol of the Cold War, but it was a global phenomenon. Beyond Europe, the war was seldom cold, as proxy conflicts consumed millions of lives around the world. The Cold War was also a struggle for the hearts and minds of people around the globe, especially in the many countries that emerged as sovereign actors on the world stage as a result of the retreat of European empires. The Americans represented themselves as the champions of liberty and freedom, even as lynchings continued in the United States and the racial terror known euphemistically as Jim Crow ruled half the country. The Soviets cast themselves as offering an alternative path to modernity—a political order that had undone the legacies of colonialism and raised former colonies to equal status.[1] The republics of Central Asia were central to these claims. They became a showcase to the so-called Third World of Soviet achievements, and Soviet Central Asians played a prominent role in this outreach. Nor was the Cold War a bipolar affair. The collapse of the Sino-Soviet alliance by the late 1950s initiated hostilities within the Communist camp that also went global. The competition between the Soviet Union and China has been called the shadow Cold War, and it created intense militarization along the two countries' long land border, a bitter war of words, and competition for influence abroad. Central Asia was at the epicenter of this conflict. The long border between Xinjiang and Kazakhstan was closed in 1962 after the exodus of tens of thousands of Kazakhs and Uyghurs to the Soviet Union and heavily militarized. And it was in Afghanistan, which borders Soviet Central Asia, that the last drama of the Cold War was played out in all its violence and brutality.

The Cold War was always an asymmetrical struggle. The United States was far wealthier and had far greater geopolitical reach than the Soviet Union. The Soviet Union was the challenger, never the driver, in the conflict. Initially, Stalin's goals were primarily geopolitical. He wanted to secure the borders of the Soviet Union and ring the country with buffer zones. Most important were the people's republics installed in Eastern Europe, but Stalin also supported an autonomous republic in Iranian Azerbaijan and forced the GMD regime in China to finally recognize the independence of Mongolia. Stalin's support for the ETR, we will remember, was part of the same calculus of power. The victory of the Communists in the Chinese revolution did not alter Stalin's calculations, for he extracted concessions from his new allies in Xinjiang and Manchuria and retained control of the Eastern Chinese Railway, the line that cut across Manchuria to link the Soviet cities of Chita and Vladivostok. This sowed the seeds of destruction for the Communist alliance, which was to collapse in spectacular fashion within a decade.

While the alliance lasted, the going was good. The Soviets made a considerable investment in it. They hosted thousands of Chinese students and sent similar numbers of advisors and experts to China, where they helped jump-start reconstruction. Soviet experts, many of them Central Asian, played a significant role in Xinjiang, where often they were the only experts who could speak with the local population: their Han Chinese counterparts, with no knowledge of Turkic languages, were reduced to communicating with hand gestures and facial expressions. Soviet experts also helped launch China's nuclear weapons program. The main test site for the Chinese nuclear program was established at Lop Nor, in eastern Xinjiang, and it was there that the first Chinese nuclear test took place on October 16, 1964. Atmospheric testing continued until 1980, during which time forty-five nuclear tests took place at Lop Nor. Central Asia thus hosted the nuclear programs of both the Soviet Union and China.

———

The beginning of the Cold War coincided with the age of decolonization, which produced new opportunities as well as challenges for Soviet diplomacy. A key challenge was to break the hold of former colonial masters on the newly independent states and to steer those states away from the global hegemony of the United States. The opportunity lay in the sentiment for independence among the new states and their aspirations to control their own destinies and resources. The Soviet Union proclaimed itself as the champion of the exploited and the guide to an alternative path to development that had raised former colonies to equality with the metropole and ostensibly ended exploitation. In many ways, this was a return to the rhetoric of the 1920s, when the Soviets had presented themselves as would-be liberators of the colonial world. In 1925, Stalin had celebrated the establishment of Tajikistan "on the gates of Hindustan" as an example for "Eastern countries."[2] He had forgotten all about such things soon after that, as his foreign policy increasingly focused on maintaining the security of the Soviet state. As Khrushchev revived (in modified form) the idea of transforming the formerly colonized world, Central Asia became central to this new diplomacy.

Khrushchev took Central Asian politicians and intellectuals with him as he toured the world. On a visit to India and Afghanistan in 1955, he could boast that "our delegation includes . . . representatives of Uzbekistan and Tajikistan, whose peoples are of the Muslim creed. But in what ways do Muslims differ from the other creeds in our country? In our country, we have no such differences, because all the peoples of our country are worthy members of the great Soviet Union and make a united family of the peoples of our country."[3] One of the members of Khrushchev's entourage was Sharaf Rashidov, the future first secretary of Uzbekistan's Communist Party. Throughout the 1950s, Rashidov traveled extensively around the decolonizing world as a Soviet emissary. Central Asians were almost never appointed to serve outside their own republics (unlike Russians and some Ukrainians, Tatars, and Armenians, whose range of service encompassed the entire Soviet Union), but many of them represented the Soviet Union abroad—especially in the Muslim world. Rashidov's travels as a Soviet cultural emissary in the 1950s were followed by the appointments of many Central Asians as Soviet ambassadors abroad. In 1956, Khrushchev transferred Bobojon Ghafurov, the first secretary of the Tajik Communist Party, to Moscow to direct the Institute of Oriental Studies. Ghafurov was a Stalin appointee, and his removal from Dushanbe was part of Khrushchev's move against Stalin loyalists in the republics. But the appointment in Moscow was more than a polite kick upstairs. Ghafurov headed the institute until shortly before his death in 1977 and had considerable input into the formulation of policy. Ghafurov was a historian, whose magnum opus—*The Tajiks*, first published in 1949—was the foundational document of the Tajik national narrative. His academic credentials allowed him to build connections with scholars in the Muslim world and beyond. In addition to the many international conferences he organized, he convened regular meetings with ambassadors from Third World countries at his institute. He was one of the most visible Central Asians in the world.

But it was the Uzbek Nuriddin Muhitdinov (1917–2008) who was the most prominent Central Asian in Soviet diplomacy. He was a veteran who had been seriously wounded at Stalingrad. After demobilization, he built a party career for himself in Uzbekistan. Khrushchev appointed him first secretary of the republic's Communist party in 1955 as part of his campaign against Stalin loyalists but then summoned Muhitdinov to Moscow in 1956 and elevated him to the Presidium of the Communist Party of the Soviet Union. He was the first Central Asian to sit in that body. "In the center, we don't have enough people from the East, or even enough people who know about it," Khrushchev told Muhitdinov. "You are an Uzbek, an Asian, from a Muslim background, hence you understand these questions. Who else but you should handle our Eastern policy?"[4] Muhitdinov did more than handle "Eastern policy," for he emerged as a key ally for Khrushchev in his struggle for control of the party. Muhitdinov also traveled abroad in the latter half of the 1950s and entertained numerous visitors in Moscow or Tashkent. When Khrushchev turned on his protégés, Muhitdinov was expelled from the presidium in 1961. He stayed in Moscow and worked in various federal-level agencies for several years. Then, in 1968, Brezhnev appointed him ambassador to Syria, a key Soviet ally. The war of 1967 had been as disastrous for Soviet goals in the Middle East as it was for Arab nationalism, and the Damascus post was of crucial importance. Muhitdinov served in Damascus until his retirement in 1978.

The claim that the Soviet Union had not just solved the national question but also raised former colonies to equality became central to the country's self-representation to the Third World early in the Cold War. Over the following decades, Soviet writers were to argue that the Central Asian experience showed that socialism could be achieved "bypassing capitalism." This was the Leninist emendation of Marx's theory of historical stages, and it was of considerable relevance to the newly independent countries of the Third World—all of which struggled with issues of modernization and development. A path to the glorious classless future of socialism that did not necessitate a lengthy sojourn in capitalism would be a great gift indeed. For many newly independent countries, the Soviet model of the planned economy, with its elements of import substitution and self-sufficiency, was highly attractive. Central Asia was now not an outpost of revolution, but an example for others to follow.

The Cold War also had a cultural front where the two superpowers fought a battle for the hearts and minds of people in the Third World. The Americans sent jazz troupes to tour the world, but they also resorted to more crass tactics, such as paying lucrative amounts to Third World writers to publish pro-American or anti-Soviet belles lettres. The Americans also provided plenty of moral and financial support for émigrés from the Soviet Union and for anticommunist organizations around the world. The Soviets did not always have fistfuls of dollars to throw around, but they could capitalize on powerful feelings. For many anticolonial intellectuals, the United States was the champion of a global status quo that had scarcely changed with the granting of formal independence to former colonies. Many people who were not Communists still saw in the Soviet Union another pole of support for their aspirations, and they were attracted to the egalitarian ideals expressed by the Soviets. The new diplomacy under Khrushchev capitalized on these affinities, with considerable help from Central Asian actors. In October 1958, Tashkent hosted a conference of Afro-Asian writers. Those in attendance included Nazım Hikmet, the Turkish poet who lived in exile in Moscow; Faiz Ahamd Faiz, the Pakistani poet who was a subject of official suspicion at home; Ousmane Sembene, the Senegalese writer and filmmaker; W. E. B. Du Bois, the African American scholar and activist; the Indonesian novelist Pramoedya Toer; the Chinese author Mao Dun; and Mulk Raj Anand, the Indian novelist. Rashidov, also a writer, was the host (see figure 20.1). The conference established the Afro-Asian Writers Association, one of the key expressions of Third World solidarity and an attempt to forge global connections not mediated by Europe or the United States. The organization lasted until the end of the Cold War and held regular conferences, including one in Almaty in 1973.

More than any other place, Tashkent became the center of Soviet engagement with the Third World. The Raduga (Rainbow) Publishing House published the works of Central Asian authors in Persian, Arabic,

FIG. 20.1. The Presidium of the Conference of Afro-Asian Writers, Tashkent, 1958.
Sharaf Rashidov (standing) was the host. The sign behind the podium is in Uzbek.
Photo: Sharaf Rashidov House Museum, Jizzax; sharafrashidov.org.

Urdu, Hindi, and other foreign languages. In 1968, the city began staging
a biennial film festival to showcase works from the countries of Asia and
Africa (and, starting in 1976, Latin America), and thousands of students
from Africa, the Middle East, and South Asia studied in its universities
and institutes. Travel was never unrestricted in the Soviet Union, a fact
that made the presence of these students in Tashkent all the more remarkable. The city itself became a showpiece of Soviet modernity, as a
constant stream of official delegations from around the world saw its
new construction (especially after the earthquake of 1966). Showing off
the region to foreign visitors also had important domestic consequences. It made Central Asians, especially those who were involved in
the visits, proud Soviet citizens and included them in the romance of
the revolution. Islam, we might note, played little if any role in this encounter. A majority of the international students who studied in Central
Asia were Muslim, but most were committed secularists. Their studies
were entirely in Russian. Most of them were Russophiles, and their sharing a religion with Central Asians did not mean much to them.

FIG. 20.2. A Writers Union conference. Left to right: the Uzbek author Komil Yashin; the Kyrgyz novelist Chingiz Aitmatov; Faiz, a frequent visitor to the Soviet Union; the Russian writer and editor Anatoly Safronov; and Rashidov. This photograph encapsulates both the great overlap between literary and political elites in the late Soviet Union and their interaction with international visitors in the cultural Cold War. Photo: Sharaf Rashidov House Museum, Jizzax; sharafrashidov.org.

Soviet diplomatic success varied. Several of the Soviet Union's closest neighbors—Turkey, Iran, and Pakistan—remained wary of it and became allied to the United States during the 1950s. Their governments suppressed domestic socialist movements, with varying degrees of intensity. The Soviets had much better relations with countries that sought a greater distance from the United States. India became a close friend. Elsewhere in the Middle East, the modernizing regimes that came to power through the overthrow of conservative monarchies (as happened in Egypt, Syria, Iraq, and Libya) were the best friends of the Soviets, whose policies of social transformation and experience of development the regimes admired. Across the Muslim world, the debate about the Soviet Union centered on its treatment of its Muslims. For anticommunists, the constraints on the practice of Islam and religious education were a clear indication that the Soviet Union oppressed religion and that its proclamations about national autonomy were mere eyewash. Those on the left focused on the economic progress of the region and its social transformation, while emphasizing the existence of religious freedom in Soviet life. The Soviets caught on to this early. In 1954, after returning from a visit to India, Pakistan, and Afghanistan, Rashidov wrote a memo to Muhitdinov, then the first secretary of the Communist Party of Uzbekistan, arguing that Uzbekistan needed to take active measures to counter the "propaganda in these countries . . . from American and English imperialists" that Muslims in the Soviet Union were oppressed. Rashidov suggested pushing back against this view by publishing a guide to Islamic sites in the republic. However, as he noted, "many mosques, shrines, and religious monuments in Uzbekistan are in a neglected state and being used not as intended." This was the harvest of the antireligious campaigns of 1927–1941. The famous Baraq Khan madrasa housed a kerosene depot, and a building on the grounds of the Tilla Shaykh mosque, where SADUM was housed, had been given to a school, which used it as a gym.[5] As a result of Rashidov's intervention, some of these buildings were repaired and handed over to SADUM, so that they could be shown off to foreign dignitaries.

SADUM had an important role to play in this contest. Its leaders hosted numerous foreign delegations, especially those from Muslim countries, and its complex was a fixture on every tourist itinerary. It was able to get rid of the school gym from its head offices, but they remained quite modest to the end. (I was one of the tourists who visited the offices in 1985. The buildings were quaint and peaceful, but they did not look as if they housed an institution of great significance.) SADUM's *ulama* also visited other countries. They were regulars at international conferences on questions of peace, disarmament, and coexistence, and they visited other Muslim countries as part of Soviet cultural diplomacy. The hope was to convince foreign Muslims that Islam flourished in Soviet Central Asia. It is doubtful if SADUM ever had much impact on the skeptics. SADUM also managed the annual hajj pilgrimage to Mecca, participation in which was allowed again starting in 1947. However, the entire Soviet delegation numbered 25–50 people each year. (By the 1980s, the annual pilgrimage attracted an average of 900,000 visitors from outside Saudi Arabia, which hosted the hajj, and contingents from Muslim countries with populations equivalent to that of Central Asia numbered in the tens of thousands.) Prospective pilgrims were carefully vetted before departure by the KGB and debriefed after their return. Saudi Arabia was rabidly anticommunist. The Soviet hajj delegations served to maintain some sort of contact between the two countries, but their minuscule size undermined any potential for public diplomacy.

———

For Central Asians, the most important front of the Cold War was the Sino-Soviet one, which traversed Central Asia. As noted above, the Sino-Soviet alliance collapsed in spectacular fashion, and by 1962, the armies of the two Communist powers were exchanging fire. Many of these skirmishes took place along the Kazakhstan–Xinjiang border. With hindsight, the collapse of the alliance is not so surprising. Throughout the twentieth century, Communism was tied to the idea of national liberation. There is no better example of this truism than China. The Chinese revolution was nationalist and anti-imperialist. From the beginning, the CCP had been motivated by the idea of recovering China's sovereignty and overcoming the century of humiliation. Soviet tutelage had been tolerated at best. Soviet assistance was indispensable, but the CCP could never forget that Russia was one of the powers that had inflicted humiliation upon China. Stalin had, we will remember, extracted concessions in Manchuria and Xinjiang, traditional zones of Russian influence, from Mao, and this rankled with Mao. In 1958, after Stalin's death, Mao complained to Khrushchev about "a man by the name of Stalin, who took Port Arthur and turned Xinjiang and Manchuria into semi-colonies, and he also created four joint companies."[6] Yet curiously, it was Khrushchev's de-Stalinization that began the process of undoing the alliance. Mao and the CCP were offended by Khrushchev's talk of coexistence with capitalism, which they saw as a betrayal of revolutionary ideals, and by Khrushchev's lack of enthusiasm for Chinese confrontations with the United States over Taiwan and with India over disputed territory in Xinjiang. In the brewing confrontation, Mao took on the mantle of Marxist orthodoxy and accused Khrushchev and the Soviets of "revisionism." Khrushchev's innovations, Mao argued, would "change the proletarian character of the Communist Party of the Soviet Union . . . and pave the way for the restoration of capitalism."[7] By the end of the 1950s, the list of grievances had lengthened to include Soviet interference in Xinjiang that was alleged to fan Uyghur nationalism with the goal of subverting Chinese sovereignty.

The rhetoric only got sharper after the split. In 1964, Mao told a Japanese delegation: "About a hundred years ago the area east of Baikal became Russian territory, and since then Vladivostok, Khabarovsk, Kamchatka and other points have become territories of the Soviet Union. We have not yet presented the bill for this list." Khrushchev was outraged. "Let us look at these things," he told the Presidium of the Communist Party of the Soviet Union. "The Russian Tsar grabbed some territories. [Today] there is no tsar, and there are no Chinese feudal lords, there is no Chinese emperor. They [the Chinese] also grabbed territories, just like the Russian Tsar. It is not the Chinese who live there, but the Kyrgyz, the Uighurs, the Kazakhs. How did it happen that they ended up in China? It is a clear thing. Mao Zedong knows that the Chinese emperor conquered these territories."[8] Khrushchev had a point, but that point had been anathema to all Chinese regimes in the twentieth century. Instead, for Mao, the Soviets were "social imperialists," who used the language of socialism to engage in imperialism. As a formerly colonized country, China was the true champion of the Third World, and its peasant-driven revolution was far more relevant to the largely agrarian countries of the decolonizing world than anything proposed by the Soviets. Chinese anti-imperialism was premised on the notion that China was a victim of imperialism, not an empire. Chinese nationalism required the categorical refusal to see Xinjiang or Tibet as colonies. It was in Xinjiang, therefore, more than any other place in the Muslim world, that the Soviet Union appeared as a champion of liberty. The Soviet system of federalism, with its territorial autonomy and a relatively decentralized party organization, appeared quite attractive to Uyghurs and Kazakhs in Xinjiang. This was the case in the 1950s, during the heyday of the Sino-Soviet alliance. The demise of the alliance set in motion a major exodus of Kazakhs and Uyghurs to the Soviet Union. Once the borders were sealed, Xinjiang was subjected to incessant propaganda from both sides. Soviet radio broadcasts in Uyghur and Kazakh extolled the virtues of life in Soviet Central Asia, while denunciations of revisionism and social imperialism became staples of Chinese political rhetoric.

———

It was in Afghanistan, of course, that the final drama of the Cold War was played out. The proxy war that began there in 1979 is, in some ways, still not over four decades later. It has remade the world in significant ways. The country traces its history back to the conquests of Ahmad Shah Durrani in the eighteenth century. Its current boundaries were established in the late nineteenth century to make it a buffer state between the Russian and the British empires. Northern Afghanistan had long been part of the same cultural and political theater as Transoxiana, but the drawing of the Russian imperial boundaries put it on a different historical trajectory. In 1919, in the turbulent aftermath of the First World War, the new king, Amanullah Khan, forced Britain to recognize his sovereignty. He then launched a program of state and nation building that achieved considerable success over the next several decades, especially during the long reign of Zahir Shah (1933–1973). Zahir Shah maintained good relations with the Soviet Union, without sharing in any of the upheavals that wracked Soviet Central Asia. During the Cold War, he kept Afghanistan neutral and received aid from both superpowers.

The decades after the Second World War saw substantial growth in the country. As in numerous other Third World countries, many members of the newly educated elites were dissatisfied with their country's backwardness and sought ways of overcoming it. The radical answer was provided by the People's Democratic Party of Afghanistan (PDPA), which was formed underground in 1965. As with many other Third World socialisms, PDPA's Marxism was secondary to its fascination with the Soviet model of social transformation. Although prone to factionalism and having no presence in the countryside, the PDPA supported Muhammad Daoud Khan, the king's cousin and brother-in-law, when he overthrew the monarchy and proclaimed a republic in 1973. As Daoud consolidated power, however, he began to move against the party. The fear of a purge led PDPA members in the army and air force to seize power through a bloody coup in April 1978. The party established a democratic republic and declared its seizure of power to be the Saur revolution, after the Afghan month in which it took place. The PDPA instituted policies of rapid transformation that included land reform, changes in family law, the provision of mass education for both boys and girls, and pushing back against the power of the old elites, including the *ulama*. Yet the revolution soured fast, as the new regime quickly fell into internecine warfare. First, the more radical and impatient Khalq (People) faction purged its Parcham (Banner) rivals. Then, the two leaders of the Khalq faction, Nur Muhammad Taraki and Hafizullah Amin, fell out. Amin won the struggle and had Taraki put to death. Even without this chaos, the new regime would have had much too small a base of support to stay in power. A massive uprising in Herat in March 1979 was followed by mutinies in the army and around the country. This turmoil came in handy to both the Americans, whose special forces entered the fray, and the Pakistanis, with whom Afghanistan had territorial disputes and permanently tense relations. Faced with this chaos, the PDPA government asked for military help from the Soviet Union.

The Soviets had been quite cautious about interventions abroad. Aside from Eastern Europe, they had sent only military advisors and experts to friends or clients. In the beginning, there was little enthusiasm in the Politburo for intervention in Afghanistan. The Soviet Union had not engineered the revolution, but it was glad to have a friendly regime in Afghanistan. Whether that friendliness was worth military intervention, which would surely inflame relations with the United States and damage the détente that had emerged between the two superpowers, was another matter. Over the course of 1979, however, Soviet opinion shifted. Amin's behavior had become increasingly erratic, and leading figures in the Politburo were afraid both that his radicalism might imperil socialism in Afghanistan and that he might cut a deal with the United States and turn on the Soviets. On December 10, 1979, the Politburo made the fateful decision to intervene in Afghanistan. Two weeks later, Soviet special forces stormed the seat of the government in Kabul. Amin was killed in the action and replaced by members of the Parcham faction, who returned from exile and were installed in power. The Soviets had intervened on behalf of the less radical socialist faction and hoped that their involvement might be limited to ensuring order while Afghan forces quelled rebellions and consolidated power.[9] Things did not go according to plan. The revolt against the government was too widespread, and the Afghan forces were too divided to restore order. Soviet forces soon found themselves fighting alongside (and often in place of) the Afghan army. They were to stay in Afghanistan for close to a decade.

The Soviet invasion produced a massive exodus of civilians into Iran and Pakistan. The refugee camps in Pakistan became the bastion of opposition to the Soviets, fueled by American, Pakistani, and Saudi resources. For the United States, the Soviet invasion, coming on the heels of the revolution in Iran, had the potential to destabilize the American position in the Middle East and its access to the region's oil. The conservative monarchies of the Arab world, led by Saudi Arabia, felt directly threatened by both the Iranian revolution and the Soviet advance, as did the military regime in Pakistan—which had long had uneasy relations with Afghanistan, the countries' common faith notwithstanding. The three sides came together to back the Afghan resistance. They defined it as a jihad against Soviet atheists and provided large amounts of aid to the warriors. The resistance fighters, known as the mujahidin, were lionized in the West as freedom fighters. Jihad carried an entirely positive connotation in the corridors of power in Washington in the 1980s. Ronald Reagan, welcoming several mujahidin leaders to the White House, compared them to the founding fathers of the United States. Throughout the Cold War, conventional wisdom in the West had seen Islam as an antidote to Communism, and thus as a strategic asset to be cultivated. Now, on the battlegrounds of Afghanistan, the West used Islamic parties as its proxies to fight the Soviets. There was also the assumption that Soviet Muslims represented a fifth column, an unassimilated population groaning under Soviet rule. Pundits spoke of an Islamic threat to the Soviet Union as something to be hoped for. Nor were the pundits alone. William Casey, director of the CIA, thought that Central Asian Muslims "could do a lot of damage to the Soviet Union."[10] The CIA had the Qur'an translated into Uzbek and smuggled into Soviet territory, along with other religious tracts from hard-line Islamist writers. The assumption was that reading the Qur'an in their own language would make Soviet Muslims rise up against the Soviet order. The war in Afghanistan did not spread Islamic zeal in Central Asia, but it did create jihadism, the idea that jihad in a primarily military sense is the answer to all problems of Muslim society. Jihadism was born in Afghanistan, a child of the Cold War.

For Soviet Central Asia, the war did not produce the results that some Western observers had hoped for. Central Asian troops fought in the war as Soviet citizens. There were no defections or desertions from their ranks. (A few Soviet army troops did defect, but many of them were Russians, who converted to Islam and began life anew. No matter how interesting their stories, their numbers were negligible.) The war was unpopular in the Soviet Union, but its unpopularity was no greater in Central Asia than anywhere else in the country. Most young men accepted the official rationale for the war: that it was being fought to assist a friendly state fight counterrevolution and foreign intervention. Even a generation after the collapse of the Soviet Union, Central Asian veterans recall fighting the war as Soviet citizens.[11] Most Central Asians fought as common soldiers, rather than as officers, but large numbers of them served as interpreters or advisors to the Afghanistan government—roles many Central Asians had filled since the 1960s. To be sure, some veterans returned with doubt in their hearts, but their numbers were not significantly different from veterans of other Soviet nationalities. To the disappointment of Western hawks, Islam did not play a part in Central Asian reactions to the war. Indeed, the Soviet leadership was largely unconcerned about any potential effect on the Muslim population in the Soviet Union. The leaders worked on the assumption, solidly in place, that Muslims were loyal Soviet citizens who had collectively demonstrated their patriotism through sacrifice in the Great Patriotic War.[12] This assumption was to change only at the end of the Soviet era. In the 1980s, Central Asians were full-fledged Soviet citizens, at home with its values and practices. From Tashkent, Almaty, or Dushanbe, Afghanistan (or Xinjiang, for that matter) appeared backward and benighted, in need of internationalist assistance by good Soviet citizens. Yet other transformations, unconnected to the war, were afoot that would throw these certainties into doubt. The Brezhnev era was coming to an end. A new generation of top leaders of the Soviet Union were to attempt to restructure the Soviet order, an attempt that would unravel the structures that held the country together.

POSTCOMMUNISM

OUR DOMINANT IMAGE of 1989 is of the massive party atop the Berlin Wall on November 9. The opening of the wall had come on the heels of a long series of capitulations by the Soviet Union in its empire during that year. In February, the last Soviet troops had withdrawn from Afghanistan. In June, Poland held multiparty elections, and in September, Hungary opened its border with West Germany. By the end of the year, "velvet revolutions" had spread throughout Eastern Europe and swept the geopolitical division of Europe into the dustbin of history. The Iron Curtain had been raised, the Cold War was over, and freedom was ascendant in Europe. All of this was the result of the series of reforms initiated in 1985 by Mikhail Gorbachev after his rise to power in Moscow. The reforms were meant to strengthen the Soviet economy and make it more competitive. The search for economic reform led Gorbachev to offer to liberalize the political and cultural order as well. This experiment in the simultaneous reform of the economy and the polity proved disastrous. As the state scaled back on censorship, it faced immense pressures from below for change. Societies mobilized to demand political rights and to renegotiate the political order. By 1988, domestic Soviet politics were unrecognizable. In 1989, the changes spilled over into the Soviet Union's empire in Eastern Europe. The Soviet state was both unwilling and unable to suppress the new demands. Before the end of 1991, the Soviet Union had ceased to exist, and the five republics of Soviet Central Asia had become sovereign states.

A few months before the fall of the Berlin Wall, the Chinese party-state had given a different response to pressures from below. A decade of reforms led by Deng Xiaoping had transformed much about the Chinese

395

economy and increased the appetite for political liberalization among the beneficiaries of those reforms. Students demanding political change occupied Tiananmen Square, the symbolic center of Beijing. The students were inspired by the reforms under way in the Soviet Union, and Gorbachev was a particular hero. The two Communist regimes had been mending fences, and as part of the process of normalization, Gorbachev had visited Beijing in May. His visit seemed to galvanize the protests, which provided a backdrop to the official meetings. Three weeks after Gorbachev left, the Chinese authorities had had enough. They ordered the students out of Tiananmen Square, and when they refused, the authorities sent in the army to clear the area. The ensuing massacre resulted in over three thousand deaths. Once order had been restored, the CCP proceeded with far-reaching economic reforms that went much beyond anything contemplated by Soviet reformers. For the CCP, economic and political reforms had to be kept separate. Today, China has a capitalist economy, for all intents and purposes, but it is led by a Leninist party that brooks no challenges to its omnipotence.

The year 1989 let loose seismic transformations in Central Asia's politics and culture. The two sets of reforms in the two regimes produced very different trajectories for the two halves of Central Asia. The five republics of Soviet Central Asia were catapulted into independence and national sovereignty. They have negotiated a place for themselves in the post–Cold War international order, while domestically they have refashioned themselves as national states that celebrate the nation and its culture. In contrast, Chinese Central Asia has been woven ever more tightly into the Chinese state, with its national and cultural specificity curtailed and its demographic composition transformed. The economic situation of the two sides has flipped as well. In 1989, Soviet Central Asia was economically much the stronger of the two parts of Central Asia, with substantial heavy industry and a robust infrastructure, but now Xinjiang has become the economic motor of the region. Chinese goods and people, shut out of Soviet space by the closed border, have become dominant in the countries of post-Soviet Central Asia, with Xinjiang playing a major role in the trade. The relationship between the two halves of Central Asia has been reversed.

21

Unwanted Independence

ON LIVE TELEVISION on December 25, 1991, Mikhail Gorbachev resigned as the president of the USSR, bringing an end not just to his
tenure in office but also to the Soviet experiment. In fact, the union had
already ceased to exist for some months, and the various republics had
all declared their independence, but the dissolution of the Soviet state
made the new status quo official. The five republics of Soviet Central
Asia emerged on the world stage as sovereign states.

The passage to independence was unexpected and, in many ways,
unwanted by both the people and the political elites of Central Asia. The
dissolution of the Soviet Union capped almost a decade of turmoil unleashed by Moscow. It was not a revolt in the periphery, but decisions
by the center that rocked the boat in the aftermath of Leonid Brezhnev's
death in November 1982. Brezhnev's successor, Yuri Andropov, had
headed the KGB from 1968 to 1982, and he made fighting corruption a
priority. The center annulled the "Brezhnev contract" that had allowed
republic-level elites great leeway in return for the fulfillment of economic
targets and made Uzbekistan the epicenter of this struggle against corruption. But it was corruption—the overlooking of legal niceties, the
prevalence of personal connections and local arrangements, and so
much more—that had kept the country functioning during the previous two decades of unparalleled stability. Andropov's sanctimonious
pursuit of legality spelled the end of that stability and opened a Pan-
dora's box of problems that could not be resolved.

———

Sharaf Rashidov was on one of his regular visits to Moscow in August 1983 when he was asked to see Yegor Ligachev, the recently appointed head of the Organizational Bureau of the Communist Party. Candidate members of the Politburo seldom received requests for appointments from mere department chiefs, but Rashidov agreed to the meeting. There, Ligachev showed him piles of letters sent to the Central Committee from ordinary people in Uzbekistan complaining about high levels of corruption and illegality in the republic. The letters had been arriving in Moscow for several years. They were sent back to party authorities in Tashkent, who usually responded either that the reports were unfounded or that appropriate measures had already been taken. Now, on Andropov's watch, the party had decided to confront Rashidov directly.[1] The confrontation was followed by the dispatch of a number of investigative teams to the republic, which uncovered a host of "negative phenomena." Personnel appointments were commonly made on the basis of personal connections—which were often based on kinship, origins in a common locality, or common educational backgrounds— thus creating support networks that became ensconced in political and administrative organs. Bribery was rife. Most importantly, investigators uncovered astonishing levels of venality in the cotton production complex. Reports of cotton production had systematically been falsified for years. Figures were inflated, and the state was charged for quantities of cotton that were produced only on paper. It turned out that between 1978 and 1983, cotton production had been overreported by 4.5 million tons, almost a full year's production quota, and hundreds of millions of rubles had been embezzled.[2] Faced with the need to fulfill ever-increasing quotas, local "commanders of production" used all sorts of methods to extort more and more from their underlings. They could force members of collective farms to work extra hours or to sign for wages they never received. Individuals could acquire enormous wealth in the form of cash or precious commodities, much of which they stashed away in basements or buried in fields. When a certain Aslanov, a former director of the consumer union in the town of Romitan, was arrested, he was found to be in the possession of 9.0 kilograms of gold, 3.5 kilograms of pearls, 974 gold coins from the Tsarist period, more than a thousand jewels, 170,000 rubles in cash, and three cars.[3] Perhaps the most notorious example was that of Ahmadjon Odilov, the director of the local agro-industrial complex in Pop district in the Ferghana valley. A former head of a collective farm, he was a much decorated member of the party (his chest bore three Orders of Lenin, an Order of the October Revolution, and a medal proclaiming him to be a Hero of Socialist Labor) who had been elected to various party congresses and served as a deputy in Uzbekistan's Supreme Soviet. He had allegedly turned much of Pop into a personal fiefdom, complete with a private jail where those who crossed him were tortured or put to forced labor.

The investigations led to a wave of arrests that spread both horizontally across the republic and vertically up the party and Soviet hierarchy. By February 1986, when the next Uzbek party congress took place, forty of the sixty-five province-level secretaries, including ten of the thirteen first secretaries, and more than 260 secretaries of party organizations at the district and city levels had been replaced. One-third of the chairmen of district and city administrations faced criminal charges. Only one-fifth of the 177 members of the republic's central committee remained from the previous congress in 1981 (the usual rate of turnover in central committees was much lower, with two-thirds or more members continuing from one congress to the next).[4] Authorities opened hundreds of criminal cases and imprisoned thousands of people. Several, including at least one province-level party secretary, were sentenced to death.[5] There were several cases of suicide among disgraced officials. Rashidov had died suddenly on October 31, 1983, just as the investigation was picking up steam. He had looked worried and depressed in the last few weeks of his life, and rumors persist to this day that he had taken his own life. The curtain came down rather suddenly and in sad circumstances on the Rashidov era. Rashidov had ruled Uzbekistan for almost half of the period of its existence by then and had presided over massive social and economic transformations. In February 1986, the Communist Party of Uzbekistan launched an attack on Rashidov and his legacy. His body was removed from his mausoleum to an ordinary cemetery, and his name became synonymous with corruption and malfeasance.

The Uzbek cotton scandal transformed Uzbekistan's relationship to the center. Many of those who were fired were replaced by cadres sent from European Russia. In 1984 alone, three hundred officials arrived from Russia, Ukraine, and Belarus to take up important positions in Uzbekistan.[6] Uzbeks lost their majority in the Bureau of the Central Committee of the Uzbek Communist Party, the republic's equivalent of the Politburo: by 1986, there were only six Uzbeks out of thirteen members, when there had been seven out of eleven in 1981.[7] The Brezhnev contract had been ripped up by his successors.

––––––

The assault on Uzbekistan's party establishment was already in high gear when Gorbachev came to power in Moscow. Gorbachev's election to the office of general secretary of the Communist Party of the Soviet Union marked a generational shift in the country's leadership, which had been in the hands of the same generation since Stalin's death in 1953. Gorbachev faced a number of problems as he took office: Soviet economic growth had slowed over the past decade and a half, global competition with the United States was stretching resources thin, and environmental problems were becoming difficult to ignore. Gorbachev was aware that the challenges required new answers. He was a Leninist and did not set out to dismantle the Soviet Union, but he unleashed forces that no one could control. His first slogan was that of *uskorenie* (acceleration), aimed at improving the slowing rates of economic growth, but he quickly realized that economic reform required the devolution of decision making and glasnost (openness) in discussing alternatives. Glasnost was the fateful campaign that relaxed censorship and made it possible to express ideas and attitudes that had hitherto been taboo. By 1987, Gorbachev was talking about the need for perestroika (restructuring). Perestroika was meant to strengthen the Soviet economy, not to dispatch it to the dustbin of history. Its initial goals were quite modest. Enterprises could set their own production targets and deal directly with foreign partners, and they had to balance their own books without subsidies from the state budget. These reforms were now to be debated in a public space that had been opened in a manner quite unprecedented in Soviet history. A highly educated populace—the great achievement of the Brezhnev era—stepped in to participate in the experiment of the simultaneous liberalization of the economic and the political realms.

Gorbachev's main goal in Central Asia was to break the hold of the old generation of local elites. He moved quickly to wring changes in the republics' leadership to install a new group of leaders. Jabbor Rasulov, the long-serving first secretary of Tajikistan's Communist party, had died in 1982, and Rashidov in 1983. Over the course of 1985, Gorbachev forced the first secretaries of the Communist parties of Kyrgyzstan and Turkmenistan (as well as Rasulov's successor, Rahmon Nabiyev) to retire, leaving Dinmuhamed Kunayev of Kazakhstan as the only Brezhnev-era leader still in power. In December 1986, Kunayev too was removed from office. He was replaced by Gennady Kolbin, an ethnic Russian who had never lived, let alone worked, in Kazakhstan. In January 1988, Inomjon Usmonxo'jayev, Rashidov's successor and the coordinator of the purge in the Uzbek party, was forced out of office. Ten months later, he was arrested on charges of corruption and bribery. Moscow had shaken up Central Asia's political elite and was rewriting the rules of the game.

All of this played out on the front pages of national newspapers and on central television. The cotton scandal became an indictment of the whole region and its culture, which had supposedly been built on corruption and illegality. Russian policy makers and academics began to talk about how Central Asia was a burden on the state and that the "subsidies" paid to the region had an impoverishing effect on Russia and other "more advanced" parts of the country. The malaise of the later Brezhnev period had produced doubts about the Soviet project among many academics and policy experts in Moscow even before Gorbachev began his moving and shaking. The ecological costs of Soviet economic policies, especially the cotton monoculture, were becoming obvious, while the massive population growth in southern Central Asia and the unwillingness of Uzbeks and Tajiks to move to cities and into industrial labor led many policy makers and scholars in Moscow to rethink certain basic assumptions.

In 1983, Yulian Bromlei, the head of the Institute of Ethnography in Moscow, argued that Soviet economic policy in Central Asia had failed to take account of the region's national traditions, which allegedly kept Central Asians from joining industries that did not accord with those traditions. Bromlei was one of the main proponents of the concept of ethnogenesis, the idea that different *ethnos* (ethnic groups) develop historically through genetic mixing, and therefore each *ethnos* is genetically distinct. The concept was controversial because it posited genetic origins for nations and emphasized their specificity, thus questioning the universality of Marxism and the Soviet project. Now, Bromlei was in effect arguing that Central Asians were genetically indisposed to perform industrial labor. The policy implications were clear: there was no point in investing in the industrial sector in the region. Other Russian anthropologists began to despair of the ability of Central Asians to leave their traditions behind and join industrial modernity. The culmination of this line of argument came in a book by Sergei Poliakov, who painted a picture of a society gripped by "traditionalism," a phenomenon that represented "a complete rejection of everything new introduced from the outside into the familiar, 'traditional' way of life. Traditionalism does not simply battle novelty; it actively demands constant correction of the life-style according to an ancient, primordial, or 'classical' model."[8] According to these pessimistic analyses, nothing had changed in Central Asia in the Soviet period, for forces of tradition had defeated all attempts at modernization. The region was alien and unassimilable. This line of analysis called into question not just Soviet policies but the nature of the Soviet project. "If the universalist vision was invalid," Artemy Kalinovsky points out, "then what was the role and purpose of the Soviet Union?"[9]

The purge in Uzbekistan had created profound resentment not just among the party elite, but also in the population at large. The investigative teams and the outsiders appointed to prominent positions came to be called a "Red invasion" (*krasnyi desant*) of the republic. It was in

Kazakhstan, however, that Moscow's assertion of power produced the first overt conflict. On December 16, 1986, a crowd of Kazakh students gathered in front of the building housing the Central Committee of the Communist Party of Kazakhstan to protest Kunayev's ouster. The fact that he had been replaced by a Russian, and someone not even from Kazakhstan, turned resentment into protest. Overnight, authorities sent in troops to disperse the crowd, which numbered in the thousands. Over the next three days, the demonstration turned into riots that were violently suppressed. There were substantial casualties, with cautious estimates putting the number of dead around two hundred. This was the first public protest in the Gorbachev era anywhere in the Soviet Union against the dictates of the center. In Kazakhstan, the protest came to be known as the Jeltoqsan (December) events. Soviet authorities hushed it up in its immediate aftermath, but a couple of years later, it was to form the basis of the platform of more than one democratic organization in Kazakhstan.

The Central Asia that encountered these reforms was vastly different from that of 1917 or 1953. Now, each republic boasted an educated populace and a national intelligentsia that could articulate public positions. In the era of glasnost, intellectuals—economists and technical experts, but also writers, poets, and filmmakers—found their voices. The journals published by various institutes and the writers' unions of each republic became tribunes of new voices in which everything was up for debate. These national intelligentsias were very much a product of the late-Soviet period: social mobility of the Soviet period had created them, and Soviet investment in the academic sector gave them employment. They were, in a sense, a very Soviet phenomenon. As such, they were loyal to the Soviet state, and they thought in Soviet categories. The critique they formulated now was also Soviet, but none the less devastating.

———

The entire Soviet economic program was put up for debate. The ecological and health consequences of the cotton monoculture took center stage in the new critique. Writers began to point out that the per capita income in Central Asia was half the all-union average, that infant mortality rates were many times higher, and the consumption of meat and dairy products half or a third of the all-union rate. Tajik economists had long argued for the creation of labor-intensive industry that would soak up the labor surplus in Tajikistan. These demands were now put forward with greater insistence. Uzbek intellectuals objected to their republic's characterization in the press as a den of corruption. It was Moscow's insatiable appetite for cotton, they argued, that had produced the cotton scandal. Odil Yaqubov, the prominent writer and then head of the republic's writers union, asked at a conference in Moscow, "Is it not the case that this esteemed organization [the State Planning Committee], which sends a plan from above for our republic, unconsciously pushes us into newer falsifications?"[10] The whole cotton economy became a matter of debate. Moscow paid a fraction of world prices for the "white gold," it was now argued, while forcing Uzbek farmers to toil in utter misery. While Moscow thus extracted Uzbekistan's resources for a pittance, it called its transfers to Uzbekistan "subsidies," making the republic appear to be a burden on the country.[11] The writer Muhammad Solih claimed that the terms on which Moscow purchased Uzbek cotton were worse than those in the Tsarist period. In that period, an Uzbek peasant received enough money for a kilogram of cotton to buy a cow, while in the mid-1980s, a kilogram of cotton paid for only fifteen boxes of matches. Uzbek writers also decried the fact that only 6 percent of the cotton fiber produced in Uzbekistan stayed in the republic. The rest was sent off to textile factories in Russia, which then sent the finished products back to Uzbekistan.[12] The republic's status as a supplier of raw materials to a Soviet textile industry based in Russia and Ukraine seemed to be a classic case of colonialism. Disgruntled Uzbek communists had complained about "Red colonialism" in the 1930s and been purged for doing so. Now the charge was made again, with greater force. In the era of glasnost, use of the term "empire" appeared to be a way of delegitimizing the Soviet order.

Glasnost also made it possible to discuss the "blank spots" in recent history. Questions that had long been taboo could now be asked and their answers sought. The history of the early Soviet period was demythologized. Names that had been consigned to oblivion returned to print. These belonged to the intellectuals of the 1920s and the first generation of Central Asian communists, who had been purged in the 1930s and expurgated from public memory. In the Khrushchev era, many of these figures were rehabilitated—that is, the legal cases against them were nullified—but that process did not rectify the tendentious and often outright fallacious depictions of their lives and works that had become the norm. The Uzbek novelist Abdulla Qodiriy, shot in 1938, was rehabilitated in 1957, and his major works reappeared in print—but little else of his writing, including his copious satirical works, ever saw the light of day. The names of Abdurauf Fitrat and Cholpan, the other major figures of Uzbek literature of the 1920s, could scarcely be mentioned in print, nor were their works reprinted. Now, their works began to reappear in print. The process was slow and piecemeal, and the lead was taken by literary scholars rather than by historians, but the return of these texts made the Soviet narrative more and more untenable. The political history of the revolutionary era began to be discussed again, and the names of Mustafa Choqay, Ähmetjan Baytursïnov, and Alikhan Bökeykhanov, leaders of the abortive autonomous governments of the revolutionary era, appeared in print again. As the blank spots were filled in, the foundations of the Soviet narrative shifted.

Nor was this just talk. Gorbachev curtailed the Communist Party's monopoly of the political realm and allowed the creation of informal public organizations. Politics moved from the offices of the party to the streets. By 1987, all sorts of "popular fronts" appeared in the European parts of the Soviet Union, with the Baltic republics leading the way. The mobilization, its form, and its methods spread around the country and provided inspiration to Central Asia as well. In Uzbekistan, a group of intellectuals in the republic's writers union formed the Birlik (Unity) organization in November 1988. Its program addressed social, economic, and ecological issues, but it also called for improvements in both the position of the Uzbek language in the republic and the republic's position in the Soviet Union.[13] In Turkmenistan, the intelligentsia likewise rallied around the hope of "a cultural renaissance" and of the improvement of the status of the Turkmen language. Its organization was also called Unity (Agzybirlik), and it also combined national with environmental concerns.[14] In Tajikistan, an organization called Rastokhez (Resurrection) was founded at a conference in December 1989 as a movement of "patriotic intellectuals" in support of perestroika in the republic. Its manifesto spoke of the need for the population of Tajikistan to control the republic's natural resources to achieve economic sovereignty. It also spoke of the necessity to elevate the status of the Tajik language in the republic. In Kazakhstan, a number of organizations appeared in 1989 to press for greater democratization and greater language and political rights for the republic. A group called Jeltoqsan (December) emerged to seek amnesty for the participants of the December 1986 uprising, while the organization Azat (Freedom) sought independence for Kazakhstan. Central Asia's Russian population, moved by anxieties about its status in a more democratic society, mobilized to protect its interests. Russian groups were strongest in Kazakhstan, where organizations such as Edinstvo (Unity) and Russkaia obshchina (Russian Community) mobilized to defend the rights of Russians and the Russian language. Across the Soviet Union, the Cossack identity had reemerged in the general turmoil of the era. A number of Cossack organizations appeared in both Kyrgyzstan and Kazakhstan. They worked for the revival of Cossack traditions, organized mutual aid, and demanded political rights for their group. In northern Kazakhstan, which the Virgin Lands campaign had transformed into a Slavic-majority area, some groups demanded secession from Kazakhstan and the creation of a South Siberian Republic that would accede to Russia in the near future.[15] Other organizations arose to defend the rights of minority nationalities in each republic. In Samarqand, Tajiks organized in groups called Sayqal (Luster) and Oftobi Sughdiyon (Sun of Sogdiana) to fight discrimination and struggle for greater rights in the republic. Uzbek cultural centers appeared in the Kyrgyzstani cities of Jalalabat and Osh.

Perhaps the most remarkable organization founded in Central Asia in the perestroika years was Nevada–Semipalatinsk, the first antinuclear movement in the Soviet Union. On February 26, 1989, Oljas Süley-menov, the preeminent Kazakh man of letters, interrupted a reading of his poetry on national television (yes, Soviet television was still broad-casting poetry readings in prime time) to speak on the matter of nuclear testing at Semipalatinsk. Two days later, thousands of demonstrators gathered outside the building of Kazakhstan's writers union to protest continued nuclear testing at the Semipalatinsk site. As it gathered steam, Nevada–Semipalatinsk sought the closure of the test site, the end to the production of nuclear weapons, and citizen control over nuclear waste. It also sought acknowledgment of the health and environmental dam-age caused by the nuclear program. Named in solidarity with Americans protesting the Nevada Test Site, Nevada–Semipalatinsk was interna-tionally oriented from the outset. It built links with U.S. antinuclear organizations and engaged in public diplomacy beyond Soviet borders. Nevada–Semipalatinsk was wildly successful in achieving its goals. The Soviet government canceled a number of planned tests, and in Decem-ber 1990, Kazakhstan's Supreme Soviet passed a bill banning nuclear weapons testing in the republic. In August 1991, the Semipalatinsk Test Site was finally closed.

Nevada–Semipalatinsk was exceptional, however. Most mobilization during perestroika took place in the name of the nation. (We might also note the complete absence of any mobilization in favor of Central Asian unity, the chimera that foreign observers had long chased.) Although Gorbachev's reforms were meant to fix the economy, the language of economic rights and class had been so thoroughly discredited by its association with official rhetoric that it was of no use to oppositional forces. The language of the nation, in contrast, was available and had wide currency in the Soviet context. National categories were relevant to people's daily lives (as noted above, nationality was listed on identity documents, and one's nationality mattered in all sorts of things, from school admissions to jobs) and provided a significant node of solidarity. Even regional disparities took on a national tinge in the non-Russian parts of the Soviet state. The intellectuals who led the debate had come to see themselves as the guardians of their nations, the keepers of mem-ory, and the seers of the future.

———

The literary sensation of 1980 in the Soviet Union was *The Day Lasts Longer than a Hundred Years*, the novel by the Kyrgyz author Chingiz Aitmatov that we briefly encountered in chapter 17. Written in Russian, it is a multilayered meditation on life, culture, and memory. One of its several lines of narrative involves the legend of a torture technique used by the ancient warriors of the Juan Juan tribe on captives taken in war. The warriors pulled the wet skin of a camel's udder over the shaven heads of their captives and left them without food or water in the hot desert sun. As the heat dried the skin, it stretched ever tighter over the skull and crushed it. Most captives died an agonizing death. The few who survived suffered a complete loss of memory and become *mankurts*. "The *mankurt* did not know who he had been, whence and from what tribe he had come, did not know his name, could not remember his childhood, father or mother—in short, he could not recognize himself as a human being."[16] Deprived of his ego, the *mankurt* became the perfect slave, loyal and submissive to his captors: "The *mankurt*, like a dog, only recognized his master. . . . All his thoughts were concerned with satisfying his belly's needs. He had no other worries. He performed the work given to him blindly, willingly and single-mindedly." Aitmatov's novel was a bestseller across the Soviet Union, and the term *mankurt* entered the vocabulary of late-Soviet culture. It is important to remember that in 1980, the story of the *mankurt* was not necessarily anti-Soviet or a veiled attack on Russification. It was much more about the costs of modernization, keeping the memory of the past alive, and cultural authenticity. These were universal questions that resonated across the Soviet Union. Especially in Central Asia, the legend of the *mankurt* resonated with anxieties about the loss of culture, especially among intellectuals who were afraid of losing their moorings in their own society. In Kyrgyzstan and Kazakhstan, where European settlement had been particularly heavy, the anxieties weighed particularly heavily.

Glasnost made it possible to discuss the national question outside the Stalinist parameters that had lasted into the Brezhnev era. Gone were the necessary paeans to the Russian elder brother, the encomia to the undying friendship of peoples, and the idea that the Tsarist conquest had been a voluntary union. Yet much of the national discourse of perestroika was a complaint about the unfulfilled promise of the Leninist nationalities policy and a plea for its implementation. The policy had promised economic equalization and territorial autonomy for the titular nationalities. In reality, the Soviet economy was hypercentralized and oblivious to national differences, while language rights were often honored in the breach. As in 1917, most national movements sought not outright independence but a renegotiation of their place in the Soviet state.

Nor was national mobilization simply an anti-Russian phenomenon. The situation was far more complex. Many of the claims for national rights were directed at other nationalities. Tajik intellectuals raised again the question of the Tajik minority in Uzbekistan and the claim to the cities of Samarqand and Bukhara. Given the scale of the dislocation, there was remarkably little violence. On the few occasions when conflicts did descend into violence, Russians were seldom the only target. Central Asia saw three episodes of mob violence during this period. In June 1989, a violent conflict broke out in the small Ferghana valley town of Kubasay between Uzbek youth and Meskhetian (or Ahıska) Turks, who had been deported to Uzbekistan in 1944. An estimated fifty-seven people were killed before security forces intervened. In the aftermath, most of the Meskhetian community was evacuated to other parts of the Soviet Union. A year later, violence broke out between Uzbek and Kyrgyz farmers over land claims in a collective farm near Osh. Widespread rioting across the area led to 300–600 deaths. In the meantime, in February 1990, mass protests had broken out in Dushanbe, the capital of Tajikistan, over rumors that Armenians fleeing Armenian-Azerbaijani violence in Baku were being given priority access to housing in the city. (Housing was in perennially short supply, and about 7 percent of the city's population was on a waiting list for apartments.) The rumors were just that (and the number of Armenian refugees was minuscule), but they served to focus anger on the government. Large crowds gathered in Dushanbe's main square, demanding the expulsion of Armenian refugees, the resignation of the Tajik government, the removal of the Communist Party from the republic, and the equitable distribution of profits from cotton production. The demonstration, again, turned violent, although the death toll was only between 15 and 25. The grievances against Armenians turned into a broader attack on all Europeans in the city. A number of Armenians, including those who had long lived there, fled Dushanbe in the immediate aftermath of the demonstration. National identities were all too real, but the conflict was not always between Central Asians and Russians.

———

This mobilization alarmed the local party elites. They had been under assault from Moscow and, with the onset of perestroika, they were also expected by Moscow to diminish their role in local politics. Over opposition from more cautious colleagues, Gorbachev pushed through competitive elections within the party and then for a new legislature, the Congress of People's Deputies, to replace the Supreme Soviet. In the autumn of 1988, he abolished the economic departments of the Central Committee, thereby ending the party's oversight of the economy. By March 1990, the party had formally ceded its leading position in society—that is, its self-proclaimed monopoly on power. All of this was terrible news for Central Asia's Communists. The only silver lining for them was that the center had also loosened its grip on the republics. The Communist Party of the Soviet Union was federalized, giving the republic-level party organizations unprecedented autonomy. In Central Asia, this situation paradoxically allowed the old party elites to dominate the new republican legislatures elected in 1990 and regain their power.

In Uzbekistan, Usmonxo'jayev had been replaced in January 1988 by Rafiq Nishanov, an old adversary of Rashidov's who had spent fifteen years abroad as Soviet ambassador to Sri Lanka and then Jordan. In June 1989, Nishanov was ousted in turn by Islom Karimov, who reestablished the hold of the party on the republic. In Kazakhstan, Kolbin, whose appointment in December 1986 had led to massive protests, was replaced by Nursultan Nazarbayev, the head of the republic's Council of Ministers. In 1990, when all republics acquired executive presidencies, the first secretaries of four of the republics managed to get themselves elected presidents without much difficulty. The only trouble came in Kyrgyzstan, where the party secretary, Absamat Masaliyev, could not defeat his opponent, Apas Jumagulov—the chairman of the Council of Ministers and thus also a member of the elite. Since neither candidate won a majority, both were disqualified according to the rules and the choice was thrown to the republic's Supreme Soviet, which chose Askar Akayev, an engineer and the president of the republic's Academy of Sciences, to be the first president on October 27, 1990. Akayev was also a member of the party, but he was not a member of the office-holding elite and thus was unique among the region's presidents. The men who came to power in 1989 and 1990 were to remain in office for a long time. With the partial exception of Kyrgyzstan, the Central Asian Communist parties managed to survive at the helm of affairs through the convulsions of the Gorbachev era.

Party elites were also wary of competition from newly organized informal groups in society. These groups were generally weak, but resolute action against them by local party organizations kept them on a short leash in any case. Although Uzbekistan's Communist Party allowed Birlik to organize rallies, it nevertheless attacked the "unhealthy moral-psychological climate" of the opposition and called for "high political vigilance" against the "extremist actions."[17] In Tajikistan, First Secretary Qahhor Mahkamov could disparage informal organizations as irrelevant as late as December 1989: "And, really, let us think—is it appropriate today to put forward suggestions about creating this or that new public organization, when we already have more than enough of them? Those who have a sincere desire to help *perestroika* can apply their energy, initiative and craving to serve their people, and transform them into practical deeds, through Party, trade-union and Komsomol organizations, newly elected Soviets and our numerous existing public associations and creative unions."[18] The going was even easier in Turkmenistan, where informal groups seem not even to have organized in any real sense. Gorbachev forced Muhammetnazar Gapurov, the Brezhnev-era head of the party, out at the end of 1985. Gapurov's successor, Saparmurat

TABLE 21.1   Perestroika-era leaders

Republic	Leaders in March 1985	Gorbachev appointments	New appointments in 1989–1990
Kazakhstan	Dinmuhammed Kunayev, since 1964	Gennady Kolbin, Dec. 1986	Nursultan Nazarbayev, 1989
Kyrgyzstan	Turdakun Usubaliyev, since 1961	Absamat Masaliyev, Nov. 1985	Askar Akayev, 1990
Tajikistan	Rahmon Nabiyev, since 1982	Qahhor Mahkamov, Nov. 1985	None
Turkmenistan	Muhammetnazar Gapurov, since 1969	Saparmurat Niyazov, Dec. 1985	None
Uzbekistan	Inomjon Usmonxo'jayev, since 1983	Rafiq Nishanov, Jan. 1988	Islom Karimov, 1989

Niyazov, hardly broke a sweat through the next six years and emerged as president of independent Turkmenistan at the end of 1991. Against all odds, the Communist elites had survived into 1991 with their control of society largely intact (see table 21.1).

———

And what of the Muslims who were supposed to make trouble for the Soviet Union? A number of Western observers, we will remember, saw Central Asia as the soft underbelly of the Soviet Union, in which a barely assimilated population was supposed to seethe under Soviet oppression. It was also conventional wisdom in the West that Islam was an antidote to Communism. Once the proxy war in Afghanistan began, Pakistan, the United States, and its allies banked on Islamic militancy to fight the Soviet occupation, and the CIA had hopes of taking the attack to the Soviet Union by radicalizing its Muslim population. None of that happened. The Afghan war did not lead to disaffection on Islamic grounds in Central Asia. Interest in Islam did soar, as glasnost allowed a general reassessment of the Soviet experiment. Mosques that had operated clandestinely came out into the open, those that had lain disused were repaired and began functioning again, and many new ones were built. Islamic education was resurrected, and the observance of

Islamic ritual became more common. None of this was necessarily anti-Soviet, however. For most people, the return to Islamic observance was part of the recovery of national values. It was not a threat to the Soviet state.

The idea that politics should be based on Islam is not ancient. It developed in the twentieth century when conservative thinkers in India and Egypt, disillusioned with secular nationalism, came up with the idea of an Islamic politics. Usually called political Islam or Islamism, this was an attempt to turn Islam into a political ideology, a key feature of the modern world. Central Asia had largely been cut off from the rest of the Muslim world since the 1920s, and these developments generally passed it by. Some of the new Islamic literature did appear in the region through SADUM's foreign contacts. SADUM's own practice was puritanical in a scripturalist sense but resolutely apolitical. It was in the milieu of the *hujra* (underground Islamic learning) that political Islam first emerged. The *hujra* was largely concerned with conserving Islamic knowledge in a hostile environment. Its major figure, Muhammadjon Hindustoniy, resolutely opposed any talk of a jihad in hostile conditions. Around 1977, some of his students dissented. The initial dispute revolved around ritual. The dissidents argued that the ritual customarily practiced in Central Asia was corrupt and in need of cleansing. The debate over ritual soon turned into a debate on Islam's place in politics. The dissidents, who styled themselves the renewers (*mujaddidlar*), accused Hindustoniy of being oblivious to politics and argued for a more assertive role of Islam in politics.[19] In 1986, the authorities arrested a certain Abdulla Saidov, an unregistered mullah, who had been calling openly for the establishment of an Islamic state in Tajikistan and urging his followers to petition the forthcoming Twenty-Seventh Congress of the Communist Party with these demands. His arrest provoked a protest at the offices of the Ministry of Internal Affairs in Qurghonteppa, the district center.[20] There was clearly support for Saidov's views (although it is not clear what he meant by an Islamic state, especially if it was to be achieved by appeal to the Communist Party). Beyond this episode, however, in Central Asia there was little political mobilization around Islam in the era of perestroika, nor were there any demands for an Islamic state until the end of 1991. Soviet authorities, blindsided by the revolution in Iran and smarting at the Islamist opposition to the Soviet occupation of Afghanistan, were still not overly worried about the possibility of an Islamist opposition in Central Asia. They were largely right.

———

Soviet federalism had largely been a legal fiction rather than a robust political reality. According to the Soviet constitution, the fifteen union republics were sovereign entities that had voluntarily joined the Soviet federation. They had all the trappings of sovereign states—flags, constitutions, anthems, legislatures, and even ministries of foreign affairs. Prompted by Gorbachev's reforms, the republics began acting more and more like actual political entities. They sought not only to claim the rights guaranteed to them in the Soviet constitution but also to expand them unilaterally. In November 1988, the Estonian Supreme Soviet issued a declaration affirming the sovereignty promised in the Soviet constitution. In the perestroika context, sovereignty meant far-reaching autonomy, in which republican laws would supersede federal ones. Other republics followed, and by 1990, a "parade of sovereignties" was in full swing. The tide hit Central Asia that summer. Uzbekistan declared its sovereignty on June 20, 1990. Turkmenistan and Tajikistan did the same in August, and they were followed by Kazakhstan in October and Kyrgyzstan in December. A year previously, each republic had declared its titular language to be the state language of the republic (similar declarations were being passed in all the other republics of the union). These moves were made by legislatures still firmly controlled by local branches of the Communist Party, for which they served two purposes. First, they loosened republics' ties with the center, which had been seeking to control them and force greater liberalization on them. Second, republican autonomy took the wind out of the sails of local public organizations. Language rights ranked near the top of the agendas for all informal groups in Central Asia. By co-opting the national agenda of their main competitors, Central Asian party leaderships ensured their continued hold on power.

Nonetheless, neither the populations nor the native Communist elites wanted complete independence. The Soviet system of national territorial autonomy had been invented as a way of preempting national forces that had figured so prominently in the Russian civil war. Territorial autonomy was primarily concerned with cultural issues such as language rights; it had never been meant to provide economic sovereignty. Central Asia occupied the unfavorable position in the centralized Soviet economy of being primarily a supplier of raw materials. It could ill afford to be severed from the structures that gave its economies their context. Yet centrifugal forces began to gain strength across the union. In June 1990, Russia declared its sovereignty from the Soviet Union, and the dissolution of the Soviet Union, once unimaginable, began to look inevitable. Gorbachev began talking about reconstituting the Soviet Union as a "renewed federation" based on a new union treaty among the republics. In March 1991, he had the question put to a union-wide referendum. The question—"Do you consider necessary the preservation of the Union of Soviet Socialist Republics as a renewed federation of equal sovereign republics, in which the rights and freedoms of persons of any nationality will be fully guaranteed?"—was ambiguous and differently worded in different republics. Gorbachev's support for preservation rested not on Communism but on history: "By virtue of history, a great many peoples, big and small, living on the vast expanse of Siberia, the flatlands and steppes of the Far East and Central Asia, in the valleys of the Caucasus and the Pamirs and on the Baltic, Caspian and Black Sea shores, have united around Russia," he said in an address to the country in February. "A huge Eurasian state with the world's largest territory and a large multilingual population has taken shape over centuries. . . . It would be madness to attempt to destroy this natural result of the flow of history."[21] There was plenty of opposition, and six of the fifteen republics refused to participate, but the five Central Asian republics voted overwhelmingly to preserve the union. The turnout rates and the majorities looked suspiciously like those of Soviet elections from before glasnost, but we can still take the results as indicative of general sentiment in the region. Far from posing an Islamic threat to the Soviet Union, Central Asians had turned out to be the most Soviet of all Soviet citizens (see table 21.2).

TABLE 21.2 Results of the March 1991 referendum on preserving the union

Republic	Total		Yes		No	
	Votes	%	Votes	%	Votes	%
Russia	79,701,169	75.4	56,860,783	71.3	21,030,753	26.4
Belarus	6,126,983	83.3	5,069,313	82.7	986,079	16.1
Ukraine	31,514,244	83.5	22,110,899	70.2	8,820,089	28.0
Azerbaijan	2,903,797	75.1	2,709,246	93.3	169,225	5.8
Abkhazia	166,544	52.3	164,231	98.6	1,566	0.9
Kazakhstan	8,816,543	88.2	8,295,519	94.1	436,560	5.0
Kyrgyzstan	2,174,593	92.9	2,057,971	94.6	86,245	4.0
Tajikistan	2,407,552	94.2	2,315,755	96.2	75,300	3.1
Turkmenistan	1,847,310	97.7	1,804,138	97.9	31,203	1.7
Uzbekistan	9,816,333	95.4	9,196,848	93.7	511,373	5.2

Source: Pravda, 27 March 1991.
Note: Abkhazia was an autonomous republic in Georgia. Although Georgia boycotted the referendum, the leadership of Abkhazia decided to participate in it.

All of this was rendered moot by events. On August 19, a conservative faction in the Politburo attempted a coup in the hopes of restoring order and stopping the centrifugal forces that had made the country ungovernable. Tanks rolled into Moscow, and troops attempted to storm the offices of the Russian government that had emerged as the main antagonist of the Soviet order. Twenty-six months after other troops in tanks had murdered thousands in Beijing, the scenario in Moscow unfolded very differently. The tanks were besieged by protesters and rendered harmless. Boris Yeltsin, the recently elected president of Russia, climbed atop one of them and gave a defiant speech. Only three people died before the coup fizzled out. Massive violence was no longer imaginable even to Soviet hard-liners.

Other than Akayev of Kyrgyzstan, all Central Asian presidents seem to have supported the coup, for they preferred a restored union. Once the failure of the coup was clear, they all hurried to declare their republics independent. The future was too chaotic to contemplate, and jumping ship was the best option. Uzbekistan and Kyrgyzstan declared themselves independent on August 31, Tajikistan on September 9, and Turkmenistan at the end of October. Kazakhstan waited until December. These declarations were not recognized internationally until the end of December, for the Soviet Union continued to exist formally until then. It ended as a result of a legal maneuver by the presidents of Russia, Ukraine, and Belarus, the three surviving signatories to the original treaty that had established the Soviet Union in 1922 (the fourth, the Transcaucasian Federative Soviet Socialist Republic, had been dissolved in 1936). On December 8, the presidents met at the Belarus government dacha in a forest near the Polish border to dissolve the union. The sovereignty of the republics had largely been a legal fiction, but legal fictions can become significant in given historical conditions. The so-called Belavezha Accords did precisely that. They provoked another round of negotiations between the remaining (former) republics. Representatives of eleven of those republics met in Almaty on December 21 to confirm the accords and establish the Commonwealth of Independent States in place of the Soviet Union. On December 25, Gorbachev resigned as president of the Soviet Union, and the country was formally dissolved. The five republics of Central Asia had become sovereign states.

22

A New Central Asia

OVER THE WINTER of 1991–1992, the five countries of Central Asia joined international organizations from the United Nations to the International Olympic Committee, and their flags began to fly alongside those of other sovereign states. Sleepy Soviet provincial towns such as Ashgabat, Bishkek (as Frunze was renamed), and Dushanbe became national capitals where the outside world showed up in many forms. Foreign embassies appeared along with foreign goods, which were now available to the few who could afford them. Foreign ministries had existed in all Soviet republics, but now they became real. They increased their staffs and opened embassies overseas. Airports were upgraded and new flight routes created. It became possible to travel to Central Asia without passing through Moscow.

Yet exhilaration at the achievement of independence was tempered by massive problems. Perestroika had unleashed an economic crisis that rivaled the Great Depression in its magnitude. All systems of exchange had been disrupted, goods were in short supply, and salaries were not being paid. Domestic output fell precipitously, as many enterprises shut down and whole sectors of the economy evaporated. Production and trade networks had taken a hit during perestroika, but the shocks were much greater with the dissolution of the Soviet state. The abandonment of the artificial prices that had governed intra-Soviet commerce benefited Kazakhstan and Turkmenistan, whose oil and natural gas exports now fetched world prices, but the other three Central Asian countries suffered from the new terms of trade. The Soviet ruble had plunged into

FIG. 22.1. Boats on the exposed bed of the Aral Sea. The retreat of the Aral Sea made possible
many such striking images. Environmental degradation was a major problem that the new
states of Central Asia faced after independence. It is tempting to see in the image a metaphor
for the Soviet project and its utopian dreams. The dreams might have been left high
and dry, but the transformations of the Soviet era still continue to shape Central Asia.
Photograph by Daniel Prudek/Shutterstock.

inflation, which ran at four-digit levels in 1992. People struggled daily to
find bare necessities and survived by relying on family connections and
informal ties. As many of the structures of Soviet modernity melted into
thin air, there was a palpable sense of demodernization, of things going
backward.

The dissolution of the Soviet Union marked the largest transformation in the geopolitics of Central Asia since the era of the colonial conquests of the mid-nineteenth century, when the region had been divided up between Russia and China. Now Russia had withdrawn, and
its part of Central Asia was open to the world as never before. Other
powers moved in, seeking trade, influence, and access to the region's
natural resources. Analysts quickly dubbed this jockeying a new Great
Game, borrowing the tired term that had never been very illuminating.
In fact, the new geopolitics was multilateral, involving a number of

powers—none of which had the ability to determine the shape of things on the ground in post-Soviet Central Asia.

A century and a half after the first British agents had visited the courts of Central Asia, Britain was finally able to open embassies in the region. Britain was no longer a great power at the end of the twentieth century, and the United States was the major new presence in the region. In the 1990s, it assisted Kazakhstan in getting rid of the nuclear weapons it had inherited from the Soviet Union and sealing bore holes and tunnels in the former test site at Semipalatinsk (now Semey). The events of 9/11 transformed the U.S. relationship to the region. In preparation for the invasion of Afghanistan in the aftermath of 9/11, the United States leased air force bases in Uzbekistan and Kyrgyzstan. Few observers noted the irony in the fact that twenty-two years after the Soviet invasion of Afghanistan, the United States was using Soviet-built bases to wage war on that country, fighting groups that were a direct product of its own proxy war of the 1980s.

Turkey was the first country to establish diplomatic ties with the new states of Central Asia. Most policy makers in Turkey assumed that Central Asians (even the Tajiks!) were fellow Turks who had long been oppressed by an alien regime and would now be happy to be guided to modernity and secularism by Turkey. They soon discovered that Central Asians had had enough of elder brothers and that they had their own notions of Turkism, in which Turkey did not play a leading role. Turkey managed to organize a summit conference of all Turkic-speaking states (Turkey, Azerbaijan, Turkmenistan, Uzbekistan, Kyrgyzstan, and Kazakhstan) in Ankara in 1992. The conference became an annual event, and in 2009 it was formalized as the Cooperation Council of Turkic-Speaking States. Yet multilateral cooperation never really took off. Far more important conduits of Turkish influence were private businesses, which expanded into Central Asia, and the transnational Hizmet (Service) movement founded by the Sufi-inspired modernist Fethüllah Gülen. Hizmet seeks the transformation of both individuals and society through education and, ultimately, the reshaping of the political sphere. It established dozens of private schools across Central Asia (they were expelled from Uzbekistan in 2000) that offered rigorous instruction in

English. Until a spectacular falling out in 2014, the movement had the tacit support of the Turkish state and helped create a small Turkish-oriented elite in Central Asia.[1]

The southern border of the former Soviet Union opened up for the first time in a century as Iran, Pakistan, and India appeared on the scene. Western fears that Iran might be a force for Islamic radicalism in the region were misguided and did not materialize. Iran has pursued trade and national security in the region, especially along its long border with Turkmenistan. Any chances of normalized relations with South Asia were stymied by the continuing chaos in Afghanistan. More than a de-cade of war had turned the country into a stateless expanse, home to jihadist outfits composed of volunteers from across the Muslim world who had come to fight the Soviets in Afghanistan. The United States, its mission accomplished following the Soviet withdrawal, lost all interest in Afghanistan, but the many factions of the mujahidin continued to receive arms and money from Saudi Arabia and Pakistan. The common enemy having vanished, the factions fell out among themselves. The Communist government in Kabul fell in early 1992 once its Soviet sup-port vanished, but the victorious mujahidin could not form a stable government, and Afghanistan descended into anarchy. Over the course of the 1990s, Afghanistan was to see the rise of both the Taliban and Al Qaeda. The war had also made Afghanistan a major source of narcotics. Drug production increased dramatically after the mujahidin takeover, and the export routes shifted north. In the 1990s, Tajikistan became a major channel for the export of Afghan drugs. More than anything else, this instability put security and Islamic radicalism firmly on the agenda for Central Asia.

Post-Soviet Russia was much diminished and historically unusual. The last time a Russian state had existed in the boundaries of the current Russian Federation was in the middle of the seventeenth century. The dissolution of the Soviet Union also created a large diaspora of ethnic Russians across the former Soviet space, who now became minority populations in states that had suddenly become foreign. Yet Russia's ties to Central Asia did not vanish. Central Asia was tied to Russia with myriad links of commerce, transportation, language, and education.

Soviet railways had their own gauge, and they all went to Moscow; all industrial goods in Central Asia were manufactured according to Soviet standards and aimed at a pan-Soviet market; and Russian was the main international language that Central Asians knew. In the 1990s, Russia was in too chaotic a condition to do very much about its retreat, although Russian troops guarded Tajikistan's border with Afghanistan until 2006.

China was the greatest beneficiary of the dissolution of the Soviet Union. Instead of facing a superpower to its west, it now had a number of small countries to contend with. Li Peng, China's prime minister, toured Central Asia in April 1994 and declared the dawn of a new era of stability, economic cooperation, and friendship. China quickly became a major trading partner with the region, and it has consolidated its relations with the states there through a series of bilateral and multilateral agreements. Until the closure of the Sino-Soviet boundary in 1962, Soviet manufactured goods had dominated in Xinjiang, which was very much the poorer and less-developed half of Central Asia. From the 1990s on, the situation was flipped. Chinese goods filled Central Asia's bazaars as Central Asia's own industrial sector shrank, and the Chinese presence became increasingly tangible during the 1990s. China shared with Russia a suspicion of the U.S. hegemony that emerged with the end of the Cold War. In 1996, China and Russia initiated a multilateral effort to build cooperation and align security policy, working with Kazakhstan, Kyrgyzstan, and Tajikistan—the three countries that share a border with China. The so-called Shanghai Five became a formal entity called the Shanghai Cooperation Organization in June 2001 (when Uzbekistan joined them). The organization has expanded since then to include India and Pakistan, and it provides the basic venue for relations among Central Asian states.

The demise of the Soviet Union also had important consequences for China's policy toward its own part of Central Asia. The CCP was alarmed at the power of national mobilization during perestroika, and it worried that the independent states of Central Asia might set an example for China's own nationalities. Uyghur discontent had been endemic, and the CCP was worried about new cross-border influences reaching Xinjiang. Xinjiang is home to more than a million Kazakhs and smaller numbers of Kyrgyz, while the newly independent Central Asian states—particularly Kazakhstan—house a sizable Uyghur diaspora, most of whose members have no fondness for Chinese rule over Xinjiang. Since 1991, the CCP has redoubled its efforts to integrate Xinjiang into the Chinese state. While the former Soviet republics became independent states, Xinjiang has gone in the other direction, being increasingly assimilated into China.

———

In three republics—Kazakhstan, Turkmenistan, and Uzbekistan—Communist leaders effortlessly transformed themselves into national leaders and emerged fully in control of the new states. Nursultan Nazarbayev of Kazakhstan was the only candidate in the presidential election of December 1991 and received a Soviet-style 98.7 percent of the vote. Saparmurat Niyazov of Turkmenistan outdid him with 99.5 percent in June 1992. Islom Karimov of Uzbekistan had an opponent—the poet Muhammad Solih, of the Erk political movement—who won 12.5 percent of the vote in December 1991. All three victors managed to get reelected several times. Niyazov and Karimov died in office and were succeeded by close associates, while Nazarbayev resigned in 2019 after almost thirty years in office. The transition was a little trickier in Kyrgyzstan, where the disarray in the party leadership was great enough that in 1990 it elected Askar Akayev, an outsider, as a compromise candidate to its leadership. Akayev went on to win an uncontested election in October 1991 (receiving 95.4 percent of the vote) and was reelected more than once. He stayed in power until massive street protests forced him to flee in 2005. Since then, the country has experienced several transfers of power, but its political elite still has links to the late-Soviet period.

Tajikistan was different. Widespread civil unrest accompanied by defections in the military and security apparatuses led to clashes that turned into a full-blown civil war by the summer of 1992. At the time, the war was seen as pitting Communists against Islamists and used as a cautionary tale about the dangers of Islamic militancy in the new Central Asia. It was only three years since Islamists had, with Western support, defeated Communists in Afghanistan, but things had changed. With the Soviets gone and the Cold War over, Tajik Communists appeared preferable to Islamists. In fact, however, the fault lines in the war were different. For much of its existence, the Tajik party elite had been recruited from the northern province of Khujand (called Leninobod during the Soviet period), which also had received the lion's share of investment from the central government. The Leninobodis had learned to share the pie with some people from other parts of the republic, primarily Kulob and Hisor. During perestroika, their control of the resources was challenged by factions of the Communist Party from other, poorer provinces; secular intellectuals; and a number of Islamic activists who had formed the Islamic Renaissance Party of Tajikistan in October 1990. This party was an alliance of unofficial reformist mullahs from the countryside, and its program had a local orientation. Its leaders argued for the creation of an Islamic state in Tajikistan, while acknowledging that this was only a long-term goal. After seven decades of Soviet rule, the main goal was to restore the basics of Islam to society and begin the process of bringing Islamic knowledge and values back into public life. As Muriel Atkin has argued, it is much more fruitful to think of the war as a struggle between "neo-Soviets" and the "opposition," or between the old guard and its challengers, than as an ideological contest.[2] The alliances between the various groups involved were profoundly pragmatic, and the parameters of the conflict were rooted squarely in the crisis of the end of the Soviet Union. The war was brutal: estimates for fatalities range from 40,000 to 100,000, with another million people displaced—all out of a population of five million. But throughout the war, the neo-Soviets held onto the capital and received international aid and recognition as the legitimate government of Tajikistan. In November 1992, in the midst of the war, Russian and Uzbekistani troops helped the neo-Soviets install Emomali Rahmonov as president of the country. Rahmonov had been the head of a state farm in his native Danghara and now found himself the head of a sovereign state with international recognition. The war ended in 1997, when a peace accord brokered by the United Nations allowed the formation of a coalition government dominated by the neo-

TABLE 22.1   Post-Soviet national leaders

Country	President	Dates in office
Kazakhstan	Nursultan Nazarbayev	1989–2019
	Qasïm-Jomart Toqayev	2019–
Kyrgyzstan	Askar Akayev	1990–2005
	Kurmanbek Bakiyev	2005–2010
	Roza Otunbayeva	2010–2011
	Almazbek Atambayev	2011–2017
	Sooronbay Jeenbekov	2017–
Tajikistan	Rahmon Nabiyev	1991–1992
	Emomali Rahmonov	1992–
Turkmenistan	Saparmurat Niyazov	1985–2006
	Gurbanguly Berdimuhamedov	2006–
Uzbekistan	Islom Karimov	1989–2016
	Shavkat Mirziyoyev	2016–

Soviets but in which the opposition acquired a minor role.[3] Thus, even the Tajik civil war did not dislodge the hold of the late-Soviet elite on the country. Instead, independence brought another period of stability at the top to rival that of the Brezhnev period, as the same men held the leadership in all five countries from 1992 to 2006. There has not been a meaningful turnover in elites since then (see table 22.1).

The Chinese government drew its own lessons from the Soviet collapse. In its analysis, the most important factor behind the dissolution of the Soviet Union was the mobilization of its nationalities: the Soviet constitution had given too much power to the republics, while Soviet policies of indigenization had promoted too many minority officials to positions of power.[4] Similar developments could not be allowed in the PRC. China was never a federal state, and territorial autonomy there, even in theory, was a lot more limited than in the Soviet Union. After 1991, even that limited autonomy shrank. The earlier emphasis on staffing local government organs with members of minority nationalities was watered down, so by 2001, it was enough that local government organs include a reasonable (*heli*) number of minority officials—and there was little enforcement of even these minimal goals. The term *minzu* was redefined. It had been adopted into Chinese from Japanese in the early twentieth century to signify "nationality," as used in Soviet-inspired discourses of nationhood and autonomy. Official Chinese documents translated it into English as "nationality." In the 2000s, the term began to be rendered into English as "ethnicity." The difference is stark. "Ethnicity" has no connotation of group rights or any claim to territory or political rights. In U.S. usage, "ethnicity" evokes pride in heritage with absolutely no connection to historical or political rights in the way that the term "nationality" has. Uyghurs as an ethnic group in China are now deemed equivalent to, say, Chinese Americans in the United States—a group that may celebrate its community and heritage but can make no claims to territory or autonomy.

The formula of "55 + 1 = 1" took on a new form. The relationship between the Han and the fifty-five minority groups was always asymmetrical, but after the turn of the millennium, the emphasis shifted increasingly toward unity, while the fifty-five groups have become largely decorative. The National Museum of China in Beijing is entirely devoted to Han Chinese history and focuses on the achievements of "Chinese ancestors." The other fifty-five *minzu*s have been shunted off to the China Ethnic Museum (Zhonghua Minzu Bowuguan) on the outskirts of the city, where each nationality has its own pavilion that includes replicas of architecture traditional to each group. Labels describe each group in highly essentialized and patronizing ways. For example, "Tibetans have made great contributions to human civilization by engaging in animal husbandry and raising yaks on the highland," while Uyghurs "are exceptional in building ditches and channels in service of their oasis agriculture. Handicraft and commerce are also well developed [among them]." Across Xinjiang, depictions of Uyghurs in folkloric costume, usually playing folk instruments and singing or dancing, are ubiquitous, and that is about the only way in which Uyghurs appear in Chinese iconography. The Soviets might have come up with the practice of representing nationality through folklore, but it is in China that the equation of nationality with frozen, ethnographic stereotypes has been fully entrenched. Such a vision of national identity emphasizes the quaint and the exotic at best. At worst, it renders nationality inherently backward. The China

Ethnic Museum packages the fifty-five groups as exotic creatures for the gaze of the Han (foreign visitors are few and far between).

This rethinking of nationalities policy was accompanied by a steely resolve to integrate Xinjiang into the PRC as never before. The 1990s saw substantial investment in Xinjiang's economy. After the split with the Soviet Union in 1962, the CCP had left the transport infrastructure of Xinjiang underdeveloped. If the Soviets invaded, they were not to be presented with good roads and an efficient railway network. In the post-Soviet age, the Chinese state acted to develop the region. The Great Western Development Strategy (Xibu Da Kaifa), launched in 2000, was an ambitious effort to steer state investment, outside expertise, foreign loans, and private capital into the PRC's west. For Xinjiang, it meant a massive ramping up of infrastructure. In 1965, Xinjiang had 368 kilometers of tarmac roads; by 1999, there were 30,000 kilometers, a number that had increased to 146,000 kilometers by 2008.[5] First-class tarmac roads now connect its many cities to each other: one can zip along from Kashgar to Yarkand in two and a half hours (a journey that took five days a century ago). The railway has finally tied Altishahr to the north, while the north is linked to China proper as never before. A high-speed train link is under construction that will cut the travel time between Beijing and Xinjiang to fifteen hours. The distance that long separated Xinjiang from China has been conquered.

A new slogan was "to speed up economic development but to downplay the national question" (jiakuai jingi fazhan, danhua minzu wenti).[6] In 1955, Säypidin Äzizi had successfully argued that autonomy is granted to peoples, not to mountains and valleys. However, the Great Western Development Strategy is all about developing mountains and valleys and deliberately ignores any national implications. This was the final outcome of a long process of integrating Xinjiang into China by transforming its demographics. The Qing, we will remember, had talked of settling the New Dominion with Han settlers but never managed to do so. It was only after the Communist occupation of Xinjiang that Han settlement began in earnest. During the first three decades of Communist rule, the vast majority of settlers were demobilized soldiers or those "sent down" (xiafang) in rustication campaigns or mobilized for revolutionary goals.

By 1978, Han constituted 42 percent of Xinjiang's population, up from a mere 6 percent in 1949. The flow was reversed in the reform era, as many Han who had been forcibly relocated to the province returned to China proper. In 1990, the Han share of the population was down to 37.5 percent, and official estimates of the time projected a decline to 25.0 percent by 2030.[7] Since 1990, the state has offered a different set of incentives—property rights, tax breaks, and job security—to attract Han migrants to Xinjiang. The logic is simple: If China is a unified multinational state, then all its citizens have equal claim to all its territory. Uyghurs, for instance, have no greater claim to Xinjiang than any Han citizen from, say, Hainan, and the government of China can move people around without regard to nationality. Han settlement in Xinjiang resumed after a lull in the 1980s and has kept pace ever since (see figure 22.2). If anything, census figures underreport the extent of the Han Chinese presence, for they include neither military personnel stationed in the region nor the "floating population"—the hundreds of thousands of people who do not reside where their official household registration (*hukou*) says they do.[8]

Han settlement is not uniform across Xinjiang. The province can be divided into three zones. First, the north (the Zungharian basin, where indigenous populations were historically nomadic) has long been the target of Han settlement. Ürümchi, the capital, is in effect a Chinese city with an Uyghur quarter, and there are pockets where the Han form the overwhelming majority of the population. For example, the city of Shihezi, established as a *bingtuan* base in the 1950s, is more than 90 percent Han. Second, the east, containing the oases of Qumul and Turpan, has the longest connection to China proper and has a substantial Han population. Third, the south, that is Altishahr, with its old cities, is the real Uyghur heartland and still largely Uyghur. Han settlers in the south are mostly concentrated in the cities, and even there they constitute small minorities, even if their political and economic power is great. There are exceptions, of course. The population of the town of Korla, the center of the new petroleum industry in Xinjiang, is more than two-thirds Han, who completely dominate that industry. Like the Russians in Soviet Central Asia, Han immigrants to Xinjiang carry their language

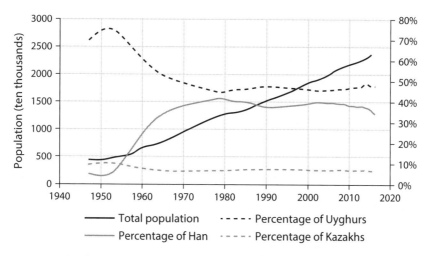

FIG. 22.2. The demographic transformation of Xinjiang since 1949. *Sources:* Rough estimate
for 1949: James A. Millward, *Eurasian Crossroads: A History of Xinjiang* (New York:
Columbia University Press, 2007), 306–307; 1953: Michael Freeberne, "Demographic and
Economic Changes in the Sinkiang Uighur Autonomous Region," *Population Studies* 20
(1966): 108; 1964 and 1982: Stanley W. Toops, "The Demography of Xinjiang," in *Xinjiang:
China's Muslim Borderland*, ed. S. Frederick Starr (Armonk, NY: M. E. Sharpe, 2004), 246;
biennial totals, 1950–1976: Ren Qiang and Yuan Xin, "Impacts of Migration to Xinjiang since
the 1950s," in *China's Minorities on the Move: Selected Case Studies*, ed. Robyn Iredale et al.
(London: Taylor and Francis, 2003), 91–92; other years: *Xinjiang Statistical Yearbook 2017*
(Beijing: China Statistics Press, 2017), table 3-8.

and culture with them. They never have the need, let alone the desire,
to learn any local language. Rather, they legitimize their presence in
Xinjiang through a number of heroic narratives: they are constructors
who are building up Xinjiang, bringing it and its backward peoples to
modernity, and ensuring stability in a region of strategic significance to
the motherland.[9]

As one might expect, this retrenchment in *minzu* policy was not welcomed by Uyghurs and other indigenous populations of Xinjiang. As
we have seen, Uyghurs in particular have always been skeptical of the
CCP regime. The gradual shrinking of *minzu* rights, already quite
limited, produced discontent that sometimes burst out into the open in
violent episodes but was always present below the surface, as we shall
see in chapter 23.

Islom Karimov had an unpleasant experience on the eve of his election as president of independent Uzbekistan in December 1991. In the city of Namangan, a group called Adolat (Justice) demanded that he meet with its members as he campaigned for election. Adolat was one of the many informal groups that had emerged during perestroika. It was part political group and part an organization of vigilante peacekeepers, in which capacity it had reportedly been helping local police in maintaining order in the city. At the meeting, Karimov was confronted by the group's leaders before a large crowd, which jostled him and presented him with a list of demands that ranged from the immediate and concrete to the far-reaching and abstract. Adolat wanted the building that housed the city committee of the Communist Party to be turned into an Islamic center, Islamic parties to be legalized, and Uzbekistan to be declared an Islamic state. Karimov talked his way out of the meeting, but he was not amused. At the same time, in neighboring Tajikistan, the Islamic Renaissance Party became a major actor in political life and played a role in the country's civil war. These developments firmly planted the Islamic threat on the security agenda for the region immediately upon its independence.

The new Central Asia emerged on the global stage at a moment when Islam was replacing Communism as the ideological threat to the established world order. The region's location next to Afghanistan, the epicenter of jihadist activity in the world, ensured that the fear of radical Islam defined the security agenda for Central Asia. Multiple interests converged on this issue: Central Asia's political elites, their Chinese counterparts, the leaders of post-Soviet Russia, and Western observers all had reason to be wary of radical Islam. The position of Central Asian elites is easy to understand. As Soviet men, they found the idea of religion meddling in politics to be unnatural. They were averse to all opposition, but they found opposition couched in religious terms particularly odious. The Chinese leaders had the same ideas. The position of Western powers is a little more difficult to explain. Up until 1989, while Soviet forces were in Afghanistan, support for the Afghan mujahidin was widespread in the West. Now, less than three years after the Soviet withdrawal from Afghanistan, minds had changed. Islam had quickly become the new ideological enemy for many. It was one thing for Islam to threaten the Soviet Union, but it was quite different for Islam to threaten a post-Soviet order. The Soviet Union's Muslims did not make much trouble for the Soviet Union, but when they made demands in the post-Soviet era, they found that they were not welcome.

In any case, Adolat and its activists were outliers in the religious landscape of the former Soviet Central Asia. The Islamic revival of the Gorbachev years was primarily concerned with reviving moral and spiritual values, reestablishing Islamic education, and recovering knowledge and ritual practices that had been forgotten in the previous three generations. The vast majority of Central Asians saw the absence of Islam from public life to be normal and natural, and for most a return to piety was a matter of reclaiming traditional values. However, Central Asian states had low tolerance for opposition, and even less for the presence of Islamic discourse in public life. Karimov drove Adolat out of the country and launched a campaign against "religious extremism." Adolat's activists ended up in Afghanistan, where they became increasingly radical and established a jihadist outfit called the Islamic Movement of Uzbekistan with the goal of overthrowing Karimov and establishing an Islamic state in Uzbekistan. The movement may have been behind a bombing in Tashkent on February 16, 1999, that killed sixteen people and damaged a number of government buildings. A few months later, an armed band belonging to the movement entered the Batken district of Kyrgyzstan from Tajikistan and took several hostages. The insurgents demanded a ransom and passage to Uzbekistani territory, where they intended to wage jihad against "the tyrannical government of Uzbekistan and the puppet Islam Karimov and his henchmen." The insurgents received the ransom and then retreated, only to return for another incursion the following summer. They did not achieve much in terms of territory or victims, but they shaped the security agenda for the region.[10]

Then came 9/11 and the Global War on Terrorism (GWOT), which produced a new global vocabulary of politics. Opposition to terrorism and religious extremism became a universal language for asserting one's position on the side of Reason, Enlightenment, and Secularism. It now provides a wonderful alibi for crackdowns by authoritarian regimes on their opponents. The regimes of Central Asia embraced this new language with alacrity, as did the Chinese government. Since 9/11, they have used the charge of terrorism and extremism to target all sorts of enemies.

23

Nationalizing States in a Globalized World

MUCH OF WESTERN COMMENTARY on the emergence of Central Asian states as sovereign actors insisted on their artificiality, weakness, and lack of coherence. Western observers assumed that the new states were merely the creation of the Soviets and had no purchase on their citizens' loyalties. The reality was quite different. The republics were over sixty years old when they became independent states, and a vast storehouse of national legitimacy was available to them. The nation was a fundamental category of Soviet practice, and much of the debate during perestroika had centered on national interests. The Communist party elites were well placed to take on the mantle of nationhood. All through the Brezhnev period, they appeared as de facto leaders of the nation, and the anticorruption campaigns unleashed by Andropov and Gorbachev only marked them as national victims of Soviet oppression. They had co-opted the agendas of the national movements that appeared in opposition to them between 1989 and 1991, and after independence, they refashioned themselves as the founding fathers of new national states. Since 1991, all Central Asian states have used national legitimacy to fashion solidarity and achieve cohesion. Many of these national ideas, as we have seen in this book, predated the Soviet Union, but they crystallized during the Soviet period around institutions and practices fashioned by the Soviet state. Since independence, Central Asian states have sought to refashion themselves into fully national states, in many ways attempting to fulfill the promises of Soviet nationalities policies without being encumbered by Soviet constraints. Even when the new states were overturning Soviet-era policies, they acted in a very Soviet fashion.

———

Since independence, all Central Asian states have acted as nationalizing states—that is, states that promise to work for the betterment of the titular nation.[1] They seek to promote the national language, make the national culture flourish, and ensure the economic well-being of the titular nation by righting the wrongs of the Soviet past. Nationalizing states have been a common phenomenon in the twentieth century, in Europe and beyond. Contemporary Western liberal thought disdains nationalism, which it equates with chauvinism—a view that it shares with past Soviet orthodoxy, which also considered "nationalism" to be a dirty word. For much of the period after the Second World War, Western liberals have sung encomiums to a postnational world in which nations and nationalism would become obsolete. Yet the liberal world order is structured around national spaces that are guarded by passports and visas, and the nation-state remains the default mode of political organization. The post-Soviet experiences of the independent states of Central Asia are best examined in this context.

Foreign observers were surprised when the statue of Karl Marx in Tashkent's main square was replaced by that of Timur, who emerged as the foundational figure of Uzbek nationhood. They clearly did not know how central Timur was to the way Uzbek identity had been imagined in the modern age, since before the Russian revolution. The Soviets had frowned upon Timur, so his reemergence was a sign of the breaking of Soviet taboos. His return was accompanied by the creation of a cult of the Timurid era. Tashkent is now adorned with new buildings in the neo-Timurid style: white stone structures topped by turquoise domes. Timurid-era buildings have been restored across the country at considerable expense. Timur's mausoleum in Samarqand dazzles visitors with the refurbished goldwork inside its dome, while across town the Bibi

Khanum mosque, commissioned by Timur but never completed, has been given a glory it never before enjoyed. In the quarter-century of independence, the state has also celebrated numerous jubilees—anniversaries of the founding of Bukhara (the 2,500th anniversary), Samarqand (2,750th), Marghilan (2,000th), and Tashkent (2,200th); the millennium of the Alpomish folk epic; and the 2,700th anniversary of the Avesta, the Zoroastrian sacred text—in addition to multiple celebrations of various anniversaries of Islamic scholars from the country's past. The past is clearly very important to contemporary Uzbekistan. Islom Karimov, the country's president, turned the Soviet slogan of building Communism into one of building up Uzbekistan as the Great State of the Future (*O'zbekiston—kelajagi buyuk davlat*). The phrase became ubiquitous in the country's public spaces. Massive, spectacular celebrations of independence day and Navroz, the Turko-Persian spring festival, further cultivated a sense of nationhood.[2]

In Kazakhstan, the nationalization of the state proceeded a little differently. Russians constituted a large chunk of the population. The far north was predominantly Russian, and there was some sentiment for secession to Russia. Nursultan Nazarbayev dealt with this challenge astutely. He left Russian as a state language and cultivated good relations with Russia. In 1996, he moved the capital from Almaty on the southern edge of the country to the town of Aqmola in the north. This policy was combined with a program of repatriation of Kazakhs from around the world to their ancestral homeland. One can think of it as the Kazakh equivalent of Israel's Law of Return, although the calamities that dispersed the Kazakhs all happened in the past century or two. This program aims to provide restitution for the great tragedies of 1916 and collectivization, which scattered Kazakhs far and wide, while also helping undo the demographic challenge posed by the large Russian population in Kazakhstan. Over the years, almost a million Kazakhs have "returned" to Kazakhstan. Most of them came from Uzbekistan, but some were from Xinjiang and Mongolia. This has transformed Kazakhstan's demographics, giving the Kazakhs a comfortable majority in the population.

In Turkmenistan, Saparmurat Niyazov, the last first secretary of the republic's Communist party, refashioned himself as the Turkmenbashy,

Head Turkmen, and presented the new regime as the fulfillment of the Turkmen people's ages-long aspirations to sovereignty and global prominence. Kyrgyz nationhood came to revolve around *Manas*, ostensibly the longest epic poem in the world and the timeless embodiment of Kyrgyz identity. It was during Soviet times that *Manas* came to be identified as the national possession of the Kyrgyz. In the post-Soviet period, it came to be the central symbol of Kyrgyzness. Bishkek's international airport is named after it, as are a number of streets and official awards. The national idea did not work so well in Tajikistan, which plunged into a civil war. But even there, after the resolution of the conflict, the government has sought to ground its legitimacy in the ancient Iranian heritage of Central Asia. Khujand province is now Sughd (Sogdiana), and the national currency is called the *somoni*, after the Samanid dynasty at whose court New Persian emerged as a literary language. The idea of Tajiks as a distinct, perhaps embattled, group in the midst of a sea of Turkicness is fundamental to Tajik identity. In each country in Central Asia, history is supremely important and politically indispensable. National symbols, often rooted in history or folklore, are ubiquitous.

If the national myths are rooted in deeper history, all five countries have also reevaluated the history of the twentieth century. The amnesia of the Soviet period lifted in the Gorbachev years, and the blank spots in history began to be filled in. After independence, many of the value judgments of the Soviet period were reversed. Those slaughtered in the purges of the 1930s became national heroes. In Uzbekistan, the Jadids were anointed leaders of a national liberation movement that sought statehood for the Uzbek people. In Kazakhstan, the leaders of Alash Orda were recognized again as founding fathers of the modern Kazakh nation. In the other three countries, the figures who had gotten the republics off the ground in the early-Soviet era but had then been purged have been brought back into memory as modernizers and national heroes. Most of the cultural heroes of the Soviet period retained their places in the pantheons, so that today's lineup of national heroes is cumulative. The literature of the 1920s, proscribed for much of the Soviet era, is now widely available in modern editions.

The new governments passed legislation to make their national languages the state languages and to downgrade the official status of Russian. Writers had already begun to reform their languages during glasnost, excising Russian loanwords and calques and coining new vocabulary or restoring words that had long ago gone out of use. Now these efforts became more formal, and attention turned to the reform of the alphabet. The Cyrillic script that had been in use since the late 1930s was now questioned. There was little interest in a return to the Arabic alphabet. It was the Latin script, used in the 1930s, that appeared as the logical choice to most reformers. The campaign for Latinization in the 1920s was rooted in the radical cultural movement of the time, as intellectuals sought ways to overcome widespread illiteracy. It was a different matter in an era when universal literacy had been achieved. Yet the symbolic value of the shift justified it. Turkmen switched to the Latin alphabet in 1993. Uzbekistan introduced a Latin alphabet in 1993, with a plan for its gradual implementation over the years. There was much less interest in the other countries, although the debate continued to simmer in Kazakhstan. Only in 2017 did the government abruptly decide to shift to the Latin script. Latinization was identified with Turkism in Tajikistan and never had any traction there, and the Cyrillic script is still in use.

These policies have nationalized space itself. The Soviets loved commemorating greatness by naming places and public spaces after important figures. Independence saw a wave of renaming, as places shed Soviet-era names and reverted to older names. Leninobod went back to being Khujand, and Frunze became Bishkek (its pre-Soviet name was Pishpek). Elsewhere, the new states insisted that place names be spelled according to local, not Russian, versions. Thus, on new maps Ashkhabad appeared as Ashgabat and Alma-Ata as Almaty. Streets, squares, and collective farms were renamed in massive numbers, shedding names with Soviet or Communist references and taking new names with national ones. Symbols of the Soviet era began to disappear and were often replaced by national markers. Urban space took new shape. Brezhnev-era apartment blocks are a clear reminder of the Soviet era, but they have been joined by new construction in self-consciously modern styles. Tashkent's neo-Timurid architecture has transformed urban space. Much more radical was the transformation of Turkmenistan's capital, Ashgabat. Niyazov decided to turn the city into a showcase of Turkmen sovereignty. In addition to its many monuments, the city acquired a host of new government buildings, multistory hotels, and apartment blocks in white marble. The construction required so much marble that world prices were affected. The city's skyline has been transformed, but most of the new apartments are too expensive for anyone to buy, and the hotels are empty because Turkmenistan retains strict visa requirements for foreign travelers.

But Kazakhstan's new capital, Astana (renamed Nur-Sultan in 2019), takes pride of place as the biggest architectural project in post-Soviet Central Asia. Moving the capital from the edge of the country to its heartland is not without precedent (Brasilia, Canberra, New Delhi, and Islamabad all come to mind). There is some irony in the case of Kazakhstan, because Khrushchev had wanted to move the capital of the republic to the same city—then called Tselinograd (Virgin Land Town)—but Kazakh elites had dragged their feet and defeated the proposal. Aqmola, as the town was renamed upon independence, was a small provincial town (its population was 281,252 at the time of the 1989 census) with an extreme continental climate: its temperatures range from -35°C to 35°C over the seasons, and it experiences savage winds from the steppe. The new capital was built on virgin territory across the river from Aqmola and is therefore not tied to the old city plan. Instead, it was built from scratch according to a master design prepared by the Japanese architect Kisho Kurokawa. It joins a long list of planned capital cities designed to showcase the aspirations of their countries to the world and build pride at home. Astana was built to be spectacular. Its architecture includes Khan Shatïr, a shopping and entertainment center built in the shape of a tent that is 150 meters high and can claim to be the largest tent in the world, even if it is made of metal; Bayterek, a 97-meter-high monument that represents the mythic tree of life from a Kazakh folktale; the pyramid-shaped Palace of Peace and Reconciliation that represents all of the world's religions; the Aq Orda, the seat of the presidency; and any number of commercial and residential buildings. It is easy to scoff at it all and dismiss it as an autocrat's folly, but we should remember that Washington is also named after a first president and has a strikingly grandiose and pompous plan. Both in its layout and in its spectacular architecture, Nur-Sultan shares much more with Dubai and Shanghai than with anything in the Soviet past. The new city also serves a nation-building purpose. Nazarbayev was not wrong when he said in 2010 that "the construction of Astana has become a national idea which has unified society and strengthened our young and independent state."[3]

————

Space also shrank. As Soviet citizens, Central Asians could travel across the thirteen time zones of the Soviet Union, and the lucky ones could go on vacation in Eastern Europe. Independence penned people in. Travel beyond the former Soviet Union was very difficult, for foreign currency and visas were not easy to obtain. Initially, travel to other former Soviet republics was not seriously disrupted, as the trains continued to run and there were few formalities for entry. By the middle of the 1990s, however, the boundaries between the republics had hardened into international borders, complete with visa regimes, border posts, and, in many cases, fences. This was a real change for many citizens: families were left divided, local commercial networks were disrupted, and mobility was diminished. The new boundaries also required new transportation routes. Soviet roads and railways routinely cut across republican boundaries. The easiest way to travel from Khujand in northern Tajikistan to Dushanbe, the republic's capital, was via Samarqand in Uzbekistan. The road from Samarqand to the Uzbek capital of Tashkent passed through Kazakhstan, while roads in the Ferghana valley crisscrossed republican boundaries as a matter of course. Uzbekistan has built new routes to ensure connections between different parts of the country without crossing international boundaries, while Tajikistan has had to construct a five-kilometer-long tunnel to connect Dushanbe to Khujand without having to go through two mountain passes over three thousand meters high. Each country now has its own currency, electrical grid, cell-phone network, and so forth.

Nationalizing states also created national minorities. Uzbeks living in Kyrgyzstan, for instance, became a minority community, as did Russians everywhere in Central Asia. The situation had existed ever since the republics were created in 1924, but now, with the broader Soviet context gone, it took on a new and very different meaning. The breakup of the Soviet Union also saw a Russian exodus from Central Asia. The outflow had begun in the 1980s, but independence swelled the tide enormously. Some of this emigration was the result of the economic crisis of perestroika, as many jobs evaporated. The deindustrialization of the region during the collapse of the Soviet economy meant that many technical jobs had vanished. But the Russian exodus was also fueled by a recognition that life would be different in a Central Asia not tied to the Russian state. A quarter-century after the end of the Soviet Union, the Russian presence in Central Asia is small. The one exception is Kazakhstan, where Russians still account for a quarter of the population. Perestroika and independence also spelled the end of Central Asia's indigenous Jewish community. The freedom to emigrate and the presence of sponsorship abroad meant that almost the entire community, which numbered around 45,000 people in 1987, emigrated to Israel or the United States.

We should be careful not to overstate the case, though. The post-Soviet regimes have been careful not to overplay the nationalist hand. The new constitutions all guarantee minority rights, and the governments have avoided making territorial claims against one another or using co-ethnic populations in neighboring countries as bargaining tools in national conflicts. There have been conflicts (the pogroms against the Uzbek population of Osh in Kyrgyzstan in 2010 being the most notable example), but generally the situation has been peaceful. The reality of the nation, however, is undeniable. In the early years of independence, Uzbekistan's president, Islom Karimov, spoke of "Turkestan as our common home" (mirroring Gorbachev's espousal of a "common European home" during perestroika), but competition over resources as well as competing national narratives have meant that regional cooperation remains a distant dream.

The survival of Soviet elites in power does not mean that nothing has changed in post-Soviet Central Asia. Many Soviet institutions have been weakened, if they did not completely disappear. The Communist Party is gone, along with its political machine, its monopoly on political power, and its youth branch. In each of the five countries, the executive dominates the state. Educational systems have had trouble maintaining their levels, as resources are stretched, and private schools and universities are firmly a part of the landscape now. Nor is Central Asia immune from outside influences. The world has come rushing in. Alongside the diplomats who staffed the new embassies came do-gooders of various sorts—missionaries, economic advisors, aid officials, and nongovernmental organizations (NGOs)—as well as merchants, bankers, and investors. Foreign goods appeared in Central Asian markets and homes as they had never done before. New kinds of stores and restaurants appeared, and new patterns of consumption became possible. By the mid-1990s, when the countries' new currencies appeared, Central Asians had learned to deal with exchange rates and world prices. Foreign books and foreign news also arrived. In the Soviet period, the shortwave radio was an instrument of subversion, for it allowed Soviet citizens to tune in to broadcasts aimed at them in their own languages by their country's adversaries. Now, satellite television brought the outside world to Central Asia (the mobile phone and internet were to follow later in the decade). Soviet schools had always taught foreign languages, but now those languages could be heard on the streets of the bigger cities. None of these novelties was universally accessible. The end of the Soviet economy also created massive inequalities that determined who had access to the benefits of this new world and who did not. The new elites could enjoy international travel and access to luxury goods, but even the lives of ordinary people were affected by these new flows. Global brands appeared, along with new ways of marketing them. Banks and financial institutions reappeared and tied the new states to the rest of the world in new ways. A private sector took root, although its success varied from country to country and within each country. Kazakhstan and Kyrgyzstan went ahead with market reforms much more willingly than the other three countries, whose governments were cautious about the social upheaval that rapid economic liberalization might bring.

For many Western observers, the demise of the Soviet Union and the end of the Cold War were supposed to usher in the triumph of liberalism worldwide. Liberated from the constraints imposed by despotic regimes, societies would automatically choose free markets and free elections and become "normal." Elections and the exercise of free will were expected to overcome the constraints of history and structures of power and inequality. None of this happened. Rather, the political and economic systems that emerged in most of the post-Soviet states are particular to their historical circumstances, in which massive transformations coexist with significant continuities with the Soviet past. The formal institutions of the new states of Central Asia are easy to describe: Each country has a constitution that affirms the equality of citizens and guarantees the usual liberal democratic freedoms of expression, assembly, conscience, and representation. All constitutions also proclaim the separation of powers, the rule of law, and the secular nature of the state. Each country has an executive presidency and legislatures, with multiparty elections for officeholders. But formal institutions tell us little about the actual exercise of power. In Central Asia, political parties are tightly controlled, and legislatures do little more than rubber-stamp decrees of the presidents, who exercise executive power untrammeled by political opposition. To understand how the presidents were able to acquire this position, we must go back to the region's Soviet legacy. During the later Soviet period, the Communist Party was a political machine that allocated resources, often on the basis of informal pacts. Communist elites in Central Asia managed to retain their control over the economy as the Soviet Union collapsed. The party is now gone, but the informal structures for the allocation of resources remain in place, although the structures' operation remains opaque. The presidents sit atop patronage networks that allow access to resources and revenue.

Observers often use the term "clan" to describe these networks of patronage. This is unfortunate, for the term invokes a traditional or primeval form of kin-based solidarity, which does not underpin the networks. Instead, they function on the basis of patronage. In return for loyalty and obedience, leaders allow their clients to use state positions for their own gain. Political economists call this a form of rent seeking. For instance, officeholders can impose fines on merchants as a perk of office or receive kickbacks, but they have to share the wealth with their superiors. These informal networks do not exist in parallel with the state but are embedded in it.[4]

Political elites retain a great deal of influence over the economy. Natural resources, especially the substantial oil and gas reserves in Kazakhstan and Turkmenistan, remain state property. In Uzbekistan, the government maintains controlling shares in key industries, including energy, telecommunications, airlines, and mining. The government also controls all silk sold in the country. Partial state ownership and influence are common in many sectors of the economy. Collective farms were turned into independent entities (*shirkat*), but their relationship to the state has not changed significantly. Moreover, across Central Asia, any business above the most modest size needs to offer kickbacks to local authorities, and many of the largest businesses are owned by government figures.

This of course is corruption, and much of the coverage of contemporary Central Asia revolves around that subject. It is easy to disdain the authoritarian rulers and their countries for their corruption, but we might want to keep a few things in mind. Informal connections affect public life everywhere, to one degree or another. Central Asia is hardly unique in this regard. Nor is the corruption in Central Asia simply a fact of local malfeasance. It is fully integrated into the global economy. Central Asia exists in a globalized world where money moves around the world with ease, even if people cannot. The Soviet Union, with its closed economy, had been a major barrier to the globalization of capitalism. Its fall internationalized Central Asia as never before. Foreign banks, corporations, and aid agencies have tied Central Asia into global flows of capital, even as they opened new sources of income to Central Asia's elites. Those who swindled the Soviet state by misreporting cotton production figures in the Brezhnev era could only buy gold or jewelry or stuff banknotes in mattresses. Today's Central Asian elites have far better options at their disposal. They quickly learned the joys of offshore accounts, shell companies, and property investment. Luxury property in central London or Geneva or offshore accounts and shell companies registered in places such as the British Virgin Islands, Cayman Islands, or the Netherlands provide Central Asian elites with new ways of pursuing their agendas on a global scale. Central Asian corruption and authoritarianism are integrally tied to the global order.[5]

———

The tragic situation in Xinjiang can also be understood through the lens of nationalization. There it is a conflict between two vastly different understandings of the nation. Uyghurs think of themselves as a distinct nation and of Eastern Turkestan as their homeland. The Chinese state asserts both that Uyghurs are part of a single Chinese nation and that China in its present boundaries is a single country that has existed across the centuries, with Xinjiang being an integral part of it. After the dissolution of the Soviet Union, the Chinese state greatly curtailed the scope of *minzu* autonomy (which had never been very extensive) and increasingly insisted that all Chinese citizens belong to a single nation with a single, all-encompassing culture. The formula of a unified multi-ethnic state reduces national minorities to mere ethnicities and denies them the rights of national minorities that post-Soviet states acknowledge. The PRC thus is also a nationalizing state, but one that has little interest in accommodating internal diversity. The views of most Uyghurs and the government are fundamentally opposed and to a large degree mutually exclusive.

In the first years of Communist rule, the Chinese state had built an infrastructure of cultural institutions on the Soviet model that allowed a space for work on folklore, ethnography, and linguistic and historical research for "minority" *minzu*s. Largely destroyed during the Cultural Revolution, these institutions were revived during the reform period. Uyghur intellectuals developed a strong sense of national identity built around a cultural heritage, an artistic and literary canon, and a pantheon of national heroes in much the same way as their counterparts in Soviet Central Asia had done in the era following the Second World War. These ideas were popularized among the Uyghurs in the 1980s and 1990s, a period of relatively lax control, through historical novels, songs, and popular music. These narratives inevitably claimed that Xinjiang was the ancestral homeland of the Uyghurs, where they had maintained a constant presence through history.

The retrenchment of *minzu* rights after 1991 created a great deal of discontent and alienation among the Uyghurs who saw the Chinese state as alien and hostile. The discontent occasionally burst out in episodes of violence, but it was always there in everyday acts of resistance and in the refusal to accept official categories and official proclamations.[6] Over the course of the 1990s, boundaries separating Uyghurs from the Han Chinese came to be reinforced. The decade witnessed an upsurge in the observance of Islamic ritual and the use of modest dress by women. Soviet Central Asia had a dual society that resulted in an ethnic division of labor. The situation in Xinjiang was far more extreme: Uyghur and Han populations remained residentially segregated, and social interaction between them was strained at best.[7] In the summer of 2001, a Hong Kong–based sociologist was able to conduct an opinion survey under enormously difficult conditions involving administrative surveillance combined with caution, if not dissimulation, on the part of the respondents. The results showed "deeply rooted mutual distrust between the Uygurs and Han Chinese" as well as widespread skepticism about the ability of government policies to maintain "healthy ethnic relations" in the province.[8]

Humor, satire, and private mockery of official slogans also gave expression to the distance between the state and the Uyghur population. The cassette tape made music publishing cheap and difficult to control in the 1980s and 1990s. Popular music became the most important vehicle for the expression of Uyghur discontent. A great many poems and popular songs carried subversive messages, often cloaked in allegorical poetic language. For example, in 1993, Abdulla Abdurähim sang:

> I stand by the waterside, longing for a drink, but when I lick my
>   lips, they smack my mouth
> As I lie on the riverbank, the stones prick me; the unjust ones
>   throw stones at me.[9]

In another popular song of the 1990s, Ömärjan Alim sang of a guest who took over his house and refused to leave:

> I brought a guest back to my house
> And laid down a cushion at the back
> Now I cannot enter
> The house I built with my own hands.
>
> By making him a guest revered
> I was separated from this house
> Receiving no place in the orchard
> I laid my cushions in the desert.
>
> I turned the desert into a garden
> And still more guests filled it up
> They lopped off the entire branch
> And took the fruits away.
>
> I brought a guest back to my house
> And laid down a cushion at the top
> He jumped into the seat of honor
> And became a boss to us
> And became a boss to us.[10]

In 2004, the writer Nurmuhämmät Yasin published a story, "The Wild Pigeon," that told of a young wild pigeon that flew into a region inhabited by tame pigeons that lived among humans and neither knew nor sought freedom. As the wild pigeon tried to escape, he was betrayed and captured; he could escape the torture of his captivity only by committing suicide.[11]

Such discontent could have been reduced if the Chinese government had been committed to more meaningful autonomy and allowed the emergence of an Uyghur political elite with some room to maneuver. But that has never really been in the cards. Uyghur cadres exist, but their power is vastly circumscribed. There is nothing like the indigenous political elite that emerged in Soviet Central Asia in the period after the Second World War and that did much to make Central Asians feel at home in the Soviet Union. Soviet party elites could claim with some justification to be national leaders, and indeed it was this claim that allowed them to negotiate independence. There was no widespread discontent against the Russians and little sense of colonial oppression by the Russians. No such possibilities exist in China. Uyghurs who work in the government or join the party are often disdained by the majority of their society as sellouts and social climbers, if not traitors. The Chinese state remains alien to most Uyghurs.

———

The state's response to Uyghur discontent was multifaceted. It made a great deal of the enormous amounts of resources it invested in Xinjiang. However, the assumption that economic well-being will make national discontent disappear is deeply flawed. The discontent is with the lack of autonomy and the suppression of culture and religion by a state that is seen as alien. It is not directly related to poverty, and prosperity is not likely to eliminate it. In addition, the investment in Xinjiang is heavily skewed along ethnic lines. An Uyghur middle class did emerge, but it remained small and poorly integrated politically. At the macro level, there is an inverse relationship between the concentration of Uyghurs and the concentration of wealth across Xinjiang (see table 23.1). The ethnic preferences that had at least nominally been in place since the beginning of Communist rule as a form of affirmative action were reversed. In Xinjiang, it is now quite common for private-sector job advertisements to openly state that only Han Chinese applicants will be considered, while state-owned enterprises often recruit Han Chinese from China proper rather than hire members of local nationalities.[12]

TABLE 23.1 Spatial and economic disparities in Xinjiang, 2017

Administrative entity	Population	Rural (%)	Uyghur population (%)	Han population (%)	Per capita GDP (yuan)
North					
Karamay (city)	304,465	0.9	15.5	74.7	137,307
Shihezi (city)	573,772	39.0	1.1	94.3	78,200
Changji Hui Autonomous Prefecture	1,400,973	57.6	4.9	72.3	70,162
Ürümchi (city)	2,678,726	18.4	12.5	73.9	69,565
Bortala Mongol Autonomous Prefecture	477,536	58.9	14.4	63.7	57,897
Tarbagatay (prefecture)	1,016,893	54.8	4.2	55.4	44,396
Altay (prefecture)	671,973	61.7	1.4	39.9	33,874
Ili Kazakh Autonomous Prefecture	4,662,016	58.3	17.9	40.6	33,120
East					
Qumul (prefecture)	561,583	39.0	19.7	65.9	65,298
Turfan (prefecture)	632,664	63.1	76.0	17.7	35,333
South					
Bayingolin Mongol Autonomous Prefecture	1,229,438	47.5	36.2	53.4	64,142
Aqsu (prefecture)	2,508,281	67.2	80.3	18.4	28,289
Kashgar (prefecture)	4,514,738	77.4	92.2	6.3	16,860
Qizilsu Kyrgyz Autonomous prefecture	602,897	77.8	65.4	6.9	16,736
Khotan (prefecture)	2,449,838	77.7	96.8	3.0	9,901

Source: *Xinjiang Statistical Yearbook 2017* (Beijing: China Statistics Press, 2017), tables 3-7, 3-9, and 20-1.

Note: GDP is gross domestic product.

These practices underpin and exacerbate the economic stratification along national lines that is obvious to any visitor and that has been extensively documented by scholars.[13]

After 2001, the state began to take a much harsher view of dissent. It ramped up censorship and began banning certain songs and arresting their singers. The limits of permissible academic research shrank. In 2002, universities in Xinjiang switched to teaching only in Chinese, and since then Chinese-language education has expanded to lower levels of education. In urban Xinjiang, children now learn Chinese in elementary school, while Uyghur or Kazakh are relegated to the status of a second language and are used to teach only those languages themselves. This is called bilingual education. The state also began to assert its own interpretation of the history of Xinjiang with increasing insistence. In 2003, the State Council issued a white paper titled "History and Development of Xinjiang" that laid down the official position of the PRC. Xinjiang, the paper stated, "has been an inseparable part of the unitary multiethnic Chinese nation" from the time of the Western Han Dynasty (206 BCE–24 CE). Since then, "Chinese central governments of all historical periods exercised military and administrative jurisdiction over Xinjiang." Granted, "the jurisdiction of the central governments over the Xinjiang region was at times strong and at other times weak, depending on the stability of the period," but Xinjiang's connection to China was unbroken. Moreover, the region's inhabitants have all been loyal to the Chinese state and "actively safeguarded their relations with the central governments," even when those governments were weak—"thus making their own contributions to the formation and consolidation of the great family of the Chinese nation."[14] Xinjiang is not part of Central Asia but constitutes the Western Regions (*Xiyu*) of China, and its history can be related only through reference to China and using Chinese categories. Since the land has always been inhabited by "many ethnic groups believing in a number of religions," Uyghurs and Islam have no prior claim to it. Instead, it has been the hard work and solicitude of Han Chinese that "promoted the local economy and regional culture" from the days of the Han dynasty, as the Xinjiang Regional Museum in Ürümchi asserts.

Maintaining this view of history requires some mental gymnastics. If the province has been an inseparable part of China for two millennia, then why is it called Xinjiang, which means "new dominion"? The white paper suggests that Xinjiang means "old territory returned to the motherland." The Manchu conquerors of China proper thus become Chinese national heroes who united the motherland. The state has also engaged in what we might call architectural rectification, by creating a new built environment that asserts this vision of history. A substantial structure outside Ghulja, built in the early 2010s, is supposed to be a reconstruction of the Qing commandery headquarters. In Qumul, the old palace of the *wangs* that was destroyed in the tumult of the 1930s was rebuilt a kilometer down the road in 2005 in a mixture of Chinese, Turkic, and Mongolian styles to represent the harmonious coexistence of different nationalities—even though it looks nothing like the old palace. A new building in Han Chinese style on the outskirts of Kashgar celebrates Ban Chao, the Chinese general who is supposed to have subdued the Xiongnu and established Chinese rule in the region in 73 CE.[15] Meanwhile, the mausoleum of Afaq Khoja, the Sufi shaykh who invited the Zunghars to invade Altishahr and whose descendants were a constant thorn in the side of the Qing empire, has been turned into the Fragrant Concubine Park. According to a legend, in the aftermath of the Qing conquest of Xinjiang, the Qianlong emperor took the wife or consort of Jahan Khoja—the descendant of Afaq Khoja whose rebellion precipitated the Qing campaigns in Altishahr—as a concubine. She was renowned for her beauty, and her body emitted a delightful fragrance without the use of any perfume. The emperor was besotted with her, but she remained steadfast and refused to give herself to the emperor. The emperor's mother grew suspicious and had her poisoned. According to one version of the legend, her body was brought back to Kashgar and buried in the memorial complex of her ancestor, Afaq Khoja. There is some factual basis to the legend—a Muslim woman from Altishahr was inducted into the Qing emperor's harem—but there is no reason to believe that she was related to Afaq Khoja or that she is buried in the complex. In any case, the story, which acquired popularity only in the early years of the Chinese republic, serves to symbolize Xinjiang's conquest by China. In the twenty-first century, it is used by the state to delineate Xinjiang's place in China. Thus, one of the most important Sufi shrines of the region is supposed to have meaning only through its spurious connection to sexual violence and imperial conquest.[16]

But the worst fate was reserved for the old city of Kashgar, one of the best preserved in Central Asia. In 2009, the Xinjiang party committee and the Kashgar municipal government decided that the old city's adobe buildings were not resistant to earthquakes and needed to be rebuilt. The renewal of the old city had been in the works since 2001, when the area was ringed by a motorway, and it had increasingly been

FIG. 23.1. The demolition of old Kashgar, July 2010.
Photo © traveladventures.org / Boris Kester.

turned into a tourist site. But the multibillion-yuan Kashgar Dangerous House Reform project launched in 2009 was a different matter altogether. It foresaw the demolition and rebuilding of 85 percent of the old city and the resettlement of more than half of its population. Over the next two years, most of the old city was bulldozed, its mosques and markets knocked down, and its population uprooted (see figure 23.1).[17] Residents were offered compensation and could choose whether to return (if their house was rebuilt) or to find housing in apartment blocks on the outskirts of the city. The bulldozing was followed by the creation of a new city plan that featured wider streets and modern building styles. The redesign was overseen by the Xinjiang Architectural Design Institute in Ürümchi, which was headed by the Han architect Wang Xiao Dong. The new design homogenized the aesthetic of the streets, which were lined with façades in a neo-Uyghur style.[18] The bulldozed city was then ringed by a city wall, complete with ceremonial gates, to create the impression of antiquity. The most modern "medieval" city wall in the world encloses what in effect is a Disneyfied version of Kashgar, served up to Han Chinese tourists looking for the exotic. (The city gate is classified as a "AAAAA National Tourist Attraction.") The newly created main thoroughfare bears a sign proclaiming it to be a "Millennium-Old Street," even if the rebuilt old city feels like a pedestrian mall in California. A column installed outside the faux-medieval city gate asserts (in three languages) that the reconstruction of the city was for the benefit of its inhabitants, with "the aim of achieving the goal of seismic prevention and disaster alleviation, facilities perfection, improvement in living standard as well as inheritance and enhancement of the Uyghur style and flavor."

There has been a lot of destruction of the old in modern China, with nary a thought of preservation. Beijing has been reshaped, with its ancient hutongs bulldozed out of existence. Old cities everywhere in the world have been reshaped and redesigned over the ages. Baron Georges-Eugène Haussmann remade Paris in the aftermath of the Commune of 1871, Stalin redesigned Moscow, and the old cities of Soviet Central Asia were greatly diminished over the course of the twentieth century. But the dynamics at work in the demolition of old Kashgar were different. The sudden destruction of Kashgar was not simply the modernization of another Chinese city. The idea that mud-brick or wooden houses were more dangerous than the steel-and-concrete apartment blocks to which most people were consigned is preposterous. For most Uyghurs in Xinjiang or the diaspora, it was clear that the demolition was an attack on Uyghur culture and punishment for Uyghur discontent. There was also a clear connection to security. Many officials feared that the old city, an internally oriented space well known to residents but opaque to outsiders, might be a space where "terrorists could hide."[19] The new "old city," with its grid plan, open spaces, and much smaller population, does not present such a threat.

———

The Chinese state's rhetoric about the threat to Xinjiang had shifted over the decades, and Islam had come to occupy a central place in it by the turn of the millennium. Some of this shift was related to an Islamic revival common to all of Central Asia. In Soviet Central Asia, Gorbachev's reforms opened a space for Islam in public life. As restrictions eased, communities rushed to rebuild what had been lost during the three generations since the antireligious campaigns of 1927–1941. The last years of the Soviet period witnessed the reopening of mosques and the construction of new ones. Islamic education returned to Central Asia, and contacts with the rest of the Muslim world were reestablished. Islamic literature appeared in Central Asia's bookshops, and the observance of Islamic rituals and dietary restrictions became much more common. Many women turned to new forms of modest dress. For many people, reclaiming Islam meant the resurrection of customary practices that were now seen as an integral part of national traditions. Soviet-era understandings of Islam thus continued to shape popular perceptions of the place of religion in society in the early years of independence. By the turn of the millennium, the Islamic landscape had become a lot more diverse. In a way, this was a normal situation, with Muslims arguing about what is proper Islamic behavior and holding a diversity of views about Islam, its place in society, and its relationship to national culture. In post-Soviet Central Asia, the gamut runs from people who believe that they have lapsed and that much about the way they practice Islam is wrong and in need for correction (usually according to practices current in Arab countries) to those for whom Islam remains an integral part of national culture. There are also those for whom Islam is of little concern.[20]

In Xinjiang, the revival took a slightly different form. The Mao era had dealt grievous blows to Islam in Xinjiang, but the devastation was shorter-lived there than in Soviet Central Asia. When official Chinese policy relented in the early 1980s, many of the survivors of the destruction of the Cultural Revolution were still alive. The displacement of Islam was less severe than in Soviet Central Asia, and the reclamation of Islamic knowledge and the rebuilding of Islamic institutions was therefore a lot easier. Islamic practice in Xinjiang was widespread and publicly visible well before glasnost and perestroika made it possible in Soviet Central Asia. However, in the 1990s Xinjiang witnessed a broad shift to greater observance of Islamic norms and public expressions of piety. This was connected both to greater contact with the wider Muslim world and to economic growth in the province. The decade saw a spate of mosque construction across Xinjiang funded in large part by newly prosperous Uyghur businessmen. Religious observance was one way for Uyghurs (and other Muslims) to distinguish themselves from the Han. Worshipping communally in mosques, refraining from the use of alcohol, and women's displaying modesty became markers of national honor and a clear boundary against Han Chinese and the Chinese state. Alcohol consumption by Uyghurs was quite common until the 1990s but dropped markedly after that, while mosque attendance soared and women in hijabs became a common sight even in affluent urban communities. The Islamic revival was directly connected to a sense of national resistance to Chinese rule.

The emergence of religion into the open put Central Asia's elites in a quandary. Their Soviet sensibilities recoiled at the presence of Islam in public life. Karimov's encounter with Adolat activists in 1991 must have seemed completely unnatural to him. At the same time, the Islamic revival changed expectations. Islam was part of the national heritage that the independent states celebrated. It could not be avoided. The new presidents took their first oaths of office on the Qur'an, and some of them even performed the hajj. Since then, Central Asian governments have had a complicated but logical position toward Islam. They make a distinction between different kinds of Islam. Islam that is part of national traditions and the local way of life is to be celebrated. Thus, the great scholars of the past—such as the imams Abu Isma'il al-Bukhari and Abu 'Isa Muhammad al-Tirmidhi, whose collections of *hadith* are considered canonical across the Muslim world, and the jurists Burhan al-Din Abu'l Hasan al-Marghinani and Abu Mansur Muhammad al-Maturidi, whose compilations of Islamic law are renowned—are considered national heroes, while the great Sufi figures of the past are seen as Central Asia's contribution to the common storehouse of world culture. They are nationally authentic. All other forms of Islam, especially those that bring influences from other countries, denote obscurantism and fanaticism and are bound to knock the nation off its path to progress. They have to be countered. Central Asian governments decide what forms of Islam are in accord with national culture and are to be permitted, and which are not.

As the independent states of Central Asia attempt to keep Islam on a tight leash, they use Soviet-style mechanisms of control. SADUM did not survive the breakup of the Soviet Union. Its Kazakh wing seceded in 1990, and by 1992 each country had its own spiritual administration. But the basic idea of having such an administration remains, and each country now has a religious directorate that is the sole venue for Islamic practice. SADUM was a tiny organization, managing fewer than two hundred mosques across the five republics on behalf of a state that was hostile to religion. The new directorates manage many more mosques and operate in a climate where Islam is part of national culture, but they are nevertheless organs of control. They have a monopoly over Islamic publishing and education, as well as the operation of mosques. They also issue fatwas that in effect define what is proper Islam and what is not. Islamic activity independent of these administrations is by definition illegal and is prosecuted. The lead was taken by Uzbekistan, where the government quickly moved to control recalcitrant religious figures. Leading Islamic figures were arrested or simply disappeared, with their mosques shut down and given over to other uses. Arrests and mosque closures became a full-blown campaign in 1998, when a new law mandated that all religious activity take place in places registered with the state. The high point of this struggle came in May 2005, when security forces massacred participants in a mass demonstration in the city of Andijon. The demonstration had been called to protest a trial of twenty-three businessmen from the city, who had been arrested on charges of extremism. Their relatives held a vigil outside the courtroom where the men were put on trial. On the night of May 12–13, 2005, demonstrators broke into the jail and freed the prisoners. They then asked the president to visit the city and hear their grievances. The Uzbek state saw the jailbreak as an attempted uprising, led by foreign fighters who wanted to impose an Islamic state on Uzbekistan. It unleashed a massive security operation that conducted the massacre on May 13. The number of casualties has never been ascertained, but the most reliable estimates put the number of dead around five hundred. Hundreds of other people fled across the border to Kyrgyzstan, while arrests continued in Uzbekistan.[21]

The peace treaty ending the Tajik civil war gave the Islamic Renaissance Party a role in the government, and for a few years Tajikistan was touted as a land of religious liberty and home to the only Islamic political party in the former Soviet Union. That changed as Emomali Rahmonov consolidated his power. The state asserted its control over the activities of the *ulama* and turned them into civil servants. Since January 2014, their salaries have been paid by the state, and they are required to wear a uniform and to read sermons that have been preapproved by the Council of Ulama, the official spiritual administration in the country. The 2009 Law on Freedom of Conscience and Religious Organizations introduced a quota for the number of mosques and mandated their registration. All unofficial mosques were shut down. In 2010, it ordered all Tajikistani citizens studying in religious institutions abroad (mostly in Egypt, Iran, and Pakistan) to return home. The following year, a law "on parental responsibility for educating and raising children" banned religious education at home and banned minors from attending mosques or participating in any religious activities, except for funerals. Parental responsibility for the well-being of children now extends to ensuring that they do not skip school to attend prayers at a mosque.[22] Tajikistan's policies toward Islam were by this point indistinguishable from those of Uzbekistan. The other countries of post-Soviet Central Asia keep the same distance from Islam and possess similar mechanisms of control.

The Chinese state's relationship to Islam is even more inimical. The former Soviet states of Central Asia regulate Islam even as they celebrate it as part of their national heritage. The Chinese nation as imagined by the state has nothing to do with Islam. Even before 2016, when the state began demanding that all religions in China Sinicize themselves, it placed strict limits on religious activity. It tolerated religion but professed not to allow any "organization or individual" to "make use of religion to engage in activities that disrupt public order, impair the health of citizens, or interfere with the educational system of the State, or in other activities that harm State or public interests, or citizens' lawful rights and interests."[23] Its mechanisms of control were similar to those in the independent states of Central Asia: the State Administration of Religious Affairs oversaw the operation of religious organizations, although in practice, local authorities bypass the legalities and deal with religious institutions themselves. Again, the difference is that the independent states have to balance their control of religion with the celebration of a national culture, while the Chinese state has no such complications. More significantly, the Chinese state began to insist that Uyghur discontent is in itself an expression of Islamic extremism. It is this diagnosis of the problem that led to the overtly anti-Islamic "de-extremification" campaign launched in 2016.

24

Are We Still Post-Soviet?

FOR ALL THEIR COMMONALITIES and their shared past, the five independent states of Central Asia have trod different paths in the generation since the dissolution of the Soviet Union. Today they have distinct physiognomies and different senses of their place in the world. Let us now take on a quick tour of the five countries to highlight this diversity and to shake ourselves out of the slothful habit of the thinking of the five "Stans" as homogeneous or interchangeable.

———

Uzbekistan is the most populous state in the region and heir to its urban civilization. Its post-Soviet development bears the distinctive stamp of Islom Karimov, the man who ran the country from 1990 until his death right after the twenty-fifth anniversary of its declaration of independence. In all, he had ruled Uzbekistan for twenty-seven of the ninety-two years since its creation in 1924. He resisted the shock therapy prescribed by international agencies during the transition in the early 1990s. Uzbekistan was spared the upheavals and stark inequality ushered in by the phenomenon elsewhere, but large parts of Uzbekistan's economy remains under state control, either direct or indirect. The government maintains controlling shares of key industries, including energy, telecommunications, airlines, and mining. Elites tied to the state dominate the substantial private sector that has emerged. As a result, there are no social forces in the country that lie outside the ambit of the state. Furthermore, cotton retains its central place in the economy. Collective farms were turned into independent entities, but their relationship to the state has not changed significantly. The Soviet-era cotton production complex not only dominated the economy but also structured political power in the countryside. It could not easily be overthrown. Although the government has made some effort to reduce the monoculture (by the mid-2010s, raw cotton production had declined to just under three million tons annually), the crop remains a major export earner and the bulwark of the rural order. The state has continued to set procurement prices and bus school and college students and state employees to help pick cotton every harvest season. Karimov also used Soviet-style political communication. Billboards peppered public spaces with slogans and exhortations, but with the words of Soviet leaders or of Communist Party resolutions replaced by those of the president. Karimov's works were put into print and were a subject of examination for schoolchildren. All scholarly work in the humanities and the social sciences had to use his wisdom to justify the significance of the research, just as in earlier generations scholarship had begun with quotations from the classics of Marxism-Leninism or the current party agenda.

Yet if the regime used Soviet methods of rule, its attitudes toward the Soviet past were decidedly ambivalent. One of the largest projects of the independence era is the memorial complex called Shahidlar Xotirasi (Martyrs' Memorial) to honor "the memory of those who died for their country [which] will live forever." The complex is built on the site where the OGPU used to execute its victims in the 1930s. But while the victims of Stalin's purges take center place, the complex commemorates all victims of the period of Russian rule, from the first Tsarist invasions of the 1850s through the cotton scandal of the 1980s. The Tsarist and the Soviet periods are thus run together as a single dark age of colonial oppression, and all their victims are claimed for Uzbekistan. There are limits to how far the Soviet past and its Uzbek heroes can be disavowed without also disavowing all modern Uzbek culture. And the Second World War remains a key feature of public memory. Like most former Soviet cities, Tashkent has a Tomb of the Unknown Soldier in its center. The memorial's postindependence redesign has made it into a specifically Uzbek national homage to the heroes. A larger-than-life statue of a grieving mother faces an eternal flame on a grassy spot, which is enclosed by a portico that houses the lists of names of all those who perished (a common practice in war memorials across former Soviet space). The portico features arches and columns in the style of a Timurid mosque, with beautiful woodwork in Uzbek national fashion. The memory of the war is nationalized, with the victory rendered as much an Uzbek achievement as a Soviet one.

Karimov staked a great deal of his legitimacy on ensuring stability and making Uzbekistan a land of peace and tranquility, unlike its neighbors (the counterexample was initially Afghanistan; then Tajikistan, with its civil war; and in the 2010s Kyrgyzstan, with its political upheavals). To ensure that tranquility, Karimov used the National Security Service, the political police in direct line of descent from the KGB, which monitored both domestic and international security. Karimov also jealously guarded Uzbekistan's sovereignty and thereby his own room to maneuver. Relations with other Central Asian countries remained tense. Uzbekistan also spurned close relations with Turkey. While Turkish businesses experienced modest success in the country, the regime had no use for Turkey's official or semiofficial cultural initiatives. The Hizmet movement of the Turkish philanthropist Fethullah Gülen—which opened private English-language schools aimed at urban elites across Central Asia—lasted only a few years in Uzbekistan. Instead, Karimov cultivated close security ties with the United States in the 1990s, a development that reached its apogee after 9/11, when the United States leased two air bases in Uzbekistan. The relationship soured quickly, however, as Karimov grew wary of constant U.S. criticism of Uzbekistan's human rights record. In 2003–2004, he forced out most foreign NGOs and aid organizations, and in 2005 he even evicted the U.S. forces from their bases. Karimov then pivoted back to Russia and led Uzbekistan into the Shanghai Cooperation Organization. Although cooperation with the United States soon resumed, Uzbekistan kept the West at arm's length in terms of diplomatic attachments.

Karimov died as Uzbekistan celebrated the twenty-fifth anniversary of its declaration of sovereignty. (He had been in a coma for several days, but the official announcement of his death was delayed so that independence celebrations could take place as planned.) The transition to his successor was smooth. Uzbekistan's constitution stipulated that the chair of the senate take over as interim president, but the incumbent, Nig'matilla Yo'ldoshev, insisted that Shavkat Mirziyoyev (b. 1957), the long-serving prime minister, be appointed interim president in recognition "of his long experience of work in executive positions and respect among the people." Parliament agreed. Three months later, Mirziyoyev defeated three other candidates in a thoroughly scripted presidential election. The transition showed how opaque the Uzbekistani state is. Still, Mirziyoyev belongs to a new generation, having had no political experience during the Soviet period. He has moved the country away from some of the diplomatic culs-de-sac into which Karimov had driven Uzbekistan and has tempered some of his predecessor's harsher policies. Since his election, Mirziyoyev has eased censorship and the surveillance of civil society, allowed greater visibility of Islam, and shut the notorious prison at Jasliq. He has also moved to improve Uzbekistan's relations with its neighbors and the world at large. Still, his presidency does not represent a structural change in Uzbek society or politics.

Meanwhile, Uzbekistan's population has continued to increase. There is considerable, if unacknowledged, unemployment—the clearest sign of which is the massive labor migration, as men and sometimes whole families travel abroad in search of jobs. What is interesting is that the bulk of the migration is to Russia and not, say, the Muslim countries of the Persian Gulf. The Uzbek labor migration thus re-creates links from the Soviet era under new conditions. Ironically, while the Soviet Union existed and Uzbeks were equal citizens in it, they showed little inclination to move to cities in Uzbekistan itself, let alone to Russia. Now, with the Soviet welfare state gone and both the push and pull factors much stronger, Uzbek citizens have become a lot more mobile. The migration has finally made Moscow a Central Asian metropolis (and made Uzbek cuisine one of the city's most popular), even as it has generated xeno-phobia and discrimination in Russia.

————

Tajikistan had the most traumatic path to independence of all the Central Asian countries. It almost fragmented during the civil war that followed independence. Both Russia and Uzbekistan intervened on behalf of the Soviet elites against their Islamic opponents. The "neo-Soviets" survived and emerged as the victors of the civil war in 1997. Tajikistan was put back together. In the decades since the end of the civil war, the neo-Soviets have consolidated their power in conditions that are distinctly non-Soviet. Emomali Rahmonov—the neo-Soviet president who in 2006 dropped the Slavic ending to his name and became Rahmon—deftly negotiated the postwar realities. He co-opted civil war commanders from both sides by promising them political positions and a share in the state's extractive capacity and consolidated his position at the center of the regime in a manner that few would have predicted during the chaos of the 1990s. The peace treaty of 1997 gave the opposition a 30 percent stake in the government, and for several years afterward the Islamic Renaissance Party constituted a real opposition in the country. Rahmon determinedly chipped away at the treaty's terms and managed to marginalize the party, so that it won only two seats in the parliamentary elections of 2010. In 2015, he declared the party a terrorist organization and banned it. The secular opposition had already been suppressed or driven into exile by the mid-2000s. Rahmon was reelected in 1999, but he then dispensed with elections and had himself appointed "leader of the nation" and president for life in 2016.

Tajik nationalism as it developed over the course of the Soviet period sees the Tajiks as heirs to the ancient indigenous Persian culture of Central Asia, and thus as the nation with the oldest roots in the region. The fact that Tajikistan today is a Persian-speaking island in a sea of Turkicness gives Tajik nationalism a sense of grievance but also a focus. The biggest rivalry is with the Uzbeks, whose nationalism also claims the heritage of sedentary Central Asia and whose republic successfully laid claim to the cities of Samarqand and Bukhara, the most ancient cities in Transoxiana, at the time of its creation. The cult of the past is therefore as great in Tajikistan as anywhere else in Central Asia. Khujand province was renamed Sughd (Sogdiana), while the Samanids, the last Persian speakers to rule in Transoxiana, are celebrated as the first dynasty to achieve statehood for the Tajiks. The Tajik currency was renamed the *somoni* in 2000 (after the Samanid dynasty), and a statue of Ismail Samani, the dynasty's founder, has replaced that of Lenin in Dushanbe's central square. Relations with Uzbekistan have been frosty since independence, although Uzbekistan's armed forces helped the Tajik regime survive the civil war. Tajikistan has sought out relations with countries outside Central Asia. Its relationship with Russia is particularly close (Russian troops protected Tajikistan's southern border until 2006), while Iran serves as a counterbalance to the Turkic presence in Central Asia. Iran's relations with Tajikistan are based on the common Persian language. Iran has spent considerable funds on promoting Tajik language and culture and has a modest presence in the Tajik economy (the distance separating the two states has been a problem), but it has always eschewed interference in the religious life of the Sunni country. Afghanistan also uses Persian (Dari, a variant of Persian, is one of the two official languages of the country), but its relations with Tajikistan have been difficult because of the chronic instability of Afghanistan and the Tajik elites' fear of Islamic insurgency. Geographic difficulties also hinder rapprochement with Pakistan or India. In contrast, China has increasingly become a major actor in Tajikistan. It is responsible for 45 percent of Tajikistan's external trade and is a generous creditor. In 2019, long-standing rumors of the existence of a small Chinese military base in Tajikistan—in the mountainous expanses of Gorno-Badakhshan, near the border with Xinjiang and Afghanistan—were confirmed.[1]

Poverty remains the single most important issue for the country. A growing population and the general lack of economic activity had created a vast labor migration by the end of the first decade of the twentieth century. Perhaps as much as 10 percent of the country's population (mostly men) work abroad, chiefly in Russia or Kazakhstan, and remittances account for 28.6 percent of the country's gross domestic product, according to official World Bank figures (the actual figure is most likely higher). During the Soviet era, officials could hardly get Tajiks to move to Dushanbe, let alone to Moscow. Now, a different economic order compels Tajiks to seek their livelihood in lands where they are now foreigners.

————

Turkmenistan became a reclusive and secretive state after independence. In 1991, there was talk that the country, with its rich deposits of natural gas, might become the Kuwait of Central Asia, a resource-rich autocracy in which the ruling elite purchases the political quiescence of its subjects by using some of the wealth to provide first-world comforts to all. That never came to pass. The autocracy did develop and the populace remained quiescent, but this was achieved not through a Kuwait-style embrace of the world economy but by drawing on certain strains of Soviet political culture—namely, the command economy and the cult of personality. Turkmenistan today is perhaps a more controlling and repressive state than any other former Soviet republic.

Turkmenistan's party organization was among the most docile in the Soviet Union. Saparmurat Niyazov, who became first secretary of the Communist Party of Turkmenistan in 1985, managed to ride out the turbulence of the Gorbachev era with considerable ease. After independence, he fashioned himself as the leader of the Turkmen people and declared independence to be the culmination of their national destiny. It was the Golden Age (*Altyn Asyr*) of Turkmen history, and Niyazov was its embodiment. Parliament bestowed on him the title of Türkmenbaşy (Head Turkmen) and named him president for life. *Beýik Saparmyrad Türkmenbaşy,* Saparmurat Türkmenbaşy the Great, became a ubiquitous presence in the country. His profile was superimposed on the upper right corner of all television broadcasts and his statues sprang up everywhere (the most famous was a fifteen-meter-high, gold-plated specimen, with arms outstretched, that revolved to face the sun). His likeness appeared on billboards and sides of buildings; in portraits in every government office, school, and hospital; and on newspapers, coins, banknotes, and bottles of vodka and brandy produced by the national monopoly. "Halk! Watan! Türkmenbaşy!" (Nation! Homeland! Türkmenbaşy!), went a ubiquitous slogan, while the refrain in the national anthem proclaimed, "The great creation of Türkmenbaşy / Native land, sovereign state / Turkmenistan, light and song of soul / Long live and prosper forever and ever!" In 2001, Niyazov took the cult to a new level when he published the *Ruhnama* (Book of the Spirit), a rambling collection of thoughts on Turkmen history, ethics, politics, and many other things. In it, he sketched a history of the Turkmen nation that combined elements of Turkmen epic poetry (which had been nationalized in the Soviet era) with concepts of Soviet historiography, such as ethnogenesis. The book presents mythical figures and events from the epic tradition as factual and narrates an uninterrupted history of the nation going back five thousand years. When they were united and followed the wisdom of the elders, the Turkmens achieved many great things and built many great states (the *Ruhnama* claims both the Seljuq and Ottoman Empires for the Turkmens). The book has little to say about the modern era. Turkmen history apparently was in limbo until it resumed with independence and Niyazov. In addition to the historical narrative, the book contains a sprinkling of moral and ethical advice. Niyazov claimed that he wrote it "with the help of inspiration sent to my heart by the God who created this wonderful universe."[2] Very quickly, it became "Holy Ruhnama," with government officials comparing its importance to that of the Qur'an and the Bible—neither of which were allegedly fully adequate for the spiritual needs of Turkmens. The book became part of the school curriculum, government servants devoted study sessions to it, and those seeking driver's licenses were tested on it. Passages from it were inscribed on the walls of the national mosque that Niyazov built in his father's village of Gypçak, outside the capital, Ashgabat. From Hitler and Stalin to Mao and Kim Il-sung, the twentieth century had seen a number of cults of personality around dictators. Niyazov's cult could trump them all.

Niyazov died of a heart attack in December 2006. The transition was surprisingly smooth, considering how he had dominated the state in his lifetime. There was some infighting among the elites, but the matter was quickly settled. According to the constitution, the chair of the parliament should have succeeded Niyazov. However, Öwezgeldi Ataýew, who occupied the post, was arrested, charged with abuse of power and immoral conduct, and sentenced to five years in prison. Power passed to Gurbanguly Berdimuhamedov, who had served as the deputy prime minister and minister for health, as well as Niyazov's dentist. After winning 89 percent of the vote in a general election that actually featured multiple candidates, Berdimuhamedov rolled back some of Niyazov's more egregious regulations, but the promise of a thaw remained unfulfilled. Berdimuhamedov proclaimed himself *Arkadag*, the Protector, and built a cult around himself. Now it is his portraits that glare at students and government servants, and it is he who receives adulatory news coverage every day. Turkmenistan has now passed from its Golden Age to the Age of Might and Happiness. Berdimuhamedov's cult borrows its iconography quite promiscuously from a number of sources. The main statue of Berdimuhamedov, which depicts him horseback riding over what looks like a stone wave, bears a striking resemblance to the one raised by Catherine the Great to Peter the Great in St. Petersburg in the eighteenth century. The Protector also displays his machismo: he appears on television playing the guitar, rapping, and acting as a DJ, and in one video, in which he performs military exercises and receives stormy applause from army officers, he is eerily reminiscent of Arnold Schwarzenegger.

Niyazov and Berdimuhamedov could pull these feats off because they managed to retain control over the machinery of the state and the loyalty of the security organs. After independence, Turkmenistan's rulers dodged most of the mantras of the new world order: human rights, an open society, freedom of the press, and privatization were all held at arm's length. The few elements of a political opposition that emerged during the Gorbachev years remained weak and were easily chased out of the country after independence. At home, the state controls the media and muzzles all dissent. Niyazov launched the country on a course of isolationism that was legitimized through the concept of "permanent neutrality." This allows the regime to eschew international entanglements and keep meddlesome international pressures at bay. The country remains reclusive, keeping its borders secure through difficult-to-obtain visas. But the outside world is not entirely absent. Turkmenistan's resources have to be exported. When the republic's reserves were first developed, Turkmenistan was connected to a pan-Soviet network of pipelines that sent its natural gas north to Russia and Ukraine. Those countries remain its main customers, although the pipelines are outdated and operate below capacity. After independence, Turkmenistan sought new routes for getting its gas to world markets. The dream of connecting to South Asian markets via TAPI, the Turkmenistan-Afghanistan-Pakistan-India pipeline, remains unfulfilled because of the instability in Afghanistan and the poor state of relations between Pakistan and India. In 2009, a Chinese-funded pipeline connected Turkmenistan to Xinjiang. Since then, China has become the largest importer of Turkmen gas. It was gas exports that have funded Turkmenistan's megalomaniacal construction projects since independence. Ashgabat is one of many cities in Asia and the Middle East that have used spectacular architecture to show themselves off to the rest of the world. However, with travel so difficult, few people from outside Turkmenistan can see the glories of the Age of Might and Happiness for themselves. Meanwhile, the agricultural sector is in some crisis. Cotton continues to be king, although its production has fallen considerably. The area under irrigation has more than doubled since independence, which puts ever greater pressure on the limited water supply, and the new lands under cultivation are of poor quality.[3] Soil degradation, salinization, and looming water shortages all speak to environmental challenges that will test the stability of the regime in the years to come.

———

Kyrgyzstan's experience has been quite the opposite. Lacking substantial natural resources, the country's leadership threw it open to the world upon independence. It privatized the economy, scaled back controls on the press, and invited in NGOs and advisors of all sorts. For a long time, the country was the poster child of the new world order of free markets, elections, and speech. Given the spectacular beauty of its mountains and the hopes for its transition to neoliberal democracy, Kyrgyzstan was dubbed "the Switzerland of Central Asia." As advisors and experts descended upon the country, its capital, Bishkek, once a sleepy provincial town, hosted enough expatriates to give rise to a sustainable nightlife. Yet the country has had the most turbulent history in all of post-Soviet space. Two presidents were overthrown by popular revolts, and in 2010 the country witnessed the worst ethnic strife anywhere in post-Soviet Central Asia. Kyrgyzstan can tell us something about the nature of the state after the Soviet Union.

Askar Akayev, Kyrgyzstan's first president, was the odd man out among Central Asia's leaders of the time in not being part of the Soviet political elite. He drove the policies that led to Kyrgyzstan's openness, but he could not prevent the plunder of public resources that privatization allowed. Kolkhoz directors and managers of industrial enterprises managed to acquire property for themselves or to sell it off. The 1990s saw a profound economic crisis in which sheep farming, one of the country's primary economic activities, collapsed, and the national livestock population went from twelve million in the late 1980s to two or three million in 2008.[4] These economic transformations were accompanied by the retreat of the state from its previous role as the provider of social services. Unlike the other countries of Central Asia, then, Kyrgyzstan had genuine pluralism in society and politics. The new elites supported Akayev, who was reelected twice. But he could not resist the temptations of the new order, and by the new millennium, his regime was deeply mired in corruption. Members of government and Akayev's own family took advantage of the privatization process to amass considerable wealth. Akayev's son and son-in-law controlled numerous enterprises, including a cement factory, the Kumtor gold mine, and Kyrgyzstan's most profitable cell-phone company.[5] Akayev also attempted to maximize his presidential powers. He acquired lifelong immunity from prosecution from the parliament in 2003, and in the run-up to parliamentary elections in 2005, he sought a pliable parliament by disqualifying opposition candidates through dubious legal maneuvers. This overreach led many of Akayev's partners to withdraw their support for him and organize mass demonstrations against him. These spread across the country and were especially numerous in the south, in the Ferghana valley. On March 24, 2005, Akayev fled with his family and ended up in exile in Moscow. His departure marked the first change in leadership in Central Asia since independence.

The largely nonviolent ouster of an unpopular president through mass public protests bore similarities to recent events in two other former Soviet states, the Rose Revolution in Georgia in 2003 and Orange Revolution in Ukraine in 2004. The Kyrgyz episode was accordingly dubbed the Tulip Revolution, after Kyrgyzstan's national flower. But if the "revolutions" in Georgia and Ukraine had replaced regimes close to Moscow with those with a pro-Western orientation, things were a little different in Kyrgyzstan. Akayev was the most pro-Western leader in Central Asia, and Kyrgyzstan's relations with the United States were warm. Akayev, an outsider to the Kyrgyz Communist elite when he was first elected in 1990, was now replaced by members of the old Soviet order. In the years before independence, Kurmanbek Bakiyev, the new president, had been a factory manager and, briefly, the secretary of the party committee in the small town of Kök-Janggak. Roza Otunbayeva, another leader of the protests, had been the head of the party committee in the city of Frunze and a member of the council of ministers of the Kyrgyz SSR. Even with Kyrgyzstan's looser political system, Soviet-era elites had not disappeared.

The Tulip Revolution was a disappointment in many ways. Bakiyev resorted to strong-arm tactics to stifle dissent and assume control of the country's resources. The protests in 2005 had been driven in part by anger at corruption, but the situation worsened considerably under the new regime. Bakiyev and his circle showed great agility in adapting to the new institutions in which Kyrgyzstan was entangled. The American airbase in Bishkek that needed a constant supply of fuel, gold mines now worked by foreign companies, and the availability of tax shelters and holding companies based in the West all allowed for moneymaking on a scale that the last Soviet generation could not have dreamed of. When another popular uprising overthrew Bakiyev in 2010, his son fled the country in a private jet for London, where the British government granted him political asylum—ignoring an extradition request from Kyrgyzstan. Maxim Bakiyev now lives in a £3.5-million mansion in suburban London and enjoys the fruits of his fortune.[6] His father found refuge in Belarus. Kyrgyzstan may be the only country in the world with two former presidents living in exile.

Bakiyev was replaced by Otunbayeva, who held office until elections in 2011. Since then, Kyrgyzstan has been stable, if ramshackle. Its leadership has shown considerable agility in balancing international commitments. It continues to host an American airbase, but it has also established a Russian military base and is (perhaps perforce) close to China, whose economic might is a key factor to contend with. The Kyrgyz economy continues to struggle, however, and large numbers of Kyrgyz citizens work abroad, mostly in Russia. Kyrgyzstan's dependence on remittances is as great as that of Tajikistan (the two countries rank second and third in the world—after Haiti—on this statistic).

The past hangs heavy in Kyrgyzstan, too. In the absence of great figures from the past, it is *Manas*, the oral epic, that serves as the node of national identity, and it does so in conditions of globalization. The epic, which runs to half a million lines, had been transmitted orally until the early twentieth century, when it was committed to paper for the first time. During the Soviet era, the epic was established as the national patrimony of the Kyrgyz. It now serves to assert the continuous existence of a Kyrgyz nation across the centuries. The Kyrgyz government declared 1995 to be the thousandth anniversary of the creation of the epic and organized a series of celebrations to mark the claim. The celebration went global when UNESCO declared 1995 to be "The Year of *Manas*" and helped fund the celebrations. (Additional sponsorship came from the Coca-Cola Company, which was hoping to conquer the new market in Kyrgyzstan.) The celebration of *Manas* as a national epic creates a sense of a long-term continuity in the existence of a distinct Kyrgyz nation and its ties to the land that it now inhabits. It also interprets the establishment of independent Kyrgyzstan (officially known as the Kyrgyz Republic) as the resumption of Kyrgyz statehood that was interrupted by accidents of history.

Kazakhstan is by far the largest country in Central Asia in terms of area, and a generation after independence, it is also the most prosperous. Extensive reserves of oil and natural gas provide the basis of economic growth. In 1991, Kazakhstan had the largest industrial base of any Central Asian country, yet the first years of independence were very turbulent. Kazakhstan's economy had been even more tightly integrated into the rest of the Soviet Union than was the case with the other republics. Its mineral resources were sent to end users in other parts of the union. Those production chains were disrupted by the dissolution of the union. Its large Russian population (38 percent of the whole in the last Soviet census of 1989) dominated the cities and formed a majority in the north, a legacy of the Virgin Lands campaign in the 1950s. Kazakhstan was also home to almost a million Germans, descendants of the Volga Germans deported during the Second World War. These Soviet Europeans dominated the industrial and technical sectors of the economy. Independence saw a large-scale exodus of Russians from the republic, while Germany offered citizenship to Soviet Germans on the basis of ethnicity, even though almost none of them spoke German. Over 1,000,000 Russians and 700,000 Germans emigrated from Kazakhstan in the first decade of independence.[7] Privatization without adequate institution building made for very difficult times, and the gross domestic product fell for much of the 1990s. Things turned around in 1999, when large-scale oil production began, and world prices for oil shot up. In the first decade of the twenty-first century, Kazakhstan was one of the fastest growing economies in the world. This booming economy funded the spectacular growth of the new capital, Astana, and transformed Almaty into a bustling metropolis.

Nursultan Nazarbayev dominated the country for thirty years, from his accession to the office of first secretary of the Communist Party of Kazakhstan in 1989 to his surprise retirement in 2019. His original term was extended by a referendum, and after that he was reelected four times by Soviet-style margins (garnering 81 percent, 91 percent, 96 percent, and 98 percent of the vote, respectively). His special status as First President and *Elbasï* (Leader of the Nation) was enshrined in law, and a cult of personality developed around him that included a number of officially funded biopics, several statues, and at least three bronze handprints in prominent locations where people can touch them and make a wish. Numerous institutions bear his name, including a lavishly funded international English-language university. After his retirement, his successor renamed the Kazakh capital Nur-Sultan in his honor. His political party, called Nur Otan (literally, Light of the Homeland, but also a play on Nazarbayev's first name), dominated parliament. In 2007, it won every seat in parliament, making Kazakhstan a de facto one-party state. It helped that the party's membership topped one million (about a tenth of the electorate) and included many government workers who could pay their membership dues through payroll deduction.[8] The Kazakh state brooks little dissent: it can run newspapers and web sites out of business, stalk political opponents through a judiciary that is independent only on paper, and rob opposition parties of any ability to function.

Yet, for all that, there is little question that Nazarbayev was popular. His global stature and the recognition he won from foreign powers mattered a lot for prestige. He also was quite adept at handling the geopolitical challenges Kazakhstan faced. At the dawn of independence, he gave up the nuclear weapons that the country had inherited from the Soviet Union, transferring them to Russia (which is the successor state of the Soviet Union in international law) and sealing the country's nuclear facilities. This was a popular move because the damage from nuclear testing had made Kazakhstan one of the most antinuclear places in the world, and antinuclear protests had been a central feature of the republic's political landscape during perestroika. After that, Nazarbayev deftly maneuvered between Russia, a rising China, and the United States.

Kazakhstan's ties with Russia remain close. The entanglement of the two economies is too great for it to be otherwise, but there are other reasons as well. Even after the exodus of the 1990s, Russians still make up 23 percent of Kazakhstan's population. Russian has official status in the country and is widely used. Nazarbayev moved the capital to the north in 1996, at least in part to reduce separatist sentiment among ethnic Russians there. Almaty, the original capital of Kazakhstan, is situated at the southern edge of the vast country, near Bishkek and Tashkent. Nur-Sultan is in a different zone altogether. From the new capital, the other Central Asian states appear distant, while Russia is much closer. From the beginning, Nazarbayev espoused his own brand of Eurasianism that emphasized economic integration into a Eurasia that was seen as a space where different religions and cultures coexisted. Among its more concrete expressions is the Eurasian Economic Union, established in 2014, that links Kazakhstan with Russia and Belarus in a customs union. At the same time, trade with China has burgeoned, making the PRC Kazakhstan's second largest trading partner. Kazakhstan is important to China as well. Xi Jinping announced the Belt and Road Initiative to the world in a speech in Astana in 2013. The town of Khorgos on the Xinjiang-Kazakhstan border is to play a key role in the initiative. It is already the largest dry port in the world. Nazarbayev cultivated good relations with China, even in the face of public suspicion of China that is not limited to the Uyghur segment of Kazakhstan's population. Nazarbayev also never squandered the esteem he acquired in the West when he gave up nuclear weapons in the 1990s. He remained in the good graces of Western governments despite his dodgy reelections, the corruption scandals, and the dubious state of civil society in the country.

Kazakhstan's government has done a reasonably good job of spreading the oil wealth around. There is inequality and maldistribution, to be sure, but Kazakhstani citizens are better off than their neighbors. The government has also managed ethnic relations quite well, ensuring that the Russians feel at home but do not have the sense of ownership that their parents might have assumed in the later Soviet period, while building up Kazakh national pride. "Kazakhstan is the land of unity and accord," goes the official slogan, and the government has put considerable effort into ensuring that different nationalities coexist in harmony. Nur-Sultan is meant to be a metaphor for the new Kazakhstan. Kazakhstan's wealth has also allowed it to implement the *oralman* (returnee) program that woos Kazakhs from other countries "back" to their homeland by offering financial help for travel and resettlement, free housing, support in finding jobs, and Kazakhstani citizenship. The program is in part a way of making up for the great dispersals of 1916 and collectivization, calamities that sent Kazakhs fleeing from their land, but it is also a way of making Kazakhstan more Kazakh. In the nearly three years since independence, more than a million Kazakhs have taken up the offer. Most of them came from Uzbekistan and other former Soviet republics, but the program has also had an impact on Kazakhs in Mongolia and Xinjiang. In addition to a sizable Uyghur diaspora, Kazakhstan now is home to many Kazakhs from Xinjiang—a fact that complicates its relationship with the PRC.

Nazarbayev surprised everyone by announcing his resignation on March 19, 2019, and handing power to Qasïm-Jomart Toqayev, the chairman of the senate and a Nazarbayev loyalist. Nazarbayev was the longest serving head of any post-Soviet state and the last of the Soviet-era Communist leaders still in office. His resignation was a way to ensure that he controlled his succession. He remained a member of Kazakhstan's Security Council, which gave him control over ministerial appointments and influence behind the scenes, while his status as Leader of the Nation gave him lifelong immunity from prosecution. We should not expect rapid shifts in policy under the new president. But Toqayev has the luxury of ruling the most prosperous and economically powerful state in Central Asia.

————

The Soviet past has been more of a blessing than a curse for the independent states of Central Asia. The Soviet infrastructure of education and transportation helped the new states negotiate the path to sovereignty, while the language of the nation, another key Soviet legacy, provided a source of stability and a legitimizing principle. The Soviet elites who retained power after independence were also an element of continuity. Yet they have taken different paths in the five states, and even the most conservative of them operate in a new world. The new states are authoritarian and corrupt according to narrow definitions of the terms, but they function in a global context, and the authoritarianism and corruption are closely tied to global phenomena. In that sense, the countries are similar to but also very different from Chinese Central Asia.

25

A Twenty-First-Century Gulag

XINJIANG'S FATE HAS BEEN RADICALLY different from that of former Soviet Central Asia. While the Soviet republics launched into statehood and sovereignty in 1991, Xinjiang became ever more subjugated to a Chinese state run by a Leninist party that had forsaken all its concerns with class struggle or economic redistribution but jealously guarded its monopoly on political life. In 2016, that state launched a campaign that expressly aimed to Sinicize both the province and its people. A rapidly built archipelago of "political reeducation camps" swallowed up large parts of the region's Muslim population—Uyghurs, Kazakhs, Kyrgyz. By the end of 2019, this Gulag held an estimated 1.5 million people, more than a tenth of the entire Muslim population of the province.

Life outside the camps was little better, for the whole province was turned into an open-air prison where the entire "minority" population was subject to constant surveillance. "Convenience security points" now sit on every other street corner and in all prominent locations (see figure 25.1). Security cameras equipped with face-recognition technology and placed on street corners, walls, and lampposts track people's progress along the street and capture license plates of cars as they pass. Checkpoints along highways, at petrol pumps, and at the "convenience security points" are equipped with machines that scan identity cards and faces and check them against biometric data stored in state-run databases. Ubiquitous police patrols carry devices that can scan irises as well as faces. In 2017, authorities began collecting DNA samples, fingerprints, iris scans, and blood types of all residents in the region

FIG. 25.1. The Heyitgah (or Idgah) mosque, the largest and most renowned in
Xinjiang, flying the Chinese flag and abutted by a "convenience security point."
Photo by the author, June 2019.

between the ages of twelve and sixty-five through compulsory programs. In some places, Uyghurs are required to download to their
phones a "web cleansing" app called Jingwang that monitors their messages and guards against illegal content and supposedly harmful information. Spot checks inspect smartphones to make sure that they do not
have forbidden software (including Facebook and WhatsApp) or carry
forbidden content; cars are required to have GPS-based tracking devices; and all knives sold in the province carry a Quick Response code
that links them to the purchaser's national identity card. Authorities
have recalled passports from Uyghur citizens and urged those living or
studying abroad to return home or risk having their passports canceled.
The entire Uyghur nation is suspect and surveilled.[1] This campaign of mass
incarceration is the most recent (final?) chapter in China's subjugation
of Xinjiang.

The path to the "reeducation" campaign passed through a number of
landmarks in the decades since 1989. The 1990s and 2000s saw several
mass protests turn into riots or attacks on police stations or other symbols of the state. There were no reliable eyewitness accounts for any of
those incidents, and even the most basic facts about them are disputed,
but they shaped the state's response. The first such episode took place
in the small town of Baren near Kashgar in April 1990, when several
hundred men occupied local government buildings for three days. The

promulgation of new laws limiting urban Uyghur families to two children (and their rural counterparts to three) seems to have been an underlying cause of the protest. The insurgents were supposed to have recited the Islamic profession of faith and called for a jihad before they were gunned down by police.[2] Another major protest took place in February 1997 a thousand kilometers to the north, in the town of Ghulja. Several hundred participants protesting the arrest of thirty men from mosques and private study groups were confronted by police who fired into the crowd, killing several people. The years between these two major episodes witnessed a number of smaller-scale riots, bombings, and gun battles between police and locals.

The government responded with resolute repression, which often begat more violence. It also began to use a new language to describe Uyghur discontent. Until the mid-1990s, the Chinese state had blamed discontent on pan-Turkism, but now it began to speak of separatism, religious extremism, and terrorism as an intertwined set of "three evils." In June 2001, China had the Shanghai Cooperation Organization ratify a convention on combating the three tendencies. Three months later, the United States launched its global war on terrorism (GWOT) and gave this language international sanction. The GWOT is waged on an abstract noun ("terrorism"), and in a unipolar world its enemies, the "terrorists," are framed as enemies of the global order and humanity itself. The United States applies the label "terrorist" with liberality and willful imprecision to nonstate actors that oppose it. A number of regimes around the world have found the designation of the enemies as terrorists (or extremists) quite useful. The regime of Islom Karimov in Uzbekistan justified its crackdown on opposition using these labels, and they have been a godsend to China, which very quickly adopted the GWOT language of antiterrorism. In November 2001, the Chinese mission at the United Nations claimed that "'Eastern Turkistan' elements," consisting of "over 40 organizations," received help from Osama bin Laden and the Taliban in Afghanistan and had "engaged themselves in terrorist violence to varying degrees" on Chinese soil over the previous decade.[3] In the following year, the U.S. government placed one of these organizations, the East Turkestan Islamic Movement (ETIM), on its list of international terrorist organizations. Since then, the Chinese state has blamed most unrest in Xinjiang on ETIM and other "Eastern Turkestan elements" and demonized all Uyghur discontent as inspired by terrorism and religious extremism.

There was a small community of Uyghurs in Afghanistan before 2001, but there is little reason to believe that they were integrally tied to Al Qaeda or other terrorist networks.[4] ETIM was completely unknown to scholars of Xinjiang at the time. Yet the organization acquired a certain notoriety when U.S. forces transported twenty-two Uyghurs to the American prison camp at Guantánamo Bay in Cuba. (Even the deeply flawed quasi-legal process in place at Guantánamo found these Uyghurs not to be "enemy combatants" and they were all released after many years of detention.)[5] Then, in 2008, a different group, the Turkestan Islamic Party (TIP), attracted global attention when it issued a video message threatening to attack the Beijing Olympic Games. TIP was aligned with Al Qaeda, although its main achievement was the production of videos and the publication of a magazine in Arabic (and thus clearly aimed at supporters in the Arab world, not at Uyghurs). There is little reason to believe that it had any ability to act inside China.

The onset of the civil war in Syria in 2011 changed the situation. That war has certain disturbing similarities with the war in Afghanistan of the previous generation: it turned large parts of the country into a haven for jihadists from around the world. By 2017, there was a significant Central Asian presence on its battlefields, with an estimated 3,000–5,000 Uyghurs among them. They had turned to radicalism in exile, as a result of their persecution by the Chinese state. However, there is still little reason to believe that foreign-based organizations can have any impact on events on Chinese territory or that all Uyghur unrest is part of a single strategy dictated from abroad. Rather, the cause lies in Xinjiang and the policies pursued by the PRC.

————

In July 2009, Ürümchi erupted into several days of violence. The chain of events began thousands of kilometers away in the town of Shaoguan, in south China. The Xuri toy factory in that town had employed several hundred Uyghur workers as part of a labor transfer program encouraged by the central government. The program, several years old by then, had its critics, who pointed to the absurdity of sending Uyghur laborers out of the province even as Han workers continued to settle in Xinjiang to take jobs there. In Shaoguan, false rumors spread by a disgruntled Han worker named Zhu accused six Uyghur men of having raped two Han women. On June 26, Han workers armed with iron bars and machetes stormed the Uyghurs' dormitory. In the murderous violence that ensued, hundreds were injured and, according to official figures, two Uyghur men were murdered. The death toll was in all likelihood much higher. The assault was recorded on cell phones and clips uploaded to the internet, where they were widely shared among Uyghurs. The videos and the lackadaisical response of local authorities (police took a long time to arrive at the scene of the assault and did not make any arrests for ten days) caused great outrage in Xinjiang. High-school and university students used social media to organize a demonstration to protest the killings and seek justice for the victims. Uyghurs from around the province traveled to Ürümchi to take part. On July 5 the protest began peacefully, with many demonstrators waving Chinese flags, but it soon turned violent when the police assaulted the protesters. Riots took on a clear ethnic dimension as they spread, with groups of Uyghurs destroying Han-owned businesses and attacking the Han in general. Fighting continued through the night. Two days later, Han vigilantes launched a counterattack on Uyghur neighborhoods, openly speaking of repaying a blood debt and expressing dissatisfaction with the state's response on the first day of rioting. The number of Uyghur deaths remains unknown. Chinese government sources put the casualties at 197 dead and over 1,700 injured, with 331 shops and 1,325 motor vehicles destroyed. Uyghur groups in exile disputed these figures, arguing that at least 400 Uyghurs were killed on the second day of the rioting.[6]

The Ürümchi riots had everything to do with Uyghur resentment and nothing at all to do with Islamic extremism. Nevertheless, they marked a turning point in the state's view of the situation in Xinjiang.

The lesson it seems to have drawn was that efforts to integrate Uyghurs into China had failed. Ürümchi is basically a Han city, and the Uyghurs there are among the most integrated in the PRC. If such a conflict could take place there, the rest of Xinjiang seemed to be beyond hope. In the months that followed, thousands of people were arrested, and twenty-four were eventually sentenced to death. The overwhelming majority of those arrested and all of those sentenced to death were Uyghurs. The authorities put the whole province in a virtual lockdown: international telephone service and text messaging were blocked until January 2010, and the internet was cut off across the province for ten months. By the time service was restored, all major Uyghur-language sites had been shut down and their administrators jailed for terms that varied from three to ten years. A new regime of surveillance emerged, with check-points, police posts, and armed patrols (conducted by mostly Han Chinese troops) becoming ubiquitous. In the longer term, the security presence of the state became pervasive. In the year after the riots, the state installed forty thousand high-definition surveillance cameras with riot-proof protective shells in the province.[7] It also increased its efforts to control Islamic practice and expression. Authorities began monitoring mosque attendance, conducted house-to-house searches for unauthorized Islamic literature, prohibited the wearing of veils by women, and monitored the size of men's beards. Any expression of Islam or Islamic observance became synonymous with extremism.

The few years after 2009 saw a number of violent episodes in the province. Some of them were, like the Ürümchi events, protests that turned violent after police intervention or ethnic riots that pitted Uyghurs against Han settlers, while others featured attacks on police stations or government buildings. In August 2010, two attackers detonated explosives in a crowd of policemen, killing seven. In July 2011, demonstrators attacked a police station in Khotan, during which the police gunned down fourteen "rioters." In July 2014, a protest in Yarkand against restrictions on the observance of Ramadan turned deadly, when police opened fire on the protesters. In the ensuing riot, twenty of them and thirteen police officers died, according to unofficial figures. (Xinhua, the official news agency, said only that "dozens of Uighur and Han civilians were killed or injured.")[8] Other attacks targeted Uyghurs who worked for the Chinese state. Juma Tahir, the imam of the landmark Heyitgah (Idgah) mosque in Kashgar, had been a vocal supporter of official policies. He was stabbed to death a few days after the Yarkand events.[9] Another imam had been stabbed to death in Turfan the previous year. Yet other attacks borrowed from the repertoire of international terrorism and targeted random civilians. In 2011, two men drove a hijacked truck into a crowd of pedestrians in Kashgar. The men jumped out of the truck and stabbed six people to death. The following day, armed assailants attacked a Chinese restaurant and killed several more people.[10] In April 2014, while Xi Jinping, the president of the PRC, was visiting Xinjiang, three people attacked the Ürümchi railway station, stabbing three people to death. The following month, five assailants in two SUVs used explosives to kill forty-three people on an Ürümchi market street. Other incidents took place outside Xinjiang. In October 2013, an Uyghur man drove an SUV into a crowd in Tiananmen Square, killing two tourists, before the SUV burst into flames. In March 2014, eight Uyghurs armed with knives killed thirty-one people at the railway station in Kunming in southwest China. Some of these attacks were indeed terrorist—that is, they were premeditated, attacked random civilians, and were meant to strike fear among the public—but most were acts of violence directed at the state or its servants. They were not coordinated from abroad or part of a broader pattern of events, and they were not driven by religious extremism.

The Chinese state responded to the violence of 2009–2014 with an iron fist. The scope and intensity of these measures expanded over the years, until in 2014 these practices were formalized into the Strike Hard Campaign against Violent Terrorism. Inaugurating the campaign, Xi exhorted the Chinese public to build a "wall of bronze and iron" against terrorism and "make terrorists become like rats scurrying across a street, with everybody shouting 'beat them.'"[11] Off the record, his message was even stronger. "We must be as harsh as them," he said in a speech to security officers in Ürümchi in the immediate aftermath of the attack on the railway station, "and show absolutely no mercy."[12] A few months later, Zhang Chunxian, the secretary of the Xinjiang bureau of the CCP,

FIG. 25.2. "Rats on the Street" by Ablet Musa, the winning entry in a Xinjiang-wide
de-extremification painting contest sponsored by the PRC Culture Ministry in 2014. The
painting is a direct response to Xi Jinping's call to "make terrorists become like rats scurrying
across a street, with everybody shouting 'beat them.'" Here, the task is being performed
by Uyghurs in national costume. The painting graphically renders the dehumanization
of the enemy implicit in the rhetoric of antiterrorism. First published on Tian Shan
Wang, the digital news platform for Xinjiang.

launched a "People's War on Terror." This was a curious combination of
GWOT rhetoric with the Maoist-style campaign politics that Xi had
begun to reintroduce all over China after several decades of routinized,
bureaucratic rule. The "people's war" involved art competitions in which
farmers and folk artists produced posters and murals depicting the dangers of extremism.[13] A number of Uyghur farmer-artists took part and
produced a set of striking images (see figure 25.2). But if the public was
invited to help fight terrorism, the main responsibility for the fight lay
with the state, which was now able to pour into it the enormous
resources—human, financial, and technical—it possessed, while it ex-

panded the definitions of terrorism and extremism to such an extent that most Uyghurs seemed to become targets of the war, rather than the state's partners in executing it.

By 2014, China was a very different country from what it had been at the time of the Tiananmen massacre. Explosive economic growth in the intervening quarter-century had made it a world power and given its government new aspirations. In late 2012, Xi, then the newly appointed general secretary of the CCP, began talking about "the Chinese dream." In the following year, he unveiled a highly ambitious project to transform the transportation infrastructure of Eurasia and remap global trade. The project has gone through a number of names and is currently called Belt and Road Initiative, but regardless of the name, it is premised on China's control of Xinjiang. The new dreams of China's greatness require unity and stability in the state and necessitate a rethinking of the policy toward so-called minorities. A "second-generation ethnic policy," debated in the early 2010s, asserted that stability requires "standardizing human behavior" across the nation. This entails replacing the "hors d'oeuvres style" policies adapted from the Soviet Union with a "melting pot" model that would emphasize intermingling among different groups. Its goal should be the creation of a single, cohesive "state-race" (*guozu*) that would be free of any particularist regional or ethnic attachments. As an article by two theorists put it, "The Bedrock of the Chinese Dream Is the Integration of the Peoples of China into a Single Nation-Race."[14] Connected to this is a new, strident emphasis on Sinicization. Xi proclaimed at the Nineteenth Party Congress in October 2017, "We will fully implement the Party's basic policy on religious affairs, insist on the Sinicization (*Hanhua*) of Chinese religions, and provide active guidance for religion and socialism to coexist." Christianity and Tibetan Buddhism should take on Chinese characteristics, and Muslims "must allow traditional Chinese culture to permeate Islam and jointly guard the homeland of the Chinese people (*Zhongguohua*)."[15] The term used here refers to the Chinese state, not the Han people, and might be translated as "Chinafication," or assimilation to an ostensibly supranational "unified multiethnic state."[16] In practice, however, China and the Han are so clearly aligned that it is impossible to distinguish between

"Chinafication" and Sinicization. Han represent China in official discourse, and there are no calls for them to "Chinafy." Sinicization is no different from Hanification. Similarly, the state-race envisioned by theorists of the "second-generation ethnic policy" is not a supranational entity or a neutral construct: it is the Han, and "intermingling" is simply assimilation into the Han.

None of this should be surprising. Since its beginning, the CCP has been a nationalist party, a prime example of how Communism has very often been tied to nationalism in the twentieth century. In the post-Mao period, the party increasingly moved away from the rhetoric of class conflict and tied its legitimacy ever more directly to its having ended China's Century of Humiliation and its record in leading China to greatness and global power. Since 2001, it has welcomed capitalists into its ranks. The Mao jacket has been consigned to the dustbin of history, and China's Communist leaders now prefer sharp business suits. There is every reason to believe that these national credentials give the party great authority among the Han majority in the country. In fact, Han nationalism is rampant on the Sinophone internet, often including strident claims of supremacy.[17] The party might not stoke these feelings, but it certainly takes advantage of them.

By the 2010s, the CCP leadership seems also to have decided that its control of the state was solid enough that it could do anything it wanted in non-Han parts of the country without regard to domestic consequences or international opinion. Any expression of disagreement with the official line on nationalism became a sign of extremism or separatism. Take the case of Ilham Tohti (b. 1969), a professor of economics at the Central Nationalities University (now the Minzu University of China) in Beijing. He did not argue for the independence of Xinjiang but was critical of official policies in the province. In 2011 authorities asked him for an analysis of the situation. However, the paper he wrote in response incensed officialdom, and he was arrested in January 2014 on charges of "separatism" and "inciting ethnic hatred." In September, a court duly sentenced him to life imprisonment and seized all his assets. Since then, he has received a number of human rights awards in the West (including those named after Andrei Sakharov and Václav Havel, as well as one from PEN International), but that recognition does not alter the fact that the Chinese state has incarcerated him for stating the obvious—that official policies in Xinjiang favor the Han at the expense of the Uyghurs and that *minzu* autonomy does not exist. It also seemed to suggest that, as far as the Chinese state is concerned, Uyghurs as a people had forsaken the obligations of citizenship and thus any rights that went with it. The price of readmission was reeducation, through which Uyghurs would be remade into worthy citizens. The three evils of separatism, extremism, and terrorism would be excised from their minds so they could become worthy members of the state-race that the unified multiethnic state of China needs. Such was the path to the political re-education camps of Xinjiang.

––––––––

The CCP has a long history of pathologizing dissent and treating it as a mental illness, and by 2016, it had classified extremism as such an illness. The cure was to be de-extremification (*qujiduanhua*), in which human minds had to be "transformed through education" and rendered less extreme. On March 29, 2017, the Xinjiang government adopted the Regulation on De-Extremification, a set of administrative measures "to contain and eradicate extremification, prevent extremist violations, and bring about social stability and lasting peace and order."[18] The goal was to change the minds and attitudes of those stricken with extremism. As Meng Jianzhu, then secretary of China's Central Political and Legal Affairs Commission, put it in 2017, through "religious guidance, legal education, skills training, psychological interventions and multiple other methods, the effectiveness of transformation through education must be increased, thoroughly reforming them towards a healthy heart attitude."[19] A booklet published by the Khotan prefectural government in April 2017 stated the matter a little differently: "Transformation through education classes are like a free hospital treatment for the masses with sick thinking." De-extremification is akin to detoxification, and it must be generally applied to all of society. "You can't uproot all the weeds hidden among the crops," said one Han official. "You need to spray chemicals to kill them all. . . . Re-educating these people is like spraying chemicals on the crops. That is why it is a general re-education, not limited to a few people."[20]

The state defines extremism so broadly that the term encompasses most forms of everyday religious practice and Uyghur norms of polite behavior. According to the Regulation on De-Extremification, signs of "extremism" include "interfering with others' freedom of religion by forcing others to participate in religious activities," "interfering with others from having communication, exchanges, mixing with, or living together, with persons of other ethnicities or other faiths," "interfering with cultural and recreational activities," "generalizing the concept of halal, to make halal expand into areas other beyond halal foods, and using the idea of something being not-halal to reject or interfere with others' secular lives," "wearing, or compelling others to wear, burqas with face coverings," and "spreading religious fanaticism through irregular beards or name selection." A number of Uyghur names had been banned for being too Islamic in 2015, and parents were required to rename children under sixteen if they bore a forbidden name.[21] In 2017, local authorities also began punishing people who had too many children, which was now deemed to be a sign of religious extremism. For the CCP, Islam is nothing more than a form of mental illness. This is proof, if one were needed, that Islamophobia is not simply a Western invention.[22]

Being accused of any of a number of activities can land one in a camp, including having a criminal history or a previous accusation of separatism, traveling abroad or having relatives abroad, and being in contact with foreigners. Travel to any of twenty-six "sensitive countries"—most of the countries on the list are Muslim-majority states, such as all of the independent states of Central Asia, Pakistan, Iran, Turkey, and the Arab states of the Middle East, but Russia and Kenya are also included—seems to guarantee incarceration.[23] Foreign connections have landed a number of Uyghurs and Kazakhs who are not even Chinese citizens in the camps, while Uyghur women married to Pakistani citizens have likewise disappeared into the Gulag.[24] Most were accused of "strong religious views" and "politically incorrect" ideas. Possessing religious literature of any kind, having unauthorized apps or religious materials on one's mobile phone, expressing suspicious or unpatriotic opinions, wearing clothes deemed too Islamic or the wrong kind of beard, not drinking alcohol or observing Islamic dietary restrictions—all have resulted in consignment to forcible re-education. The "de-extremification" campaign has particularly targeted intellectual and political elites. The arrest of Tohti in 2014 was a precursor to a much larger purge of Uyghur intellectuals that started in 2017. The writer and poet Abduqadir Jalalidin, the anthropologist Rahile Dawut, the poets Perhat Tursun and Chimängul Awut, the veteran head of Kashgar Publishing House, Mämätjan Abliz Boriyar, and many others have been arrested and not heard from since. Tashpolat Täyip, the president of Xinjiang University, disappeared as he prepared to travel to Germany to attend a conference. He was later sentenced to death, although the sentence is suspended as of this writing. Similarly, the professional football player Erfan Häzim, the pop star Ablajan Äyup, the popular comedian Adil Mijit, the master *dotar* player Abdurähim Heyit, and the iconic singer and musicologist Sänubär Tursun have all disappeared into the Gulag.[25]

Testimony from those few who have been released and managed to leave China and a few leaked documents give us some sense of what happens inside the camps. At their best, the camps provide mandatory daily instruction in Chinese and intensive political indoctrination, where inmates sing songs in praise of China and the CCP and thank Chairman Xi for their daily bread. By all accounts, conditions are crowded, and punishments—which range from solitary confinement to sexual assault and torture—are common.[26] Treating sick minds apparently requires assaulting bodies as well.

———

Uyghur society, of course, is not homogeneous. The urban middle classes are not the same as the rural majority. A substantial number of people in the former group have all their education in Chinese, rather than Uyghur, and there are secular or nonobservant sections of the population that are less invested than others in Islamic ritual. Many intellectuals have a fraught relationship with Islam and Islamic elites. Afaq Khoja, the Sufi sheikh who asked the fifth Dalai Lama for help in regaining his power in Altishahr, might be considered to be a holy man by ordinary Uyghurs, but intellectuals have consistently seen him as a national villain who invited foreign conquest for personal gain.[27] Many secular Uyghurs might also be unhappy with the new piety that has emerged since the 1990s. Then there are the party and state cadres and people such as Ablet Musa, who created the poster shown in figure 25.2, who have no sympathy for the increasing Islamization of Uyghur society and may even have welcomed the campaign against it. Yet the state's assault has been so general that clearly the state has little interest in making use of cleavages in Uyghur society or cultivating a base in it.

The campaign has targeted the most thoroughly assimilated Uyghur elites—those who are not religiously observant, are fluent in Chinese, and have been model citizens of the new China—as much as those supposedly afflicted with religious extremism. Cadres at all levels have been punished. Jälil Mätniyaz, the head of a village party cell in Khotan prefecture, was publicly shamed and demoted in 2017 for not smoking in front of elders (refraining from smoking in that context is a basic point of Uyghur etiquette). This sign of adherence to etiquette was deemed to indicate an insufficient "commitment to secularization."[28] Halmurat Ghopur, president of the Xinjiang Food and Drug Administration's Department of Inspection and Supervision and former president of Xinjiang Medical University Hospital in Ürümchi, was given a two-year suspended death sentence for exhibiting "separatist tendencies" and "plotting to create a Muslim Caliphate" in Xinjiang by 2030.[29] Ghalip Qurban, deputy head of the Intermediate People's Court in Ürümchi, complained to central authorities about the mass arrests in Xinjiang. He was also arrested—for being two-faced.[30] Past leaders are not exempt either. Säypidin Äzizi, the great survivor of the first decades of CCP rule, is now under a cloud, and his books have been withdrawn from libraries (and Säypidin is one of the names now banned by Chinese authorities for being too Islamic).[31] More pertinent is the case of Nur Bäkri, chairman of Xinjiang's government from 2008 to 2014 (during which time he condemned the Ürümchi riots of 2009) and director of the National Energy Administration in Beijing in 2014–2018, who was arrested in September 2018 for graft, expelled from the party, and, a year later, sentenced to life imprisonment. The state's persecution of even its own Uyghur officials has clearly diminished internal divisions within Uyghur society.

To become properly patriotic Chinese, Uyghurs need to speak the "national language" (as Mandarin Chinese is now called), adopt Chinese food culture, intermarry with Han, and abandon their traditional codes of honor and respect. Officials in many places have sent out circulars requiring Uyghurs to conduct all public interaction in the national language, to eschew the Uyghur greeting of *assalamu aläykum* (an Arabic phrase that has been thoroughly indigenized) and use instead the Chinese *nin hao,* and not to pray in public spaces. A meeting at Kashgar University in October 2018 exhorted students to "remain committed to removing extremism from eating"—that is, to not avoid pork.[32] The state is willing to help Uyghurs achieve these goals. In 2014, it began sending Han public officials and party members to stay in Uyghur homes "in a bid to enhance ethnic unity in the region." The program is called Becoming Family, and in it the Han cadres act as big brothers and big sisters to their hosts. In 2017, the program was ratcheted up, and as many as a million "relatives" invaded Uyghur and Kazakh homes across Xinjiang. These "relatives" stay for a whole week, during which they share meals, watch television, converse in Mandarin, sing patriotic songs . . . and observe. Do their "younger siblings" avoid pork or alcohol? Do they have any religious books or decorations in their house? Do the women veil or wear dresses that are too long? Are the men's beards too long? The "relatives" can also quiz children about the behavior of their elders. One can only imagine how disruptive these homestays can be—even without the fear of surveillance—for they fly in the face of Uyghur notions of gender propriety and undermine the authority of parents in the family.[33] Meanwhile, the children of those interned in the reeducation camps can be sent to "centers for the protection of disadvantaged children" (essentially orphanages), where they are separated from their families and given a patriotic education in Chinese only.[34] They will grow up with no connection to their families, language, or religion.

Controls over mosques are of long standing in Xinjiang, and it was illegal for minors to enter them. After 2009, authorities also sought to restrict fasting during Ramadan, forbidding it for party members, civil servants, students, and minors. Restaurants were forced to stay open during the daytime and students detained at school during the month to ensure that they did not fast. In 2016, the state stepped up the pressure with a mosque rectification campaign, which began with inspections of mosques for their architectural soundness. Thousands were found to be unsafe and demolished. These included some of the largest and most historic mosques in the region: the thirteenth-century Heyitgah mosque in Keriyä, one of the largest in Eastern Turkestan; the seventeenth-century Grand Mosque in Qaghiliq; and the eighteenth-century Reste mosque in Aqsu have all been demolished.[35]

Other mosques have been shut down or converted to other uses such as art galleries—or in one case in the new "old city" of Kashgar, a bar (called "Dream of Kashgar").[36] Those that remain open are required to hoist a Chinese flag, remove Islamic inscriptions from their walls, and replace them with large red banners inscribed with party slogans. On Monday mornings, mosques hold flag-raising ceremonies accompanied by the singing of the Chinese national anthem and a patriotic song titled "Without the Communist Party, There Is No New China."[37] The demolition of mosques has been accompanied by the destruction of dozens of Muslim cemeteries across the province. A major cemetery in Khotan was bulldozed and replaced by a car park. Another in Aqsu, where Lutpulla Mütellip, an iconic modernist poet, is buried, was turned into a "Happiness Park," complete with children's rides, an artificial lake, and giant statues of pandas.[38] In June 2020, the Bulaqtagh cemetery in Ürümchi was demolished (although in this case, the remains were to be moved elsewhere).[39] Uyghurs are literally being ripped out from their land.

By 2018, the Sinicization campaign had gone beyond Xinjiang and engulfed all Muslims in China, including the Hui—who until then had not been considered a threat at all. Mosques in Ningxia and Gansu were told to remove their crescents and domes, while halal restaurants in China proper, long a fixture in the Chinese urban landscape, were forced to remove signage indicating their halal status. These policies bank on an increasingly popular Islamophobia among the Han population, which incorporates themes from broader, global articulations of it and applies them to China's Muslim populations and which has peculiarly Chinese characteristics as well. As for Xinjiang, official rhetoric has taken an increasingly blunt form since 2016. A white paper released in July 2019 asserted that "Uighur conversion to Islam was not a voluntary choice made by the common people, but a result of religious wars and imposition by the ruling class. . . . Islam is neither an indigenous nor the sole belief system of the Uygur people."[40] Not only do the Uyghurs have no claim to Xinjiang, but they also have no claim to Islam.

————

All this has taken place in full view of a world tied together by instantaneous communication. While Chinese authorities flatly denied the existence of these camps until late 2018, meticulous detective work using satellite imagery and Google Earth by scholars and journalists provided proof of the construction of these camps.[41] Uyghur activists abroad have used this information to try to influence international opinion. Xinjiang was largely absent from the international limelight until the turn of the millennium, but it has increasingly been recognized as an important flash point. Until the dissolution of the Soviet Union, the main center for Uyghur exile activism was Turkey. Isa Yusuf Alptekin and Mehmed Emin Bughra, two of the Three Gentlemen who had cooperated with the GMD in the 1940s, moved there after the Communist victory and engaged in a persistent, if not very successful, campaign to keep the Eastern Turkestan issue in the international spotlight. Since the end of the Cold War, Uyghur activism has been based in the West. Its flagship is the World Uyghur Congress, an umbrella group headquartered in Munich, that does as much as it can to publicize Uyghur causes. The Uyghurs have received considerable attention in the international press since the turn of the millennium—in part because of the diligence of the Uyghur diaspora. But such goodwill in the West cannot match the might of the Chinese state and the resources at its disposal.

The PRC aggressively rebuts all international attention to Xinjiang (and to Tibet, for that matter) as interference in its internal affairs. It also harasses Uyghurs who have managed to leave the country. Chinese embassies refuse to renew passports of Uyghur citizens living or studying abroad, thus forcing them to return or else become stateless. Families of Uyghurs who have sought asylum elsewhere also find themselves targeted. And the Chinese state strong-arms other states into yielding up Uyghurs. The reaction from other Central Asian states and the broader Muslim world has been muted. Kazakhstan, home to a substantial Uyghur population as well as a beacon for many of Xinjiang's Kazakhs, was briefly a center of Uyghur activism. But China's diplomatic heft and its soft (and not-so-soft) power ensured that Kazakhstan did not become a platform for Uyghur dissent. By 2019, the Kazakh government was arresting Uyghur activists and, in some cases, deporting them to China. The response from other Muslim countries has been largely silence (most of those countries are obliged in various degrees to accept Chinese aid), and the only protests have come from the West. The ability of such protests to achieve any change in Chinese policies is, of course, very limited.

––––––

In 2018, Chinese authorities stopped denying the existence of the camps and claimed instead that they were "vocational training institutes" or free boarding schools. During 2019, they invited foreign journalists to take highly controlled tours of the facilities. The world thus got to see videos of Uyghur detainees practicing Uyghur folk dances, singing songs in Chinese, and explaining the benefits of their confinement to their visitors. In December 2019, Shohrät Zakir, the Uyghur head of Xinjiang's government, announced that all detainees had graduated from their vocational training. However, there was no news of detainees returning home. Instead, leaked documents suggested that detainees were being transferred to factories across China as forced laborers. (The central government touts this as a program to alleviate poverty in Xinjiang.) Such laborers live in segregated dormitories, where they have to take compulsory lessons in Chinese and patriotic education and are subject to constant surveillance—which, among other things, makes it impossible to perform Islamic rituals.[42] Other reports suggested that an increasing number of detainees are being tried in the regular criminal system and given jail terms.[43] There are credible reports of Uyghur women being forcibly sterilized.[44] All along, there have been persistent fears of organ harvesting in the camps and prisons of Xinjiang.

I visited Xinjiang in June 2019 on what was the strangest research trip of my career. Security cameras were everywhere, as were checkpoints and convenience police stations. Red banners emblazoned with official slogans in the style of campaigns in the eras of Mao and Stalin were ubiquitous, not just in public spaces but also on Uyghur-owned businesses. Uyghur-owned shops made a point of advertising that they sold alcohol, and at least one Uyghur fast-food restaurant I visited offered pork noodles alongside burgers and *döner*. The hijab had disappeared from the streets. The imposing Baytulla mosque in Ghulja, built in the 1990s and representing both the new piety and the rise of an Uyghur middle class, was locked up, but it flew the Chinese flag and was draped with a banner proclaiming (in Chinese only), "Actively Bring on the Mutual Adaptation of Religion and Socialism." The Heyitgah mosque in Kashgar was open for worship (although the Friday afternoon crowd consisted of fewer than two hundred people in a mosque that can accommodate ten thousand), but outside prayer time it was a tourist attraction, accessible only after purchasing a ticket that cost forty-five yuan. Kashgar's famed night market was now an open-air food court (where all vendors accepted WeChat Pay, the Chinese digital wallet service) with plenty of Chinese food and beer available. The Dream of Kashgar, the bar in a mosque, was well stocked but not very busy. Uyghur-language radio and television continued to broadcast, but Uyghur books had disappeared from bookstores. I visited numerous bookstores in three cities and found that the only Uyghur-language titles for sale were two books on horticulture and a translation of volume 2 of Xi Jinping's immortal *Governance of China*. An Uyghur interlocutor told me in a moment of candor: "They declared all books published between 2003 and 2016 illegal and did house-to-house searches looking for them.

People burned their books." The one surprising thing was the number of Uyghurs who staffed the apparatus of surveillance.

———

As I write these lines, a tenth of Xinjiang's Muslim population is incarcerated, children are being separated from their families and sent to boarding schools, women are being forcibly sterilized, and intellectuals purged. It is impossible to say where this campaign will go or when it might end. However, it is important to ask where it belongs in the history of state violence in Central Asia and beyond. Its scope and ambition are astonishing. The independent states of Central Asia also show little tolerance for dissent and deem Islamic extremism to be a great danger, but their stances are quite different and the scale of their suppression not nearly as expansive as is the case in China. This is because the independent countries of Central Asia are national states of indigenous populations. Islam represents part of the national cultural heritage that they profess to promote. With the turn to Sinicization, China is without question the national state of the Han, in which Uyghurs and Kazakhs are minorities and Islam an alien religion. The suppression of Islam and Uyghur and Kazakh culture in the PRC therefore comes from a very different position than it does in the independent states of Central Asia.

The current campaign is sometimes compared to the Cultural Revolution, but the comparison is flawed. The Cultural Revolution was a vast upheaval, initiated by Mao but driven from below. The mayhem it caused shook everything up, and there were no specific targets. Today's de-extremification campaign is driven by the state and targets particular national groups. We can think of other precursors. The notion of reform through education can be traced back to Soviet Marxism as well as to the Confucian tradition, both of which offer the possibility of remaking the human soul through proper education and labor. Indeed, the archipelago of camps that dot Xinjiang is reminiscent of the Soviet Gulag (and its Chinese counterpart, the *laogai*), which also attempted to reform and reforge the human soul through labor. The Stalinist terror also saw categories of crime that were flexible and expansive, much like the way extremism is construed today in Xinjiang. Nevertheless, the Soviet Gulag's victims were defined by their social class (the bourgeois were enemies of the Soviet order by virtue of their class position, and *kulaks* were to be liquidated as a class), not by their nationality. The most direct comparison of the targeting of Uyghurs as a nationality is with the Stalinist deportations that targeted entire national groups (Chechens, Crimean Tatars, Koreans, Poles) regardless of their class position or political views. The destruction of mosques and the arrests of intellectuals and academics is eerily reminiscent of the Stalinist 1930s. But the atrocities of Stalinism and Maoism took place in secretive societies in ages when information was at a premium. The current Chinese campaign takes place in the full glare of a perpetually interconnected world. It is systematic and orderly in a frightening manner and directed by a state authority that has enormous financial and technological resources at its disposal.

Several scholars have suggested a different set of comparisons, those with the destruction of indigenous populations in North America and Australia by settler colonial regimes. We do not (yet) see the physical destruction of the Uyghur people, but there can be little doubt that Chinese state policies aim to destroy their culture, language, and identity. "Cultural genocide" is not a term recognized by international law, but a number of scholars have argued that the "purposeful weakening and ultimate destruction of cultural values of feared out-groups" is an important part of destroying an enemy group by impairing its ability to exist as a group, let alone resist domination.[45] The current PRC campaign in Xinjiang is little less than that—it is cultural genocide and a war on the Uyghurs.[46]

Finally, the current regime of surveillance is fully imbricated in global networks of commerce and science. The forced labor of the "graduates" of the camps is part of the supply chains for numerous global brands from Amazon and Apple through H&M and Victoria's Secret to Volkswagen and Zegna.[47] The surveillance technology itself is big business. "Controlling the Uyghurs has also become a test case for marketing Chinese technological prowess to authoritarian nations around the world," writes Darren Byler. The annual China-Eurasia Security Expo in Ürümchi draws a hundred government agencies and companies from two dozen countries, including the United States, France, and Israel.[48] Facial recognition technology and forensic genetics are prestigious fields of inquiry, and scientists and companies from around the world are eager to participate in the new technology being developed and proven in Xinjiang. The Chinese state itself is a major customer. The Xinjiang government's spending on information technology and computer equipment quintupled between 2013 and 2017. The Chinese state, now richer than ever before, can pour resources and capabilities into surveillance and control that previous generations could not even have dreamed of. It also uses advanced technology that previous dictatorial regimes could not even imagine. This is high-tech totalitarianism. What is taking shape in Xinjiang is a twenty-first-century security state that may well be the future of other places in coming decades. Once again, Central Asia is at the cutting edge of global developments.

Conclusion

WE HAVE SURVEYED two and a half centuries of enormous transformation in Central Asia. The region has experienced all the currents of the modern age: colonialism, anticolonialism, development, social revolution, nationalism, state-led modernization, and social engineering. It has been the site of massive schemes of transforming nature and nuclear testing and the launch pad of the Space Age. There is nothing exotic or isolated about Central Asia. In fact, its history is depressingly normal.

Conquest and colonization were the fate of many societies around the world in the eighteenth and nineteenth centuries, including Central Asia. The fact that it became part of overland empires, rather than overseas ones, made the conquest seem more natural to outsiders, but it was no less colonial for that. As I have argued in this book, colonialism is an inherently diverse phenomenon, and we cannot use a standard definition of it to judge whether Central Asia was colonial or not. It was distance—moral and political, much more than physical—that set Central Asia apart from the imperial heartlands and made its relationship to them colonial. Both the Qing and Russian empires took difference for granted and granted legal sanction to local peculiarities, yet in Central Asia that difference was greater than anywhere else in those empires. By the end of the nineteenth century, the Qing itself was being imperialized, and Xinjiang was as much a colony of the Russian empire as it was of the Qing.

Colonial empires also ushered in modernity in their colonies. Central Asians found themselves connected to new global exchanges of goods and ideas but also confronted with new questions. Why had they been conquered? What did the future hold? What was to be done? Neither the questions nor the answers were straightforward or unanimous, and the result was new debates and contention within Central Asian society as much as between it and its colonizers. The new, increasingly modern context shaped by colonial conquest in its turn shaped the way questions were posed and debates took place. This context produced new political and communal projects that are still with us. The idea that the nation was the normal and most efficacious form of political organization arrived in Central Asia (and China) at the turn of the twentieth century, and it has been a significant force in the region ever since.

Both the Qing and Russian empires collapsed in the 1910s, but the paths of their successors diverged. The Russian empire fell in the face of a crisis of imperial legitimacy ushered in by a disastrous war. Revolution brought imperial collapse and civil war, from which emerged the world's first Communist regime—which proceeded to put most of the former empire together, but under a different dispensation. The Soviet regime institutionalized the concept of nationality and grounded it in a promise of territorial autonomy to the non-Russian peoples of the new state. The collapse of the Qing empire was also followed by political fragmentation, as well as a slow-motion civil war that lasted thirty-seven years. There were multiple possibilities afoot in those decades, but all sides in China proper agreed that the former empire was a single, indivisible national state. The GMD and its Communist rivals both saw the non-Han peoples of the empire as Chinese and permanently tied to the state. The Communist regime that emerged in 1949 instituted certain policies of national autonomy that were diluted versions of their Soviet equivalents, but the state remained resolutely unitary.

The Tsarist empire was run by a multinational service elite, and its opposition was also multinational. Non-Russians were overrepresented in the ranks of the Bolsheviks who established the Soviet Union. Russians accounted for only a little more than half the population of the union (their share of the population was 52.9 percent in the 1926 census and reached a high of 58.4 percent in 1939, before postwar annexations on the western borderlands reduced that proportion). The Russians dominated the state, but they could never lay claim to its ownership. The Union of Soviet Socialist Republics was the only country in the world without a geographic or ethnic indicator in its name. "Soviet" was an ethnically neutral category that could (and did) coexist with national labels, such as Turkmen or Kyrgyz. The postwar decades saw an enormous transformation in Soviet Central Asia. Its people became full citizens of the Soviet Union and came to identify with it and its myths. The common experience of the Second World War was one path to common citizenship in a country that aspired to certain universal values. Central Asians were active participants in the Soviet project and took ownership of it. They represented the country overseas and fought for it as citizens. More than half the current population of the independent states of Central Asia was born after the demise of the Soviet Union, but most members of the older generation remember the Soviet Union with fondness—as a place where the "friendship of peoples" was a reality, where opportunity and equality existed, even as a place that was meritocratic.[1] To be sure, nostalgia plays a part, but the Soviet past is very much present in post-Soviet Central Asia.

In Chinese Central Asia, developments took a different direction. The Uyghurs and other indigenous Muslim groups in Xinjiang were incorporated into a state that was resoundingly Han Chinese and where they were condemned to be mere minorities. A pan-national patriotism never became a possibility in the PRC, and consequently there was never a space for the emergence of non-Han political elites. The Han have always accounted for well over 90 percent of the population in the PRC, and their sense of ownership of the country is foundational. This demographic preponderance allows the PRC to transform the demographic balance in the minority areas through Han settlement without much effort. Today, the state might try to make a distinction between *Zhongguohua* ("Chinafication") and *Hanhua* ("Sinicization"), but in practical terms the two are the same. China (Zhongguo) is not ethnically neutral (as "Soviet" was), and being, say, Uyghur and Chinese at the same time seems to be impossible both for the Uyghurs and for the state. The Uyghur national narrative could not find a place in a Chinese framework; it could only be antithetical to it. The cultural genocide currently in progress in Xinjiang is the state's heavy-handed response to this contradiction.

We should always keep in mind that the course of Central Asia's history was neither preordained nor inevitable. Things turned out the way they did because of historical situations and accidents. There are any number of points at which developments in Central Asia could have taken a different route. What if the Qing had not thought that Burhan and Jahangir Khoja were important enough to be chased across the Tien-Shan? Or if those who considered Xinjiang a burden on the Qing treasury had won out and the province had not been reconquered? Or if the First World War had gone differently? The Bolsheviks were barely on the political map when Tsarism fell in February 1917 and there was nothing that foretold their victory. Or if the Soviet Union had collapsed in 1941 in the face of the Nazi assault, as Hitler had reason to believe it would? Many of the Soviet transformations explored in this book took place after the Second World War. The interwar years were full of haste and waste, in which the destruction of the old outpaced the construction of the new. The year 1941 was only three years after the murderous violence of the purges that had taken many Central Asian elites prematurely to their graves. Postwar developments, too, were often the unintended consequences of Soviet policies, not their intended ones. The Brezhnev contract that allowed republic-level elites their autonomy was ultimately extraconstitutional. Late-Soviet Central Asia was not created by design. Contingencies mattered.

We can close with two sets of thoughts about what the history of Central Asia can tell us about two global forces, Communism and Islam. In the triumphalism at the end of the Cold War, conventional wisdom in the West labeled Communism a historical mistake and consigned it to oblivion. This required forgetting that a Communist party still ruled the world's most populous state. (Indeed, if the CCP survives in power until the end of 2023, it will have been in power longer than the Soviet Communists were.) Such triumphalism also obscures the fact that Communism arose in the bosom of Western civilization, as an internal critique of it, and shared many of its values and assumptions. That was the source of its enormous appeal around the world over the course of the twentieth century. Communism was always larger than the Soviet Union and never controlled by it. It was seen by many as an antidote to colonialism and a path to national salvation. In Soviet Central Asia, Communism was the annihilation of nomadism and old elites, but it was also the social state that leveled social differences, provided universal education, and brought ordinary people into public life. Most importantly, Communism was always tied to the nation. Marx's philosophical moorings never completely disappeared, but for most of those who experienced it, lived Communism was a path to national betterment. The Russian revolution was not national, but by the early 1930s, Communism had come to be tied to a Soviet patriotism. That patriotism was multinational, and especially in the post-Stalin era, it had space for national communisms of the non-Russian peoples of the Soviet Union. It was for this reason that the rhetoric of Communism could so easily be abandoned in the twilight years of the Cold War and replaced by a search for national destinies. This was the case in China as much as in post-Soviet Central Asia, for the CCP has from its origins been a party of national salvation. But if in Soviet Central Asia, local Communist elites could use the language of the nation against the center, in Chinese Central Asia, that was never possible. Uyghurs are the victims of a Communist party that seeks the advancement of a nation defined as Han Chinese and to which they do not belong.

Islamic danger looms large in contemporary security debates about Central Asia, and the PRC has explicitly invoked it to justify its ongoing cultural genocide of the Uyghurs. It is all the more important, then, to recognize that Islam is not a single, homogeneous entity. Islam has taken many forms over its long history and is a site of constant contestation. Until the turn of the twentieth century, Islam was part of everyday life, completely integrated into it to the point where most Muslims did not think of it as something separate. Those who wielded Islamic authority, usually by virtue of their birth or education, tended to be politically quiescent, willing to throw their support to rulers who allowed them to maintain their authority in society. They came up with all sorts of agreements with Muslim rulers in Central Asia to maintain order, and they found it quite easy to strike similar relationships with non-Muslim rulers. Afaq Khoja actively invited the Zunghar invasion. The *ulama* of Turkestan found ways to get along with the Tsarist regime, and their descendants found it possible to work with the Soviet regime—even after being persecuted during the antireligious campaigns of 1927–1941. Islamic trouble has come from various groups that question its orthodoxy and the hold of traditional elites on it. Jadidism started as a movement of religious reform before it took anticolonial and national positions. Central Asia missed most mid-century developments that produced Islamism as a political ideology, but when Islamism arrived in Central Asia, it came on the shoulders not of the classically trained *ulama* but of new actors who disdained the traditional elites. Today, numerous struggles go on around Islam. Governments in the independent states of Central Asia seek to sculpt Islam in a national image, while the CCP considers Islam to be a mental illness. The contestedness and indeterminacy of Islam is acutely visible in Central Asia.

———

I finish this book in the midst of a global pandemic that has altered the global economy and cast everything in a different light. The crisis has tested institutions around the world, and very few countries have come through it well. The independent states of Central Asia seem to have done no worse than most (the exception again being Turkmenistan, whose government has refused to acknowledge the existence of the virus and has reported no cases). In Xinjiang, the official figures for cases in the first six months were very low. A new outbreak in Ürümchi in July 2020 was more serious and rekindled fear that the disease might spread through the overcrowded internment camps that still hold a large chunk of the region's Muslim population. The pandemic has added another layer of intensity to the cultural genocide in that region that has been in progress since 2017.

NOTES

Introduction

1. Information Office of the State Council, "History and Development of Xinjiang," May 26, 2003, http://en.people.cn/200305/26/eng20030526_117240.shtml. This argument was repeated even more forcefully in another white paper issued by the State Council in July 2019, according to which the various "ethnic cultures" of Xinjiang are "part of Chinese culture" and have no independent existence of their own (Information Office of the State Council, "Historical Matters Concerning Xinjiang," July 22, 2019, http://english.scio.gov.cn/2019-07/22/content_75017992_6.htm).

2. The precise location of this point depends on the definition of "open water" and the nearest coastline. The point described above is the most widely accepted, but alternative continental poles are in the same neighborhood. For a discussion of other alternatives, see Daniel Garcia-Castellanos and Umberto Lombardo, "Poles of Inaccessibility: A Calculation Algorithm for the Remotest Places on Earth," *Scottish Geographical Journal* 123 (2007): 227–233.

Chapter 1

1. James A. Millward, *The Silk Road: A Very Short Introduction* (Oxford: Oxford University Press, 2013).

2. ʿAla-ad-Din ʿAta Malik Juvaini, *The History of the World Conqueror*, trans. J. A. Boyle (Cambridge, MA: Harvard University Press, 1958), 1:97–98.

3. Hafiz Abru, *A Persian Embassy to China, Being an Extract from* Zubdatuʾt Tawarikh *of Hafiz Abru*, trans. K. M. Mitra (Lahore, 1934; repr., New York: Paragon, 1970), 12–15.

4. Juvaini, *The History of the World Conqueror*, 1:104–105.

5. Scott C. Levi, *The Bukharan Crisis: A Connected History of 18th-Century Central Asia* (Pittsburgh, PA: University of Pittsburgh Press, 2020), chap. 3; Erica Monahan, *The Merchants of Siberia: Trade in Early Modern Eurasia* (Ithaca, NY: Cornell University Press, 2016).

6. Devin DeWeese, *Islamization and Native Religion in the Golden Horde: Baba Tükles and Conversion to Islam in Historical and Epic Tradition* (University Park: Pennsylvania State University Press, 1994), 541–543.

7. Mirza Haidar Dughlat, *Tarikh-i-Rashidi: A History of the Khans of Moghulistan*, in *Classical Writings of the Medieval Islamic World: Persian Histories of the Mongol Dynasties*, trans. Wheeler Thackston (London: I. B. Tauris, 2012), 1:6.

8. Mahmūd al-Kāšγarī, *Compendium of the Turkic Dialects (Dīwān Luγāt at-Turk)*, ed. and trans. Robert Dankoff (Cambridge, MA: Harvard University Printing Office, 1982), 1:82.

Chapter 2

1. Muḥammad Ṣadiq Kashghari, *In Remembrance of the Saints: Muḥammad Ṣadiq Kashghari's Tazkira-i ʿAzizan*, trans. David Brophy (New York: Columbia University Press, 2020), 34.

2. James A. Millward, *Beyond the Pass: Economy, Ethnicity, and Empire in Qing Central Asia, 1759–1864* (Stanford, CA: Stanford University Press,1998), 92; Henry G. Schwartz, "The Khwājas of Eastern Turkestan," *Central Asiatic Journal* 20 (1976): 266–296.

3. Alexandre Papas, *Soufisme et politique entre Chine, Tibet et Turkestan: Etude sur les Khwâjas naqshbandîs du Turkestan oriental* (Paris: Librairie d'Amérique et d'Orient, 2005).

4. Peter C. Perdue, *China Marches West: The Qing Conquest of Central Eurasia* (Cambridge, MA: Belknap Press of Harvard University Press, 2005), 283.

5. Ibid., 285.

6. Laura J. Newby, *The Empire and the Khanate: A Political History of Qing Relations with Khoqand, c. 1760–1860* (Leiden: Brill, 2005), 21–27.

7. Millward, *Beyond the Pass*, 201.

8. Hodong Kim, *Holy War in China: The Muslim Rebellion and State in Chinese Central Asia, 1864–1877* (Stanford, CA: Stanford University Press, 2004), 69.

9. Millward, *Beyond the Pass*, 51.

10. Kwangmin Kim, "Profit and Protection: Emin Khwaja and the Qing Conquest of Central Asia, 1759–1777," *Journal of Asian Studies* 71 (2012): 603–626; David Brophy, "The Kings of Xinjiang: Muslim Elites and the Qing Empire," *Études orientales* 25 (2008): 69–90.

11. Quoted in Millward, *Beyond the Pass*, 133.

12. Brophy, "The Kings of Xinjiang," 84.

13. Molla Musa Sayrami, *Tarikhi äminiyä*, ed. Mähämmät Zunun (Ürümchi: Shinjang Khälq Näshriyati, 1989), 28 (see 38–42 for the legend of the emperors' conversion).

14. Millward, *Beyond the Pass*, 205–208.

Chapter 3

1. Scott C. Levi, *The Bukharan Crisis: A Connected History of 18th-Century Central Asia* (Pittsburgh, PA: University of Pittsburgh Press, 2020).

2. James Pickett, *Polymaths of Islam: Power and Networks of Knowledge in Central Asia* (Ithaca, NY: Cornell University Press, 2020).

3. Tōru Saguchi, "The Eastern Trade of the Khoqand Khanate," *Memoirs of the Research Department of the Toyo Bunko*, no. 24 (1965): 51.

4. Scott C. Levi, *The Rise and Fall of Khoqand, 1709–1876: Central Asia in the Global Age* (Pittsburgh, PA: University of Pittsburgh Press, 2017).

5. Ibid., 148–149.

6. Laura J. Newby, *The Empire and the Khanate: A Political History of Qing Relations with Khoqand, c. 1760–1860* (Leiden: Brill, 2005), 55.

7. Hājjī Muḥammad Ḥākim Khān, *Muntakhab al-tavārīkh*, trans. Scott C. Levi, in *Islamic Central Asia: An Anthology of Historical Sources*, ed. Scott C. Levi and Ron Sela (Bloomington: Indiana University Press, 2010), 276–277.

8. Quoted in Newby, *The Empire and the Khanate*, 94.

9. Quoted in ibid., 110.

10. Millward, *Beyond the Pass*, 59.

11. Gong Zizhen, "Xiyu zhi xingsheng yi," in Gong Zizhen, *Gong Zizhen quanji* (Shanghai: Shanghai renmin chubanshe, 1975), 105–112. For an English translation, see David C. Wright, "Gong Zizhen and His Essay on the 'Western Regions,'" in *Opuscula Altaica: Essays Presented in Honor of Henry Schwarz*, ed. Edward H. Kaplan and Donald W. Whisenhunt (Bellingham: Center for East Asian Studies, Western Washington University, 1994), 655–685.

12. Meer Izzut-oollah, *Travels in Central Asia in the Years 1812–13*, trans. P. D. Henderson (Calcutta: Foreign Department, 1872), 60–61.

13. N. Khanykov, *Bokhara: Its Amír and Its People*, trans. Clement de Bode (London: James Madden, 1845); Wolfgang Holzwarth, "Bukharan Armies and Uzbek Military Power, 1670–1870: Coping with the Legacy of a Nomadic Conquest," in *Nomad Military Power in Iran and Adjacent Areas in the Islamic World*, ed. Kurt Franz and Wolfgang Holzwarth (Wiesbaden: Reichert, 2015), 273–274.

14. T. K. Beisembiev, "Farghana's Contacts with India in the 18th and 19th Centuries," *Journal of Asian History* 28 (1994): 126.

15. Joseph Wolff, *Narrative of a Mission to Bokhara, in the Years 1843–1845, to Ascertain the Fate of Colonel Stoddart and Captain Conolly* (London: J. W. Parker, 1845), 1:351–352.

Chapter 4

1. S. V. Zhukovskii, *Snosheniia Rossii s Bukharoi i Khivoi za poslednee trekhsotletie* (Petrograd, 1915), 45–59.

2. Erica Monahan, *The Merchants of Siberia: Trade in Early Modern Eurasia* (Ithaca, NY: Cornell University Press, 2016).

3. Michael Khodarkovsky, *Russia's Steppe Frontier: The Making of a Colonial Empire, 1500–1800* (Bloomington: Indiana University Press, 2002).

4. Yuriy Malikov, *Tsars, Cossacks, and Nomads: The Formation of a Borderland Culture in Northern Kazakhstan in the 18th and 19th Centuries* (Berlin: Klaus Schwarz Verlag, 2011).

5. Joo-Yup Lee, *Qazaqlïq, or Ambitious Brigandage, and the Formation of the Qazaqs: State and Identity in Post-Mongol Central Eurasia* (Leiden: Brill, 2016).

6. Gregory Afinogenov, "Languages of Hegemony on the Eighteenth-Century Kazakh Steppe," *International History Review* 41 (2018): 1020–1038.

7. Khodarkovsky, *Russia's Steppe Frontier*, 153.

8. Jin Noda, *The Kazakh Khanates between the Russian and Qing Empires* (Leiden: Brill, 2016).

9. Alexander Morrison, *The Russian Conquest of Central Asia: A Study in Imperial Expansion, 1814–1914* (Cambridge: Cambridge University Press, 2020), 10.

10. M. A. Yapp, "The Legend of the Great Game," *Proceedings of the British Academy* 111 (2000): 189–190.

Chapter 5

1. Alexander Morrison, *The Russian Conquest of Central Asia: A Study in Imperial Expansion, 1814–1914* (Cambridge: Cambridge University Press, 2020), chap. 5.

2. Ibid., 13–24.

3. Scott C. Levi, *The Rise and Fall of Khoqand, 1709–1876* (Pittsburgh, PA: University of Pittsburgh Press, 2017).

4. Quoted in ibid., 174.

5. Hodong Kim, *Holy War in China: The Muslim Rebellion and State in Chinese Central Asia, 1864–1877* (Stanford, CA: Stanford University Press, 2004).

6. Mulla Muhammad Yunus Jan Tashkandi, *The Life of 'Alimqul: A Native Chronicle of Nineteenth Century Central Asia*, ed. and trans. Timur K. Beisembiev (London: Routledge, 2003), 70.

7. Ibid., 62–63.

8. The quotation is from an English translation of the treaty in Seymour Becker, *Russia's Protectorates in Central Asia: Bukhara and Khiva, 1865–1924* (Cambridge, MA: Harvard University Press, 1968), 316.

9. Quoted in Morrison, *The Russian Conquest of Central Asia*, 409.

10. *Afganskoe razgranichenie: Peregovory mezhdu Rossiei i Velikobritaniei, 1872–1885* (St. Petersburg: Izd. Ministerstva inostrannykh del, 1886).

11. Kim, *Holy War in China*, 187.

12. R. B. Shaw, *Visits to High Tartary, Yarkand, and Kashgar* (London: John Murray, 1871).

13. Kim, *Holy War in China*, 144–146 and 189–193 (quote on 189).

14. Zuo Zongtang, "Zun zhi tong chou quan ju zhe," in Zuo Zongtang, *Zuo Zongtang quanji* (Shanghai: Shanghai shudian, 1986), 9:7894–7896.

15. Zuo Zongtang, letter to Liu Dian, governor of Shaanxi (1875), in Zuo Zongtang, *Zuo Zongtang quanji* (Shanghai: Shanghai shudian, 1986), 14: 11839–11841.

16. James A. Millward, *Eurasian Crossroads: A History of Xinjiang* (New York: Columbia University Press, 2007), 125–130; Immanuel C. Y. Hsü, "The Late Ch'ing Reconquest of Sinkiang: A Reappraisal of Tso Tsung-T'ang's Role," *Central Asiatic Journal* 12 (1968): 50–63.

17. Immanuel C.Y. Hsü, *The Ili Crisis: A Study in Sino-Russian Diplomacy, 1871–1881* (Oxford: Clarendon Press of Oxford University Press, 1965); S. C. M. Paine, *Imperial Rivals: China, Russia, and their Disputed Frontier* (Armonk, NY: M. E. Sharpe, 1996), 132–173.

18. David Brophy, *Uyghur Nation: Reform and Revolution on the Russia-China Frontier* (Cambridge, MA: Harvard University Press, 2016), 68–72.

Chapter 6

1. Eugene Schuyler, *Turkistan: Notes of a Journey in Russian Turkistan, Khokand, Bukhara, and Kuldja* (New York: Scribner, Armstrong & Co., 1876), 1:76.

2. Great Britain, *Central Asia, No. 2 (1873): Correspondence Respecting Central Asia*, C. 704 (London: Her Majesty's Stationery Office, 1873), 70–75.

3. George N. Curzon, *Russia in Central Asia in 1889 and the Anglo-Russian Question* (London: Longmans, Green and Co., 1889), 12.

4. Jeff Sahadeo, *Russian Colonial Society in Tashkent, 1865–1923* (Bloomington: Indiana University Press, 2007), 69–78.

5. Ch. E. de Ujfalvy de Mező-Kovesd, *Expédition scientifique française en Russie, en Sibérie et dans le Turkestan* (Paris: Ernest Leroux, 1878), 2:14.

6. T. V. Kotiukova, *Okraina na osobom polozhenii . . . : Turkestan v preddverii dramy* (Moscow, 2016), chap. 1.

7. F. Azadaev, *Tashkent vo vtoroi polovine XIX v.* (Tashkent: Izd. AN UzSSR, 1959), 72–75.

8. James Pickett, "Written into Submission: Reassessing Sovereignty through a Forgotten Eurasian Dynasty," *American Historical Review* 123 (2018): 817–845.

9. Ekaterina Pravilova, "River of Empire: Geopolitics, Irrigation, and the Amu Darya in the Late XIXth Century," *Cahiers d'Asie centrale*, no. 17–18 (2009): 255–287.

10. Quoted in Daniel R. Brower, *Turkestan and the Fate of the Russian Empire* (London: RoutledgeCurzon, 2003), 44.

11. Allen J. Frank, *Muslim Religious Institutions in Imperial Russia: The Islamic World of Novouzensk District and the Kazakh Inner Horde, 1780–1910* (Leiden: Brill, 2001); Charles Steinwedel, *Threads of Empire: Loyalty and Tsarist Authority in Bashkiria, 1552–1917* (Bloomington: Indiana University Press, 2016), 82–88.

12. K. P. fon-Kaufman, *Proekt vsepoddanneishogo otcheta General-ad"iutanta K. P. fon-Kaufmana po grazhdanskomu upravleniiu i ustroistvu v oblastiakh Turkestanskogo general-gubernatorstva 7 noiabria 1867–25 marta 1881 g.* (St. Petersburg, 1885), 82.

13. A. A. Tatishchev, *Zemli i liudi: V gushche pereselencheskogo dvizheniia (1906–1921)* (Moscow: Russkii put', 2001), 178.

14. Quoted in Richard A. Pierce, *Russian Central Asia, 1867–1917: A Study in Colonial Rule* (Berkeley: University of California Press, 1960), 181–182.

15. Eric Schluessel, *Land of Strangers: The Civilizing Project in Qing Central Asia* (New York: Columbia University Press, 2020).

16. David Brophy, *Uyghur Nation: Reform and Revolution on the Russia-China Frontier* (Cambridge, MA: Harvard University Press, 2016), 84–85.

Chapter 7

1. Munavvar qori Abdurashidxon o'g'li, "What Is Reform?," trans. Adeeb Khalid, in *Modernist Islam: A Sourcebook, 1840–1940*, ed. Charles Kurzman (New York: Oxford University Press, 2002), 227–228.

2. The following pages offer a distillation of my work over the years, best presented in Adeeb Khalid, *The Politics of Muslim Cultural Reform: Jadidism in Central Asia* (Berkeley: University of California Press, 1998).

3. Benedict Anderson, *Imagined Communities: Reflections on the Origins and Spread of Nationalism*, rev. ed. (London: Verso, 1991), 7.

4. Fiṭrat Bukhārā'ī, *Sayḥa* (Istanbul, 1911), excerpted in Ṣadr al-Dīn 'Aynī, *Namūna-yi adabiyāt-i tājīk* (Moscow: Nashriyāt-i Markazī-yi Khalq-i Ittiḥād-i Jamāhīr-i Shūravī-yi Sūsiyālistī, 1926), 535. The Ka'ba is the shrine at the center of the Sacred Mosque in Mecca, the holiest shrine in Islam. The *qibla* is the direction of the Ka'ba. All Muslim ritual worship (*namaz* or *salat*) is performed facing in the direction of the Ka'ba.

5. Muhammad Sālih Khwāja Tāshkandī, "Ta'rikh-i jadīda-yi Tāshkand" (ms., ca. 1908), 2a–2b.

6. Quoted in 'Abdul 'Azīm Būstānī, *Tuḥfa-yi shāhī*, ed. Nādira Jalālī (Tehran: Anjuman-i Āsār va Mafākhir-i Farhang, 1388/2010), 203.

7. Fozilbek Otabek o'g'li, *Dukchi Eshon voqeasi: Farg'onada istibdod jallodlari* (Tashkent: Cho'lpon, 1992 [orig. 1927]); Hisao Komatsu, "The Andijan Uprising Reconsidered," in *Muslim Societies: Historical and Comparative Aspects*, ed. Tsugitaka Sato (London: RoutledgeCurzon, 2004), 50–54; Aftandil Erkinov, "The Andijan Uprising of 1898 and Its Leader Dukchi-Ishan Described by Contemporary Poets," TIAS Central Eurasian Research Series, no. 3 (Tokyo: Department of Islamic Area Studies, University of Tokyo, 2009).

8. Eric Schluessel, *Land of Strangers: The Civilizing Project in Qing Central Asia* (New York: Columbia University Press, 2020).

9. David Brophy, *Uyghur Nation: Reform and Revolution on the Russia-China Frontier* (Cambridge, MA: Harvard University Press, 2016), 94–112.

10. Rian Thum, *The Sacred Routes of Uyghur History* (Cambridge, MA: Harvard University Press, 2014), 177–182.

11. Quoted in Brophy, *Uyghur Nation*, 130.

12. Peter Rottier, "Creating the Kazak Nation: The Intelligentsia's Quest for Acceptance in the Russian Empire, 1905–1920," PhD diss., University of Wisconsin, 2005, chap. 4.

13. Mirjaqïp Dulatulï, "Oyan, Qazaq!" My translation is based on that of Gulnar Kendirbay ("The National Liberation Movement of the Kazakh Intelligentsia at the Beginning of the 20th Century," *Central Asian Survey* 16 [1997]:496). The original text is one of the most famous pieces of modern Kazakh poetry and widely available on the internet.

Chapter 8

1. Quoted in Edward J. M. Rhoads, *Manchus and Han Ethnic Relations and Political Power in Late Qing and Early Republican China, 1861–1928* (Seattle: University of Washington Press, 2000), 14.

2. Young-tsu Wong, *Search for Modern Nationalism: Zhang Binglin and Revolutionary China, 1869–1936* (Hong Kong: Oxford University Press, 1989), 61–66.

3. Quoted in Melvyn C. Goldstein and Gelek Rimpoche, *A History of Modern Tibet* (Berkeley: University of California Press, 1991), 60.

4. Gang Zhao, "Reinventing *China*: Imperial Qing Ideology and the Rise of Modern Chinese National Identity in the Early Twentieth Century," *Modern China* 32 (2006): 3–30. For a somewhat different argument, see William C. Kirby, "When Did China Become China? Thoughts on the Twentieth Century," in *The Teleology of the Modern Nation-State: Japan and China*, ed. Joshua A. Fogel (Philadelphia: University of Pennsylvania Press, 2005), 105–114.

5. Quoted in David Brophy, *Uyghur Nation: Reform and Revolution on the Russia-China Frontier* (Cambridge, MA: Harvard University Press, 2016), 128.

6. Judd C. Kinzley, *Natural Resources and the New Frontier: Constructing Modern China's Borderlands* (Chicago: University of Chicago Press, 2018), 61.

7. Salavat M. Iskhakov, "Turkic Muslims in the Russian Army: From the Beginning of the First World War to the Revolutions of 1917," in *Combatants of Muslim Origin in European Armies*

in the Twentieth Century: Far from Jihad, ed. Xavier Bougarel, Raphaëlle Branche, and Cloé Drieu (London: Bloomsbury, 2017), 95–120.

8. Mahmudxo'ja Behbudiy, "Rusiya va Turkiya arasinda harb," *Oyina*, November 6, 1914, 3.

9. Peter Rottier, "Creating the Kazak Nation: The Intelligentsia's Quest for Acceptance in the Russian Empire, 1905–1920," PhD diss., University of Wisconsin, 2005, 269–282.

10. Peter Gatrell, *A Whole Empire Walking* (Bloomington: Indiana University Press, 1999), 56.

11. Jeff Sahadeo, *Russian Colonial Society in Tashkent, 1865–1923* (Bloomington: Indiana University Press, 2007), 170–176.

12. See the documents collected in *Qaharlï 1916 jïl/Groznyi 1916-i god* (Almaty: Qazaqstan, 1998), 2:70–90.

13. Niccolò Pianciola, "Scales of Violence: The 1916 Central Asian Uprising in the Context of Wars and Revolutions (1914–1923)," in *The Central Asian Revolt of 1916: A Collapsing Empire in the Age of War and Revolution*, ed. Aminat Chokobaeva, Cloé Drieu, and Alexander Morrison (Manchester: Manchester University Press, 2020), 169–190. On the broader context of the war, see also Joshua A. Sanborn, *Imperial Apocalypse: The Great War and the Destruction of the Russian Empire* (Oxford: Oxford University Press, 2014), esp. 175–183.

Chapter 9

1. Sirojiddin Maxdum Sidqiy, *Toza hurriyat* (Tashkent, 1917), 2.

2. *Alash qozghalïsï / Dvizhenie Alash: Sbornik dokumentov i materialov* (Almaty: Alash, 2004), 1:219.

3. For a fuller discussion of the events of 1917 in Turkestan, see Adeeb Khalid, *Making Uzbekistan: Nation, Empire, and Revolution in the Early USSR* (Ithaca, NY: Cornell University Press, 2015), chap. 2.

4. Sharīfjān Makhdūm Ṣadr-i Żiyā, *Rūznāma-yi Ṣadr-i Żiyā: Vaqāyi'-nigārī-yi taḥavullāt-i siyāsī-ijtimā'ī-yi Bukhārā-yi sharīf*, ed. Muḥammadjān Shakūrī Bukhārāyī (Tehran: Markaz-i asnād va khidmāt-i pazhūhashī, 1382/2004), 266.

5. Quoted in F. Kasymov and B. Ergashev, "Bukharskaia revoliutsiia: Dorogu vybral kurul-tai," *Rodina*, 1989, no. 10: 33.

6. Niccolò Pianciola, "Scales of Violence: The 1916 Central Asian Uprising in the Context of Wars and Revolutions (1914–1923)," in *The Central Asian Revolt of 1916: A Collapsing Empire in the Age of War and Revolution*, ed. Aminat Chokobaeva, Cloé Drieu, and Alexander Morrison (Manchester: Manchester University Press, 2020), 177.

7. Quoted in Khalid, *Making Uzbekistan*, 72.

8. Marco Buttino, *La rivoluzione capovolta: L'Asia centrale tra il crollo dell'impero Zarista e la formazione dell'URSS* (Naples: L'Ancora del Mediterraneo, 2003).

9. Cho'lpon, "Ozod turk bayrami," in Cho'lpon, *Asarlar*, vol. 1 (Tashkent: Sharq, 1994), 1:126–127.

10. *Alash qozghalïsï*, 1:472–482.

11. Quoted in V. Semeniuta, "Golod v Turkestane v 1917–1920 godakh," *Chelovek i politika*, 1991, no. 12: 72–78.

12. Marco Buttino, "Study of the Economic Crisis and Depopulation in Turkestan, 1917–1920," *Central Asian Survey* 9, no. 4 (1990): 61–69.

13. *Dekrety sovetskoi vlasti* (Moscow: Izd. Politisheskoi literatury, 1957), 113.

14. V. I. Lenin, *Polnoe sobranie sochinenii*, 5th ed. (Moscow: Izd. Politisheskoi literatury, 1965), 53:190 (all emphasis in the original).

15. Quoted in Khalid, *Making Uzbekistan*, 93–94.

16. Dina Amanzholova, *Na izlome: Alash v etnopoliticheskoi istorii Kazakhstana* (Almaty: Taymas, 2009), 330.

Chapter 10

1. Fitrat, *Sharq siyosati* (Tashkent, 1919), 40.

2. Erez Manela, *The Wilsonian Moment: Self-Determination and the International Origins of Anticolonial Nationalism* (New York: Oxford University Press, 2007).

3. T. R. Ryskulov, *Sobranie sochinenii v trekh tomakh* (Almaty: Qazaqstan, 1997), 3:175.

4. Quoted in Adeeb Khalid, *Making Uzbekistan: Nation, Empire, and Revolution in the Early USSR* (Ithaca, NY: Cornell University Press, 2015), 108.

5. Lev Trotsky to the Central Committee of the Russian Communist Party, August 5, 1919, in Jan M. Meijer, ed., *The Trotsky Papers, 1917–1922* (The Hague: Mouton, 1964), 1:625.

6. Richard H. Ullman, *Anglo-Soviet Relations, 1917–1921*, vol. 3: *The Anglo-Soviet Accord* (Princeton, NJ: Princeton University Press, 1972), 474.

7. Sherali Turdiyev, *Ular Germaniyada o'qigan edilar* (Tashkent, 2006).

8. Niccolò Pianciola, "Décoloniser l'Asie centrale? Bolcheviks et colons au Semireč'e (1920–1922)," *Cahiers du monde russe* 49 (2008): 101–144.

9. V. L. Genis, "Deportatsiia russkikh iz Turkestana v 1921 godu ('Delo Safarova')," *Voprosy istorii*, 1998, no. 1: 44–58.

10. A. Khalid, "Turkestan v 1917–1922 godakh: Bor'ba za vlast' na okraine Rossii," in *Tragediia velikoi derzhavy: Natsional'nyi vopros i raspad Sovetskogo Soiuza*, ed. G. N. Sevost'ianov (Moscow: Izd. "Sotsial'no-politicheskaia mysl'," 2005), 211–215.

11. Quoted in Justin M. Jacobs, *Xinjiang and the Modern Chinese State* (Seattle: University of Washington Press, 2016), 62.

12. David Brophy, *Uyghur Nation: Reform and Revolution on the Russia-China Frontier* (Cambridge, MA: Harvard University Press, 2016), 146–150; Ablet Kamalov, "Links across Time: Taranchis during the Uprising of 1916 in Semirech'e and the 'Atu' Massacre of 1918," in *The Central Asian Revolt of 1916: A Collapsing Empire in the Age of War and Revolution*, ed. Aminat Chokobaeva, Cloé Drieu, and Alexander Morrison (Manchester: Manchester University Press, 2020), 245–249.

13. Michael Share, "The Russian Civil War in Chinese Turkestan (Xinjiang), 1918–1921: A Little Known and Explored Front," *Europe-Asia Studies* 62 (2010): 389–420; V. I. Petrov, *Miatezhnoe "serdtse" Azii: Sin'tszian. Kratkaia istoriia narodnykh dvizhenii i vospominanii* (Moscow: Kraft+, 2003), 278–283.

14. Brophy, *Uyghur Nation*, 206.

15. Maurice Meisner, *Li Ta-chao and the Origins of Chinese Marxism* (Cambridge, MA: Harvard University Press, 1967), 144.

Chapter 11

1. I. V. Stalin, "Nashi zadachi na Vostoke," *Pravda*, March 2, 1919.

2. A more sustained explication of the themes introduced in this chapter may be found in Adeeb Khalid, *Making Uzbekistan: Nation, Empire, and Revolution in the Early USSR* (Ithaca, NY: Cornell University Press, 2015).

3. Terry Martin, *The Affirmative Action Empire: Nations and Nationalism in the Soviet Union, 1923–1939* (Ithaca, NY: Cornell University Press, 2001).

4. Abdurauf Fitrat, "'Tadrij'ga qorshu," *Tong*, no. 3 (1920): 78–80.

5. *1921 yil yanvarda bo'lgan birinchi o'lka o'zbek til va imlo qurultoyining chiqorgan qarorlari* (Tashkent, 1922).

6. Marianne Kamp, *The New Woman in Uzbekistan: Islam, Modernity, and Unveiling under Communism* (Seattle: University of Washington Press, 2006).

7. Sharīfjān Makhdūm Ṣadr-i Żiyā, *Rūznāma-yi Ṣadr-i Żiyā: Vaqāyiʿ-nigārī-yi taḥavullāt-i siyāsī-ijtimāʿī-yi Bukhārā-yi sharīf*, ed. Muḥammadjān Shakūrī Bukhārāyī (Tehran: Markaz-i asnād va khidmāt-i pazhūhashī, 1382/2004), 290.

8. Fitrat, *Qiyomat: Xayoli hikoya* (Moscow: Markaziy Sharq Nashriyoti, 1923).

9. Fitrat, *Shaytonning tangriga isyoni* (Tashkent: O'rta Osiya Davlat Nashriyoti, 1924), 19–20. I have provided more extended analyses of this text and the one cited in the previous note in Khalid, *Making Uzbekistan*, chap. 7.

10. Quoted in Khalid, *Making Uzbekistan*, 176.

Chapter 12

1. Malise Ruthven, *Historical Atlas of Islam* (Cambridge, MA: Harvard University Press, 2004), 103.

2. Olivier Roy, *La nouvelle Asie centrale, ou la fabrication des nations* (Paris: Seuil, 1997), 101 and 117.

3. J. V. Stalin, *Marxism and the National Question* (1913).

4. Juozas Vareikis to Stalin, March 27, 1924, in *TsK RKP(b)–VKP(b) i natsional'nyi vopros* (Moscow: Rosspen, 2005), 1:190.

5. Fitrat, "Yurt qayg'usi (Temur oldinda)," *Hurriyat*, October 31, 1917. This work also appears in Abdurauf Fitrat, *Tanlangan asarlar*, vol. 1 (Tashkent: Sharq, 2000), 33–35.

6. Fitrat, "Yurt qayg'usi," *Hurriyat*, July 28, 1917.

7. Fitrat, "Yurt qayg'usi (Temur oldinda)."

8. Adrienne L. Edgar, *Tribal Nation: The Making of Soviet Turkmenistan* (Princeton, NJ: Princeton University Press, 2004).

9. Daniel Prior, *The Šabdan Baatïr Codex: Epic and the Writing of Northern Kirghiz History* (Leiden: Brill, 2013).

10. Rian Thum, *The Sacred Routes of Uyghur History* (Cambridge, MA: Harvard University Press, 2014).

11. David Brophy, *Uyghur Nation: Reform and Revolution on the Russia-China Frontier* (Cambridge, MA: Harvard University Press, 2016), 178–181.

12. Adeeb Khalid, *Making Uzbekistan: Nation, Empire, and Revolution in the Early USSR* (Ithaca, NY: Cornell University Press, 2015), 272.

13. Russian State Archive of Sociopolitical History (RGASPI), f. 62, op. 2, d. 101, ll. 1–4. For a translation of the document, see Adeeb Khalid, "National Consolidation as Soviet Work: The Origins of Uzbekistan," *Ab Imperio*, 2016, no. 4: 185–205.

14. The verbatim records are available in RGASPI, f. 62, op. 2, dd. 100–110. Arne Haugen, *The Establishment of National Republics in Soviet Central Asia* (London: Palgrave Macmillan, 2003), provides a connected narrative of the process.

Chapter 13

1. Robert Kindler, *Stalin's Nomads: Power and Famine in Kazakhstan*, trans. Cynthia Klohr (Pittsburgh, PA: University of Pittsburgh Press, 2018), 78–87.

2. Ingeborg Baldauf, *Schriftreform und Schriftwechsel bei den muslimischen Russland- und Sowjettürken (1850–1937): Ein Symptom ideengeschichtlicher und kulturpolitischer Entwicklungen* (Budapest: Akadémiai Kiadó, 1993).

3. Marianne Kamp, *The New Woman in Uzbekistan: Islam, Modernity, and Unveiling under Communism* (Seattle: University of Washington Press, 2006).

4. Adeeb Khalid, *Making Uzbekistan: Nation, Empire, and Revolution in the Early USSR* (Ithaca, NY: Cornell University Press, 2015), chap. 11.

5. Kamp, *The New Woman in Uzbekistan*, 187.

6. Adrienne L. Edgar, *Tribal Nation: The Making of Soviet Turkmenistan* (Princeton, NJ: Princeton University Press, 2004), 209–212; Turganbek Allaniiazov, *Krasnye Karakumy: Ocherki istorii bor'by s antisovetskim povstancheskim dvizhenii v Turkmenistane (mart–oktiabr' 1931 goda)* (Jezkezgan: 2006).

7. RGASPI, f. 558, op. 11, d. 46, l. 117 (March 13, 1934).

8. Sarah Cameron, *The Hungry Steppe: Famine, Violence, and the Making of Soviet Kazakhstan* (Ithaca, NY: Cornell University Press, 2018), 5.

9. Isabelle Ohayon, *La sédentarisation des Kazakhs dans l'URSS de Staline: Collectivisation et changement social (1928–1945)* (Paris: Maisonneuve & Larose, 2006), 218.

10. Niccolò Pianciola, "Stalinist Spatial Hierarchies: Placing the Kazakhs and Kyrgyz in Soviet Economic Regionalization," *Central Asian Survey* 36 (2017): 84.

11. Niccolò Pianciola, *Stalinismo di frontiera: Colonizzazione agricola, sterminio dei nomadi e construzione statale in Asia centrale (1905–1936)* (Rome: Viella, 2009), 392–393.

12. Cameron, *The Hungry Steppe*, chap. 5.

13. Ibid., 170.

14. Yousof Mamoor, *In Quest of a Homeland: Recollections of an Emigrant* (Istanbul: Çitlembik, 2005), 92–113. Mamoor was the surname Yousof took in emigration, which took him, over the course of his life, from Kashgar to Peshawar to Kabul, and eventually, to New York.

15. Joshua Kunitz, *Dawn over Samarkand: The Rebirth of Central Asia* (New York: Covici Friede, 1935), 13.

16. Langston Hughes, *A Negro Looks at Soviet Central Asia* (Moscow: Co-Operative Publishing Society of Foreign Workers in the USSR, 1934), 7–8.

17. Langston Hughes, "Letter to the Academy," in Langston Hughes, *The Collected Poems of Langston Hughes*, ed. Arnold Rampersad and David Roessel (New York: Knopf, 1994), 169.

18. Quoted in Mambet Koigeldiev, "The Alash Movement and the Soviet Government: A Difference of Positions," in *Empire, Islam, and Politics in Central Eurasia*, ed. Tomohiko Uyama (Sapporo: Slavic Research Center, Hokkaido University, 2007), 170–171.

19. RGASPI, f. 17, op. 67, d. 480, l. 27 (October 1929).

20. *Report of Court Proceedings in the Case of the Anti-Soviet "Bloc of Rights and Trotskyites," Heard before the Military Collegium of the Supreme Court of the USSR . . . : Verbatim Report* (Moscow, 1938).

21. Edgar, *Tribal Nation*, 127.

22. V. M. Ustinov, *Turar Ryskulov: Ocherki politicheskoi biografii* (Almaty: Qazaqstan, 1996), 399–405.

23. Quoted in Terry Martin, *The Affirmative Action Empire: Nations and Nationalism in the Soviet Union, 1923–1939* (Ithaca, NY: Cornell University Press, 2001), 438.

24. A. Iu. Iakubovskii, *K voprosu ob etnogeneze uzbekskogo naroda* (Tashkent, 1941), 18–19.

Chapter 14

1. "Sharqiy Türkistan dävlät qurulishi," *Istiqlal*, no. 1–2 (November 1933), 14–15; *Erkin Türkistan*, November 15, 1933; Hamidullah Tarim, *Turkistan tarikhi* (Istanbul: Doğu Türkistan Dergisi, 1983), 151–153; Abduqadir Haji, "1933- yildin 1937- yilghichä Qäshqär, Khotän, Aqsularda bolub ötkän väqälär," *Shinjang tarikh matiriyalliri*, no. 17 (Ürümchi: Shinjang Khälq Näshriyati, 1986), 62–63.

2. "Milli gazetälär maqsadi," *Shärqi Türkistan häyati*, July 21, 1933.

3. Quoted in Justin M. Jacobs, *Xinjiang and the Modern Chinese State* (Seattle: University of Washington Press, 2016), 65.

4. Quoted in David Brophy, *Uyghur Nation: Reform and Revolution on the Russia-China Frontier* (Cambridge, MA: Harvard University Press, 2016), 218.

5. Muhämmät Shaniyaz, *Baldur oyghanghan adäm Abdukhaliq Uyghur* (Ürümchi: Shinjang Yashlar-Ösmürlär Näshriyati, 2001).

6. Abdukhaliq Uyghur, "Oyghan," in Abdukhaliq Uyghur, *Abdukhaliq Uyghur she'irliri*, ed. Mähmut Zäyidi, Mähmut Äkbär, and Ismayil Tömüri (Ürümchi: Shinjang Khälq Näshriyati, 2000), 8.

7. Uyghur, untitled poem, in Uyghur, *Abdukhaliq Uyghur she'irliri*, 90.

8. Uyghur, "Ghäzäp vä zar," in Uyghur, *Abdukhaliq Uyghur she'irliri*, 35.

9. Muhammad Emin Bughra, *Sharqiy Türkistan tarikhi* (Ankara, 1987 [orig. Srinagar, 1940]), 553.

10. Jacobs, *Xinjiang and the Modern Chinese State*, 82–83.

11. David Brophy, "The Qumul Rebels' Appeal to Outer Mongolia," *Turcica* 42 (2010): 334 (Brophy's translation).

12. Yolbars's memoirs were published in exile in Taiwan in 1969. The quote is from Andrew D. W. Forbes, *Warlords and Muslims in Chinese Central Asia: A Political History of Republican Sinkiang, 1911–1949* (Cambridge: Cambridge University Press, 1986), 54 (some spellings modified).

13. Tarim, *Turkistan tarikhi*, 27.

14. *Shärqiy Türkistan häyati*, July 28, 1933.

15. Abduqadir Haji, "1933- yildin 1937- yilghichä Qäshqär, Khotän, Aqsularda bolub ötkän väqälär," 53.

16. An image of an ETR passport appears in Bughra, *Sharqiy Turkistan tarikhi*, 600.

17. "Qanun-i asasiy," *Istiqlal*, no. 1–2 (November 1933), 21–41. An incomplete and indirect English translation of the constitution may be found in Forbes, *Warlords and Muslims in Chinese Central Asia*, 255–258.

18. Forbes, *Warlords and Muslims in Chinese Central Asia*, 115.

19. Dzhamil' Gasanly, *Sin'tszian v orbite sovetskoi politiki: Stalin i musul'manskoe dvizhenie v Vostochnom Turkestane, 1931–1949* (Moscow: Nauka, 2015), 21–25.

20. Tarim, *Turkistan tarikhi*, 131.

21. James A. Millward, *Eurasian Crossroads: A History of Xinjiang* (New York: Columbia University Press, 2007), 200. Millward cites a Xinjiang source. The figures are, as always, difficult to ascertain. The British consul at the time estimated the number of deaths at 1,700–2,000. See Forbes, *Warlords and Muslims in Chinese Central Asia*, 122.

22. Judd C. Kinzley, *Natural Resources and the New Frontier: Constructing Modern China's Borderlands* (Chicago: Chicago University Press, 2018), 86–121.

23. "Letter of Governor Shicai Sheng to Cdes. Stalin, Molotov, and Voroshilov" (June 1934), trans. Gary Goldberg, Wilson Center, http://digitalarchive.wilsoncenter.org/document /121894.

24. "Letter from Stalin to Cde. G. Apresov, Consul General in Urumqi" (July 27, 1934), trans. Gary Goldberg, Wilson Center, http://digitalarchive.wilsoncenter.org/document/121898.

25. "Telegram from Cdes. Stalin, Molotov, and Voroshilov to G. Apresov, Consul General in Urumqi" (1936), trans. Gray Goldberg, Wilson Center, http://digitalarchive.wilsoncenter.org /document/121892.

26. *Yängi häyat*, August 30, 1934.

27. Brophy, *Uyghur Nation*, 255.

28. *Xinjiang minzhong fandi lianhehui ziliao huibian* (Ürümchi: Xinjiang qingshaonian chubanshe, 1986), 51–53.

29. Bao Erhan [Burhan Shähidi], *Xinjiang wushi nian: Bao Erhan huiyi lu* (Beijing: Zhongguo wenshi chubanshe, 1994), 193–194.

30. Gasanly, *Sin'tszian v orbite sovetskoi politiki*, 72.

31. Brophy, *Uyghur Nation*, 257; Bao, *Xinjiang wushi nian*, 244.

32. Quoted in Brophy, *Uyghur Nation*, 257.

33. See, for instance, "Concerning the 36th Division of the NRA's Appeals to the Soviet Government" (September 1937), trans. Gary Goldberg, Wilson Center, http://digitalarchive .wilsoncenter.org/document/121870.

34. Forbes, *Warlords and Muslims in Chinese Central Asia*, 130.

35. Ibid., 141.

36. Ibid., 141–144 (the note to the British consulate is quoted on 143).

37. Gasanly, *Sin'tszian v orbite sovetskoi politiki*, 83–84.

38. "Translation of a Letter from Governor Shicai Sheng to Cdes. Stalin, Molotov, and Voroshilov" (January 4, 1939), Wilson Center, http://digitalarchive.wilsoncenter.org/document /121890.

Chapter 15

1. Flora Roberts, "A Time for Feasting? Autarky in the Tajik Ferghana Valley at War, 1941–45," *Central Asian Survey* 36 (2017): 37–54.

2. David Motadel, *Islam and Nazi Germany's War* (Cambridge, MA: Belknap Press of Harvard University Press, 2014), 174.

3. Bakhtiyor Babadjanov, "Sredneaziatskoe Dukhovnoe Upravlenie Musul'man: Predystoriia i posledstviia raspada," in *Mnogomernye granitsy Tsentral'noi Azii*, ed. M. B. Olcott and A. Malashenko (Moscow, 2000), 66n.

4. RGASPI, f. 17, op. 162, d. 37, l. 79 (June 10, 1943).

5. Amirsaid Usmankhodzhaev, *Zhizn' muftiev Babakhanovykh: Sluzhenie vozrozhdeniiu islama v Sovetskom Soiuze* (Nizhnii Novgorod: Medina, 2008).

6. Jeff Eden, "A Soviet Jihad against Hitler: Ishan Babakhan Calls Central Asian Muslims to War," *Journal of the Economic and Social History of the Orient* 59 (2016): 256–257.

7. Ibid., 256–257.

8. *O'zbekiston tarixi (1917–1991 yillari)*, vol. 2 (Tashkent: O'zbekiston, 2019), 60.

9. Roberto J. Carmack, *Kazakhstan in World War II: Mobilization and Ethnicity in the Soviet Empire* (Lawrence: University of Kansas Press, 2019), 12.

10. G. F. Krivosheev, *Rossiia i SSSR v voinakh XX veka: Poteri vooruzhennykh sil. Statisticheskoe issledovanie* (Moscow: OLMA-Press, 2001), 238.

11. Charles Shaw, "Making Ivan-Uzbek: War, Friendship of Peoples, and the Creation of Soviet Uzbekistan, 1941–1945," PhD diss., University of California, 2015, chaps. 3–4.

12. N. E. Masanov et al., *Istoriia Kazakhstana: Narody i kul'tury* (Almaty: Daik-Press, 2001), 306–316; *O'zbekistonning yangi tarixi* (Tashkent, 2000), 2:445.

13. Moritz Florin, "Becoming Soviet through War: The Kyrgyz and the Great Fatherland War," *Kritika* 17 (2016): 495.

14. Brandon Schechter, "'The People's Instructions': Indigenizing the Great Patriotic War among 'Non-Russians,'" *Ab Imperio*, 2012, no. 3: 109–133.

15. "O'zbek xalqining jangchilariga ularning el-yurtlaridan maktub," *Pravda*, October 31, 1942.

16. "Pis'mo boitsam-tadzhikam ot tadzhikskogo naroda," *Pravda*, March 20, 1943.

17. Rustam Qobil, "Why Were 101 Uzbeks Killed in the Netherlands in 1942?," BBC News, May 9, 2017, http://www.bbc.com/news/magazine-39849088.

18. Mustafa Choqay to Vali Qayum-Khan, October 1941, Archives Mustafa Chokay Bey, Institut national des langues et civilisations orientales, Paris, carton 2, dossier 4, p. 8.

19. Ibid., 10.

20. *Millij Turkistan*, November 1942, 3, quoted in Abdulhamid Ismoil, *Turkiston Legioni: Tarixning o'qilmagan varaqlari* (Bishkek: Vagant-Profit, 2007), 8.

21. Bakhyt Sadykova, *Istoriia Turkestanskogo Legiona v dokumentakh* (Almaty: Qaynar, 2002), 83–84.

22. Shaw, "Making Ivan-Uzbek."

23. Quoted in Paul Stronski, *Tashkent: Forging a Soviet City, 1930–1966* (Pittsburgh, PA: University of Pittsburgh Press, 2010), 133.

24. "Prikaz SVGK SSSR ot 16.08.1941 no. 270," text available at https://www.1000dokumente .de/index.html?c=dokument_ru&dokument=0033_obe&object=translation&l=ru.

25. Enver Altaylı, *A Dark Path to Freedom: Ruzi Nazar, from the Red Army to the CIA*, trans. David Barchard (London: Hurst & Co., 2017); Jeffrey B. Lilley, *Have the Mountains Fallen? Two Journeys of Loss and Redemption in the Cold War* (Bloomington: Indiana University Press, 2018).

Chapter 16

1. Roostam Sadri, "The Islamic Republic of Eastern Turkestan: A Commemorative Review," *Journal of the Institute of Muslim Minority Affairs* 5 (1984): 300.

2. The most definitive list of the members of the original government is in Shü Yüchi et al., *Shinjang üch vilayät inqilabi tarikhi* (Beijing: Millätlär Näshriyati, 2000), 74–75.

3. Quoted in Linda Benson, *The Ili Rebellion: The Moslem Challenge to Chinese Authority in Xinjiang, 1944–1949* (Armonk, NY: M. E. Sharpe, 1990), 45–46.

4. "Why Are We Fighting," a pamphlet that circulated in the summer of 1945, translated by the U.S. consulate in Ürümchi, quoted in ibid., 201.

5. Max Oidtmann, "Imperial Legacies and Revolutionary Legends: The Sibe Cavalry Company, the Eastern Turkestan Republic, and Historical Memories in Xinjiang," *Saksaha* 12 (2014): 49–87.

6. Dzhamil' Gasanly, *Sin'tszian v orbite sovetskoi politiki: Stalin i musul'manskoe dvizhenie v Vostochnom Turkestane, 1931–1949* (Moscow: Nauka, 2015), 110.

7. "Letter from Governor Shicai Sheng to Cdes. Stalin, Molotov, and Voroshilov" (May 10, 1942), trans. Gary Goldberg, Wilson Center, https://digitalarchive.wilsoncenter.org/document /121902.

8. Sheng Shih-ts'ai [Sheng Shicai], "Red Failure in Sinkiang," in Allen S. Whiting and Sheng Shih-ts'ai, *Sinkiang: Pawn or Pivot?* (East Lansing: Michigan State University Press, 1958), 239. This is an excerpt from Sheng's unapologetic and nakedly self-serving autobiography penned in exile.

9. James Leibold, *Reconfiguring Chinese Nationalism: How the Qing Frontier and Its Indigenes Became Chinese* (New York: Palgrave Macmillan, 2007), 56.

10. Chiang Kai-shek, *China's Destiny*, trans. Wang Chung-hui (New York: Macmillan, 1947), 4. On Tao's authorship, see Leibold, *Reconfiguring Chinese Nationalism*, 52.

11. These are the words of a modern historian highly sympathetic to Wu: Justin M. Jacobs, *Xinjiang and the Modern Chinese State* (Seattle: University of Washington Press, 2016), 145.

12. "Excerpt on Xinjiang from Minutes No. 40 of the VKP(B) CC Politburo Meetings" (April 5, 1943), trans. Gary Goldberg, Wilson Center, http://digitalarchive.wilsoncenter.org /document/121806.

13. Gasanly, *Sin'tszian v orbite sovetskoi politiki*, 6.

14. Ibid., 136.

15. Quoted in ibid., 176.

16. "Letter from Alihan Tore to Commander-In-Chief Marshal Stalin" (April 22, 1945), trans. Gary Goldberg, Wilson Center, http://digitalarchive.wilsoncenter.org/document/121726.

17. Uvaysxon Shokirov, *Alixonto'ra Sog'uniy* (Tashkent: Navro'z, 2014), 236–238 and 259ff.

18. Muhammät Imin Ömärov and Tursun Yasin, *Äkhmätjan Qasimi* (Ürümchi: Shinjang Yashlar-Ösmürlär Näshriyati, 1987); Abdurakhman Abdulla, *Tashkäntchilär* (Ürümchi: Shinjang Khälq Näshriyati, 2004), 2:1–31.

19. Benson, *The Ili Rebellion*, 185–187.

20. Ibid., 151.

21. David D. Wang, *Under the Soviet Shadow. The Yining Incident: Ethnic Conflicts and International Rivalry in Xinjiang, 1944–1949* (Hong Kong: Chinese University Press, 1999), 268–269.

22. İsa Yusuf Alptekin, *Esir Doğu Türkistan İçin: İsa Yusuf Alptekin'in Mücadele Hatıraları*, ed. M. Ali Taşçı (Istanbul: Doğu Türkistan Neşriyat Merkezi, 1985).

23. Linda Benson, "Uygur Politicians of the 1940s: Mehmet Emin Buğra, Isa Yusuf Alptekin and Mesut Sabri," *Central Asian Survey* 10, no. 4 (1991): 93–94.

24. Ondřej Klimeš, *Struggle by the Pen: The Uyghur Discourse of Nation and National Interest, c. 1900–1949* (Leiden: Brill, 2015), 188–226.

25. Chang Chih-chung [Zhang Zhizhong], "Dilemma in Sinkiang," *Pacific Affairs* 20 (1947): 428.

26. Alptekin, *Esir Doğu Türkistan İçin*, 464–465.

27. "Appeal to the Peoples of Xinjiang" (1948), trans. Gary Goldberg, Wilson Center, http:// digitalarchive.wilsoncenter.org/document/121813.

28. Alptekin, *Esir Doğu Türkistan İçin*, 470.

29. Äkhmätjan Qasimi, "Uluschilar kimlär vä ular öz millitigä qandaq khiyanät qilidu?," in Äkhmätjan Qasimi, *Maqalä vä nutuqlar*, ed. Tursun Qahhariy (Almaty: Qazaqstan, 1992), 74.

30. Many details of Shähidi's life are shrouded in mystery. For this account, I have followed Yulduz Khalilullin, "Kto vy, Burkhan Shakhidi?," *Tatarstan*, no. 11 (2002), http://tatmsk .tatarstan.ru/kto-vi-burhan-shahidi.htm. Shähidi was understandably coy about his Russian birth in his memoirs (see *Shinjangdiki 50 yilim* [Beijing: Millätlär Näshriyati, 1986]).

31. Gasanly, *Sin'tszian v orbite sovetskoi politiki*, 329; İsa Alptekin, *Doğu Türkistan dâvâsı* (Istanbul: Otağ Yayınevi, 1973), 219; Alptekin, *Esir Doğu Türkistan İçin*, 534.

32. Gasanly, *Sin'tszian v orbite sovetskoi politiki*, 331.

33. "Ciphered Telegram No. 4159 from Filipov [Stalin] to Kovalev" (October 14, 1949), trans. Gary Goldberg, Wilson Center, https://digitalarchive.wilsoncenter.org/document/176342; Charles Kraus, "How Stalin Elevated the Chinese Communist Party to Power in Xinjiang in 1949" (May 11, 2018), *Sources and Methods* (blog): Wilson Center, https://www.wilsoncenter.org /blog-post/how-stalin-elevated-the-chinese-communist-party-to-power-xinjiang-1949.

34. Gasanly, *Sin'tszian v orbite sovetskoi politiki*, 319.

35. Quoted in ibid.

36. Quotes from Oidtmann, "Imperial Legacies and Revolutionary Legends," 55–57; Gardner Bovingdon, "Contested Histories," in *Xinjiang: China's Muslim Borderland*, ed. S. Frederick Starr (Armonk, NY: M.E. Sharpe, 2004), 354–357. This attitude is not limited to official Chinese historiography: David Wang bases his account of the ETR on these assumptions and sees its leaders as "docile pawns" of the Soviet Union (*Under the Soviet Shadow*, 18).

Chapter 17

1. Togzhan Kassenova, "The Lasting Toll of Semipalatinsk's Nuclear Testing," *Bulletin of the Atomic Scientists*, September 28, 2009, http://thebulletin.org/lasting-toll-semipalatinsks -nuclear-testing.

2. Claus Bech Hansen, "Ambivalent Empire: Soviet Rule in the Uzbek Soviet Socialist Republic, 1945–1964," PhD diss., European University Institute, 2013.

3. J. V. Stalin, "Toast to the Russian People at a Reception in Honour of Red Army Commanders Given by the Soviet Government in the Kremlin on Thursday, May 24, 1945," Stalin Archive, https://www.marxists.org/reference/archive/stalin/works/1945/05/24.htm.

4. Quoted in Alexandre Bennigsen, "The Crisis of the Turkic National Epics, 1951–1952: Local Nationalism or Internationalism?," *Canadian Slavonic Papers* 17 (1975): 463–474.

5. Alan Barenberg, *Gulag Town, Company Town: Forced Labor and Its Legacy in Vorkuta* (New Haven, CT: Yale University Press, 2014).

6. *Regional'naia politika N. S. Khrushcheva: TsK KPSS i regional'nye partiinye komitety 1953–1964 gg.* (Moscow: Rosspen, 2009), 211–222.

7. Fedor Razzakov, *Korruptsiia v Politbiuro: Delo "krasnogo uzbeka"* (Moscow: Eksmo, 2009), 110–111.

8. Quoted in Artemy Kalinovsky, *Laboratory of Socialist Development: Cold War Politics and Decolonization in Soviet Tajikistan* (Ithaca, NY: Cornell University Press, 2018), 34.

9. Sergei Abashin, *Sovetskii kishlak: Mezhdu kolonializmom i modernizatsiei* (Moscow: NLO, 2015), 351.

10. Robert Craumer, "Agricultural Change, Labor Supply, and Rural Out-Migration in Soviet Central Asia," in *Geographic Perspectives on Soviet Central Asia*, ed. Robert A. Lewis (New York: Routledge, 1992), 143–144.

11. Grey Hodnett, "Technology and Social Change in Soviet Central Asia: The Politics of Cotton Growing," in *Soviet Politics and Society in the 1970's*, ed. Henry W. Morton and Rudolf L. Tőkés (New York: Free Press, 1974), 62–64.

12. Russell Zanca, *Life in a Muslim Uzbek Village: Cotton Farming after Communism* (Belmont, CA: Wadsworth, 2011), 163; Shoshana Keller, "The Puzzle of the Manual Harvest in Uzbekistan: Economics, Status and Labour in the Khrushchev Era," *Central Asian Survey* 34 (2015): 296–309.

13. Craumer, "Agricultural Change, Labor Supply, and Rural Out-Migration in Soviet Central Asia," 147.

14. Boris Rumer, *Soviet Central Asia: "A Tragic Experiment"* (Boston: Unwin Hyman, 1989), 72.

15. Erika Weinthal, *State Making and Environmental Cooperation: Linking Domestic and International Politics in Central Asia* (Cambridge, MA: Harvard University Press, 2002), 82–102.

16. Nancy Lubin, *Labour and Nationality in Soviet Central Asia: An Uneasy Compromise* (London: St. Martin's Press, 1984), chap. 2; Kalinovsky, *Laboratory of Socialist Development*, 136 and 177.

17. Paul Stronski, *Tashkent: Forging a Soviet City, 1930–1966* (Pittsburgh, PA: University of Pittsburgh Press, 2010).

18. Philipp Meuser, *Seismic Modernism: Architecture and Housing in Soviet Tashkent* (Berlin: Dom, 2016).

19. Ronald D. Liebowitz, "Soviet Geographical Imbalances and Soviet Central Asia," in *Geographical Perspectives on Soviet Central Asia*, ed. Robert A. Lewis (London: Routledge, 1992), 122.

20. Nancy Lubin, "Implications of Ethnic and Demographic Trends," in *Soviet Central Asia: The Failed Transformation*, ed. William Fierman (Boulder, CO: Westview, 1991), 57.

21. *Uzbekistan–Nechernozem'iu* (Moscow: Politizdat, 1979).

22. Philip P. Micklin, "Aral Sea Basin Water Resources and the Changing Aral Water Balance," in *The Aral Sea: The Devastation and Partial Rehabilitation of a Great Lake*, ed. Philip Micklin, Nikolay V. Aladin, and Igor Plotnikov (Berlin: Springer, 2014), 125.

23. Philip P. Micklin, "Desiccation of the Aral Sea: A Water Management Disaster in the Soviet Union," *Science* 241 (September 2, 1988): 1170–1176.

24. Julia Obertreis, *Imperial Desert Dreams: Cotton Growing and Irrigation in Central Asia, 1860–1991* (Göttingen: V&R unipress, 2017), 343–347 and 448. The figures for chemical use are from Lubin, "Implications of Ethnic and Demographic Trends," 56.

Chapter 18

1. Vincent Fourniau, *Transformations soviétiques et mémoires en Asie centrale: De l'indigénisation à l'indépendance* (Paris: Indes Savantes, 2019), 21.

2. Kathryn Dooley, "Selling Socialism, Consuming Difference: Ethnicity and Consumer Culture in Soviet Central Asia, 1945–1985," PhD diss., Harvard University, 2016, chap. 1.

3. Sergei Abashin, *Sovetskii kishlak: Mezhdu kolonializmom i modernizatsiei* (Moscow: NLO, 2015).

4. Gillian Tett, "'Guardians of the Faith'? Gender and Religion in an (ex) Soviet Tajik Village," in *Muslim Women's Choices: Religious Belief and Social Reality*, ed. Camillia Fawzi El-Solh and Judy Mabro (Oxford: Berg, 1994), 144.

5. Abdulla Qahhor, "To'yda aza," in Abdulla Qahhor, *Tanlangan asarlar* (Tashkent: G'afur G'ulom, 2007), 117–121. I owe the reference and the analysis to Dooley, "Selling Socialism, Consuming Difference," 351–353.

6. Jeff Sahadeo, *Voices from the Soviet Edge: Southern Migrants in Leningrad and Moscow* (Ithaca, NY: Cornell University Press, 2019).

7. Adrienne L. Edgar, *Intermarriage and the Friendship of Peoples: Ethnic Mixing in Soviet Central Asia*, forthcoming.

8. Shaken Aymanov, dir., *Zemlia ottsov/Atalar mekeni* (Almaty: Kazakhfilm, 1966).

9. Dooley, "Selling Socialism, Consuming Difference," 330–347.

10. Chingiz Aitmatov, *The Day Lasts More than a Hundred Years*, trans. John French (London: Futura, 1983), 21. Aitmatov's vision in the novel was more complicated, as we shall see when we return to this novel in chapter 21, but this point stands.

11. Ziyauddin Khan Ibn Ishan Babakhan, *Islam and the Muslims in the Land of Soviets*, trans. Richard Dixon (Moscow: Progress, 1980); Adeeb Khalid, *Islam after Communism: Religion and Politics in Central Asia* (Berkeley: University of California Press, 2007), chap. 4.

12. Bakhtiiar Babadzhanov, "O fetvakh SADUM protiv 'neislamskikh obychaev,'" in *Islam na postsovetskom prostranstve: vzgliad iznutri*, ed. Martha Brill Olcott and Aleksei Malashenko (Moscow: Tsentr Karnegi, 2001), 170–184.

13. On Hindustoniy, see B. M. Babadzhanov, A. K. Muminov, and M. B. Olkott, "Mukhamadzhan Khindustani (1892–1989) i religioznaia sreda ego epokhi (predvaritel'nye razmyshleniia o formirovanii 'sovetskogo islama' v Srednei Azii)," *Vostok*, 2004, no. 5: 43–49. His autobiography was published posthumously by his disciples as *Yodnoma: Hazrati Mavlono Muhammadjon Qo'qandiy (Hindustoniy) farzandlar, shogirdlar va do'stlar xotirasida* (Dushanbe, 2003). On Alikhan Tora, see Uvaysxon Shokirov, *Alixonto'ra Sog'uniy* (Tashkent: Navro'z, 2014).

Chapter 19

1. Milton J. Clark, "How the Kazakhs Fled to Freedom," *National Geographic Magazine* 106 (1954), 621–644; Godfrey Lias, *Kazak Exodus* (London: Evans, 1956).

2. Zhe Wu, "Caught between Opposing Han Chauvinism and Opposing Local Nationalism: The Drift toward Ethnic Antagonism in Xinjiang Society, 1952–1963," in *Maoism at the Grassroots: Everyday Life in China's Era of High Socialism*, ed. Jeremy Brown and Matthew D. Johnson (Cambridge, Mass.: Harvard University Press, 2015), 313.

3. Donald H. McMillen, *Chinese Communist Power and Policy in Xinjiang, 1949–1977* (Boulder, Colo.: Westview, 1979), 57–60.

4. Quoted in ibid., 114.

5. Xiaoyuan Liu, *Frontier Passages: Ethnopolitics and the Rise of Chinese Communism, 1921–1945* (Washington: Woodrow Wilson Center Press, 2004), 64.

6. Quoted in James Leibold, *Reconfiguring Chinese Nationalism: How the Qing Frontier and Its Indigenes Became Chinese* (New York: Palgrave Macmillan, 2007), 90.

7. Quoted in ibid., 91.

8. Ibid., 148.

9. "Memorandum of Conversation between Anastas Mikoyan and Mao Zedong" (January 31, 1949), trans. Sergey Radchenko, Wilson Center, https://digitalarchive.wilsoncenter.org/document/112436.

10. Mao Zedong, "On the Ten Major Relationships" (April 25, 1956), in Mao Tsetung, *Selected Works of Mao Tsetung* (Peking: Foreign Languages Press, 1977), 5:295.

11. Zhiyi Zhang, *A Discussion of the National Question in the Chinese Revolution and of Actual Nationalities Policy (Draft)*, in George Moseley, *The Party and the National Question in China* (Cambridge, MA: MIT Press, 1966), 81–82.

12. Thomas S. Mullaney, *Coming to Terms with the Nation: Ethnic Classification in Modern China* (Berkeley: University of California Press, 2011).

13. Gardner Bovingdon, *The Uyghurs: Strangers in Their Own Land* (New York: Columbia University Press, 2010), 199n.

14. David Brophy, "The 1957–58 Xinjiang Committee Plenum and the Attack on 'Local Nationalism'" (December 11, 2017), document 5, *Sources and Methods* (blog), Wilson Center, https://www.wilsoncenter.org/blog-post/the-1957-58-xinjiang-committee-plenum-and-the-attack-local-nationalism.

15. Abdulla Abdurākhman, *Tashkäntchilär*, 2 vols. (Ürümchi: Shinjang Khälq Näshriyati, 2004).

16. Zhihua Shen and Danhui Li, *After Leaning to One Side: China and Its Allies in the Cold War* (Washington: Woodrow Wilson Center Press, 2011), 142.

17. Brophy, "The 1957–58 Xinjiang Committee Plenum and the Attack on 'Local Nationalism,'" document 3.2.

18. Linda Benson and Ingvar Svanberg, *China's Last Nomads: The History and Culture of China's Kazaks* (Armonk, NY: M. E. Sharpe, 1998), 166.

19. McMillen, *Chinese Communist Power*, 142.

20. Quoted in George Moseley, *A Sino-Soviet Cultural Frontier: The Ili Kazakh Autonomous Chou* (Cambridge, MA: Harvard East Asian Research Center, 1966), 105.

21. Bruce F. Adams, "Reemigration from Western China to the USSR, 1954–1962," in *Migration, Homeland, and Belonging in Eurasia*, ed. Cynthia J. Buckley and Blair A. Ruble, with Erin Trouth Hofmann (Washington: Woodrow Wilson Center Press, 2008), 191.

22. William Clark and Ablet Kamalov, "Uighur Migration across Central Asian Frontiers," *Central Asian Survey* 23 (2004): 167–182.

23. Quoted in James A. Millward, *Eurasian Crossroads: A History of Xinjiang* (New York: Columbia University Press, 2007), 275.

24. Benson and Svanberg, *China's Last Nomads*, 185.

25. Ibid.

26. Quoted in Minglang Zhou, *Multilingualism in China: The Politics of Writing Reforms for Minority Languages 1949–2002* (Berlin: Mouton de Gruyter, 2003), 301.

27. William Clark, "Ibrahim's Story," *Asian Ethnicity* 12 (2011): 216.

28. *Tianshan nanbei jin zhaohui: Xinjiang zai fanxiu fangxiu douzheng zhong qianjin* (Shanghai: Shanghai renmin chubanshe, 1976), 74–75.

29. Gardner Bovingdon, "The Not-So-Silent Majority: Uyghur Resistance to Han Rule in Xinjiang," *Modern China* 28 (2002), 60–61.

Chapter 20

1. Odd Arne Westad, *The Global Cold War: Third World Interventions and the Making of Our Times* (Cambridge: Cambridge University Press, 2011).

2. *Pravda Vostoka*, March 12, 1925.

3. Quoted in Hannah Jansen, "Peoples' Internationalism: Central Asian Modernisers, Soviet Oriental Studies and Cultural Revolution in the East (1936–1977)," PhD diss., University of Amsterdam, 2020, 127.

4. N. A. Mukhitdinov, *Gody provedënnye v Kremle* (Tashkent, 1994), 312.

5. S. Rizaev, *Sharaf Rashidov: Shtrikhi k portretu* (Tashkent: Yozuvchi, 1992), 24–28.

6. Vladislav M. Zubok, "The Mao-Khrushchev Conversations, 31 July–3 August 1958 and 2 October 1959," *Cold War International History Project Bulletin*, no. 12–13 (2002): 254.

7. Mao Tsetung, "On Khrushchov's Phoney Communism and Its Historical Lessons for the World" (July 1964), https://www.marxists.org/reference/archive/mao/works/1964/phnycom.htm.

8. All of the quotes are from Sergey Radchenko, "The Sino-Soviet Split," *Cambridge History of the Cold War*, ed. Melvyn P. Leffler and Odd Arne Westad, vol. 2 (Cambridge: Cambridge University Press, 2010), 356–357.

9. Artemy Kalinovsky, *A Long Goodbye: The Soviet Withdrawal from Afghanistan* (Cambridge, MA: Harvard University Press, 2011), chap. 1.

10. Steve Coll, *Ghost Wars: The Secret History of the CIA, Afghanistan, and Bin Laden, from the Soviet Invasion to September 10, 2001* (New York: Penguin, 2004), 104–105; Mohammad Yousaf and Mark Adkin, *The Bear Trap: Afghanistan's Untold Story* (London: Leo Cooper, 1992), 192–195.

11. See the interviews collected in Marlène Laruelle and Botagoz Rakieva, *Pamiat' iz plameni Afganistana: Interv'iu s voinami-internatsionalistami Afganskoi voiny 1979–1989 godov* (Washington: Central Asia Program, George Washington University, 2015). A number of memoirs from Tajikistan, several of which touch on military service in Afghanistan, have been collected and

are available online. See Artemy Kalinovsky, Isaac Scarborough, Marlene Laruelle, and Vadim Staklo, "Central Asian Memoirs of the Soviet Era," *Russian Perspectives on Islam*, https://islamperspectives.org/rpi/collections/show/18.

12. Yaacov Ro'i, *Islam in the Soviet Union: From the Second World War to Gorbachev* (New York: Columbia University Press, 2000), 560.

Chapter 21

1. Yegor Ligachev, *Inside Gorbachev's Kremlin* (New York: Random House, 1993), 214.

2. Leslie Holmes, *The End of Communist Power: Anti-Corruption Campaigns and Legitimation Crisis* (New York: Oxford University Press, 1993), 101.

3. Riccardo Mario Cucciola, "The Crisis of Soviet Power in Central Asia: The 'Uzbek Cotton Affair' (1975–1991)," PhD diss., IMT School for Advanced Studies Lucca, 2017, 284.

4. Anne Sheehy, "Slav Presence Increased in Uzbek Party Buro and Secretariat," *Radio Liberty Research Bulletin*, February 24, 1986.

5. James Critchlow, "Prelude to 'Independence': How the Uzbek Party Apparatus Broke Moscow's Grip on Elite Recruitment," in *Soviet Central Asia: The Failed Transformation*, ed. William Fierman (Boulder, CO: Westview, 1991), 135–154.

6. Rafik Nishanov, as told to Marina Zavade and Iurii Kulikov, *Derev'ia zeleneiut do metelei* (Moscow: Molodaia gvardiia, 2012), 258.

7. Cucciola, "The Crisis of Soviet Power in Central Asia," 360n.

8. Sergei P. Poliakov, *Everyday Islam: Religion and Tradition in Rural Central Asia*, trans. Anthony Olcott (Armonk, NY: M. E. Sharpe, 1992), 4.

9. Artemy Kalinovsky, *Laboratory of Socialist Development: Cold War Politics and Decolonization in Soviet Tajikistan* (Ithaca, NY: Cornell University Press, 2018), 226–227.

10. Quoted in Patricia Carley, "The Price of the Plan: Perceptions of Cotton and Health in Uzbekistan and Turkmenistan," *Central Asian Survey* 8, no. 4 (1989): 23.

11. S. Rizaev, *Sharaf Rashidov: Shtrikhi k portretu* (Tashkent: Yozuvchi, 1992), 78–79.

12. Boris Rumer, "Central Asia's Cotton Economy and Its Costs," in *Soviet Central Asia: The Failed Transformation*, ed. William Fierman (Boulder, CO: Westview, 1991), 84–87.

13. William Fierman, "Political Development in Uzbekistan: Democratization?," in *Conflict, Cleavage and Change in Central Asia and the Caucasus*, ed. Karen Dawisha and Bruce Parrott (Cambridge: Cambridge University Press, 1997), 367.

14. Victoria Clement, *Learning to Become Turkmen: Literacy, Language, and Power, 1914–2014* (Pittsburgh, PA: University of Pittsburgh Press, 2018), 117–118.

15. Vladimir Babak, "The Formation of Political Parties and Movements in Central Asia," in *Democracy and Pluralism in Muslim Eurasia*, ed. Yaacov Ro'i (London: Frank Cass, 2004), 152–154.

16. Chingiz Aitmatov, *The Day Lasts More than a Hundred Years*, trans. John French (London: Futura, 1983), 126.

17. Fierman, "Political Development in Uzbekistan," 368.

18. Quoted in Kirill Nourzhanov and Christian Bleuer, *Tajikistan: A Political and Social History* (Canberra: Australian National University Press, 2013), 178–179.

19. Bakhtiyar Babadjanov and Muzaffar Kamilov, "Muhammadjân Hindûstânî (1892–1989) and the Beginning of the Great Schism among the Muslims of Uzbekistan," in *Islam in Politics in Russia and Central Asia (Early Eighteenth to Late Twentieth Centuries)*, ed. Stéphane A. Dudoignon and Hisao Komatsu (London: Kegan Paul, 2001), 195–219.

20. Adeeb Khalid, *Islam after Communism: Religion and Politics in Central Asia* (Berkeley: University of California Press, 2007), 146.

21. *Pravda*, February 7, 1991. The translation is from *The Rise and Fall of the Soviet Union, 1917–1991*, ed. Richard Sakwa (London: Routledge, 1999), 471–473.

Chapter 22

1. Bayram Balci, *Missionaires de l'Islam en Asie centrale: Les écoles turques de Fethullah Gülen* (Paris: Maisonneuve & Larose, 2003).

2. Muriel Atkin, "Thwarted Democratization in Tajikistan," in *Conflict, Cleavage and Change in Central Asia and the Caucasus*, ed. Karen Dawisha and Bruce Parrott (Cambridge: Cambridge University Press, 1997), 277–311.

3. On the Tajik civil war, see Tim Epkenhans, *The Origins of the Civil War in Tajikistan: Nationalism, Islamism, and Violent Conflict in Post-Soviet Space* (Lanham, MD: Lexington Books, 2016); Jesse Driscoll, *Warlords and Coalition Politics in Post-Soviet States* (Cambridge: Cambridge University Press, 2015).

4. Minglang Zhou, "The Fate of the Soviet Model of Multinational State-Building in the People's Republic of China," in *China Learns from the Soviet Union, 1949–Present*, ed. Thomas P. Bernstein and Hua-Yu Li (Lanham, MD: Lexington Books, 2010), 488–490.

5. Agnieszka Joniak-Lüthi, "Roads in China's Borderlands: Interfaces of Spatial Representations, Perceptions, Practices, and Knowledges," *Modern Asian Studies* 50 (2016): 118–140.

6. Zhou, "The Fate of the Soviet Model," 492.

7. Nicolas Becquelin, "Xinjiang in the Nineties," *China Journal* 44 (2000): 69.

8. Stanley W. Toops, "The Demography of Xinjiang," in *Xinjiang: China's Muslim Borderland*, ed. S. Frederick Starr (Armonk, NY: M. E. Sharpe, 2004), 241–263.

9. Tom Cliff, *Oil and Water: Being Han in Xinjiang* (Chicago: University of Chicago Press, 2016).

10. Adeeb Khalid, *Islam after Communism: Religion and Politics in Central Asia* (Berkeley: University of California Press, 2007), chap. 6.

Chapter 23

1. Rogers Brubaker, *Nationalism Reframed: Nationhood and the National Question in the New Europe* (Cambridge: Cambridge University Press, 1996), 83–84.

2. Laura L. Adams, *The Spectacular State: Culture and National Identity in Uzbekistan* (Durham, NC: Duke University Press, 2010).

3. Quoted in Natalie Koch, *The Geopolitics of Spectacle: Space, Synecdoche, and the New Capitals of Asia* (Ithaca, NY: Cornell University Press, 2018), 47.

4. Henry E. Hale, *Patronal Politics: Eurasian Regime Dynamics in Comparative Perspective* (Cambridge: Cambridge University Press, 2014); Lawrence P. Markowitz, *State Erosion: Unlootable Resources and Unruly Elites in Central Asia* (Ithaca, NY: Cornell University Press, 2013).

5. Alexander Cooley and John Heathershaw, *Dictators without Borders: Power and Money in Central Asia* (New Haven, CT: Yale University Press, 2017).

6. Gardner Bovingdon, *The Uyghurs: Strangers in Their Own Land* (New York: Columbia University Press, 2010), chap. 3; Joanne Smith Finley, *The Arts of Symbolic Resistance: Uyghur Identities and Uyghur-Han Relations in Contemporary Xinjiang* (Leiden: Brill, 2013), chaps. 3–4.

7. Jay Dautcher, *Down a Narrow Road: Identity and Masculinity in a Uyghur Community in Xinjiang, China* (Cambridge, MA: Harvard University East Asia Center, 2009).

8. Herbert S. Yee, "Ethnic Consciousness and Identity: A Research Report on Uygur-Han Relations in Xinjiang," *Asian Ethnicity* 6 (2005): 35–50.

9. Quoted in Bovingdon, *The Uyghurs*, 95. The translation is by Bovingdon.

10. Quoted in Smith Finley, *The Arts of Symbolic Resistance*, 193. I have taken the liberty of altering Smith Finley's translation a little.

11. Bovingdon, *The Uyghurs*, 100–101.

12. Ilham Tohti, "Present-Day Ethnic Problems in Xinjiang Uighur Autonomous Region: Overview and Recommendations," trans. Cindy Carter, April 22–May 19, 2015, China Change, https://chinachange.org/wp-content/uploads/2015/05/ilham-tohti_present-day-ethnic-problems-in-xinjiang-uighur-autonomous-region-overview-and-recommendations_complete-translation3.pdf; Andrew Jacobs, "Uighurs in China Say Bias Is Growing," *NYT*, October 7, 2013.

13. Emily Hannum and Yu Xie, "Ethnic Stratification in Northwest China: Occupational Differences between Han Chinese and National Minorities in Xinjiang, 1982–1990," *Demography* 35 (1998): 323–333; Ben Hopper and Michael Webber, "Modernisation and Ethnic Estrangement: Uyghur Migration to Urumqi, Xinjiang Uyghur Autonomous Region, PRC," *Inner Asia* 11 (2009): 173–203; Xiaogang Wu and Xi Song, "Ethnic Stratification amid China's Economic Transition: Evidence from the Xinjiang Uyghur Autonomous Region," *Social Science Research* 44 (2014): 158–172.

14. Information Office of the State Council, "History and Development of Xinjiang," May 26, 2003, http://en.people.cn/200305/26/print20030526_117240.html.

15. Ildikó Bellér-Hann, "The Bulldozer State: Chinese Socialist Development in Xinjiang," in *Ethnographies of the State in Central Asia: Performing Politics*, ed. Madeleine Reeves, Johan Rasanayagam, and Judith Beyer (Bloomington: Indiana University Press, 2014), 181; Gardner Bovingdon, "The History of History in Xinjiang," *Twentieth-Century China* 26 (2001): 95.

16. The classic analysis of the legend of the fragrant concubine is by James Millward, "A Uyghur Muslim in Qianlong's Court: The Meanings of the Fragrant Concubine," *Journal of Asian Studies* 53 (1994): 427–458.

17. Joshua Hammer, "Demolishing Kashgar's History," *Smithsonian Magazine*, March 2010, 24–33.

18. Jean-Paul Loubes, *La Chine et la ville au XXIe siècle: La sinisation urbaine au Xinjiang ouïghour et en Mongolie intérieur* (Paris: Éditions du Sextant, 2015), 119–134.

19. Tianyang Liu and Zhenjie Yuan, "Making a Safer Space? Rethinking Space and Securitization in the Old Town Redevelopment Project of Kashgar, China," *Political Geography* 69 (2019): 30–42.

20. Bayram Balci, *Islam in Central Asia and the Caucasus since the Fall of the Soviet Union* (London: Hurst, 2018).

21. Peter Boehm and Andrew Osborn, "Uzbekistan: 'In the Narrow Lane, the Machine Guns Clattered Remorselessly for Two Hours,'" *Independent on Sunday* (London), May 22, 2005; Human Rights Watch, "'Bullets Were Falling Like Rain': The Andijan Massacre, May 13, 2005" (June 2005), https://www.hrw.org/report/2005/06/06/bullets-were-falling-rain/andijan -massacre-may-13-2005.

22. Igor Rotar, "Political Islam in Tajikistan after the Formation of the IS," CERIA Brief no. 8, October 2015, https://app.box.com/s/f8f5s98pd6pkd2l1xaxipdnnvzwnzrvq .

23. Quoted in Rémi Castets, "The Modern Chinese State and Strategies of Control over Uyghur Islam," *Central Asian Affairs* 2 (2015): 237–238.

Chapter 24

1. Gerry Shih, "Chinese Troops Sit on Afghan Doorstep," *Washington Post*, February 19, 2019.

2. Saparmyrat Turkmenbashy, *Rukhnama: Reflections on the Spiritual Values of the Turkmen* (Ashgabat, Turkmenistan, 2003), 9.

3. Sebastien Peyrouse, *Turkmenistan: Strategies of Power, Dilemmas of Development* (Armonk, NY: M. E. Sharpe, 2012), 146–154.

4. Boris Petric, *Where Are All Our Sheep? Kyrgyzstan, a Global Political Arena*, trans. Cynthia Schoch (New York: Berghahn, 2015), 11.

5. Scott Radnitz, *Weapons of the Wealthy: Predatory Regimes and Elite-Led Protests in Central Asia* (Ithaca, NY: Cornell University Press, 2010), 63–64; Erica Marat, "Extent of Akayev Regime Corruption Becoming Clearer," *Eurasia Daily Monitor*, April 26, 2005, https://jamestown .org/program/extent-of-akayev-regime-corruption-becoming-clearer/.

6. Global Witness, "Blood Red Carpet," March 2015, available for download from https:// www.globalwitness.org/en/reports/surrey-mansion-used-hide-suspect-funds/; Alexander Cooley and John Heathershaw, *Dictators without Borders: Power and Money in Central Asia* (New Haven, CT: Yale University Press, 2017), chap. 5.

7. Richard Pomfret, *The Central Asian Economies in the Twenty-First Century: Paving a New Silk Road* (Princeton, NJ: Princeton University Press, 2019), 71–72.

8. Joanna Lillis, *Dark Shadows: Inside the Secret World of Kazakhstan* (London: I. B. Tauris, 2019), 81.

Chapter 25

1. Megha Rajagopalan, "This Is What a 21st-Century Police State Really Looks Like," *BuzzFeed News*, October 17, 2017, https://www.buzzfeednews.com/article/meghara/the -police-state-of-the-future-is-already-here; James Millward, "'Re-Educating' Xinjiang's Muslims," *New York Review of Books*, February 7, 2019, 38–41.

2. Gardner Bovingdon, *The Uyghurs: Strangers in Their Own Land* (New York: Columbia University Press, 2010), 123–128; James A. Millward, *Eurasian Crossroads: A History of Xinjiang* (New York: Columbia University Press, 2007), 325–328.

3. Permanent Mission of the People's Republic of China to the UN, "Terrorist Activities Perpetrated by 'Eastern Turkistan' Organizations and Their Links with Osama bin Laden and the Taliban," November 29, 2001, https://www.fmprc.gov.cn/ce/ceee/eng/ztlm/fdkbzy/t112733.htm.

4. Sean R. Roberts, *The War on the Uyghurs: China's Campaign against Xinjiang's Muslims* (Princeton, NJ: Princeton University Press, 2020), chaps. 2–3.

5. Richard Bernstein, "When China Convinced the U.S. That Uighurs Were Waging Jihad," *Atlantic*, March 19, 2019, https://www.theatlantic.com/international/archive/2019/03/us-uighurs-guantanamo-china-terror/584107/.

6. James Millward, "Does the 2009 Urumchi Violence Mark a Turning Point?" *Central Asian Survey* 28 (2009): 347–360.

7. "China Puts Urumqi under 'Full Surveillance,'" *Guardian*, January 25, 2011.

8. Quoted in Andrew Jacobs, "After Deadly Clash, China and Uighurs Disagree on Events That Led to Violence," *NYT*, July 30, 2014.

9. Andrew Jacobs, "Imam in China Who Defended Party's Policies in Xinjiang Is Stabbed to Death," *NYT*, July 31, 2014.

10. "China: Unrest in Kashgar, Xinjiang, Leaves 15 Dead," BBC News, July 31, 2011.

11. Reuters, "China's President Warns against Growing Threats to National Security," April 26, 2014.

12. Austin Ramzy and Chris Buckley, "'Absolutely No Mercy': Leaked Files Expose How China Organized Mass Detentions of Muslims," *NYT*, November 16, 2019.

13. See the images in Darren Byler, "Imagining Re-Engineered Muslims in Northwest China," April 26, 2017, *The Art of Life in Chinese Central Asia* (blog), https://livingotherwise.com/2017/04/26/imagining-re-engineered-muslims-northwest-china/.

14. Mark Elliott, "The Case of the Missing Indigene: Debate over a 'Second-Generation' Ethnic Policy," *China Journal*, no. 73 (2015): 186–213. See also James Leibold, *Ethnic Policy in China: Is Reform Inevitable?* (Honolulu, HI: East-West Center, 2013), and "Hu the Uniter: Hu Lianhe and the Radical Turn in China's Xinjiang Policy," *China Brief* 18, no. 16 (2018): 7–11.

15. Quoted in Julia Bowie and David Gitter, "The CCP's Plan to 'Sinicize' Religions," *Diplomat*, June 14, 2018.

16. I am grateful to Max Oidtmann for helping me make this distinction.

17. James Leibold, "More Than a Category: Han Supremacism on the Chinese Internet," *China Quarterly* no. 203 (2010): 539–559; Kevin Carrico, *The Great Han: Race, Nationalism, and Tradition in China Today* (Oakland: University of California Press, 2017).

18. "Xinjiang Uyghur Autonomous Region Regulation on De-Extremification," March 29, 2017, https://www.chinalawtranslate.com/en/xinjiang-uyghur-autonomous-region-regulation-on-de-extremification/ The translation is unofficial.

19. Quoted in Adrian Zenz, "'Thoroughly Reforming Them Towards a Healthy Heart Attitude': China's Political Re-Education Campaign in Xinjiang," *Central Asian Survey* 38 (2019): 116.

20. Quoted in Shohret Hoshur, "Chinese Authorities Jail Four Wealthiest Uyghurs in Xinjiang's Kashgar in New Purge," Radio Free Asia (RFA), January 5, 2018.

21. "Xinjiang's 'List of Forbidden Names' Forces Uyghurs to Change Names of Children Under 16," RFA (2017), https://www.rfa.org/english/news/special/uyghur-oppression/ChenPolicy6.html.

22. Timothy Grose, "'Once Their Mental State Is Healthy, They Will Be Able to Live Happily in Society': How China's Government Conflates Uighur Identity with Mental Illness," ChinaFile, August 2, 2019, https://www.chinafile.com/reporting-opinion/viewpoint/once-their-mental-state-healthy-they-will-be-able-live-happily-society.

23. Human Rights Watch, *"Eradicating Ideological Viruses": China's Campaign of Repression Against Xinjiang's Muslims* (New York: Human Rights Watch, 2018), 15.

24. BBC Urdu, November 18, 2018.

25. Uyghur Human Rights Project, "The Persecution of the Intellectuals in the Uyghur Region: Disappeared Forever?," Uyghur Human Rights Project, October 2018, https://docs.uhrp.org/pdf/UHRP_Disappeared_Forever_.pdf. Expatriates maintain an online database of those who have been disappeared. See "Xinjiang Victims Database," https://www.shahit.biz/eng/.

26. John Sudworth, "China Uighurs: A Model's Video Gives a Rare Glimpse inside Internment," BBC News, August 4, 2020; Merdan Ghappar, "Wear Your Mask under Your Hood: An Eyewitness Account of Arbitrary Detention in Xinjiang during the 2020 Coronavirus Pandemic," trans. James A. Millward, Medium, August 4, 2020, https://medium.com/@millwarj/wear-your-mask-under-your-hood-an-account-of-prisoner-abuse-in-xinjiang-during-the-2020-3007a1f7437d; David Stavrou, "A Million People Are Jailed at China's Gulags. I Managed to Escape. Here's What Really Goes on Inside," *Haaretz*, October 17, 2019; Bruce Pannier, "Kazakh Man Recounts 'Reeducation' In Western Chinese Camp," *Qishloq Ovozi*, April 26, 2018, https://www.rferl.org/a/kazakh-recounts-reeducation-in-western-chinese-camp/29194106.html.

27. Edmund Waite, "From Holy Man to National Villain: Popular Historical Narratives about Apaq Khoja amongst Uyghurs in Contemporary Xinjiang," *Inner Asia* 8 (2006): 5–28; Rian Thum, *The Sacred Routes of Uyghur History* (Cambridge, MA: Harvard University Press, 2014), 236–244.

28. "China Punishes Xinjiang Official for Refusing to Smoke near Muslim Elders," *South China Morning Post*, April 11, 2017.

29. Shohret Hoshur, "Prominent Uyghur Intellectual Given Two-Year Suspended Death Sentence for 'Separatism,'" RFA, September 28, 2018.

30. Shohret Hoshur, "Xinjiang Authorities Arrest Uyghur Court Official Who Denounced Political Re-Education Camps," RFA, December 18, 2018.

31. Eset Sulaiman, "Xinjiang Authorities Ban Books by Uyghur Former Chairman of Region," RFA, August 15, 2017.

32. Quoted in Mihray Abdilim, "Xinjiang's Kashgar University Students, Teachers Forced to Give up Muslim Dietary Restrictions," RFA, November 6, 2018.

33. Darren Byler, "China's Government Has Ordered a Million Citizens to Occupy Uighur Homes. Here's What They Think They're Doing," ChinaFile, October 24, 2018, http://www.chinafile.com/reporting-opinion/postcard/million-citizens-occupy-uighur-homes-xinjiang.

34. "China Is Putting Uighur Children in 'Orphanages' Even If Their Parents Are Alive," *Independent* (London), September 21, 2018.

35. For satellite images that document the destruction, see Bahram K. Sintash, *Demolishing Faith: The Destruction and Desecration of Uyghur Mosques and Shrines* (Washington: Uyghur Human Rights Project, 2019).

36. Joanne Smith Finley, "'Now We Don't Talk Anymore': Inside the 'Cleansing' of Xinjiang," ChinaFile, December 28, 2018, http://www.chinafile.com/reporting-opinion/viewpoint/now -we-dont-talk-anymore.

37. Kurban Niyaz and Shohret Hoshur, "Xinjiang Authorities Convert Uyghur Mosques into Propaganda Centers," RFA, August 3, 2017.

38. Sintash, *Demolishing Faith*; Lily Kuo, "Revealed: New Evidence of China's Mission to Raze the Mosques of Xinjiang," *Guardian*, May 7, 2019. The latter contains lots of satellite images.

39. Mihray Abdilim, "Authorities to Destroy Uyghur Cemetery in Xinjiang Capital," RFA, June 4, 2020.

40. State Council Information Office of the People's Republic of China, "Historical Matters Concerning Xinjiang" (July 22, 2019), http://english.scio.gov.cn/2019-07/22/content_75017992.htm.

41. Shawn Zhang, "Detention Camp Construction Is Booming in Xinjiang," June 18, 2018, Medium, https://medium.com/@shawnwzhang/detention-camp-construction-is-booming -in-xinjiang-a2525044c6b1; John Sudworth, "China's Hidden Camps: What's Happened to the Vanished Uighurs of Xinjiang?," BBC, October 24, 2018, https://bbc.in/2ytNBMY.

42. Vicky Xiuzhong Xu et al., *Uyghurs for Sale: 'Re-Education,' Forced Labour and Surveillance beyond Xinjiang* (Canberra: Australian Strategic Policy Institute, 2020).

43. Chris Buckley, "China's Prisons Swell after Deluge of Arrests Engulfs Muslims," *NYT*, August 31, 2019.

44. Adrian Zenz, *Sterilizations, IUDs, and Mandatory Birth Control: The CCP's Campaign to Suppress Uyghur Birthrates in Xinjiang* (Washington: Jamestown Foundation, 2020).

45. Lawrence Davidson, *Cultural Genocide* (New Brunswick, NJ: Rutgers University Press, 2012).

46. Roberts, *The War on the Uyghurs*, makes this point very thoughtfully.

47. Xu et al., *Uyghurs for Sale*, 5.

48. Darren Byler, "China's Hi-Tech War on Its Muslim Minority," *Guardian*, April 11, 2019.

Conclusion

1. Jeff Sahadeo, *Voices from the Soviet Edge: Southern Migrants in Leningrad and Moscow* (Ithaca, NY: Cornell University Press, 2019), 212; Timur Dadabaev, *Identity and Memory in Post-Soviet Central Asia* (London: Routledge, 2018).

SUGGESTIONS
FOR FURTHER READING

THE WRITING OF CENTRAL ASIAN HISTORY has been utterly transformed in the generation since the end of the Cold War. Travel into and out of Central Asia became easier than ever before, and it became possible to conduct academic research there in ways that were scarcely imaginable during the Cold War. Central Asian scholars established links with worlds of scholarship beyond the former Soviet Union, and all scholars gained access to vast storehouses of source material. Both the Tsarist empire and the Soviet Union were bureaucratic states that took documents very seriously and made great efforts to collect and store them. The Soviets created an intricate network of archives that spanned the country. One of the key developments of glasnost was the opening up of these archives to researchers, both foreign and domestic. After the dissolution of the Soviet Union, different countries have offered different levels of access to their archives, but—apart from Turkmenistan, where the archives were never opened—the situation is radically different than it was when Mikhail Gorbachev came to power. Archives, of course, contain only documents, not truth, and many documents are quite mundane (contrary to popular belief, "smoking gun" documents are almost nonexistent). The opening of the archives did not reveal the truth to us, but it allowed us to talk about Central Asia's past at a level of detail that we had only dreamed of before. At the same time, the end of the Cold War allowed scholars to ask new questions and think in ways not burdened with the political struggles of the Cold War. Finally, more and more scholars began to use sources in the languages of Central Asia, rather than simply working with Russian or Chinese sources. Scholars have been able to think about the course of Central Asia's history apart from the politically fraught categories that structured most analysis during the Cold War. This book would have looked very different without all these changes.

The situation in the PRC is not quite as rosy. The reform period after 1978 included China's opening up to international scholars, and archival work became possible. But since Xinjiang remains a sensitive part of the Chinese state (rather than an independent state like Kazakhstan), provincial archives were never opened up to international scholars. Indeed, since the turn of the millennium the Chinese state has been wary of foreign scholars working on Xinjiang. A number of leading Xinjiang specialists have been denied visas, and those who are let in work under difficult conditions, knowing that any Uyghurs or Kazakhs they contact might end up in trouble with the state. Since 2017, all international visitors, including journalists and scholars, have been subject to unprecedented surveillance.

Below I list the most impressive works of modern scholarship on Central Asia, including some that are not mentioned in the notes. I emphasize works in English, but the reader should keep in mind that the literature on Central Asia is multilingual, and the best works are often written in languages other than English. The list below is in no way comprehensive, but it should serve as a gateway to a broader understanding of the region.

———

There often seems to be a clear trade-off between accessibility and quality in works that survey the history of Central Asia. The best works are often impenetrable to nonspecialists, while popular works make cringe-inducing generalizations. There are few works in this category to endorse wholeheartedly, except for James A. Millward's *Eurasian Crossroads: A History of Xinjiang* (New York: Columbia University Press, 2007), and Shoshana Keller's account of Russia's long relationship with Central Asia, *Russia and Central Asia: Coexistence, Conquest, Convergence* (Toronto: University of Toronto Press, 2019). The four-volume work by the Swiss archaeologist Christoph Baumer, *The History of Central Asia* (London: I. B. Tauris, 2012–2018), is richly illustrated and provides a strong focus on ancient history. The concept of the Silk Road is best approached through the very fine (and concise) analysis by James A. Millward, *The Silk Road: A Very Short Introduction* (Oxford: Oxford University Press, 2013). For critiques of the way the Silk Road is talked about, see Scott C. Levi, *The Bukharan Crisis: A Connected History of 18th-Century Central Asia* (Pittsburgh, PA: University of Pittsburgh Press, 2020), chap. 2; Khodadad Rezakhani, "The Road That Never Was: The Silk Road and Trans-Eurasian Exchange," *Comparative Studies of South Asia, Africa and the Middle East* 30 (2010): 420–433; and Tamara Chen, "The Invention of the Silk Road, 1877," *Critical Inquiry* 40 (2013): 194–219.

Alain Cariou, *L'Asie centrale: Territoires, sociétés et environnement* (Paris: Armand Colin, 2015), provides an excellent overview of the geography and environment of Central Asia using the same definition of the region that I use. For the history of the period before the Mongol conquests, V. V. Bartol'd's classic *Turkestan down to the Mongol Invasion* (trans. T. Minorsky [London: Luzac, 1928]), originally defended as a doctoral dissertation in 1898, is still useful, especially if the reader keeps in mind the caveats offered by Levi (in *The Bukharan Crisis*, cited above). See also Peter Golden, *Central Asia in World History* (New York: Oxford University Press, 2011), for a broad comparative perspective. On the advent of Islam and what Islamization meant, see Devin DeWeese, *Islamization and Native Religion in the Golden Horde: Baba Tükles and Conversion to Islam in Historical and Epic Tradition* (University Park: Pennsylvania State University Press, 1994). DeWeese tends to bury the nuggets of his insight in very large haystacks of detail, but the effort to find the nuggets is usually worthwhile. On post-Mongol developments, see Azfar Moin, *The Millennial Sovereign: Sacred Kingship and Sainthood in Islam* (New York: Columbia University Press, 2012). The period between the fall of the Timurids and the imperial conquests is still only spottily covered, but there are some very fine works available: Alexandre Papas, *Soufisme et politique entre Chine, Tibet et Turkestan: Etude sur les Khwâjas naqshbandîs du Turkestan oriental* (Paris: Librairie d'Amérique et d'Orient, 2005); Scott C. Levi, *The Rise and Fall of Khoqand, 1709–1876: Central Asia in the Global Age* (Pittsburgh, PA: University of Pittsburgh

Press, 2017); and James Pickett, *The Polymaths of Islam: Power and Networks of Knowledge in Central Asia* (Ithaca, NY: Cornell University Press, 2020).

The study of the Qing empire has undergone seismic changes in the past generation, as scholars began to take the Manchu origins of the dynasty seriously. My analysis banks on the new Qing historiography that has emerged since the 1990s. Its main landmarks are: Evelyn S. Rawski, "Reenvisioning the Qing: The Significance of the Qing Period in Chinese History," *Journal of Asian Studies* 55 (1996): 829–850; James A. Millward, *Beyond the Pass: Economy, Ethnicity, and Empire in Qing Central Asia, 1759–1864* (Stanford, CA: Stanford University Press, 1998); Mark C. Elliott, *The Manchu Way: The Eight Banners and Ethnic Identity in Late Imperial China* (Stanford, CA: Stanford University Press, 2001); Pamela Kyle Crossley, *A Translucent Mirror: History and Identity in Qing Imperial Ideology* (Berkeley: University of California Press, 2002); and Max Oidtmann, *Forging the Golden Urn: The Qing Empire and the Politics of Reincarnation in Tibet* (New York: Columbia University Press, 2018). For our purposes, however, the most significant work in this corpus is Peter C. Purdue's magisterial *China Marches West: The Qing Conquest of Central Eurasia* (Cambridge, MA: Belknap Press of Harvard University Press, 2005).

On the aftermath of the Qing conquests, see Laura J. Newby, *The Empire and the Khanate: A Political History of the Qing Relations with Khoqand, c. 1760–1860* (Leiden: Brill, 2005), and Jin Noda, *The Kazakh Khanates between the Russian and Qing Empires* (Leiden: Brill, 2016). For the Russian conquest, we finally have a comprehensive account: Alexander Morrison, *The Russian Conquest of Central Asia: A Study in Imperial Expansion, 1814–1914* (Cambridge: Cambridge University Press, 2020), a delightful work based on a mastery of both Russian and Central Asian sources that is always keenly aware of the comparative perspective of European imperialism. (Morrison also explains why the Great Game is a useless concept.) The best account of the collapse of Qing rule in Xinjiang in the 1860s and of Yaqub Beg's short-lived state is Hodong Kim, *Holy War in China: The Muslim Rebellion and State in Chinese Central Asia, 1864–1877* (Stanford, CA: Stanford University Press, 2004).

On imperial rule in Central Asia, see Virginia Martin, *Law and Custom in the Steppe: The Kazakhs of the Middle Horde and Russian Colonialism in the Nineteenth Century* (Richmond: Curzon, 2001); Ian W. Campbell, *Knowledge and the Ends of Empire: Kazak Intermediaries and Russian Rule on the Steppe, 1731–1917* (Ithaca, NY: Cornell University Press, 2017); Jeff Sahadeo, *Russian Colonial Society in Tashkent, 1865–1923* (Bloomington: Indiana University Press, 2007); T. V. Kotiukova, *Okraina na osobom polozhenii . . . : Turkestan v preddverii dramy* (Moscow: Nauchno-politicheskaia kniga, 2016); and Eric Schluessel, *Land of Strangers: The Civilizing Project in Qing Central Asia* (New York: Columbia University Press, 2020). Julia Obertreis, *Imperial Desert Dreams: Cotton Growing and Irrigation in Central Asia, 1860–1991* (Göttingen: V&R unipress, 2017), and Maya K. Peterson, *Pipe Dreams: Water and Empire in Central Asia's Aral Sea Basin* (Cambridge: Cambridge University Press, 2019), offer fundamental accounts of the economic and environmental transformation set in motion by the Russian conquest. On the dramatic impact of the conquest on how Central Asians imagined the world, see Adeeb Khalid, *The Politics of Muslim Cultural Reform: Jadidism in Central Asia* (Berkeley: University of California Press, 1998). On the way identities were reshaped in this period, see the ingenious book by Rian Thum, *The Sacred Routes of Uyghur History* (Cambridge, MA: Harvard University Press, 2014), and the amazingly researched work of David Brophy, *Uyghur Nation: Reform and Revolution on the Russia-China Frontier* (Cambridge, MA: Harvard University Press, 2016).

The 1916 uprising in Russian Central Asia has been understudied, but a new volume, *The Central Asian Uprising of 1916*, edited by Aminat Chokobaeva, Cloé Drieu, and Alexander Morrison (Manchester: Manchester University Press, 2020) makes up for that lack by bringing together top-notch scholarship from three continents. The period of the Russian revolution has been studied by Marco Buttino, *La rivoluzione capovolta: L'Asia centrale tra il crollo dell'impero zarista e la formazione dell'URSS* (Naples: L'Ancora del Mediterraneo, 2003); Saidakbar Agzamkhodzhaev, *Istoriia Turkestanskoi avtonomii: Turkiston muxtoryiati* (Tashkent: Toshkent Islom universteti, 2006); and Dina Amanzholova, *Na izlome: Alash v etnopoliticheskoi istorii Kazakhstana* (Almaty: Taymas,

2009). For the early Soviet period, see Adeeb Khalid, *Making Uzbekistan: Nation, Empire, and Revolution in the Early USSR* (Ithaca, NY: Cornell University Press, 2015). Marianne Kamp, *The New Woman in Uzbekistan: Islam, Modernity, and Unveiling under Communism* (Seattle: University of Washington Press, 2006), and Douglas Northrop, *Veiled Empire: Gender and Power in Stalinist Central Asia* (Ithaca, NY: Cornell University Press, 2004), offer contrasting takes on the *hujum*. Cloé Drieu, *Cinema, Nation, and Empire in Uzbekistan, 1919–1937* (trans. Adrian Morfee) [Bloomington: Indiana University Press, 2018]), provides wonderful insights into questions of representation in the early Soviet period. On Kazakhstan, Niccolò Pianciola, *Stalinismo di frontiera: Colonizzazione agricola, stermino dei nomadi e construzione statale in Asia centrale (1905–1936)* (Rome: Viella, 2009), offers a sweeping account that spans the revolution. Excellent work has recently appeared on collectivization and the disasters that it produced: Isabelle Ohayon, *Le sédentarisation des Kazakhs dans l'URSS de Staline: Collectivisation et changement social (1928–1945)* (Paris: Maisonneuve et Larose, 2006); Robert Kindler, *Stalin's Nomads: Power and Famine in Kazakhstan* (trans. Cynthia Klohr [Pittsburgh, PA: University of Pittsburgh Press, 2018]); and Sarah Cameron, *The Hungry Steppe: Famine, Violence, and the Making of Soviet Kazakhstan* (Ithaca, NY: Cornell University Press, 2018). Excellent studies also exist on the other republics in the early Soviet period. See Adrienne L. Edgar, *Tribal Nation: The Making of Soviet Turkmenistan* (Princeton, NJ: Princeton University Press, 2004); Ali İğmen, *Speaking Soviet with an Accent: Culture and Power in Kyrgyzstan* (Pittsburgh, PA: University of Pittsburgh Press, 2012). Victoria Clement, *Learning to Become Turkmen: Literacy, Language, and Power, 1914–2014* (Pittsburgh, PA: University of Pittsburgh Press, 2018), and Kirill Nourzhanov and Christian Bleuer, *Tajikistan: A Political and Social History* (Canberra: Australian National University Press, 2013), offer expansive coverage of individual countries across the revolutionary divide. Sergei Abashin, *Sovetskii kishlak: Mezhdu kolonializmom i modernizatsiei* (Moscow: NLO, 2015), offers a fascinating study of a single village in Tajikistan over the course of a century and a half.

For the interwar period in Xinjiang, Andrew D. W. Forbes, *Warlords and Muslims in Chinese Central Asia: A Political History of Republican*

Sinkiang, 1911–1949 (Cambridge: Cambridge University Press, 1986), remains essential, especially for the first ETR. The Azerbaijani scholar Cemil Hesenli has combed through Soviet archives to write the most thorough account to date of the politics of the era: Dzhamil' Gasanly, *Sin'tszian v orbite sovetskoi politiki: Stalin i musul'manskoe dvizhenie v Vostochnom Turkestane, 1931–1949* (Moscow, 2015). Ondřej Klimeš, *Struggle by the Pen: The Uyghur Discourse of Nation and National Interest, c. 1900–1949* (Leiden: Brill, 2015), is based on a thorough reading of the Uyghur-language materials of the period. James Leibold, *Reconfiguring Chinese Nationalism: How the Qing Frontier and Its Indigenes Became Chinese* (New York: Palgrave Macmillan, 2007), is indispensable for understanding the evolution of Chinese nationalism over the course of the twentieth century and its fraught relationship with the peoples conquered by the Qing. See also the critical approaches to Chinese nationalism in Joshua A. Fogel's edited volume, *The Teleology of the Modern Nation-State: Japan and China* (Philadelphia: University of Pennsylvania Press, 2005).

The Second World War transformed Central Asia in many ways, but work on the region in the period is only now beginning to appear in book form. Paul Stronski offers important insights on wartime in his history of mid-century Tashkent: *Tashkent: Forging a Soviet City, 1930–1966* (Pittsburgh, PA: University of Pittsburgh Press, 2010), while Roberto J. Carmack, *Kazakhstan in World War II: Mobilization and Ethnicity in the Soviet Empire* (Lawrence: University of Kansas Press, 2019), provides a solid account of the home front in Kazakhstan. Similarly, historians have only recently turned their attention to the postwar period in the region. Excellent studies of the transformations of that period include Vincent Fourniau, *Transformations soviétiques et mémoires en Asie centrale: De l'indigénisation à l'indépendance* (Paris: Indes Savantes, 2019), and Artemy Kalinovsky, *Laboratory of Socialist Development: Cold War Politics and Decolonization in Soviet Tajikistan* (Ithaca, NY: Cornell University Press 2018). Oral histories have yielded important insights into the late-Soviet period. See especially Jeff Sahadeo, *Voices from the Soviet Edge: Southern Migrants in Leningrad and Moscow* (Ithaca, NY: Cornell University Press, 2019), and Adrienne L. Edgar, *Intermarriage and the Friendship of Peoples: Ethnic Mixing in Soviet Central Asia*, forthcoming.

On Islam in the late-Soviet period, see Adeeb Khalid, *Islam after Communism: Religion and Politics in Central Asia*, rev. ed. (Berkeley: University of California Press, 2014). Islam has become a central theme in writing about Central Asia. During the Cold War, the conventional wisdom in the West held that Soviet efforts at secularization and modernization had produced few successes and that Central Asians remained Muslims. A number of scholars who come to Central Asian history with training in Islamic studies have reverted to that argument and have insisted, often in spite of the evidence that they provide, that Islam remained the most salient aspect of Central Asian life and that the region can be understood only through the perspective of Islam as expressed by conventional Islamic elites. Paolo Sartori had made this argument for continuity with the greatest persistence. For example, see his "Of Saints, Shrines, and Tractors: Untangling the Meaning of Islam in Soviet Central Asia," *Journal of Islamic Studies* 30 (2019): 367–405. Eren Tasar, *Soviet and Muslim: The Institutionalization of Islam in Central Asia* (New York: Oxford University Press, 2017), makes the argument even more stridently and presents the late-Soviet era almost as a time of religious freedom. I find these views deeply problematic and prefer the more nuanced view of the lived reality of Islam in this period presented by the contributors to a volume edited by Stéphane A. Dudoignon and Christian Noack, *Allah's Kolkhozes: Migration, De-Stalinisation, Privatisation and the New Muslim Congregations in the Soviet Realm (1950s–2000s)* (Berlin: Klaus Schwarz, 2014).

Philip Micklin has studied the environmental disaster of the Aral Sea since the 1980s. His work is scattered across different scientific journals, but see the volume he edited with Nikolay V. Aladin and Igor Plotnikov: *The Aral Sea: The Devastation and Partial Rehabilitation of a Great Lake* (Berlin: Springer, 2014). The gold standard for the study of Central Asia's economies is set by Richard Pomfret, who has published extensively. His latest work is *The Central Asian Economies in the Twenty-First Century: Paving a New Silk Road* (Princeton, NJ: Princeton University Press, 2019).

The study of Xinjiang did not experience the archival bonanza that reshaped the historiography of Russian Central Asia. For the Maoist period, Donald H. McMillen, *Chinese Communist Power and Policy in Xinjiang, 1949–1977* (Boulder, CO: Westview, 1979), is still unsurpassed. The best guide to the post-Mao period is a volume edited by S. Frederick Starr, *Xinjiang: China's Muslim Borderland* (Armonk, NY: M. E. Sharpe, 2004). The Chinese government was offended enough by the book that it has not granted visas to any of the thirteen contributors since publication. See also Gardner Bovingdon, *The Uyghurs: Strangers in Their Own Land* (New York: Columbia University Press, 2010), and Joanne Smith Finley, *The Arts of Symbolic Resistance: Uyghur Identities and Uyghur-Han Relations in Contemporary Xinjiang* (Leiden: Brill, 2013). Nathan Light, *Intimate Heritage: Creating Uyghur Muqam Song in Xinjiang* (Münster: Lit Verlag, 2008), provides an excellent account of the crystallization of a modern Uyghur cultural canon in this period. Tom Cliff's *Oil and Water: Being Han in Xinjiang* (Chicago: University of Chicago Press, 2016) is a fine ethnography of Han settlers in the region. Sean R. Roberts, *The War on the Uyghurs: China's Campaign against Xinjiang's Muslims* (Princeton, NJ: Princeton University Press, 2020), is indispensable for understanding the PRC's descent into its current campaign against the Uyghurs.

Post-Soviet Central Asia has unfortunately not benefited from good journalistic reportage. The exceptions are Monica Whitlock, *Beyond the Oxus: The Central Asians* (London: John Murray, 2002), and Joanna Lillis, *Dark Shadows: Inside the Secret World of Kazakhstan* (London: I. B. Tauris, 2019). However, we have a substantial amount of social science literature on the region. See Laura L. Adams, *The Spectacular State: Culture and National Identity in Uzbekistan* (Durham, NC: Duke University Press, 2010), on celebrations and national identity, as well as Madeleine Reeves, *Border Work: Spatial Lives of the State in Rural Central Asia* (Ithaca, NY: Cornell University Press, 2014), and Nick Megoran, *Nationalism in Central Asia: A Biography of the Uzbekistan-Kyrgyzstan Boundary* (Pittsburgh, PA: University of Pittsburgh Press, 2017), on how the new states and their boundaries affect citizens. The nature of the new states is explored by Scott Radnitz, *Weapons of the Wealthy: Predatory Regimes and Elite-Led Protests in Central Asia* (Ithaca, NY: Cornell University Press, 2010); Lawrence P. Markowitz, *State Erosion: Unlootable*

Resources and Unruly Elites in Central Asia (Ithaca, NY: Cornell University Press, 2013); and Jesse Driscoll, *Warlords and Coalition Politics in Post-Soviet States* (Cambridge: Cambridge University Press, 2015). Alexander Cooley and John Heathershaw, *Dictators without Borders: Power and Money in Central Asia* (New Haven, CT: Yale University Press, 2017), provide a trenchant analysis of the conections between globalization and the corruption of Central Asia's new states. For an overview of the place of Islam in the new states, see Bayram Balci, *Islam in Central Asia and the Caucasus since the Fall of the Soviet Union* (London: Hurst, 2018). Thoughtful ethnographic accounts of the multiple meanings of Islam in post-Soviet Central Asia include: Maria Elisabeth Louw, *Everyday Islam in Post-Soviet Central Asia* (London: Routledge, 2007); Krisztina Kehl-Bodrogi, *"Religion Is Not So Strong Here": Muslim Religious Life in Khorezm after Socialism* (Berlin: Lit Verlag, 2008); David W. Montgomery, *Practicing Islam: Knowledge, Experience, and Social Navigation in Kyrgyzstan* (Pittsburgh, PA: University of Pittsburgh Press, 2016); and Julie McBrien, *From Belonging to Belief: Modern Secularisms and the Construction of Religion in Kyrgyzstan* (Pittsburgh, PA: University of Pittsburgh Press, 2017).

The voices of Central Asians still remain difficult to find in translation. We now have a fine English translation of Cholpan's 1935 Uzbek novel *Night* (trans. Christopher Fort [Boston: Academic Studies Press, 2019]), and almost the entire corpus of the Kyrgyz novelist Chingiz Aitmatov is available in English—including his most significant work, *The Day Lasts More than a Hundred Years* (trans. John French [London: Futura, 1983]). The Uzbek author Hamid Ismoilov, born in Kyrgyzstan and exiled from Uzbekistan in 1992, has produced a number of stunning novels in Russian or Uzbek. I enthusiastically recommend *The Railway*, written in Russian (trans. Robert Chandler [London: Vintage, 2006]), and *The Devils' Dance*, written in Uzbek (trans. Donald Rayfield [London: Tilted Axis Press, 2017]), a brilliant novel that juxtaposes the Khoqand of Madali Khan with a Tashkent in which the secret police terrorize Abdulla Qodiriy and Cholpan.

INDEX

Italic page numbers indicate illustrations.